FIFTH EDITION

MICROSOFT®
VISUAL BASIC® 2012:
RELOADED

DIANE ZAK

CENGAGE
Learning®

Australia • Brazil • Japan • Korea • Mexico • Singapore • Spain • United Kingdom • United States

Microsoft® Visual Basic® 2012: RELOADED, Fifth Edition
Diane Zak

Product Director: Kathleen McMahon

Senior Product Manager: Jim Gish

Senior Content Developer: Alyssa Pratt

Content Product Manager:
  Jennifer Feltri-George

Product Assistant: Sarah Timm

Art Director: Cheryl Pearl, GEX

Manuscript Quality Assurance: Nicole Spoto

Cover Designer: GEX, Inc.

Cover Photo Credit ©Nik Merkulov/
  Shutterstock

Manufacturing Planner: Julio Esperas

Proofreader: Suzanne Huizenga

Indexer: Constance A. Angelo

Compositor: Integra Software Services Pvt. Ltd.

For product information and technology assistance, contact us at **Cengage Learning Customer & Sales Support, www.cengage.com/support**

For permission to use material from this text or product, submit all requests online at **cengage.com/permissions** Further permissions questions can be emailed to **permissionrequest@cengage.com**

Library of Congress Control Number: 2013945551

ISBN-13: 978-1-285-08416-9

Cengage Learning
20 Channel Center Street
Boston, MA 02210
USA

Some of the product names and company names used in this book have been used for identification purposes only and may be trademarks or registered trademarks of their respective manufacturers and sellers.

Cengage Learning reserves the right to revise this publication and make changes from time to time in its content without notice.

Cengage Learning is a leading provider of customized learning solutions with office locations around the globe, including Singapore, the United Kingdom, Australia, Mexico, Brazil, and Japan. Locate your local office at: **www.cengage.com/global**

Cengage Learning products are represented in Canada by Nelson Education, Ltd.

Purchase any of our products at your local college store or at our preferred online store **www.cengagebrain.com**

Printed in the United States of America
1 2 3 4 5 6 7 19 18 17 16 15 14 13

Brief Contents

Contents

vi

CHAPTER 4   Making Decisions in a Program 186

CHAPTER 5   More on the Selection Structure 240

Preface

Microsoft Visual Basic 2012: RELOADED, Fifth Edition uses Visual Basic 2012, an object-oriented language, to teach programming concepts. This book is designed for a beginning programming course; however, it assumes students are familiar with basic Windows skills and file management.

Organization and Coverage

Microsoft Visual Basic 2012: RELOADED, Fifth Edition contains 14 chapters and five appendices (A through E). In the chapters, students with no previous programming experience learn how to plan and create their own interactive Windows applications. By the end of the book, students will have learned how to use TOE charts, pseudocode, and flowcharts to plan an application. They also will learn how to work with objects and write Visual Basic statements such as If...Then...Else, Select Case, Do...Loop, For...Next, and For Each...Next. Students also will learn how to manipulate variables, constants, strings, sequential access files, structures, and arrays. In Chapter 12, they will learn how to connect an application to a Microsoft Access database, and then use Language Integrated Query (LINQ) to query the database. Chapter 13 shows students how to create simple Web applications, and Chapter 14 shows them how to create their own classes and objects.

Approach

Like the previous editions, *Microsoft Visual Basic 2012: RELOADED, Fifth Edition* is distinguished from other textbooks because of its unique approach, which motivates students by demonstrating why they need to learn the concepts and skills presented. Each chapter begins with an introduction to one or more programming concepts. The concepts are illustrated with code examples and sample programs. The sample programs are provided to students to allow them to observe how the current concept can be utilized before they are introduced to the next concept. Following the concept portion in each chapter are two Programming Tutorials. Each Programming Tutorial guides students through the process of creating an application using the concepts covered in the chapter. A Programming Example follows the Programming Tutorials in each chapter. The Programming Example contains a completed application that demonstrates the chapter concepts. Following the Programming Example are the Summary, Key Terms, Review Questions, Exercises, and Case Projects sections.

Features

Microsoft Visual Basic 2012: RELOADED, Fifth Edition is an exceptional textbook because it also includes the following features:

READ THIS BEFORE YOU BEGIN This section is consistent with Cengage's commitment to helping instructors introduce technology into the classroom. Technical considerations and assumptions about hardware, software, and default settings are listed in one place to help instructors save time and eliminate unnecessary aggravation.

DESIGNED FOR THE DIFFERENT LEARNING STYLES The three most common learning styles are visual, auditory, and kinesthetic. This book contains videos for visual and auditory learners, and Try It! files for kinesthetic learners.

 VIDEOS These notes direct students to videos that explain and/or demonstrate one or more of the chapter's concepts, provide additional information about the concepts, or cover topics related to the concepts. The videos are available online at *www.cengagebrain.com*. Search for the ISBN of your title (from the back cover of your book) using the search box at the top of the page. This will take you to the product page where free companion resources can be found.

 TRY IT! FILES Each chapter has accompanying Try It! files that allow the student to practice a concept before moving on to the next concept.

MINI-QUIZZES Mini-Quizzes are strategically placed to test students' knowledge at various points in the chapter. Answers to the quiz questions are provided in Appendix A, allowing students to determine whether they have mastered the material covered thus far before continuing with the chapter.

HOW TO BOXES The How To boxes in each chapter summarize important concepts and provide a quick reference for students. The How To boxes that introduce new statements, functions, or methods contain the syntax and examples of using the syntax. Many of the How To boxes contain the steps for performing common tasks.

TIP These notes provide additional information about the current concept. Examples include alternative ways of writing statements or performing tasks, as well as warnings about common mistakes made when using a particular command and reminders of related concepts learned in previous chapters.

PROGRAMMING TUTORIALS Each chapter contains two Programming Tutorials that provide step-by-step instructions for using the chapter's concepts in an application. In most cases, the first tutorial in each chapter is easier than the second because it contains more detailed steps. Typically, one of the tutorial applications is a simple game, while the other is a business application. Game applications are used because research shows that the fun and exciting nature of games helps motivate students to learn.

PROGRAMMING EXAMPLE A Programming Example follows the Programming Tutorials in each chapter. The Programming Example shows the TOE chart and pseudocode used to plan the application. It also shows the user interface and Visual Basic code.

SUMMARY Each chapter contains a Summary section that recaps the concepts covered in the chapter.

KEY TERMS Following the Summary section in each chapter is a listing of the key terms introduced throughout the chapter, along with their definitions.

REVIEW QUESTIONS Each chapter contains Review Questions designed to test a student's understanding of the chapter's concepts.

 PENCIL AND PAPER EXERCISES Following the Review Questions in each chapter are Pencil and Paper Exercises. The Exercises are designated as Modify This, Introductory, Intermediate, Advanced, Discovery, and Swat the Bugs. The Advanced and Discovery Exercises provide practice in applying cumulative programming knowledge. They also allow students to explore alternative solutions to programming tasks. The Swat the Bugs Exercises provide an opportunity for students to detect and correct errors in one or more lines of code.

 COMPUTER EXERCISES The Computer Exercises, which follow the Pencil and Paper Exercises in each chapter, provide students with additional practice of the skills and concepts they learned in the chapter. The Exercises are designated as Modify This, Introductory, Intermediate, Advanced, Discovery, and Swat the Bugs. The Advanced and Discovery Exercises provide practice in applying cumulative programming knowledge. They also allow students to explore alternative solutions to programming tasks. The Swat the Bugs Exercises provide an opportunity for students to detect and correct errors in an existing application.

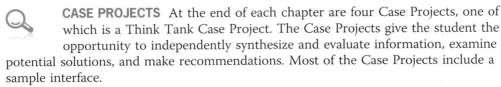 **CASE PROJECTS** At the end of each chapter are four Case Projects, one of which is a Think Tank Case Project. The Case Projects give the student the opportunity to independently synthesize and evaluate information, examine potential solutions, and make recommendations. Most of the Case Projects include a sample interface.

THINK TANK CASE PROJECTS The last Case Project in each chapter is designated by the "Think Tank" icon. The Think Tank Case Projects are more challenging than the other Case Projects.

New to this Edition!

READING/STUDY GUIDE Each chapter is accompanied by a Reading/Study Guide filled with interactive, fun, and motivational learning activities. The activities are designed to help students focus on the important concepts in the chapter. The Reading/Study Guides are available at *www.cengagebrain.com.*

OBJECTIVES The Review Questions, Exercises, and Case Projects are now associated with one or more of the objectives listed at the beginning of the chapter.

NEW EXAMPLES, SAMPLE PROGRAMS, TUTORIALS, AND EXERCISES Each chapter has been updated with new examples, sample programs, tutorials, and/or exercises.

 VIDEOS The videos that accompany the book have been updated from the previous edition.

Instructor Resources

All of the resources available with this book can be found at *www.cengagebrain.com.* At the CengageBrain.com home page, search for the ISBN of your title (from the back cover of your book) using the search box at the top of the page. This will take you to the product page where free companion resources can be found.

ELECTRONIC INSTRUCTOR'S MANUAL The Instructor's Manual that accompanies this textbook includes additional instructional material to assist in class preparation, including items such as Sample Syllabi, Chapter Outlines, Technical Notes, Lecture Notes, Quick Quizzes, Teaching Tips, Discussion Topics, and Additional Case Projects.

EXAMVIEW® This textbook is accompanied by ExamView, a powerful testing software package that allows instructors to create and administer printed, computer (LAN-based), and Internet exams. ExamView includes hundreds of questions that correspond to the topics covered in this text, enabling students to generate detailed study guides that include page references for further review. The computer-based and Internet testing components allow students to take exams at their computers, and also save the instructor time by grading each exam automatically.

POWERPOINT® PRESENTATIONS This book offers Microsoft PowerPoint slides for each chapter. These are included as a teaching aid for classroom presentation, to make available to students on the network for chapter review, or to be printed for classroom distribution. Instructors can add their own slides for additional topics they introduce to the class.

DATA FILES Data Files are necessary for completing many of the computer activities in this book. The Data Files can be downloaded by students at *www.cengagebrain.com.*

SOLUTION FILES Solutions to the Review Questions, Pencil and Paper Exercises, Computer Exercises, and Case Projects, as well as to the sample programs that appear in the figures throughout the book, are available for instructors.

Acknowledgments

Writing a book is a team effort rather than an individual one. I would like to take this opportunity to thank my team, especially Alyssa Pratt (Senior Content Developer), Sreejith Govindan (Full Service Project Manager), Jennifer Feltri-George (Content Project Manager), Suzanne Huizenga (Proofreader), Nicole Spoto (Quality Assurance), and the compositors at Integra. Thank you for your support, enthusiasm, patience, and hard work. Last, but certainly not least, I want to thank the following reviewers for their invaluable ideas and comments: Lorraine Bergkvist, University of Baltimore and David Taylor, Seminole State College of Florida.

Diane Zak

Read This Before You Begin

Technical Information

Data Files

You will need data files to complete some of the computer activities in this book. Your instructor may provide the data files to you. You may obtain the files electronically at *www.cengagebrain.com*, and then navigating to the page for this book.

Each chapter in this book has its own set of data files, which are stored in a separate folder within the VbReloaded2012 folder. The files for Chapter 1 are stored in the VbReloaded2012\Chap01 folder. Similarly, the files for Chapter 2 are stored in the VbReloaded2012\Chap02 folder. Throughout this book, you will be instructed to open files from or save files to these folders.

You can use a computer in your school lab or your own computer to complete the computer activities in this book.

Using Your Own Computer

To use your own computer to complete the computer activities in this book, you will need the following:

- A Pentium® 4 processor, 1.6 GHz or higher, personal computer running Microsoft Windows. This book was written and Quality Assurance tested using Microsoft Windows 8.

- Either Microsoft Visual Studio 2012 or the Express Editions of Microsoft Visual Studio 2012 (namely, Microsoft Visual Studio Express 2012 for Windows Desktop and Microsoft Visual Studio Express 2012 for Web) installed on your computer. This book was written using Microsoft Visual Studio Professional 2012, and Quality Assurance tested using the Express Editions of Microsoft Visual Studio 2012. At the time of this writing, you can download a free copy of the Express Editions at *www.microsoft.com/visualstudio/eng/products/visual-studio-express-products*.

Figures

The figures in this book reflect how your screen will look if you are using Microsoft Visual Studio Professional 2012 and a Microsoft Windows 8 system. Your screen may appear slightly different in some instances if you are using another version of either Microsoft Visual Studio or Microsoft Windows.

Visit Our Web Site

Additional materials designed for this textbook might be available at *www.cengagebrain.com*. Search this site for more details.

To the Instructor

To complete the computer activities in this book, your students must use a set of data files. These files can be obtained electronically at *www.cengagebrain.com*.

The material in this book was written using Microsoft Visual Studio Professional 2012 on a Microsoft Windows 8 system. It was Quality Assurance tested using Microsoft Visual Studio Express 2012 for Windows Desktop and Microsoft Visual Studio Express 2012 for Web.

Data Files

You are granted a license to copy the data files to any computer or computer network used by individuals who have purchased this book.

An Introduction to Programming

After studying this Overview, you should be able to:

◎ Define the terminology used in programming

◎ Explain the tasks performed by a programmer

◎ Understand the employment opportunities for programmers and software developers

◎ Use the chapters effectively

◎ Run a Visual Basic 2012 application

Programming a Computer

In essence, the word **programming** means *giving a mechanism the directions to accomplish a task*. If you are like most people, you've already programmed several mechanisms, such as your digital video recorder (DVR), cell phone, or coffee maker. Like these devices, a computer also is a mechanism that can be programmed.

The directions given to a computer are called **computer programs** or, more simply, **programs**. The people who write programs are called **programmers**. Programmers use a variety of special languages, called **programming languages**, to communicate with the computer. Some popular programming languages are Visual Basic, C#, C++, and Java. In this book, you will use the Visual Basic programming language.

The Programmer's Job

When a company has a problem that requires a computer solution, typically it is a programmer who comes to the rescue. The programmer might be an employee of the company; or he or she might be a freelance programmer (or programming consultant), which is a programmer who works on temporary contracts rather than for a long-term employer.

Overview-
Programmers

First the programmer meets with the user, which is the person (or people) responsible for describing the problem. In many cases, this person (or these people) will eventually use the solution. Depending on the complexity of the problem, multiple programmers may be involved, and they may need to meet with the user several times. Programming teams often contain subject matter experts, who may or may not be programmers. For example, an accountant might be part of a team working on a program that requires accounting expertise. The purpose of the initial meetings with the user is to determine the exact problem and to agree on the desired solution.

After the programmer and user agree on the solution, the programmer begins converting the solution into a computer program. During the conversion phase, the programmer meets periodically with the user to determine whether the program fulfills the user's needs and to refine any details of the solution. When the user is satisfied that the program does what he or she wants it to do, the programmer rigorously tests the program with sample data before releasing it to the user. In many cases, the programmer also provides the user with a manual that explains how to use the program. As this process indicates, the creation of a good computer solution to a problem—in other words, the creation of a good program—requires a great deal of interaction between the programmer and the user.

Employment Opportunities

When searching for a job in computer programming, you will encounter ads for "computer programmers" as well as for "software developers." Although job titles and descriptions vary, software developers typically are responsible for designing an appropriate solution to a user's problem, while computer programmers are responsible for translating the solution into a language that the computer can understand. The process of translating the solution is called **coding**.

Overview-
Programmer
Qualities

Keep in mind that, depending on the employer and the size and complexity of the user's problem, the design and coding tasks may be performed by the same employee, no matter what his or her job title is. In other words, it's not unusual for a software developer to code her solution, just as it's not unusual for a programmer to have designed the solution he is coding.

Programmers and software developers need to have strong problem-solving and analytical skills, as well as the ability to communicate effectively with team members, end users, and other nontechnical personnel. Typically, software developers are expected to have at least a bachelor's degree in computer science, along with practical work experience, especially in the industry in which they are employed. Computer programmers usually need at least an associate's degree in computer science, mathematics, or information systems, as well as proficiency in one or more programming languages.

Computer programmers and software developers are employed in almost every industry, such as telecommunications companies, software publishers, financial institutions, insurance carriers, educational institutions, and government agencies. The Bureau of Labor Statistics predicts that employment of software developers will increase by 30% from 2010 to 2020. The employment of computer programmers, on the other hand, will increase by 12% over the same period. Consulting opportunities for freelance programmers and software developers are also expected to increase as companies look for ways to reduce their payroll expenses.

There is a great deal of competition for programming and software developer jobs, so jobseekers will need to keep up to date with the latest programming languages and technologies. A competitive edge may be gained by obtaining vendor-specific and/or language-specific certifications. More information about computer programmers and software developers can be found on the Bureau of Labor Statistics Web site at *www.bls.gov*.

Using the Chapters Effectively

The chapters in this book teach you how to write programs using the Visual Basic programming language. Each chapter focuses on programming concepts, which are first introduced using simple examples and then utilized in larger applications at the end of the chapter. Two Programming Tutorials follow the concepts section in each chapter. Each Programming Tutorial guides you through the process of creating an application using the concepts covered in the chapter. In most cases, the first tutorial in each chapter is easier than the second one because it contains more detailed steps. Many of the applications created in the Programming Tutorials are simple games, while others are business applications. A Programming Example follows the Programming Tutorials in each chapter. The Programming Example contains a completed application that demonstrates the chapter concepts. A Reading and Study Guide is provided for each chapter to help you master the chapter's concepts.

After reading the concepts section, be sure to complete one or both of the Programming Tutorials and the Programming Example. Doing this will help you complete the Computer Exercises and Case Projects at the end of the chapter. In addition, some of the Computer Exercises require you to modify the applications created in the Programming Tutorials and Programming Example.

To run a sample application that you will create in this book:

The Windows logo key looks like this: .

1. Press and hold down the **Windows logo** key on your keyboard as you tap the letter **r**. When the Run dialog box opens, release the logo key.

2. Click the **Browse** button to open the Browse dialog box. Locate and then open the VbReloaded2012\Overview folder on the disk that contains the data files for this book.

3. Click **TicTacToe** (**TicTacToe.exe**) in the list of filenames. (Depending on how Windows is set up on your computer, you may see the .exe extension on the filename.) Click the **Open** button. The Browse dialog box closes and the Run dialog box appears again.

4. Click the **OK** button in the Run dialog box. (If an Open File - Security Warning dialog box appears, click the Run button.) After a few moments, the Tic-Tac-Toe application's user interface appears on the screen. Click the **middle square**. See Figure O-1.

4

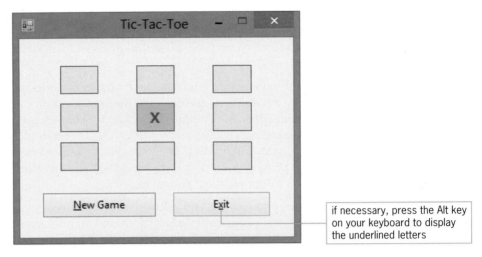

if necessary, press the Alt key on your keyboard to display the underlined letters

Figure O-1 Tic-Tac-Toe application

5. Click the **first square** in the top row, click the **middle square** in the top row, and then click the **last square** in the top row.

6. Finally, click the **middle square** in the bottom row. The "Game over! X wins." message appears in a message box. Click the **OK** button to close the message box. See Figure O-2.

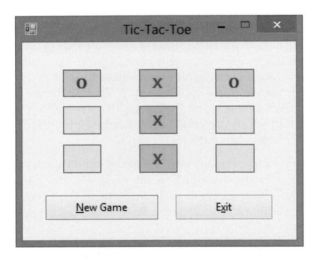

Figure O-2 Os and Xs in the interface

7. If you want to play the game again, click the **New Game** button; otherwise, click the **Exit** button.

Throughout each chapter, you will find How To boxes. Some How To boxes, like the one in Figure O-3, contain numbered steps that show you how to accomplish a task, such as how to open an existing solution in Visual Basic. You are not expected to follow the steps in these How To boxes while you are reading the chapter. Rather, these How To boxes are intended to provide a quick reference that you can use when completing the end-of-chapter Programming Tutorials, Programming Example, Computer Exercises, and Case Projects. Feel free to skim these How To boxes and use them only if and when you need to do so. The same holds true for How To boxes containing bulleted items, like the one shown in Figure O-4.

HOW TO Open an Existing Solution

1. Click FILE on the menu bar and then click Open Project.

2. Locate and then click the solution filename, which is contained in the application's solution folder. (The solution filename has an .sln filename extension, which stands for "solution.")

3. Click the Open button in the Open Project dialog box.

4. If the designer window is not open, click VIEW on the menu bar and then click Designer. Or, you can right-click the form file's name in the Solution Explorer window and then click View Designer.

Figure O-3 How to open an existing solution
© 2013 Cengage Learning

HOW TO Start an Application

- Save the solution, click DEBUG on the menu bar, and then click Start Debugging.

- Save the solution and then press the F5 key on your keyboard.

- Save the solution and then click the Start button on the Standard toolbar.

Figure O-4 How to start an application
© 2013 Cengage Learning

Other How To boxes contain information pertaining to a Visual Basic instruction. The How To box in Figure O-5, for example, contains the syntax and examples of assigning a value to an object's property while an application is running. You should study the information in these How To boxes while you are reading the chapter.

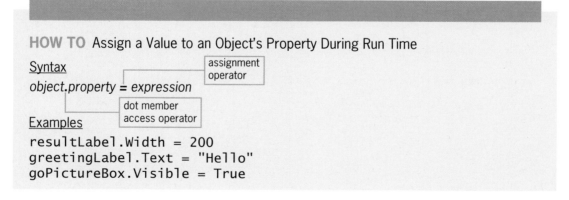

HOW TO Assign a Value to an Object's Property During Run Time

Syntax

object.property = expression

    assignment operator

    dot member access operator

Examples

```
resultLabel.Width = 200
greetingLabel.Text = "Hello"
goPictureBox.Visible = True
```

Figure O-5 How to assign a value to an object's property during run time
© 2013 Cengage Learning

The three most common learning styles are visual, auditory, and kinesthetic. Briefly, visual learners learn by watching, auditory learners learn by listening, and kinesthetic learners learn by doing. This book contains special elements designed specifically for each of the different learning styles. For example, each chapter contains videos for visual and auditory learners. The videos demonstrate and explain the concepts covered in the chapter. In addition to the Programming Tutorials, most chapters contain Try It! files for kinesthetic learners. The Try It! files allow the learner to practice with a concept before moving on to the next concept.

Summary

- Programs are the step-by-step instructions that tell a computer how to perform a task.

- Programmers use various programming languages to communicate with the computer.

- In most cases, a programmer meets with the user several times to determine the exact problem to be solved and to agree on a solution. He or she also gets together periodically with the user to verify that the solution meets the user's needs and to refine any details.

- Programmers rigorously test a program with sample data before releasing the program to the user.

- It's not unusual for the same person to perform the duties of both a software developer and a computer programmer.

Key Terms

Coding—the process of translating a solution into a language that the computer can understand

Computer programs—the directions given to computers; also called programs

Programmers—the people who write computer programs

Programming—the process of giving a mechanism the directions to accomplish a task

Programming languages—languages used to communicate with a computer

Programs—the directions given to computers; also called computer programs

CHAPTER 1

An Introduction to Visual Basic 2012

After studying Chapter 1, you should be able to:

1 Define some of the terms used in object-oriented programming
2 Create, start, and end a Visual Basic 2012 Windows application
3 Manage the windows in the integrated development environment (IDE)
4 Set the properties of an object
5 Manipulate controls
6 Use label, button, and picture box controls
7 Use the options on the FORMAT menu
8 Write Visual Basic code
9 Save, close, and open a solution
10 Run a project's executable file
11 Write an assignment statement
12 Print an application's code and interface
13 Find and correct a syntax error

Reading and Study Guide

Before you begin reading Chapter 1, view the Ch01_ReadingStudyGuide.pdf file. You can open the file using Adobe Reader, which is available for free on the Adobe Web site at *www.adobe.com/downloads/*.

Visual Basic 2012

In this book, you will learn how to create programs using the Visual Basic 2012 programming language. Visual Basic 2012 is an **object-oriented programming language**, which is a language that allows the programmer to use objects to accomplish a program's goal. An **object** is anything that can be seen, touched, or used. In other words, an object is nearly any *thing*. The objects in an object-oriented program can take on many different forms. Programs written for the Windows environment typically use objects such as check boxes, list boxes, and buttons. A payroll program, on the other hand, might utilize objects found in the real world, such as a time card object, an employee object, and a check object. Object-oriented programming is more simply referred to as **OOP**.

Every object in an object-oriented program is created from a **class**, which is a pattern that the computer uses to create the object. The class contains the instructions that tell the computer how the object should look and behave. An object created from a class is called an **instance** of the class and is said to be **instantiated** from the class. An analogy involving a cookie cutter and cookies is often used to describe a class and its objects: The class is the cookie cutter, and the objects instantiated from the class are the cookies, as illustrated in Figure 1-1. You will learn more about classes and objects throughout this book.

Figure 1-1   Illustration of a class and objects
OpenClipArt.org/jarda

Visual Basic 2012 is one of the languages included in Visual Studio 2012, which is available in many different editions, such as Ultimate, Premium, Professional, and Express. Each of these products includes an **integrated development environment (IDE)**, which is an environment that contains all the tools and features you need to create, run, and test your programs. (At the time of this writing, you can download a free copy of one or more of the Express editions on the Microsoft Web site at *www.microsoft.com/visualstudio/eng/downloads*.)

You can use Visual Basic to create programs, called **applications**, for the Windows environment or for the Web. A Windows application has a Windows user interface and runs on a personal computer. A **user interface** is what the user sees and interacts with while an application is running. Examples of Windows applications include graphics programs, data-entry systems, and games. A Web application, on the other hand, has a Web user interface and runs on a server. You access a Web application using your computer's browser. Examples of Web applications include e-commerce applications available on the Internet, and employee handbook applications accessible on a company's intranet. You can also use Visual Basic to create applications for tablet PCs and mobile devices, such as cell phones and PDAs (personal digital assistants).

Creating a Visual Basic Windows Application

Windows applications in Visual Basic are composed of solutions, projects, and files. A solution is a container that stores the projects and files for an entire application. Although the solutions in this book contain only one project, a solution can contain several projects. A project also is a container, but it stores only the files associated with that particular project.

Before you can create a Windows application in Visual Basic, you must start Visual Studio; the steps for doing this are listed in the How To box shown in Figure 1-2. As mentioned in the Overview, you are not expected to follow the steps listed in a How To box right now. Rather, the steps are intended to be used as a quick reference when you are completing the Programming Tutorials, Programming Example, Exercises, and Case Projects located at the end of each chapter. For now, simply skim the How To box to see what it contains.

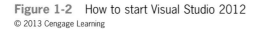

HOW TO Start Visual Studio 2012

1. *Windows 8*: If necessary, tap the Windows logo key to switch to the Windows 8 tile-based mode. *If you are using Visual Studio Professional 2012*, click the Visual Studio 2012 tile. *If you are using Visual Studio Express 2012 for Windows Desktop*, click the VS Express for Desktop tile.

   Windows 7: Click the Start button on the Windows 7 taskbar and then point to All Programs. *If you are using Visual Studio Professional 2012*, click Microsoft Visual Studio 2012 on the All Programs menu and then click Visual Studio 2012. *If you are using Visual Studio Express 2012 for Windows Desktop*, click Microsoft Visual Studio 2012 Express on the All Programs menu and then click VS Express for Desktop.

2. *If the Choose Default Environment Settings dialog box appears*, click Visual Basic Development Settings and then click Start Visual Studio. *If the Choose Default Environment Settings dialog box does not appear*, you can select the appropriate settings (if necessary) as follows: Click TOOLS on the menu bar, click Import and Export Settings, select the Reset all settings radio button, click the Next button, and then select the appropriate radio button. If the Next button is available, click it and then click Visual Basic Development Settings. Click the Finish button and then click the Close button.

3. To reset the IDE to the default layout for Visual Basic, click WINDOW on the menu bar, click Reset Window Layout, and then click the Yes button.

4. To show/hide the underlined letters, called access keys, press the Alt key on your keyboard.

 Ch01-Start
Visual Studio

Figure 1-2   How to start Visual Studio 2012
© 2013 Cengage Learning

When you start Visual Studio 2012 on a Windows 8 system, your screen will appear similar to either Figure 1-3 or Figure 1-4, depending on the edition of Visual Studio you are using. (If you are using a Windows 7 system, the text in the title bar will be left-aligned rather than centered.) However, your Recent list might include the names of projects or solutions with which you have recently worked. In addition, your menu bar may contain underlined letters, called access keys. The access keys, which are shown in Figure 1-4, can be displayed and also hidden by pressing the Alt key on your keyboard. You will learn about access keys in Chapter 2.

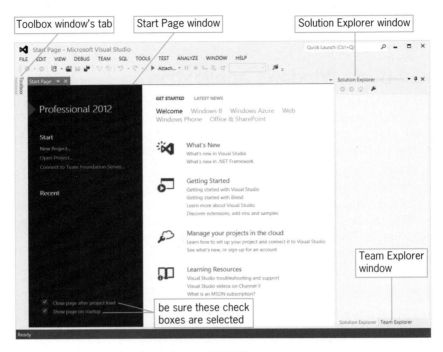

Figure 1-3   Visual Studio Professional 2012 startup screen

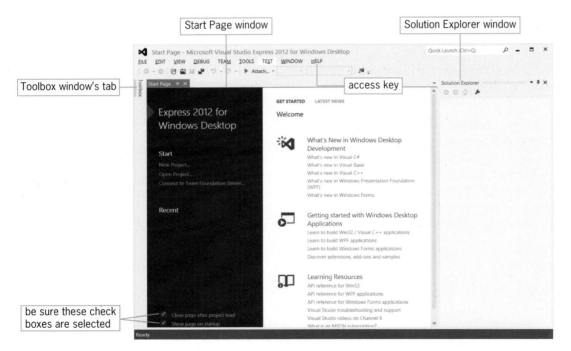

Figure 1-4   Visual Studio Express 2012 for Windows Desktop startup screen

As Figures 1-3 and 1-4 indicate, the IDE contains several windows. The Toolbox window in both figures is auto-hidden. (You will learn how to auto-hide a window in the *Managing the Windows in the IDE* section of this chapter.)

The steps for creating a Visual Basic 2012 Windows application are shown in Figure 1-5. Here again, you don't need to perform the steps right now; just glance over the figure to familiarize yourself with its contents. Figure 1-6 shows an example of the Options dialog box mentioned in the steps. Figures 1-7 and 1-8 show an example of a completed New Project dialog box in Visual Studio Professional 2012 and in Visual Studio Express 2012 for Windows Desktop, respectively.

HOW TO Create a Visual Basic 2012 Windows Application

1. If necessary, start Visual Studio 2012.

2. This step is necessary so that your screen agrees with the figures and tutorial instructions in this book. Click TOOLS on the menu bar and then click Options to open the Options dialog box. Click the Projects and Solutions node. Use the information shown in Figure 1-6 to select and deselect the appropriate check boxes. (Your dialog box will look slightly different if you are using the Express edition of Visual Studio 2012. It will also look slightly different if you are using Windows 7.) When you are finished, click the OK button to close the Options dialog box.

3. Click FILE on the menu bar and then click New Project to open the New Project dialog box.

4. If necessary, expand the Visual Basic node in the Installed Templates list, and then (if necessary) click Windows.

5. If necessary, click Windows Forms Application in the middle column of the dialog box.

6. Enter an appropriate name and location in the Name and Location boxes, respectively. (You can use the Browse button to enter the location.)

7. If necessary, select the Create directory for solution check box.

8. Enter an appropriate name in the Solution name box. Examples of completed New Project dialog boxes are shown in Figures 1-7 (Visual Studio Professional 2012) and 1-8 (Visual Studio Express 2012 for Windows Desktop).

9. Click the OK button.

Ch01-Create
Windows
Application

Figure 1-5 How to create a Visual Basic 2012 Windows application
© 2013 Cengage Learning

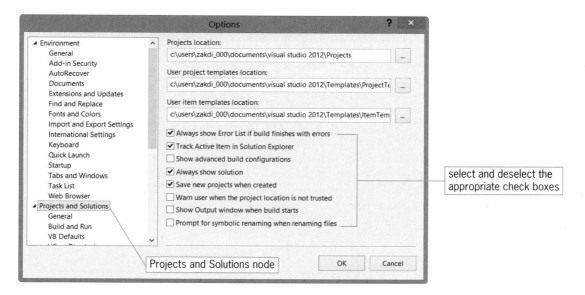

Figure 1-6 Options dialog box

Figure 1-7   New Project dialog box (Visual Studio Professional 2012)

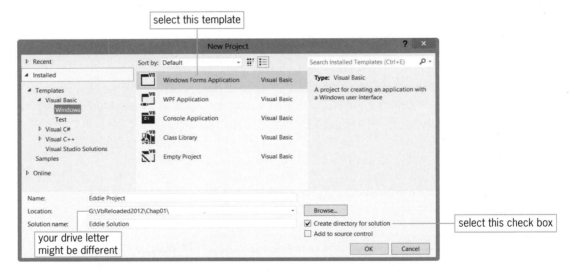

Figure 1-8   New Project dialog box (Visual Studio Express 2012 for Windows Desktop)

When you click the OK button in the New Project dialog box, the computer creates a solution and adds a Visual Basic project to the solution. The names of the solution and project, along with other information pertaining to the project, appear in the Solution Explorer window, as shown in Figure 1-9. Also notice that, in addition to the windows shown earlier in Figures 1-3 and 1-4, three other windows appear in the IDE: Windows Form Designer, Properties, and Data Sources. (If you are using the Express edition of Visual Studio, you will not have the Team Explorer window, and the menu bar will not contain the SQL and ANALYZE items.)

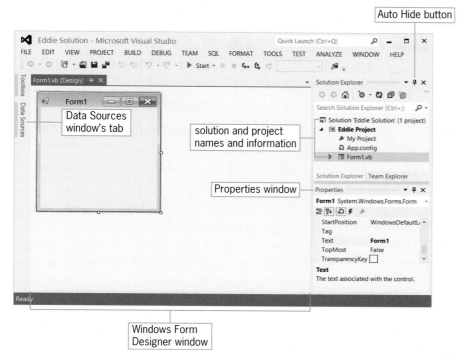

Figure 1-9   Solution and Visual Basic project

Managing the Windows in the IDE

You will usually find it easier to work in the IDE if you either close or auto-hide the windows you are not currently using. The easiest way to close an open window is to click the Close button on the window's title bar. In most cases, the VIEW menu provides an appropriate option for opening a closed window.

Rather than closing a window, you can auto-hide it using the Auto Hide button (shown earlier in Figure 1-9) on its title bar. The Auto Hide button is a toggle button: Clicking it once activates it, and clicking it again deactivates it. The Toolbox and Data Sources windows shown earlier in Figure 1-9 are auto-hidden windows.

Figure 1-10 lists various ways of managing the windows in the IDE. As mentioned in the Overview, you don't need to read every bulleted item in a How To box right now. But you should browse the How To box to get familiar with its contents.

HOW TO Manage the Windows in the IDE

- To close an open window, click the Close button on its title bar.
- To open a closed window, use an option on the VIEW menu.
- To auto-hide a window, click the Auto Hide (vertical pushpin) button on its title bar.
- To temporarily display an auto-hidden window, click the window's tab. To subsequently hide the window, click the tab again.
- To permanently display an auto-hidden window, click the Auto Hide (horizontal pushpin) button on its title bar.
- To reset the window layout, click WINDOW on the menu bar, click Reset Window Layout, and then click the Yes button.

ChO1-Manage
Windows

Figure 1-10   How to manage the windows in the IDE
© 2013 Cengage Learning

In the next several sections, you will take a closer look at the Windows Form Designer, Solution Explorer, Properties, and Toolbox windows.

The Windows Form Designer Window

Figure 1-11 shows the **Windows Form Designer window**, where you create (or design) your application's graphical user interface, more simply referred to as a **GUI**. Only a Windows Form object appears in the designer window shown in the figure. A **Windows Form object**, or **form**, is the foundation for the user interface in a Windows application. You create the user interface by adding other objects, such as buttons and text boxes, to the form. The title bar, which appears at the top of the form, contains a default caption (Form1) along with Minimize, Maximize, and Close buttons. (The title bar text will be left-aligned in Windows 7.) At the top of the designer window is a tab labeled Form1.vb [Design]. Form1.vb is the name of the file (on your computer's hard disk or on another device) that contains the Visual Basic instructions associated with the form, and [Design] identifies the window as the designer window.

name of the disk file
containing the instructions
associated with the form

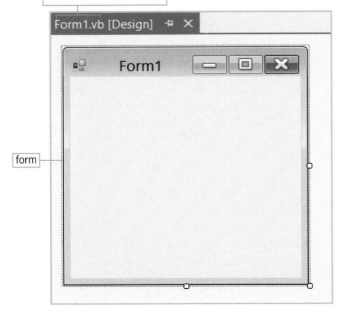

form

Figure 1-11   Windows Form Designer window

As you learned earlier in this chapter, all objects in an object-oriented program are instantiated (created) from a class. A form, for example, is an instance of the Windows Form class. The form is automatically instantiated for you when you create a Windows application.

The Solution Explorer Window

The **Solution Explorer window** displays a list of the projects contained in the current solution and the items contained in each project. Figure 1-12 shows the Solution Explorer window for the Eddie Solution, which contains one project named Eddie Project. Within the Eddie Project are the My Project folder and two files named App.config and Form1.vb. The project also contains other items, which are typically kept hidden. However, you can display and also subsequently hide the additional items by clicking the Show All Files button. The .vb in the Form1.vb filename indicates that the file is a Visual Basic source file. A **source file** is a file that contains program instructions, called **code**. The Form1.vb file contains the code associated with the form displayed in the designer window. You can view the code using the Code Editor window, which you will learn about in the *The Code Editor Window* section of this chapter.

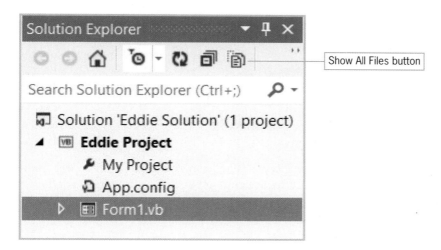

Figure 1-12 Solution Explorer window

The Form1.vb source file is referred to as a **form file** because it contains the code associated with a form. The code associated with the first form included in a project is automatically stored in a form file named Form1.vb. The code associated with the second form in the same project is stored in a form file named Form2.vb, and so on. Because a project can contain many forms and, therefore, many form files, you should give each form file a more meaningful name. Doing this will help you keep track of the various form files in the project. You can use the Properties window to change the filename.

The Properties Window

As is everything in an object-oriented language, a file is an object. Each object has a set of attributes, called **properties**, that determine its appearance and behavior. The names of the properties appear in the **Properties window** along with each property's current value (or setting). When an object is created, a default value is assigned to each of its properties. The Properties window shown in Figure 1-13 lists the default values assigned to the properties of the Form1.vb file. You can tell that the properties refer to the Form1.vb file because Form1.vb appears in the Object box in the window; the Object box always contains the name of the selected object. In this case, the Form1.vb file is selected in the Solution Explorer window, as shown earlier in Figure 1-12. To change the value of a property, you first select the property in the Properties list. A brief description of the selected property appears in the Description pane, which is located at the bottom of the Properties window. You then either type the new value in the property's Settings box or select the new value from a list or dialog box. (To restore a property to its default value, right-click the property in the Properties list and then click Reset on the context menu.)

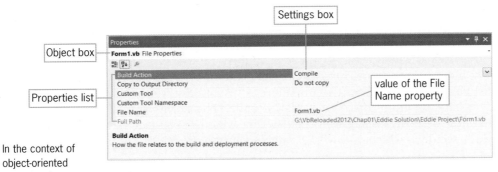

Figure 1-13   Properties window

In the context of object-oriented programming (OOP), the Properties window "exposes" an object's attributes (properties) to the programmer, allowing the programmer to change one or more default values.

You can display the property names either alphabetically (using the second button below the Object box) or by category (using the first button below the Object box). However, it's usually easier to work with the Properties window when the properties are listed in alphabetical order, as they are in Figure 1-13.

Properties of a Windows Form

Like a file, a Windows form also has a set of properties. The form's properties will appear in the Properties window when you select the form in the designer window. The Properties window in Figure 1-14 shows some of the properties of a Windows form. The vertical scroll bar on the Properties window indicates that there are more properties to view.

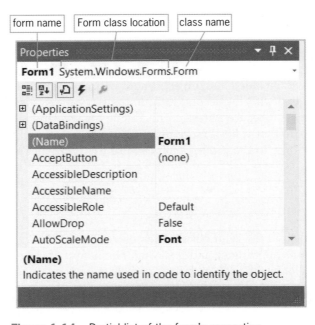

Figure 1-14   Partial list of the form's properties

Notice that Form1 System.Windows.Forms.Form appears in the Object box in Figure 1-14. Form1 is the default name assigned to the first form in a project. The name is automatically assigned when the form is instantiated (created). In System.Windows.Forms.Form, Form is the name of the class (pattern) used to instantiate the form. System.Windows.Forms is the namespace that contains the Form class definition. A **class definition** is a block of code that specifies (or defines) an object's appearance and behavior. All class definitions in Visual Basic 2012 are contained in namespaces, which you can picture as blocks of memory cells inside the computer. Each **namespace** contains the code that defines a group of related classes. The System.Windows.Forms namespace contains the definition of the Windows Form class. It also contains the class definitions for objects you add to a form, such as buttons and text boxes.

The period that separates each word in System.Windows.Forms.Form is called the **dot member access operator**. Similar to the backslash (\) in a folder path, the dot member access operator indicates a hierarchy, but of namespaces rather than folders. In other words, the backslash in the path G:\VbReloaded2012\Chap01\Eddie Solution\Eddie Project\Form1.vb (shown earlier in Figure 1-13) indicates that the Form1.vb file is contained in (or is a member of) the Eddie Project folder, which is a member of the Eddie Solution folder, which is a member of the Chap01 folder, which is a member of the VbReloaded2012 folder, which is a member of the G: drive. Likewise, the name System.Windows.Forms.Form indicates that the Form class is a member of the Forms namespace, which is a member of the Windows namespace, which is a member of the System namespace. The dot member access operator allows the computer to locate the Form class in the computer's internal memory, similar to the way the backslash (\) allows it to locate the Form1.vb file on your computer's disk.

Name and Text Properties

As you do to a form file, you should assign a more meaningful name to a Windows form because doing so will help you keep track of the various forms in a project. Unlike a file, a Windows form has a Name property rather than a File Name property. You use the name entered in an object's Name property to refer to the object in code, so each object must have a unique name. The name you assign to an object must begin with a letter and contain only letters, numbers, and the underscore character. The name cannot include punctuation characters or spaces.

There are several conventions for naming objects in Visual Basic. In this book, you will use a naming convention that begins each object's name with the object's purpose, followed by the name of its class. In addition, form names will be entered using **Pascal case**, which capitalizes the first letter in the name and the first letter of each subsequent word in the name. Following this naming convention, you would assign the name MainForm to the main form in an application. "Main" reminds you of the form's purpose, and "Form" indicates the class used to create the form. Similarly, a secondary form used to access an employee database might be named EmployeeDataForm or PersonnelForm.

 Pascal is a programming language named in honor of the seventeenth-century French mathematician Blaise Pascal.

In addition to changing the form's Name property, you should change its Text property, which controls the text displayed in the form's title bar. Form1 is the default value assigned to the Text property of the first form in a project. Better and more descriptive values for the Text property of a form include Commission Calculator and Employee Information.

The Name and Text properties of a Windows form should always be changed to more meaningful values. The Name property is used by the programmer when coding the application. The Text property, on the other hand, is read by the user while the application is running.

StartPosition Property

When an application is started, the computer uses the form's StartPosition property to determine the form's initial position on the screen. To display a form in the middle of the screen, you change its StartPosition property from WindowsDefaultLocation to CenterScreen.

Font Property

A form's Font property determines the type, style, and size of the font used to display the text on the form. A font is the general shape of the characters in the text. Segoe UI, Tahoma, and Microsoft Sans Serif are examples of font types. Font styles include regular, bold, and italic. The numbers 9, 12, and 18 are examples of font sizes, which are typically measured in points, with one point (pt) equaling 1/72 of an inch. The recommended font type for applications created for systems running either Windows 8 or Windows 7 is Segoe UI because it offers improved readability on a computer screen. Segoe is pronounced SEE-go, and UI stands for user interface. The recommended font size is 9pt. (However, to make the figures in the book more readable, some of the interfaces created in this book will use a larger font size.)

Size Property

Like any Windows object, you can size a form by selecting it and then dragging its sizing handles. You also can size an object by selecting it and then pressing and holding down the Shift key as you press the up, down, right, or left arrow key on your keyboard. In addition, you can set the object's Size property. The Size property contains two numbers separated by a comma and a space. The first number represents the object's width, and the second number represents its height. Both measurements are stated in pixels. A pixel, which is short for "picture element," is one spot in a grid of thousands of such spots that form an image either produced on the screen by a computer or printed on a page by a printer.

The answers to Mini-Quiz questions are located in Appendix A. Each question is associated with one or more objectives listed at the beginning of the chapter.

Mini-Quiz 1-1

1. Windows applications created in Visual Studio 2012 are composed of _____. (2)

   a. solutions
   b. projects
   c. files
   d. all of the above

2. How do you auto-hide a window? (3)

3. How do you temporarily display an auto-hidden window? (3)

4. How do you reset the windows in the IDE? (3)

5. The value assigned to a form's _____ property appears in the form's title bar. (4)

   a. Caption
   b. Name
   c. Text
   d. Title

6. You can display a form in the middle of the screen by setting the form's _____ property to CenterScreen. (4)

   a. StartPosition
   b. ScreenLocation
   c. StartLocation
   d. CenterScreen

The Toolbox Window

Figure 1-15 shows a portion of the Toolbox window that appears when you are using the Windows Form designer. The **Toolbox window**, referred to more simply as the **toolbox**, contains the tools you use when creating your application's user interface. Each tool represents a class from which an object, such as a button or check box, can be instantiated. The instantiated objects, called **controls**, will appear on the form. Figure 1-16 lists the steps for adding a control to a form. When a control is added to a form, its Font property will be assigned the same value as the form's Font property.

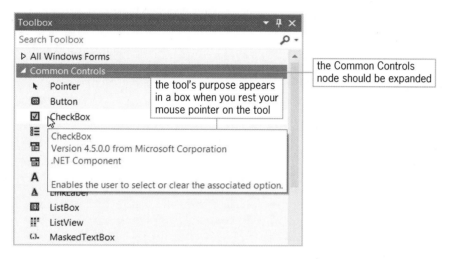

Figure 1-15   Toolbox window

> Using OOP terminology, the control's Font property "inherits" the value stored in the form's Font property.

HOW TO Add a Control to a Form

1. Click a tool in the toolbox, but do not release the mouse button.

2. Hold down the mouse button as you drag the mouse pointer to the form. You will see a solid box, an outline of a rectangle, and a plus box following the mouse pointer.

3. Release the mouse button.

Additional ways:

- Click a tool in the toolbox and then click the form.

- Click a tool in the toolbox, place the mouse pointer on the form, and then press the left mouse button and drag the mouse pointer until the control is the desired size.

- Double-click a tool in the toolbox.

 Ch01-Adding a Control

Figure 1-16   How to add a control to a form
© 2013 Cengage Learning

Controls on a form can be selected, sized, moved, deleted, restored, locked, and unlocked. Locking a control prevents it from being moved inadvertently as you are working in the IDE. When a control is locked, a small lock appears in the upper-left corner of the control. Figure 1-17 summarizes the methods used to manipulate the controls on a form.

Ch01-
Manipulating
Controls

HOW TO Manipulate the Controls on a Form

- To select a control, click it in the designer window. You can also click the list arrow button in the Properties window's Object box and then click the control's name.

- To size a control, use the sizing handles that appear on the control when it is selected; or, set its Size property.

- To move a control, drag the control to the desired location; or, set its Location property.

- To delete a control, select the control in the designer window and then press the Delete key on your keyboard. To restore the control, click EDIT on the menu bar and then click Undo.

- To lock and unlock the controls, right-click the form (or any control on the form) and then click Lock Controls on the context menu. The Lock Controls option is a toggle option: Clicking it once activates it, and clicking it again deactivates it. You can also click FORMAT on the menu bar and then click Lock Controls.

Figure 1-17 How to manipulate the controls on a form
© 2013 Cengage Learning

In the next three sections, you will learn about the Label control, the Button control, and the Picture box control, all of which appear in the user interface shown in Figure 1-18. (As you will learn in Programming Tutorial 1, the interface actually contains two picture boxes; one is hidden behind the other in the figure.)

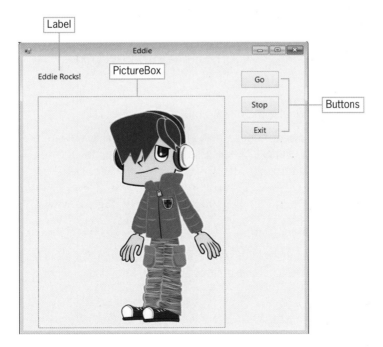

Figure 1-18 Eddie application's user interface
Image by Diane Zak; Created with Reallusion CrazyTalk Animator

The Label Control

You use the Label tool to add a label control to a form. The purpose of a **label control** is to display text that the user is not allowed to edit while the application is running. Label controls are used in an interface to identify the contents of other controls, such as the contents of text boxes and list boxes. The label control in Figure 1-18 identifies the contents of a picture box control. Label controls are also used to display program output, such as the result of a calculation.

You use the Name property to give a label control a more meaningful name. You use the Text property to specify the text to display inside the control. The Name property is used by the programmer when coding the application, whereas the Text property is read by the user while the application is running.

Some programmers assign meaningful names to all of the label controls in an interface, while others do so only for label controls that display program output; this book follows the latter practice. In the naming convention used in this book, control names are made up of the control's purpose followed by the control's class (in this case, Label). Unlike form names, which are entered using Pascal case, control names are entered using **camel case**. This means that you enter the first word in the control's name in lowercase and then capitalize the first letter of each subsequent word in the name, like this: `salesTaxLabel`. Camel case refers to the fact that the uppercase letters appear as "humps" in the name because they are taller than the lowercase letters.

The Button Control

You use the Button tool to instantiate a **button control**, whose purpose is to perform an immediate action when clicked. The OK and Cancel buttons are examples of button controls found in many Windows applications. Each button in the interface shown earlier in Figure 1-18 will perform an action when it is clicked: The Go button will display an animated image of a character named Eddie, the Stop button will display a static image of Eddie, and the Exit button will close the application. Here, too, you use the Name property to give a button control a more meaningful name. The name should end with the word "Button," which is the class from which a button control is created. You use the Text property to specify the text to display on the button's face.

The Picture Box Control

The PictureBox tool instantiates a **picture box control** for displaying an image on the form, such as the image of Eddie shown earlier in Figure 1-18. You use the control's Name property to assign a more meaningful name (which should end with PictureBox) to the control, and use its Image property to specify the image to display. A PictureBox control's SizeMode property handles how the image will be displayed and can be set to Normal, StretchImage, AutoSize, CenterImage, or Zoom.

Using the FORMAT Menu

The FORMAT menu provides options for aligning and sizing two or more controls, as well as centering one or more controls on the form. Three of the options are listed and explained in Figure 1-19.

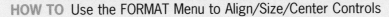

HOW TO Use the FORMAT Menu to Align/Size/Center Controls

● To align/size two or more controls: Click the reference control and then press and hold down the Ctrl (Control) key as you click the other controls you want to align/size. Click FORMAT on the menu bar and then click one of the following options:

✔ Align option: aligns two or more controls by their left, right, top, or bottom borders

✔ Make Same Size option: makes two or more controls the same width and/or height

● To center one or more controls either horizontally or vertically on the form: Click a control that you want to center and then (if necessary) press and hold down the Ctrl (Control) key as you click the other controls you want to center. Click FORMAT on the menu bar and then click the following option:

✔ Center in Form option: centers one or more controls either horizontally or vertically on the form

Note: To select a group of controls on the form, place the mouse pointer slightly above and to the left of the first control you want to select. Press and hold down the left mouse button as you drag the mouse pointer. A dotted rectangle appears as you are dragging. When all of the controls you want to select are within (or at least touched by) the dotted rectangle, release the mouse button.

Ch01-
FORMAT
menu

Figure 1-19   How to use the FORMAT menu to align/size/center controls
© 2013 Cengage Learning

When aligning and sizing controls, the first control you select should always be the one whose location and/or size you want to match. For example, to align the left border of the Label2 control with the left border of the Label1 control, you select the Label1 control first and then select the Label2 control. However, to make the Label1 control the same size as the Label2 control, you must select the Label2 control before selecting the Label1 control. The first control you select is referred to as the **reference control**. The reference control will have white sizing handles, whereas the other selected controls will have black sizing handles. You will experiment with the FORMAT menu in both Programming Tutorials at the end of this chapter.

The answers to Mini-Quiz questions are located in Appendix A. Each question is associated with one or more objectives listed at the beginning of the chapter.

Mini-Quiz 1-2

1. How do you delete a control from the form? (5)

2. Amounts calculated by an application should be displayed in a _____ control on the form. (4, 6)

   a. button

   b. form

   c. label

   d. text

3. Using the naming convention you learned in this book, which of the following is a valid name for a control? (4, 6)

   a. calcButton

   b. salesTaxLabel

   c. birthdayPictureBox

   d. all of the above

4. Which of the following properties determines the image that appears in a picture box? (4, 6)

 a. Icon

 b. Image

 c. Picture

 d. none of the above

5. If you want to use the FORMAT menu to align the top border of the Label5 control with the top border of the Label4 control, which of the two controls should you select first? (7)

The Code Editor Window

After creating your application's user interface, you can begin entering the Visual Basic instructions (code) that tell the controls how to respond to the user's actions. Those actions—such as clicking, double-clicking, and scrolling—are called **events**. You tell a control how to respond to an event by writing an **event procedure**, which is a set of Visual Basic instructions that are processed only when the event occurs. You enter an event procedure's code in the **Code Editor window**. Figure 1-20 lists various ways to open the Code Editor window, and Figure 1-21 shows the Code Editor window opened in the IDE.

In object-oriented programming (OOP), an event is considered a behavior of an object because it represents an action to which the object can respond. The Code Editor window "exposes" an object's behaviors to the programmer.

HOW TO Open the Code Editor Window

- Right-click the form and then click View Code on the context menu.

- Verify that the designer window is the active window. Click VIEW on the menu bar and then click Code.

- Verify that the designer window is the active window. Press the F7 key on your keyboard.

- Click the form or a control on the form, click the Events button in the Properties window, and then double-click the desired event.

Note: To display line numbers in the Code Editor window, click TOOLS on the menu bar and then click Options. Click the arrow next to Text Editor to expand the node, click Basic, select the Line numbers check box, and then click the OK button.

Figure 1-20   How to open the Code Editor window
© 2013 Cengage Learning

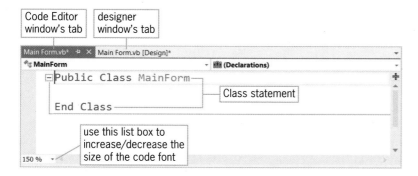

Figure 1-21   Code Editor window

The `Public` keyword indicates that the class can be used by code defined outside of the class.

The Code Editor window contains the Class statement, which is used to define a class in Visual Basic. Between the statement's Public Class and End Class clauses, you enter the code to tell the form and its objects how to react to the user's actions.

As indicated in Figure 1-22, the Code Editor window also contains a Class Name list box and a Method Name list box. The **Class Name list box** lists the names of the objects included in the user interface, and the **Method Name list box** lists the events to which the selected object is capable of responding. You use the Class Name and Method Name list boxes to select the object and event, respectively, that you want to code. For example, to code the exitButton's Click event, you first select exitButton in the Class Name list box and then select Click in the Method Name list box. When you do this, a code template for the exitButton's Click event procedure appears in the Code Editor window, as shown in Figure 1-22. The code template helps you follow the rules of the Visual Basic language. The rules of a programming language are called its **syntax**.

Figure 1-22   Code template for the exitButton_Click procedure

The first line in the code template is called the **procedure header**, and the last line is called the **procedure footer**. The procedure header begins with the two keywords `Private Sub`. A **keyword** is a word that has a special meaning in a programming language. Keywords appear in a different color from the rest of the code. The `Private` keyword in Figure 1-22 indicates that the button's Click event procedure can be used only within the current Code Editor window. The `Sub` keyword is an abbreviation of the term **sub procedure**, which is a block of code that performs a specific task.

Following the `Sub` keyword is the name of the object, an underscore, the name of the event, and parentheses containing some text. For now, you do not have to be concerned with the text that appears between the parentheses. After the closing parenthesis is `Handles exitButton.Click`. This part of the procedure header indicates that the procedure handles (or is associated with) the exitButton's Click event. It tells the computer to process the procedure only when the exitButton is clicked.

The code template ends with the procedure footer, which contains the keywords `End Sub`. You enter your Visual Basic instructions at the location of the insertion point, which appears between the Private Sub and End Sub clauses in Figure 1-22. The Code Editor automatically indents the line between the procedure header and footer. Indenting the lines within a procedure makes the instructions easier to read and is a common programming practice.

When the user clicks an Exit button on a form, it usually indicates that he or she wants to end the application. You can stop an application using the `Me.Close()` instruction.

The Me.Close() Instruction

The `Me.Close()` instruction tells the computer to close the current form. If the current form is the only form in the application, closing it terminates the entire application. In the instruction, `Me` is a keyword that refers to the current form, and `Close` is one of the methods available in Visual Basic. A **method** is a predefined procedure that you can call (or invoke) when needed. For example, if you want the computer to close the current form when the user clicks the Exit button, you enter the `Me.Close()` instruction in the exitButton's Click event procedure, as shown in Figure 1-23. Notice the empty set of parentheses after the method's name in the instruction. The parentheses are required when calling some Visual Basic methods. However, depending on the method, the parentheses may or may not be empty. If you forget to enter the parentheses, the Code Editor will enter them for you when you move the insertion point to another line in the Code Editor window.

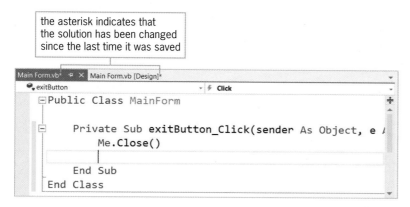

Figure 1-23 `Me.Close()` instruction entered in the exitButton_Click procedure

When the user clicks the Exit button while the application is running, the computer processes the instructions shown in the exitButton_Click procedure one after another in the order in which they appear in the procedure. In programming, this is referred to as **sequential processing** or as the **sequence structure**. (You will learn about two other programming structures, called selection and repetition, in later chapters.)

Saving a Solution

The asterisk (*) that appears on the designer and Code Editor tabs in Figure 1-23 indicates that a change was made to the solution since the last time it was saved. It is a good idea to save the current solution every 10 or 15 minutes so that you will not lose a lot of your work if the computer loses power. When you save a solution, the computer saves any changes made to the files included in the solution. It also removes the asterisk that appears on the designer and Code Editor tabs. Figure 1-24 lists two ways to save a solution.

HOW TO Save a Solution

- Click FILE on the menu bar and then click Save All.
- Click the Save All button on the Standard toolbar.

Figure 1-24 How to save a solution
© 2013 Cengage Learning

Starting and Ending an Application

Before you start an application for the first time, you should open the Project Designer window and verify the name of the **startup form**, which is the form that the computer automatically displays each time the application is started. Figure 1-25 shows the steps you follow to specify the startup form's name, and Figure 1-26 shows the name of the startup form (in this case, MainForm) selected in the Project Designer window.

HOW TO Specify the Startup Form

1. Use one of the following ways to open the Project Designer window:
   - ✔ Right-click My Project in the Solution Explorer window and then click Open on the context menu.
   - ✔ Click PROJECT on the menu bar and then click *<project name>* Properties on the menu.
   - ✔ Right-click the project's name in the Solution Explorer window and then click Properties.
2. Click the Application tab, if necessary.
3. If the startup form's name does not appear in the Startup form list box, click the Startup form list arrow and then click the appropriate form name in the list.
4. Click the Close button on the Project Designer window.

Figure 1-25 How to specify the startup form
© 2013 Cengage Learning

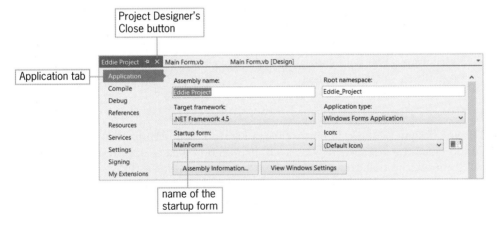

Figure 1-26 Project Designer window

Figure 1-27 shows various ways to start an application, and Figure 1-28 shows the result of starting the Eddie application. The computer automatically displays the startup form, which in this case is the MainForm.

HOW TO Start an Application

- Save the solution, click DEBUG on the menu bar and then click Start Debugging.
- Save the solution and then press the F5 key on your keyboard.
- Save the solution and then click the Start button on the Standard toolbar.

Figure 1-27 How to start an application
© 2013 Cengage Learning

Figure 1-28 Result of starting the Eddie application
Image by Diane Zak; Created with Reallusion CrazyTalk Animator

When you start a Visual Basic application, the computer automatically creates a file that can be run outside of the IDE (such as from the Run dialog box in Windows). The file is referred to as an **executable file**. The executable file's name is the same as the project's name, except it ends with .exe. The name of the executable file for the Eddie Project, for example, is Eddie Project.exe. You can use the Project Designer window to change the executable file's name; or, you can use Windows to rename the file. The steps for using the Project Designer window are listed in Figure 1-29.

HOW TO Change the Executable File's Name in the Project Designer Window

1. Open the Project Designer window using one of the ways listed earlier in Figure 1-25.

2. Click the Application tab, if necessary.

3. Replace the current name in the Assembly name box with the new name. For example, to change the executable file's name from Eddie Project.exe to Eddie.exe, replace the Eddie Project text in the Assembly name box with Eddie. Visual Basic will automatically append the .exe extension to the filename when the application is started.

4. Click the Close button on the Project Designer window.

Figure 1-29 How to change the executable file's name in the Project Designer window
© 2013 Cengage Learning

The computer stores the executable file in the project's bin\Debug folder. In this case, the file will be stored in the VbReloaded2012\Chap01\Eddie Solution\Eddie Project\bin\Debug folder. When you are finished with an application, you typically give the user only the executable file because it does not allow the user to modify the application's code. To allow someone to modify the code, you need to provide the entire solution.

The way you end (or close) a running application depends on the application's interface. To end the Eddie application shown in Figure 1-28, you can click either the Exit button in the interface or the Close button on the application's title bar. To close Visual Studio 2012, you can use either the Exit option on Visual Studio's FILE menu or the Close button on its title bar. Figure 1-30 lists various ways of ending an application.

HOW TO End a Running Application
- Click an Exit button in the interface.
- Click FILE on the application's menu bar and then click Exit.
- Click the Close button on the application's title bar.
- Click the designer window to make it the active window, click DEBUG on the menu bar, and then click Stop Debugging.
- Click the Stop Debugging button on the Standard toolbar.

Figure 1-30 How to end a running application
© 2013 Cengage Learning

Assigning a Value to a Property During Run Time

As you learned earlier, you use the Properties window to set an object's properties during design time, which is when you are building the interface. You can also set an object's properties during run time, which occurs while an application is running; you do this using an assignment statement. An **assignment statement** is one of many different types of Visual Basic instructions. Its purpose is to assign a value to something (such as to the property of an object) while an application is running.

Figure 1-31 shows the syntax of an assignment statement that assigns a value to an object's property. In the syntax, *object* and *property* are the names of the object and property, respectively, to which you want the value of the *expression* assigned. The *expression* can be numeric, as shown in the first example in the figure. It can also be a string, as shown in the second example. A **string** is zero or more characters enclosed in quotation marks. The expression can also be a keyword, as shown in the third example in the figure. Notice that the assignment statement's syntax contains the dot member access operator (a period) and an equal sign. The operator indicates that the *property* is a member of the *object*. When used in an assignment statement, the equal sign is called the **assignment operator**.

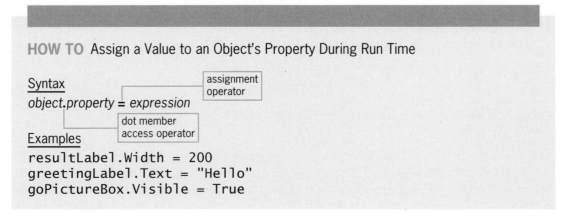

HOW TO Assign a Value to an Object's Property During Run Time

Syntax
object.property = expression

assignment operator

dot member access operator

Examples
```
resultLabel.Width = 200
greetingLabel.Text = "Hello"
goPictureBox.Visible = True
```

Figure 1-31 How to assign a value to an object's property during run time
© 2013 Cengage Learning

When the computer processes an assignment statement, it assigns the value of the expression that appears on the right side of the assignment operator to the object and property that appear on the left side of the operator. The assignment statement `resultLabel.Width = 200`, for example, assigns the number 200 to the label's Width property. Likewise, the assignment statement `greetingLabel.Text = "Hello"` assigns the string "Hello" to the Text property of the greetingLabel. Recall that a control's Text property specifies the text to display inside the control. The assignment statement `goPictureBox.Visible = True` assigns the keyword `True` to the Visible property of the goPictureBox. When a control's Visible property is set to True, the control is visible on the form while the application is running. To make a control invisible during run time, you set its Visible property to False, like this: `goPictureBox.Visible = False`. Figure 1-32 shows the appropriate assignment statements entered in the Eddie application's Code Editor window. (Recall that the application's interface contains two picture boxes. The picture boxes are named stopPictureBox and goPictureBox. You will create the Eddie application in Programming Tutorial 1.)

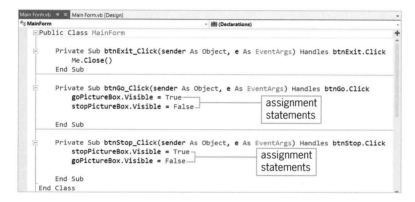

Figure 1-32 Assignment statements entered in the Code Editor window

Printing the Code and User Interface

You should always print a copy of your application's code and user interface because the printout will help you understand and maintain the application in the future. Figure 1-33 shows the steps you follow to print the code and the interface during design time. (In Chapter 2, you will learn how to print the interface during run time.)

HOW TO Print the Code and Interface During Design Time

To print the code:

1. Make the Code Editor window the active window. Collapse any code that you do not want to print. You collapse the code by clicking the minus box that appears next to the code.

2. Click FILE on the menu bar and then click Print to open the Print dialog box. If you don't want to print the collapsed code, select the Hide collapsed regions check box. To print line numbers, select the Include line numbers check box.

3. Click the OK button to begin printing.

To use the Windows Snipping Tool to print the interface during design time:

1. Make the designer window the active window.

Figure 1-33 How to print the code and interface during design time (*continues*)

(continued)

2. *If you are using Windows 8*, press the Windows key to switch to tile-based mode. Begin typing the words "snipping tool" (without the quotes). When you see Snipping Tool in the list of applications, click Snipping Tool.

   If you are using Windows 7, click the Start button on the taskbar, click All Programs, click the Accessories folder to open it, and then click Snipping Tool.

3. Click the New button. Drag the cursor around the area you want to capture and then release the mouse button. Click File and then click Save As.

Ch01-
Snipping
Tool

Figure 1-33   How to print the code and interface during design time
© 2013 Cengage Learning

Closing the Current Solution

When you are finished working on a solution, you should close it using the steps listed in Figure 1-34. Closing a solution closes all projects and files contained in the solution.

HOW TO Close a Solution

1. Click FILE on the menu bar.

2. Click Close Solution.

Note: Be sure to use the Close Solution option rather than the Close option. The Close option does not close the solution. Instead, it closes only the open windows (such as the designer and Code Editor windows) in the IDE.

Figure 1-34   How to close a solution
© 2013 Cengage Learning

Opening an Existing Solution

Figure 1-35 shows the steps you follow to open an existing solution. The names of solution files end with .sln. If a solution is already open in the IDE, you will be given the option of closing it before another solution is opened.

HOW TO Open an Existing Solution

1. Click FILE on the menu bar and then click Open Project.

2. Locate and then click the solution filename, which is contained in the application's solution folder. (The solution filename has an .sln filename extension, which stands for "solution.")

3. Click the Open button in the Open Project dialog box.

4. If the designer window is not open, click VIEW on the menu bar and then click Designer. Or, you can right-click the form file's name in the Solution Explorer window and then click View Designer.

Figure 1-35   How to open an existing solution
© 2013 Cengage Learning

Syntax Errors

As the amount of code you need to enter increases, so does the likelihood for errors. An error in a program's code is referred to as a **bug**. The process of locating and correcting any bugs in a program is called **debugging**. Program bugs are typically categorized as syntax errors, logic errors, or run time errors. In this chapter, you'll learn about syntax errors only. Logic errors and run time errors are covered later in this book.

A **syntax error** occurs when you break one of the programming language's rules. Most syntax errors are a result of typing errors that occur when entering instructions, such as typing Me.Clse() instead of Me.Close(). The Code Editor detects most syntax errors as you enter the instructions. Figure 1-36 shows the result of typing Me.Clse() in the exitButton_Click procedure. The jagged blue line indicates that the statement contains a syntax error.

Figure 1-36   Syntax error in the exitButton_Click procedure

You can find out more information about the syntax error by positioning your mouse pointer on the mistyped instruction. When you do so, the Code Editor displays a box that contains an appropriate error message, as shown in Figure 1-37. In this case, the message indicates that the Code Editor does not recognize Clse.

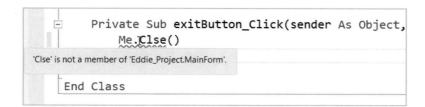

Figure 1-37   Result of placing the mouse pointer on the jagged blue line

Usually, you correct any syntax errors before starting an application. However, if you inadvertently start an application that contains a syntax error, the dialog box shown in Figure 1-38 will appear. Clicking the No button opens the Error List window shown in Figure 1-39. The window provides both the description and location of the error in the code.

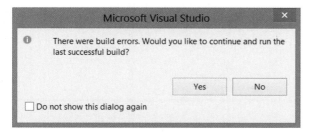

Figure 1-38   Message dialog box

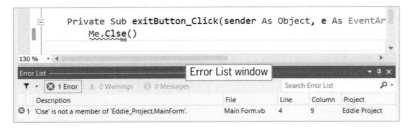

Figure 1-39 Result of starting an application that contains a syntax error

Mini-Quiz 1-3

1. The proper way to close a solution is to click the _____ option on the FILE menu. (9)

   a. Close

   b. Close Solution

   c. Close All

   d. either a or b

2. The form that appears automatically when an application is started is called the _____ form. (2)

   a. beginning

   b. main

   c. startup

   d. none of the above

3. Which of the following instructions can be used to end an application? (8)

   a. `Close.Me()`

   b. `Me.Close()`

   c. `Me.End()`

   d. `Me.Stop()`

4. Which of the following assigns the string "Nashville" to the cityLabel control? (4, 8, 11)

   a. `cityLabel.Label = "Nashville"`

   b. `cityLabel.String = "Nashville"`

   c. `cityLabel.Text = "Nashville"`

   d. none of the above

5. The process of locating and fixing the errors in a program is called _____. (13)

   a. bug-proofing

   b. bug-eliminating

   c. debugging

   d. error removal

You have completed the concepts section of Chapter 1. The next section is the Programming Tutorial section, which contains two tutorials. The tutorials give you step-by-step instructions for completing applications that use the chapter's concepts. In most cases, the first tutorial in each chapter is easier than the second tutorial because it contains more detailed step-by-step instructions. A Programming Example follows the tutorials. The Programming Example is a completed program that demonstrates the concepts taught in the chapter. Following the Programming Example are the Summary, Key Terms, Review Questions, Exercises, and Case Projects sections.

PROGRAMMING TUTORIAL 1

Creating the Eddie Application

This tutorial contains the steps for creating, running, and testing the Eddie application from the chapter. The interface contains a label, two picture boxes, and three buttons. The first button displays an animated image of a character named Eddie. The second button displays a static image of Eddie, and the third button ends the application.

To begin creating the Eddie application:

1. *Windows 8*: If necessary, tap the **Windows logo** key to switch to the Windows 8 tile-based mode. *If you are using Visual Studio Professional 2012*, click the **Visual Studio 2012** tile. *If you are using Visual Studio Express 2012 for Windows Desktop*, click the **VS Express for Desktop** tile.

   Windows 7: Click the **Start** button on the Windows 7 taskbar and then point to **All Programs**. *If you are using Visual Studio Professional 2012*, click **Microsoft Visual Studio 2012** on the All Programs menu and then click **Visual Studio 2012**. *If you are using Visual Studio Express 2012 for Windows Desktop*, click **Microsoft Visual Studio 2012 Express** on the All Programs menu and then click **VS Express for Desktop**.

2. *If the Choose Default Environment Settings dialog box appears*, click **Visual Basic Development Settings** and then click **Start Visual Studio**.

3. Click **WINDOW** on the menu bar, click **Reset Window Layout**, and then click the **Yes** button. *If you are using Visual Studio Professional 2012 on a Windows 8 system*, your screen will appear similar to Figure 1-40. *If you are using Visual Studio Express 2012 for Windows Desktop on a Windows 8 system*, your screen will appear similar to Figure 1-41. (*If you are using a Windows 7 system*, the text in the title bar in each figure will be left-aligned rather than centered.)

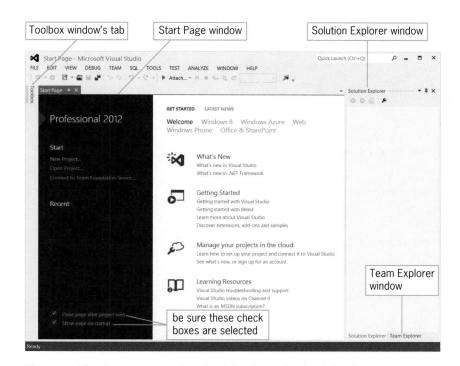

Figure 1-40 Startup screen for Visual Studio Professional 2012

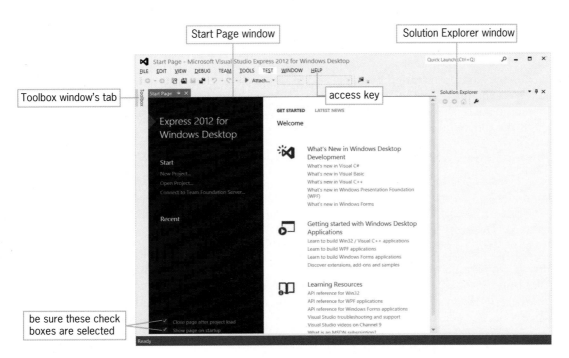

Figure 1-41 Startup screen for Visual Studio Express 2012 for Windows Desktop

4. Click **TOOLS** on the menu bar, click **Options**, and then click the **Projects and Solutions** node. Use the information shown in Figure 1-42 to select and deselect the appropriate check boxes. (Your dialog box will look slightly different if you are using the Express edition of Visual Studio 2012. It will also look slightly different if you are using Windows 7.)

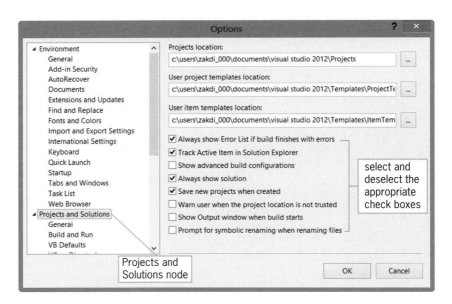

Figure 1-42 Options dialog box

5. Click the **OK** button to close the Options dialog box.

6. Click **FILE** on the menu bar and then click **New Project**. If necessary, expand the **Visual Basic** node in the Installed Templates list, and then (if necessary) click **Windows**.

7. If necessary, click **Windows Forms Application** in the middle column of the dialog box.

8. Change the name entered in the Name box to **Eddie Project**. Click the **Browse** button to open the Project Location dialog box. Locate and then click the **VbReloaded2012\ Chap01** folder. Click the **Select Folder** button to close the Project Location dialog box.

9. If necessary, select the **Create directory for solution** check box in the New Project dialog box. Change the name entered in the Solution name box to **Eddie Solution**. Figures 1-43 and 1-44 show the completed New Project dialog box in Visual Studio Professional 2012 and in Visual Studio Express 2012 for Windows Desktop, respectively.

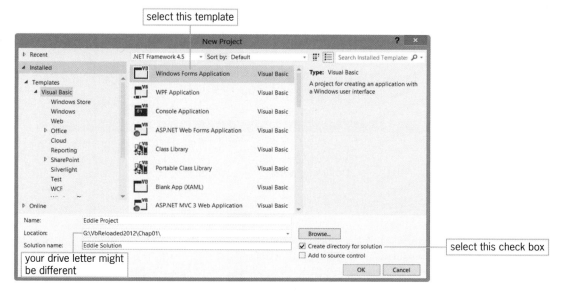

Figure 1-43 New Project dialog box (Visual Studio Professional 2012)

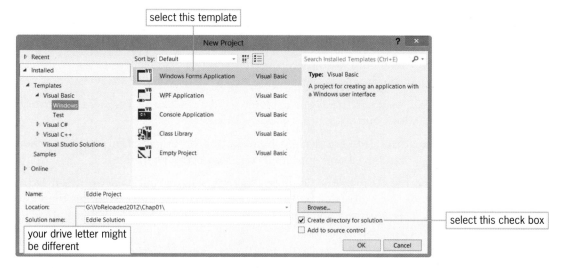

Figure 1-44 New Project dialog box (Visual Studio Express 2012 for Windows Desktop)

10. Click the **OK** button to close the New Project dialog box. The computer creates a solution and adds a Visual Basic project to the solution. See Figure 1-45. (If you are using the Express edition of Visual Studio, you will not have the Team Explorer window, and the menu bar will not contain the SQL and ANALYZE items.)

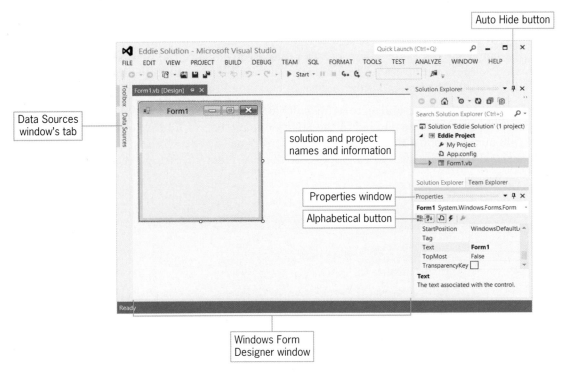

Figure 1-45   Solution and Visual Basic project

11. If necessary, click the **Alphabetical** button in the Properties window to display the property names in alphabetical order.

Managing the Windows in the IDE

In the next set of steps, you will practice closing, opening, auto-hiding, and displaying the windows in the IDE.

To close, open, auto-hide, and display the windows in the IDE:

1. Click the **Close** button on the Properties window's title bar to close the window. Now, click **VIEW** on the menu bar and then click **Properties Window** to open the window.

2. If your IDE contains the Team Explorer window, click the **Team Explorer** tab and then click the **Close** button on the window's title bar.

3. Click the **Auto Hide** (vertical pushpin) button on the Solution Explorer window. The window is minimized and appears as a tab on the edge of the IDE.

4. To temporarily display the Solution Explorer window, click the **Solution Explorer** tab. Notice that the Auto Hide button is now a horizontal pushpin rather than a vertical pushpin. To return the Solution Explorer window to its auto-hidden state, click the **Solution Explorer** tab again.

5. On your own, close the Data Sources window. Then, permanently display the Toolbox window by clicking its tab and then clicking its Auto Hide button. If necessary, expand the **Common Controls** node in the Toolbox window.

Adding and Manipulating Controls

In the next set of steps, you will add three buttons to the form. You will also practice sizing, moving, deleting, and restoring a control.

To add controls to the form and then manipulate the controls:

1. Click the **Button** tool in the toolbox, but do not release the mouse button. Hold down the mouse button as you drag the mouse pointer to the lower-left corner of the form. As you drag the mouse pointer, you will see a solid box, an outline of a rectangle, and a plus box following the mouse pointer. The blue lines that appear between the form's borders and the button's borders are called margin lines because their size is determined by the contents of the button's Margin property. The purpose of the margin lines is to assist you in spacing the controls properly on a form. See Figure 1-46.

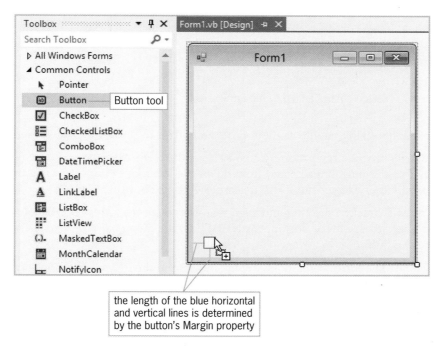

the length of the blue horizontal and vertical lines is determined by the button's Margin property

Figure 1-46 Button tool being dragged to the form

2. Release the mouse button. A button control appears on the form. See Figure 1-47. The sizing handles on the button indicate that it is selected. You can use the sizing handles to make a control bigger or smaller.

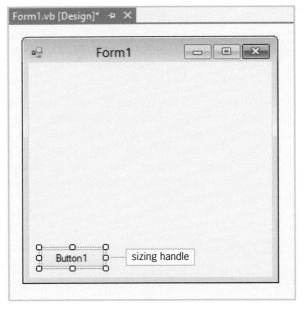

Figure 1-47 Button control added to the form

3. Use the middle sizing handle at the top of the button to make the button taller.

4. Now you will practice repositioning a control on the form. Place your mouse pointer on the center of the button. Press and hold down the left mouse button as you drag the button to another area of the form. Release the mouse button.

5. Next, you will practice deleting and then restoring a control. Press the **Delete** key on your keyboard to delete the button. Click **EDIT** on the menu bar and then click **Undo** to reinstate the button.

6. Drag the button control back to its original location in the lower-left corner of the form.

7. Another way to add a control to a form is by clicking the appropriate tool and then clicking the form. Click the **Button** tool in the toolbox and then click anywhere on the **form**.

8. Drag the second button until its top border is aligned with the top border of the first button, but don't release the mouse button. When the tops of both controls are aligned, the designer displays a blue snap line. See Figure 1-48.

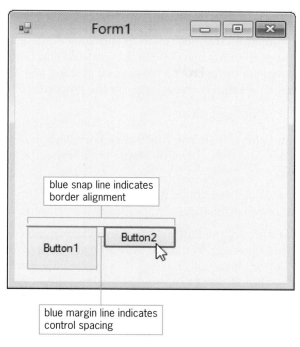

Figure 1-48 Controls aligned by their top borders

9. Now drag the second button down slightly, until the Button2 text is aligned with the Button1 text, but don't release the mouse button. When the text in both controls is aligned, the designer displays a pink snap line. See Figure 1-49.

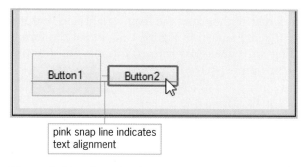

Figure 1-49 Controls aligned by their text

10. Release the mouse button.

11. You can also add a control to a form by clicking the appropriate tool, placing the mouse pointer on the form, and then pressing the left mouse button and dragging the mouse pointer until the control is the desired size. Click the **Button** tool in the toolbox and then place the mouse pointer anywhere on the form. Press the left mouse button and drag the mouse pointer until the control is the desired size, and then release the mouse button. (You do not need to worry about the exact location and size of the button.)

12. Click the **Button1** control to select it. Press and hold down the **Ctrl** (Control) key as you click the **Button2** and **Button3** controls. Press the **Delete** key to remove the three buttons from the form.

Using the Properties Window to Change an Object's Properties

Each object in Visual Basic has a set of properties that determine its appearance and behavior, and each property has a default value assigned to it when the object is created. You can use the Properties window to assign a different value to a property. In the next set of steps, you will change the form file object's File Name property. You will also change some of the properties of the form.

To change the properties of the form file and form:

1. Permanently display the Solution Explorer window. Right-click **Form1.vb** in the Solution Explorer window, click **Properties**, and then click **File Name** in the Properties list. Type **Main Form.vb** and press **Enter**.

2. Click the **form** in the designer window. Sizing handles appear on the form to indicate that it is selected, and the form's properties appear in the Properties window.

3. First, you will change the type and size of the font used to display text in the controls on the form. (You will add the controls later in this tutorial.) Click **Font** in the Properties list and then click the **...** (ellipsis) button in the Settings box. When the Font dialog box opens, click **Segoe UI** in the Font box. Click **11** in the Size box and then click the **OK** button. When a control is added to the form, its Font property will be assigned the same value as the form's Font property.

4. Click **StartPosition** in the Properties list. Recall that this property determines the location of the form when the application is run and the form first appears on the screen. Click the **list arrow** in the Settings box and then click **CenterScreen**.

5. Click **Text** in the Properties list. Recall that this property specifies the text to display in the form's title bar. Type **Eddie** and press **Enter**.

6. Now you will give the form a more meaningful name. Scroll to the top of the Properties window and then click **(Name)** in the Properties list. Type **MainForm** and press **Enter**.

7. Finally, you will make the form larger. Either drag the form's right and bottom borders until the form is approximately the size shown in Figure 1-50, or set the form's Size property to **565, 590**. (Depending on your display screen, you may need to use slightly different values for your form's Size property.)

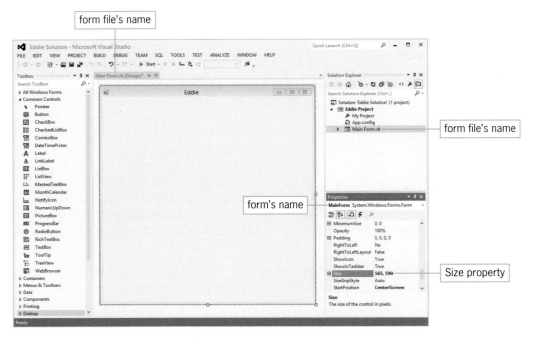

Figure 1-50   Correct size for the form

Adding Label and Button Controls to the Form

In the next set of steps, you will add label and button controls to the form and then set some of their properties.

To add label and button controls and then set some of their properties:

1. Add a label control and three buttons to the form. Position the controls as shown in Figure 1-51.

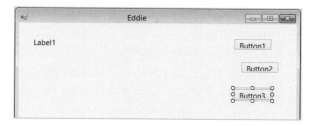

Figure 1-51 Label and buttons added to the form

2. Click the **Label1** control on the form. Verify that the label's Font property contains the same value as the form's Font property.

3. With the Label1 control still selected, click **Text** in the Properties list. Type **Eddie Rocks!** and press **Enter**. Notice that the label's size automatically adjusts to fit its contents; this occurs because the default value for the control's AutoSize property is True.

4. Click the **Button1** control on the form. Here again, verify that the button's Font property contains the same value as the form's Font property.

5. Now, set the Button1 control's Name property to **goButton** and set its Text property to **Go**. For now, don't worry about the size and location of the buttons on the form.

6. Click the **Button2** control on the form. Set its Name and Text properties to **stopButton** and **Stop**, respectively.

7. Click the **Button3** control on the form. Set its Name and Text properties to **exitButton** and **Exit**, respectively.

Using the FORMAT Menu

In this set of steps, you will set the goButton's Location and Size properties. You then will use the FORMAT menu to align the left borders of the three buttons and also make the buttons the same size.

To set the goButton's size and location, and then use the FORMAT menu:

1. The goButton will be the reference control, which is the control whose size and/or location you want the other buttons to match. Click the **goButton**. Set its Size and Location properties to approximately **75, 35** and **425, 30**, respectively.

2. With the goButton still selected, press and hold down the **Ctrl (Control)** key as you click the **Stop** and **Exit** buttons, and then release the Ctrl key. The three buttons are now selected. You can tell that the Go button is the reference control because its sizing handles are white; the sizing handles on the other selected controls are black. See Figure 1-52.

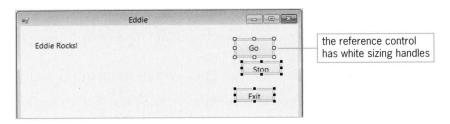

Figure 1-52 Buttons selected on the form

the reference control
has white sizing handles

3. Click **FORMAT** on the menu bar, point to **Make Same Size**, and then click **Both**. The Stop and Exit buttons are now the same size as the Go button.

4. Click **FORMAT** on the menu bar, point to **Align**, and then click **Lefts**. The left borders of the Stop and Exit buttons are now aligned with the left border of the Go button.

5. On your own, use the FORMAT menu to equalize the vertical spacing between the three buttons.

6. Click the **form** to deselect the buttons.

Coding the Exit Button's Click Event Procedure

When the user clicks the Exit button in the interface, the button's Click event procedure should end the application.

To code the Exit button's Click event procedure:

1. Right-click the **form** and then click **View Code** to open the Code Editor window.

2. Click the **Class Name** list arrow and then click **exitButton** in the list. Click the **Method Name** list arrow and then click **Click** in the list. The code template for the exitButton's Click event procedure appears in the Code Editor window. See Figure 1-53. You can use the sizing list box, which appears in the lower-left corner of the window, to either increase or decrease the size of the font used to display the code.

Class Name list arrow

Method Name list arrow

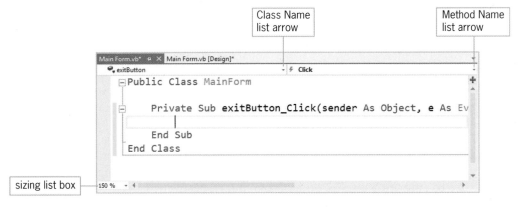

sizing list box

Figure 1-53 Code template for the exitButton's Click event procedure

3. The Exit button should end the application when it is clicked; therefore, the appropriate instruction to enter in its Click event procedure is Me.Close(). You can type the instruction on your own or use the Code Editor window's IntelliSense feature. In this set of steps, you will use the IntelliSense feature. Type **me.** (be sure to type the period, but don't press Enter). When you type the period, the IntelliSense feature displays a list of properties, methods, and so on from which you can select.

Note: If the list of choices does not appear, the IntelliSense feature may have been turned off on your computer system. To turn it on, click TOOLS on the menu bar and then click Options. Expand the Text Editor node and then click Basic. Select the Auto list members check box and then click the OK button.

4. If necessary, click the **Common** tab. The Common tab displays the most commonly used items, whereas the All tab displays all of the items. Type **cl** (but don't press Enter). The IntelliSense feature highlights the Close method in the list. (If Close is not highlighted, type the letter o.) See Figure 1-54.

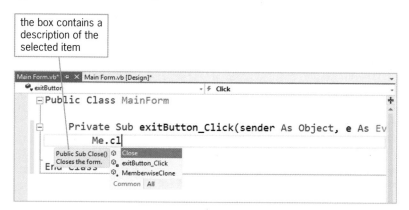

the box contains a description of the selected item

Figure 1-54   List displayed by the IntelliSense feature

5. Press the **Tab** key on your keyboard to include the Close method in the instruction, and then press **Enter**. See Figure 1-55.

Figure 1-55   Completed exitButton_Click procedure

Adding a Picture Box Control to the Form

In the next set of steps, you will add a picture box to the form and then set some of its properties.

To add a picture box to the form and then set some of its properties:

1. Click the **Main Form.vb [Design]** tab to return to the designer window. Add a picture box to the form. Position it as shown in Figure 1-56.

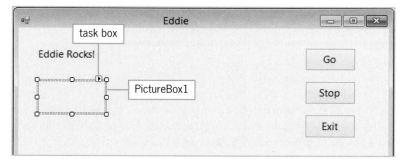

Figure 1-56   Picture box added to the form

2. Notice that a box containing a triangle appears in the upper-right corner of the control. The box is referred to as the task box because when you click it, it displays a list of the tasks associated with the control. Each task in the list is associated with one or more properties. You can set the properties using the task list or the Properties window. Click the **task box** on the PictureBox1 control. See Figure 1-57.

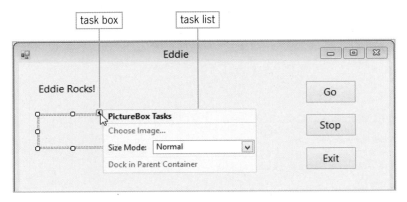

Figure 1-57 PictureBox1 control's task list

3. Click **Choose Image** to open the Select Resource dialog box. The Choose Image task is associated with the Image property in the Properties window.

4. To include the image file within the project itself, the Project resource file radio button must be selected in the Select Resource dialog box. Verify that the radio button is selected, and then click the **Import** button to open the Open dialog box.

5. Open the VbReloaded2012\Chap01 folder, if necessary. Click **EddieGo** (**EddieGo.gif**) in the list of filenames and then click the **Open** button. The completed Select Resource dialog box is shown in Figure 1-58.

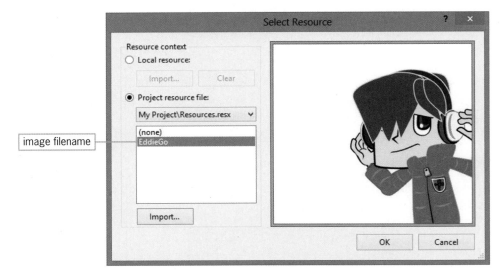

Figure 1-58 Completed Select Resource dialog box
Image by Diane Zak; Created with Reallusion CrazyTalk Animator

6. Click the **OK** button. Click the **picture box** control to close its task list. Drag the picture box's sizing handles until the picture box is approximately the size shown in Figure 1-59. (Or, set its Size property to approximately **365, 465**.)

Figure 1-59 Correct size for the picture box
Image by Diane Zak; Created with Reallusion CrazyTalk Animator

7. Use the Properties window to set the picture box's Name property to **goPictureBox**.

8. When the application is started, the goPictureBox control should be invisible. To view the control, the user will need to click the Go button. Use the Properties window to set the picture box's Visible property to **False**.

9. Click **FILE** on the menu bar and then click **Save All**.

Coding the Go and Stop Buttons' Click Event Procedures

When the user clicks the Go button in the interface, its Click event procedure should make the goPictureBox visible. You can accomplish this task by assigning the keyword `True` to the goPictureBox's Visible property, like this: `goPictureBox.Visible = True`. When the user clicks the Stop button, on the other hand, its Click event procedure should make the goPictureBox invisible again. This is accomplished using the following assignment statement: `goPictureBox.Visible = False`.

 Ch01-Using
IntelliSense

To begin coding the Click event procedures and then test the code:

1. Click the **Main Form.vb** tab to return to the Code Editor window. Use the Class Name and Method Name list boxes to open the code template for the goButton's Click event procedure.

2. Type **gopi** to highlight the goPictureBox entry in the IntelliSense list. Press **Tab** to include the entry in the instruction.

3. The next character in the instruction is a period. Type **.** (a period), and then type the letter **v** to select the Visible entry in the list. Press **Tab** and then type **=** (an equal sign).

4. Type the letter **t** to select the `True` keyword in the list. Press **Tab** and then press **Enter**. The procedure now contains the `goPictureBox.Visible = True` assignment statement.

5. Open the code template for the stopButton's Click event procedure. On your own, use the IntelliSense feature to enter the following assignment statement in the procedure:

goPictureBox.Visible = False

6. Save the solution by clicking **FILE** on the menu bar and then clicking **Save All**.

7. Now you will start the application and test the code entered so far. Recall that before you start the application the first time, you should verify the name of the startup form in the Project Designer window. Right-click **My Project** in the Solution Explorer window and then click **Open** on the context menu. If necessary, click the **Application** tab. If MainForm does not appear in the Startup form box, click the **Startup form** list arrow, click **MainForm** in the list, and then save the solution.

8. Close the Project Designer window by clicking the **Close** button on its tab.

9. Click **DEBUG** on the menu bar and then click **Start Debugging**. The interface appears on the screen. (Do not be concerned about any windows that appear at the bottom of the screen.) Notice that the goPictureBox is invisible.

10. Click the **Go** button to make the goPictureBox visible, and then click the **Stop** button to make it invisible. Click the **Exit** button to stop the application.

Completing the User Interface

In the next set of steps, you will complete the user interface.

To complete the user interface:

1. Return to the designer window. Add another picture box to the form. (You don't need to worry about the exact location.) Change its name to **stopPictureBox**.

2. Click the stopPictureBox's **task box**. Click **Choose Image** to open the Select Resource dialog box. Verify that the Project resource file radio button is selected, and then click the **Import** button to open the Open dialog box.

3. Open the VbReloaded2012\Chap01 folder, if necessary. Click **EddieStop** (**EddieStop.gif**) in the list of filenames, click the **Open** button, and then click the **OK** button.

4. Now you will make the stopPictureBox the same size as the goPictureBox, and then align their left and top borders. Click the **goPictureBox** control (the reference control) and then Ctrl+click the **stopPictureBox** control. Use the FORMAT menu to make the stopPictureBox the same height and width as the reference control. Also use the FORMAT menu to align the left and top borders of the stopPictureBox with the reference control.

5. Now that the interface is complete, you can lock the controls on the form. Right-click the **form** and then click **Lock Controls** on the context menu. Notice that a small lock appears in the upper-left corner of the form. (You can also lock the controls by clicking FORMAT on the menu bar and then clicking Lock Controls.)

6. Click the **Go** button. The small lock in the upper-left corner of the control indicates that the control is locked.

7. Try dragging one of the controls to a different location on the form. You will not be able to do so.

If you need to move a control after you have locked the controls in place, you can change the control's Location property setting in the Properties window. You also can unlock the control by changing its Locked property to False. Or, you can unlock all of the controls by clicking FORMAT on the menu bar and then clicking Lock Controls. The Lock Controls option is a toggle option: Clicking it once activates it, and clicking it again deactivates it.

Completing the Code

In the next set of steps, you will finish coding the Go and Stop buttons' Click event procedures.

To complete the code and then test it:

1. Return to the Code Editor window. After making the goPictureBox visible, the goButton_Click procedure will make the stopPictureBox invisible. Similarly, before making the goPictureBox invisible, the stopButton's Click event procedure will make the stopPictureBox visible.

2. Enter the additional assignment statements shown in Figure 1-60.

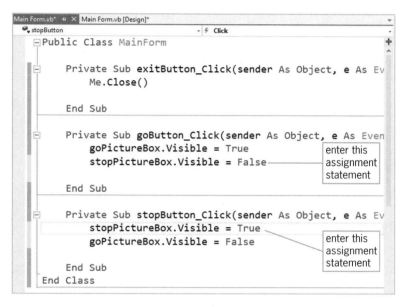

Figure 1-60 Completed Click event procedures

3. Now you will save the solution and then start the application. Click **FILE** on the menu bar and then click **Save All**. Click **DEBUG** on the menu bar and then click **Start Debugging**. (You can also press the F5 key on your keyboard.)

4. Click the **Go** button and then click the **Stop** button. Click the **Go** button again and then click the **Stop** button again. Click the **Exit** button.

Displaying Line Numbers in the Code Editor Window

At times, you may want to display line numbers in the Code Editor window.

To display line numbers in the Code Editor window:

1. Click **TOOLS** on the menu bar and then click **Options**. Expand the **Text Editor** node in the Options dialog box (if necessary) and then click **Basic**. Select the **Line numbers** check box and then click the **OK** button. See Figure 1-61.

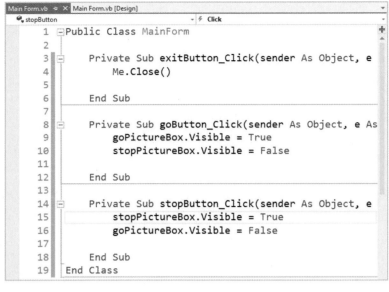

```
Main Form.vb  -₪ X  Main Form.vb [Design]
 ⚲ stopButton                                    ▾  ⚡ Click
   1  ⊟Public Class MainForm
   2
   3  ⊟    Private Sub exitButton_Click(sender As Object, e
   4          Me.Close()
   5
   6        End Sub
   7
   8  ⊟    Private Sub goButton_Click(sender As Object, e As
   9          goPictureBox.Visible = True
  10          stopPictureBox.Visible = False
  11
  12        End Sub
  13
  14  ⊟    Private Sub stopButton_Click(sender As Object, e
  15          stopPictureBox.Visible = True
  16          goPictureBox.Visible = False
  17
  18        End Sub
  19  End Class
```

Figure 1-61   Line numbers shown in the Code Editor window

Closing the Current Solution

When you are finished working with a solution, you should use the Close Solution option on the FILE menu to close it. When you close a solution, all projects and files contained in the solution are also closed.

To close the current solution:

1. Close the Code Editor window. Click **FILE** on the menu bar and then click **Close Solution**.

2. Use the Solution Explorer window to verify that no solutions are open in the IDE.

Opening an Existing Solution

You can use the FILE menu to open an existing solution.

To open the Eddie Solution:

1. If necessary, permanently display the Solution Explorer window.

2. Click **FILE** on the menu bar and then click **Open Project** to open the Open Project dialog box.

3. Locate and then open the VbReloaded2012\Chap01\Eddie Solution folder. Click **Eddie Solution** (**Eddie Solution.sln**) in the list of filenames (if necessary) and then click the **Open** button.

4. If you do not see the form in the designer window, click **VIEW** on the menu bar and then click **Designer**.

Printing the Application's Interface

To print the application's interface during design time, the Windows Form designer window must be the active window.

To print the Eddie application's interface:

1. *If you are using Windows 8,* press the Windows key to switch to tile-based mode. Begin typing the words "snipping tool" (without the quotes). When you see Snipping Tool in the list of applications, click **Snipping Tool**.

   If you are using Windows 7, click the **Start** button on the taskbar, click **All Programs**, click the **Accessories** folder to open it, and then click **Snipping Tool**.

2. Click the **New** button. Drag the cursor around the form and then release the mouse button.

3. Click **File** and then click **Save As**. Locate and then open the VbReloaded2012\Chap01\ Eddie Solution folder. You can save the file using any one of the following formats: .png, .gif, .jpg, or .mht. In this case, you will save it as a .png file. If necessary, change the entry in the Save as type box to **Portable Network Graphic file (PNG) (*.PNG)**. Type **Eddie** in the File name box and then click the **Save** button. Close the Snipping Tool application.

4. If your computer is connected to a printer, use Windows to open the VbReloaded2012\Chap01\Eddie Solution folder. Right-click **Eddie.png**, point to **Open with**, and then click **Paint**. Click **File**, point to **Print**, click **Print**, and then click the **Print** button. Close Paint.

Printing the Application's Code

For your future reference, you should always print a copy of the application's code. To print the code, the Code Editor window must be the active (current) window.

To print the application's code:

1. Open the Code Editor window by right-clicking the **form** and then clicking **View Code**.

2. First, you will remove the line numbers from the Code Editor window. Click **TOOLS** on the menu bar and then click **Options**. If necessary, expand the **Text Editor** node in the Options dialog box and then click **Basic**. Click the **Line numbers** check box to deselect it and then click the **OK** button.

3. Click **FILE** on the menu bar and then click **Print** to open the Print dialog box. If you select the Include line numbers check box, line numbers will be printed even if they do not appear in the Code Editor window. If the Include line numbers check box is not selected, no line numbers will appear on the printout, even though they may appear in the Code Editor window.

4. Select the **Include line numbers** check box.

5. If your computer is connected to a printer, click the **OK** button to begin printing; otherwise, click the **Cancel** button. If you clicked the OK button, your printer prints the code.

Syntax Errors in Code

In this section, you will introduce a syntax error in the Go button's Click event procedure. You then will debug the procedure by locating and fixing the error.

To introduce a syntax error in the code:

1. Locate the goButton_Click procedure. Change the word `False` in the assignment statement to **Flse**, and then click the **blank line** below the assignment statement. The jagged blue line that appears below the mistyped word indicates that the instruction contains a syntax error.

2. Position your mouse pointer on the jagged blue line, as shown in Figure 1-62. The error message indicates that the Code Editor does not recognize the word `Flse`.

Figure 1-62   Jagged blue line and message indicate a syntax error

3. Now observe what happens when you start the application without correcting the syntax error. Save the solution and then start the application. The message box shown in Figure 1-63 appears.

Figure 1-63   Result of running an application that contains a syntax error

4. Click the **No** button. The Error List window shown in Figure 1-64 opens. The window indicates that the code has one error, which occurs on Line 10.

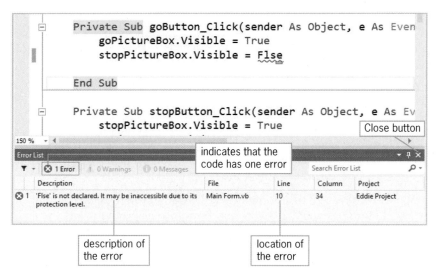

Figure 1-64   Error List window

5. Change F1se in Line 10's assignment statement to **False** and then click the **blank line** below the assignment statement. The Error List window shows that the code is now free of any errors.

6. Close the Error List window. Save the solution and then start the application. Click the **Go** button to verify that it is working correctly.

7. Click the **Exit** button to end the application, and then close the Code Editor window.

Exiting Visual Studio 2012

You can exit Visual Studio using either the Close button on its title bar or the Exit option on its FILE menu.

To exit Visual Studio:

1. First, close the current solution. Click **FILE** on the menu bar and then click **Close Solution**.

2. Click **FILE** on the menu bar and then click **Exit**.

Running the Application's Executable File

Earlier you learned that when you start a Visual Basic application, the computer automatically creates a file that can be run outside of the IDE. Unless you change the file's name, it has the same name as the project, but with an .exe filename extension. The computer stores the file in the project's bin\Debug folder.

To run the Eddie Project.exe file:

1. Press and hold down the **Windows logo** key on your keyboard as you tap the letter **r**. When the Run dialog box opens, release the logo key.

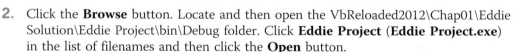

The Windows logo key looks like this:

2. Click the **Browse** button. Locate and then open the VbReloaded2012\Chap01\Eddie Solution\Eddie Project\bin\Debug folder. Click **Eddie Project** (**Eddie Project.exe**) in the list of filenames and then click the **Open** button.

3. Click the **OK** button in the Run dialog box. After a few moments, the Eddie application's interface appears on the screen. Click the **Go** and **Stop** buttons to test the application, and then click the **Exit** button.

PROGRAMMING TUTORIAL 2

Creating the Jerrod Realty Application

In this tutorial, you create the Jerrod Realty application shown in Figure 1-65. The interface contains a label, three picture boxes, and three buttons. The maplePictureBox and elmPictureBox controls contain images of houses. The images are stored in the 65Maple.png and 2323Elm.png files contained in the VbReloaded2012\Chap01 folder. (The images were downloaded from the Open Clip Art Library at *http://openclipart.org*.) The mapleButton and elmButton controls each display one of the house images in the displayPictureBox. Each also displays the address of its respective house (either 65 Maple or 2323 Elm) in the addressLabel control. The exitButton ends the application.

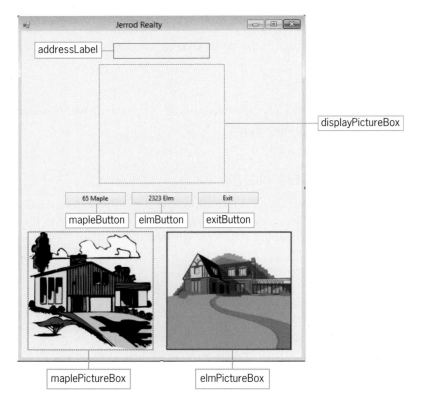

Figure 1-65   Jerrod Realty application's user interface
OpenClipArt.org/Francesco Rollandin

To begin creating the Jerrod Realty application:

1. Start Visual Studio 2012. If you need help, refer to the How To box shown earlier in Figure 1-2.

2. Click **WINDOW** on the menu bar, click **Reset Window Layout**, and then click the **Yes** button.

3. Click **TOOLS** on the menu bar and then click **Options** to open the Options dialog box. Use the information shown earlier in Figure 1-6 to select and deselect the appropriate check boxes, and then close the dialog box.

4. Use the **New Project** option on the FILE menu to create a new Visual Basic Windows application. Use the following names for the solution and project, respectively: **Jerrod Solution** and **Jerrod Project**. Save the solution in the VbReloaded2012\Chap01 folder. If you need help, refer to the How To box shown earlier in Figure 1-5.

5. Use the Properties window to change the form file's name from Form1.vb to **Main Form.vb**. (If you do not see the form file's properties in the Properties window, click Form1.vb in the Solution Explorer window.)

6. Click the **form**. Change the form's name to **MainForm**. Also change the form's Font property to **Segoe UI, 9pt**.

7. Change the form's StartPosition property so that the form will be centered on the screen when the application is started.

8. Change the form's Text property to display "Jerrod Realty" (without the quotes) in its title bar.

9. Change the form's Size property to **540, 675**.

Managing the Windows in the IDE

In the next set of steps, you will practice closing, opening, auto-hiding, and displaying the windows in the IDE. If you need help while performing the steps, refer to the How To box shown earlier in Figure 1-10.

To close, open, auto-hide, and display the windows in the IDE:

1. Close the Properties window and then open it again.

2. If necessary, close the Team Explorer and Data Sources windows.

3. Auto-hide the Solution Explorer window, and then temporarily display the window.

4. Permanently display the Solution Explorer window. Also, permanently display the Toolbox window (if necessary).

Adding Controls to a Form

In the next set of steps, you will add the seven controls to the form. You will also size, move, delete, and undelete a control.

To add controls to the form and then manipulate the controls:

1. Use the Label tool in the toolbox to add a label to the form. If you need help, refer to the How To box shown earlier in Figure 1-16.

2. Next, add three picture boxes and three buttons to the form. Position the controls as shown in Figure 1-66. If you need help, refer to the How To box shown earlier in Figure 1-17. (If necessary, use the form's sizing handles to make the form larger or smaller.)

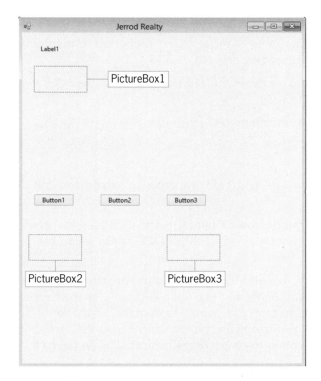

Figure 1-66   Controls added to the form

3. Click the **Label1** control. Change the label's name to **addressLabel**. Set its BorderStyle and AutoSize properties to **FixedSingle** and **False**, respectively.

4. Click **Text** in the label's Properties list, press the **Backspace** key, and then press **Enter** to remove the Label1 text from the control. Now change the label's Size property to **180, 30**.

5. Click **TextAlign** in the Properties list, click the **list arrow** in the Settings box, and then click the **rectangle** located in the second row, second column. This will center the text within the label control.

6. Click the **PictureBox2** control at the bottom of the form. Change its name to **maplePictureBox**. Click the control's **task box** and then use its task list to display the image stored in the **65Maple.png** file, which is contained in the VbReloaded2012\ Chap01 folder. Also use the task list to set the Size Mode to **StretchImage**. If you need help, refer to the *Adding a Picture Box Control to the Form* section in Programming Tutorial 1.

7. Use the Properties window to set the maplePictureBox control's Size property to **235, 230**.

8. Use the Make Same Size option on the FORMAT menu to make the other two picture boxes the same size as the maplePictureBox. If you need help, refer to the How To box shown earlier in Figure 1-19.

9. Click the **form** to deselect the three picture boxes.

10. Click the **PictureBox3** control at the bottom of the form. Change its name to **elmPictureBox**. Use the control's task list to display the image stored in the **2323Elm.png** file, which is contained in the VbReloaded2012\Chap01 folder. Also use the task list to set the Size Mode to **StretchImage**.

11. Click the **PictureBox1** control at the top of the form. Use the Properties window to change the control's Name and SizeMode properties to **displayPictureBox** and **StretchImage**, respectively.

12. Click the **Button1** control. Change its Name and Text properties to **mapleButton** and **65 Maple**, respectively. Change its Size property to **115, 25**.

13. Use the Make Same Size option on the FORMAT menu to make the other two buttons the same size as the mapleButton.

14. Click the **form** to deselect the three buttons.

15. Change the Button2 control's Name and Text properties to **elmButton** and **2323 Elm**, respectively.

16. Change the Button3 control's Name and Text properties to **exitButton** and **Exit**, respectively.

17. Just for practice, click the **mapleButton** on the form and then press the **Delete** key on your keyboard. To restore the control, click **EDIT** on the menu bar and then click **Undo**.

18. Position the controls as shown in Figure 1-67. If necessary, use the Align option on the FORMAT menu to align the top borders of the three buttons. Use the Center in Form option on the FORMAT menu to center the label, horizontally, on the form. Then use it to center the displayPictureBox, horizontally, on the form. Select the three buttons and then use the Center in Form option to center them, horizontally, on the form. Click the **form** to deselect the buttons.

Figure 1-67 Completed user interface
OpenClipArt.org/Francesco Rollandin

19. Place your mouse pointer on the sizing handle that appears at the bottom of the form. Press and hold down the left mouse button as you drag the bottom border up. When you no longer see the maplePictureBox and elmPictureBox controls, release the mouse button.

20. Right-click the **form** and then click **Lock Controls**.

21. Save the solution. If you need help, refer to the How To box shown earlier in Figure 1-24.

Coding the Jerrod Realty Application

At this point, the buttons in the interface do not know the tasks they should perform when they are clicked by the user. You tell a button what to do by writing an event procedure for it. You write the event procedure in the Code Editor window.

To code the Exit button's Click event procedure:

1. Auto-hide the Toolbox, Solution Explorer, and Properties windows.

2. Open the Code Editor window. If you need help, refer to the How To box shown earlier in Figure 1-20.

3. Use the Class Name and Method Name list boxes to open the code template for the exitButton's Click event procedure.

4. The Exit button should end the application when it is clicked. Type **me.** (be sure to type the period, but don't press Enter). When you type the period, the Code Editor's IntelliSense feature displays a list of properties, methods, and so on from which you can select.

56

Note: If the list of choices does not appear, the IntelliSense feature may have been turned off on your computer system. To turn it on, click TOOLS on the menu bar and then click Options. If necessary, expand the Text Editor node and then click Basic. Select the Auto list members check box and then click the OK button.

5. If necessary, click the **Common** tab. The Common tab displays the most commonly used items, whereas the All tab displays all of the items. Type **cl** (but don't press Enter). The IntelliSense feature highlights the Close method in the list. (If Close is not highlighted, type the letter o.)

6. Press the **Tab** key on your keyboard to include the Close method in the instruction, and then press **Enter**.

When the user clicks the 65 Maple button, its Click event procedure should display the image from the maplePictureBox in the displayPictureBox. You can accomplish this task using an assignment statement that assigns the Image property of the maplePictureBox to the Image property of the displayPictureBox, like this: `displayPictureBox.Image = maplePictureBox.Image`. The Click event procedure should also display the address "65 Maple" in the addressLabel. This task requires the following assignment statement, which assigns the string "65 Maple" to the Text property of the addressLabel: `addressLabel.Text = "65 Maple"`.

To code the 65 Maple button's Click event procedure:

1. Open the code template for the mapleButton's Click event procedure.

2. Type **displ** to select displayPictureBox in the list. Press the **Tab** key to enter displayPictureBox in the procedure.

3. Type **.** (a period) and then type the letter **i** to select the Image property in the list. Press **Tab** to include the Image property in the statement.

4. Type **=maplep** to select maplePictureBox in the list, and then press **Tab**.

5. Type **.** (a period). The Image property should be highlighted in the list. (If Image is not highlighted, type the letter i.) Press **Tab** and then press **Enter**. The procedure now contains the `displayPictureBox.Image = maplePictureBox.Image` statement.

6. Next, use the IntelliSense feature to type the **addressLabel.Text = "65 Maple"** statement in the procedure. Press **Enter** after typing the statement.

When the user clicks the 2323 Elm button, its Click event procedure should display the image from the elmPictureBox in the displayPictureBox. It should also display the address "2323 Elm" in the addressLabel.

To code the 2323 Elm button's Click event procedure:

1. Open the code template for the elmButton's Click event procedure and then enter the appropriate assignment statements.

2. If line numbers do not appear in the Code Editor window, click **TOOLS** on the menu bar and then click **Options**. If necessary, expand the **Text Editor** node in the Options dialog box and then click **Basic**. Select the **Line numbers** check box and then click the **OK** button. The completed code is shown in Figure 1-68.

PROGRAMMING TUTORIAL 2

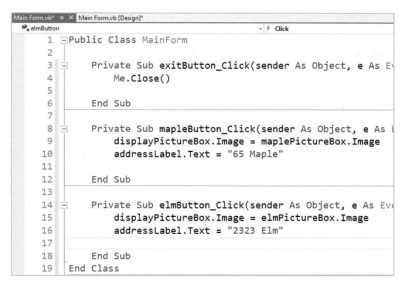

Figure 1-68 Jerrod Realty application's code

3. To remove the line numbers from the Code Editor window, click **TOOLS** on the menu bar and then click **Options**. If necessary, expand the **Text Editor** node in the Options dialog box and then click **Basic**. Deselect the **Line numbers** check box and then click the **OK** button.

Testing an Application

In the following set of steps, you will test the application to determine whether the buttons respond correctly to the user.

To start and end the current application:

1. Open the Project Designer window and verify that MainForm is the name of the startup form. Also change the executable file's name to **Jerrod Realty**. If you need help accomplishing either of these tasks, refer to the How To boxes shown earlier in Figures 1-25 and 1-29.

2. Save the solution and then close the Project Designer window.

3. Start the application. If you need help, refer to the How To box shown earlier in Figure 1-27. (Do not be concerned about any windows that appear at the bottom of the screen.)

4. Click the **65 Maple** button. The picture of the house at 65 Maple appears in the displayPictureBox, and the address "65 Maple" appears in the label control. See Figure 1-69.

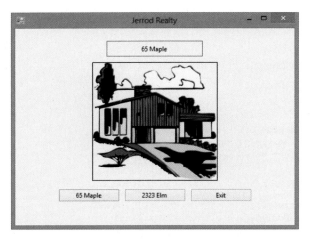

Figure 1-69   Sample run of the application
OpenClipArt.org/Francesco Rollandin

5. Click the **2323 Elm** button. The picture of the house at 2323 Elm appears in the displayPictureBox, and the address "2323 Elm" appears in the label control.

6. Click the **Exit** button.

Printing the Application's Code and Interface

For your future reference, you should always print a copy of the application's code and its interface. To print the code, the Code Editor window must be the active (current) window. To print the interface during design time, the Windows Form designer window must be the active window.

To print the current application's code and interface:

1. If necessary, make the Code Editor window the active window. If your computer is connected to a printer, print the code with line numbers. If you need help, refer to the How To box shown earlier in Figure 1-33.

2. Make the designer window the active window. If your computer is connected to a printer, print the application's interface. If you need help, refer to the How To box shown earlier in Figure 1-33.

Closing and Opening a Solution

When you are finished working with a solution, you should close it using the Close Solution option on the FILE menu. Closing a solution closes all projects and files contained in the solution. You can open an existing solution using the Open Project option on the FILE menu.

To close and then open the current solution:

1. First, close the Code Editor window.

2. Next, close the Jerrod Realty solution. If you need help, refer to the How To box shown earlier in Figure 1-34.

3. Temporarily display the Solution Explorer window to verify that no solutions are open.

4. Now, open the Jerrod Realty solution. If you need help, refer to the How To box shown earlier in Figure 1-35.

5. Temporarily display the Solution Explorer window to verify that the solution is open.

Syntax Errors in Code

In this section, you will introduce a syntax error in the 65 Maple button's Click event procedure. You will then debug the procedure by locating and fixing the error.

To introduce a syntax error in the code:

1. Open the Code Editor window and locate the mapleButton_Click procedure. Delete **.Text** in the second assignment statement and then click the **blank line** below the assignment statement. The jagged blue line that appears below the string "65 Maple" indicates that the assignment statement contains a syntax error.

2. Position your mouse pointer on the jagged blue line. The error message shown in Figure 1-70 indicates that the string "65 Maple" cannot be converted to a label. In other words, it cannot be assigned to the label itself. Instead, it must be assigned to one of the label's properties—in this case, its Text property.

```
Private Sub mapleButton_Click(sender As Object, e As
    displayPictureBox.Image = maplePictureBox.Image
    addressLabel = "65 Maple"
Value of type 'String' cannot be converted to 'System.Windows.Forms.Label'.
    End Sub
```

Figure 1-70 Jagged line and message indicate a syntax error

3. Now observe what happens when you start the application without correcting the syntax error. Save the solution and then start the application. A message box appears and indicates that the code contains errors. The message asks whether you want to continue.

4. Click the **No** button. The Error List window opens at the bottom of the IDE. The Error List window indicates that Line 10 contains an error.

5. Type **.Text** after addressLabel to correct the error, and then click **another line** in the Code Editor window. The Error List window shows that the code is now free of errors.

6. Close the Error List window. Save the solution and then start the application. Click the **65 Maple** button to verify that it is working correctly.

7. Click the **Exit** button to end the application. Close the Code Editor window and then close the solution.

Exiting Visual Studio 2012

You can exit Visual Studio using either the Close button on its title bar or the Exit option on its FILE menu.

To exit Visual Studio:

1. Click **FILE** on the menu bar and then click **Exit** on the menu.

Running the Application's Executable File

Earlier you learned that when you start a Visual Basic application, the computer automatically creates a file that can be run outside of the IDE. The file's name ends with .exe. The computer stores the file in the project's bin\Debug folder.

To run the Jerrod Realty.exe file:

1. Press and hold down the **Windows logo** key on your keyboard as you tap the letter **r**. When the Run dialog box opens, release the logo key.

2. Click the **Browse** button. Locate and then open the VbReloaded2012\Chap01\Jerrod Solution\Jerrod Project\bin\Debug folder. Click **Jerrod Realty** (**Jerrod Realty.exe**) in the list of filenames and then click the **Open** button.

3. Click the **OK** button in the Run dialog box. After a few moments, the Jerrod Realty application's interface appears on the screen. Click the **2323 Elm** and **65 Maple** buttons to test the application, and then click the **Exit** button.

PROGRAMMING EXAMPLE

State Capitals

Create an application that displays the state capital in a label when a button with the state's name is clicked. Use the following names for the solution and project, respectively: State Capitals Solution and State Capitals Project. Save the files in the VbReloaded2012\Chap01 folder. Change the form file's name to Main Form.vb. Remember to lock the controls in the interface. See Figures 1-71 through 1-73. The image in the picture box is contained in the VbReloaded2012\Chap01\USMap.png file. (The image was downloaded from the Open Clip Art Library at *http://OpenClipart.org*.)

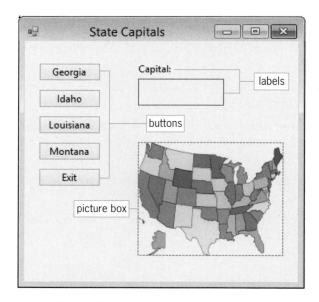

Figure 1-71 User interface
OpenClipArt.org/bnielsen

Object	Property	Setting
Form1	Name	MainForm
	Font	Segoe UI, 9pt
	StartPosition	CenterScreen
	Text	State Capitals
Button1	Name	georgiaButton
	Text	Georgia
Button2	Name	idahoButton
	Text	Idaho
Button3	Name	louisianaButton
	Text	Louisiana
Button4	Name	montanaButton
	Text	Montana
Button5	Name	exitButton
	Text	Exit
Label1	Text	Capital:
Label2	Name	capitalLabel
	AutoSize	False
	BorderStyle	FixedSingle
	Text	(empty)
	TextAlign	MiddleCenter
PictureBox1	Image	USMap.png
	SizeMode	StretchImage

Figure 1-72   Objects, properties, and settings
© 2013 Cengage Learning

```
1 Public Class MainForm
2
3    Private Sub exitButton_Click(sender As Object,
     e As EventArgs) Handles exitButton.Click
4        Me.Close()
5
6    End Sub
7
8    Private Sub georgiaButton_Click(sender As Object,
     e As EventArgs) Handles georgiaButton.Click
9        capitalLabel.Text = "Atlanta"
10
11   End Sub
12
13   Private Sub idahoButton_Click(sender As Object,
     e As EventArgs) Handles idahoButton.Click
14       capitalLabel.Text = "Boise"
15
16   End Sub
17
18   Private Sub louisianaButton_Click(sender As Object,
     e As EventArgs) Handles louisianaButton.Click
19       capitalLabel.Text = "Baton Rouge"
20
21   End Sub
22
23   Private Sub montanaButton_Click(sender As Object,
     e As EventArgs) Handles montanaButton.Click
24       capitalLabel.Text = "Helena"
25
26   End Sub
27 End Class
```

Figure 1-73   Code
© 2013 Cengage Learning

Summary

- An object-oriented programming language, such as Visual Basic 2012, allows programmers to use objects to accomplish a program's goal.

- An object is anything that can be seen, touched, or used. Every object has attributes, called properties, that control its appearance and behavior.

- Every object in an object-oriented program is instantiated (created) from a class, which is a pattern that tells the computer how the object should look and behave. An object is referred to as an instance of the class.

- Applications created in Visual Studio 2012 are composed of solutions, projects, and files.

- You create your application's GUI in the Windows Form Designer window.

- A form is the foundation for the user interface in a Windows application.

- A Windows Form object is instantiated from the Windows Form class.

- The Solution Explorer window displays the names of projects and files contained in the current solution.

- The Properties window lists the selected object's properties.

- The System.Windows.Forms namespace contains the definition of the Windows Form class, as well as the class definitions for objects you add to a form.

- You use the value stored in an object's Name property to refer to the object in code.

- The value stored in the form's Text property appears in the form's title bar.

- The form's StartPosition property determines the position of the form when it first appears on the screen when the application is started.

- The recommended font for applications created for either the Windows 8 or Windows 7 environment is the 9-point size of the Segoe UI font.

- The Toolbox window contains the tools you use when creating your application's GUI.

- The value stored in a control's Text property appears inside the control.

- Controls on a form can be selected, sized, moved, deleted, restored, locked, and unlocked.

- A label control displays text that the user is not allowed to edit while the application is running.

- Button controls are commonly used to perform an immediate action when clicked.

- You use a picture box control to display an image on the form.

- The FORMAT menu provides options for aligning, sizing, and centering the controls on a form.

- You tell an object how to respond to an event by coding an event procedure. You enter the code in the Code Editor window.

- You use the Class Name and Method Name list boxes in the Code Editor window to select the object and event, respectively, that you want to code.

- The Code Editor provides a code template for each of an object's event procedures. The code template begins with the Private Sub clause and ends with the End Sub clause. You enter your Visual Basic instructions between those clauses.

- You can use the `Me.Close()` instruction to terminate an application.

- You should save the solution every 10 or 15 minutes.

- When you start a Visual Basic application, the computer automatically creates an executable file and saves it in the project's bin\Debug folder. This is the file typically given to the user. You can run this file from the Run dialog box in Windows.

- You can use an assignment statement to assign a value to a property while an application is running.

- You should print an application's code and its user interface.

- Closing a solution closes all projects and files contained in the solution.

- The process of locating and correcting the errors (bugs) in a program is called debugging.

Key Terms

Applications—programs created for the Windows environment, the Web, or mobile devices

Assignment operator—the equal sign in an assignment statement

Assignment statement—an instruction that assigns a value to something, such as to the property of an object

Bug—an error in a program's code

Button control—the control commonly used to perform an immediate action when clicked

Camel case—the practice of entering the first word in an object's name in lowercase and then capitalizing the first letter of each subsequent word in the name

Class—the term used in object-oriented programming (OOP) to refer to a pattern that the computer uses to instantiate an object

Class definition—a block of code that specifies (or defines) an object's appearance and behavior

Class Name list box—appears in the Code Editor window; lists the names of the objects included in the user interface

Code—program instructions

Code Editor window—the window in which you enter your application's code

Controls—objects (such as a label, a picture box, or a button) added to a form

Debugging—the process of locating and correcting the errors (bugs) in a program

Dot member access operator—a period; used to indicate a hierarchy

Event procedure—a set of Visual Basic instructions that tell an object how to respond to an event

Events—actions to which an object can respond; examples include clicking, double-clicking, and scrolling

Executable file—a file that can be run outside of the Visual Studio IDE, such as from the Run dialog box in Windows; the file has an .exe extension on its filename

Form—the foundation for the user interface in a Windows application; also called a Windows form object

Form file—a file that contains the code associated with a Windows form

GUI—a graphical user interface

IDE—an integrated development environment

Instance—the term used in object-oriented programming (OOP) to refer to an object instantiated (created) from a class

Instantiated—the term used in object-oriented programming (OOP) to refer to the process of creating an object from a class

Integrated development environment—an environment that contains all the tools and features needed to create, run, and test a program; also called an IDE

Keyword—a word that has a special meaning in a programming language

Label control—the control used to display text that the user is not allowed to edit during run time

Method—a predefined Visual Basic procedure that you can call (or invoke) when needed

Method Name list box—appears in the Code Editor window; lists the events to which the selected object is capable of responding

Namespace—a block of memory cells inside the computer; the memory cells contain the code that defines a group of related classes

Object—in object-oriented programming (OOP), anything that can be seen, touched, or used

Object-oriented programming language—a language that allows the programmer to use objects to accomplish a program's goal

OOP—object-oriented programming

Pascal case—the practice of capitalizing the first letter in a name and the first letter of each subsequent word in the name

Picture box control—the control used to display an image on a form

Procedure footer—the last line in a code template

Procedure header—the first line in a code template

Properties—the attributes that control an object's appearance and behavior

Properties window—the window that lists an object's attributes (properties)

Reference control—the first control selected in a group of controls; this is the control whose size and/or location you want the other selected controls to match

Sequence structure—refers to the fact that the computer processes a procedure's instructions one after another in the order in which they appear in the procedure; also referred to as sequential processing

Sequential processing—see sequence structure

Solution Explorer window—the window that displays a list of the projects contained in the current solution and the items contained in each project

Source file—a file that contains code

Startup form—the form that appears automatically when an application is started

String—zero or more characters enclosed in quotation marks

Sub procedure—a block of code that performs a specific task

Syntax—the rules of a programming language

Syntax error—occurs when an instruction in your code breaks one of a programming language's rules

Toolbox—see Toolbox window

Toolbox window—the window that contains the tools used when creating an interface; each tool represents a class; referred to more simply as the toolbox

User interface—what the user sees and interacts with while an application is running

Windows Form Designer window—the window in which you create your application's GUI

Windows Form object—the foundation for the user interface in a Windows application; referred to more simply as a form

Review Questions

Each Review Question is associated with one or more objectives listed at the beginning of the chapter.

1. When a form has been modified since the last time it was saved, what appears on its tab in the designer window? (9)

    a. an ampersand (&)   c. a percent sign (%)
    b. an asterisk (*)   d. a plus sign (+)

2. Which of the following assigns the string "785.23" to the amountLabel control? (4, 8, 11)

    a. `amountLabel = "785.23"`
    b. `amountLabel.String = "785.23"`
    c. `amountLabel.Text = '785.23'`
    d. `amountLabel.Text = "785.23"`

3. Which of the following is a pattern for creating an object? (1)

    a. an attribute   c. a class
    b. a behavior   d. an instance

4. Which window is used to set the characteristics that control an object's appearance and behavior? (4)

    a. Characteristics   c. Properties
    b. Object   d. Toolbox

5. Which of the following instructions makes the soLongLabel invisible? (4, 8, 11)

    a. `soLongLabel.Visible = False`
    b. `soLongLabel.Visible = True`
    c. `soLongLabel.Invisible = False`
    d. `soLongLabel.Invisible = True`

6. Which property contains the text that appears on the face of a button? (4, 6)

    a. Caption   c. Name
    b. Label   d. Text

7. Actions such as clicking and double-clicking are called _____. (1)

    a. actionEvents   c. happenings
    b. events   d. procedures

8. The equal sign in an assignment statement is called the _____ operator. (11)

    a. assignment   c. equality
    b. dot member access   d. equation

9. If a project is stored in the F:\Chap01\First Solution\First Project folder, where will the computer store the project's executable file? (2, 10)

    a. F:\Chap01\First Solution\First Project
    b. F:\Chap01\First Solution\First Project\bin\Debug
    c. F:\Chap01\First Solution\First Project\bin\Executable
    d. F:\Chap01\First Solution\First Project\Executable

Each Exercise is associated with one or more objectives listed at the beginning of the chapter.

66

10. Which property does the programmer use to refer to an object in code? (4, 8)

   a. Caption   c. Name

   b. Label   d. Text

Exercises

Pencil and Paper

INTRODUCTORY

1. Explain the difference between an object's Text property and its Name property. (4, 6, 8)

INTRODUCTORY

2. Explain the process of using the FORMAT menu to align the left border of the Button1 and Button2 controls with the left border of the Button3 control. (5, 7)

INTERMEDIATE

3. Write an assignment statement to assign the string "Visual Basic" to the languageLabel control. (8, 11)

ADVANCED

4. Write an assignment statement to assign the contents of the firstLabel control to the secondLabel control. (8, 11)

SWAT THE BUGS

5. Correct the errors in the following line of code: `myButton.Visibel = Yes` (4, 11, 13)

SWAT THE BUGS

6. Correct the errors in the following line of code: `nameLabel = Jake Smith` (4, 11, 13)

Computer

MODIFY THIS

7. If necessary, create the Jerrod Realty application from this chapter's Programming Tutorial 2. Use Windows to make a copy of the Jerrod Solution folder. Rename the copy Jerrod Solution-ModifyThis. Open the Jerrod Solution (Jerrod Solution.sln) file contained in the Jerrod Solution-ModifyThis folder. Add another button and picture box to the form; name the controls mainButton and mainPictureBox, respectively. In the mainPictureBox control, display the image stored in the VbReloaded2012\Chap01\123Main.png file. (The image is courtesy of openclipart.org/Francesco Rollandin.) When the user clicks the mainButton, the button's Click event procedure should display the mainPictureBox's image in the displayPictureBox, and display the address "123 Main" in the addressLabel. Make the appropriate modifications to the application's interface and code. Save the solution and then start and test the application. Close the solution. Locate the application's .exe file. Run the file from the Run dialog box in Windows. Print the application's code and interface. (1-12)

MODIFY THIS

8. If necessary, create the State Capitals application from this chapter's Programming Example. Use Windows to make a copy of the State Capitals Solution folder. Rename the copy State Capitals Solution-ModifyThis. Open the State Capitals Solution (State Capitals Solution.sln) file contained in the State Capitals Solution-ModifyThis folder. Add another label control to the form. Assign the name signingOrderLabel to the control. Modify the application so that it displays a message indicating the state's U.S. Constitution signing order. For example, when the user clicks the Georgia button, the button's Click event procedure should display the message "Georgia was the 4th state to sign the U.S. Constitution." (Idaho was the 43rd state to sign, Louisiana was the 18th state, and Montana was the 41st state.) Save the solution and then start and test the application. Close the solution. Locate the application's .exe file. Run the file from the Run dialog box in Windows. (1-11)

9. In this exercise, you add label and button controls to a form. You also change the properties of the form and its controls. (1-11)

    INTRODUCTORY

    a. Open the Carpenters Solution (Carpenters Solution.sln) file contained in the VbReloaded2012\Chap01\Carpenters Solution folder.

    b. Change the form file's name to Main Form.vb. Change the form's name to MainForm. Change the form's Font property to Segoe UI, 9pt. The form's title bar should say ICA; set the appropriate property. The form should be centered on the screen when it first appears; set the appropriate property.

    c. Add a label to the form. The label should contain the text "International Carpenters Association" (without the quotes); set the appropriate property. Display the label's text in italic using the Segoe UI, 16pt font. Position the label near the top of the form and then center it, horizontally, on the form.

    d. Add a picture box to the form. The control should display the image stored in the ICA.png file contained in the VbReloaded2012\Chap01 folder. Set the picture box's SizeMode property to StretchImage. Change the picture box's size to 290, 110. Center the picture box on the form, both vertically and horizontally.

    e. Add a button to the form. Position the button in the lower-right corner of the form. Change the button's name to exitButton. The button should display the text "Exit" (without the quotation marks); set the appropriate property.

    f. Lock the controls on the form.

    g. The Exit button should terminate the application when clicked. Enter the appropriate code in the Code Editor window.

    h. Verify that MainForm is the project's startup form. Also, change the executable file's name to ICA. Close the Project Designer window.

    i. Save the solution and then start and test the application. Close the Code Editor window and then close the solution.

    j. Use the Run dialog box in Windows to run the project's executable file, which is contained in the project's bin\Debug folder.

10. Create a Visual Basic Windows application. Use the following names for the solution and project, respectively: Costello Solution and Costello Project. Save the application in the VbReloaded2012\Chap01 folder. Change the form file's name to Main Form.vb. Create the user interface shown in Figure 1-74. You will need to set the messageLabel's AutoSize and BorderStyle properties. The picture box should display the image stored in the DollarSign.png file contained in the VbReloaded2012\Chap01 folder. Change the form's Font property to Segoe UI, 9pt. You can use any font style and font size for the labels. The form should be centered on the screen when the application is started. The Exit button should terminate the application when it is clicked. When the Display button is clicked, it should display the message "We have the best deals in town!" in the messageLabel. Enter the appropriate code in the Code Editor window. Change the executable file's name to Costello Motors. Close the Project Designer window. Save the solution and then start and test the application. Close the Code Editor window and then close the solution. Use the Run dialog box in Windows to run the project's executable file, which is contained in the project's bin\Debug folder. (1-11)

    INTERMEDIATE

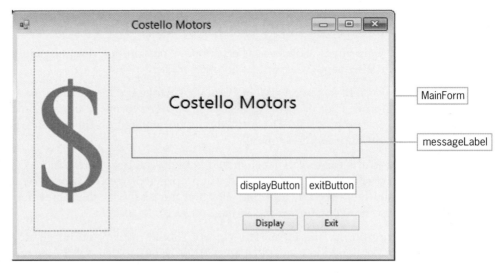

Figure 1-74   Interface for the Costello Motors application

SWAT THE BUGS

11. Open the Debug Solution (Debug Solution.sln) file contained in the VbReloaded2012\ Chap01\Debug Solution folder. Start the application. Click the Exit button. Notice that the Exit button does not end the application. Click the Close button on the form's title bar to end the application. Open the Code Editor window. Locate and then correct the error. Save the solution and then start and test the application. Close the Code Editor window and then close the solution. (13)

Case Projects

 Castle's Ice Cream Parlor

Create an application that displays the price of an item in a label when a button with the item's name is clicked. Include a button that allows the user to terminate the application. Be sure to assign meaningful names to the form, the buttons, and the label that contains the price. Use the following names for the solution and project, respectively: Castle Solution and Castle Project. Save the application in the VbReloaded2012\Chap01 folder. Change the form file's name to Main Form.vb. You can either create your own interface or create the one shown in Figure 1-75. The image in the picture box was downloaded from the Open Clip Art Library at *http://openclipart.org*. The image is stored in the VbReloaded2012\ Chap01\IceCream.png file. The item names are shown in the figure. Use your own prices for the items. (1-9, 11)

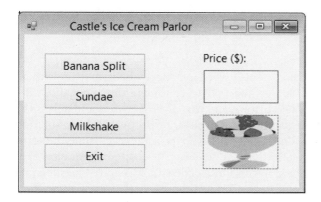

Figure 1-75 Sample interface for the Castle's Ice Cream Parlor application
OpenClipArt.org/Machovka

 Allen School District

Create an application that displays the name of the principal and the school's phone number in labels when a button with the school's name is clicked. Include a button that allows the user to terminate the application. Be sure to assign meaningful names to the form, the buttons, and the label controls that contain the name and phone number. Use the following names for the solution and project, respectively: Allen Solution and Allen Project. Save the application in the VbReloaded2012\Chap01 folder. Change the form file's name to Main Form.vb. You can either create your own interface or create the one shown in Figure 1-76. The image in the picture box was downloaded from the Open Clip Art Library at *http://openclipart.org*. The image is stored in the VbReloaded2012\Chap01\School.png file. The school names are shown in the figure. You provide the names for the principals and the phone numbers for the schools. (1-9, 11)

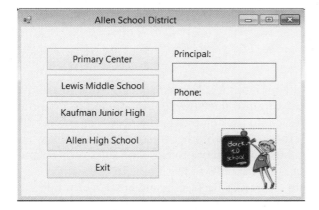

Figure 1-76 Sample interface for the Allen School District application
OpenClipArt.org/sammo241

Elvira Learning Center

Create an application that displays the equivalent Spanish word in a label when a button with an English word is clicked. Include a button that allows the user to terminate the application. Be sure to assign meaningful names to the form, the buttons, and the label control that displays the Spanish word. Use the following names for the solution and project, respectively: Elvira Solution and Elvira Project. Save the application in the VbReloaded2012\Chap01 folder. Change the form file's name to Main Form.vb. You can either create your own interface or create the one shown in Figure 1-77. The image in the picture box is stored in the VbReloaded2012\Chap01\Question.png file. The English words are shown in the figure. If necessary, use the Internet to determine the equivalent Spanish words. (1-9, 11)

Figure 1-77 Sample interface for the Elvira Learning Center application

Mary Golds Flower Shop

Create an eye-catching splash screen for the flower shop. A splash screen is the first image that appears when an application is started. It is used to introduce the application and to hold the user's attention while the application is being read into the computer's memory. You can use the tools you learned in this chapter, or you can experiment with other tools from the toolbox. For example, the Timer tool creates a timer control that you can use to close the splash screen after a specified period of time. (You can look ahead to Chapter 8 to learn how to use a timer control.) You may also want to experiment with a control's BackColor and ForeColor properties. Be sure to include one or more images in the interface. You can use either your own image file(s) or download one or more free images from the Open Clip Art Library at *http://openclipart.org*. Use the following names for the solution and project, respectively: Mary Golds Solution and Mary Golds Project. Save the application in the VbReloaded2012\Chap01 folder. Change the form file's name to Main Form.vb. Save the application in the VbReloaded2012\Chap01 folder. Print the application's code and interface. (1-9, 11, 12)

CHAPTER 2

Creating a User Interface

After studying Chapter 2, you should be able to:

1 Plan an application using a TOE chart

2 Use a text box and a table layout panel

3 Follow the Windows standards regarding the layout and labeling of controls

4 Follow the Windows standards regarding the use of graphics, fonts, and color

5 Assign access keys to controls

6 Set the tab order

7 Add a splash screen to a project

8 Use the Font and Color dialog boxes

9 Change an object's color and font from code

10 Designate a default button

11 Print the interface from code

12 Play an audio file

Reading and Study Guide

Before you begin reading Chapter 2, view the Ch02_ReadingStudyGuide.pdf file. You can open the file using Adobe Reader, which is available for free on the Adobe Web site at *www.adobe.com/downloads/*.

Planning an Application

Before you create the user interface for a Visual Basic Windows application, you should plan the application. The plan should be developed jointly with the user to ensure that the application meets the user's needs. It cannot be stressed enough that the only way to guarantee the success of an application is to actively involve the user in the planning phase. Figure 2-1 lists the steps to follow when planning an application.

HOW TO Plan an Application

1. Identify the tasks the application needs to perform.

2. Identify the objects to which you will assign those tasks.

3. Identify the events required to trigger an object into performing its assigned tasks.

4. Design the user interface.

Figure 2-1   How to plan an application
© 2013 Cengage Learning

You can use a TOE (Task, Object, Event) chart to record the application's tasks, objects, and events, which are identified in the first three steps of the planning phase. In the next several sections, you will complete a TOE chart for a small company named Sophie's Teddy Bears.

Sophie's Teddy Bears

Sophie's Teddy Bears takes orders for teddy bears by phone. The bears are priced at $50 each and are available in two styles: Bowtie Bear and Hearts Bear. The company employs 10 salespeople to answer the phones. The salespeople record each order on a form that contains the customer's name and address, and the number of each style of bear ordered. The salespeople then calculate the total number of bears ordered and the total price of the order, including a 5% sales tax. The company's sales manager feels that having the salespeople manually perform the necessary calculations is much too time-consuming and prone to errors. He wants you to create a computerized application that will solve the problems of the current order-taking system. The first step in planning this application is to identify the application's tasks.

Identifying the Application's Tasks

Realizing that it is essential to involve the user when planning the application, you meet with the sales manager to determine his requirements. You ask the sales manager to bring the form the salespeople currently use to record the orders. Viewing the current forms and procedures will help you gain a better understanding of the application. You also may be able to use the current form as a guide when designing the user interface. Figure 2-2 shows the current order form used by Sophie's Teddy Bears.

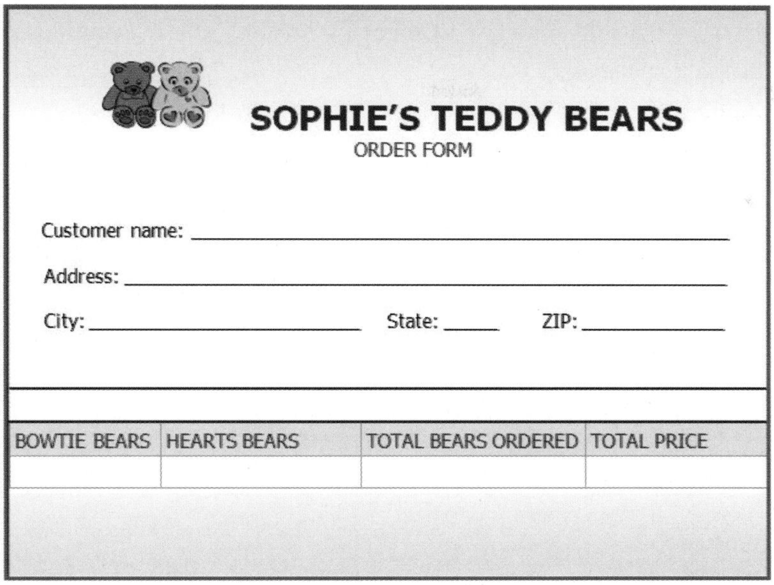

SOPHIE'S TEDDY BEARS
ORDER FORM

Customer name: ______________________________

Address: ______________________________

City: ______________ State: _____ ZIP: __________

BOWTIE BEARS	HEARTS BEARS	TOTAL BEARS ORDERED	TOTAL PRICE

Figure 2-2 Current order form
OpenClipArt.org/Gerald_G

When identifying the tasks an application needs to perform, it is helpful to ask the questions italicized in the following bulleted items. The answers pertaining to the Sophie's Teddy Bears application follow each question.

- *What information will the application need to display on the screen and/or print on the printer?* The application should both display and print the customer's name, street address, city, state, ZIP code, number of Bowtie Bears ordered, number of Hearts Bears ordered, total number of bears ordered, and total price of the order.
- *What information will the user need to enter into the user interface to display and/or print the desired information?* The salesperson (the user) must enter the customer's name, street address, city, state, ZIP code, number of Bowtie Bears ordered, and number of Hearts Bears ordered.
- *What information will the application need to calculate to display and/or print the desired information?* The application needs to calculate the total number of bears ordered and the total price of the order.
- *How will the user end the application?* The application will use an Exit button.
- *Will previous information need to be cleared from the screen before new information is entered?* The order information will need to be cleared from the screen before the next customer's information is entered.

Figure 2-3 shows the application's tasks listed in a TOE chart. The tasks do not need to be listed in any particular order. In this case, the data entry tasks are listed first, followed by the calculation tasks, the display and printing tasks, the application ending task, and the screen clearing task.

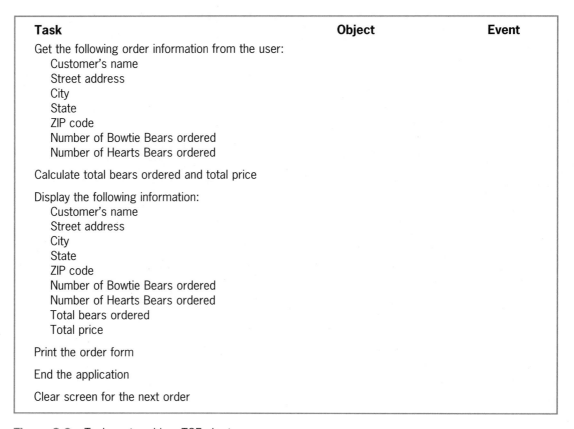

Task	Object	Event
Get the following order information from the user: Customer's name Street address City State ZIP code Number of Bowtie Bears ordered Number of Hearts Bears ordered		
Calculate total bears ordered and total price		
Display the following information: Customer's name Street address City State ZIP code Number of Bowtie Bears ordered Number of Hearts Bears ordered Total bears ordered Total price		
Print the order form		
End the application		
Clear screen for the next order		

Figure 2-3   Tasks entered in a TOE chart
© 2013 Cengage Learning

Identifying the Objects

After completing the Task column of the TOE chart, you then assign each task to an object in the user interface. For this application, the only objects you will use besides the Windows form itself are the button, label, and text box controls. As you already know, you use a label control to display information that you do not want the user to change while the application is running, and you use a button control to perform an action immediately after the user clicks it. You use a **text box** to give the user an area in which to enter data.

The first task listed in the TOE chart gets the order information from the user. Because you need to provide the salesperson with areas in which to enter the information, you will assign the first task to seven text boxes—one for each item of information.

The TOE chart's second task calculates both the total number of bears ordered and the total price. So that the salesperson can calculate these amounts at any time, you will assign the task to a button named calcButton.

The third task in the TOE chart displays the order information, the total number of bears ordered, and the total price. The order information is displayed automatically when the user enters that information in the seven text boxes. The total bears ordered and total price, however, are not entered by the user. Instead, those amounts are calculated by the calcButton. Because the user should not be allowed to change the calculated results, you will have the calcButton display the total bears ordered and total price in two label controls named totalBearsLabel and totalPriceLabel, respectively. If you look ahead to Figure 2-4, you will notice that "(from calcButton)" was added to the Task column for both display tasks.

The TOE chart's fourth task prints the order form. Here again, you will assign the task to a button so that the salesperson has control over when (and if) the order form is printed. You will name the button printButton.

The last two tasks listed in the TOE chart are "End the application" and "Clear screen for the next order." You will assign the tasks to buttons named exitButton and clearButton, respectively; doing this gives the user control over when the tasks are performed. Figure 2-4 shows the TOE chart with the Task and Object columns completed.

Task	Object	Event
Get the following order information from the user:		
Customer's name	nameTextBox	
Street address	addressTextBox	
City	cityTextBox	
State	stateTextBox	
ZIP code	zipTextBox	
Number of Bowtie Bears ordered	bowtieTextBox	
Number of Hearts Bears ordered	heartsTextBox	
Calculate total bears ordered and total price	calcButton	
Display the following information:		
Customer's name	nameTextBox	
Street address	addressTextBox	
City	cityTextBox	
State	stateTextBox	
ZIP code	zipTextBox	
Number of Bowtie Bears ordered	bowtieTextBox	
Number of Hearts Bears ordered	heartsTextBox	
Total bears ordered (from calcButton)	totalBearsLabel	
Total price (from calcButton)	totalPriceLabel	
Print the order form	printButton	
End the application	exitButton	
Clear screen for the next order	clearButton	

Figure 2-4   Tasks and objects entered in a TOE chart
© 2013 Cengage Learning

Identifying the Events

After defining the application's tasks and assigning the tasks to objects in the interface, you then determine which event (if any) must occur for an object to carry out its assigned task. The seven text boxes listed in the TOE chart in Figure 2-4 are assigned the task of getting and displaying the order information. Text boxes accept and display information automatically, so no special event is necessary for them to carry out their assigned task.

The two label controls listed in the TOE chart are assigned the task of displaying the total number of bears ordered and the total price of the order. Label controls automatically display their contents; so, here again, no special event needs to occur. (Recall that the two label controls will get their values from the calcButton.)

The remaining objects listed in the TOE chart are the four buttons. You will have each button perform its assigned task(s) when the user clicks it. Figure 2-5 shows the completed TOE chart.

Task	Object	Event
Get the following order information from the user:		
Customer's name	nameTextBox	None
Street address	addressTextBox	None
City	cityTextBox	None
State	stateTextBox	None
ZIP code	zipTextBox	None
Number of Bowtie Bears ordered	bowtieTextBox	None
Number of Hearts Bears ordered	heartsTextBox	None
Calculate total bears ordered and total price	calcButton	Click
Display the following information:		
Customer's name	nameTextBox	None
Street address	addressTextBox	None
City	cityTextBox	None
State	stateTextBox	None
ZIP code	zipTextBox	None
Number of Bowtie Bears ordered	bowtieTextBox	None
Number of Hearts Bears ordered	heartsTextBox	None
Total bears ordered (from calcButton)	totalBearsLabel	None
Total price (from calcButton)	totalPriceLabel	None
Print the order form	printButton	Click
End the application	exitButton	Click
Clear screen for the next order	clearButton	Click

Figure 2-5   Completed TOE chart ordered by task
© 2013 Cengage Learning

If the application you are creating is small, as is the Sophie's Teddy Bears application, you can use the TOE chart in its current form to help you write the Visual Basic code. When the application is large, however, it is often helpful to rearrange the TOE chart so that it is ordered by object rather than by task. To do so, you list all of the objects in the Object column of a new TOE chart, being sure to list each object only once. You then list each object's tasks and events in the Task and Event columns, respectively. Figure 2-6 shows the rearranged TOE chart ordered by object rather than by task.

Task	Object	Event
1. Calculate total bears ordered and total price 2. Display total bears ordered and total price in totalBearsLabel and totalPriceLabel	calcButton	Click
Print the order form	printButton	Click
End the application	exitButton	Click
Clear screen for the next order	clearButton	Click
Display total bears ordered (from calcButton)	totalBearsLabel	None
Display total price (from calcButton)	totalPriceLabel	None
Get and display the order information	nameTextBox, addressTextBox, cityTextBox, stateTextBox, zipTextBox, bowtieTextBox, heartsTextBox	None

Figure 2-6   Completed TOE chart ordered by object
© 2013 Cengage Learning

Mini-Quiz 2-1

1. When planning an application, what is the first thing you need to identify? (1)

   a. code

   b. events

   c. objects

   d. tasks

2. Every object in a user interface needs an event to occur in order for it to perform its assigned task. (1)

   a. True

   b. False

3. The task of getting a sales tax rate from the user should be assigned to what type of control? (1, 2)

   a. button

   b. label

   c. text box

   d. either b or c

 The answers to Mini-Quiz questions are located in Appendix A. Each question is associated with one or more objectives listed at the beginning of the chapter.

Designing the User Interface

After completing the TOE chart, the next step is to design the user interface. Although the TOE chart lists the objects to include in the interface, it does not indicate *where* the objects should be placed on the form. While the design of an interface is open to creativity, there are some guidelines to which you should adhere so that your application is consistent with the Windows standards. This consistency will give your interface a familiar look, which will make your application easier to both learn and use. The guidelines are referred to as GUI (graphical user interface) guidelines. The first GUI guidelines you will learn in this chapter relate to the placement of the controls in the interface.

 Some companies have their own standards for interfaces used within the company. A company's standards supersede the Windows standards.

Control Placement

In Western countries, the user interface should be organized so that the information flows either vertically or horizontally, with the most important information always located in the upper-left corner of the interface. In a vertical arrangement, the information flows from top to bottom: The essential information is located in the first column, while secondary information is placed in subsequent columns. In a horizontal arrangement, on the other hand, the information flows from left to right: The essential information is placed in the first row, with secondary information placed in subsequent rows.

Related controls should be grouped together using either white (empty) space or one of the tools located in the Containers section of the toolbox. Examples of tools found in the Containers section include the GroupBox, Panel, and TableLayoutPanel tools. The difference between a panel and a group box is that, unlike a group box, a panel can have scroll bars. However, unlike a panel, a group box has a Text property that you can use to indicate the contents of the control. Unlike the panel and group box controls, the table layout panel control provides a table structure in which you place other controls. You will learn how to use a table layout panel in this chapter's Programming Tutorial 1.

Ch02-
Container
Controls

Figures 2-7 and 2-8 show two different interfaces for the Sophie's Teddy Bears application. In Figure 2-7 the information is arranged vertically, and white space is used to group related controls together. In Figure 2-8 the information is arranged horizontally, with related controls grouped together using a group box, panel, and table layout panel. Each text box and button in both interfaces is labeled so the user knows the control's purpose. For example, the "Name:" label tells the user the type of information to enter in the text box that appears below it. Similarly, the "Calculate" text on the calcButton's face indicates the action the button will perform when it is clicked.

Figure 2-7   Vertical arrangement of the interface
OpenClipArt.org/Gerald_G

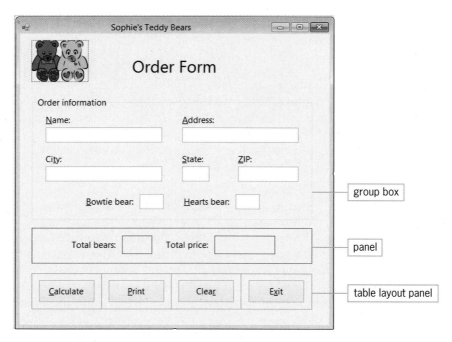

Figure 2-8   Horizontal arrangement of the interface
OpenClipArt.org/Gerald_G

Label controls that display program output, such as the result of calculations, should be labeled to make their contents obvious to the user. In the interfaces shown in Figures 2-7 and 2-8, the "Total bears:" and "Total price:" labels identify the contents of the totalBearsLabel and totalPriceLabel controls, respectively.

The text contained in an identifying label should be meaningful and left-aligned within the label. In most cases, an identifying label should be from one to three words only and appear on one line. In addition, the identifying label should be positioned either above or to the left of the control it identifies. An identifying label should end with a colon (:), which distinguishes it from other text in the user interface (such as the heading text "Order Form"). Some assistive technologies, which are technologies that provide assistance to individuals with disabilities, rely on the colons to make this distinction. The Windows standard is to use sentence capitalization for identifying labels. **Sentence capitalization** means you capitalize only the first letter in the first word and in any words that are customarily capitalized.

As you learned in Chapter 1, a button is identified by the text that appears on its face. The text is often referred to as the button's caption. The caption should be meaningful, be from one to three words only, and appear on one line. A button's caption should be entered using **book title capitalization**, which means you capitalize the first letter in each word, except for articles, conjunctions, and prepositions that do not occur at either the beginning or end of the caption. If the buttons are stacked vertically, as they are in Figure 2-7, all the buttons should be the same height and width. If the buttons are positioned horizontally, as they are in Figure 2-8, all the buttons should be the same height, but their widths may vary if necessary. In a group of buttons, the most commonly used button typically appears first—either on the top (in a vertical arrangement) or on the left (in a horizontal arrangement).

When positioning the controls in the interface, place related controls close to each other and be sure to maintain a consistent margin from the edges of the form. Also, it's helpful to align the borders of the controls wherever possible to minimize the number of different margins appearing in the interface. Doing this allows the user to more easily scan the information. You can align the borders using the snap lines that appear as you are building the interface. Or, you can use the FORMAT menu to align (and also size) the controls.

Graphics, Fonts, and Color

When designing a user interface, keep in mind that you want to create a screen that no one notices. Interfaces that contain a lot of different colors, fonts, and graphics may get "oohs" and "aahs" during their initial use, but they become tiresome after a while. The most important point to remember is that the interface should not distract the user from doing his or her work. In this section, you will learn some guidelines to follow regarding the use of graphics, fonts, and color in an interface.

 The graphics, font, and color guidelines do not pertain to game applications.

The human eye is attracted to pictures before text, so use graphics sparingly in an interface. Designers typically include graphics to either emphasize or clarify a portion of the screen. However, a graphic also can be used merely for aesthetic purposes, as long as it is small and placed in a location that does not distract the user. The small graphic in the Sophie's Teddy Bears interfaces is included for aesthetics only. The graphic is purposely located in the upper-left corner of each interface, which is where you want the user's eye to be drawn first anyway. The graphic adds a personal touch to the order form without distracting the user.

As you learned in Chapter 1, an object's Font property determines the type, style, and size of the font used to display the object's text. You should use only one font type (typically Segoe UI) for all of the text in an interface, and use no more than two different font sizes. In addition, avoid using italics and underlining because both font styles make text difficult to read. The use of bold text should be limited to titles, headings, and key items that you want to emphasize.

The human eye is attracted to color before black and white; therefore, use color sparingly in an interface. It is a good practice to build the interface using black, white, and gray first, and then add color only if you have a good reason to do so. Keep the following three points in mind when deciding whether to include color in an interface:

1. People who have some form of either color blindness or color confusion will have trouble distinguishing colors.

2. Color is very subjective: A color that looks pretty to you may be hideous to someone else.

3. A color may have a different meaning in a different culture.

Usually, it is best to use black text on a white, off-white, or light gray background because dark text on a light background is the easiest to read. You should never use a dark color for the background or a light color for the text. This is because a dark background is hard on the eyes, and light-colored text can appear blurry.

If you are going to include color in the interface, limit the number of colors to three, not including white, black, and gray. Be sure that the colors you choose complement each other. Although color can be used to identify an important element in the interface, you should never use it as the only means of identification. In the interfaces shown earlier in Figures 2-7 and 2-8, for example, the colored box helps the salesperson quickly locate the total price. However, color is not the only means of identifying the contents of that box; the box also has an identifying label, "Total price:". (You can change the background color of an object by setting its BackColor property.)

Borders, Sizing, and Text Alignment

A control's border is determined by its BorderStyle property, which can be set to None, FixedSingle, or Fixed3D. Controls with a BorderStyle property set to None have no border. Setting the BorderStyle property to FixedSingle surrounds the control with a thin line, and setting it to Fixed3D gives the control a three-dimensional appearance. In most cases, a text box's BorderStyle property should be left at its default setting: Fixed3D.

The appropriate setting for a label control's BorderStyle property depends on the control's purpose. Label controls that identify other controls (such as those that identify text boxes) should have a BorderStyle property setting of None, which is the default setting. On the other hand, label controls that display program output (such as those that display the result of a calculation) typically have a BorderStyle property setting of FixedSingle. You should avoid setting a label control's BorderStyle property to Fixed3D because, in Windows applications, a control with a three-dimensional appearance implies that it can accept user input.

A label control's AutoSize property determines whether the control automatically sizes to fit its current contents. Here, too, the appropriate setting depends on the label's purpose. Label controls that identify other controls use the default setting: True. However, you typically set to False the AutoSize property of label controls that display program output.

A label control's TextAlign property determines the alignment of the text within the label. The TextAlign property can be set to nine different values, such as TopLeft, MiddleCenter, and BottomRight.

If you remove the contents of a label's Text property when its AutoSize and BorderStyle properties are set to True and None, respectively, you will not see the label on the form. You will need to use the Properties window's Object box to access the label.

The answers to Mini-Quiz questions are located in Appendix A. Each question is associated with one or more objectives listed at the beginning of the chapter.

Mini-Quiz 2-2

1. The text on a button's face should be entered using _____. (3)

   a. book title capitalization

   b. lowercase letters

   c. sentence capitalization

   d. uppercase letters

2. Which of the following controls can be used to group together other controls? (2, 3)

   a. group box

   b. panel

   c. table layout panel

   d. all of the above

3. Label controls that identify text boxes usually have their BorderStyle and AutoSize properties set to ———————— and ————————, respectively. (3)

   a. None, False

   b. None, True

   c. False, No

   d. FixedSingle, Yes

Assigning Access Keys

The text in many of the controls shown in Figure 2-9 contains an underlined letter. The underlined letter is called an **access key**, and it allows the user to select an object using the Alt key in combination with a letter or number. For example, you can select the Exit button by pressing Alt+x because the letter x is the Exit button's access key. Access keys are not case sensitive; therefore, you can select the Exit button by pressing either Alt+x or Alt+X. If you do not see the underlined access keys while an application is running, you can show them temporarily by pressing the Alt key. You can subsequently hide them by pressing the Alt key again.

Figure 2-9 Sophie's Teddy Bears interface

OpenClipArt.org/Gerald_G

You should assign access keys to each of the controls (in the interface) that can accept user input. Examples of such controls include text boxes and buttons. This is because the user can enter information in a text box and also click a button. The only exceptions to this rule are the OK and Cancel buttons, which typically do not have access keys in Windows applications. It is important to assign access keys to controls for the following reasons:

1. They allow a user to work with the application even when the mouse becomes inoperative.

2. They allow users who are fast typists to keep their hands on the keyboard.

3. They allow people who cannot work with a mouse, such as people with disabilities, to use the application.

You assign an access key by including an ampersand (&) in the control's caption or identifying label. If the control is a button, you include the ampersand in the button's Text property, which is where a button's caption is stored. If the control is a text box, you include the ampersand in the Text property of its identifying label. (As you will learn later in this chapter, you also must set the TabIndex properties of the text box and its identifying label appropriately.) You enter the ampersand to the immediate left of the character you want to designate as the access key. For example, to assign the letter x as the access key for the Exit button, you enter E&xit in the button's Text property. To assign the letter N as the access key for the nameTextBox, you enter &Name: in the Text property of its identifying label.

Notice that the "Total bears:" and "Total price:" labels in Figure 2-9 do not have access keys. This is because those labels do not identify controls that accept user input; rather, they identify other label controls. Users cannot access label controls while an application is running, so it is inappropriate to include an access key in their identifying labels.

Each access key in the interface should be unique. The first choice for an access key is the first letter of the caption or identifying label, unless another letter provides a more meaningful association. For example, the letter x is the access key for an Exit button because it provides a more meaningful association than does the letter E. If you can't use the first letter (perhaps because it is already used as the access key for another control) and no other letter provides a more meaningful association, then use a distinctive consonant in the caption or label. The last choices for an access key are a vowel or a number.

Controlling the Tab Order

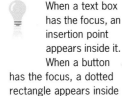

When a text box has the focus, an insertion point appears inside it. When a button has the focus, a dotted rectangle appears inside its darkened border.

While you are creating the interface, each control's TabIndex property contains a number that represents the order in which the control was added to the form. The first control added to a form has a TabIndex value of 0; the second control has a TabIndex value of 1; and so on. The TabIndex values determine the tab order, which is the order that each control receives the **focus** when the user either presses the Tab key or employs an access key while an application is running. A control whose TabIndex is 2 will receive the focus immediately after the control whose TabIndex is 1, and so on. When a control has the focus, it can accept user input. Not all controls have a TabIndex property. A picture box control, for example, does not have a TabIndex property. You can tell whether a control has a TabIndex property by viewing its Properties list.

Most times you will need to reset the TabIndex values for an interface. This is because controls are rarely added to a form in the desired tab order. To determine the appropriate TabIndex values, you first make a list of the controls that can accept user input. The list should reflect the order in which the user will want to access the controls. In the Sophie's Teddy Bears interface, the salesperson will typically want to access the nameTextBox first, followed by the addressTextBox, cityTextBox, and so on.

If a control that accepts user input is identified by a label control, you also include the label control in the list. (A text box is an example of a control that accepts user input and is identified by a label control.) You place the name of the label control immediately above the name of the control it identifies in the list. In the Sophie's Teddy Bears interface, the Label1 control (which displays <u>N</u>ame:) identifies the nameTextBox. Therefore, Label1 should appear immediately above nameTextBox in the list.

The names of controls that do not accept user input and are not used to identify controls that do should be placed at the bottom of the list; these names do not need to appear in any specific order. After listing the control names, you then assign each control in the list a TabIndex value, beginning with the number 0. If a control does not have a TabIndex property, you do not assign it a TabIndex value in the list.

Figure 2-10 shows the list of controls and TabIndex values for the Sophie's Teddy Bears interface. Notice that the TabIndex value assigned to each text box's identifying label is one number less than the value assigned to the text box itself. This is necessary for a text box's access key (which is defined in the identifying label) to work appropriately.

Controls that accept user input, along with their identifying labels	TabIndex value
Label1 (Name:)	0
nameTextBox	1
Label2 (Address:)	2
addressTextBox	3
Label3 (City:)	4
cityTextBox	5
Label4 (State:)	6
stateTextBox	7
Label5 (ZIP:)	8
zipTextBox	9
Label6 (Bowtie bears:)	10
bowtieTextBox	11
Label7 (Hearts bears:)	12
heartsTextBox	13
calcButton	14
printButton	15
clearButton	16
exitButton	17
Other controls	
Label10 (Order Form)	18
Label8 (Total bears:)	19
totalBearsLabel	20
Label9 (Total price:)	21
totalPriceLabel	22
PictureBox1	N/A

Figure 2-10 List of controls and TabIndex values
© 2013 Cengage Learning

Although you can use the Properties window to set each control's TabIndex property, it is easier to use the Tab Order option on the VIEW menu. Figure 2-11 shows the steps for using that option, and Figure 2-12 shows the correct TabIndex values for the Sophie's Teddy Bears interface.

HOW TO Set the TabIndex Property Using the Tab Order Option

1. If necessary, make the designer window the active window.

2. Click VIEW on the menu bar and then click Tab Order. The current TabIndex values appear in blue boxes on the form.

3. Click the first control you want in the tab order. The color of the box changes to white, and the number 0 appears in the box.

4. Click the second control you want in the tab order, and so on. If you make a mistake when specifying the tab order, press the Esc key to remove the boxes from the form, and then start over again.

5. When you have finished setting all of the TabIndex values, the color of the boxes will automatically change from white to blue. See Figure 2-12.

6. Press the Esc key to remove the blue boxes from the form. (You also can click VIEW on the menu bar and then click Tab Order.)

Figure 2-11 How to set the TabIndex property using the Tab Order option

© 2013 Cengage Learning

If you want to try setting the tab order, open the solution contained in the Try It 1! folder. Then use the information in Figures 2-11 and 2-12.

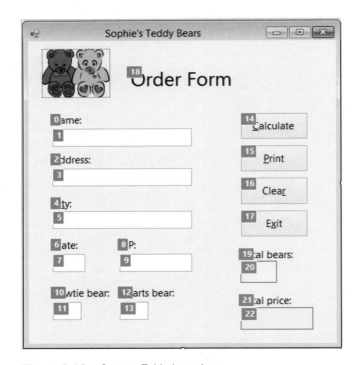

Figure 2-12 Correct TabIndex values

OpenClipArt.org/Gerald_G

Mini-Quiz 2-3

1. What is the first TabIndex value on a form? (6)

   a. 0

   b. 1

2. If a label's TabIndex value is 2, the TabIndex value of the text box it identifies should be ⎯⎯⎯⎯⎯⎯. (6)

   a. 1

   b. 2

   c. 3

3. You can select the Calculate <u>T</u>ax button by pressing ⎯⎯⎯⎯⎯⎯. (5)

   a. Shift+t

   b. Ctrl+t

   c. Alt+t

   d. none of the above

4. Every control in an interface has a TabIndex property. (5, 6)

   a. True

   b. False

85

The answers to Mini-Quiz questions are located in Appendix A. Each question is associated with one or more objectives listed at the beginning of the chapter.

Splash Screens

Many times, a splash screen appears when an application is started. Developers use a splash screen to introduce the application and to hold the user's attention as the application is being read into the computer's internal memory. Figure 2-13 lists the steps for adding a new splash screen to a project, and Figure 2-14 shows an example of a completed Add New Item dialog box.

HOW TO Add a New Splash Screen to a Project

1. Click PROJECT on the menu bar and then click Add New Item to open the Add New Item dialog box.

2. Expand the Common Items node in the Installed list (if necessary) and then click Windows Forms.

3. Click Splash Screen in the middle column of the dialog box. Enter an appropriate name in the Name box. Figure 2-14 shows an example of a completed Add New Item dialog box. (Your dialog box will look slightly different if you are using Visual Studio Express 2012 for Windows Desktop.)

4. Click the Add button. See Figure 2-15.

Ch02-Splash Screen

Figure 2-13 How to add a new splash screen to a project
© 2013 Cengage Learning

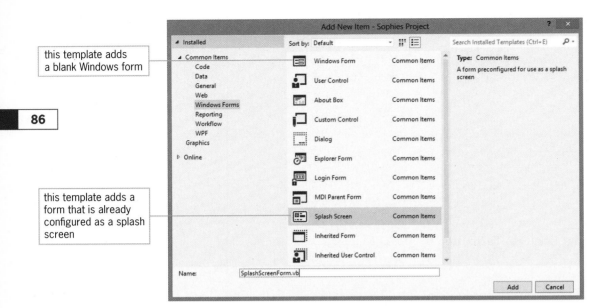

this template adds a blank Windows form

this template adds a form that is already configured as a splash screen

Figure 2-14 Completed Add New Item dialog box

You can use the templates listed in the Add New Item dialog box to add many different items to a project. The Splash Screen template adds a Windows form that is already configured for use as a splash screen. If you prefer to create your splash screen from scratch, you can use the Windows Form template to add a blank Windows form to the project. You then would set the form's FormBorderStyle property to either None or FixedSingle. However, if you set it to FixedSingle, you would also need to set the form's ControlBox property to False and then remove the text from the form's Text property. Setting the ControlBox property to False removes the Control menu box, as well as the Minimize, Maximize, and Close buttons, from the title bar. (The Control menu box appears in the left corner of a form's title bar. When clicked, it opens a menu containing the following options: Restore, Move, Size, Minimize, Maximize, and Close.)

Figure 2-15 shows the form created by the Splash Screen template during design time. The form contains five controls: two table layout panels and three labels. You can modify the form by adding controls to it or deleting controls from it. You also can use the Properties window to change the properties of the form and its controls.

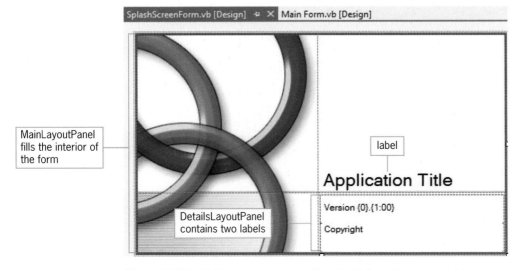

MainLayoutPanel fills the interior of the form

label

DetailsLayoutPanel contains two labels

Figure 2-15 Splash screen created by the Splash Screen template

In addition to automatically displaying an application's startup form, the computer also automatically displays an application's splash screen, as long as the splash screen's name is selected in the Project Designer window. Figure 2-16 shows the steps you follow to indicate the name of the splash screen, and Figure 2-17 shows the name (in this case, SplashScreenForm) selected in the Project Designer window. When the application is started, the splash screen will appear first. After a few seconds, the splash screen will disappear automatically and the startup form will appear.

HOW TO Specify the Splash Screen

1. Use one of the following ways to open the Project Designer window:
   ✔ Right-click My Project in the Solution Explorer window and then click Open on the context menu.
   ✔ Click PROJECT on the menu bar and then click *<project name>* Properties on the menu.
   ✔ Right-click the project's name in the Solution Explorer window and then click Properties.
2. Click the Application tab (if necessary) and then click the Splash screen list arrow in the Application pane.
3. Click the name of the splash screen in the list. Figure 2-17 shows an example of the Project Designer window.
4. Click the Close button on the Project Designer window.

 If you want to try adding a splash screen to a project, open the solution contained in the Try It 2! folder. Then use the information in Figures 2-13 through 2-17.

Figure 2-16 How to specify the splash screen
© 2013 Cengage Learning

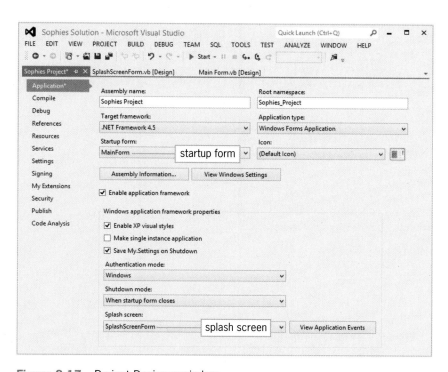

Figure 2-17 Project Designer window

Figure 2-18 shows the SplashScreenForm during run time. The values that appear in the three labels are determined by the entries in the Assembly Information dialog box, which is shown in Figure 2-19. You would need to use this dialog box, rather than the Properties window, to make changes to those values. To open the dialog box, you first open the Project Designer window. You then click the Assembly Information button in the window's Application pane.

Sophie's Teddy Bears

Version 1.00

Copyright © 2014

this information comes from the Assembly Information dialog box

Figure 2-18   SplashScreenForm during run time

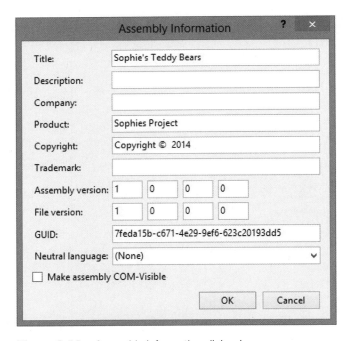

Figure 2-19   Assembly Information dialog box

Dialog Boxes

Most Windows applications consist of at least one main window (referred to as a primary window) and one or more secondary windows (called dialog boxes). You use the **primary window** to view and edit your application's data. The primary window shown in Figure 2-20, for example, allows you to view and edit documents created using the Notepad application. **Dialog**

boxes, on the other hand, support and supplement a user's activities in a primary window. For instance, you can use the Font dialog box in Figure 2-20 to specify the font of the text selected in the primary window.

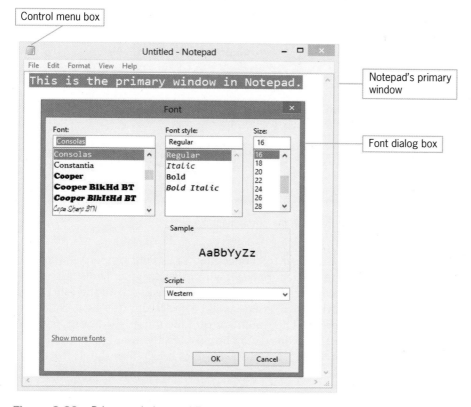

Figure 2-20   Primary window and Font dialog box in Notepad

The Dialog template in the Add New Item dialog box creates a Windows form that is already configured for use as a dialog box. If you prefer to create your dialog box from scratch, you can use the Windows Form template to add a blank Windows form to the project. You then would set the form's FormBorderStyle property to FixedDialog, and set its MinimizeBox and MaximizeBox properties to False.

In addition to the Dialog template, Visual Basic also provides several tools for creating commonly-used dialog boxes, such as the Color, Font, and Save As dialog boxes. The tools are located in the Dialogs section of the toolbox. When you drag one of these tools to the form, its instantiated control does not appear on the form. Instead, the control is placed in the component tray in the IDE. The component tray stores controls that do not appear in the user interface during run time. The component tray shown in Figure 2-21 contains the font and color dialog controls.

ChO2-Font and Color Dialogs

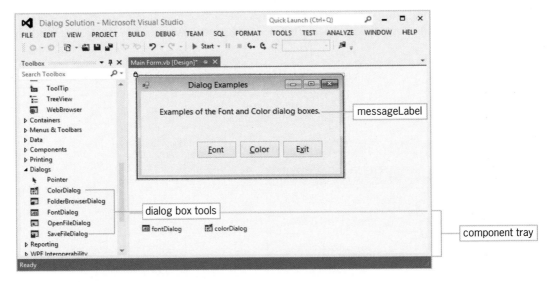

90

If you want to try creating the Font and Color dialog boxes, open the solution contained in the Try It 3! folder. Then use the information in Figures 2-21 through 2-25.

Figure 2-21   Font and Color dialog box controls in the component tray

The Font button in the interface allows the user to change the form's Font property values. The code entered in the button's Click event procedure is shown in Figure 2-22. The statement on Line 8 assigns the form's Font property values (name, style, size, and so on) to the fontDialog control's Font property. By doing this, the form's values will be selected in the Font dialog box when the dialog box appears on the screen. The statement on Line 9 uses the ShowDialog method to show (in other words, open) the Font dialog box. When the user closes the Font dialog box, the last statement in the procedure assigns the values selected in the dialog box to the form's Font property.

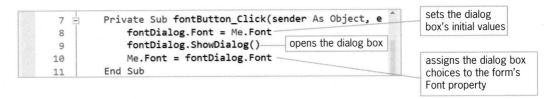

Figure 2-22   Font button's Click event procedure

Figure 2-23 shows an example of an open Font dialog box. As are all of the dialog boxes created by the dialog tools in the toolbox, the Font dialog box is **modal**, which means it remains on the screen until the user closes it. While it is on the screen, no input from the keyboard or mouse can occur in the application's primary window; however, you can access other applications. You close a modal dialog box by selecting either the OK button or the Cancel button, or by clicking the Close button on the dialog box's title bar.

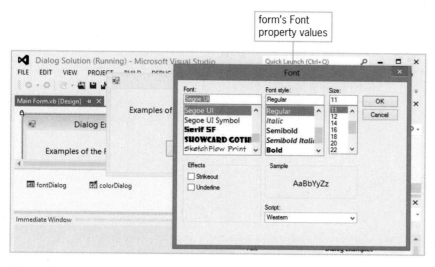

form's Font property values

Figure 2-23   Font dialog box created by the FontDialog tool

The Color button shown earlier in Figure 2-21 allows the user to change the color of the messageLabel's text. The color of an object's text is determined by the object's ForeColor property. (The background color of an object is determined by the object's BackColor property.) The code entered in the Color button's Click event procedure is shown in Figure 2-24. The statement on Line 14 assigns the current value of the messageLabel's ForeColor property to the colorDialog control's Color property. This assignment statement ensures that the ForeColor's value is selected in the Color dialog box when the dialog box appears on the screen. The statement on Line 15 shows (opens) the Color dialog box. When the user closes the Color dialog box, the last statement in the procedure assigns the color selected in the dialog box to the messageLabel's ForeColor property.

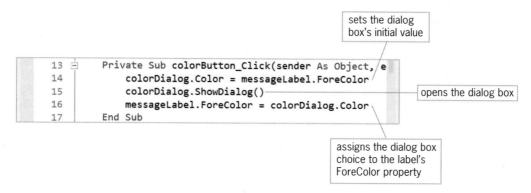

sets the dialog box's initial value

```
13    Private Sub colorButton_Click(sender As Object, e
14         colorDialog.Color = messageLabel.ForeColor
15         colorDialog.ShowDialog()
16         messageLabel.ForeColor = colorDialog.Color
17    End Sub
```

opens the dialog box

assigns the dialog box choice to the label's ForeColor property

Figure 2-24   Color button's Click event procedure

An example of an open Color dialog box is shown in Figure 2-25. Notice that the OK button in the dialog box has a darkened border, even though it does not have the focus. (The black square in the color palette has the focus.) This is because the OK button is the dialog box's default button. Like other buttons, a default button can be selected by clicking it or by pressing the Enter key when the button has the focus. However, unlike other buttons, a **default button** can also be selected by pressing the Enter key when the button does *not* have the focus. Not all default buttons are captioned OK. For example, Open and Save As dialog boxes typically use default buttons that are captioned Open and Save, respectively.

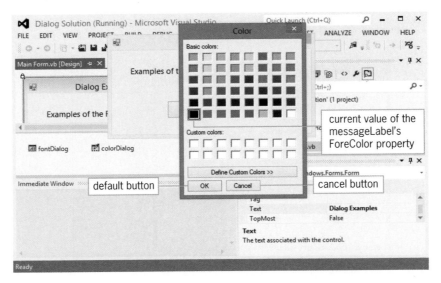

Figure 2-25   Color dialog box created by the ColorDialog tool

In addition to a default button, most dialog boxes also have a cancel button, which is usually captioned Cancel. A **cancel button** can be selected in one of three ways: by clicking it, by pressing the Enter key when the button has the focus, or by pressing the Esc key when the button does *not* have the focus.

Designating the Default Button on a Form

Like dialog boxes, Windows forms can have a default button. You specify the default button by setting the form's AcceptButton property to the name of the button. For example, to make the Calculate button the default button on the MainForm in the Sophie's Teddy Bears application, you set the MainForm's AcceptButton property to calcButton. Doing this allows the user to select the Calculate button without having to take his or her hands off the keyboard.

A form does not have to have a default button. However, if one is used, it should be the button that is most often selected by the user, except in cases where the tasks performed by the button are both destructive and irreversible. For example, a button that deletes information should not be designated as the default button. A form can have only one default button. The default button has a darkened border during design time, as shown in Figure 2-26, and also during run time.

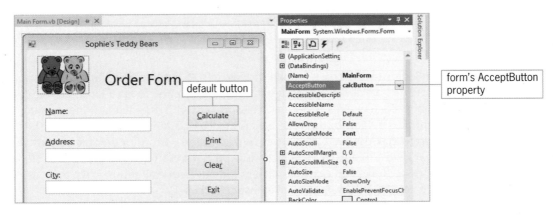

Figure 2-26   Default button on the MainForm
OpenClipArt.org/Gerald_G

Printing an Interface from Code

You can use Visual Basic's PrintForm tool, which is contained in the Visual Basic PowerPacks section of the toolbox, to print an interface from code. When you drag the PrintForm tool to the form, the instantiated print form control appears in the component tray, as shown in Figure 2-27.

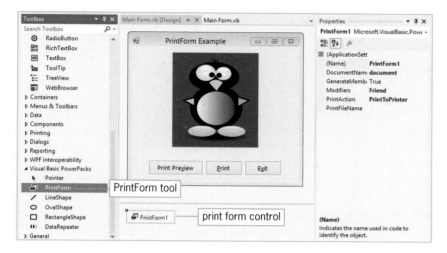

Figure 2-27 PrintForm Example application's interface
OpenClipArt.org/vojtam

 If you want to try using the PrintForm tool, open the solution contained in the Try It 4! folder. Then use the information in Figures 2-27 and 2-28.

The Print Preview button in Figure 2-27 sends the printer output to the Print preview window, whereas the Print button sends it directly to the printer. Figure 2-28 shows the code entered in the Click event procedures for both of these buttons. The first line in each procedure specifies the output destination, and the second line starts the print operation.

```
 7    Private Sub previewButton_Click(sender As Object, e As EventArgs) Ha
 8        PrintForm1.PrintAction = Printing.PrintAction.PrintToPreview
 9        PrintForm1.Print()
10    End Sub                                           destination
11
12    Private Sub printButton_Click(sender As Object, e As EventArgs) Hand
13        PrintForm1.PrintAction = Printing.PrintAction.PrintToPrinter
14        PrintForm1.Print()
15    End Sub

                                                      destination
```

Figure 2-28 Print Preview and Print buttons' Click event procedures

We'll wrap up this chapter with a fun and easy topic, and one that you will use in both programming tutorials at the end of this chapter: playing audio files.

Playing Audio Files

Some applications contain an audio component, such as music, sound effects, or spoken text. Figure 2-29 shows the syntax you use to include audio in a Visual Basic application. The figure also contains an example of using the syntax to play an audio file named GoodMorning.wav. (As mentioned in the Overview, you should study the information in How To boxes that contain syntax and examples *while* you are reading the chapter.)

94

If you want to try playing an audio file, open the solution contained in the Try It 5! folder. Then use the information in Figure 2-29.

HOW TO Play an Audio File

Syntax

My.Computer.Audio.Play(*fileName***)**

Example

```
My.Computer.Audio.Play("GoodMorning.wav")
```

Figure 2-29   How to play an audio file
© 2013 Cengage Learning

The keyword My in the syntax refers to Visual Basic's **My feature**—a feature that exposes a set of commonly-used objects to the programmer. One of the objects exposed by the My feature is the Computer object, which represents your computer. The Computer object provides access to other objects available on your computer, such as your computer's Audio object. As the syntax shows, you use the Audio object's Play method to play an audio file.

Following the Play method in the syntax is a set of parentheses containing the text *fileName*. Items within parentheses after a method's name are called **arguments** and represent information that the method needs to perform its task. In this case, the *fileName* argument represents the name of the audio file you want played. The file must be a WAV file, which is an audio file whose filename extension is .wav. You enclose the *fileName* argument in quotation marks. If the audio file is not in the project's bin\Debug folder, you will need to include the path to the file in the *fileName* argument.

The answers to Mini-Quiz questions are located in Appendix A. Each question is associated with one or more objectives listed at the beginning of the chapter.

Mini-Quiz 2-4

1. In most cases, a dialog box's title bar contains which of the following? (8)

    a.   the Control menu box

    b.   Minimize and Maximize buttons

    c.   the Close button

    d.   all of the above

2. How can the default button on a form be selected? (10)

    a.   by clicking it

    b.   by pressing the Enter key when the button has the focus

    c.   by pressing the Enter key when the button does *not* have the focus

    d.   all of the above

3. If a form contains the PrintForm1 control, which of the following statements can be used to start the print operation? (11)

    a.   `PrintForm1.Go()`

    b.   `PrintForm1.Print()`

    c.   `PrintForm1.Start()`

    d.   none of the above

4. The My.Computer.Audio object can play which of the following types of files? (12)

    a. .aud

    b. .avi

    c. .wav

    d. .wmv

You have completed the concepts section of Chapter 2. The Programming Tutorial section is next. Recall that the first tutorial in each chapter contains more detailed step-by-step instructions than does the second tutorial.

PROGRAMMING TUTORIAL 1

Creating the Color Game Application

In this tutorial, you will create an application that can be used to teach the Spanish names for nine different colors. The application's TOE chart, MainForm, and splash screen are shown in Figures 2-30, 2-31, and 2-32, respectively. The MainForm contains a table layout panel, a label, and 13 buttons. The application also uses a print form control and a font dialog control, which do not appear on the form.

Note: If you are in a computer lab, your instructor (or the lab supervisor) may not want you to play the audio files for this tutorial because doing so might be disruptive to other students. You may need to use earphones or mute your computer's speakers.

Task	Object	Event
1. Change the button's background to the appropriate color 2. Display the appropriate Spanish word on the button's face 3. Play an audio file of the Spanish word's pronunciation	redButton, blueButton, greenButton, yellowButton, brownButton, pinkButton, purpleButton, grayButton, orangeButton	Click
Change the background of the nine color buttons to white	startOverButton	Click
Print the interface (use a print form control)	printButton	Click
Show the Font dialog box to allow the user to change the form's font (use a font dialog control)	fontButton	Click
End the application	exitButton	Click

Figure 2-30 TOE chart for the Color Game application
© 2013 Cengage Learning

Figure 2-31   MainForm for the Color Game application

Figure 2-32   SplashScreenForm for the Color Game application

Adding a Table Layout Panel Control to the Form

Included in the data files for this book is a partially completed Color Game application. Before you begin coding the application, you will need to add a table layout panel control to the form. You will also need to include a font dialog control and a print form control in the application.

To add a table layout panel control to the form:

1. Start Visual Studio and open the Toolbox and Solution Explorer windows.

2. Open the **Color Game Solution** (**Color Game Solution.sln**) file contained in the VbReloaded2012\Chap02\Color Game Solution folder. If necessary, open the designer window. The partially completed MainForm appears on the screen.

3. If necessary, open the Properties window. In this application, you will not allow the user to maximize the MainForm. Set the MainForm's MaximizeBox property to **False**.

4. Use the TableLayoutPanel tool, which is located in the Containers section of the toolbox, to add a table layout panel control to the form. You can move the control to a different location on the form by placing your mouse pointer on the control's move box and then dragging the control to the desired location. If necessary, click the **task box** to open the task list. See Figure 2-33.

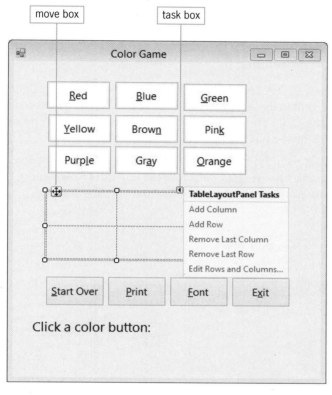

Figure 2-33 Table layout panel added to the form

5. Click **Add Column** on the task list, and then click **Add Row**. The control now contains three rows and three columns.

6. Next, you will make each column the same size. Click **Edit Rows and Columns** on the task list to open the Column and Row Styles dialog box.

7. Now select the three entries in the Member list by holding down the **Shift** key as you click **Column3**. Click the **Percent** radio button in the Size Type section of the dialog box. As Figure 2-34 shows, the Value column in the dialog box indicates that each of the three columns will occupy 50.00% (one-half) of the table, which is impossible. The three columns, if sized the same, would each occupy 33.33% (one-third) of the table.

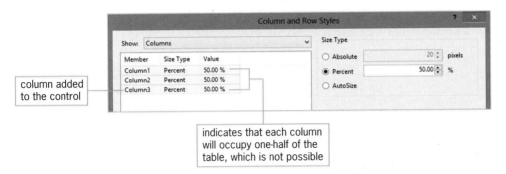

column added
to the control

indicates that each column
will occupy one-half of the
table, which is not possible

Figure 2-34   Column and Row Styles dialog box

8. You can enter the appropriate percentage for each column manually, using the text box that appears next to the Percent radio button. Or, you can let the computer change the percentages for you. Click the **OK** button to have the computer change the percentages. The Column and Row Styles dialog box closes.

9. Now verify that the computer changed the percentages to 33.33%. If necessary, click the table layout panel control's **task box** to open its task list. Click **Edit Rows and Columns** on the task list. The Column and Row Styles dialog box now contains the correct percentages. See Figure 2-35.

Show box's
list arrow

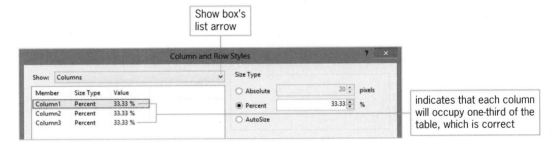

indicates that each column
will occupy one-third of the
table, which is correct

Figure 2-35   Correct percentages shown in the dialog box

10. Next, you will make the rows the same size. Click the **list arrow** in the Show box and then click **Rows**. Press and hold down the **Shift** key as you click **Row3** in the Member list. Click the **Percent** radio button and then click the **OK** button.

11. Next, you will put a border around each of the nine cells in the table layout panel. A cell is an intersection of a row and a column. Use the Properties window to change the control's CellBorderStyle property to **OutsetDouble**.

12. Now you will make the table layout panel larger. Click **Size** in the Properties window. Type **347, 200** and press **Enter**.

13. Drag the Red button into the first cell in the table layout panel. The button appears in the upper-left corner of the cell because its Anchor property is set to the default, which is "Top, Left". The Anchor property determines how a control is anchored to its container. To center the Red button within its container (in this case, the cell), you change its Anchor property to None. To have the button fill the entire cell, on the other hand, you change its Anchor property to "Top, Bottom, Left, Right"; this setting anchors each of the button's borders to its associated border within the cell. In the next step, you will have the button fill the entire cell.

14. Click **Anchor** in the Properties window and then click the property's **list arrow**. The left and top bars are already selected. Click the **right and bottom bars**. All four bars are now selected, as shown in Figure 2-36.

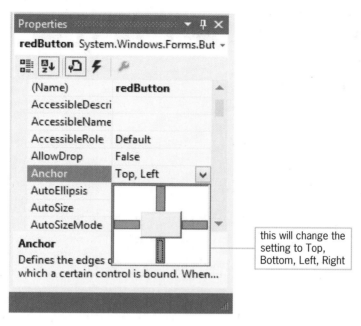

this will change the setting to Top, Bottom, Left, Right

Figure 2-36   Bars selected in the Anchor property

15. Press **Enter** to close the Anchor property's box. The Anchor property is now set to "Top, Bottom, Left, Right", and the Red button fills the cell.

16. Select the remaining eight color buttons and then set their Anchor properties to **Top, Bottom, Left, Right**.

17. Click the **form** to deselect the buttons. Next, drag each of the remaining eight color buttons into its own cell, as shown in Figure 2-37.

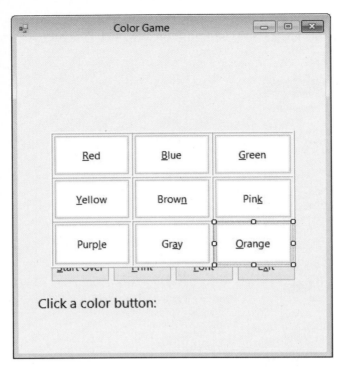

Figure 2-37   Color buttons positioned in the table layout panel

18.   Now you will position the controls appropriately on the form. Click the **table layout panel** and then set its Location property to **41, 95**. Click the **Label1** control, which contains the "Click a color button:" text, and then set its Location property to **35, 60**.

19.   Right-click the **form**, and then click **Lock Controls**.

20.   Next, use the Tab Order option on the VIEW menu to set each control's TabIndex property to the values shown in Figure 2-38. Notice that the TabIndex values of the color buttons begin with the number 4, which is the TabIndex value of the table layout panel. (The table layout panel's TabIndex value is not visible because the Red button fills the entire first cell.) The number 4 indicates that the buttons belong to the table layout panel rather than to the form. If you move or delete the table layout panel, the controls that belong to it will also be moved or deleted. The numbers that appear after the period in the color buttons' TabIndex values indicate the order in which each button will receive the focus within the table layout panel.

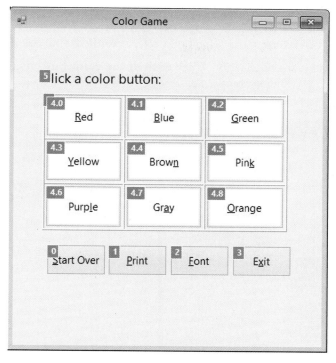

Figure 2-38   Tab order

21. Press the **Esc** key to remove the tab order boxes from the form.

Including the Font Dialog and Print Form Controls

To include the font dialog and print form controls in the application:

1. Click **FontDialog** in the Dialogs section of the toolbox and then drag a font dialog control to the form. When you release the mouse button, the control appears in the component tray. Change the control's name to **fontDialog**.

2. Click **PrintForm** in the Visual Basic PowerPacks section of the toolbox and then drag a print form control to the form. When you release the mouse button, the control appears in the component tray.

3. Auto-hide the Toolbox, Solution Explorer, and Properties windows, and then save the solution.

Coding the Color Buttons

According to the TOE chart shown earlier in Figure 2-30, each color button's Click event procedure must perform three tasks. The first task changes the button's background to the appropriate color. The background color of an object is specified in the object's BackColor property. To change the value stored in the BackColor property while an application is running, you use an assignment statement in the following format: *objectName*.**BackColor** = *color*.

To begin coding the color buttons' Click event procedures:

1. Open the Code Editor window. The exitButton_Click procedure already contains the `Me.Close()` instruction.

2. Open the code template for the blueButton's Click event procedure. Type **blueButton.BackColor = Color.LightBlue** and press **Enter**.

101

3. On your own, code the Click event procedures for the remaining eight color buttons. Assign the following colors to the buttons' BackColor properties: Color.Brown, Color.Gray, Color.Green, Color.Orange, Color.Pink, Color.MediumPurple, Color.Red, and Color.Yellow.

4. Save the solution and then start the application. Click **each of the color buttons** to verify that the code you entered is working correctly. See Figure 2-39.

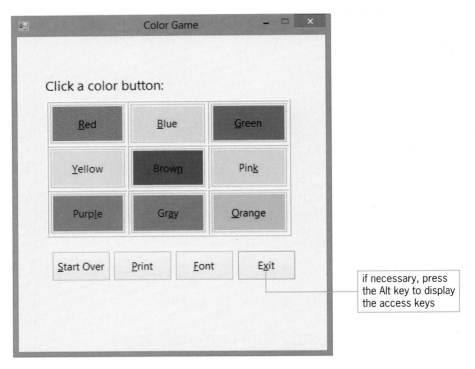

Figure 2-39   Result of clicking each color button

5. Click the **Exit** button to end the application.

In addition to changing its background color, each color button should also display the appropriate Spanish word on its face and then play an audio file containing the pronunciation of the Spanish word. The audio files are located in the current project's bin\Debug folder. Figure 2-40 lists the Spanish words and the names of the audio files associated with each button.

Button	Spanish word	Audio file
Blue	Azul	blue.wav
Brown	Marron	brown.wav
Gray	Gris	gray.wav
Green	Verde	green.wav
Orange	Anaranjado	orange.wav
Pink	Rosa	pink.wav
Purple	Morado	purple.wav
Red	Rojo	red.wav
Yellow	Amarillo	yellow.wav

Figure 2-40   Spanish words and audio files for the color buttons

© 2013 Cengage Learning

Note: If you are in a computer lab, your instructor (or the lab supervisor) may not want you to play the audio files for this tutorial because doing so might be disruptive to other students. You may need to use earphones or mute your computer's speakers.

To finish coding each color button's Click event procedure:

1. Locate the blueButton_Click procedure. Click the **blank line** above the End Sub clause and then enter the following two lines of code:

   blueButton.Text = "Azul"
   My.Computer.Audio.Play("blue.wav")

2. Save the solution, and then start the application. Click the **Blue** button. Azul, which is the Spanish word for "blue," appears on the button's face. In addition, you hear the message "Blue, Azul."

3. Click the **Exit** button.

4. Use the information listed in Figure 2-40 to finish coding the Click event procedures for the remaining eight color buttons.

5. Save the solution and then start the application. Click **each of the color buttons** to verify that the code you entered is working correctly.

Coding the Start Over, Print, and Font Buttons

According to the application's TOE chart, the Start Over button should change each color button's background to white, and the Print button should print the interface. You will send the printout to the Print preview window. The Font button should show the Font dialog box and allow the user to change the font used to display the text on the form.

To code the Start Over button's Click event procedure:

1. Open the code template for the startOverButton's Click event procedure. Type **blueButton.BackColor = Color.White** and press **Enter**.

2. On your own, assign Color.White to the BackColor property of the remaining eight color buttons, which are named brownButton, grayButton, greenButton, orangeButton, pinkButton, purpleButton, redButton, and yellowButton.

3. Save the solution and then start the application. Click **each of the color buttons** and then click the **Start Over** button. The background of each color button is now white.

4. Click the **Exit** button to end the application.

To code the Print button's Click event procedure:

1. Open the code template for the printButton's Click event procedure and then enter the following code:

   PrintForm1.PrintAction =
       Printing.PrintAction.PrintToPreview
   PrintForm1.Print()

2. Save the solution and then start the application. Click the **Print** button. The printout of the interface appears in the Print preview window. Click the **Zoom button** list arrow and then click **75%**. See Figure 2-41.

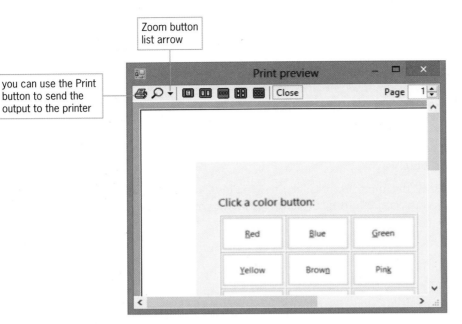

Zoom button
list arrow

you can use the Print
button to send the
output to the printer

Figure 2-41   Print preview window

3. Click the **Close** button in the Print preview window and then click the **Exit** button.

To code the Font button's Click event procedure:

1. Open the code template for the fontButton's Click event procedure. First, the procedure should assign the current values of the form's Font property to the font dialog control. By doing this, the values will be selected in the Font dialog box when it opens. Next, the procedure should show the dialog box. Finally, the procedure should assign the values selected in the dialog box to the form's Font property. Enter the following lines of code:

```
fontDialog.Font = Me.Font
fontDialog.ShowDialog()
Me.Font = fontDialog.Font
```

2. Save the solution and then start the application. Click the **Font** button, which opens the Font dialog box. Select a different font, style, or size and then click the **OK** button. Your changes affect all of the text except the text in the Label1 control. This is because the Label1 control's Font property was changed individually when the interface was created.

3. Click the **Exit** button to end the application.

Adding a Splash Screen to the Color Game Project

In the next set of steps, you will add a splash screen to the application. Recall that the Add New Item dialog box provides a template that is already configured as a splash screen.

To add a new splash screen to the Color Game project:

1. Display the Solution Explorer and Properties windows.

2. Click **PROJECT** on the menu bar and then click **Add New Item**. Expand the Common Items node in the Installed Templates list (if necessary) and then click **Windows Forms**. Click **Splash Screen** in the middle column of the dialog box.

3. Change the Name box entry to **SplashScreenForm.vb** and then click the **Add** button. Included on the SplashScreenForm are three labels and two table layout panels.

4. Click the **ApplicationTitle** label control and then set its Font property to **Segoe UI, 18pt**.

5. Set the Font properties for the Version and Copyright label controls to **Segoe UI, 9pt**.

6. Right-click **My Project** in the Solution Explorer window, and then click **Open** to open the Project Designer window. Click the **Splash screen** list arrow in the Application pane and then click **SplashScreenForm** in the list.

7. Change the name in the Assembly name box to **Color Game**. Recall that the Assembly name box specifies the name of the project's executable file.

8. Click the **Assembly Information** button to open the Assembly Information dialog box. Change the text in the Title box to **Color Game**. If necessary, change the year in the Copyright box to **2014**. See Figure 2-42.

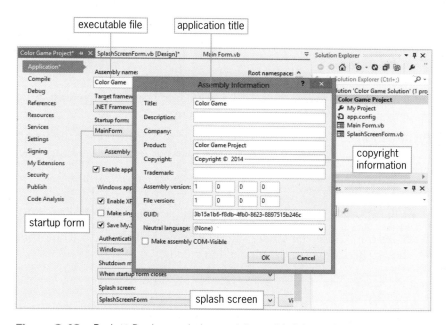

Figure 2-42   Project Designer window and Assembly Information dialog box

9. Click the **OK** button to close the Assembly Information dialog box. Save the solution and then close the Project Designer window.

Testing the Application

To test the application:

1. Start the application. The splash screen shown in Figure 2-43 appears first.

Figure 2-43 Splash screen

2. After a few seconds have elapsed, the splash screen disappears and the startup form (MainForm) appears. Click **each of the color buttons**.

3. Click the **Print** button. If your computer is connected to a printer, click the **Print** button in the Print preview window and then click the **Close** button; otherwise, just click the **Close** button.

4. Click the **Start Over** button.

5. Click the **Font** button. Select a different font, style, or size and then click the **OK** button.

6. Click the **Exit** button. Close the Code Editor window and then close the solution. Figure 2-44 shows the Color Game application's code.

```
1 Public Class MainForm
2
3    Private Sub exitButton_Click(sender As Object,
     e As EventArgs) Handles exitButton.Click
4        Me.Close()
5    End Sub
6
7    Private Sub blueButton_Click(sender As Object,
     e As EventArgs) Handles blueButton.Click
8        blueButton.BackColor = Color.LightBlue
9        blueButton.Text = "Azul"
10       My.Computer.Audio.Play("blue.wav")
11
12   End Sub
13
```

Figure 2-44 Color Game application's code *(continues)*

(continued)

```
14      Private Sub brownButton_Click(sender As Object,
        e As EventArgs) Handles brownButton.Click
15          brownButton.BackColor = Color.Brown
16          brownButton.Text = "Marron"
17          My.Computer.Audio.Play("brown.wav")
18
19      End Sub
20
21      Private Sub grayButton_Click(sender As Object,
        e As EventArgs) Handles grayButton.Click
22          grayButton.BackColor = Color.Gray
23          grayButton.Text = "Gris"
24          My.Computer.Audio.Play("gray.wav")
25
26      End Sub
27
28      Private Sub greenButton_Click(sender As Object,
        e As EventArgs) Handles greenButton.Click
29          greenButton.BackColor = Color.Green
30          greenButton.Text = "Verde"
31          My.Computer.Audio.Play("green.wav")
32
33      End Sub
34
35      Private Sub orangeButton_Click(sender As Object,
        e As EventArgs) Handles orangeButton.Click
36          orangeButton.BackColor = Color.Orange
37          orangeButton.Text = "Anaranjado"
38          My.Computer.Audio.Play("orange.wav")
39
40      End Sub
41
42      Private Sub pinkButton_Click(sender As Object,
        e As EventArgs) Handles pinkButton.Click
43          pinkButton.BackColor = Color.Pink
44          pinkButton.Text = "Rosa"
45          My.Computer.Audio.Play("pink.wav")
46
47      End Sub
48
49      Private Sub purpleButton_Click(sender As Object,
        e As EventArgs) Handles purpleButton.Click
50          purpleButton.BackColor = Color.MediumPurple
51          purpleButton.Text = "Morado"
52          My.Computer.Audio.Play("purple.wav")
53
54      End Sub
55
56      Private Sub redButton_Click(sender As Object,
        e As EventArgs) Handles redButton.Click
57          redButton.BackColor = Color.Red
58          redButton.Text = "Rojo"
59          My.Computer.Audio.Play("red.wav")
60
61      End Sub
62
63      Private Sub yellowButton_Click(sender As Object,
        e As EventArgs) Handles yellowButton.Click
64          yellowButton.BackColor = Color.Yellow
65          yellowButton.Text = "Amarillo"
66          My.Computer.Audio.Play("yellow.wav")
67
68      End Sub
```

Figure 2-44   Color Game application's code *(continues)*

(continued)

```
69
70     Private Sub startOverButton_Click(sender As Object,
         e As EventArgs) Handles startOverButton.Click
71         blueButton.BackColor = Color.White
72         brownButton.BackColor = Color.White
73         grayButton.BackColor = Color.White
74         greenButton.BackColor = Color.White
75         orangeButton.BackColor = Color.White
76         pinkButton.BackColor = Color.White
77         purpleButton.BackColor = Color.White
78         redButton.BackColor = Color.White
79         yellowButton.BackColor = Color.White
80
81     End Sub
82
83     Private Sub printButton_Click(sender As Object,
         e As EventArgs) Handles printButton.Click
84         PrintForm1.PrintAction =
85             Printing.PrintAction.PrintToPreview
86         PrintForm1.Print()
87
88     End Sub
89
90     Private Sub fontButton_Click(sender As Object,
         e As EventArgs) Handles fontButton.Click
91         fontDialog.Font = Me.Font
92         fontDialog.ShowDialog()
93         Me.Font = fontDialog.Font
94
95     End Sub
96 End Class
```

Figure 2-44   Color Game application's code
© 2013 Cengage Learning

PROGRAMMING TUTORIAL 2

Creating the Music Sampler Application

In this tutorial, you will create an application that allows the user to preview a song by playing several seconds of it. The application's TOE chart, MainForm, and splash screen are shown in Figures 2-45, 2-46, and 2-47, respectively. The MainForm contains a table layout panel, seven labels, and nine buttons.

Note: If you are in a computer lab, your instructor (or the lab supervisor) may not want you to play the audio files for this tutorial because doing so might be disruptive to other students. You may need to use earphones or mute your computer's speakers.

Task	Object	Event
Play an audio file that contains a preview of the song associated with the button	everythingPictureBox, invisiblePictureBox, magicPictureBox, threePictureBox, unclaimedPictureBox	Click
Show the Color dialog box to allow the user to change the background color of the form (use a color dialog control)	colorButton	Click
Print the interface (use a print form control)	printButton	Click
End the application	exitButton	Click

Figure 2-45   TOE chart for the Music Sampler application
© 2013 Cengage Learning

Figure 2-46   MainForm for the Music Sampler application
OpenClipArt.org/mightyman; Music by Dan-O at DanoSongs.com

Figure 2-47   SplashScreenForm for the Music Sampler application

Adding a Table Layout Panel Control to the Form

Included in the data files for this book is a partially completed Music Sampler application. Before you begin coding the application, you will need to add a table layout panel control to the form. You will also need to include a color dialog control and a print form control in the application.

To add a table layout panel control to the form:

1. Start Visual Studio and open the Toolbox and Solution Explorer windows.

2. Open the **Music Sampler Solution** (**Music Sampler Solution.sln**) file contained in the VbReloaded2012\Chap02\Music Sampler Solution folder. If necessary, open the designer window. The partially completed MainForm appears on the screen.

3. If necessary, open the Properties window. In this application, you will not allow the user to maximize the MainForm. Set the MainForm's MaximizeBox property to **False**.

4. Use the TableLayoutPanel tool, which is contained in the Containers section of the toolbox, to add a table layout panel control to the form. You can move the control to a different location on the form by placing your mouse pointer on the control's move box and then dragging the control to the desired location.

5. Using the table layout panel control's task list, add three additional rows to the control.

6. Click **Edit Rows and Columns** on the task list to open the Column and Row Styles dialog box. Change the entry in the Percent box for Column1 to **80.00**, and then change the entry in the Percent box for Column2 to **20.00**.

7. Click the **list arrow** in the Show box and then click **Rows**. Press and hold down the **Shift** key as you click **Row5** in the Member list. Click the **Percent** radio button in the Size Type section of the dialog box and then click the **OK** button.

8. Open the Column and Row Styles dialog box again. Verify that the Column1 and Column2 percentages are 80.00% and 20.00%, respectively. Also verify that each row's percentage is 20.00%. See Figure 2-48.

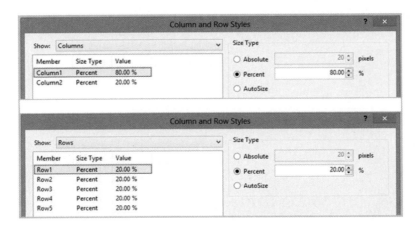

Figure 2-48 Column and row percentages

9. Click the **OK** button to close the Column and Row Styles dialog box.

10. Use the Properties window to change the table layout panel's CellBorderStyle property to **Single**.

11. Make the table layout panel larger by dragging its bottom and right borders. (Or, set its Size property to **220, 300**.) See Figure 2-49.

Figure 2-49 Correct size of the table layout panel
OpenClipArt.org/mightyman; Music by Dan-O at DanoSongs.com

12. Drag the **Label1** control into the first cell in the table layout panel. The label appears in the upper-left corner of the cell because its Anchor property is set to the default, which is "Top, Left". The Anchor property determines how a control is anchored to its container. To have the Label1 control fill the entire cell (its container), you would change its Anchor property to "Top, Bottom, Left, Right"; this setting anchors each of the label's borders to its associated border within the cell. However, to center the Label1 control within the cell, you would change its Anchor property to None. In the next step, you will anchor the Label1 control to the cell's left border.

13. Click **Anchor** in the Properties list and then click the property's **list arrow**. Click the **top bar** to deselect it, and then press **Enter** to close the Anchor property's box. The Anchor property is now set to Left.

14. Select the remaining four music labels and then set their Anchor properties to **Left**.

15. Click the **form** to deselect the labels. Now select the five picture boxes. Use the Properties window to set their Anchor properties to **None**.

16. Click the **form** to deselect the picture boxes. Now drag each of the remaining four music labels and the five picture boxes into its own cell in the table layout panel. Figure 2-50 shows the correct placement of the labels and picture boxes.

Figure 2-50 Correct placement of the labels and picture boxes
OpenClipArt.org/mightyman; Music by Dan-O at DanoSongs.com

17. Next, size the form as shown in Figure 2-51, and then use the Center in Form option on the FORMAT menu to center the table layout panel and the "Try Before You Buy!" text, horizontally, on the form. Also use the Tab Order option on the VIEW menu to set each control's TabIndex property to the values shown in the figure. Notice that the TabIndex values of the controls within the table layout panel begin with the number 3, which is the TabIndex value of the table layout panel. The number 3 indicates that the controls belong to the table layout panel rather than to the form. If you move or delete the table layout panel, the controls that belong to it will also be moved or deleted. The numbers that appear after the period in the controls' TabIndex values indicate the order of the controls within the table layout panel.

the table layout panel's TabIndex value is 3

Figure 2-51　Correct form size and TabIndex values
OpenClipArt.org/mightyman; Music by Dan-O at DanoSongs.com

18.　Remove the tab order boxes from the form and then lock the controls.

Including the Color Dialog and Print Form Controls

To include the color dialog and print form controls in the application:

1.　Click **ColorDialog** in the Dialogs section of the toolbox and then drag a color dialog control to the form. When you release the mouse button, the control appears in the component tray. Change the control's name to **colorDialog**.

2.　Click **PrintForm** in the Visual Basic PowerPacks section of the toolbox and then drag a print form control to the form. When you release the mouse button, the control appears in the component tray.

3.　Auto-hide the Toolbox, Solution Explorer, and Properties windows, and then save the solution.

Coding the Picture Boxes

According to the TOE chart shown earlier in Figure 2-45, each picture box should play an audio file when it is clicked. The audio files are contained in the current project's bin\Debug folder.

Note: If you are in a computer lab, your instructor (or the lab supervisor) may not want you to play the audio files for this tutorial because doing so might be disruptive to other students. You may need to use earphones or mute your computer's speakers.

To code each picture box's Click event procedure:

1. Open the Code Editor window. The exitButton_Click procedure already contains the `Me.Close()` instruction.

2. Open the code template for the everythingPictureBox's Click event procedure and then enter the instruction to play the Everything-Begins-by-danosongs.com.wav file. If you need help, refer to the How To box shown earlier in Figure 2-29.

3. On your own, code the Click event procedures for the remaining four picture boxes. The audio files associated with these picture boxes are listed in Figure 2-52.

Picture box	File
invisiblePictureBox	Invisible-Love-by-danosongs.com.wav
magicPictureBox	Magic-Ghost-by-danosongs.com.wav
threePictureBox	Three-Drops-by-danosongs.com.wav
unclaimedPictureBox	Unclaimed-Territory-by-danosongs.com.wav

Figure 2-52   Files associated with four of the picture boxes
© 2013 Cengage Learning

4. Save the solution and then start the application. Click **each of the buttons within the table layout panel** to verify that the code you entered is working correctly.

5. Click the **Exit** button to end the application.

Coding the Color and Print Buttons

According to the application's TOE chart, the Color button should show the Color dialog box and allow the user to change the background color of the form. The background color of an object is specified in the object's BackColor property. The Print button should print the interface. You will send the printout to the Print preview window.

To code the Color button's Click event procedure:

1. Open the code template for the colorButton's Click event procedure. Enter the instruction to assign the current value of the form's BackColor property to the color dialog control's Color property. (Recall that you refer to the form using the keyword Me.)

2. Next, enter the instruction to show the Color dialog box.

3. Finally, enter the instruction to assign the value selected in the Color dialog box to the form's BackColor property.

4. Save the solution and then start the application. Click the **Color** button to open the Color dialog box. Select a different color square and then click the **OK** button. The background color of the form changes to the color you selected.

5. Click the **Exit** button to end the application.

To code the Print button's Click event procedure:

1. Open the code template for the printButton's Click event procedure. Enter the instruction to specify that the printout should be sent to the Print preview window. If you need help, refer to the code shown earlier in Figure 2-28.

2. Next, enter the instruction to tell the computer to start the print operation.

3. Save the solution and then start the application. Click the **Print** button. The printout of the interface appears in the Print preview window. Click the **Zoom button** list arrow and then click **75%**. See Figure 2-53.

you can use the Print button to send the output to the printer

Zoom button list arrow

Figure 2-53 Print preview window
OpenClipArt.org/mightyman; Music by Dan-O at DanoSongs.com

4. Click the **Close** button in the Print preview window and then click the **Exit** button.

Adding a Splash Screen to the Music Sampler Project

In the next set of steps, you will add a splash screen to the application. Recall that the Add New Item dialog box provides a template that is already configured as a splash screen.

To add a new splash screen to the Music Sampler project:

1. Add a new splash screen named **SplashScreenForm.vb** to the project. If you need help, refer to the How To box shown earlier in Figure 2-13.

2. Set the Font property of the ApplicationTitle label control to **Segoe UI, 18pt**.

3. Set the Font properties of the Version and Copyright label controls to **Segoe UI, 9pt**.

4. Specify that the SplashScreenForm is the splash screen for the project. If you need help, refer to the How To box shown earlier in Figure 2-16.

5. Open the Project Designer window, if necessary. Change the executable file's name to **Music Sampler**. Next, open the Assembly Information dialog box by clicking the **Assembly Information** button in the Application pane. Change the text in the Title box to **Music Sampler**. If necessary, change the year in the Copyright box to **2014**.

6. Click the **OK** button to close the Assembly Information dialog box. Save the solution and then close the Project Designer window.

Testing the Application

To test the application:

1. Start the application. The splash screen shown earlier in Figure 2-47 appears first. After a few seconds have elapsed, the splash screen disappears and the startup form (MainForm) appears.

2. Click **each of the buttons within the table layout panel**.

3. Click the **Color** button. Select a different color and then click the **OK** button.

4. Click the **Print** button. If your computer is connected to a printer, click the **Print** button in the Print preview window and then click the **Close** button; otherwise, just click the **Close** button.

5. Click the **Exit** button. Close the Code Editor window and then close the solution. Figure 2-54 shows the Music Sampler application's code.

```
 1 Public Class MainForm
 2
 3    Private Sub exitButton_Click(sender As Object,
      e As EventArgs) Handles exitButton.Click
 4        Me.Close()
 5    End Sub
 6
 7    Private Sub everythingPictureBox_Click(sender As Object,
      e As EventArgs) Handles everythingPictureBox.Click
 8        My.Computer.Audio.Play(
                 "Everything-Begins-by-danosongs.com.wav")
 9
10    End Sub
11
12    Private Sub invisiblePictureBox_Click(sender As Object,
      e As EventArgs) Handles invisiblePictureBox.Click
13        My.Computer.Audio.Play(
                 "Invisible-Love-by-danosongs.com.wav")
14
15    End Sub
16
17    Private Sub magicPictureBox_Click(sender As Object,
      e As EventArgs) Handles magicPictureBox.Click
18        My.Computer.Audio.Play("Magic-Ghost-by-danosongs.com.wav")
19
20    End Sub
21
22    Private Sub threePictureBox_Click(sender As Object,
      e As EventArgs) Handles threePictureBox.Click
23        My.Computer.Audio.Play("Three-Drops-by-danosongs.com.wav")
24
25    End Sub
26
27    Private Sub unclaimedPictureBox_Click(sender As Object,
      e As EventArgs) Handles unclaimedPictureBox.Click
28        My.Computer.Audio.Play(
                 "Unclaimed-Territory-by-danosongs.com.wav")
29
30    End Sub
31
32    Private Sub colorButton_Click(sender As Object,
      e As EventArgs) Handles colorButton.Click
33        colorDialog.Color = Me.BackColor
34        colorDialog.ShowDialog()
35        Me.BackColor = colorDialog.Color
36
37    End Sub
```

Figure 2-54 Music Sampler application's code *(continues)*

(continued)

```
38
39    Private Sub printButton_Click(sender As Object,
         e As EventArgs) Handles printButton.Click
40        PrintForm1.PrintAction =
41            Printing.PrintAction.PrintToPreview
42        PrintForm1.Print()
43
44    End Sub
45 End Class
```

Figure 2-54   Music Sampler application's code
© 2013 Cengage Learning

PROGRAMMING EXAMPLE

Just Paper

Create an interface that allows the user to enter the following customer information: name, address, city, state, ZIP code, the number of cases of standard size paper ordered, and the number of cases of legal size paper ordered. The interface will need to display the total number of cases ordered and the total price of the order. Use the following names for the solution and project, respectively: Just Paper Solution and Just Paper Project. Save the files in the VbReloaded2012\Chap02 folder. Change the form file's name to Main Form.vb. Remember to lock the controls in the interface. See Figures 2-55 through 2-59. In this chapter, you will code only the Exit and Print Order buttons' Click event procedures. You will code the Click event procedures for the Calculate Order and Clear Order buttons in Chapter 3.

Task	Object	Event
1. Calculate the total number of cases ordered and the total price of the order 2. Display the total number of cases ordered and the total price of the order in totalCasesLabel and totalPriceLabel	calcButton	Click
Print the order form (use a print form control)	printButton	Click
Clear screen for the next order	clearButton	Click
End the application	exitButton	Click
Display the total number of cases ordered (from calcButton)	totalCasesLabel	None
Display the total price of the order (from calcButton)	totalPriceLabel	None
Get and display the order information	nameTextBox, addressTextBox, cityTextBox, stateTextBox, zipTextBox, standardTextBox, legalTextBox	None

Figure 2-55   TOE chart
© 2013 Cengage Learning

Figure 2-56   User interface

Object	Property	Setting
Form1	Name	MainForm
	AcceptButton	calcButton
	Font	Segoe UI, 9pt
	MaximizeBox	False
	StartPosition	CenterScreen
	Text	Just Paper
Label1	Font	Segoe UI, 16pt
	Text	Order Form
Label2	Text	&Name:
Label3	Text	&Address:
Label4	Text	Cit&y:
Label5	Text	S&tate:
Label6	Text	&ZIP:
Label7	Text	&Standard (8.5 X 11):
Label8	Text	&Legal (8.5 X 14):
Label9	Text	Cases ordered:
Label10	Text	Total price:
Label11	Name	totalCasesLabel
	AutoSize	False
	BorderStyle	FixedSingle
	Text	(empty)
	TextAlign	MiddleCenter
Label12	Name	totalPriceLabel
	AutoSize	False
	BorderStyle	FixedSingle
	Text	(empty)
	TextAlign	MiddleCenter
TextBox1	Name	nameTextBox
TextBox2	Name	addressTextBox
TextBox3	Name	cityTextBox
TextBox4	Name	stateTextBox
	CharacterCasing	Upper (changes entry to uppercase)
	MaxLength	2 (accepts a maximum of 2 characters)

Figure 2-57   Objects, properties, and settings *(continues)*

(continued)

Object	Property	Setting
TextBox5	Name	zipTextBox
TextBox6	Name	standardTextBox
TextBox7	Name	legalTextBox
Button1	Name	calcButton
	Text	&Calculate Order
Button2	Name	printButton
	Text	&Print Order
Button3	Name	clearButton
	Text	Clea&r Order
Button4	Name	exitButton
	Text	E&xit
PrintForm1		

Figure 2-57 Objects, properties, and settings
© 2013 Cengage Learning

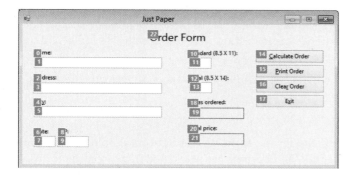

Figure 2-58 Tab order

Figure 2-59 Code

Summary

- You should plan an application jointly with the user to ensure that the application meets the user's needs.

- Planning an application requires that you identify the application's tasks, objects, and events. You then build the interface. You can record the tasks, objects, and events in a TOE chart.

- Not all objects will need an event to occur for them to perform their assigned task.

- You use a text box control to give the user an area in which to enter data.

- In Western countries, you should organize the user interface so that the information flows either vertically or horizontally, with the most important information always located in the upper-left corner of the screen.

- You can group related controls together using either white (empty) space or one of the tools located in the Containers section of the toolbox.

- The text contained in identifying labels should be left-aligned within the label. Identifying labels should be positioned either above or to the left of the control they identify.

- Identifying labels and button captions should contain only one to three words, which should appear on one line.

- Identifying labels and button captions should be meaningful. Identifying labels should end with a colon and be entered using sentence capitalization. Button captions should be entered using book title capitalization.

- When positioning the controls, you should maintain a consistent margin from the edges of the form.

- Related controls are typically placed close together in the interface.

- When buttons are positioned horizontally on the form, all the buttons should be the same height; their widths, however, may vary. When buttons are stacked vertically on the form, all the buttons should be the same height and the same width.

- Align the borders of the controls wherever possible to minimize the number of different margins used in the interface.

- Graphics and color should be used sparingly in an interface.

- Avoid using italic and underlining in an interface, and limit the use of bold text to titles, headings, and key items that you want to emphasize.

- You should use only one font type and not more than two different font sizes for the text in an interface. Segoe UI (9pt) is the recommended font for Windows 8 and Windows 7 applications. It's helpful to change the form's Font property *before* adding controls to the form.

- In most cases, an identifying label's BorderStyle and AutoSize properties are set to None and True, respectively. A label control that displays program output, on the other hand, usually has its BorderStyle and AutoSize properties set to FixedSingle and False, respectively.

- A label's TextAlign property determines the alignment of the text within the label.

- You should assign access keys to each of the controls that can accept user input (such as text boxes and buttons). You assign an access key by including an ampersand (&) in the control's caption or identifying label.

- The TabIndex property determines the order in which a control receives the focus when the user either presses the Tab key or employs an access key during run time. A text box's

TabIndex property should be set to a value that is one number more than the TabIndex value of its identifying label.

- You can use the Add New Item dialog box to add a splash screen to a project. You specify the name of a project's splash screen in the Project Designer window.

- You use an application's primary window to view and edit the application's data. Dialog boxes are used to support and supplement a user's activities in a primary window.

- The form's FormBorderStyle property specifies its border style. The form's ControlBox, MinimizeBox, and MaximizeBox properties determine the status of the form's Control menu box, Minimize button, and Maximize button.

- The Dialogs section of the toolbox provides tools for creating commonly-used dialog boxes. The dialog boxes are modal and contain both default and cancel buttons. The controls instantiated from these tools appear in the component tray in the IDE.

- You use a form's AcceptButton property to designate a default button. A form can have only one default button.

- The Visual Basic PowerPacks section of the toolbox provides the PrintForm tool for instantiating a print form control, which you can use to print the interface during run time. The instantiated control appears in the component tray in the IDE.

- You can use the Play method of the My.Computer.Audio object to play a WAV file during run time.

Key Terms

Access key—the underlined character in an object's identifying label or caption; allows the user to select the object using the Alt key in combination with the underlined character

Arguments—the items within parentheses after a method's name; represent information that the method needs to perform its task

Book title capitalization—the capitalization used for a button's caption; refers to capitalizing the first letter in each word, except for articles, conjunctions, and prepositions that do not occur at either the beginning or the end of the caption

Cancel button—a button that can be selected by pressing the Esc key

Default button—a button that can be selected by pressing the Enter key even when it does not have the focus

Dialog boxes—windows that support and supplement a user's activities in a primary window

Focus—indicates that a control is ready to accept user input

Modal—refers to the fact that the dialog box remains on the screen until the user closes it; while it is on the screen, no input from the keyboard or mouse can occur in the application's primary window; however, you can access other applications

My feature—the Visual Basic feature that exposes a set of commonly-used objects (such as the Computer object) to the programmer

Primary window—the window in which you view and edit an application's data

Sentence capitalization—the capitalization used for identifying labels; refers to capitalizing only the first letter in the first word and in any words that are customarily capitalized

Text box—a control that provides an area in the form for the user to enter data

Review Questions

1. Which of the following statements is false? (3)

   a. A button's caption should appear on one line.

   b. A button's caption should be from one to three words only.

   c. A button's caption should be entered using book title capitalization.

   d. A button's caption should end with a colon (:).

2. Which of the following statements is false? (3)

   a. The text that identifies a text box should be left-aligned within a label control.

   b. An identifying label should be positioned either above or to the left of the control it identifies.

   c. Labels that identify controls should be entered using book title capitalization.

   d. Labels that identify text boxes should end with a colon (:).

3. Which property determines the order in which a control receives the focus when the user presses the Tab key? (6)

   a. OrderTab   c. TabIndex

   b. SetOrder   d. TabOrder

4. Which property is used to assign an access key? (5)

   a. Access   c. KeyAccess

   b. Caption   d. Text

5. Which property is used to designate a default button in the interface? (10)

   a. button's AcceptButton   c. form's AcceptButton

   b. button's DefaultButton   d. form's DefaultButton

6. If a text box's TabIndex value is 7, its identifying label's TabIndex value should be _____. (5, 6)

   a. 6   c. 8

   b. 7   d. 9

7. Which of the following changes the background color of the totalTextBox to the color selected in the colorDialog control? (8, 9)

   a. `totalTextBox.BackGround = colorDialog.Color`

   b. `totalTextBox.BackGround = colorDialog.Selected`

   c. `totalTextBox.BackGroundColor = colorDialog.Color`

   d. `totalTextBox.BackColor = colorDialog.Color`

8. A _____ dialog box remains on the screen until the user closes it. (8)

   a. modal   c. sticky

   b. perpetual   d. none of the above

9. Which of the following tells the PrintForm1 control to start the print operation? (11)

   a. `Print.PrintForm1()`   c. `PrintForm1.Print()`

   b. `PrintForm1.BeginPrint()`   d. `PrintForm1.Start()`

10. Which of the following tells the computer to play the Hello.wav file contained in the project's bin\Debug folder? (12)

    a. `My.Audio.Play("Hello.wav")`

    b. `My.Computer.Audio.Play("Hello.wav")`

    c. `My.Computer.Play.Audio("Hello.wav")`

    d. `My.Computer.Play.AudioFile("Hello.wav")`

Each Exercise, except the DISCOVERY exercises, is associated with one or more objectives listed at the beginning of the chapter.

123

Exercises

Pencil and Paper

1. Define the following two terms: book title capitalization and sentence capitalization. (3)

    INTRODUCTORY

2. List the four steps you should follow when planning a Visual Basic application. (1)

    INTRODUCTORY

3. Explain the procedure for choosing a control's access key. (5)

    INTRODUCTORY

4. Explain how you give users keyboard access to a text box. (5, 6)

    INTRODUCTORY

5. Write the Visual Basic instruction to change the redLabel's font to the font selected in the fontDialog control. (8, 9)

    INTERMEDIATE

6. Write the Visual Basic instruction to specify that the PrintForm1 control should send a printout of the interface directly to the printer. (11)

    INTERMEDIATE

7. Write the Visual Basic instruction to change the redLabel's text to red. (9)

    ADVANCED

8. Five of the labels in Figure 2-49 contain two lines of text. How do you enter more than one line of text in a label?

    DISCOVERY

9. Correct the following line of code, which should play the Intro.wav file contained in the Music folder on the F drive: `My.Computer.Music.Play("Intro.wav")`. (12)

    SWAT THE BUGS

Computer

10. If necessary, create the Color Game application from this chapter's Programming Tutorial 1, and then close the solution. Use Windows to make a copy of the Color Game Solution folder. Rename the copy Color Game Solution-ModifyThis. Open the Color Game Solution (Color Game Solution.sln) file contained in the Color Game Solution-ModifyThis folder. (2, 3, 5, 6, 9, 12)

    MODIFY THIS

    a. Add three buttons to the form. Change their Anchor properties to "Top, Bottom, Left, Right". Make the buttons the same size and color as the Red button. Name the buttons goldButton, maroonButton, and turquoiseButton. Use the following captions for the buttons: Gold, Maroon, Turquoise.

    b. Add another row to the table layout panel. Adjust the size of the table layout panel and its rows. You may also need to adjust the size of the form and the location of the Start Over, Print, Font, and Exit buttons. Drag the Gold, Maroon, and Turquoise buttons into the new cells in the table layout panel. Reset the tab order, if necessary.

c. Code the new buttons using the following Spanish words and WAV files: Dorado, gold.wav, Granate, maroon.wav, Turquesa, turquoise.wav. The WAV files are contained in the VbReloaded2012\Chap02 folder. You will need to use Windows to copy the files to the current project's bin\Debug folder. Also make the necessary modifications to the Start Over button's Click event procedure.

d. Save the solution and then start and test the application. Close the Code Editor window and then close the solution.

MODIFY THIS   11. If necessary, create the Music Sampler application from this chapter's Programming Tutorial 2, and then close the solution. Use Windows to make a copy of the Music Sampler Solution folder. Rename the copy Music Sampler Solution-ModifyThis. Open the Music Sampler Solution (Music Sampler Solution.sln) file contained in the Music Sampler Solution-ModifyThis folder. (2, 3, 12)

a. Add a label and a picture box to the form. Name the picture box inkarnationPictureBox. Display the image stored in the VbReloaded2012\Chap02\PlayButton.png file. (The image was downloaded from the Open Clip Art Library at *www.openclipart.org*.) Enter Inkarnation on the first line in the label and Dan-O on the second line.

b. Set the label's Anchor property to Left. Set the picture box's Anchor property to None.

c. Add another row to the table layout panel. Adjust the size of the table layout panel and its rows. You may also need to adjust the location of the Color, Print, and Exit buttons. Drag the label and picture box into the table layout panel.

d. Code the inkarnationPictureBox using the VbReloaded2012\Chap02\Inkarnation-by-danosongs.com.wav file. You will need to use Windows to copy the file to the current project's bin\Debug folder.

e. Save the solution and then start and test the application. Close the Code Editor window and then close the solution.

MODIFY THIS   12. If necessary, create the Just Paper application from this chapter's Programming Example, and then close the solution. Use Windows to make a copy of the Just Paper Solution folder. Rename the copy Just Paper Solution-ModifyThis. Open the Just Paper Solution (Just Paper Solution.sln) file contained in the VbReloaded2012\Chap02\Just Paper Solution-ModifyThis folder. (1-3, 6)

a. Add four labels to the form. Two of the labels will display the price of the order without any sales tax and the sales tax amount. The other two labels will be identifying labels. Use appropriate captions for the identifying labels.

b. Place the four labels from Step a, as well as the four labels associated with the total number of cases ordered and total price, in a table layout panel. If necessary, reset the tab order.

c. Make the appropriate modifications to the TOE chart shown earlier in Figure 2-55.

d. Save the solution and then start the application. If your computer is connected to a printer, use the Print Order button to print the interface. Click the Exit button. Close the Code Editor window and then close the solution. (You do not need to code the Calculate Order or Clear Order buttons.)

MODIFY THIS   13. Open the Time Solution (Time Solution.sln) file contained in the VbReloaded2012\Chap02\Time Solution folder. Lay out and organize the interface so that it follows all of the design guidelines specified in this chapter. (You do not need to code the Calculate

Hours button.) Save the solution and then start the application. Click the Exit button and then close the solution. (3-6)

14. Karen Scott wants an application that calculates and displays the amount to tip a waiter at a restaurant. The application should allow Karen to enter her total bill and the tip percentage (in decimal format). It should also allow her to send a printout of the interface to the Print preview window. Prepare a TOE chart ordered by object. Create a Windows application. Use the following names for the solution and project, respectively: Tip Solution and Tip Project. Save the application in the VbReloaded2012\Chap02 folder. Change the form file's name to Main Form.vb. Code only the Print and Exit buttons. Save the solution and then start and test the application. Close the Code Editor window and then close the solution. (1-6, 11)   INTRODUCTORY

15. Party-On sells individual hot/cold cups and dessert plates for parties. The store manager wants an application that allows him to enter the price of a cup, the price of a plate, the number of cups purchased, and the number of plates purchased. The application will need to calculate and display the total cost of the purchase. It should also allow the store manager to send a printout of the interface to the Print preview window. In addition, the store manager should be allowed to change the background color of the form. Prepare a TOE chart ordered by object. Create a Windows application. Use the following names for the solution and project, respectively: Party Solution and Party Project. Save the application in the VbReloaded2012\Chap02 folder. Change the form file's name to Main Form.vb. Include a table layout panel in the interface. The button that calculates and displays the total cost should be the default button. Code only the Print, Color, and Exit buttons. Save the solution and then start and test the application. Close the Code Editor window and then close the solution. (1-6, 8-11)   INTRODUCTORY

16. The manager of Rent A Van wants an application that calculates and displays the total cost of renting a van. Customers pay a base fee plus a charge per mile driven. The application should allow the manager to send a printout of the interface to the Print preview window. In addition, the manager should be allowed to change the form's font. Prepare a TOE chart ordered by object. Create a Windows application. Use the following names for the solution and project, respectively: Van Solution and Van Project. Save the application in the VbReloaded2012\Chap02 folder. Change the form file's name to Main Form.vb. Include a splash screen in the application. Code only the Print, Font, and Exit buttons. Save the solution and then start and test the application. Close the Code Editor window and then close the solution. (1-9, 11)   INTERMEDIATE

17. The manager of Carson Carpets wants an application that calculates and displays the area of a rectangle in both square feet and square yards. The manager will enter the length and width of the rectangle in feet. The application should allow the manager to send a printout of the interface to the Print preview window. Prepare a TOE chart ordered by object. Create a Windows application. Use the following names for the solution and project, respectively: Carson Solution and Carson Project. Save the application in the VbReloaded2012\Chap02 folder. Change the form file's name to Main Form.vb. The button that calculates and displays the output should be the default button. Include a splash screen in the application. Code only the Print and Exit buttons. Save the solution and then start and test the application. Close the Code Editor window and then close the solution. (1-7, 10, 11)   INTERMEDIATE

18. Create an application that plays five quotes from either a movie or a TV show. Download any five WAV files from the Internet. You can find free WAV files at *www.thefreesite.com/Free_Sounds/Free_WAVs*. Create a Windows application that allows the user to play each WAV file. Use the following names for the solution and project, respectively: Quotes Solution and Quotes Project. Save the application in the VbReloaded2012\Chap02 folder. Change the form file's name to Main Form.vb. Code   ADVANCED

the application. Save the solution and then start and test the application. Close the Code Editor window and then close the solution. (1, 3-6, 12)

DISCOVERY

19. In this exercise, you learn how to bypass a control in the tab order when the user is tabbing. Open the Johnson Solution (Johnson Solution.sln) file contained in the VbReloaded2012\Chap02\Johnson Solution folder. Start the application. Press the Tab key several times and notice where the focus is placed each time. Click the Exit button. Most of Johnson's customers are located in California. Enter CA in the stateTextBox's Text property. Find a property that will bypass (skip over) the stateTextBox when the user is tabbing. If the user needs to place the focus in the stateTextBox (for example, to change the control's contents), he or she will need to either click the control or use its access key. Save the solution and then start and test the application. Click the Exit button and then close the solution.

SWAT THE BUGS

20. Open the Debug Solution (Debug Solution.sln) file contained in the VbReloaded2012\ Chap02\Debug Solution folder. Start the application. Test all of the access keys in the interface. So that you can test its access key, the Calculate Total button's Click event procedure contains a line of code. Notice that not all of the access keys are working. Stop the application. Locate and then correct any errors. Save the solution and then start and test the application. Close the solution. (5, 6)

Case Projects

 Crispies Bagels and Bites

Create a TOE chart and interface for an application that allows the user to enter the number of bagels, donuts, and cups of coffee a customer orders. The interface will need to display the total price of the order. Use the following names for the solution and project, respectively: Crispies Solution and Crispies Project. Save the application in the VbReloaded2012\Chap02 folder. Change the form file's name to Main Form.vb. You can either create your own interface or create the one shown in Figure 2-60. The image in the picture box was downloaded from the Open Clip Art Library at *www.openclipart.org* and is stored in the VbReloaded2012\Chap02\ Crispies.png file. The Color button should allow the user to change the background color of the label that displays the total price of the order. The Font button should allow the user to change the form's font. Code the Click event procedures for the Color, Font, and Exit buttons only. (1-6, 8-10)

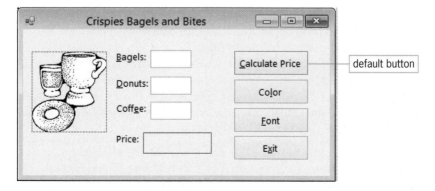

Figure 2-60   Sample interface for the Crispies Bagels and Bites application
OpenClipArt.org/johnny_automatic

Basket Haven

Create a TOE chart and interface for an application that allows the user to enter a customer's name, address, city, state, ZIP code, number of small baskets ordered, number of medium baskets ordered, and number of large baskets ordered. The interface will need to display the total number of baskets ordered and the total price of the order. Use the following names for the solution and project, respectively: Basket Haven Solution and Basket Haven Project. Save the application in the VbReloaded2012\Chap02 folder. Change the form file's name to Main Form.vb. You can either create your own interface or create the one shown in Figure 2-61. The image in the picture box was downloaded from the Open Clip Art Library at *www.openclipart.org* and is stored in the VbReloaded2012\Chap02\Basket.png file. The Print Order button should send a printout of the interface to the Print preview window. Code the Click event procedures for the Print Order and Exit buttons only. Include a splash screen in the application. (1-7, 10, 11)

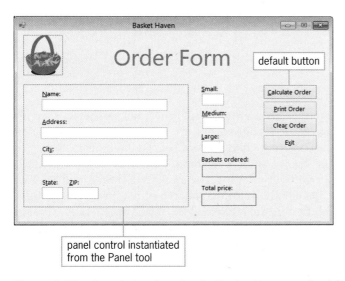

Figure 2-61 Sample interface for the Basket Haven application
OpenClipArt.org/Jose Mourinho/centroacademico

 Kingston Sales

Create a TOE chart and interface for an application that allows the user to enter the sales amounts for five stores. The interface will need to display the total sales amount and the total commission earned by the salespeople. Use the following names for the solution and project, respectively: Kingston Solution and Kingston Project. Save the solution in the VbReloaded2012\Chap02 folder. Change the form file's name to Main Form.vb. You can either create your own interface or create the one shown in Figure 2-62. The Print button should send a printout of the interface to the Print preview window. Code the Click event procedures for the Print and Exit buttons only. Include a splash screen in the application. (1-7, 10, 11)

group box control
instantiated from
the GroupBox tool

128

Figure 2-62   Sample interface for the Kingston Sales application

Sophia's Italian Deli

Sophia's offers the following items on its lunch menu: Italian sub, meatball sandwich, slice of pizza, sausage sandwich, meatball/sausage combo, chicken fingers, ravioli plate, lasagna plate, bowl of soup, Caesar salad, calamari, spumoni, and cheesecake. Create a TOE chart and interface for an application that allows the user to enter a customer's lunch order. The interface will need to display the price of the order without sales tax, the sales tax amount, and the total price of the order. Use the following names for the solution and project, respectively: Sophia Solution and Sophia Project. Save the solution in the VbReloaded2012\Chap02 folder. Change the form file's name to Main Form.vb. Include Calculate, Clear, About, and Exit buttons in the interface. Also include a splash screen in the application. Use the Windows Forms About Box template in the Add New Item dialog box to include an About Box form in the application. The form should display as a modal form when the user clicks the About button. Code the Click event procedures for the About and Exit buttons only. (1-7)

CHAPTER 3

Memory Locations and Calculations

After studying Chapter 3, you should be able to:

1 Declare variables and named constants

2 Assign data to an existing variable

3 Convert data to the appropriate type using the TryParse method, Convert class methods, and a literal type character

4 Write and evaluate arithmetic expressions

5 Understand the scope and lifetime of variables and named constants

6 Understand the purpose of the Option statements

7 Use a TOE chart, pseudocode, and a flowchart to code an application

8 Format an application's numeric output

9 Clear the contents of a control's Text property during run time

10 Send the focus to a control during run time

11 Explain the different types of program errors

12 Use the FromArgb method (Programming Tutorial 1)

Reading and Study Guide

Before you begin reading Chapter 3, view the Ch03_ReadingStudyGuide.pdf file. You can open the file using Adobe Reader, which is available for free on the Adobe Web site at *www.adobe.com/downloads/*.

Internal Memory

Inside every computer is a component called internal memory. The internal memory of a computer is composed of memory locations. It may be helpful to picture memory locations as shoe boxes, similar to the ones illustrated in Figure 3-1. As you know, shoe boxes come in different types and sizes. There are small boxes for children's sandals, larger boxes for adult sneakers, and even larger boxes for boots. The type and size of the footwear determine the appropriate type and size of the box. Like shoe boxes, memory locations come in different types and sizes. Here too, the type and size of the item you want to store determine the appropriate type and size of the memory location. Just as shoe boxes are designed to hold only one pair of footwear, memory locations are designed to store only one item at a time. Examples of items stored in memory locations include numbers, strings, Boolean values, and Visual Basic instructions.

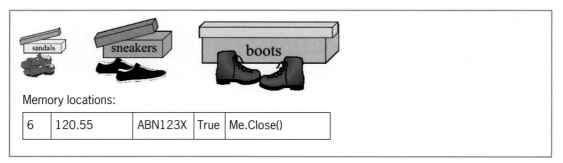

Figure 3-1 Illustration of shoe boxes and memory locations
OpenClipArt.org/jarekadam; OpenClipArt.org/drunken_duck; OpenClipArt.org/pawnk

Some of the memory locations inside the computer are automatically filled with data while you use your computer. For example, when you enter the number 6 at your keyboard, the computer saves the number 6 in a memory location for you. Likewise, when you start an application, each program instruction is placed in a memory location, where it awaits processing.

Memory locations can also be reserved by a programmer for use in a program. Reserving a memory location is also referred to as declaring the memory location. You declare a memory location using a Visual Basic instruction that assigns a name, a data type, and an initial value to the location. The name allows the programmer to refer to the memory location in code. The **data type** indicates the type of data—for example, numeric or string—the memory location will store.

A memory location declared in a program can be either a variable or a named constant. You will learn about variables first. Named constants are covered in the *Named Constants* section in this chapter.

Variables

A **variable** is a computer memory location that a programmer uses to temporarily store data while an application is running. The data might be entered by the user at the keyboard. It also might be read from a file or be the result of a calculation made by the computer. The memory location is called a variable because its contents can change (vary) during run time.

The programmer must assign a name to each variable he or she wants to use in a program. The name, which is typically entered using camel case, should describe the variable's contents. Besides being descriptive, a variable name must follow the rules listed in Figure 3-2. The figure also includes examples of valid and invalid variable names.

HOW TO Name a Variable

1. The name must begin with a letter or an underscore.

2. The name can contain only letters, numbers, and the underscore character. No punctuation characters, special characters, or spaces are allowed in the name.

3. Although the name can contain thousands of characters, 32 is the recommended maximum number of characters to use.

4. The name cannot be a reserved word, such as Sub or Private.

Valid names
income2014, lastName, northSales, taxRate, region1_2ndQtr

Invalid names	Problem
2014Income	the name must begin with a letter or an underscore
last Name	the name cannot contain a space
north.Sales	the name cannot contain punctuation
north$Sales	the name cannot contain a special character
r2Q	valid, but not descriptive

Figure 3-2 How to name a variable
© 2013 Cengage Learning

The item that a memory location will accept for storage is determined by the location's data type, which the programmer assigns to the location when he or she declares it in code. Figure 3-3 describes most of the basic data types available in Visual Basic. Each data type listed in the figure is a class, which means that each data type is a pattern from which objects—in this case, variables—are instantiated.

Data type	Stores	Memory required
Boolean	a logical value (True, False)	2 bytes
Char	one Unicode character	2 bytes
Date	date and time information Date range: January 1, 0001 to December 31, 9999 Time range: 0:00:00 (midnight) to 23:59:59	8 bytes
Decimal	a number with a decimal place Range with no decimal place: +/−79,228,162,514,264,337,593,543,950,335 Range with a decimal place: +/−7.9228162514264337593543950335	16 bytes
Double	a number with a decimal place Range: +/−4.94065645841247 X 10^{-324} to +/−1.79769313486231 X 10^{308}	8 bytes

Figure 3-3 Basic data types in Visual Basic (*continues*)

(continued)

Data type	Stores	Memory required
Integer	integer Range: –2,147,483,648 to 2,147,483,647	4 bytes
Long	integer Range: –9,223,372,036,854,775,808 to 9,223,372,036,854,775,807	8 bytes
Object	data of any type	4 bytes
Short	integer Range: –32,768 to 32,767	2 bytes
Single	a number with a decimal place Range: +/–1.401298 X 10^{-45} to +/–3.402823 X 10^{38}	4 bytes
String	text; 0 to approximately 2 billion characters	

Figure 3-3   Basic data types in Visual Basic
© 2013 Cengage Learning

As Figure 3-3 indicates, variables assigned the Integer, Long, or Short data type can store **integers**, which are positive or negative numbers that do not have any decimal places. The differences among these three data types are in the range of integers each type can store and the amount of memory each type needs to store the integer.

Variables assigned the Decimal, Double, or Single data type, on the other hand, can store **real numbers**, which are numbers that contain a decimal place. Here again, the differences among these three data types are in the range of numbers each type can store and the amount of memory each type needs to store the numbers. However, calculations involving Decimal variables are not subject to the small rounding errors that may occur when using Double or Single variables. In most cases, the small rounding errors do not create any problems in an application. One exception to this is when the application contains complex equations dealing with money, where you need accuracy to the penny. In those cases, the Decimal data type is the best type to use.

The Char data type can store one Unicode character, while the String data type can store from zero to approximately two billion Unicode characters. Unicode is the universal coding scheme for characters. It assigns a unique numeric value to each character used in the written languages of the world. (For more information, see The Unicode Standard at *www.unicode.org*.)

Also listed in Figure 3-3 are the Boolean, Date, and Object data types. You use a Boolean variable to store a Boolean value (either True or False), and use a Date variable to store date and time information. The Object data type can store any type of data. However, your application will pay a price for this flexibility: It will run more slowly because the computer has to determine the type of data currently stored in the variable. It is best to avoid using the Object data type.

The applications in this book will use the Integer data type for variables that will store integers used in calculations, even when the integers are small enough to fit into a Short variable. This is because a calculation containing Integer variables takes less time to process than the equivalent calculation containing Short variables. Either the Decimal data type or the Double data type will be used for real numbers involved in calculations. The applications will use the String data type for variables that contain either text or numbers not involved in calculations, and the Boolean data type to store Boolean values.

Declaring a Variable in Code

Figure 3-4 shows the syntax of the statement used to declare a variable. The declaration statement tells the computer to set aside a small section of its internal memory, and it allows the programmer to refer to the section by the variable's name. The size of the section is determined by the variable's data type. The {Dim | Private | Static} portion of the syntax indicates that you can select only one of the keywords appearing within the braces. In most instances, you declare a variable using the Dim keyword. (You will learn about the Private and Static keywords in the *Variables with Class Scope* and *Static Variables* sections, respectively, in this chapter.)

HOW TO Declare a Variable

Syntax
{Dim | Private | Static} *variableName* **As** *dataType* [= *initialValue*]

Example 1
Dim hours As Integer
Dim payRate As Double

declares an Integer variable named **hours** and a Double variable named **payRate**; the variables are automatically initialized to 0

Example 2
Dim discount As Decimal

declares a Decimal variable named **discount**; the variable is automatically initialized to 0

Example 3
Dim isDataOk As Boolean = True

declares a Boolean variable named **isDataOk** and initializes it using the keyword **True**

Example 4
Dim message As String = "Good Morning"

declares a String variable named **message** and initializes it using the string "Good Morning"

Figure 3-4 How to declare a variable
© 2013 Cengage Learning

"Dim" comes from the word "dimension," which is how programmers in the 1960s referred to the process of allocating the computer's memory. "Dimension" refers to the size of something.

As mentioned earlier, a variable is considered an object in Visual Basic. The variable is an instance of the class specified in the *dataType* portion of its declaration statement. The Dim hours As Integer statement, for example, creates (instantiates) a variable (object) named hours. The hours variable (object) is an instance of the Integer class.

InitialValue in the syntax is the value you want stored in the variable when it is created in the computer's internal memory. The square brackets in the syntax indicate that the "= *initialValue*" part of the syntax is optional. If you do not assign an initial value to a variable when it is declared, the computer stores a default value in the variable. The default value depends on the variable's data type. A variable declared using one of the numeric data types is automatically initialized to—in other words, given a beginning value of—the number 0. The computer automatically initializes a Boolean variable using the keyword False, and a Date variable to 1/1/0001 12:00:00 AM. Object and String variables are automatically initialized using the keyword Nothing. Variables initialized to Nothing do not actually contain the word "Nothing"; rather, they contain no value at all.

Mini-Quiz 3-1

1. A variable can store ——————— at a time. (1)

    a. only one item

    b. a maximum of two items

    c. an unlimited number of items

2. Which of the following is a valid name for a variable? (1)

    a. `jan.Sales`

    b. `2ndQuarterIncome`

    c. `commission_rate`

    d. `march$`

3. Write a Dim statement that declares a Double variable named `pricePerItem`. (1)

4. Write a Dim statement that declares an Integer variable named `counter` and initializes the variable to the number 1. (1)

The answers to Mini-Quiz questions are located in Appendix A. Each question is associated with one or more objectives listed at the beginning of the chapter.

134

Assigning Data to an Existing Variable

In the previous chapters, you used an assignment statement to assign a value to a control's property during run time. You can also use an assignment statement to assign a value to a variable during run time; the syntax for doing this is shown in Figure 3-5. In the syntax, *expression* represents the value you want assigned to the variable. The expression can contain items such as literal constants, object properties, variables, keywords, or arithmetic operators. A **literal constant** is an item of data whose value does not change during run time; examples include the numeric literal constant 650 and the string literal constant "James". When the computer processes an assignment statement, it first evaluates the expression that appears on the right side of the assignment operator (=). It then assigns the result to the variable (memory location) that appears on the left side of the assignment operator, replacing the variable's existing data. (Recall that a variable can store only one item of data at a time.) The data type of the value assigned to a variable should be the same data type as the variable itself, as shown in the examples included in Figure 3-5.

HOW TO Assign a Value to an Existing Variable

<u>Syntax</u>
variableName = *expression*

<u>Example 1</u>
```
Dim quantity As Integer
quantity = 650
```
The assignment statement assigns the integer 650 to the `quantity` variable.

<u>Example 2</u>
```
Dim firstName As String
firstName = "James"
```
The assignment statement assigns the string "James" to the `firstName` variable.

Figure 3-5   How to assign a value to an existing variable *(continues)*

(continued)

Example 3
```
Dim zipCode As String
zipCode = zipTextBox.Text
```
The assignment statement assigns the string contained in the zipTextBox's Text property to the zipCode variable.

Example 4
```
Dim discountRate As Double
discountRate = .05
```
The assignment statement assigns the Double number .05 to the discountRate variable.

Figure 3-5 How to assign a value to an existing variable
© 2013 Cengage Learning

The assignment statement in Example 1 stores the numeric literal constant 650, an integer, in an Integer variable named quantity. Similarly, the assignment statement in Example 2 stores the string literal constant "James" in a String variable named firstName. Notice that string literal constants are enclosed in quotation marks, but numeric literal constants and variable names are not. The quotation marks differentiate a string from both a number and a variable name. In other words, "650" is a string, but 650 is a number. Similarly, "James" is a string, but James (without the quotation marks) would be interpreted by the computer as the name of a memory location. When the computer processes an assignment statement that assigns a string to a String variable, it assigns only the characters that appear between the quotation marks; it does not assign the quotation marks themselves.

The assignment statement in Example 3 in Figure 3-5 assigns the contents of the zipTextBox to a String variable named zipCode. A String variable is appropriate in this case because the value contained in an object's Text property is always treated as a string in Visual Basic. The assignment statement in Example 4 assigns the Double number .05 to a Double variable named discountRate. This is because a numeric literal constant that has a decimal place is automatically treated as a Double number in Visual Basic. When entering a numeric literal constant, you do not enter a comma or special characters, such as the dollar sign or percent sign. If you want to include a percentage in an assignment statement, you do so using its decimal equivalent; for example, you enter .05 rather than 5%.

In all of the assignment statements in Figure 3-5, the data type of the value matches the data type of the variable to which the value is assigned. At times, however, the value's data type might be different from the variable's data type. You can change the value's data type to match the variable's data type using either the TryParse method or one of the methods in the Convert class.

Using the TryParse Method

As you learned earlier, each data type in Visual Basic is a class. Most classes have one or more methods that perform a specific task for the class. For example, all of the Visual Basic numeric data types (such as Double, Decimal, or Integer) have a **TryParse method** whose task is to convert a string to that particular data type. Figure 3-6 shows the basic syntax of the TryParse method along with examples of using the method. In the syntax, *dataType* is one of the numeric data types available in Visual Basic.

HOW TO Use the Basic Syntax of the TryParse Method

Basic syntax
dataType.**TryParse**(*string*, *numericVariableName*)

Example 1
```
Dim sales As Double
Double.TryParse(salesTextBox.Text, sales)
```
If the string contained in the Text property can be converted to a Double number, the TryParse method converts the string and then stores the result in the `sales` variable; otherwise, it stores 0 in the variable.

Example 2
```
Dim gross As Decimal
Decimal.TryParse(grossLabel.Text, gross)
```
If the string contained in the Text property can be converted to a Decimal number, the TryParse method converts the string and then stores the result in the `gross` variable; otherwise, it stores 0 in the variable.

Example 3
```
Dim inputNumber As String = "34"
Dim number As Integer
Integer.TryParse(inputNumber, number)
```
The TryParse method converts the string contained in the `inputNumber` variable to an Integer number and then stores the result (34) in the `number` variable.

Ch03-
TryParse

Figure 3-6   How to use the basic syntax of the TryParse method
© 2013 Cengage Learning

The dot member access operator in the syntax indicates that the TryParse method is a member of the *dataType* class. The method's arguments (*string* and *numericVariableName*) represent information that the method needs to perform its task. The *string* argument is the string you want converted to a number of the *dataType* type and typically is either the Text property of a control or the name of a String variable. The *numericVariableName* argument is the name of a numeric variable in which the TryParse method can store the number. The numeric variable must have the same data type as specified in the *dataType* portion of the syntax.

The TryParse method parses its *string* argument to determine whether the string can be converted to a number of the specified data type. In this case, the term "parse" means to look at each character in the string. If the string can be converted, the TryParse method converts the string to a number and stores the number in the variable specified in the *numericVariableName* argument. If the TryParse method determines that the string cannot be converted to the appropriate data type, it assigns the number 0 to the variable.

Figure 3-7 shows how the TryParse method of the Double, Decimal, and Integer data types would convert various strings. As the figure indicates, the three methods can convert a string that contains only numbers. They can also convert a string that contains a leading sign, as well as one that contains leading or trailing spaces. In addition, the Double.TryParse and Decimal. TryParse methods can convert a string that contains a decimal point or a comma. However, none of the three methods can convert an empty string or a string that contains a dollar sign, a percent sign, a letter, or a space within the string. An **empty string**, also referred to as a **zero-length string**, is a set of quotation marks with nothing between them.

String	Double.TryParse	Decimal.TryParse	Integer.TryParse
"62"	62	62	62
"–9"	–9	–9	–9
"12.55"	12.55	12.55	0
"–4.23"	–4.23	–4.23	0
"1,457"	1457	1457	0
" 33 "	33	33	33
"" (empty string)	0	0	0
"$5"	0	0	0
"7%"	0	0	0
"122a"	0	0	0
"1 345"	0	0	0

Figure 3-7   Results of the TryParse method for the Double, Decimal, and Integer data types
© 2013 Cengage Learning

Using the Convert Class Methods

At times, you may need to convert a number (rather than a string) from one data type to another. Visual Basic provides several ways of accomplishing this task. For example, you can use the Visual Basic conversion functions, which are listed in Appendix D in this book. Or, you can use one of the methods defined in the **Convert class**. In this book you will use the Convert class methods because unlike the conversion functions, which can be used only in the Visual Basic language, the methods can be used in any of the languages built into Visual Studio.

Figure 3-8 describes the more commonly used Convert class methods and includes the syntax for using them. The dot member access operator indicates that the *method* is a member of the Convert class. In most cases, the method's *value* argument is a numeric value that you want converted either to the String data type or to a different numeric data type (for example, from Double to Decimal).

HOW TO Use the Convert Class Methods

Syntax
Convert.*method*(*value*)

Method	Purpose
ToDecimal	convert the *value* argument to the Decimal data type
ToDouble	convert the *value* argument to the Double data type
ToInt32	convert the *value* argument to the Integer data type
ToString	convert the *value* argument to the String data type

Example 1
```
Dim taxRate As Decimal
taxRate = Convert.ToDecimal(.15)
```
The Convert method converts the Double number .15 to Decimal. (Recall that a number with a decimal place is automatically treated as a Double number in Visual Basic.) The assignment statement then assigns the result to the **taxRate** variable.

Figure 3-8   How to use the Convert class methods *(continues)*

(continued)

<u>Example 2</u>
```
Dim totalScore As Integer
totalScore = 100
totalLabel.Text = Convert.ToString(totalScore)
```
The Convert method converts the integer stored in the `totalScore` variable to String. The assignment statement then assigns the result to the totalLabel's Text property.

Note: Although you can use the Convert methods to convert a string to a numeric data type, the TryParse method is the recommended method to use for that task because, unlike the Convert methods, the TryParse method does not produce an error when it tries to convert the empty string. Instead, the TryParse method assigns the number 0 to its *numericVaria-bleName* argument.

Figure 3-8   How to use the Convert class methods
© 2013 Cengage Learning

The answers to Mini-Quiz questions are located in Appendix A. Each question is associated with one or more objectives listed at the beginning of the chapter.

Mini-Quiz 3-2

1. Which of the following assigns the city name Paris to a String variable named `city`? (2)

    a. `city = 'Paris'`

    b. `city = "Paris"`

    c. `city = Paris`

    d. `city As String = "Paris"`

2. Which of the following assigns the number 50 to an Integer variable named `amount`? (2)

    a. `amount = '50'`

    b. `amount = "50"`

    c. `amount = 50`

    d. `amount As Integer = 50`

3. Which of the following can be used to store the contents of a String variable named `inputPop` in an Integer variable named `population`? (2, 3)

    a. `inputPop.TryParse(String, population)`

    b. `Integer.TryParse(inputPop, population)`

    c. `String.TryParse(inputPop, population)`

    d. `inputPop = TryParse(String, population)`

4. Which of the following assigns the number 25.67 to a Decimal variable named `cost`? (2, 3)

    a. `cost = Convert.ToDecimal(25.67)`

    b. `Convert.ToDecimal(25.67, cost)`

    c. `cost = TryParse.ToDecimal(25.67)`

    d. `TryParse.ToDecimal(25.67, cost)`

Arithmetic Expressions

Most applications require the computer to perform at least one calculation. You instruct the computer to perform a calculation by writing an arithmetic expression, which is an expression that contains one or more arithmetic operators along with any of the following: variables, literal constants, named constants, or methods. When an expression contains a variable or named constant, the computer uses the value stored inside the memory location to process the expression.

Figure 3-9 lists the most commonly used arithmetic operators available in Visual Basic and includes their precedence numbers. The precedence numbers indicate the order in which the computer performs the operation in an expression. Operations with a precedence number of 1 are performed before operations with a precedence number of 2, and so on. However, you can use parentheses to override the order of precedence because operations within parentheses are always performed before operations outside of parentheses.

Operator	Operation	Precedence number
^	exponentiation (raises a number to a power)	1
–	negation (reverses the sign of a number)	2
*, /	multiplication and division	3
\	integer division	4
Mod	modulus (remainder) arithmetic	5
+, –	addition and subtraction	6

Figure 3-9   Most commonly used arithmetic operators
© 2013 Cengage Learning

Although the negation and subtraction operators use the same symbol (a hyphen), there is a difference between these operators: The negation operator is unary, whereas the subtraction operator is binary. Unary and binary refer to the number of operands required by the operator. Unary operators require one operand; binary operators require two operands. For example, the expression −7 uses the negation operator to turn its one operand (the positive number 7) into a negative number. The expression 9 − 4, on the other hand, uses the subtraction operator to subtract its second operand (the number 4) from its first operand (the number 9).

Two of the arithmetic operators listed in Figure 3-9 might be less familiar to you: the integer division operator (\) and the modulus operator (Mod). You use the **integer division operator** to divide two integers and then return the result as an integer. For instance, the expression 211 \ 4 results in 52, which is the integer result of dividing 211 by 4. (If you use the standard division operator [/] to divide 211 by 4, the result is 52.75 rather than 52.) You might use the integer division operator in a program that determines the number of quarters, dimes, and nickels to return as change to a customer. For example, the expression 53 \ 25 will determine the number of quarters to return when the change is 53 cents; the expression evaluates to 2.

The **modulus operator** (sometimes referred to as the remainder operator) is also used to divide two numbers, but the numbers do not have to be integers. After dividing the numbers, the modulus operator returns the remainder of the division. For instance, 211 Mod 4 equals 3, which is the remainder of 211 divided by 4. A common use for the modulus operator is to determine whether a number is even or odd. If you divide the number by 2 and the remainder is 0, the number is even; if the remainder is 1, however, the number is odd. Figure 3-10 shows several examples of using the integer division and Mod operators.

HOW TO Use the Integer Division and Mod Operators

Examples	Results
211 \ 4	52
211 Mod 4	3
53 \ 25	2
53 Mod 25	3
75 \ 2	37
75 Mod 2	1
100 \ 2	50
100 Mod 2	0

Figure 3-10 How to use the integer division and Mod operators
© 2013 Cengage Learning

You may have noticed that some of the operators listed in Figure 3-9, like the multiplication and division operators, have the same precedence number. When an expression contains more than one operator having the same priority, those operators are evaluated from left to right. In the expression 20 + 8 / 4 − 3 * 6, for instance, the division is performed first, followed by the multiplication, addition, and subtraction. The result of the expression is the number 4, as shown in Example 1 in Figure 3-11. However, as Example 2 shows, you can use parentheses to change the order in which the operators in an expression are evaluated. Notice that the expression (20 + 8) / 4 − 3 * 6 evaluates to −11 rather than to 4. This is because the parentheses tell the computer to perform the addition first, followed by the division, multiplication, and subtraction.

HOW TO Evaluate Expressions Containing Operators with the Same Precedence

Example 1

Original expression	20 + 8 / 4 − 3 * 6
The division is performed first.	20 + 2 − 3 * 6
The multiplication is performed second.	20 + 2 − 18
The addition is performed third.	22 − 18
The subtraction is performed last.	4

Example 2

Original expression	(20 + 8) / 4 − 3 * 6
The addition is performed first.	28 / 4 − 3 * 6
The division is performed second.	7 − 3 * 6
The multiplication is performed third.	7 − 18
The subtraction is performed last.	−11

Ch03-
Expressions

Figure 3-11 How to evaluate expressions containing operators with the same precedence
© 2013 Cengage Learning

You can save the result of an arithmetic expression by assigning it to a variable. The variable should have the same data type as the value being assigned to it, as shown in the examples in Figure 3-12.

HOW TO Assign the Result of an Arithmetic Expression to a Variable

Example 1
```
Dim age As Integer = 35
age = age + 1
```
The assignment statement adds the integer 1 to the contents of the Integer `age` variable and then assigns the result (36) to the variable.

Example 2
```
Dim dimes As Integer
Dim change As Integer = 123
dimes = change \ 10
```
The assignment statement divides the contents of the Integer `change` variable by the integer 10 and then assigns the result (12) to the Integer `dimes` variable.

Example 3
```
Dim sales As Double = 2075
Dim bonus As Double
bonus = sales * .1
```
The assignment statement multiplies the contents of the Double `sales` variable by the Double number .1 and then assigns the result (207.5) to the Double `bonus` variable.

Example 4
```
Dim price As Decimal = 20
price = price * Convert.ToDecimal(1.04)
```
The Convert method converts the Double number 1.04 to Decimal. The assignment statement then multiplies the Decimal result by the contents of the Decimal `price` variable and then assigns the result (20.8) to the variable.

Example 5
```
Dim sales As Double = 2075
bonusLabel.Text = Convert.ToString(sales * .1)
```
The Convert method multiplies the contents of the Double `sales` variable by the Double number .1 and then converts the result (207.5) to the String data type. The assignment statement then assigns the string ("207.5") to the bonusLabel's Text property.

Figure 3-12 How to assign the result of an arithmetic expression to a variable
© 2013 Cengage Learning

If you want to practice writing assignment statements that contain arithmetic expressions, open the solution contained in the Try It 1! folder. For now, ignore the Option statements in the Code Editor window.

Arithmetic Assignment Operators

In addition to the standard arithmetic operators listed earlier in Figure 3-9, Visual Basic also provides several arithmetic assignment operators. You can use the **arithmetic assignment operators** to abbreviate an assignment statement that contains an arithmetic operator. However, the assignment statement must have the following format, in which *variableName* is the name of the same variable: *variableName = variableName arithmeticOperator value*. For example, you can use the addition assignment operator (+=) to abbreviate the statement `age = age + 1` as follows: `age += 1`. Both statements tell the computer to add the number 1 to the contents of the `age` variable and then store the result in the variable.

Figure 3-13 shows the syntax for using an arithmetic assignment operator. Notice that each operator listed in the figure consists of an arithmetic operator followed immediately by the assignment operator (=). The arithmetic assignment operators do not contain a space; in other words, the addition assignment operator is +=, not + =. Figure 3-13 also includes examples of using arithmetic assignment operators to abbreviate assignment statements.

142

HOW TO Use the Arithmetic Assignment Operators

Syntax
variableName arithmeticAssignmentOperator value

Operator	Purpose
+=	addition assignment
-=	subtraction assignment
*=	multiplication assignment
/=	division assignment

Example 1
Original assignment statement: age = age + 1
Abbreviated statement: age += 1
Both statements add 1 to the number stored in the Integer `age` variable and then assign the result to the variable.

Example 2
Original assignment statement: `price = price - discount`
Abbreviated statement: `price -= discount`
Both statements subtract the number stored in the Decimal `discount` variable from the number stored in the Decimal `price` variable and then assign the result to the `price` variable.

Example 3
Original assignment statement: `sales = sales * 1.05`
Abbreviated statement: `sales *= 1.05`
Both statements multiply the number stored in the Double `sales` variable by 1.05 and then assign the result to the variable.

Example 4
Original assignment statement: `payment = payment / 2`
Abbreviated statement: `payment /= 2`
Both statements divide the number stored in the Double `payment` variable by 2 and then assign the result to the variable.

Note: To abbreviate an assignment statement, remove the variable name that appears on the left side of the assignment operator (=), and then put the assignment operator immediately after the arithmetic operator.

Figure 3-13   How to use the arithmetic assignment operators
© 2013 Cengage Learning

The answers to Mini-Quiz questions are located in Appendix A. Each question is associated with one or more objectives listed at the beginning of the chapter.

Mini-Quiz 3-3

1. The expression 7 + 4 / 2 * 4.5 evaluates to which of the following? (4)

    a.   1.222222

    b.   7.444444

    c.   16

    d.   24.75

2. The expression 131 \ 4 evaluates to which of the following? (4)

   a. 3

   b. 32

   c. 32.75

   d. 33

3. The statement `counter = counter + 1` is equivalent to which of the following statements? (4)

   a. `counter += 1`

   b. `counter =+ 1`

   c. `1 += counter`

   d. both a and c

Scope and Lifetime

Besides a name, a data type, and an initial value, every variable also has a scope and a lifetime. A variable's **scope** indicates where the variable can be used in an application's code, and its **lifetime** indicates how long the variable remains in the computer's internal memory. Variables can have class scope, procedure scope, or block scope. However, most of the variables used in an application will have procedure scope. This is because fewer unintentional errors occur in applications when the variables are declared using the minimum scope needed, which usually is procedure scope. (Variables can also have namespace scope and are referred to as public variables. Such variables can lead to unintentional errors in a program and should be avoided, if possible. For this reason, they are not covered in this book.)

A variable's scope and lifetime are determined by where you declare the variable—in other words, where you enter the variable's declaration statement. Typically, you enter the declaration statement either in a procedure (such as an event procedure) or in the Declarations section of a form. A form's Declarations section begins with the Public Class clause and ends with the End Class clause in the Code Editor window. Variables declared in a form's Declarations section have class scope. Variables declared in a procedure, on the other hand, have either procedure scope or block scope, depending on where in the procedure they are declared. In the next two sections, you will learn about procedure scope variables and class scope variables. Variables having block scope are covered in Chapter 4.

Variables with Procedure Scope

Variables declared in a procedure are called **procedure-level variables**. A procedure-level variable has **procedure scope** because it can be used only within the procedure in which it is declared. Procedure-level variables are typically declared at the beginning of a procedure, and they remain in the computer's internal memory only while the procedure is running. Procedure-level variables are removed from memory when the procedure in which they are declared ends. In other words, a procedure-level variable has the same lifetime as the procedure that declares it. (One exception to this rule is a static procedure-level variable, which you will learn about in the *Static Variables* section of this chapter.) As mentioned earlier, most of the variables in your applications will be procedure-level variables.

The Discount Calculator application that you view next illustrates the use of procedure-level variables. As the interface shown in Figure 3-14 indicates, the application allows the user to enter a sales amount. It then calculates and displays either a 15% discount or a 20% discount, depending on the button selected by the user.

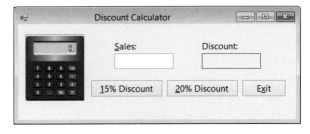

Figure 3-14 Discount Calculator application's interface
OpenClipArt.org/Cristian Pozzessere/ilnanny

If you want to experiment with the Discount Calculator application, open the solution contained in the Try It 2! folder. For now, ignore the Option statements in the Code Editor window.

Figure 3-15 shows the Click event procedures for the two discount buttons. The green lines of text in each procedure are called comments. Programmers use **comments** to document a procedure's purpose and also to explain various sections of a procedure's code. Including comments in your code will make the code more readable and easier to understand by anyone viewing it. You create a comment by typing an apostrophe (') before the text that represents the comment. The computer ignores everything that appears after the apostrophe on that line. Although it is not required, some programmers use a space to separate the apostrophe from the comment text, as shown in the figure.

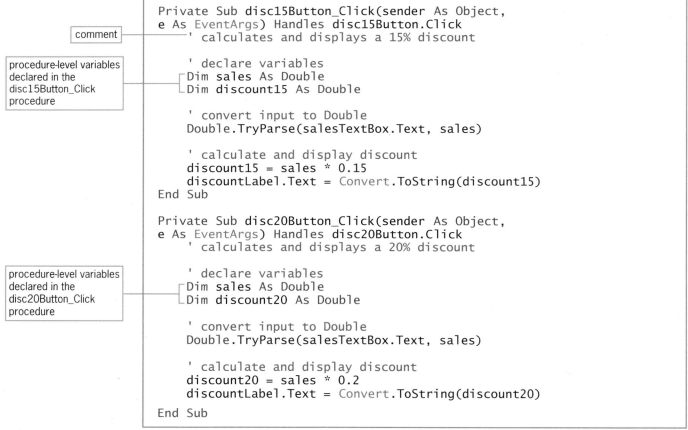

```
Private Sub disc15Button_Click(sender As Object,
e As EventArgs) Handles disc15Button.Click
    ' calculates and displays a 15% discount

    ' declare variables
    Dim sales As Double
    Dim discount15 As Double

    ' convert input to Double
    Double.TryParse(salesTextBox.Text, sales)

    ' calculate and display discount
    discount15 = sales * 0.15
    discountLabel.Text = Convert.ToString(discount15)
End Sub

Private Sub disc20Button_Click(sender As Object,
e As EventArgs) Handles disc20Button.Click
    ' calculates and displays a 20% discount

    ' declare variables
    Dim sales As Double
    Dim discount20 As Double

    ' convert input to Double
    Double.TryParse(salesTextBox.Text, sales)

    ' calculate and display discount
    discount20 = sales * 0.2
    discountLabel.Text = Convert.ToString(discount20)
End Sub
```

comment

procedure-level variables declared in the disc15Button_Click procedure

procedure-level variables declared in the disc20Button_Click procedure

Figure 3-15 Click event procedures using procedure-level variables
© 2013 Cengage Learning

When the user clicks the 15% Discount button, the Dim statements in the disc15Button_Click procedure create and initialize two procedure-level Double variables named `sales` and `discount15`; both variables can be used only within that procedure. Next, the TryParse method converts the sales amount entered in the salesTextBox to Double and then stores the result in the `sales` variable. The first assignment statement in the procedure multiplies the contents of the `sales` variable by the Double number .15 and then stores the result in the `discount15` variable. The Convert method in the second assignment statement converts the contents of the `discount15` variable to String. The assignment statement then assigns the result to the discountLabel's Text property. When the disc15Button_Click procedure ends, the computer removes the `sales` and `discount15` variables from memory. The variables will be created again the next time the user clicks the 15% Discount button. A similar process is followed when the user clicks the 20% Discount button, except the variable that stores the discount amount is named `discount20` rather than `discount15`, and the discount is calculated using a rate of .2 rather than .15.

Notice that both procedures in Figure 3-15 declare a variable named `sales`. When you use the same name to declare a variable in more than one procedure, each procedure creates its own variable when the procedure is invoked. Each procedure also destroys its own variable when the procedure ends. In other words, although both procedures declare a variable named `sales`, each `sales` variable will refer to a different section in the computer's internal memory, and each will be both created and destroyed independently from the other. This concept can be illustrated using the shoe box analogy from the beginning of the chapter. Just as both shoe boxes in Figure 3-16 have the same name (sneakers), both variables in the figure also have the same name (`sales`). However, like each shoe box, each variable has a different owner, different contents, and a different location.

Figure 3-16 Illustration of shoe boxes and variables
OpenClipArt.org/drunken_duck

Variables with Class Scope

In addition to declaring a variable in a procedure, you can declare a variable in the form's Declarations section, which begins with the Public Class clause and ends with the End Class clause. Variables declared in a form's Declarations section are called **class-level variables** and have **class scope**. Class-level variables can be used by all of the procedures in the form, including the procedures associated with the controls contained on the form. Class-level variables retain their values and remain in the computer's internal memory until the application ends. In other words, a class-level variable has the same lifetime as the application itself.

Unlike a procedure-level variable, which is declared using the `Dim` keyword, you declare a class-level variable using the `Private` keyword. You typically use a class-level variable when you need more than one procedure in the same form to use the same memory location. However, a class-level variable can also be used when only one procedure needs to retain a memory location's value after the procedure ends. The Total Calories application, which you view next, illustrates this use of a class-level variable. The application's interface, which is shown in Figure 3-17, provides a text box for the user to enter the number of calories consumed in a day. Each time the user clicks the Add to Total button, the button's Click event procedure will add the daily amount to the grand total and then display the grand total in the interface.

Figure 3-17   Total Calories application's interface
OpenClipArt.org/johnny_automatic

Figure 3-18 shows the application's code. The code uses a class-level variable named `totalCalories` to accumulate (add together) the daily calorie amounts entered by the user. Class-level variables are declared after the Public Class clause, but before the first Private Sub clause. For now, don't be concerned about the three Option statements that appear in the code. You will learn about the Option statements later in this chapter. However, notice the comments at the beginning of the Code Editor window. The comments document the project's name and purpose, the programmer's name, and the date the program was either created or revised.

you will learn about these statements later in this chapter

class-level variable declared in the form's Declarations section

procedure-level variable declared in the addButton_Click procedure

you can also use `totalCalories += dailyCalories`

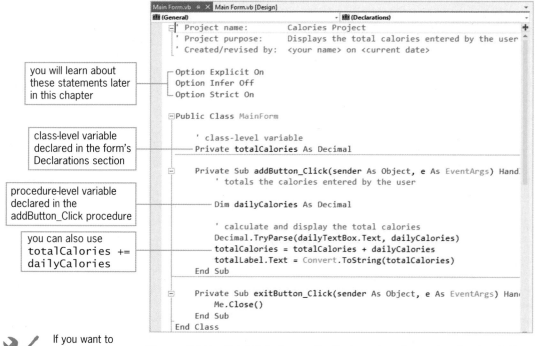

Figure 3-18   Total Calories application's code using a class-level variable

If you want to experiment with the Total Calories application, open the solution contained in the Try It 3! folder.

When the user starts the Total Calories application, the computer will process the `Private totalCalories As Decimal` statement first. The statement creates and initializes the class-level `totalCalories` variable. The variable is created and initialized only once, when the application starts. It remains in the computer's internal memory until the application ends.

Each time the user clicks the Add to Total button, the button's Click event procedure creates and initializes a procedure-level variable named dailyCalories. The TryParse method then converts the contents of the dailyTextBox to Decimal, storing the result in the dailyCalories variable. The first assignment statement in the procedure adds the contents of the procedure-level dailyCalories variable to the contents of the class-level totalCalories variable. At this point, the totalCalories variable contains the sum of the daily calorie amounts entered so far. The last assignment statement in the procedure converts the contents of the totalCalories variable to String and then assigns the result to the totalLabel. When the addButton_Click procedure ends, the computer removes the procedure-level dailyCalories variable from its memory. However, it does not remove the class-level totalCalories variable. The totalCalories variable is removed from the computer's memory only when the application ends.

Static Variables

Recall that you can declare a variable using the Dim, Private, or Static keywords. You already know how to use the Dim and Private keywords to declare procedure-level and class-level variables, respectively. In this section, you will learn how to use the Static keyword to declare a special type of procedure-level variable, called a static variable.

A **static variable** is a procedure-level variable that remains in memory, and also retains its value, even when the procedure in which it is declared ends. Like a class-level variable, a static variable is not removed from the computer's internal memory until the application ends. However, unlike a class-level variable, which can be used by all the procedures in a form, a static variable can be used only by the procedure in which it is declared. In other words, a static variable has a narrower (or more restrictive) scope than does a class-level variable. As mentioned earlier, you can prevent many unintentional errors from occurring in an application by declaring the variables using the minimum scope needed.

In the previous section, you viewed the interface and code for the Total Calories application, which uses a class-level variable to accumulate the daily calorie amounts entered by the user. Rather than using a class-level variable for that purpose, you can use a static variable, as shown in the code in Figure 3-19.

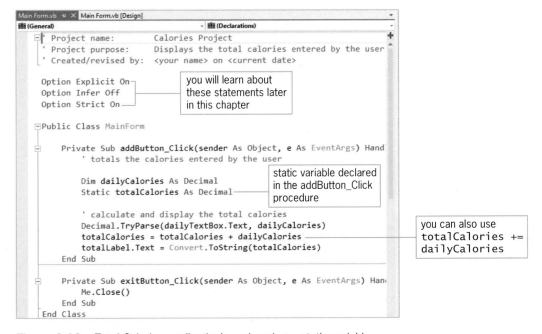

If you want to experiment with this version of the Total Calories application, open the solution contained in the Try It 4! folder.

Figure 3-19 Total Calories application's code using a static variable

The first time the user clicks the Add to Total button in the application's interface, the button's Click event procedure creates and initializes a procedure-level variable named `dailyCalories` and a static variable named `totalCalories`. The TryParse method then converts the contents of the dailyTextBox to Decimal, storing the result in the `dailyCalories` variable. The first assignment statement in the procedure adds the contents of the `dailyCalories` variable to the contents of the `totalCalories` variable. The last assignment statement in the procedure converts the contents of the `totalCalories` variable to String and assigns the result to the totalLabel. When the addButton_Click procedure ends, the computer removes the variable declared using the `Dim` keyword (`dailyCalories`) from its internal memory. But it does not remove the variable declared using the `Static` keyword (`totalCalories`).

Each subsequent time the user clicks the Add to Total button, the computer re-creates and re-initializes the `dailyCalories` variable declared in the button's Click event procedure. However, it does not re-create or re-initialize the `totalCalories` variable because that variable, as well as its current value, is still in the computer's memory. After re-creating and re-initializing the `dailyCalories` variable, the computer processes the remaining instructions contained in the button's Click event procedure. Here again, each time the procedure ends, the `dailyCalories` variable is removed from the computer's internal memory. The `totalCalories` variable is removed only when the application ends.

Ch03-
Scope and
Lifetime

Named Constants

In addition to using literal constants and variables in your code, you can use named constants. Like a variable, a **named constant** is a memory location inside the computer. However, unlike the value stored in a variable, the value stored in a named constant cannot be changed while the application is running.

You create a named constant using the **Const statement**. The statement's syntax is shown in Figure 3-20. In the syntax, *expression* is the value you want stored in the named constant when it is created in the computer's internal memory. The expression's value must have the same data type as the named constant. The expression can contain a literal constant, another named constant, or an arithmetic operator; however, it cannot contain a variable or a method.

HOW TO Declare a Named Constant

Syntax
[Private] Const *constantName* **As** *dataType* = *expression*

Example 1
`Const Pi As Double = 3.141593`
declares `Pi` as a Double named constant and initializes it to the Double number 3.141593

Example 2
`Const MaxHours As Integer = 40`
declares `MaxHours` as an Integer named constant and initializes it to the integer 40

Example 3
`Const Heading As String = "ABC Company"`
declares `Heading` as a String named constant and initializes it to the string "ABC Company"

Example 4

the D literal type character changes the number from Double to Decimal

`Private Const TaxRate As Decimal = .05D`
declares `TaxRate` as a Decimal named constant and initializes it to the Decimal number .05

Figure 3-20 How to declare a named constant
© 2013 Cengage Learning

To differentiate the name of a constant from the name of a variable, many programmers enter the names of constants using Pascal case (rather than camel case), as shown in the examples in Figure 3-20. When entered in a procedure, the Const statements shown in the first three examples create procedure-level named constants. To create a class-level named constant, you precede the Const keyword with the Private keyword, as shown in Example 4. In addition, you enter the Const statement in the form's Declarations section.

The D that follows the number .05 in Example 4 is one of the literal type characters in Visual Basic. A **literal type character** forces a literal constant to assume a data type other than the one its form indicates. In this case, the D forces the Double number .05 to assume the Decimal data type. The Convert.ToDecimal method was not used for this purpose because, as mentioned earlier, the expression assigned to a named constant cannot contain a method.

Named constants make code more self-documenting and easier to modify because they allow a programmer to use meaningful words in place of values that are less clear. The named constant Pi, for example, is much more meaningful than the number 3.141593, which is the value of pi rounded to six decimal places. Once you create a named constant, you can use the constant's name, rather than its value, in the application's code. For example, instead of using the statement area = 3.141593 * radius * radius to calculate the area of a circle, you can use area = Pi * radius * radius.

Unlike the value stored in a variable, the value stored in a named constant cannot be inadvertently changed while the application is running. Using a named constant to represent a value has another advantage: If the value changes in the future, you will need to modify only the Const statement in the program, rather than all the program statements that use the value.

Mini-Quiz 3-4

The answers to Mini-Quiz questions are located in Appendix A. Each question is associated with one or more objectives listed at the beginning of the chapter.

1. Most of the variables used in an application will have _____ scope. (1, 5)

    a. block

    b. class

    c. general

    d. procedure

2. _____ variables are declared in the form's Declarations section using the Private keyword. (1, 5)

    a. Block-level

    b. Class-level

    c. General-level

    d. Procedure-level

3. Which of the following declares a procedure-level variable that retains its value until the application ends? (1, 5)

    a. `Dim Static score As Integer`

    b. `Private Static score As Integer`

    c. `Static score As Integer`

    d. `Static Dim score As Integer`

4. Which of the following declares and initializes a class-level named constant called Title? (1, 5)

    a. `Private Const Title As String = "Coach"`

    b. `Static Title As String = "Coach"`

    c. `Const Private Title As String = "Coach"`

    d. `Const Class Title As String = "Coach"`

Note: You have learned a lot so far in this chapter. You may want to take a break at this point before continuing.

Option Statements

In the following two sections, you will learn about the Option statements shown earlier in Figures 3-18 and 3-19. As you may remember, the figures contain the code for both versions of the Total Calories application. Although not shown in any figures, the Option statements are also included in the code for the Discount Calculator application, which you viewed earlier in the chapter. You will learn about the Option Explicit and Option Infer statements first.

Note: Rather than entering the Option statements in the Code Editor window, as shown in Figures 3-18 and 3-19, you can set the options using either the Project Designer window or the Options dialog box. However, it is strongly recommended that you enter the Option statements in the Code Editor window because doing so makes your code more self-documenting and ensures that the options are set appropriately. The steps for setting the options in the Project Designer window and Options dialog box are included in the Summary section at the end of this chapter. In Visual Basic 2012, the default setting for Option Explicit and Option Infer is On, whereas the default setting for Option Strict is Off.

Option Explicit and Option Infer

It is important to declare every variable used in your code. This means that every variable should appear in a declaration statement, such as a Dim, Private, or Static statement. The declaration statement is important because it allows you to control the variable's data type. Declaration statements also make your code more self-documenting. However, a word of caution is in order at this point: In Visual Basic you can create variables "on the fly." This means that if a statement in your code refers to an undeclared variable, Visual Basic will create the variable for you and assign the Object data type to it. Recall that the Object data type is not a very efficient data type, and its use should be limited.

Because it is so easy to forget to declare a variable—and so easy to misspell a variable's name while coding, thereby inadvertently creating an undeclared variable—Visual Basic provides a statement that tells the Code Editor to flag any undeclared variables in your code. The statement, `Option Explicit On`, must be entered in the Code Editor window's General Declarations section, which is located above the Public Class clause. When you also enter the `Option Infer Off` statement in the General Declarations section, the Code Editor ensures that every variable and named constant is declared with a data type. In other words, the `Option Infer Off` statement tells the computer not to infer (or assume) a memory location's data type based on the data assigned to the memory location.

Option Strict

As you learned earlier, the data type of the value assigned to a memory location should be the same as the data type of the memory location itself. If the value's data type does not match the memory location's data type, the computer uses a process called **implicit type conversion** to convert the value to fit the memory location. For example, when processing the statement `Dim sales As Double = 453`, the computer converts the integer 453 to the Double number 453.0 before storing the value in the `sales` variable. When a value is converted from one data type to another data type that can store either larger numbers or numbers with greater precision, the value is said to be **promoted**. In this case, if the `sales` variable is used subsequently in a calculation, the results of the calculation will not be adversely affected by the implicit promotion of the number 453 to the number 453.0.

On the other hand, if you inadvertently assign a Double number to a memory location that can store only integers, the computer converts the Double number to an integer before storing the value in the memory location. It does this by rounding the number to the nearest whole number and then truncating (dropping off) the decimal portion of the number. When processing the statement `Dim price As Integer = 75.4`, for example, the computer converts the Double number 75.4 to the integer 75 before storing the integer in the `price` variable. When a value is converted from one data type to another data type that can store only smaller numbers or numbers with less precision, the value is said to be **demoted**. If the `price` variable is used subsequently in a calculation, the implicit demotion of the number 75.4 to the number 75 will probably cause the calculated results to be incorrect.

With implicit type conversions, data loss can occur when a value is converted from one data type to a narrower data type, which is a data type with less precision or smaller capacity. You can eliminate the problems that occur as a result of implicit type conversions by entering the `Option Strict On` statement in the Code Editor window's General Declarations section. When the `Option Strict On` statement appears in an application's code, the computer uses the type conversion rules listed in Figure 3-21. The figure also includes examples of these rules.

HOW TO Use the Type Conversion Rules with Option Strict On

<u>Rules and examples</u>

1. Strings will not be implicitly converted to numbers. The Code Editor will display a warning message when a statement attempts to use a string where a number is expected.

```
            Dim hours As Double
Incorrect:  hours = hoursTextBox.Text
Correct:    Double.TryParse(hoursTextBox.Text, hours)
```

2. Numbers will not be implicitly converted to strings. The Code Editor will display a warning message when a statement attempts to use a number where a string is expected.

```
            Dim grossPay As Decimal = 235.67
Incorrect:  grossLabel.Text = grossPay
Correct:    grossLabel.Text = Convert.ToString(grossPay) [As you
            will learn later in this chapter, you can also use grossLabel.Text
            = grossPay.ToString.]
```

3. Wider data types will not be implicitly demoted to narrower data types. The Code Editor will display a warning message when a statement attempts to use a wider data type where a narrower data type is expected. (Recall that a number with a decimal place is assumed to be a Double number.)

```
Incorrect:  Const TaxRate As Decimal = .075
Correct:    Const TaxRate As Decimal = .075D
```

4. Narrower data types will be implicitly promoted to wider data types. In this case, the `hoursWkd` variable will be promoted to the Double data type before being multiplied by the `PayRate` named constant.

```
            Dim hoursWkd As Integer
            Const PayRate As Double = 45.15
            Dim pay As Double
Correct:    pay = hoursWkd * PayRate
```

Figure 3-21 How to use the type conversion rules with Option Strict On
© 2013 Cengage Learning

According to the first rule, the computer will not implicitly convert a string to a number. As a result, the Code Editor will issue the warning "Option Strict On disallows implicit conversions from 'String' to 'Double'" when your code contains the statement `hours = hoursTextBox.Text`. This is because the statement tells the computer to store a string in a Double variable. As you learned earlier, you should use the TryParse method to explicitly convert a string to the Double data type before assigning it to a Double variable. In this case, the appropriate statement to use is `Double.TryParse(hoursTextBox.Text, hours)`.

According to the second rule, the computer will not implicitly convert a number to a string. Therefore, the Code Editor will issue an appropriate warning message when your code contains the statement `grossLabel.Text = grossPay`; this is because the statement assigns a number to a string. Recall that you can use the Convert.ToString method to explicitly convert a number to the String data type. An appropriate statement to use here is `grossLabel.Text = Convert.ToString(grossPay)`.

The third rule states that wider data types will not be implicitly demoted to narrower data types. A data type is wider than another data type if it can store either larger numbers or numbers with greater precision. Because of this rule, a Double number will not be implicitly demoted to the Decimal or Integer data types. If your code contains the statement `Const TaxRate As Decimal = .075`, the Code Editor will issue an appropriate warning message because the statement assigns a Double number to a Decimal named constant. The correct statement to use in this case is `Const TaxRate As Decimal = .075D`.

According to the last rule listed in Figure 3-21, the computer will implicitly convert narrower data types to wider data types. For example, when processing the `pay = hoursWkd * PayRate` statement, the computer will implicitly promote the integer stored in the `hoursWkd` variable to Double before multiplying it by the contents of the `PayRate` named constant. The result, a Double number, will be assigned to the Double `pay` variable.

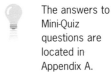

The answers to Mini-Quiz questions are located in Appendix A. Each question is associated with one or more objectives listed at the beginning of the chapter.

Mini-Quiz 3-5

1. When entered in the Code Editor window's General Declarations section, which of the following does not allow an undeclared variable in your code? (6)

   a. `Option Explicit On`

   b. `Option Infer On`

   c. `Option Undeclared Off`

   d. `Option Declared On`

2. If your code contains the `Option Strict On` statement, which of the following is the correct way to assign the contents of the salesTextBox to a Double variable named `sales`? (2, 3, 6)

   a. `sales = salesTextBox.Text`

   b. `sales = Double.TryParse(salesTextBox.Text)`

   c. `Double.TryParse(salesTextBox.Text, sales)`

   d. `Double.TryParse(sales, salesTextBox.Text)`

3. The `sales` and `commission` variables in the following assignment statement have the Double data type, whereas the `commRate` variable has the Decimal data type: `commission = sales * commRate`. If your code contains the `Option Strict On` statement, how will the computer process the assignment statement? (2, 4, 6)

Circle Area Application

In this section, you will use what you learned about variables, constants, calculations, and the Option statements to code the Circle Area application, which calculates and displays the area of a circle. You will also learn how programmers plan a procedure's code. The application's interface and TOE chart are shown in Figures 3-22 and 3-23, respectively.

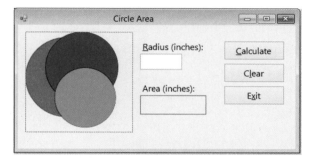

Figure 3-22   Circle Area application's interface

Task	Object	Event
1. Calculate the area 2. Display the area in areaLabel	calcButton	Click
End the application	exitButton	Click
Prepare screen for the next calculation	clearButton	Click
Display the area (from calcButton)	areaLabel	None
Get and display the radius	radiusTextBox	None

Figure 3-23   Circle Area application's TOE chart
© 2013 Cengage Learning

After planning an application and building its interface, you then can begin coding the application. You code an application so that the objects in the interface perform their assigned tasks when the appropriate event occurs. The objects and events that need to be coded, as well as the tasks assigned to each object and event, are listed in the application's TOE chart. The TOE chart in Figure 3-23 indicates that only the three buttons require coding, as they are the only objects with an event listed in the Event column.

You should always plan a procedure before you begin coding it. Many programmers use planning tools such as pseudocode or flowcharts. You do not need to create both a flowchart and pseudocode for a procedure; you need to use only one of these planning tools. The tool you use is really a matter of personal preference. For simple procedures, pseudocode works just fine. When a procedure becomes more complex, however, the procedure's steps may be easier to understand in a flowchart. The programmer uses either the procedure's pseudocode or its flowchart as a guide when coding the procedure.

Using Pseudocode to Plan a Procedure

Pseudocode uses short phrases to describe the steps a procedure must take to accomplish its goal. Even though the word "pseudocode" might be unfamiliar to you, you have already written pseudocode without even realizing it. Consider the last time you gave directions to someone. You wrote each direction down on paper, in your own words; your directions were a form of pseudocode.

Figure 3-24 shows the pseudocode for the procedures that need to be coded in the Circle Area application. The exitButton's Click event procedure will simply end the application. The calcButton's Click event procedure will calculate the circle's area and then display the result in the areaLabel. The clearButton's Click event procedure will prepare the screen for the next calculation. It will do this by removing the current radius and area from the appropriate controls in the interface. It then will send the focus to the radiusTextBox so the user can begin entering the radius for the next calculation.

exitButton Click event procedure
end the application

calcButton Click event procedure
1. assign user input (radius) to a variable
2. area = pi * radius * radius, where pi is 3.141593
3. display area in areaLabel

clearButton Click event procedure
1. clear the Text property of the radiusTextBox
2. clear the Text property of the areaLabel
3. send the focus to the radiusTextBox

Figure 3-24   Pseudocode for the Circle Area application
© 2013 Cengage Learning

Using a Flowchart to Plan a Procedure

Unlike pseudocode, which consists of short phrases, a **flowchart** uses standardized symbols to show the steps a procedure must follow to reach its goal. Figure 3-25 shows the flowcharts for the procedures that need to be coded in the Circle Area application. The logic illustrated in the flowcharts is the same as the logic shown in the pseudocode in Figure 3-24.

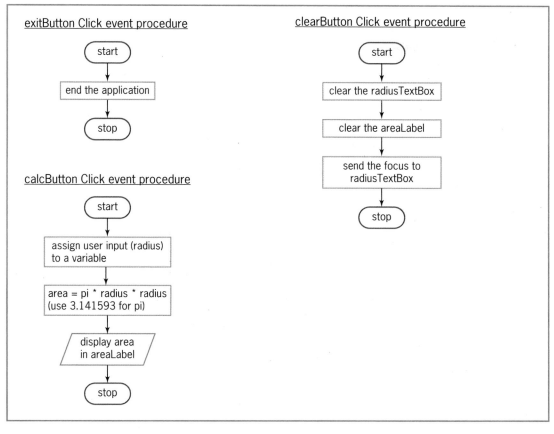

Figure 3-25 Flowcharts for the Circle Area application
© 2013 Cengage Learning

The flowcharts in Figure 3-25 contain three different symbols: an oval, a rectangle, and a parallelogram. The oval symbol is called the **start/stop symbol**. The start and stop ovals indicate the beginning and end, respectively, of the flowchart. The rectangles are called **process symbols**. You use the process symbol to represent tasks such as making assignments and calculations. The parallelogram in a flowchart is called the **input/output symbol** and is used to represent input tasks (such as getting information from the user) and output tasks (such as displaying information). The parallelogram in Figure 3-25 represents an output task. The lines connecting the symbols in a flowchart are called **flowlines**.

Coding the calcButton's Click Event Procedure

The programmer uses either the procedure's pseudocode or its flowchart as a guide when coding the procedure; in this chapter, you will use the pseudocode. We'll begin by coding the calcButton's Click event procedure, whose pseudocode appears in Figure 3-26.

calcButton Click event procedure
1. assign user input (radius) to a variable
2. area = pi * radius * radius, where pi is 3.141593
3. display area in areaLabel

Figure 3-26 Pseudocode for the calcButton_Click procedure
© 2013 Cengage Learning

Before you begin coding a procedure, you first study its pseudocode (or flowchart) to determine the variables and named constants (if any) the procedure will require. When determining the named constants, look for items whose value should be the same each time the procedure is invoked. In the calcButton's Click event procedure, the value of pi will always be 3.141593; therefore, you will assign the value to a Double named constant.

When determining a procedure's variables, look in the pseudocode (or flowchart) for items whose value is allowed to change during run time. In the calcButton's Click event procedure, the radius provided by the user will likely be different each time the procedure is processed. As a result, the area's value will also vary because it is based on the radius. Therefore, you will assign the radius and area values to variables. Assuming the radius's value can contain a decimal place, you will use Double variables to store both values. Figure 3-27 lists the memory locations that the procedure will use.

Named constant	Data type	Value
Pi	Double	3.141593

Variables	Data type	Value source
radius	Double	user input (radiusTextBox)
area	Double	procedure calculation

Figure 3-27   Memory locations for the calcButton_Click procedure
© 2013 Cengage Learning

Figure 3-28 shows the declaration statements entered in the procedure. The green jagged lines indicate that, at this point, the named constant and variables do not appear in any other statement in the code.

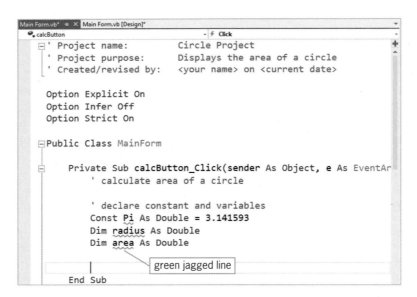

Figure 3-28   Declaration statements entered in the procedure

Next, you code each of the steps in the pseudocode (or each symbol in the flowchart), one at a time. However, keep in mind that some steps (symbols) may require more than one line of code. The first step in the pseudocode shown earlier in Figure 3-26 assigns the user input—in this case, the radius entered in the radiusTextBox—to a variable. You can code the first step using the TryParse method shown in Figure 3-29. The method converts the text box's Text property to the Double data type and then stores the result in the **radius** variable.

```
' assign user input to a variable
Double.TryParse(radiusTextBox.Text, radius)

|
End Sub
```

Figure 3-29 Radius stored in a variable

The second step in the pseudocode calculates the area. You can perform this task using the statement area = Pi * radius * radius. The last step in the pseudocode displays the area in the areaLabel. You accomplish this task using an assignment statement along with the Convert.ToString method. Figure 3-30 shows the code entered in the calcButton_Click procedure, and Figure 3-31 shows a sample run of the application. Notice that the output contained in the Area box contains six decimal places. In the next section, you will learn how to specify the number of decimal places to display in a number.

```
Private Sub calcButton_Click(sender As Object, e As EventAr
    ' calculate area of a circle

    ' declare constant and variables
    Const Pi As Double = 3.141593
    Dim radius As Double
    Dim area As Double

    ' assign user input to a variable
    Double.TryParse(radiusTextBox.Text, radius)

    ' calculate and display area                you can also use
    area = Pi * radius * radius                  area = Pi *
    areaLabel.Text = Convert.ToString(area)      radius ^ 2
End Sub
```

Figure 3-30 calcButton_Click procedure

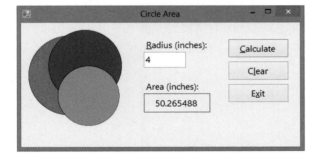

Figure 3-31 Sample run of the application

Formatting Numeric Output

Many times, you will want an application's numeric output to contain a specific number of decimal places and an optional special character (such as a dollar sign). Specifying the number of decimal places and the special characters to display in a number is called **formatting**. You can format a number in Visual Basic using the ToString method.

Figure 3-32 shows the ToString method's syntax and includes examples of using the method. In the syntax, *numericVariableName* is the name of a numeric variable. The **ToString method** places a copy of the variable's contents in a temporary memory location, where it converts the copy to a string. The method formats the string using the information in its *formatString* argument and then returns the result as a string. The *formatString* argument must take the form "*Axx*", where *A* is an alphabetic character called the format specifier, and *xx* is a sequence of digits called the precision specifier. The format specifier must be one of the built-in format characters. The most commonly used format characters are listed in the figure; these characters can be entered in either uppercase or lowercase. When used with one of the format characters listed in the figure, the precision specifier determines the number of digits that will appear after the decimal point in the formatted number. You can also use the ToString method without its *formatString* argument, as shown in Example 4 in the figure. The statement in Example 4 is equivalent to the statement `maxLabel.Text = Convert.ToString(MaxScore)`.

HOW TO Format a Number Using the ToString Method

Syntax
numericVariableName.**ToString**[(*formatString*)]

Format specifier (Name)	Description
C or c (Currency)	displays the string with a dollar sign; includes a thousands separator (if appropriate); negative values are enclosed in parentheses
N or n (Number)	similar to the Currency format, but does not include a dollar sign and negative values are preceded by a minus sign
F or f (Fixed-point)	same as the Number format, but does not include a thousands separator
P or p (Percent)	multiplies the value by 100 and displays the result with a percent sign; negative values are preceded by a minus sign

Example 1
```
Dim commission As Integer = 1250
commissionLabel.Text = commission.ToString("C2")
```
assigns the string "$1,250.00" to the commissionLabel's Text property

Example 2
```
Dim total As Decimal = 123.675
totalLabel.Text = total.ToString("N2")
```
assigns the string "123.68" to the totalLabel's Text property

Example 3
```
Dim rate As Double = .06
rateLabel.Text = rate.ToString("P0")
```
assigns the string "6 %" to the rateLabel's Text property

Example 4
```
Const MaxScore As Integer = 100
maxLabel.Text = MaxScore.ToString
```
assigns the string "100" to the maxLabel's Text property

> the expression is equivalent to `Convert.ToString(MaxScore)`

Figure 3-32 How to format a number using the ToString method
© 2013 Cengage Learning

In the Circle Area application, you will have the calcButton_Click procedure display the area with two decimal places, rather than the six decimal places shown earlier in Figure 3-31, and a thousands separator (if necessary). You can accomplish this by changing the

Convert.ToString(area) expression in the last assignment statement to area.ToString("N2").
Figure 3-33 shows the modified procedure, and Figure 3-34 shows the formatted output in
the interface.

```
Private Sub calcButton_Click(sender As Object, e As EventAr
    ' calculate area of a circle

    ' declare constant and variables
    Const Pi As Double = 3.141593
    Dim radius As Double
    Dim area As Double

    ' assign user input to a variable
    Double.TryParse(radiusTextBox.Text, radius)

    ' calculate and display area
    area = Pi * radius * radius
    areaLabel.Text = area.ToString("N2")
End Sub
```

formats the area with two
decimal places and an optional
thousands separator

If you want to
experiment
with the
Circle Area
application,
open the solution
contained in the Try It 5!
folder.

Figure 3-33   Modified calcButton_Click procedure

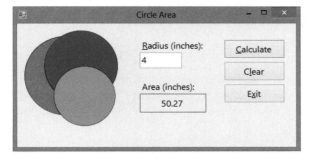

Figure 3-34   Formatted output shown in the interface

Coding the exitButton's Click Event Procedure

According to its pseudocode, the exitButton's Click event procedure should end the application.
You accomplish that task by entering the Me.Close() statement in the procedure, as shown in
Figure 3-35.

```
Private Sub exitButton_Click(sender As Object, e As EventAr
    Me.Close()
End Sub
```

Figure 3-35   Completed exitButton_Click procedure

Coding the clearButton's Click Event Procedure

The pseudocode for the clearButton's Click event procedure is shown in Figure 3-36. The
procedure does not perform any tasks that require user input or calculations, so it will not need
any named constants or variables.

> clearButton Click event procedure
> 1. clear the Text property of the radiusTextBox
> 2. clear the Text property of the areaLabel
> 3. send the focus to the radiusTextBox

Figure 3-36   Pseudocode for the clearButton_Click procedure
© 2013 Cengage Learning

The first two steps in the pseudocode clear the Text property of the radiusTextBox and areaLabel. Figure 3-37 shows two ways of clearing the Text property of a control. Example 1 assigns an empty (or zero-length) string to the property. Example 2 assigns the value **String.Empty** to the property. The value represents the empty string in Visual Basic.

HOW TO Clear the Text Property of a Control

Example 1
```
radiusTextBox.Text = ""
areaLabel.Text = ""
```

Example 2
```
radiusTextBox.Text = String.Empty
areaLabel.Text = String.Empty
```

Figure 3-37   How to clear the Text property of a control
© 2013 Cengage Learning

The last step in the pseudocode sends the focus to the radiusTextBox. You can accomplish this task using the **Focus method**. The method's syntax is shown in Figure 3-38 along with an example of using the method. In the syntax, *object* is the name of the object to which you want the focus sent.

HOW TO Send the Focus to a Control

Syntax
object.**Focus()**

Example
```
radiusTextBox.Focus()
```

Figure 3-38   How to send the focus to a control
© 2013 Cengage Learning

Figure 3-39 shows the code entered in the clearButton's Click event procedure.

```
Private Sub clearButton_Click(sender As Object, e As EventA
    ' prepare screen for next calculation

    radiusTextBox.Text = String.Empty
    areaLabel.Text = String.Empty
    radiusTextBox.Focus()
End Sub
```

Figure 3-39   Completed clearButton_Click procedure

Testing and Debugging the Application

After coding an application, you must test it to verify that the code works correctly. You begin by choosing a set of sample data for the input values. You then use the sample data to manually compute the expected output. Next, you start the application and enter your sample data. You then compare the actual output with the expected output; both should be the same. If they are not the same, it indicates that your code contains one or more errors. You will need to locate and then correct the errors before giving the application to the user.

Recall that errors in a program's code are called bugs, and the process of locating and correcting the bugs is referred to as debugging. As you learned in Chapter 1, the bugs in a program are typically categorized as syntax errors, logic errors, or run time errors. You learned about syntax errors in Chapter 1. In this chapter, you will learn about logic errors and run time errors.

Unlike syntax errors, logic errors are much more difficult to find because they do not trigger an error message from the Code Editor. The only way to determine whether your code contains a logic error is by comparing its output with your manually calculated results; if they are not the same, chances are the code contains a logic error. A **logic error** can occur for a variety of reasons, such as forgetting to enter an instruction or entering the instructions in the wrong order. Some logic errors occur as a result of calculation statements that are correct syntactically but incorrect mathematically. For example, consider the statement numSquared = num + num, which is supposed to square the number stored in the num variable. The statement's syntax is correct; however, the statement is incorrect mathematically because you square a value by multiplying it by itself, not by adding it to itself. For tips on finding and fixing logic errors, refer to the *Finding and Fixing Logic Errors* and *Setting Breakpoints* sections in Appendix E.

A **run time error** is an error that occurs while an application is running, and it causes the application to end abruptly. An expression that attempts to divide a value by the number 0, for example, will result in a run time error. This is because, as in math, division by zero is not allowed. You will learn how to prevent this run time error from occurring in Chapter 4. For now, if a run time error occurs in your applications, click DEBUG on the Visual Studio menu bar and then click Stop Debugging.

Your sample input data should include both valid and invalid data. **Valid data** is data that the application is expecting the user to enter. **Invalid data**, which is typically the result of a typing error made by the user, is data that the application is *not* expecting the user to enter. The Circle Area application, for example, expects to find a number in the Radius box; it does not expect the box to contain a letter or a special character. Therefore, you should test the application using one or more numbers, letters, and special characters. Doing this helps to ensure that the application displays the correct output when valid data is entered, and does not end abruptly when invalid data is entered.

Mini-Quiz 3-6

The answers to Mini-Quiz questions are located in Appendix A. Each question is associated with one or more objectives listed at the beginning of the chapter.

1. The rectangle in a flowchart is called the _____ symbol. (7)

    a. input

    b. output

    c. process

    d. start/stop

2. Which of the following can be used to clear the contents of the salesTextBox? (9)

    a. `salesTextBox.Text = ""`
    b. `salesTextBox.Text = String.Empty`
    c. `salesTextBox.Text = String.Clear`
    d. both a and b

3. Which of the following sends the focus to the clearButton? (10)

    a. `clearButton.Focus()`
    b. `clearButton.SendFocus()`
    c. `clearButton.SetFocus()`
    d. none of the above

4. If the `commission` variable contains the number 1325.5, which of the following assigns the string "1,325.50" to the commLabel? (8)

    a. `commLabel.Text = commission.Format("N2")`
    b. `commLabel.Text = commission.ToString("N2")`
    c. `commLabel.Text = commission.ToFormat("C2")`
    d. `commLabel.Text = commission.ToString("C2")`

You have completed the concepts section of Chapter 3. The Programming Tutorial section is next.

PROGRAMMING TUTORIAL 1

PROGRAMMING TUTORIAL 1

Creating the Color Mixer Application

The colors displayed on a computer screen are created using a mixture of three primary colors: red, green, and blue. The difference in each screen color is due to the amount (or intensity) of each primary color it contains. The intensity can range from 0 through 255, with 0 meaning an absence of the primary color. Figure 3-40 lists several colors along with their red, green, and blue values. The combination of a color's red, green, and blue values is called its RGB value. The color yellow's RGB value, for example, is 255, 255, 0. You can make the yellow lighter by adding some blue to its RGB value, like this: 255, 255, 100.

Color	Red value	Green value	Blue value
Black	0	0	0
White	255	255	255
Red	255	0	0
Green	0	255	0
Blue	0	0	255
Yellow	255	255	0
Light yellow	255	255	100
Light gray	192	192	192

Figure 3-40   Colors and their RGB values
© 2013 Cengage Learning

In this tutorial, you will create an application that allows the user to enter an RGB value. The value will determine the color of an oval shape in the interface. You can specify an object's color by assigning the RGB value to the object's BackColor property. You do this using the Color class's **FromArgb method**, whose syntax is `Color.FromArgb(redValue, greenValue, blueValue)`. Each of the method's three arguments must be an integer from 0 through 255.

The application's TOE chart and MainForm are shown in Figures 3-41 and 3-42, respectively. The MainForm contains three labels, three text boxes, two buttons, and an oval shape.

Task	Object	Event
Change the background color of the colorOvalShape to match the RGB values entered in the text boxes	viewButton	Click
End the application	exitButton	Click
Get and display the RGB values	redTextBox, greenTextBox, blueTextBox	None
Show the appropriate color	colorOvalShape	None

Figure 3-41 TOE chart for the Color Mixer application
© 2013 Cengage Learning

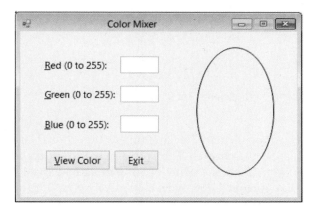

Figure 3-42 MainForm for the Color Mixer application

Completing the MainForm's Interface

Included in the data files for this book is a partially completed Color Mixer application. Before you begin coding the application, you will need to add an oval shape to the MainForm's interface.

To complete the MainForm's interface:

1. Start Visual Studio and open the Toolbox and Solution Explorer windows.

2. Open the **Color Mixer Solution (Color Mixer Solution.sln)** file contained in the VbReloaded2012\Chap03\Color Mixer Solution folder. If necessary, open the designer window. The partially completed MainForm appears on the screen.

3. Use the OvalShape tool, which is located in the Visual Basic PowerPacks section of the toolbox, to add an oval shape control to the form. Refer to Figure 3-42 for the appropriate size and location for the control.

4. If necessary, open the Properties window. Set the oval shape's Name and BackStyle properties to **colorOvalShape** and **Opaque**, respectively.

5. Lock the controls on the form. Auto-hide the Toolbox, Solution Explorer, and Properties windows, and then save the solution.

Including Comments and the Option Statements in the General Declarations Section

In the Code Editor window's General Declarations section, many programmers include comments that document the project's name and purpose, the programmer's name, and the date the program was either created or revised.

To include comments in the General Declarations section:

1. Open the Code Editor window. Insert a blank line above the Public Class clause.

2. Enter the comments shown in Figure 3-43 and then position the insertion point as shown in the figure. Be sure to replace <your name> and <current date> with your name and the current date, respectively.

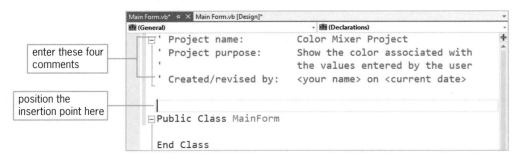

enter these four comments

position the insertion point here

Figure 3-43   Comments entered in the General Declarations section

The Color Mixer application will use variables, so the General Declarations section should also contain the three Option statements you learned in the chapter. The `Option Explicit On` and `Option Infer Off` statements tell the Code Editor to flag the name of an undeclared variable and warn you if a declaration statement does not contain a data type, respectively. The `Option Strict On` statement tells the computer not to perform any implicit type conversions that may lead to a loss of data.

To include the Option statements in the General Declarations section:

1. Enter the three Option statements shown in Figure 3-44 and then save the solution.

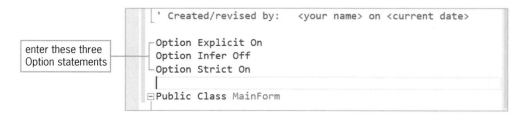

enter these three Option statements

Figure 3-44   Option statements entered in the General Declarations section

Coding the exitButton and viewButton Click Event Procedures

According to the application's TOE chart, the exitButton should end the application when it is clicked.

To code the exitButton_Click procedure:

1. Open the code template for the exitButton's Click event procedure. Type **Me.Close()** and press **Enter**.

The application's TOE chart indicates that the viewButton should change the background color of the colorOvalShape to match the RGB values entered in the text boxes. The pseudocode for the button's Click event procedure is shown in Figure 3-45.

viewButton Click event procedure
1. assign the user input (red, green, and blue values) to Integer variables
2. assign the values stored in the Integer variables to the colorOvalShape's BackColor property

Figure 3-45   Pseudocode for the viewButton_Click procedure
© 2013 Cengage Learning

Before you begin coding a procedure, you first study the procedure's pseudocode (or flowchart) to determine the variables and named constants (if any) the procedure will require. In this case, the viewButton_Click procedure will not need any named constants. However, it will need three Integer variables to store the RGB values entered in the text boxes. The variables are listed in Figure 3-46.

Variables	Data type	Value source
inputRed	Integer	user input (redTextBox)
inputGreen	Integer	user input (greenTextBox)
inputBlue	Integer	user input (blueTextBox)

Figure 3-46   Variables for the viewButton_Click procedure
© 2013 Cengage Learning

To code the viewButton_Click procedure:

1. Open the code template for the viewButton's Click event procedure. Type ' **change the oval's color** and press **Enter** twice.

2. Enter the comment and declaration statements shown in Figure 3-47, and then position the insertion point as shown in the figure.

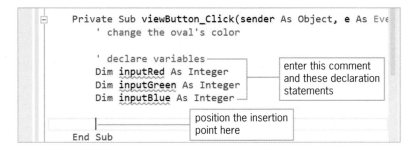

Figure 3-47   Comment and declaration statements entered in the procedure

3. First, the pseudocode assigns the contents of the three text boxes to the Integer variables. Enter the comment and three TryParse methods shown in Figure 3-48, and then position the insertion point as shown in the figure.

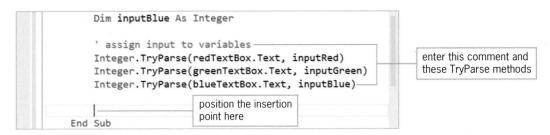

```
Dim inputBlue As Integer

' assign input to variables
Integer.TryParse(redTextBox.Text, inputRed)
Integer.TryParse(greenTextBox.Text, inputGreen)
Integer.TryParse(blueTextBox.Text, inputBlue)

|
End Sub
```

enter this comment and these TryParse methods

position the insertion point here

Figure 3-48   Comment and TryParse methods entered in the procedure

4. Next, the pseudocode assigns the values stored in the Integer variables to the colorOvalShape's BackColor property. Enter the comment and assignment statement shown in Figure 3-49.

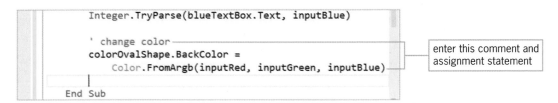

```
Integer.TryParse(blueTextBox.Text, inputBlue)

' change color
colorOvalShape.BackColor =
    Color.FromArgb(inputRed, inputGreen, inputBlue)
|
End Sub
```

enter this comment and assignment statement

Figure 3-49   Comment and assignment statement entered in the procedure

Testing and Debugging the Application

After coding an application, you must test it to verify that the code works correctly. You should use both valid and invalid test data.

To test the application:

1. Save the solution and then start the application. First, you will test the application using valid data. Type **255** in the Red box, **255** in the Green box, and **0** in the Blue box. Click the **View Color** button. The background color of the oval shape is now yellow. See Figure 3-50.

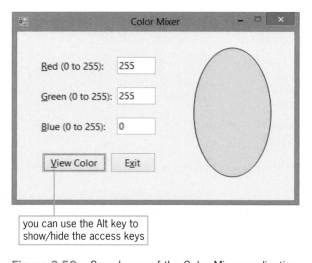

you can use the Alt key to show/hide the access keys

Figure 3-50   Sample run of the Color Mixer application

2. Change the contents of the Blue box from 0 to **100** and then click the **View Color** button. The background color of the oval shape turns to a light yellow.

3. Now, you will use invalid data. Change the contents of the Red box to **256** and then click the **View Color** button. A run time error occurs, which causes the application to end abruptly and display the error message "Value of '256' is not valid for 'red'. 'red' should be greater than or equal to 0 and less than or equal to 255." See Figure 3-51. Note: If you are using the Express Edition, the error message appears in a box along with a Break button. Click the Break button and then go to Step 4.

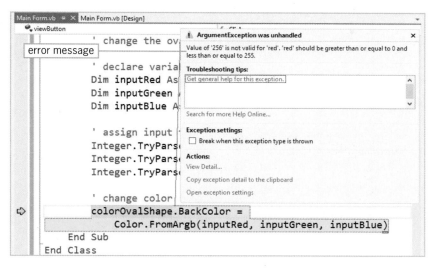

Figure 3-51   Result of entering 256 in the Red box

4. Click **DEBUG** on the menu bar and then click **Stop Debugging**. In Chapter 4, you will learn how to prevent the application from ending abruptly with an error when the user enters an invalid RGB value.

5. Start the application again. On your own, test the application using different RGB values. However, be sure to use numbers from 0 through 255 only.

6. Click the **Exit** button to end the application. Close the Code Editor window and then close the solution. Figure 3-52 shows the Color Mixer application's code.

```
1  ' Project name:          Color Mixer Project
2  ' Project purpose:       Show the color associated with
3  '                        the values entered by the user
4  ' Created/revised by:    <your name> on <current date>
5
6  Option Explicit On
7  Option Infer Off
8  Option Strict On
9
10 Public Class MainForm
11
12     Private Sub exitButton_Click(sender As Object,
       e As EventArgs) Handles exitButton.Click
13         Me.Close()
14
15     End Sub
16
17     Private Sub viewButton_Click(sender As Object,
       e As EventArgs) Handles viewButton.Click
18         ' change the oval's color
19
```

Figure 3-52   Color Mixer application's code *(continues)*

(continued)

```
20          ' declare variables
21          Dim inputRed As Integer
22          Dim inputGreen As Integer
23          Dim inputBlue As Integer
24
25          ' assign input to variables
26          Integer.TryParse(redTextBox.Text, inputRed)
27          Integer.TryParse(greenTextBox.Text, inputGreen)
28          Integer.TryParse(blueTextBox.Text, inputBlue)
29
30          ' change color
31          colorOvalShape.BackColor =
32              Color.FromArgb(inputRed, inputGreen, inputBlue)
33      End Sub
34 End Class
```

Figure 3-52   Color Mixer application's code
© 2013 Cengage Learning

PROGRAMMING TUTORIAL 2

Coding the Vans & More Depot Application

In this tutorial, you will create an application for Vans & More Depot, which rents vans for company outings. Each van can transport 10 people. The interface should allow the user to enter the number of people attending the outing. The application should calculate and display both the number of vans that can be filled completely and the number of people who will need to arrange for their own transportation. The application's TOE chart and MainForm are shown in Figures 3-53 and 3-54, respectively. The MainForm contains five labels, one text box, two buttons, and one picture box.

Task	Object	Event
Get and display the number of attendees	attendeesTextBox	None
1. Calculate the number of filled vans 2. Calculate the number of people remaining 3. Display the calculated results in the vansLabel and remainingLabel 4. Send the focus to the attendeesTextBox	calcButton	Click
End the application	exitButton	Click
Display the number of filled vans (from calcButton)	vansLabel	None
Display the number of people remaining (from calcButton)	remainingLabel	None

Figure 3-53   TOE chart for the Vans & More Depot application
© 2013 Cengage Learning

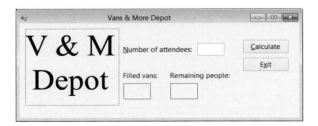

Figure 3-54   MainForm for the Vans & More Depot application

Opening the Vans & More Depot Solution

Included in the data files for this book is a partially completed Vans & More Depot application. To complete the application, you just need to code it.

To open the Vans & More Depot solution:

1. Start Visual Studio and open the Solution Explorer window.

2. Open the **Vans Solution** (**Vans Solution.sln**) file contained in the VbReloaded2012\ Chap03\Vans Solution folder. If necessary, open the designer window. The MainForm shown earlier in Figure 3-54 appears on the screen.

Entering Comments and the Option Statements in the General Declarations Section

In the Code Editor window's General Declarations section, you will enter comments that document the project's name and purpose, the programmer's name, and the date the program was either created or revised. The application will use variables, so you will also enter the three Option statements you learned in the chapter.

To enter the comments and Option statements:

1. Auto-hide the Solution Explorer window and then open the Code Editor window.

2. Enter the comments and Option statements shown in Figure 3-55, and then position the insertion point as shown in the figure. Be sure to replace <your name> and <current date> with your name and the current date, respectively.

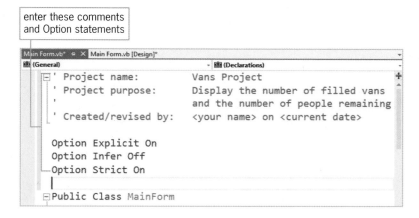

Figure 3-55   *General Declarations section*

Coding the exitButton and calcButton Click Event Procedures

According to the application's TOE chart, the exitButton should end the application when it is clicked.

To code the exitButton_Click procedure:

1. Open the code template for the exitButton's Click event procedure and then enter the appropriate instruction.

The application's TOE chart indicates that the calcButton's Click event procedure should calculate and display two values: the number of filled vans and the number of people remaining. The procedure's pseudocode is shown in Figure 3-56. The second step in the pseudocode calculates the number of filled vans by dividing the number of attendees by the maximum number of people that a van can transport (in this case, 10). The division operation is performed using the integer division operator (\) rather than the standard division operator (/) because you are interested only in the integer result of the division. For example, using the integer division operator, the quotient will be 4 when the number of attendees is 48; however, it would be 4.8 using the standard division operator. The third step in the pseudocode uses the Mod operator to calculate the number of people remaining. The Mod operator will return the remainder after dividing the number of attendees by the maximum number of people that a van can transport.

---

calcButton Click event procedure
1. assign the number of attendees to an Integer variable
2. number of filled vans = number of attendees \ maximum number of people that a van can transport
3. number of people remaining = number of attendees Mod maximum number of people that a van can transport
4. display number of filled vans and number of people remaining in vansLabel and remainingLabel
5. send the focus to the attendeesTextBox

Figure 3-56   Pseudocode for the calcButton_Click procedure
© 2013 Cengage Learning

Before you begin coding a procedure, you first study the procedure's pseudocode (or flowchart) to determine the variables and named constants (if any) the procedure will require. In this case, the calcButton_Click procedure will use one named constant to store the maximum number of people that a van can transport: 10. It will also use three Integer variables to store the number of attendees, the number of filled vans, and the number of people remaining. The named constant and variables are listed in Figure 3-57.

Named constant	Data type	Value
MaxInVan	Integer	10
Variables	**Data type**	**Value source**
attendees	Integer	user input (attendeesTextBox)
vans	Integer	procedure calculation
remaining	Integer	procedure calculation

Figure 3-57   Memory locations for the calcButton_Click procedure
© 2013 Cengage Learning

To code the calcButton_Click procedure:

1. Open the code template for the calcButton's Click event procedure. Enter the comments shown in Figure 3-58.

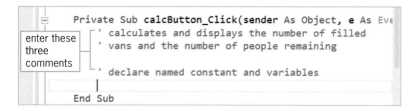

Figure 3-58   Comments entered in the calcButton_Click procedure

2. Now, enter the statements to declare the named constant and variables listed in Figure 3-57. Press **Enter** twice after typing the last declaration statement.

3. The first step in the procedure's pseudocode assigns the number of attendees to a variable. Type ' **store user input in a variable** and press **Enter**. Now, enter a TryParse method that converts the contents of the attendeesTextBox to Integer and then stores the result in the `attendees` variable. Press **Enter** twice after typing the TryParse method.

4. The second step in the pseudocode calculates the number of filled vans. Type ' **calculate number of filled vans** and press **Enter**. Now, enter the appropriate assignment statement.

5. The third step in the pseudocode calculates the number of people remaining. Type ' **calculate number remaining** and press **Enter**. Now, type the appropriate assignment statement and then press **Enter** twice.

6. The fourth step in the pseudocode displays the number of filled vans and the number of people remaining. Type ' **display output** and press **Enter**, and then enter the appropriate assignment statements. Press **Enter** twice after typing the last assignment statement.

7. The last step in the pseudocode is to send the focus to the attendeesTextBox. Enter the appropriate statement.

Testing and Debugging the Application

After coding an application, you must test it to verify that the code works correctly. You should use both valid and invalid test data.

To test the application:

1. Save the solution and then start the application. First, you will test the application using valid data. Type **48** in the Number of attendees box and then click the **Calculate** button. The interface indicates that 4 vans can be filled completely, and 8 people will need to arrange for their own transportation. See Figure 3-59.

Figure 3-59   Sample run of the application using valid data

2. Now, you will test the application using invalid data. Change the contents of the Number of attendees box to **4$a** and then click the **Calculate** button. The number 0 appears in the label controls, as shown in Figure 3-60.

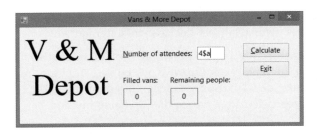

Figure 3-60 Sample run of the application using invalid data

3. Click the **Exit** button to end the application. Close the Code Editor window and then close the solution. Figure 3-61 shows the Vans & More Depot application's code. (Instead of using the ToString method in Lines 35 and 36, you can use the Convert.ToString method, like this: `Convert.ToString(vans)` and `Convert.ToString(remaining)`.)

```vb
 1 ' Project name:        Vans Project
 2 ' Project purpose:     Display the number of filled vans
 3 '                      and the number of people remaining
 4 ' Created/revised by:  <your name> on <current date>
 5
 6 Option Explicit On
 7 Option Infer Off
 8 Option Strict On
 9
10 Public Class MainForm
11
12     Private Sub exitButton_Click(sender As Object,
        e As EventArgs) Handles exitButton.Click
13         Me.Close()
14     End Sub
15
16     Private Sub calcButton_Click(sender As Object,
        e As EventArgs) Handles calcButton.Click
17         ' calculates and displays the number of filled
18         ' vans and the number of people remaining
19
20         ' declare named constant and variables
21         Const MaxInVan As Integer = 10
22         Dim attendees As Integer
23         Dim vans As Integer
24         Dim remaining As Integer
25
26         ' store user input in a variable
27         Integer.TryParse(attendeesTextBox.Text, attendees)
28
29         ' calculate number of filled vans
30         vans = attendees \ MaxInVan
31         ' calculate number remaining
32         remaining = attendees Mod MaxInVan
33
34         ' display output
35         vansLabel.Text = vans.ToString
36         remainingLabel.Text = remaining.ToString
37
38         attendeesTextBox.Focus()
39
40     End Sub
41 End Class
```

Figure 3-61 Vans & More Depot application's code
© 2013 Cengage Learning

PROGRAMMING EXAMPLE

Completing the Just Paper Application

In this Programming Example, you will finish coding the Just Paper application from Chapter 2's Programming Example. The application's TOE chart and user interface are shown in Figures 2-55 and 2-56, respectively, in Chapter 2. According to the TOE chart, the Click event procedures for the four buttons need to be coded. You coded the printButton_Click and exitButton_Click procedures in Chapter 2, so you just need to code the clearButton_Click and calcButton_Click procedures.

The pseudocode for the clearButton_Click and calcButton_Click procedures is shown in Figure 3-62. Figure 3-63 lists the named constant and variables used in the calcButton_Click procedure. (Just Paper charges $27.99 for a case of paper.) Open the Just Paper Solution (Just Paper Solution.sln) file contained in the VbReloaded2012\Chap03\Just Paper Solution folder. Open the designer window (if necessary) and then open the Code Editor window. In the General Declarations section, enter the comments and Option statements shown in Figure 3-64. Also enter the appropriate code in the Click event procedures for the clearButton and calcButton. Save the solution and then start and test the application. Figure 3-65 shows a sample run of the application.

---

clearButton Click event procedure
1. clear the Text property of the seven text boxes
2. clear the Text property of the totalCasesLabel and totalPriceLabel
3. send the focus to the nameTextBox

calcButton Click event procedure
1. assign the user input (number of standard cases and number of legal cases) to Integer variables
2. total cases = number of standard cases + number of legal cases
3. total price = total cases * price per case
4. display total cases and total price in totalCasesLabel and totalPriceLabel
5. send the focus to the printButton

Figure 3-62 Pseudocode
© 2013 Cengage Learning

Named constant	Data type	Value
PricePerCase	Double	27.99

Variables	Data type	Value source
standard	Integer	user input (standardTextBox)
legal	Integer	user input (legalTextBox)
totalCases	Integer	procedure calculation
totalPrice	Double	procedure calculation

Figure 3-63 Memory locations for the calcButton_Click procedure
© 2013 Cengage Learning

```
 1 ' Project name:        Just Paper Project
 2 ' Project purpose:     Display the total number of cases
 3 '                      ordered and the total price
 4 ' Created/revised by:  <your name> on <current date>
 5
 6 Option Explicit On
 7 Option Infer Off
 8 Option Strict On
 9
10 Public Class MainForm
11
12     Private Sub exitButton_Click(sender As Object,
       e As EventArgs) Handles exitButton.Click
13         Me.Close()
14
15     End Sub
16
17     Private Sub printButton_Click(sender As Object,
       e As EventArgs) Handles printButton.Click
18         PrintForm1.PrintAction = Printing.PrintAction.PrintToPreview
19         PrintForm1.Print()
20
21     End Sub
22
23     Private Sub clearButton_Click(sender As Object,
       e As EventArgs) Handles clearButton.Click
24         ' prepares the screen for the next order
25
26         nameTextBox.Text = String.Empty
27         addressTextBox.Text = String.Empty
28         cityTextBox.Text = String.Empty
29         stateTextBox.Text = String.Empty
30         zipTextBox.Text = String.Empty
31         standardTextBox.Text = String.Empty
32         legalTextBox.Text = String.Empty
33         totalCasesLabel.Text = String.Empty
34         totalPriceLabel.Text = String.Empty
35         nameTextBox.Focus()
36
37     End Sub
38
39     Private Sub calcButton_Click(sender As Object,
       e As EventArgs) Handles calcButton.Click
40         ' calculates the total cases and total price
41
42         ' declare constant and variables
43         Const PricePerCase As Double = 27.99
44         Dim standard As Integer
45         Dim legal As Integer
46         Dim totalCases As Integer
47         Dim totalPrice As Double
48
49         ' assign input to variables
50         Integer.TryParse(standardTextBox.Text, standard)
51         Integer.TryParse(legalTextBox.Text, legal)
52
53         ' perform calculations
54         totalCases = standard + legal
55         totalPrice = totalCases * PricePerCase
```

Figure 3-64   Just Paper application's code (continues)

(continued)

```
56
57            ' display calculated results
58            totalCasesLabel.Text = Convert.ToString(totalCases)
59            totalPriceLabel.Text = totalPrice.ToString("C2")
60
61            printButton.Focus()
62
63        End Sub
64 End Class
```

Figure 3-64 Just Paper application's code
© 2013 Cengage Learning

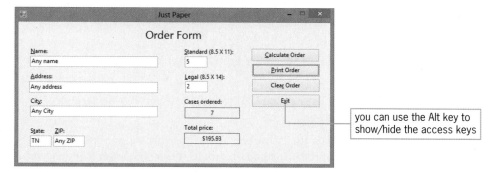

Figure 3-65 Sample run of the Just Paper application

Summary

- Each memory location in the computer's internal memory can store only one item at a time.

- Variables and named constants are computer memory locations that the programmer uses to store data while an application is running. During run time, the contents of a variable can change, whereas the contents of a named constant cannot change.

- All variables and named constants have a name, data type, initial value, scope, and lifetime.

- The name assigned to a memory location (variable or named constant) should describe the memory location's contents.

- A variable declared in a procedure has procedure scope, and its declaration statement begins with either the keyword Dim or the keyword Static. A variable declared in a form's Declarations section has class scope, and its declaration statement begins with the keyword Private.

- You can use an assignment statement to assign a value to an existing variable during run time. The data type of the value should be the same as the data type of the variable.

- Unlike variables and named constants, which are computer memory locations, a literal constant is an item of data. The value of a literal constant does not change during run time.

- String literal constants are enclosed in quotation marks ("").

- You can use the TryParse method to convert a string to a number.

- The Convert class contains methods that convert values to a specified data type.

175

- When an arithmetic expression contains the name of a memory location (variable or named constant), the computer uses the value stored inside the memory location to process the expression.

- You can use the arithmetic assignment operators to abbreviate some assignment statements.

- A procedure-level memory location can be used only by the procedure in which it is declared. Procedure-level variables declared with the Dim keyword are removed from memory when the procedure ends. Procedure-level variables declared with the Static keyword remain in memory, and also retain their value, until the application ends.

- A class-level memory location can be used by all the procedures in the form, including the procedures associated with the controls contained on the form. Class-level variables are removed from memory when the application ends.

- Programmers use comments to internally document an application's code. Comments begin with an apostrophe.

- You use the Const statement to declare a named constant.

- The Option Explicit On statement tells the Code Editor to flag the name of an undeclared variable in the code.

- The Option Infer Off statement tells the Code Editor to warn you if a declaration statement does not contain a data type.

- The Option Strict On statement tells the computer not to perform any implicit type conversions that may lead to a loss of data. Instead, it should follow the rules listed earlier in Figure 3-21.

- Programmers commonly use either pseudocode (short phrases) or a flowchart (standardized symbols) when planning a procedure's code.

- You can use the ToString method to format an application's numeric output so that it displays special characters (such as dollar signs and commas) and a specified number of decimal places.

- While an application is running, you can remove the contents of a text box or label by assigning either the empty string ("") or the String.Empty value to the control's Text property.

- You can use the Focus method to move the focus to a control during run time.

- After coding an application, you should test it to verify that the code is working correctly. Your sample data should include both valid and invalid values.

- Programs can contain syntax errors, logic errors, or run time errors.

- To set the Option statements for the current project only, open the Project Designer window, click the Compile tab, set the options, and then close the Project Designer window.

- To set the Option statements for all of your projects, click TOOLS on the Visual Studio menu bar, click Options, expand the Project and Solutions node, click VB Defaults, set the options, and then click the OK button.

Key Terms

Arithmetic assignment operators—composed of an arithmetic operator followed by the assignment operator; used to abbreviate an assignment statement that has the following format, in which *variableName* is the name of the same variable: *variableName = variableName arithmeticOperator value*

Class scope—the scope of a class-level variable; refers to the fact that the variable can be used by any procedure in the form

Class-level variables—variables declared in the form's Declarations section; the variables have class scope

Comments—used to document a program internally; created by placing an apostrophe (') before the text you want to treat as a comment

Const statement—used to create a named constant

Convert class—contains methods that convert a value to a specified data type and then return the result

Data type—indicates the type of data a memory location (variable or named constant) can store

Demoted—the process of converting a value from one data type to another data type that can store only smaller numbers or numbers with less precision

Empty string—a set of quotation marks with nothing between them (""); also called a zero-length string

Flowchart—a planning tool that uses standardized symbols to show the steps a procedure must take to accomplish its goal

Flowlines—the lines connecting the symbols in a flowchart

Focus method—used to move the focus to a control during run time

Formatting—specifying the number of decimal places and the special characters to display in numeric output

FromArgb method—a member of the Color class; used to assign RGB values; covered in Programming Tutorial 1

Implicit type conversion—the process by which a value is automatically converted to fit the memory location to which it is assigned

Input/output symbol—the parallelogram in a flowchart; used to represent input and output tasks

Integer division operator—represented by a backslash (\); divides two integers and then returns the quotient as an integer

Integers—positive or negative numbers without any decimal places

Invalid data—data that an application is not expecting the user to enter

Lifetime—indicates how long a variable or named constant remains in the computer's internal memory

Literal constant—an item of data whose value does not change during run time

Literal type character—a character (such as the letter D) appended to a literal constant for the purpose of forcing the literal constant to assume a different data type (such as Decimal)

Logic error—occurs when you neglect to enter an instruction, when you enter the instructions in the wrong order, or as a result of calculation statements that are correct syntactically but incorrect mathematically

Modulus operator—represented by the keyword Mod; divides two numbers and then returns the remainder of the division

Named constant—a computer memory location whose contents cannot be changed during run time; created using the Const statement

Procedure scope—the scope of a procedure-level variable; refers to the fact that the variable can be used only within the procedure in which it is declared

Procedure-level variables—variables declared in a procedure; the variables have procedure scope

Process symbols—the rectangle symbols in a flowchart; used to represent assignment and calculation tasks

Promoted—the process of converting a value from one data type to another data type that can store either larger numbers or numbers with greater precision

Pseudocode—a planning tool that uses phrases to describe the steps a procedure must take to accomplish its goal

Real numbers—numbers that contain a decimal place

Run time error—an error that occurs while an application is running

Scope—indicates where a memory location (variable or named constant) can be used in the application's code

Start/stop symbol—the oval symbol in a flowchart; used to indicate the beginning and end of the flowchart

Static variable—a procedure-level variable that remains in memory, and also retains its value, until the application (rather than the procedure) ends

String.Empty—the value that represents the empty string in Visual Basic

ToString method—formats a number stored in a numeric variable and then returns the result as a string

TryParse method—used to convert a string to a number

Valid data—data that an application is expecting the user to enter

Variable—a computer memory location where programmers can temporarily store data, as well as change the data, while an application is running

Zero-length string—a set of quotation marks with nothing between them (""); also called an empty string

Review Questions

Each Review Question is associated with one or more objectives listed at the beginning of the chapter.

1. Every variable and named constant has ——————. (1, 5)

    a. a data type   c. a scope
    b. a lifetime   d. all of the above

2. Which of the following statements stores the string contained in the `inputValue` variable in a Double variable named `number`? (2, 3)

    a. `Double.TryParse(number, inputValue)`
    b. `Double.TryParse(inputValue, number)`
    c. `number = Double.TryParse(inputValue)`
    d. `number = TryParse.Double(inputValue)`

3. What will be assigned to the Integer `answer` variable when the `answer = 45 Mod 6` statement is processed? (2, 4)

    a. 3   c. 7.5
    b. 7   d. none of the above

4. Static variables can be declared in ——————. (1, 5)

    a. the form's Declarations section   c. a procedure
    b. the General Declarations section   d. all of the above

5. Which of the following is a valid variable name? (1)

   a. `income.94`

   b. `inc_94`

   c. `income$Tax`

   d. all of the above

6. Which of the following displays the contents of the **bonus** variable with a dollar sign and two decimal places? (8)

   a. `bonusTextBox.Text = Convert.ToString(bonus, "C2")`

   b. `bonusTextBox.Text = ToString(bonus, "C2")`

   c. `bonusTextBox.Text = bonus.ToString("C2")`

   d. none of the above

7. If an application contains the `Option Strict On` statement, which of the following is the appropriate way to display the sum of the `score1` and `score2` variables in the answerTextBox? (2, 3, 4, 6)

   a. `answerTextBox.Text = Convert.ToString(score1) + Convert.ToString(score2)`

   b. `answerTextBox.Text = Convert.ToString(score1 + score2)`

   c. `answerTextBox.Text = score1 + score2`

   d. all of the above

8. If an application contains the `Option Strict On` statement, which of the following is the appropriate way to declare the `Rate` named constant? (1, 3, 6)

   a. `Const Rate As Decimal = .09`

   b. `Const Rate As Decimal = Convert.ToDecimal(.09)`

   c. `Const Rate As Decimal = .09D`

   d. both b and c

9. Which of the following statements adds the number 5 to the contents of the **order** variable? (2, 4)

   a. `order += 5`

   b. `order =+ 5`

   c. `5 += order`

   d. both a and c

10. Which of the following sends the focus to the numberTextBox? (10)

   a. `numberTextBox.Focus()`

   b. `numberTextBox.SendFocus()`

   c. `numberTextBox.SetFocus()`

   d. `SetFocus(numberTextBox)`

Exercises

Pencil and Paper

Each Exercise is associated with one or more objectives listed at the beginning of the chapter.

1. A procedure needs to store an employee's name and net pay amount, which may have a decimal place. Write the Dim statements to declare the necessary procedure-level variables. (1)

INTRODUCTORY

2. Write an assignment statement that multiplies the contents of the **sales** variable by the contents of the **BonusRate** constant and then assigns the result to the **bonus** variable. The three memory locations have the Decimal data type. (2, 4)

INTRODUCTORY

INTRODUCTORY

3. Write the statement to declare the procedure-level `TaxRate` constant whose data type and value are Double and .09, respectively. (1)

INTRODUCTORY

4. Write the statement to store the contents of the unitsTextBox in an Integer variable named `numberOfUnits`. (2, 3)

INTRODUCTORY

5. Write the statement to display the contents of an Integer variable named `total` in the totalLabel. Display the output with a dollar sign and no decimal places. (8)

INTERMEDIATE

6. Write the statement to declare the class-level `CommRate` constant whose data type and value are Decimal and .12, respectively. (1, 3)

INTERMEDIATE

7. Write the statement to declare a String variable that can be used by two procedures in the same form. Name the variable `employeeName`. Also specify where you will need to enter the statement and whether the variable is a procedure-level or class-level variable. (1, 5)

INTERMEDIATE

8. Write the statement to assign to the payLabel the value stored in a Decimal variable named `grossPay`. The value should be displayed with a dollar sign and two decimal places. (8)

INTERMEDIATE

9. Write two versions of an assignment statement that multiplies the contents of the `salary` variable by the number 1.5 and then assigns the result to the `salary` variable. The `salary` variable has the Decimal data type. Use the standard multiplication and assignment operators in one of the statements. Use the appropriate arithmetic assignment operator in the other statement. (2, 4)

ADVANCED

10. Write the statement to add together the contents of two Decimal variables named `westSales` and `eastSales` and then assign the sum to a String variable named `totalSales`. (2, 3, 4)

Computer

MODIFY THIS

11. If necessary, complete the Vans & More Depot application from this chapter's Programming Tutorial 2, and then close the solution. Use Windows to make a copy of the Vans Solution folder. Rename the copy Vans Solution-ModifyThis. Open the Vans Solution (Vans Solution.sln) file contained in the Vans Solution-ModifyThis folder. Open the designer and Code Editor windows. Locate the calcButton_Click procedure. Rewrite the statement that calculates the number of people remaining without using the Mod operator. Save the solution and then start and test the application. Close the solution. (4)

MODIFY THIS

12. Open the Static Solution (Static Solution.sln) file contained in the VbReloaded2012\ Chap03\Static Solution folder. Start the application. Click the Count button several times. The message indicates the number of times the Count button was clicked. Click the Exit button. Modify the application's code so that it uses a static variable rather than a class-level variable. Save the solution and then start and test the application. Close the solution. (1, 5)

MODIFY THIS

13. Open the Circle Solution (Circle Solution.sln) file contained in the VbReloaded2012\ Chap03\Circle Solution folder. Change the text in the form's title bar to Circle Math. Modify the application's interface so that it also displays the circle's circumference. Make the appropriate modifications to the code. Display the circumference with one decimal place. Save the solution and then start and test the application. Close the solution. (1-4, 8, 9)

14. If necessary, complete the Just Paper application from this chapter's Programming Example, and then close the solution. Use Windows to make a copy of the Just Paper Solution folder. Rename the copy Just Paper Solution-ModifyThis. Open the Just Paper Solution (Just Paper Solution.sln) file contained in the Just Paper Solution-Modify This folder. Just Paper has raised the price of a case of legal-size paper to $29.99. In addition, it now needs to charge customers a 4% sales tax and a $7 shipping charge. Modify the code accordingly. (Don't charge sales tax on the shipping.) Save the solution and then start and test the application. (If the customer orders two standard-size cases and three legal-size cases, the total price should be $158.79.) Close the solution. (1, 2, 4)

MODIFY THIS

15. Open the Shiloh Solution (Shiloh Solution.sln) file contained in the VbReloaded2012\ Chap03\Shiloh Solution folder. At the end of each year, each salesperson at Shiloh Products is paid a bonus of 10% of his or her annual sales. Code the application. Display the bonus with a dollar sign and two decimal places. Be sure to include comments and the Option statements. Save the solution and then start and test the application. Close the solution. (1-10)

INTRODUCTORY

16. Open the Time Solution (Time Solution.sln) file contained in the VbReloaded2012\ Chap03\Time Solution folder. Open the Code Editor window and enter the appropriate Option statements. The application should calculate and display the total number of weekday hours and the total number of weekend hours. Write the pseudocode for the Calculate Hours button and then code the application. Save the solution and then start and test the application. Close the solution. (1-7, 10)

INTRODUCTORY

17. Open the Happy Flooring Solution (Happy Flooring Solution.sln) file contained in the VbReloaded2012\Chap03\Happy Flooring Solution folder. The application should calculate and display the area of a floor in square yards. Code the application. Display the calculated result with one decimal place. Be sure to include comments and the Option statements. Save the solution and then start and test the application. Close the solution. (1-8)

INTRODUCTORY

18. Open the Property Tax Solution (Property Tax Solution.sln) file contained in the VbReloaded2012\Chap03\Property Tax Solution folder. Open the Code Editor window and enter the appropriate Option statements. The application should calculate the annual property tax. Currently, the property tax rate is $1.02 for each $100 of a property's assessed value. Write the pseudocode for the Calculate button and then code the application. Display the tax with a dollar sign and two decimal places. Save the solution and then start and test the application. Close the solution. (1-8, 10)

INTRODUCTORY

19. Colfax Industries needs an application that allows the shipping clerk to enter the quantity of an item in inventory and the quantity that can be packed in a box for shipping. When the shipping clerk clicks a button, the application should compute and display the number of full boxes that can be packed and the number of items left over. Prepare a TOE chart ordered by object. Create a Windows application. Use the following names for the solution and project, respectively: Colfax Solution and Colfax Project. Save the application in the VbReloaded2012\Chap03 folder. Change the form file's name to Main Form.vb. Build the interface. Write the pseudocode and then code the application. Be sure to include comments and the Option statements. Save the solution and then start and test the application. Colfax has 45 skateboards in inventory. If six skateboards can fit into a box for shipping, how many full boxes could the company ship, and how many skateboards will remain in inventory? Close the solution. (1-8, 10)

INTRODUCTORY

20. In this exercise, you create an application that calculates the amount to tip a waiter at a restaurant. The interface should allow the user to enter the amount of the bill. The application should calculate and display a 10% tip, 15% tip, and 20% tip. Prepare a TOE chart ordered by object. Create a Windows application. Use the following names for the solution and project, respectively: Tip Solution and Tip Project. Save the

INTRODUCTORY

application in the VbReloaded2012\Chap03 folder. Change the form file's name to Main Form.vb. Build the interface. Write the pseudocode and then code the application. Be sure to include comments and the Option statements. Save the solution and then start and test the application. Close the solution. (1-8, 10)

INTERMEDIATE

21. Open the Mason Solution (Mason Solution.sln) file contained in the VbReloaded2012\ Chap03\Mason Solution folder. The application should calculate the projected sales for each sales region. Code the application. Display the calculated results with two decimal places. Be sure to include comments and the Option statements. (1-8, 10)

a. Save the solution and then start the application. Test the application using the following valid data:

Region 1 sales and percentage: 150000, .15
Region 2 sales and percentage: 175500, .12
Region 3 sales and percentage: 100300, .11

b. Now, test the application without entering any data. Also test it using letters as the sales and percentage amounts.

c. Close the solution.

INTERMEDIATE

22. The River Bend Hotel needs an application that calculates a customer's total bill. Each customer pays a room charge that is based on a per-night rate of $55. For example, if the customer stays two nights, the room charge is $110. Customers also may be billed a room service charge and a telephone charge. In addition, each customer pays an entertainment tax, which is 10% of the room charge only. The application's interface should allow the hotel manager to enter the number of nights, the total charge for room service, and the total charge for using the telephone. It should display the room charge, the entertainment tax, and the total bill. The application should allow the manager to send a printout of the interface to the Print preview window. It should also allow the user to clear the screen for the next calculation. Prepare a TOE chart ordered by object. Create a Windows application. Use the following names for the solution and project, respectively: River Bend Solution and River Bend Project. Save the application in the VbReloaded2012\Chap03 folder. Change the form file's name to Main Form.vb. Build the interface. Draw the flowcharts and then code the application. Save the solution and then start and test the application. Close the solution. (1-10)

INTERMEDIATE

23. If necessary, create the Vans & More Depot application from this chapter's Programming Tutorial 2, and then close the solution. Use Windows to make a copy of the Vans Solution folder. Rename the folder Vans Solution-Intermediate. Open the Vans Solution (Vans Solution.sln) file contained in the Vans Solution-Intermediate folder. In addition to renting vans, Vans & More Depot also rents cars. Each van can transport 10 people, and each car can transport five people. The modified application should calculate and display three values: the number of filled vans, the number of filled cars, and the number of people remaining. Make the appropriate modifications to the interface and code. Save the solution and then start and test the application. Close the solution. (1-4)

ADVANCED

24. Create an application that allows your friend Miranda to enter the number of pennies she has in a jar. The application should calculate the number of dollars, quarters, dimes, nickels, and pennies she will receive when she cashes in the pennies at a bank. Use the following names for the solution and project, respectively: Pennies Solution and Pennies Project. Save the application in the VbReloaded2012\Chap03 folder. Change the form file's name to Main Form.vb. Be sure to include a button that will prepare the screen for the next calculation. Code the application. Save the solution and then start and test the application. Close the solution. (1-10)

25. In this exercise, you will finish coding the Crispies Bagels and Bites application from Chapter 2's Case Projects section. If you did not complete that Case Project, you will need to do so before you can complete this exercise. After completing the Case Project, copy the Crispies Solution folder from the VbReloaded2012\Chap02 folder to the VbReloaded2012\Chap03 folder, and then open the solution. The Calculate Price button should calculate the total price of the order. Bagels are $1.75, donuts are $1.05, and coffee is $2. Code the procedure. Save the solution and then start and test the application. Close the solution. (1-8)

ADVANCED

26. In this exercise, you will finish coding the Basket Haven application from Chapter 2's Case Projects section. If you did not complete that Case Project, you will need to do so before you can complete this exercise. After completing the Case Project, copy the Basket Haven Solution folder from the VbReloaded2012\Chap02 folder to the VbReloaded2012\Chap03 folder, and then open the solution. Code the Calculate Order and Clear Order buttons. Use your own prices for the different sizes of baskets. Save the solution and then start and test the application. Close the solution. (1-10)

ADVANCED

27. Open the Debug Solution (Debug Solution.sln) file contained in the VbReloaded2012\Chap03\Debug Solution folder. Start and then test the application. Locate and then correct any errors. When the application is working correctly, close the solution. (4, 11)

SWAT THE BUGS

Case Projects

Myran Music Hall

Create an application that allows the user to enter the number of concert tickets sold in each of three seating categories: Orchestra, Main floor, and Balcony. The application should calculate the amount of revenue generated by each category, the total revenue, and the percentage of the total revenue contributed by each category. Use the following names for the solution and project, respectively: Myran Solution and Myran Project. Save the application in the VbReloaded2012\Chap03 folder. Change the form file's name to Main Form.vb. You can either create your own interface or create the one shown in Figure 3-66. The image in the picture box is stored in the VbReloaded2012\Chap03\Notes.png file. Use your own prices for the tickets in each category; however, be sure each category has a different price. (1-8)

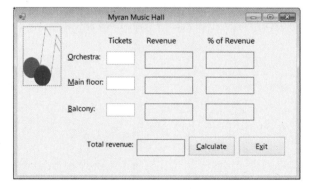

Figure 3-66   Sample interface for the Myran Music Hall application

Exercise Tracker

Carol Jones exercises at her local health club every day. Her favorite machines are the stair stepper, elliptical trainer, and stationary bicycle. The stair stepper burns 446 calories per hour, the elliptical trainer burns 670 calories per hour, and the stationary bicycle burns 520 calories per hour. Carol needs to burn 3,500 calories for every pound she wants to lose. She wants an application that allows her to enter the number of hours she spends on each machine. The application should calculate and display the number of pounds that she exercised off. Use the following names for the solution and project, respectively: Exercise Solution and Exercise Project. Save the application in the VbReloaded2012\Chap03 folder. Change the form file's name to Main Form.vb. You can either create your own interface or create the one shown in Figure 3-67. The image in the picture box is stored in the VbReloaded2012\Chap03\Exercise.png file. (1-8)

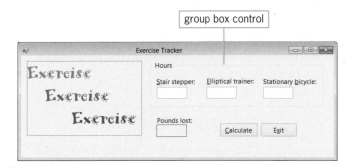

Figure 3-67 Sample interface for the Exercise Tracker application

 Credit Card Charges

Create an application that allows the user to enter the total monthly amount charged to his or her credit card for the following six categories of expenses: Merchandise, Restaurants, Gasoline, Travel/Entertainment, Services, and Supermarkets. The application should calculate and display each month's total charges, as well as the total annual amount the user charged. The application should also calculate and display the percentage that each category contributed to the total annual amount charged. Use the following names for the solution and project, respectively: Credit Solution and Credit Project. Save the application in the VbReloaded2012\ Chap03 folder. Change the form file's name to Main Form.vb. You can either create your own interface or create the one shown in Figure 3-68. (1-8)

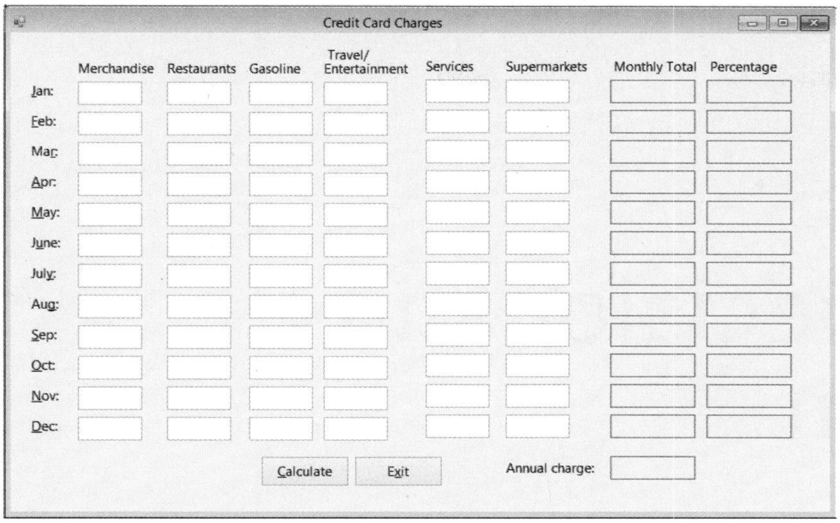

Figure 3-68   Sample interface for the Credit Card Charges application

Warren County

Warren County's Property Tax Administrator wants an application that calculates the amount of property tax owed based on a property's assessed value. Seven different tax rates are involved in the calculation. Each tax rate is per $100 of assessed value. The state rate is .124, the county rate is .096, and the school rate is .557. The remaining four rates are for special services as follows: ambulance is .1, health is .038, library is .093, and soil conservation is .02. The application's interface should allow the user to enter the assessed value. The application should calculate and display each of the seven taxes and the total tax. Use the following names for the solution and project, respectively: Warren Solution and Warren Project. Save the application in the VbReloaded2012\Chap03 folder. Change the form file's name to Main Form.vb. Code the application. Display the seven taxes with two decimal places, and display the total tax with a dollar sign and two decimal places. Now, save the solution and start the application. Test the application using an assessed value of $105,000. The total property tax should be $1,079.40. Now test the application using an assessed value of $121,920. Notice that when you total the seven taxes, the sum differs by a penny from the total property tax displayed in the interface. Why do the amounts differ? How can you fix the problem? (Hint: Research Visual Basic's Math.Round method.) (1-8)

CHAPTER 4

Making Decisions in a Program

After studying Chapter 4, you should be able to:

1 Include the selection structure in pseudocode and in a flowchart

2 Explain the difference between single-alternative and dual-alternative selection structures

3 Code a selection structure using the If...Then...Else statement

4 Include comparison and logical operators in a selection structure's condition

5 Prevent the division by zero run time error

6 Swap two values

7 Create a block-level variable

8 Concatenate strings

9 Use the ControlChars.NewLine constant

10 Change the case of a string

11 Include a check box in an interface

12 Generate random numbers

Before you begin reading Chapter 4, view the Ch04_ReadingStudyGuide.pdf file. You can open the file using Adobe Reader, which is available for free on the Adobe Web site at *www.adobe.com/downloads/*.

The Selection Structure

All of the procedures in an application are written using one or more of three basic control structures: sequence, selection, and repetition. The procedures in the previous chapters used the sequence structure only. When one of the procedures was invoked during run time, the computer processed its instructions sequentially—in other words, in the order the instructions appeared in the procedure. Every procedure you write will contain the sequence structure.

Many times, however, you will also need to use the selection structure in a procedure. The **selection structure** (also called the decision structure) indicates that a decision needs to be made before any further processing can occur. The decision is based on a **condition** that must be evaluated to determine the next instruction to process. The condition must evaluate to either True or False only. For example, a procedure that calculates an employee's gross pay would typically use a selection structure whose condition determines whether the employee worked more than 40 hours. If the condition evaluates to True, the computer would process the instruction that computes regular pay plus overtime pay. If the condition evaluates to False, on the other hand, the computer would process the instruction that computes regular pay only.

There are three types of selection structures: single-alternative, dual-alternative, and multiple-alternative. You will learn about single-alternative and dual-alternative selection structures in this chapter. Multiple-alternative selection structures are covered in Chapter 5.

Single-Alternative and Dual-Alternative Selection Structures

A **single-alternative selection structure** has a specific set of instructions to follow *only* when its condition evaluates to True. Example 1 in Figure 4-1 contains a single-alternative selection structure. A **dual-alternative selection structure**, on the other hand, has one set of instructions to follow when the condition evaluates to True, but a different set of instructions to follow when the condition evaluates to False. Examples 2 and 3 in Figure 4-1 contain a dual-alternative selection structure; both of these examples produce the same result.

Example 1 – single-alternative selection structure

1. drop a game token into the token slot
2. pull the yellow lever to shoot the rocket at the ghost
3. if the rocket hits the ghost
    - say "I got him!"
    - watch the ghost get destroyed   ← True path
    - take the game ticket from the ticket slot
    end if

Example 2 – dual-alternative selection structure

1. drop a game token into the token slot
2. pull the yellow lever to shoot the rocket at the ghost
3. if the rocket hits the ghost
    - say "I got him!"
    - watch the ghost get destroyed   ← True path
    - take the game ticket from the ticket slot
    else
    - say "I missed him!"   ← False path
    - watch the ghost turn into a red monster
    end if

Example 3 – another way to write the dual-alternative selection structure

1. drop a game token into the token slot
2. pull the yellow lever to shoot the rocket at the ghost
3. if the rocket misses the ghost
    - say "I missed him!"   ← True path
    - watch the ghost turn into a red monster
    else
    - say "I got him!"   ← False path
    - watch the ghost get destroyed
    - take the game ticket from the ticket slot
    end if

Figure 4-1   Single-alternative and dual-alternative selection structures

Image by Diane Zak; Created with Reallusion CrazyTalk Animator; OpenClipArt.org/lemmling; OpenClipArt.org/mystica; OpenClipArt.org/rg1024; OpenClipArt.org/rduris

As indicated in Figure 4-1, the instructions to follow when the condition evaluates to True are called the **True path**. The instructions to follow when the condition evaluates to False are called the **False path**. When writing pseudocode, most programmers use the words "if" and "end if" to denote the beginning and end, respectively, of a selection structure, and the word "else" to denote the beginning of the False path. They also indent the instructions within the selection structure, as shown in the figure.

The only way to determine whether a procedure requires a selection structure, and whether the structure should be single-alternative or dual-alternative, is by studying the problem specification. The first problem specification you will examine in this chapter is for Rosebud Roses, a small flower store that sells roses by the dozen. The problem specification is shown in Figure 4-2 along with an appropriate interface. The figure also includes the pseudocode for the Calculate button's Click event procedure. The procedure requires only the sequence structure. It does not need a selection structure because no decisions are necessary to calculate and display the total amount owed.

Problem specification
The store manager at Rosebud Roses wants an application that allows the store clerk to enter two items: the price for a dozen roses and the number of dozens ordered by the customer. The application should calculate and display the total amount the customer owes.

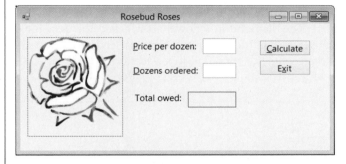

calcButton Click event procedure
1. store user input (price per dozen and dozens ordered) in variables
2. total owed = price per dozen * dozens ordered
3. display total owed in totalOwedLabel

Figure 4-2   Rosebud Roses application (sequence structure only)
OpenClipArt.org/Unomano/Viktar Palstsiuk

Now we'll make a slight change to the problem specification from Figure 4-2. Rosebud Roses now offers a 10% discount when the customer orders more than two dozen roses. Consider the changes you will need to make to the pseudocode shown in Figure 4-2. The first two steps in the original pseudocode store the user input in variables and then calculate the total owed by multiplying the price per dozen by the number of dozens ordered. The modified pseudocode will still need both of these steps.

Step 3 in the original pseudocode displays the total owed in the totalOwedLabel. Before the modified procedure can display the total owed, it must determine whether the customer ordered more than two dozen roses. It will make this determination using a selection structure whose condition compares the number ordered to the number 2. If the number ordered is greater than 2 (a True condition), the modified procedure should calculate the discount and then subtract the discount from the total owed.

The modified problem specification and pseudocode are shown in Figure 4-3. The pseudocode contains a single-alternative selection structure. In this case, a single-alternative selection structure is appropriate because the procedure needs to follow a special set of instructions *only* when the condition evaluates to True.

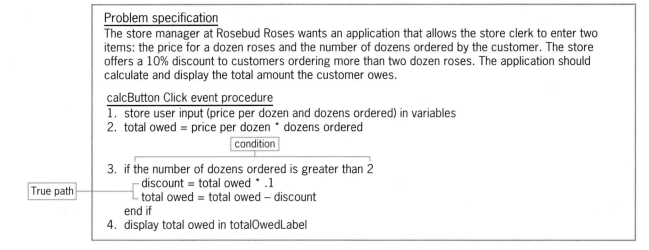

Figure 4-3   Modified Rosebud Roses application (single-alternative selection structure)
© 2013 Cengage Learning

Figure 4-4 shows the Calculate button's Click event procedure in flowchart form. Recall that the oval in a flowchart is the start/stop symbol, the rectangle is the process symbol, and the parallelogram is the input/output symbol. The diamond in a flowchart is called the **decision symbol** because it is used to represent the condition (decision) in both the selection and repetition structures. The diamond in Figure 4-4 represents the condition in a selection structure. (You will learn how to use the diamond to represent a repetition structure's condition in Chapter 6.)

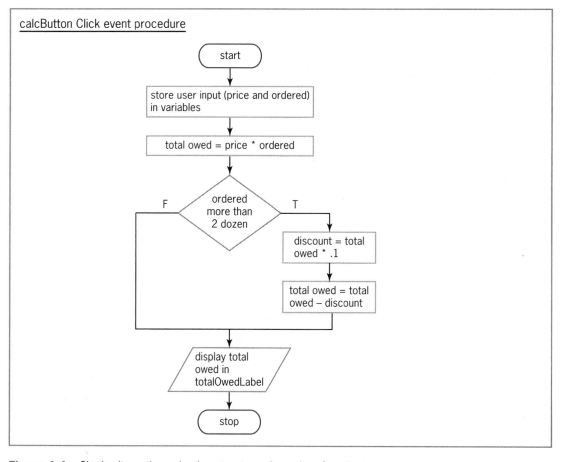

Figure 4-4   Single-alternative selection structure shown in a flowchart
© 2013 Cengage Learning

The condition in Figure 4-4's diamond checks whether the customer ordered more than two dozen roses. Notice that the condition results in an answer of either True or False only. Also notice that the diamond has one flowline entering it and two flowlines leaving it. One of the flowlines leading out of a diamond in a flowchart should be marked with a T (for True) and the other should be marked with an F (for False). The T flowline points to the next instruction to be processed when the condition evaluates to True. In Figure 4-4, the next instruction calculates the 10% discount. The F flowline points to the next instruction to be processed when the condition evaluates to False. In Figure 4-4, that instruction displays the total owed. You can tell that the selection structure in Figure 4-4 is a single-alternative selection structure because only its True path contains a special set of instructions.

Next, we'll modify the Rosebud Roses problem specification one more time. In addition to the 10% discount for ordering more than two dozen roses, Rosebud Roses is now offering a 5% discount when the customer orders either one or two dozen roses. The modified problem specification, pseudocode, and flowchart are shown in Figure 4-5. The pseudocode and flowchart contain a dual-alternative selection structure. In this case, a dual-alternative selection structure is appropriate because the procedure needs to follow one instruction when the condition evaluates to True, but a different instruction when the condition evaluates to False. You can tell that the selection structure in Figure 4-5 is a dual-alternative selection structure because both of its paths contain a special instruction.

You can also mark the flowlines with a Y and an N (for yes and no).

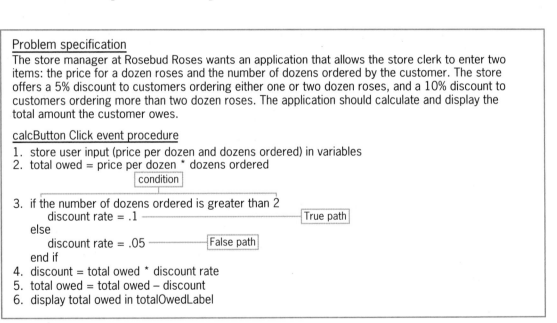

Figure 4-5   Modified Rosebud Roses application (dual-alternative selection structure) *(continues)*

(continued)

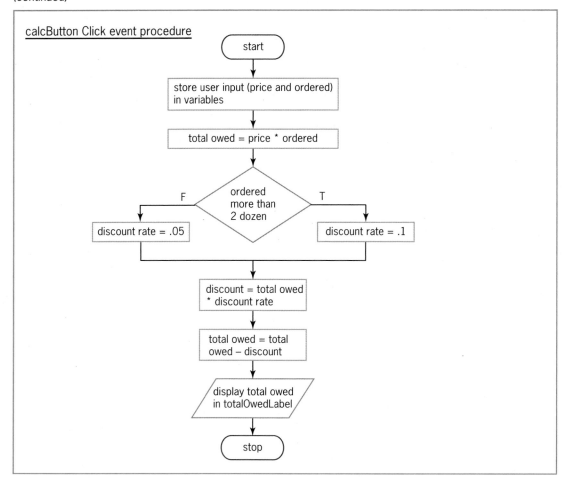

calcButton Click event procedure

Figure 4-5 Modified Rosebud Roses application (dual-alternative selection structure)
© 2013 Cengage Learning

Mini-Quiz 4-1

1. Every procedure in an application contains the selection structure. (1)

   a. True

   b. False

2. A dual-alternative selection structure contains instructions in _____. (2)

   a. its True path only

   b. its False path only

   c. both its True and False paths

3. In a flowchart, a hexagon is used to represent a selection structure's condition. (1)

   a. True

   b. False

4.   Which of the following is the decision symbol in a flowchart? (1)

   a.   diamond

   b.   oval

   c.   parallelogram

   d.   rectangle

Coding Single-Alternative and Dual-Alternative Selection Structures

Visual Basic provides the **If…Then…Else statement** for coding single-alternative and dual-alternative selection structures. The statement's syntax is shown in Figure 4-6. The square brackets in the syntax indicate that the Else portion, referred to as the Else clause, is optional. Boldfaced items in a statement's syntax are required. In this case, the keywords **If**, **Then**, and **End If** are required. The **Else** keyword is necessary only in a dual-alternative selection structure.

Italicized items in a statement's syntax indicate where the programmer must supply information. In the If…Then…Else statement, the programmer must supply the *condition* that the computer needs to evaluate before further processing can occur. The condition must be a Boolean expression, which is an expression that results in a Boolean value (either True or False). The programmer must also provide the statements to be processed in the True path and (optionally) in the False path. The set of statements contained in each path is referred to as a **statement block**. Also included in Figure 4-6 are two examples of using the If…Then…Else statement. Example 1 shows how you use the statement to code the single-alternative selection structure shown earlier in Figures 4-3 and 4-4. Example 2 shows how you use the statement to code the dual-alternative selection structure shown earlier in Figure 4-5.

HOW TO Use the If…Then…Else Statement

Syntax
If *condition* **Then**
    statement block to be processed when the condition evaluates to True
[Else
    statement block to be processed when the condition evaluates to False]
End If

Example 1
```
Dim pricePerDoz As Double
Dim ordered As Integer
Dim totalOwed As Double
Dim discount As Double
Double.TryParse(priceTextBox.Text, pricePerDoz)
Integer.TryParse(orderedTextBox.Text, ordered)

totalOwed = pricePerDoz * ordered
If ordered > 2 Then
    discount = totalOwed * .1
    totalOwed = totalOwed - discount
End If
totalOwedLabel.Text = totalOwed.ToString("C2")
```

single-alternative selection structure

If you want to experiment with the Rosebud Roses application, open the solution contained in the Try It 1! folder.

Figure 4-6   How to use the If…Then…Else statement *(continues)*

(continued)

```
Example 2
Dim pricePerDoz As Double
Dim ordered As Integer
Dim totalOwed As Double
Dim discount As Double
Dim discountRate As Double
Double.TryParse(priceTextBox.Text, pricePerDoz)
Integer.TryParse(orderedTextBox.Text, ordered)

totalOwed = pricePerDoz * ordered
If ordered > 2 Then
    discountRate = .1
Else
    discountRate = .05
End If
discount = totalOwed * discountRate
totalOwed = totalOwed - discount
totalOwedLabel.Text = totalOwed.ToString("C2")
```

dual-alternative selection structure

Figure 4-6   How to use the If...Then...Else statement
© 2013 Cengage Learning

An If...Then...Else statement's condition can contain items with which you are already familiar—namely, variables, constants, properties, methods, keywords, and arithmetic operators. The condition can also contain comparison operators and logical operators, which you will learn about in this chapter.

Comparison Operators

Figure 4-7 lists the most commonly used **comparison operators** (also referred to as relational operators) in Visual Basic. Each comparison operator can be used to compare two values, and the comparison always results in a Boolean value: either True or False. When comparing values, keep in mind that equal to (=) is the opposite of not equal to (<>), greater than (>) is the opposite of less than or equal to (<=), and less than (<) is the opposite of greater than or equal to (>=). Also included in Figure 4-7 are examples of using comparison operators in an If...Then...Else statement's condition.

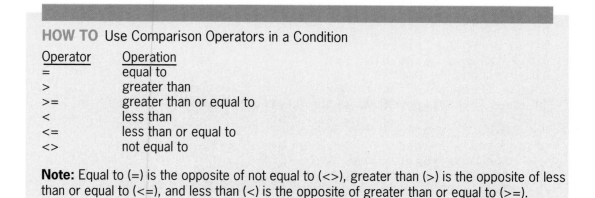

HOW TO Use Comparison Operators in a Condition

Operator	Operation
=	equal to
>	greater than
>=	greater than or equal to
<	less than
<=	less than or equal to
<>	not equal to

Note: Equal to (=) is the opposite of not equal to (<>), greater than (>) is the opposite of less than or equal to (<=), and less than (<) is the opposite of greater than or equal to (>=).

Figure 4-7   How to use comparison operators in a condition *(continues)*

(continued)

Example 1
```
If northSales = southSales Then
```
The condition evaluates to True when both variables contain the same value; otherwise, it evaluates to False.

Example 2
```
If age >= 21 Then
```
The condition evaluates to True when the value stored in the `age` variable is greater than or equal to 21; otherwise, it evaluates to False.

Example 3
```
If price < 35.99D Then
```
The condition evaluates to True when the value stored in the Decimal `price` variable is less than 35.99; otherwise, it evaluates to False. You can also write the condition as `price < Convert.ToDecimal(35.99)`.

Example 4
```
If state <> "TN" Then
```
The condition evaluates to True when the `state` variable does not contain the string "TN"; otherwise, it evaluates to False.

Figure 4-7 How to use comparison operators in a condition
© 2013 Cengage Learning

Unlike arithmetic operators, comparison operators do not have an order of precedence. When an expression contains more than one comparison operator, the computer evaluates the comparison operators from left to right in the expression. Comparison operators are evaluated after any arithmetic operators in an expression. For example, when processing the expression $6 < 2 + 5$, the computer first adds the number 2 to the number 5, giving 7. It then compares the number 6 to the number 7. Because 6 is less than 7, the expression evaluates to True, as shown in Figure 4-8. The figure also shows the evaluation steps for two other expressions that contain arithmetic and comparison operators.

HOW TO Evaluate Expressions Containing Arithmetic and Comparison Operators

Example 1	Result
Original expression	$6 < 2 + 5$
The addition is performed first.	$6 < 7$
The < comparison is performed last.	True

Example 2	Result
Original expression	$14 / 2 + 3 > 7 * 4$
The division is performed first.	$7 + 3 > 7 * 4$
The multiplication is performed next.	$7 + 3 > 28$
The addition is performed next.	$10 > 28$
The > comparison is performed last.	False

Figure 4-8 How to evaluate expressions containing arithmetic and comparison operators *(continues)*

(continued)

Example 3	Result
Original expression	7 + 6 * 4 * 2 – 1 > 50
The first multiplication is performed first.	7 + 24 * 2 – 1 > 50
The remaining multiplication is performed next.	7 + 48 – 1 > 50
The addition is performed next.	55 – 1 > 50
The subtraction is performed next.	54 > 50
The > comparison is performed last.	True

Figure 4-8   How to evaluate expressions containing arithmetic and comparison operators
© 2013 Cengage Learning

Preventing the Division by Zero Error

In Chapter 3 you learned that a run time error occurs when an expression attempts to divide a value by the number 0. This is because, as in math, division by zero is not allowed. You can prevent the run time error from occurring by using a selection structure whose condition compares the expression's denominator with the number 0, as shown in the examples in Figure 4-9.

HOW TO Prevent the Division by Zero Run Time Error

Rule
Use a selection structure whose condition compares the denominator in the expression with the number 0.

Original code
```
Dim num1 As Decimal
Dim num2 As Decimal
Dim quotient As Decimal
Decimal.TryParse(num1TextBox.Text, num1)
Decimal.TryParse(num2TextBox.Text, num2)
[place selection structure here]
quotientLabel.Text = quotient.ToString("N2")
```

Example 1 – single-alternative selection structure
```
If num2 <> 0 Then
     quotient = num1 / num2
End If
```

Example 2 – dual-alternative selection structure
```
If num2 <> 0 Then
     quotient = num1 / num2
Else
     quotient = 0
End If
```
unnecessary in this case

Example 3 – single-alternative selection structure
```
If num2 > 0 Then
     quotient = num1 / num2
End If
```
use when the denominator must be a positive number

Figure 4-9   How to prevent the division by zero run time error
© 2013 Cengage Learning

196

The selection structures in Examples 1 and 2 calculate the quotient *only* when the num2 variable (the denominator) does not contain the number 0. However, notice that the single-alternative structure in Example 1 assigns a value to the quotient variable only when the num2 variable's value is not 0. The dual-alternative structure, on the other hand, always assigns a value to the quotient variable: either the result of the division or the number 0. Although the two selection structures will produce the same result, the Else portion in Example 2 is not really necessary in this case because the quotient variable already contains the number 0 from its Dim statement. However, there is nothing wrong with using the dual-alternative structure. Some programmers would argue that it makes the code clearer.

You can use the single-alternative structure shown in Example 3 in Figure 4-9 to prevent the division by zero run time error when the denominator must be a positive number. You do this using a condition that determines whether the denominator's value is greater than 0.

Swapping Numeric Values

Figure 4-10 shows a sample run of the Auction House application, which displays the lowest and highest of two bids entered by the user. The figure also includes the pseudocode and flowchart for the Display button's Click event procedure. The procedure contains a single-alternative selection structure whose condition determines whether the first bid entered by the user is greater than the second bid. If it is, the selection structure's True path takes the appropriate action.

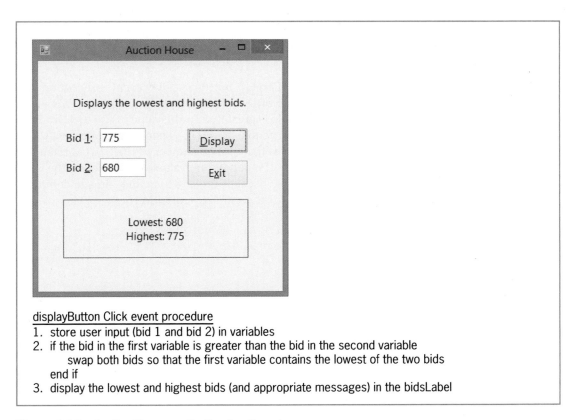

displayButton Click event procedure
1. store user input (bid 1 and bid 2) in variables
2. if the bid in the first variable is greater than the bid in the second variable
    swap both bids so that the first variable contains the lowest of the two bids
   end if
3. display the lowest and highest bids (and appropriate messages) in the bidsLabel

Figure 4-10 Auction House application *(continues)*

(continued)

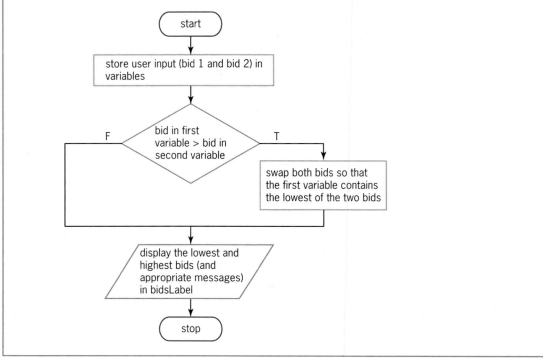

Figure 4-10   Auction House application
© 2013 Cengage Learning

Figure 4-11 shows the code entered in the Display button's Click event procedure. The condition in the If clause compares the contents of the **bid1** variable with the contents of the **bid2** variable. If the value in the **bid1** variable is greater than the value in the **bid2** variable, the condition evaluates to True and the four instructions in the If...Then...Else statement's True path swap both values. Swapping the values places the smaller number in the **bid1** variable and places the larger number in the **bid2** variable. If the condition evaluates to False, on the other hand, the True path instructions are skipped over because the **bid1** variable already contains a number that is smaller than (or possibly equal to) the number stored in the **bid2** variable.

```
Private Sub displayButton_Click(sender As Object,
e As EventArgs) Handles displayButton.Click
    ' displays the lowest and highest bids

    Dim bid1 As Integer
    Dim bid2 As Integer

    ' assign input to variables
    Integer.TryParse(bid1TextBox.Text, bid1)
    Integer.TryParse(bid2TextBox.Text, bid2)

    ' swap bids, if necessary
    If bid1 > bid2 Then
        Dim temp As Integer
        temp = bid1
        bid1 = bid2
        bid2 = temp
    End If

    ' display bids
    bidsLabel.Text = "Lowest: " & bid1.ToString &
        ControlChars.NewLine & "Highest: " & bid2.ToString
End Sub
```

single-alternative
selection structure

you will learn about
this statement in the
String Concatenation
section of the chapter

Figure 4-11 Display button's Click event procedure
© 2013 Cengage Learning

If you want to
experiment
with the
Auction House
application,
open the solution
contained in the Try It 2!
folder.

The first instruction in the If...Then...Else statement's True path declares and initializes a variable named temp. Like a variable declared at the beginning of a procedure, a variable declared within a statement block—referred to as a **block-level variable**—remains in memory until the procedure ends. However, unlike a variable declared at the beginning of a procedure, block-level variables have block scope rather than procedure scope. A variable that has **block scope** can be used only within the statement block in which it is declared. More specifically, it can be used only below its declaration statement within the statement block. In this case, the procedure-level bid1 and bid2 variables can be used anywhere below their Dim statements within the displayButton_Click procedure, but the block-level temp variable can be used only after its Dim statement within the If...Then...Else statement's True path.

You may be wondering why the temp variable was not declared at the beginning of the procedure, along with the other variables. Although there is nothing wrong with declaring the temp variable in that location, there is no reason to create the variable until it is needed, which (in this case) is only when a swap is necessary.

The second instruction in the If...Then...Else statement's True path assigns the value in the bid1 variable to the temp variable. If you do not store the bid1 variable's value in the temp variable, the value will be lost when the computer processes the bid1 = bid2 statement, which replaces the contents of the bid1 variable with the contents of the bid2 variable. Finally, the bid2 = temp instruction assigns the temp variable's value to the bid2 variable; this completes the swap.

Figure 4-12 lists the steps for swapping the contents of two variables. It also contains an example that illustrates the swapping concept, assuming the user enters the numbers 775 and 680 in the bid1TextBox and bid2TextBox, respectively.

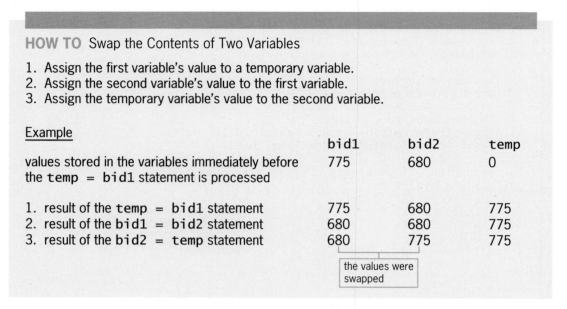

HOW TO Swap the Contents of Two Variables

1. Assign the first variable's value to a temporary variable.
2. Assign the second variable's value to the first variable.
3. Assign the temporary variable's value to the second variable.

Example

	bid1	bid2	temp
values stored in the variables immediately before the `temp = bid1` statement is processed	775	680	0
1. result of the `temp = bid1` statement	775	680	775
2. result of the `bid1 = bid2` statement	680	680	775
3. result of the `bid2 = temp` statement	680	775	775

the values were swapped

Ch04-
Swapping

Figure 4-12 How to swap the contents of two variables
© 2013 Cengage Learning

String Concatenation

The code shown earlier in Figure 4-11 contains two items that were not covered in the previous three chapters: the `ControlChars.NewLine` constant and the concatenation operator. The **ControlChars.NewLine constant** advances the insertion point to the next line in the bidsLabel and is the reason that the "Highest: 775" text appears on the second line in the label, as shown earlier in Figure 4-10. You use the **concatenation operator**, which is the ampersand (**&**), to concatenate (connect or link together) strings. For the Code Editor to recognize the ampersand as the concatenation operator, the ampersand must be both preceded and followed by a space. The last assignment statement shown earlier in Figure 4-11 concatenates five strings: the string "Lowest: ", the contents of the `bid1` variable converted to a string, the `ControlChars.NewLine` constant, the string "Highest: ", and the contents of the `bid2` variable converted to a string. Figure 4-13 shows other examples of string concatenation.

HOW TO Concatenate Strings

Variables/Constant	Contents
city	Bowling Green
state	KY
people	58300
CoName	Sun Products

Concatenated string	Result
city & state	Bowling GreenKY
city & ", " & state	Bowling Green, KY
"She lives in " & city & "."	She lives in Bowling Green.
"Population: " & Convert.ToString(people)	Population: 58300
"Population: " & people.ToString("N0")	Population: 58,300
"He works for " & CoName & "."	He works for Sun Products.

 If you want to practice concatenating strings, open the solution contained in the Try It 3! folder.

Figure 4-13 How to concatenate strings
© 2013 Cengage Learning

Comparing Strings

As is true in many programming languages, string comparisons in Visual Basic are case-sensitive, which means that the uppercase letters of the alphabet are not equal to their lowercase counterparts. Because of this, each of the following three string comparisons will evaluate to False: "A" = "a", "Yes" = "yes", and "Yes" = "YES".

At times, your code may need to compare strings whose case cannot be determined until run time, such as strings either entered by the user or read from a file. When comparing two strings whose case is unknown, you can temporarily convert the strings to the same case (either uppercase or lowercase) and then use the converted strings in the comparison. You use Visual Basic's **ToUpper method** to temporarily convert a string to uppercase, and use its **ToLower method** to temporarily convert a string to lowercase. Both methods affect only letters of the alphabet because they are the only characters that have uppercase and lowercase forms.

 Each uppercase letter is stored in internal memory using a different Unicode value than its lowercase counterpart.

Figure 4-14 shows the syntax of the ToUpper and ToLower methods and includes examples of using the methods. In each syntax, *string* is usually either the name of a String variable or the Text property of an object. Both methods copy the contents of the *string* to a temporary location in the computer's internal memory. The methods convert the temporary string to the appropriate case (if necessary) and then return the temporary string. Keep in mind that the ToUpper and ToLower methods do not change the contents of the original *string*; they change the contents of the temporary location only.

HOW TO Use the ToUpper and ToLower Methods

Syntax
string.**ToUpper**
string.**ToLower**

Example 1
`If senior.ToUpper = "Y" Then`
compares the uppercase version of the string stored in the `senior` variable with the uppercase letter Y

Example 2
`If item1.ToUpper = item2.ToUpper Then`
compares the uppercase version of the string stored in the `item1` variable with the uppercase version of the string stored in the `item2` variable

Example 3
`If senior.ToLower <> "y" Then`
compares the lowercase version of the string stored in the `senior` variable with the lowercase letter y

Example 4
`If "madrid" = cityTextBox.Text.ToLower Then`
compares the lowercase string "madrid" with the lowercase version of the string stored in the cityTextBox's Text property

Example 5
`nameLabel.Text = customer.ToUpper`
assigns the uppercase version of the string stored in the `customer` variable to the nameLabel's Text property

Example 6
`firstName = firstName.ToUpper`
`stateTextBox.Text = stateTextBox.Text.ToLower`
changes the contents of the `firstName` variable to uppercase, and changes the contents of the stateTextBox's Text property to lowercase

Figure 4-14 How to use the ToUpper and ToLower methods
© 2013 Cengage Learning

When using the ToUpper method in a comparison, be sure that the strings you are comparing are uppercase, as shown in Examples 1 and 2; otherwise, the comparison will not evaluate correctly. Likewise, when using the ToLower method in a comparison, be sure that the strings you are comparing are lowercase, as shown in Examples 3 and 4. The statement in Example 5 temporarily converts the contents of the **customer** variable to uppercase and then assigns the result to the nameLabel. As Example 6 indicates, you can also use the ToUpper and ToLower methods to permanently convert the contents of either a String variable or a control's Text property to uppercase or lowercase, respectively. You will use the ToUpper method in the Math Calculator application, which you view in the next section.

The Math Calculator Application

Figure 4-15 shows a sample run of the Math Calculator application, which displays either the sum or the product of two numbers entered by the user. The figure also includes the pseudocode and flowchart for the Calculate button's Click event procedure. The procedure contains two dual-alternative selection structures: one to determine the arithmetic operation to perform, and one to determine the number of decimal places to display in the answer.

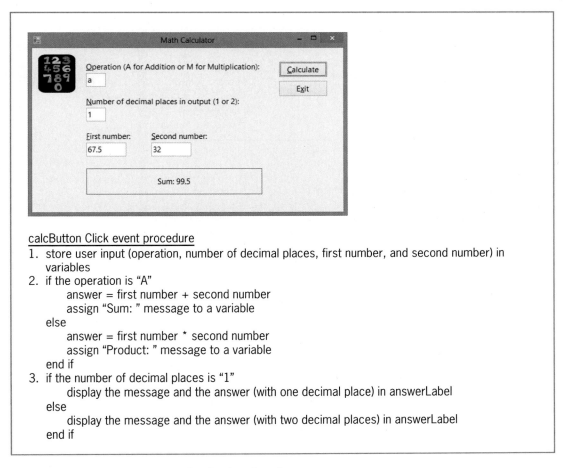

calcButton Click event procedure
1. store user input (operation, number of decimal places, first number, and second number) in variables
2. if the operation is "A"
      answer = first number + second number
      assign "Sum: " message to a variable
   else
      answer = first number * second number
      assign "Product: " message to a variable
   end if
3. if the number of decimal places is "1"
      display the message and the answer (with one decimal place) in answerLabel
   else
      display the message and the answer (with two decimal places) in answerLabel
   end if

Figure 4-15   Math Calculator application *(continues)*

(continued)

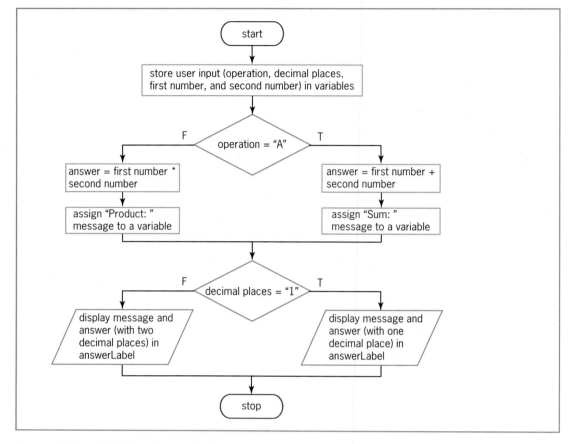

Figure 4-15 Math Calculator application
OpenClipArt.org/kablam/George Supreeth; © 2013 Cengage Learning

Figure 4-16 shows two versions of the code for the Calculate button's Click event procedure. The ToUpper method is shaded in each version. In Version 1, the ToUpper method is included in the statement that assigns the text box value to the `operation` variable. After the statement is processed, the variable will contain an uppercase letter (assuming the user entered a letter). In Version 2, the ToUpper method is included in the If...Then...Else statement's condition. The `operation.ToUpper` portion of the condition will change the `operation` variable's value to uppercase only temporarily. After the comparison is made, the variable will still contain its original value. In this instance, neither version of the code is better than the other; both simply represent two different ways of performing the same task.

```
Version 1 – ToUpper in assignment statement
Private Sub calcButton_Click(sender As Object,
e As EventArgs) Handles calcButton.Click
    ' calculates the sum or product of two numbers

    Dim operation As String
    Dim decimalPlaces As String
    Dim firstNum As Double
    Dim secondNum As Double
    Dim answer As Double
    Dim operationMsg As String
```

Figure 4-16 Two versions of the calcButton_Click procedure *(continues)*

(continued)

```
      ' store input in variables
      operation = operationTextBox.Text.ToUpper
      decimalPlaces = decimalPlacesTextBox.Text
      Double.TryParse(firstTextBox.Text, firstNum)
      Double.TryParse(secondTextBox.Text, secondNum)

      ' determine operation and perform calculation
      If operation = "A" Then
          answer = firstNum + secondNum
          operationMsg = "Sum: "
      Else
          answer = firstNum * secondNum
          operationMsg = "Product: "
      End If

      ' determine number of decimal places and display answer
      If decimalPlaces = "1" Then
          answerLabel.Text =
              operationMsg & answer.ToString("N1")
      Else
          answerLabel.Text =
              operationMsg & answer.ToString("N2")
      End If
End Sub
```

Version 2 – ToUpper in If...Then...Else statement's condition

```
Private Sub calcButton_Click(sender As Object,
e As EventArgs) Handles calcButton.Click
      ' calculates the sum or product of two numbers

      Dim operation As String
      Dim decimalPlaces As String
      Dim firstNum As Double
      Dim secondNum As Double
      Dim answer As Double
      Dim operationMsg As String

      ' store input in variables
      operation = operationTextBox.Text
      decimalPlaces = decimalPlacesTextBox.Text
      Double.TryParse(firstTextBox.Text, firstNum)
      Double.TryParse(secondTextBox.Text, secondNum)

      ' determine operation and perform calculation
      If operation.ToUpper = "A" Then
          answer = firstNum + secondNum
          operationMsg = "Sum: "
      Else
          answer = firstNum * secondNum
          operationMsg = "Product: "
      End If

      ' determine number of decimal places and display answer
      If decimalPlaces = "1" Then
          answerLabel.Text =
              operationMsg & answer.ToString("N1")
      Else
          answerLabel.Text =
              operationMsg & answer.ToString("N2")
      End If
End Sub
```

 If you want to experiment with the Math Calculator application, open the solution contained in the Try It 4! folder.

Figure 4-16 Two versions of the calcButton_Click procedure

You can also code the Calculate button's Click event procedure without using the ToUpper or ToLower methods. To do this, you must change the operationTextBox's CharacterCasing property from Normal to either Upper or Lower; you do this in the Properties window. A text box's **CharacterCasing property** indicates whether the text inside the control should remain as typed, or be converted to either uppercase or lowercase as the user is typing. For example, if the operationTextBox's CharacterCasing property is set to Upper, an uppercase letter A will appear in the text box even when the user types the lowercase letter a. As a result, the `operation = operationTextBox.Text` statement will assign an uppercase letter A to the `operation` variable. The CharacterCasing property allows you to control the case of the input. (If you want to try using the CharacterCasing property, complete Exercise 14 at the end of the chapter.)

Comparing Boolean Values

Figure 4-17 shows a sample run of the Halloway Products application, which displays the total amount a customer owes. The interface provides a check box for specifying whether the customer is entitled to the 10% employee discount. You add a check box to an interface using the CheckBox tool in the toolbox. In Windows applications, **check boxes** provide one or more independent and nonexclusive items from which the user can choose. An interface can contain any number of check boxes, and any number of them can be selected at the same time. Each check box should be labeled to make its purpose obvious. You enter the label using sentence capitalization in the check box's Text property. Each check box should also have a unique access key. During run time, you can determine whether a check box is selected by looking at the Boolean value in its Checked property: A True value indicates that the check box is selected, whereas a False value indicates that it is not selected.

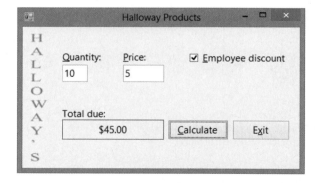

Figure 4-17 Sample run of the Halloway Products application

Figure 4-18 shows two versions of the code for the Calculate button's Click event procedure. Version 1 contains a single-alternative selection structure; Version 2 contains a dual-alternative selection structure. The condition in each selection structure is shaded in the figure. Because the Checked property contains a Boolean value, you can omit the `= True` in the If clause's condition, as shown in Version 2.

```
Version 1 – single-alternative selection structure
Private Sub calcButton_Click(sender As Object,
e As EventArgs) Handles calcButton.Click
    ' calculates the total owed

    Const DiscRate As Decimal = 0.1D
    Dim quantity As Integer
    Dim price As Decimal
    Dim subtotal As Decimal
    Dim discount As Decimal
    Dim totalDue As Decimal

    ' store input in variables
    Integer.TryParse(quantityTextBox.Text, quantity)
    Decimal.TryParse(priceTextBox.Text, price)

    ' calculate subtotal, discount, and total due
    subtotal = quantity * price
    If employeeCheckBox.Checked = True Then
        discount = subtotal * DiscRate
    End If
    totalDue = subtotal - discount

    totalDueLabel.Text = totalDue.ToString("C2")
End Sub

Version 2 – dual-alternative selection structure
Private Sub calcButton_Click(sender As Object,
e As EventArgs) Handles calcButton.Click
    ' calculates the total owed

    Const DiscRate As Decimal = 0.1D
    Dim quantity As Integer
    Dim price As Decimal
    Dim subtotal As Decimal
    Dim discount As Decimal
    Dim totalDue As Decimal

    ' store input in variables
    Integer.TryParse(quantityTextBox.Text, quantity)
    Decimal.TryParse(priceTextBox.Text, price)

    ' calculate subtotal, discount, and total due
    subtotal = quantity * price
    If employeeCheckBox.Checked Then
        discount = subtotal * DiscRate
    Else
        discount = 0
    End If
    totalDue = subtotal - discount

    totalDueLabel.Text = totalDue.ToString("C2")
End Sub
```

you can omit the = True when comparing Boolean values

 If you want to experiment with the Halloway Products application, open the solution contained in the Try It 5! folder.

Figure 4-18 Calculate button's Click event procedure
© 2013 Cengage Learning

Mini-Quiz 4-2

1. What is the scope of a variable declared in an If...Then...Else statement's False path? (3, 7)

    a. the entire application
    b. the procedure in which the If...Then...Else statement appears
    c. the entire If...Then...Else statement
    d. only the False path in the If...Then...Else statement

The answers to Mini-Quiz questions are located in Appendix A. Each question is associated with one or more objectives listed at the beginning of the chapter.

2. Which of the following determines whether the value contained in the **sales** variable is at least $450.67? (3, 4)

    a. `If sales >= 450.67 Then`
    b. `If sales <= 450.67 Then`
    c. `If sales > 450.67 Then`
    d. `If sales < 450.67 Then`

3. Which of the following concatenates the "Do they live in " message, the contents of the String **state** variable, and a question mark? (8)

    a. `"Do they live in " & state & "?"`
    b. `"Do they live in & state & ?"`
    c. `Do they live in & state & ?`
    d. `"Do they live in " # state # "?"`

4. Which of the following methods temporarily converts the string stored in the **item** variable to lowercase? (10)

    a. `item.Lower`
    b. `item.ToLower`
    c. `LowerCase(item)`
    d. `Lower(item)`

5. If a check box is selected, its _____ property contains the Boolean value True. (11)

    a. Checked
    b. Checkbox
    c. Selected
    d. Selection

Logical Operators

As mentioned earlier, you can also include logical operators in an If...Then...Else statement's condition. **Logical operators** allow you to combine two or more sub-conditions into one compound condition. The compound condition will always evaluate to a Boolean value: either True or False. You already are familiar with the concept of logical operators because you use logical operators—namely, *and* and *or*—in your daily conversations. Examples of this are shown in Figure 4-19.

Logical _and_ and _or_ examples

- If you finished your homework _and_ you studied for tomorrow's exam, you can watch a movie.

- If your cell phone rings _and_ (it's your spouse calling _or_ it's your child calling), you should answer your phone.

- If you are driving your car _and_ (it's raining _or_ it's foggy _or_ there is bug splatter on your windshield), you should turn your car's wipers on.

Figure 4-19   Examples of the English logical operators
© 2013 Cengage Learning

The Visual Basic language provides six logical operators. The two most commonly used are listed in Figure 4-20 along with their order of precedence. The figure also contains examples of using the operators in an If…Then…Else statement's condition. Notice that the compound condition in each example evaluates to either True or False. Also notice that a complete expression appears on both sides of the logical operator.

HOW TO Use Logical Operators in a Condition

Logical operator	Operation	Precedence number
AndAlso	all sub-conditions must be true for the compound condition to evaluate to True	1
OrElse	only one of the sub-conditions needs to be true for the compound condition to evaluate to True	2

Example 1
```
Dim quantity As Integer
Integer.TryParse(quantityTextBox.Text, quantity)
If quantity > 0 AndAlso quantity < 50 Then
```
The compound condition evaluates to True when the number stored in the `quantity` variable is greater than 0 and, at the same time, less than 50; otherwise, it evaluates to False.

Example 2
```
Dim sales As Double
Double.TryParse(salesTextBox.Text, sales)
If bonusCheckBox.Checked AndAlso sales >= 500 Then
```
The compound condition evaluates to True when the bonusCheckBox is selected and, at the same time, the number stored in the `sales` variable is greater than or equal to 500; otherwise, it evaluates to False. (You can also write the first sub-condition as `bonusCheckBox.Checked = True`.)

Figure 4-20   How to use logical operators in a condition _(continues)_

(continued)

Example 3
```
Dim age As Integer
Integer.TryParse(ageTextBox.Text, age)
If age = 21 OrElse age > 55 Then
```
The compound condition evaluates to True when the number stored in the `age` variable is either equal to 21 or greater than 55; otherwise, it evaluates to False.

Example 4
```
Dim rating As Integer
Dim cost As Decimal
Integer.TryParse(ratingTextBox.Text, rating)
Decimal.TryParse(costTextBox.Text, cost)
If rating = 3 OrElse cost < 75.99 Then
```
The compound condition evaluates to True when either (or both) of the following is true: The number stored in the `rating` variable is 3 or the number stored in the `cost` variable is less than 75.99; otherwise, it evaluates to False.

Example 5
```
Dim num As Integer
Dim state As String
Integer.TryParse(numTextBox.Text, num)
state = stateTextBox.Text.ToUpper
If state = "KY" OrElse num > 0 AndAlso num < 100 Then
```
The compound condition evaluates to True when either (or both) of the following is true: The `state` variable contains the string "KY" or the number stored in the `num` variable is between 0 and 100; otherwise, it evaluates to False. (The AndAlso operator is evaluated before the OrElse operator because it has a higher precedence.)

Figure 4-20   How to use logical operators in a condition
© 2013 Cengage Learning

The tables shown in Figure 4-21, called **truth tables**, summarize how the computer evaluates expressions containing a logical operator. Notice that sub-condition2 is not always evaluated. Because both sub-conditions combined with the **AndAlso operator** need to be True for the compound condition to be True, there is no need to evaluate sub-condition2 when sub-condition1 is False. Similarly, because only one of the sub-conditions combined with the **OrElse operator** needs to be True for the compound condition to be True, there is no need to evaluate sub-condition2 when sub-condition1 is True. The concept of evaluating sub-condition2 based on the result of sub-condition1 is referred to as **short-circuit evaluation**.

HOW TO Evaluate Expressions Containing a Logical Operator

Truth table for the AndAlso operator

sub-condition1	sub-condition2	sub-condition1 AndAlso sub-condition2
True	True	True
True	False	False
False	(not evaluated)	False

Truth table for the OrElse operator

sub-condition1	sub-condition2	sub-condition1 OrElse sub-condition2
True	(not evaluated)	True
False	True	True
False	False	False

Figure 4-21   How to evaluate expressions containing a logical operator
© 2013 Cengage Learning

Using the Truth Tables

When ordering from Warren's Web site, customers using their Warren credit card to pay for their order receive free shipping on order amounts over $100. In the procedure that determines the free-shipping eligibility, the order amount and credit card name are stored in variables named orderAmount and creditCard, respectively. Therefore, you can phrase sub-condition1 in the If...Then...Else statement as orderAmount > 100, and phrase sub-condition2 as creditCard = "Warren". Which logical operator should you use to combine both sub-conditions into one compound condition? We'll use the truth tables from Figure 4-21 to answer this question.

For a customer to receive free shipping at Warren's, both sub-conditions must be True. If at least one of the sub-conditions is False, then the compound condition should be False and the customer should not receive free shipping. According to the truth tables, both logical operators evaluate the compound condition as True when both sub-conditions are True. However, only the AndAlso operator evaluates it as False when at least one of the sub-conditions is False. Therefore, the correct compound condition to use here is orderAmount > 100 AndAlso creditCard = "Warren".

Unlike Warren's Web site, Houston's Web site has the following shipping policy: Customers who are members of Houston's free shipping club are always entitled to free shipping; all other customers receive free shipping only when their order amount is over $100. In the procedure that determines the free-shipping eligibility, the order amount and club information are stored in variables named orderAmount and club, respectively. Therefore, you can phrase sub-condition1 in the If...Then...Else statement as orderAmount > 100, and phrase sub-condition2 as club = "Member". Now which logical operator should you use to combine both sub-conditions into one compound condition? Again, we'll use the truth tables from Figure 4-21 to answer this question.

For a customer to receive free shipping at Houston's, at least one of the sub-conditions must be True: Either the customer's order needs to be over $100, or the customer needs to be a member of the free shipping club. According to the truth tables, the OrElse operator is the only operator that evaluates the compound condition as True when at least one of the sub-conditions is True. Therefore, the correct compound condition to use here is orderAmount > 100 OrElse club = "Member".

The Carroll Company Application

Carroll Company wants an application that calculates and displays an employee's gross pay. No one at the company works more than 40 hours per week, and everyone earns the same hourly rate: $10.65. Before making the gross pay calculation, the procedure should verify that the number of hours entered by the user is greater than or equal to 0 but less than or equal to 40. Programmers refer to the process of verifying that the input data is within the expected range as **data validation**. If the number of hours is valid, the procedure should calculate and display the gross pay. Otherwise, it should display an error message alerting the user that the number of hours is incorrect. Figure 4-22 shows two sample runs of the application: one using valid data and one using invalid data.

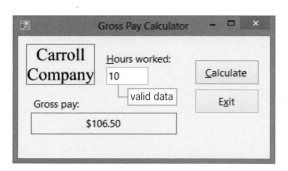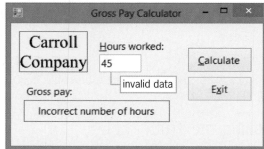

Figure 4-22   Sample runs of the Carroll Company application

Figure 4-23 shows two versions of the Calculate button's Click event procedure. Both versions contain a dual-alternative selection structure whose compound condition includes a logical operator. The compound conditions are shaded in the figure. The compound condition in Version 1 uses the AndAlso operator to determine whether the value stored in the **hours** variable is greater than or equal to 0 and, at the same time, less than or equal to 40. The compound condition in Version 2, on the other hand, uses the OrElse operator to determine whether the value stored in the **hours** variable is either less than 0 or greater than 40. Both versions produce the same result and simply represent two different ways of performing the same task.

```
Version 1 – using the AndAlso operator
Private Sub calcButton_Click(sender As Object,
e As EventArgs) Handles calcButton.Click
    ' calculates the gross pay

    Const RatePerHour As Double = 10.65
    Dim hours As Double
    Dim gross As Double

    ' store input in a variable
    Double.TryParse(hoursTextBox.Text, hours)

    If hours >= 0 AndAlso hours <= 40 Then
        ' calculate and display gross pay
        gross = hours * RatePerHour
        grossLabel.Text = gross.ToString("C2")
    Else     ' display error message
        grossLabel.Text = "Incorrect number of hours"
    End If
End Sub
```

Figure 4-23   Two versions of the Calculate button's Click event procedure *(continues)*

(continued)

```
Version 2 – using the OrElse operator
Private Sub calcButton_Click(sender As Object,
e As EventArgs) Handles calcButton.Click
    ' calculates the gross pay

    Const RatePerHour As Double = 10.65
    Dim hours As Double
    Dim gross As Double

    ' store input in a variable
    Double.TryParse(hoursTextBox.Text, hours)

    If hours < 0 OrElse hours > 40 Then
        ' display error message
        grossLabel.Text = "Incorrect number of hours"
    Else
        ' calculate and display gross pay
        gross = hours * RatePerHour
        grossLabel.Text = gross.ToString("C2")
    End If
End Sub
```

Figure 4-23   Two versions of the Calculate button's Click event procedure
© 2013 Cengage Learning

If you want to experiment with the Carroll Company application, open the solution contained in the Try It 6! folder.

213

Summary of Operators

Figure 4-24 shows the order of precedence for the arithmetic, concatenation, comparison, and logical operators you have learned so far. Recall that operators with the same precedence number are evaluated from left to right in an expression. Notice that arithmetic operators are evaluated first, followed by the concatenation operator, comparison operators, and logical operators. As a result, the expression 12 > 0 AndAlso 12 < 10 * 2 evaluates to True, as shown in Figure 4-24. Keep in mind, however, that you can use parentheses to override the order of precedence.

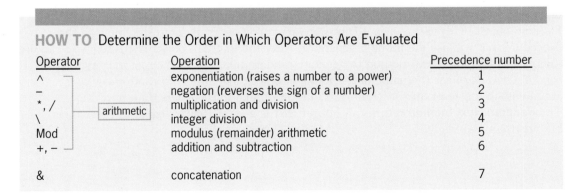

HOW TO Determine the Order in Which Operators Are Evaluated

Operator	Operation	Precedence number
^	exponentiation (raises a number to a power)	1
−	negation (reverses the sign of a number)	2
*, /	multiplication and division	3
\	integer division	4
Mod	modulus (remainder) arithmetic	5
+, −	addition and subtraction	6
&	concatenation	7

*(arithmetic: ^, −, *, /, \, Mod, +, −)*

Ch04-Operators

Figure 4-24   How to determine the order in which operators are evaluated *(continues)*

(continued)

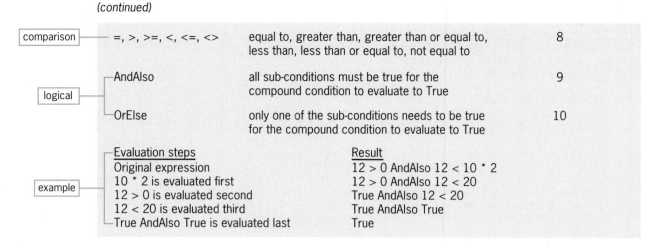

comparison	=, >, >=, <, <=, <>	equal to, greater than, greater than or equal to, less than, less than or equal to, not equal to	8
logical	AndAlso	all sub-conditions must be true for the compound condition to evaluate to True	9
	OrElse	only one of the sub-conditions needs to be true for the compound condition to evaluate to True	10

	Evaluation steps	Result
example	Original expression	12 > 0 AndAlso 12 < 10 * 2
	10 * 2 is evaluated first	12 > 0 AndAlso 12 < 20
	12 > 0 is evaluated second	True AndAlso 12 < 20
	12 < 20 is evaluated third	True AndAlso True
	True AndAlso True is evaluated last	True

Figure 4-24　How to determine the order in which operators are evaluated
© 2013 Cengage Learning

The last concept covered in this chapter is how to generate random integers. You will use random integers in the game application coded in Programming Tutorial 1.

Generating Random Integers

Some applications require the use of random numbers; examples include game applications, lottery applications, and applications used to practice elementary math skills. Most programming languages provide a **pseudo-random number generator**, which is a device that produces a sequence of numbers that meet certain statistical requirements for randomness. Pseudo-random numbers are chosen with equal probability from a finite set of numbers. The chosen numbers are not completely random. This is because a definite mathematical algorithm is used to select them. However, they are sufficiently random for practical purposes. The pseudo-random number generator in Visual Basic is an object whose data type is Random.

Figure 4-25 shows the syntax for generating random integers in Visual Basic, and it includes examples of using the syntax. As the figure indicates, you first create a **Random object** to represent the pseudo-random number generator in your application's code. You create the Random object by declaring it in a Dim statement. You enter the Dim statement in the procedure that will use the number generator. After the Random object is created, you can use the object's Random.Next method to generate random integers. In the method's syntax, *randomObjectName* is the name of the Random object. The *minValue* and *maxValue* arguments in the syntax must be integers, and minValue must be less than maxValue. The **Random.Next method** returns an integer that is greater than or equal to minValue, but less than maxValue.

HOW TO Generate Random Integers

Syntax
Dim *randomObjectName* **As New Random**
randomObjectName.**Next(***minValue, maxValue***)**

Example 1
```
Dim number As Integer
Dim randGen As New Random
number = randGen.Next(1, 51)
```
The Dim statements create an Integer variable named **number** and a Random object named **randGen**. The **randGen.Next(1, 51)** expression generates a random integer that is greater than or equal to 1, but less than 51. The assignment statement assigns the random integer to the **number** variable.

Example 2
```
Dim number As Integer
Dim randGen As New Random
number = randGen.Next(-10, 0)
```
The Dim statements create an Integer variable named **number** and a Random object named **randGen**. The **randGen.Next(-10, 0)** expression generates a random integer that is greater than or equal to –10, but less than 0. The assignment statement assigns the random integer to the **number** variable.

In Computer Exercise 29, you will learn how to generate random real numbers.

Figure 4-25   How to generate random integers
© 2013 Cengage Learning

Figure 4-26 shows a sample run of the Random Integer application. It also contains the code for the Generate Random Integer button's Click event procedure, which generates and displays a random number from 1 through 10.

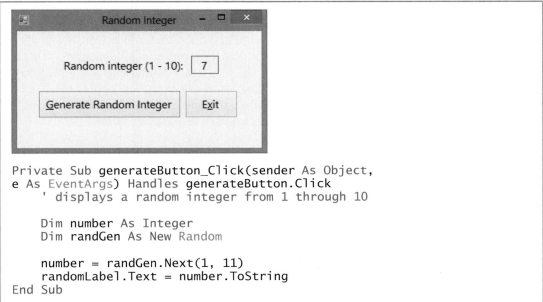

```
Private Sub generateButton_Click(sender As Object,
e As EventArgs) Handles generateButton.Click
    ' displays a random integer from 1 through 10

    Dim number As Integer
    Dim randGen As New Random

    number = randGen.Next(1, 11)
    randomLabel.Text = number.ToString
End Sub
```

If you want to experiment with the Random Integer application, open the solution contained in the Try It 7! folder.

Figure 4-26   Sample run and code for the Random Integer application
© 2013 Cengage Learning

Mini-Quiz 4-3

1. If the value of sub-condition1 is True and the value of sub-condition2 is False, the compound condition sub-condition1 OrElse sub-condition2 will evaluate to _____. (4)

    a. True

    b. False

2. The compound condition 7 > 3 AndAlso 5 < 2 will evaluate to _____. (4)

3. The compound condition 3 + 4 * 2 > 12 AndAlso 4 < 15 will evaluate to _____. (4)

4. Which of the following declares an object to represent the pseudo-random number generator? (12)

    a. `Dim randGen As New Generator`

    b. `Dim randGen As New Random`

    c. `Dim randGen As New RandomGenerator`

    d. `Dim randGen As New RandomObject`

The answers to Mini-Quiz questions are located in Appendix A. Each question is associated with one or more objectives listed at the beginning of the chapter.

216

You have completed the concepts section of Chapter 4. The Programming Tutorial section is next.

PROGRAMMING TUTORIAL 1

Creating the Find the Robot Application

In this tutorial, you will create the Find the Robot application. The application's TOE chart and MainForm are shown in Figures 4-27 and 4-28, respectively. The form's BackgroundImage property displays the image stored in the Room.png file, which is contained in the project's Resources folder. The form's BackgroundImageLayout property is set to Stretch.

The form contains six picture boxes, a label, and two buttons. The openPictureBox, robotPictureBox, and closedPictureBox controls will be invisible when the application is started. When the user clicks the Hide button, the button's Click event procedure will display the closed door image in the door1PictureBox, door2PictureBox, and door3PictureBox controls. It will also generate a random number from 1 through 3. The random number will indicate which of those three picture boxes will display the robot image when clicked. For example, if the random number is 1 and the user clicks the door1PictureBox, the robot image will appear in the picture box. However, if the user clicks the door2PictureBox, the open door image will appear in the picture box. The player's task is to find the robot, using as few guesses as possible.

Task	Object	Event
1. Generate a random integer from 1 through 3 2. Display the closed door image in door1PictureBox, door2PictureBox, and door3PictureBox	hideButton	Click
Use the random integer generated by the hideButton to display either the robot image or the open door image	door1PictureBox, door2PictureBox, door3PictureBox	Click
End the application	exitButton	Click
Store the closed door image	closedPictureBox	None
Store the open door image	openPictureBox	None
Store the robot image	robotPictureBox	None

Figure 4-27   TOE chart for the Find the Robot application
© 2013 Cengage Learning

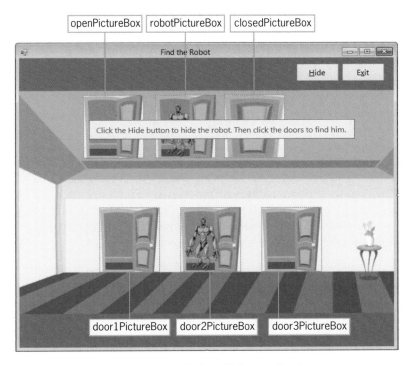

Figure 4-28   MainForm for the Find the Robot application
Image by Diane Zak; Created with Reallusion CrazyTalk Animator

Coding the Find the Robot Application

According to the application's TOE chart, the Click event procedures for the hideButton, the exitButton, and three of the picture boxes need to be coded.

To begin coding the application:

   1.   Start Visual Studio. Open the **Robot Solution** (**Robot Solution.sln**) file contained in the VbReloaded2012\Chap04\Robot Solution folder. If necessary, open the designer window.

2. Open the Code Editor window. Notice that the exitButton's Click event procedure has already been coded for you.

3. In the comments that appear in the General Declarations section, replace <your name> and <current date> with your name and the current date, respectively.

4. The application will use variables, so you should enter the appropriate Option statements in the General Declarations section. Click the **blank line** above the Public Class clause and then enter the following three statements:

Option Explicit On
Option Infer Off
Option Strict On

The hideButton's Click event procedure is responsible for generating a random number from 1 through 3 and also displaying the closed door image in three of the picture boxes. Figure 4-29 shows the procedure's pseudocode.

---

hideButton Click event procedure
1. assign a random integer from 1 through 3 to a class-level Integer variable
2. assign the closed door image, which is contained in the closedPictureBox, to the door1PictureBox, door2PictureBox, and door3PictureBox controls

---

Figure 4-29　Pseudocode for the hideButton_Click procedure
© 2013 Cengage Learning

The procedure will use two variables: a Random variable to represent the pseudo-random number generator, and an Integer variable to store the random integer. You will use the names `randGen` and `randomInteger` for the Random and Integer variables, respectively. The `randGen` variable can be a procedure-level variable because it is needed only within the hideButton_Click procedure. The `randomInteger` variable, however, will need to be a class-level variable because it will be used by four different procedures: The hideButton_Click procedure will set the variable's value, and the door1PictureBox_Click, door2PictureBox_Click, and door3PictureBox_Click procedures will use the value to determine the appropriate image to display (either the robot image or the open door image).

To declare the class-level variable and then code the hideButton_Click procedure:

1. Click the **blank line** below the `' class-level variable` comment and then enter the following Private statement:

Private randomInteger As Integer

2. Open the code template for the hideButton's Click event procedure. Type the following comment and then press **Enter** twice:

' prepares the interface

3. Next, type the following Dim statement and then press **Enter** twice:

Dim randGen As New Random

4. The first step in the pseudocode assigns a random integer from 1 through 3 to the class-level variable, which is named `randomInteger`. Enter the following comment and assignment statement. Press **Enter** twice after typing the assignment statement.

```
' generate a random integer from 1 through 3
randomInteger = randGen.Next(1, 4)
```

5. The second step in the pseudocode assigns the image contained in the closedPictureBox to three picture boxes. Enter the following comment and code:

```
' display the closed door image
door1PictureBox.Image = closedPictureBox.Image
door2PictureBox.Image = closedPictureBox.Image
door3PictureBox.Image = closedPictureBox.Image
```

6. Save the solution.

According to the application's TOE chart, the door1PictureBox's Click event procedure will use the random integer generated by the hideButton to display either the robot image or the closed door image in the picture box. The procedure's pseudocode is shown in Figure 4-30.

```
door1PictureBox Click event procedure
if the random integer generated by the hideButton is 1
    assign the image contained in the robotPictureBox to the door1PictureBox
else
    assign the image contained in the openPictureBox to the door1PictureBox
end if
```

Figure 4-30   Pseudocode for the door1PictureBox_Click procedure
© 2013 Cengage Learning

To code the door1PictureBox's Click event procedure:

1. Open the code template for the door1PictureBox's Click event procedure. Type the following comment and then press **Enter** twice:

   ' displays the appropriate image

2. Now, enter the following If...Then...Else statement. You will notice that when you press Enter after typing the If clause, the Code Editor will automatically enter the End If clause for you.

```
If randomInteger = 1 Then
    door1PictureBox.Image = robotPictureBox.Image
Else
    door1PictureBox.Image = openPictureBox.Image
End If
```

3. Save the solution.

The door2PictureBox_Click and door3PictureBox_Click procedures will be almost identical to the door1PictureBox_Click procedure. The only exception is that the door2PictureBox_Click procedure will display the robot image in the door2PictureBox when the random number is 2. Similarly, the door3PictureBox_Click procedure will display the robot image in the door3PictureBox when the random number is 3.

To finish coding the application and then test it:

1. Open the code template for the door2PictureBox's Click event procedure. Also open the code template for the door3PictureBox's Click event procedure.

2. Copy the comment and the If...Then...Else statement from the door1PictureBox_Click procedure to the door2PictureBox_Click and door3PictureBox_Click procedures.

3. In the door2PictureBox_Click procedure, change the number 1 in the If...Then...Else statement's condition to **2**. Also change door1PictureBox in the True and False paths to **door2PictureBox**.

4. On your own, make the appropriate modifications to the door3PictureBox_Click procedure.

5. Save the solution and then start the application. Click the **Hide** button. The closed door image appears in the three visible picture boxes, as shown in Figure 4-31.

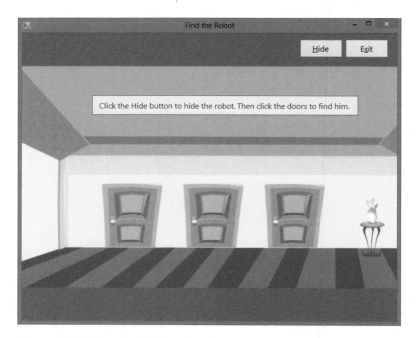

Figure 4-31   Result of clicking the Hide button
Image by Diane Zak; Created with Reallusion CrazyTalk Animator

6. Click **one of the closed doors**. Either the robot image or the open door image appears.

7. Click **each of the remaining two doors**. Figure 4-32 shows a sample run of the application. Because the application uses a random number, the robot image may be in a different location on your screen.

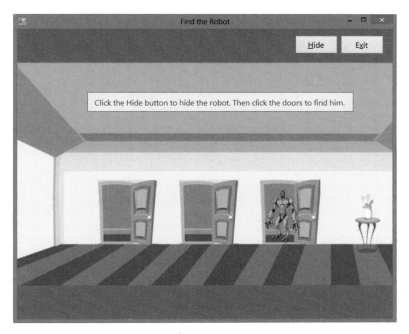

Figure 4-32 Sample run of the Find the Robot application
Image by Diane Zak; Created with Reallusion CrazyTalk Animator

8. Click the **Hide** button. The closed door image appears in the three visible picture boxes. Try to find the robot again.

9. Click the **Exit** button. Close the Code Editor window and then close the solution. Figure 4-33 shows the application's code.

```
1 ' Project name:        Robot Project
2 ' Project purpose:     Guess where a robot is hiding
3 ' Created/revised by: <your name> on <current date>
4
5 Option Explicit On
6 Option Infer Off
7 Option Strict On
8
9 Public Class MainForm
10
11     ' class-level variable
12     Private randomInteger As Integer
13
14     Private Sub exitButton_Click(sender As Object,
        e As EventArgs) Handles exitButton.Click
15         Me.Close()
16     End Sub
17
18     Private Sub hideButton_Click(sender As Object,
        e As EventArgs) Handles hideButton.Click
19         ' prepares the interface
20
```

Figure 4-33 Find the Robot application's code *(continues)*

(continued)

```
21          Dim randGen As New Random
22
23          ' generate a random integer from 1 through 3
24          randomInteger = randGen.Next(1, 4)
25
26          ' display the closed door image
27          door1PictureBox.Image = closedPictureBox.Image
28          door2PictureBox.Image = closedPictureBox.Image
29          door3PictureBox.Image = closedPictureBox.Image
30
31      End Sub
32
33      Private Sub door1PictureBox_Click(sender As Object,
        e As EventArgs) Handles door1PictureBox.Click
34          ' displays the appropriate image
35
36          If randomInteger = 1 Then
37              door1PictureBox.Image = robotPictureBox.Image
38          Else
39              door1PictureBox.Image = openPictureBox.Image
40          End If
41      End Sub
42
43      Private Sub door2PictureBox_Click(sender As Object,
        e As EventArgs) Handles door2PictureBox.Click
44          ' displays the appropriate image
45
46          If randomInteger = 2 Then
47              door2PictureBox.Image = robotPictureBox.Image
48          Else
49              door2PictureBox.Image = openPictureBox.Image
50          End If
51      End Sub
52
53      Private Sub door3PictureBox_Click(sender As Object,
        e As EventArgs) Handles door3PictureBox.Click
54          ' displays the appropriate image
55
56          If randomInteger = 3 Then
57              door3PictureBox.Image = robotPictureBox.Image
58          Else
59              door3PictureBox.Image = openPictureBox.Image
60          End If
61      End Sub
62  End Class
```

Figure 4-33   Find the Robot application's code
© 2013 Cengage Learning

PROGRAMMING TUTORIAL 2

Coding the Greenview Health Club Application

In this tutorial, you will create the Greenview Health Club application, which calculates and displays a club member's monthly dues. The interface provides a text box for entering the member's basic monthly fee. It also provides check boxes for specifying whether the member wants to use the club's tennis and/or racquetball courts. The additional monthly charge for using the tennis court is $20. The additional monthly charge for using the racquetball court is $10. The application's TOE chart and MainForm are shown in Figures 4-34 and 4-35, respectively. The MainForm contains three labels, one text box, two check boxes, two buttons, and a picture box.

Task	Object	Event
Get and display the basic monthly fee	basicFeeTextBox	None
Specify whether the member should be charged for using the tennis and/or racquetball courts	tennisCheckBox, racquetballCheckBox	None
1. Calculate the monthly dues, which include the basic monthly fee and optional additional charges for tennis and racquetball 2. Display the monthly dues in the duesLabel	calcButton	Click
End the application	exitButton	Click
Display the monthly dues (from calcButton)	duesLabel	None

Figure 4-34   TOE chart for the Greenview Health Club application
© 2013 Cengage Learning

Figure 4-35   MainForm for the Greenview Health Club application

Coding the Greenview Health Club Application

According to the application's TOE chart, the Click event procedures for the calcButton and exitButton need to be coded.

To begin coding the application:

1. Start Visual Studio. Open the **Greenview Solution (Greenview Solution.sln)** file contained in the VbReloaded2012\Chap04\Greenview Solution folder. If necessary, open the designer window.

2. Open the Code Editor window. Notice that the exitButton's Click event procedure has already been coded for you.

3. In the comments that appear in the General Declarations section, replace <your name> and <current date> with your name and the current date, respectively.

4. Enter the appropriate Option statements in the General Declarations section.

The calcButton's Click event procedure is responsible for calculating and displaying the monthly dues. Figure 4-36 shows the procedure's pseudocode along with the memory locations it requires.

---

calcButton Click event procedure
1. assign the basic fee, which is entered in the basicFeeTextBox, as the monthly dues
2. if the Tennis check box is selected
        add the additional tennis charge to the monthly dues
    end if
3. if the Racquetball check box is selected
        add the additional racquetball charge to the monthly dues
    end if
4. display the monthly dues in the duesLabel

Named constants	Data type	Value
TennisChg	Integer	20
RacquetballChg	Integer	10

Variable	Data type	Value source
monthlyDues	Integer	user input (basicFeeTextBox and procedure calculation)

Figure 4-36 Pseudocode and memory locations for the calcButton_Click procedure
© 2013 Cengage Learning

To code the calcButton_Click procedure and then test the application:

1. Open the code template for the calcButton's Click event procedure. Enter the following two comments. Press **Enter** twice after typing the second comment.

    ' calculates the monthly dues, which include
    ' a basic fee and optional additional charges

2. Enter the statements to declare the three memory locations listed in Figure 4-36. Press **Enter** twice after typing the last declaration statement.

3. The first step in the pseudocode assigns the basic fee, which is entered in the basicFeeTextBox, as the monthly dues. Enter a TryParse method that converts the contents of the text box to Integer and then stores the result in the monthlyDues variable. Press **Enter** twice after typing the TryParse method.

4. The second step in the pseudocode is a single-alternative selection structure that determines whether the Tennis check box is selected. If it is selected, the selection structure's True path should add the tennis charge to the monthly dues. Type **' add any additional charges to the monthly dues** and press **Enter**. Now enter the appropriate If...Then...Else statement.

5. Step 3 in the pseudocode is another single-alternative selection structure. This selection structure determines whether the Racquetball check box is selected. If it is selected, the selection structure's True path should add the racquetball charge to the monthly dues. Insert a **blank line** between the End If clause and the End Sub clause, and then enter the appropriate If...Then...Else statement.

6. The last step in the pseudocode displays the monthly dues in the duesLabel. Insert **two blank lines** between the second End If clause and the End Sub clause. In the blank line above the End Sub clause, type **' display the monthly dues** and press **Enter**. Now, enter the assignment statement to display the monthly dues, formatted with a dollar sign and two decimal places.

7. Save the solution and then start the application. Type **50** in the Basic monthly fee box and then click the **Racquetball** check box. Click the **Calculate Dues** button. $60.00 appears in the Monthly dues box, as shown in Figure 4-37.

Figure 4-37 Sample run of the application

8. Click the **Tennis** check box and then click the **Calculate Dues** button. The monthly dues are now $80.00.

9. Click the **Racquetball** check box to deselect it, and then click the **Calculate Dues** button. The monthly dues are now $70.00.

10. Click the **Tennis** check box to deselect it, and then click the **Calculate Dues** button. The monthly dues are now $50.00.

11. Click the **Exit** button to end the application. Close the Code Editor window and then close the solution.

Figure 4-38 shows the Greenview Health Club application's code. (You can also write the assignment statements in Lines 27 and 30 as monthlyDues = monthlyDues + TennisChg and monthlyDues = monthlyDues + RacquetballChg, respectively. Also, you can omit the "= True" from the If clause's condition in Lines 26 and 29.)

```
1 ' Project name:        Greenview Project
2 ' Project purpose:     Displays a member's monthly dues
3 ' Created/revised by:  <your name> on <current date>
4
5 Option Explicit On
6 Option Infer Off
7 Option Strict On
8
9 Public Class MainForm
10
11     Private Sub exitButton_Click(sender As Object,
        e As EventArgs) Handles exitButton.Click
12         Me.Close()
13     End Sub
14
15     Private Sub calcButton_Click(sender As Object,
        e As EventArgs) Handles calcButton.Click
16         ' calculates the monthly dues, which include
17         ' a basic fee and optional additional charges
18
19         Const TennisChg As Integer = 20
20         Const RacquetballChg As Integer = 10
21         Dim monthlyDues As Integer
22
23         Integer.TryParse(basicFeeTextBox.Text, monthlyDues)
24
25         ' add any additional charges to the monthly dues
26         If tennisCheckBox.Checked = True Then
27             monthlyDues += TennisChg
28         End If
29         If racquetballCheckBox.Checked = True Then
30             monthlyDues += RacquetballChg
31         End If
32
33         ' display the monthly dues
34         duesLabel.Text = monthlyDues.ToString("C2")
35
36     End Sub
37 End Class
```

Figure 4-38   Greenview Health Club application's code
© 2013 Cengage Learning

PROGRAMMING EXAMPLE

Edwards and Son Application

Create an interface that allows the user to enter a company's sales revenue and expenses. The interface will need to display either the company's net income (using a black font) or its net loss (using a red font). It should also display one of two messages: either "The company made a profit of *x*." or "The company experienced a loss of *x*." In both messages, *x* represents the amount of the company's profit or loss. Use the following names for the solution and project, respectively: Edwards Solution and Edwards Project. Save the application in the VbReloaded2012\Chap04 folder. Change the form file's name to Main Form.vb. See Figures 4-39 through 4-44. The image in the picture box in Figure 4-40 is stored in the VbReloaded2012\Chap04\EdwardsAndSon.png file.

Task	Object	Event
Get and display the revenue and expenses	revenueTextBox, expensesTextBox	None
1. Calculate the net income/loss 2. Display the net income (using a black font) or the net loss (using a red font) in the netLabel 3. Display an appropriate message in the messageLabel	calcButton	Click
End the application	exitButton	Click
Display the net income or net loss (from calcButton)	netLabel	None
Display the message (from calcButton)	messageLabel	None

Figure 4-39 TOE chart
© 2013 Cengage Learning

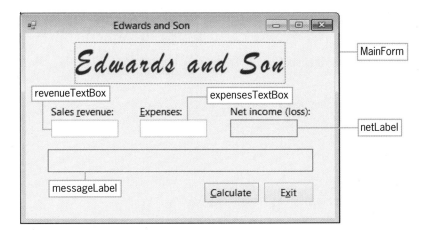

Figure 4-40 User interface

Object	Property	Setting
MainForm	AcceptButton	calcButton
	Font	Segoe UI, 11pt
	StartPosition	CenterScreen
	Text	Edwards and Son
netLabel	AutoSize	False
	BorderStyle	FixedSingle
	Text	(empty)
	TextAlign	MiddleCenter
messageLabel	AutoSize	False
	BorderStyle	FixedSingle
	Text	(empty)
	TextAlign	MiddleCenter

Figure 4-41 Objects, properties, and settings
© 2013 Cengage Learning

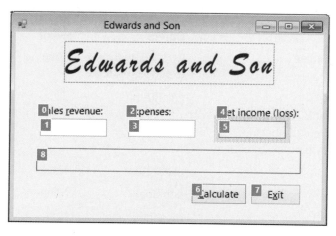

Figure 4-42 Tab order

---

calcButton Click event procedure

1. assign user input (revenue and expenses) to variables
2. calculate net = revenue − expenses
3. if net is less than 0
     display loss message and net in messageLabel
     change netLabel's font color to red
   else
     display profit message and net in messageLabel
     change netLabel's font color to black
   end if
4. display net in netLabel

Named constants	Data type	Value
ProfitMsg	String	"The company made a profit of "
LossMsg	String	"The company experienced a loss of "

Variable	Data type	Value source
revenue	Decimal	user input (revenueTextBox)
expenses	Decimal	user input (expensesTextBox)
net	Decimal	procedure calculation

Figure 4-43 Pseudocode and memory locations

© 2013 Cengage Learning

```
 1 ' Project name:          Edwards Project
 2 ' Project purpose:       Display the net income or net loss
 3 ' Created/revised by:    <your name> on <current date>
 4
 5 Option Explicit On
 6 Option Infer Off
 7 Option Strict On
 8
 9 Public Class MainForm
10
11     Private Sub exitButton_Click(sender As Object,
        e As EventArgs) Handles exitButton.Click
12         Me.Close()
13     End Sub
14
15     Private Sub calcButton_Click(sender As Object,
        e As EventArgs) Handles calcButton.Click
16         ' calculates and displays the annual net income
17
18         Const ProfitMsg As String = "The company made a profit of "
19         Const LossMsg As String = "The company experienced a loss of "
20         Dim revenue As Decimal
21         Dim expenses As Decimal
22         Dim net As Decimal
23
24         ' assign input to variables
25         Decimal.TryParse(revenueTextBox.Text, revenue)
26         Decimal.TryParse(expensesTextBox.Text, expenses)
27
28         ' calculate net
29         net = revenue - expenses
30
31         ' display net using appropriate color      be sure to enter
32         If net < 0 Then                            the negation operator
33             messageLabel.Text = LossMsg & (-net).ToString("C2") & "."
34             netLabel.ForeColor = Color.Red
35         Else
36             messageLabel.Text = ProfitMsg & net.ToString("C2") & "."
37             netLabel.ForeColor = Color.Black
38         End If
39         netLabel.Text = net.ToString("C2")
40     End Sub
41 End Class
```

Figure 4-44 Code
© 2013 Cengage Learning

Summary

- The selection structure allows a procedure to make a decision (based on some condition) and then take the appropriate action.

- There are three types of selection structures: single-alternative, dual-alternative, and multiple-alternative.

- The condition in a selection structure must evaluate to either True or False. In a single-alternative selection structure, a specific set of tasks is performed only when the condition evaluates to True. In a dual-alternative selection structure, one set of tasks is performed when the condition evaluates to True, but a different set of tasks is performed when it evaluates to False.

- A selection structure's condition is represented in a flowchart by a diamond, which is called the decision symbol. The decision symbol has one flowline entering the symbol, and two flowlines (marked with a T and an F) leaving the symbol.

- Visual Basic provides the If...Then...Else statement for coding single-alternative and dual-alternative selection structures.

- All expressions containing a comparison operator evaluate to a Boolean value: either True or False.

- Comparison operators do not have an order of precedence in Visual Basic. If an expression contains more than one comparison operator, the comparison operators are evaluated from left to right. Comparison operators are evaluated after any arithmetic operators in an expression.

- Variables declared in a statement block (for example, in the True or False path of a selection structure) have block scope and are referred to as block-level variables. A block-level variable can be used only within the statement block in which it is defined, and only after its declaration statement.

- You connect (or link) strings together using the concatenation operator, which is the ampersand (&).

- The ControlChars.NewLine constant advances the insertion point to the next line in a control.

- String comparisons in Visual Basic are case-sensitive. When comparing strings, you can use either the ToUpper method or the ToLower method to temporarily convert the strings to uppercase or lowercase, respectively.

- You can use check boxes in an interface to provide the user with one or more independent and nonexclusive items from which to choose. The value in a check box's Checked property indicates whether the check box is selected (True) or unselected (False).

- You use logical operators to combine two or more sub-conditions into one compound condition. The compound condition always evaluates to a Boolean value: either True or False.

- The AndAlso logical operator is evaluated before the OrElse logical operator in an expression.

- Logical operators are evaluated after any arithmetic and comparison operators in an expression.

- You use the pseudo-random number generator in Visual Basic to generate random numbers. The pseudo-random number generator is an object whose data type is Random.

Key Terms

&—the concatenation operator in Visual Basic

AndAlso operator—one of the logical operators in Visual Basic; when used to combine two sub-conditions, the resulting compound condition evaluates to True only when both sub-conditions evaluate to True

Block scope—the scope of a variable declared within a statement block; a variable with block scope can be used only within the statement block in which it is declared, and only after its declaration statement

Block-level variable—a variable declared within a statement block; the variable has block scope

CharacterCasing property—indicates whether the case of the text in a text box should remain as typed or be converted to either uppercase or lowercase as the user is typing

Check boxes—used in an interface to provide one or more independent and nonexclusive choices

Comparison operators—used to compare values in an expression; also called relational operators

Concatenation operator—the ampersand (&); used to concatenate strings; must be both preceded and followed by a space character

Condition—specifies the decision that must be made before further processing can occur; must be phrased so that it evaluates to a Boolean value (either True or False)

ControlChars.NewLine constant—used to advance the insertion point to the next line in a control

Data validation—the process of verifying that a program's input data is within the expected range

Decision symbol—the diamond in a flowchart; used to represent the condition in selection and repetition structures

Dual-alternative selection structure—a selection structure that requires the computer to follow one set of instructions when the structure's condition evaluates to True, but a different set of instructions when the structure's condition evaluates to False

False path—contains the instructions to be processed when a selection structure's condition evaluates to False

If...Then...Else statement—used to code single-alternative and dual-alternative selection structures in Visual Basic

Logical operators—used to combine two or more sub-conditions into one compound condition

OrElse operator—one of the logical operators in Visual Basic; when used to combine two sub-conditions, the resulting compound condition evaluates to False only when both sub-conditions evaluate to False

Pseudo-random number generator—a device that produces a sequence of numbers that meet certain statistical requirements for randomness; the pseudo-random number generator in Visual Basic is an object whose data type is Random

Random object—represents the pseudo-random number generator in Visual Basic

Random.Next method—used to generate a random integer that is greater than or equal to a minimum value, but less than a maximum value

Selection structure—one of the three basic control structures; tells the computer to make a decision based on some condition and then select the appropriate action; also called the decision structure

Short-circuit evaluation—refers to the way the computer evaluates the second of two sub-conditions connected by a logical operator; when the logical operator is AndAlso, the computer does not evaluate sub-condition2 when sub-condition1 evaluates to False; when the logical operator is OrElse, the computer does not evaluate sub-condition2 when sub-condition1 evaluates to True

Single-alternative selection structure—a selection structure that requires the computer to follow a special set of instructions *only* when the structure's condition evaluates to True

Statement block—in a selection structure, the set of statements terminated by either an Else clause or an End If clause

ToLower method—temporarily converts a string to lowercase

ToUpper method—temporarily converts a string to uppercase

True path—contains the instructions to be processed when a selection structure's condition evaluates to True

Truth tables—tables that summarize how the computer evaluates the logical operators in an expression

Each Review Question is associated with one or more objectives listed at the beginning of the chapter.

Review Questions

1. Which of the following is a valid condition for an If...Then...Else statement? (3, 4, 10)

   a. `priceLabel.Text > 0 AndAlso priceLabel.Text < 10`

   b. `age > 30 OrElse < 50`

   c. `number > 100 AndAlso number <= 1000`

   d. `state.ToUpper = "Alaska" OrElse state.ToUpper = "Hawaii"`

2. Which of the following conditions should you use to compare the contents of the firstTextBox with the name Joe? Be sure the condition will handle Joe, JOE, joe, and so on. (3, 4, 10)

   a. `firstTextBox.Text = ToUpper("JOE")`

   b. `firstTextBox.Text = ToUpper("Joe")`

   c. `ToUpper(firstTextBox.Text) = "JOE"`

   d. `firstTextBox.Text.ToUpper = "JOE"`

3. The expression 3 < 6 AndAlso 7 > 4 evaluates to _____. (4)

   a. True

   b. False

4. The computer will perform short-circuit evaluation when processing which of the following If clauses? (3, 4)

   a. `If 3 * 2 < 4 AndAlso 5 > 3 Then`

   b. `If 6 < 9 OrElse 5 > 3 Then`

   c. `If 12 > 4 * 4 AndAlso 6 < 2 Then`

   d. all of the above

5. The expression 7 >= 3 + 4 AndAlso 6 < 4 OrElse 2 < 5 evaluates to _____. (4)

   a. True

   b. False

6. The expression 5 * 3 > 3 ^ 2 AndAlso True OrElse False evaluates to _____. (4)

   a. True

   b. False

7. Which of the following generates a random integer from 10 to 55, inclusive? The Random object is named randGen. (12)

   a. `randGen.Next(10, 56)`

   b. `randGen.Next(10, 55)`

   c. `randGen.Next(9, 55)`

   d. `randGen.Next(9, 56)`

8. The city and state variables contain the strings "Boston" and "MA", respectively. Which of the following will display the string "Boston, MA" (the city, a comma, a space, and the state) in the addressLabel? (8)

   a. `addressLabel.Text = "city" & ", " & "state"`

   b. `addressLabel.Text = city $ ", " $ state`

   c. `addressLabel.Text = city & ", " & state`

   d. `addressLabel.Text = "city," & "state"`

9. A procedure contains an If...Then...Else statement. If the **x** variable is declared immediately after the statement's `Else` clause, where can the variable be used? (3, 7)

   a. in any instruction in the entire procedure
   b. in any instruction after the declaration statement in the procedure
   c. in any instruction in the False path
   d. in any instruction in the If...Then...Else statement

10. Which of the following conditions evaluates to True when the `initial` variable contains the letter A in either uppercase or lowercase? (4)

    a. `initial = "A" OrElse initial = "a"`
    b. `initial = "A" AndAlso initial = "a"`
    c. `initial = "A" OrElse "a"`
    d. `initial = "A" AndAlso "a"`

Each Exercise, except the DISCOVERY exercise, is associated with one or more objectives listed at the beginning of the chapter.

Exercises

 Pencil and Paper

1. Draw the flowchart that corresponds to the pseudocode shown here. (1, 3, 4)

   INTRODUCTORY

   if the years employed are less than or equal to 2
       display "1 week vacation"
   else
       display "2 weeks vacation"
   end if

2. Write the If...Then...Else statement that corresponds to the partial flowchart shown in Figure 4-45. Use the following variable names: **sold** and **bonus**. Display the appropriate message and bonus amount (formatted with a dollar sign and two decimal places) in the messageLabel. (1, 3, 4)

   INTRODUCTORY

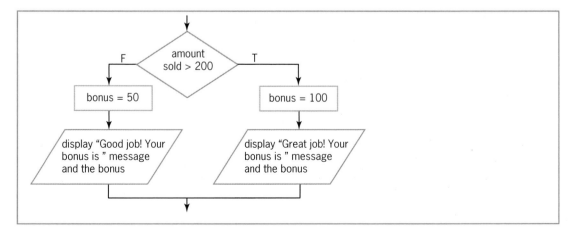

Figure 4-45 Partial flowchart
© 2013 Cengage Learning

INTRODUCTORY

3. Write an If...Then...Else statement that displays the string "350Z" in the carLabel when the carTextBox contains the string "Nissan" (entered using any case). (3, 4, 10)

INTRODUCTORY

4. Write an If...Then...Else statement that displays the string "Reorder" in the messageLabel when the quantity variable's value is less than 10; otherwise, display the string "Sufficient quantity". (3, 4)

INTRODUCTORY

5. Write an If...Then...Else statement that assigns the number 25 to the bonus variable when the sales variable's value is less than or equal to $500; otherwise, assign the number 40. (3, 4)

INTRODUCTORY

6. Write an If...Then...Else statement that assigns the number 100 to the shipping variable when the state variable contains the string "Hawaii" (entered using any case); otherwise, assign the number 65. (3, 4, 10)

INTRODUCTORY

7. Write an If...Then...Else statement that assigns the number 15 to the reward variable when the state variable contains the string "IL" (entered using any case) and the sales variable contains a number that is greater than 2000; otherwise, assign the number 5. (3, 4, 10)

INTRODUCTORY

8. Write an If...Then...Else statement that displays the string "Winner" in the messageLabel when the status variable contains either the uppercase letter X or the uppercase letter Y. (3, 4, 10)

INTERMEDIATE

9. Write an If...Then...Else statement that displays the string "Please enter your ZIP code" in the messageLabel when the zipTextBox does not contain any data. (3, 4)

INTERMEDIATE

10. Write an If...Then...Else statement that calculates a 5% sales tax when the code variable contains the string "3", and calculates a 4.5% sales tax when the code variable contains anything other than "3". Calculate the sales tax by multiplying the tax rate by the contents of the Double sales variable. Assign the sales tax to the Double tax variable. Also write the code to display the sales tax in the taxLabel. Display the sales tax with a dollar sign and two decimal places. (3, 4)

ADVANCED

11. Figure 4-18 in the chapter shows two versions of the calcButton_Click procedure for the Halloway Products application. Research the Not logical operator. Then use it to rewrite the If...Then...Else statement shown in Version 2 in Figure 4-18. (3, 4, 11)

Computer

MODIFY THIS

12. If necessary, complete the Greenview Health Club application from this chapter's Programming Tutorial 2, and then close the solution. Use Windows to make a copy of the Greenview Solution folder. Rename the folder Greenview Solution-ModifyThis. Open the Greenview Solution (Greenview Solution.sln) file contained in the Greenview Solution-ModifyThis folder. Include a Golf check box in the interface. The monthly charge for using the golf course is $35. Modify the application's code. Save the solution and then start and test the application. Close the solution. (3, 4, 11)

MODIFY THIS

13. In this exercise, you modify the Color Mixer application from Chapter 3's Programming Tutorial 1. Open the Color Mixer Solution (Color Mixer Solution.sln) file contained in the VbReloaded2012\Chap04\Color Mixer Solution folder. Add a label at the bottom of the form. Change the label's Name property to messageLabel, and then remove its Text property value. (If necessary, you can use the Properties window's Object box to access the label.) Modify the View Color button's Click event procedure so that it uses one dual-alternative selection structure to determine whether the RGB entries are valid. A valid entry is a number from 0 through 255. If one or more entries are not valid, display the message "Invalid color code" in the messageLabel; otherwise, change the oval shape

to the appropriate color and remove any message from the messageLabel. Save the solution and then start and test the application. Close the solution. (3, 4)

14. Open the Math Solution (Math Solution.sln) file contained in the VbReloaded2012\ Chap04\ Math Solution folder. Change the operationTextBox's CharacterCasing property to Upper. Open the Code Editor window and remove the ToUpper method from the assignment statement. Save the solution and then start and test the application. Close the solution. (10)

MODIFY THIS

15. Open the Random Swap Solution (Random Swap Solution.sln) file contained in the VbReloaded2012\Chap04\Random Swap Solution folder. The application should generate two random integers from 1 through 250. It then should display the lowest and highest integer in the interface. Draw the flowchart for the generateButton_Click procedure and then code the procedure. Save the solution and then start and test the application. Close the solution. (1-4, 6, 7, 12)

INTRODUCTORY

16. Open the Bonus Solution (Bonus Solution.sln) file contained in the VbReloaded2012\ Chap04\Bonus Solution folder. The application should calculate and display a salesperson's bonus. Salespeople selling more than $3,500 receive a 5% bonus; otherwise, the bonus rate is 4%. Display the bonus with a dollar sign and two decimal places. Write the pseudocode for the calcButton_Click procedure and then code the procedure. Save the solution and then start and test the application. Close the solution. (1-4)

INTRODUCTORY

17. Open the Quotient Solution (Quotient Solution.sln) file contained in the VbReloaded2012\ Chap04\Quotient Solution folder. The application should display the result of dividing the number contained in the first text box by the number contained in the second text box. Display the result with two decimal places. Write the pseudocode for the Calculate button's Click event procedure and then code the procedure. Save the solution and then start and test the application. Be sure to test the application using both valid and invalid data. Close the solution. (1-5)

INTRODUCTORY

18. Open the Mount Rushmore Solution (Mount Rushmore Solution.sln) file contained in the VbReloaded2012\Chap04\Mount Rushmore Solution folder. The Display (AndAlso) and Display (OrElse) buttons should display the message "On Mount Rushmore" when the user enters the name of any of the four Mount Rushmore presidents; otherwise, they should display the message "Not on Mount Rushmore". Use the AndAlso operator in the Display (AndAlso) button's Click event procedure. Use the OrElse operator in the Display (OrElse) button's Click event procedure. Save the solution and then start and test the application. Close the solution. (2-4, 10)

INTRODUCTORY

19. Open the Computer Workshop Solution (Computer Workshop Solution.sln) file contained in the VbReloaded2012\Chap04\Computer Workshop Solution folder. Computer Workshop offers programming seminars to companies. The price per person depends on the number of people the company registers. The price for the first 10 registrants is $80 per person; thereafter, it is $70 per person. Therefore, if the company registers seven people, the total cost is $560. If the company registers 12 people, the total cost is $940. Display the total cost (formatted with a dollar sign and no decimal places) in the totalLabel. Save the solution and then start and test the application. Close the solution. (2-4)

INTERMEDIATE

20. Tea Time Company wants an application that allows a clerk to enter the number of pounds of tea ordered. The price per pound is $11.25. Use a check box to specify whether the customer should receive a 10% discount on his or her purchase. Also use a check box to specify whether the customer should be charged a $5 shipping fee. The application should calculate and display the total amount the customer owes. Create a Visual Basic Windows application. Use the following names for the solution and project, respectively: Tea Time Solution and Tea Time Project. Save the application in the VbReloaded2012\Chap04 folder. Change the form file's name to Main Form.vb. Code the application. Save the solution and then start and test the application. Close the Code Editor window and then close the solution. (1-4, 11)

INTERMEDIATE

INTERMEDIATE

21. Create an application that generates and displays six lottery numbers. Each lottery number can range from 1 through 54 only. (An example of six lottery numbers would be: 4, 8, 35, 15, 20, 3.) Create a Windows application. Use the following names for the solution and project, respectively: Lottery Solution and Lottery Project. Save the application in the VbReloaded2012\Chap04 folder. Change the form file's name to Main Form.vb. Build an appropriate interface. Code the application. For now, do not worry if the lottery numbers are not unique. You will learn how to display unique numbers in Chapter 9 in this book. Save the solution and then start and test the application. Close the solution. (8, 12)

INTERMEDIATE

22. Open the Shipping Solution (Shipping Solution.sln) file contained in the VbReloaded2012\Chap04\Shipping Solution folder. The application should display the appropriate shipping charge. The shipping charge for the following ZIP codes is $32: 60618, 60620, and 60632. All other ZIP codes are charged $37.75. Code the application. Save the solution and then start and test the application. Close the solution. (2-4)

INTERMEDIATE

23. In this exercise, you modify the Just Paper application from Chapter 3's Programming Example. Open the Just Paper Solution (Just Paper Solution.sln) file contained in the VbReloaded2012\Chap04\Just Paper Solution folder. Add a check box to the form. Change the text box's Name property to discountCheckBox, and change its Text property to &20% discount. Modify the code to give customers a 20% discount when the check box is selected. Deselect the check box when the Clear Order button is clicked. Save the solution and then start and test the application. Close the solution. (2-4, 11)

INTERMEDIATE

24. In this exercise, you modify the Color Game application from Chapter 2's Programming Tutorial 1. Open the Color Game Solution (Color Game Solution.sln) file contained in the VbReloaded2012\Chap04\Color Game Solution folder. Add a check box to the form. When the user selects the check box, its Click event procedure should change the Text property of each color button to the appropriate Spanish word, and also change each color button's BackColor property to Color.White. When the user deselects the check box, its Click event procedure should change the Text property of each color button to the appropriate English word, and also change each color button's BackColor property to Color.White. If the check box is not selected, each color button's Click event procedure should display the appropriate Spanish word (as each does now). However, if the check box is selected, each color button's Click event procedure should display the appropriate English word. The Start Over button should also display the appropriate English or Spanish words when it is clicked. Make the appropriate modifications to the code. Save the solution and then start and test the application. Close the solution. (2-4, 11)

INTERMEDIATE

25. Create an application that calculates and displays the area of a floor in either one or both of the following measurements: square feet or square yards. Use two check boxes to allow the user to select the measurement type: one labeled Square feet and one labeled Square yards. The user will enter the floor's measurements in feet. Create a Visual Basic Windows application. Use the following names for the solution and project, respectively: Carpet Solution and Carpet Project. Save the application in the VbReloaded2012\Chap04 folder. Change the form file's name to Main Form.vb. Create the interface and then code the application. Save the solution and then start and test the application. Close the solution. (1-4, 11)

INTERMEDIATE

26. Create an application that calculates a customer's water bill for the Canton Water Department. The user will enter the current meter reading and the previous meter reading. The application should calculate and display the number of gallons of water used and the total charge for the water. The charge for water is $1.75 per 1000 gallons, or .00175 per gallon. However, there is a minimum charge of $19.50. In other words, every customer must pay at least $19.50. Display the total charge with a dollar sign and two decimal places. Use the following names for the solution and project, respectively: Canton Solution and Canton Project. Save the solution in the VbReloaded2012\Chap04 folder. Change the form

file's name to Main Form.vb. Create the interface and then code the application. Save the solution and then start and test the application. Close the solution. (1-4)

27. Marcy's is having a BoGoHo (Buy One, Get One Half Off) sale. Create an application that allows the user to enter the prices of two items. The application should calculate the total owed and the amount the customer saved. The half-off should always be taken on the item having the lowest price. For example, if one item costs $24.99 and the second item costs $12.50, the $12.50 item would be half off. (In other words, the item would cost $6.25.) Use the following names for the solution and project, respectively: Marcy Solution and Marcy Project. Save the solution in the VbReloaded2012\Chap04 folder. Change the form file's name to Main Form.vb. Create the interface and then code the application. Save the solution and then start and test the application. Close the solution. (1-4)

INTERMEDIATE

28. Open the Color Mixer Solution (Color Mixer Solution.sln) file contained in the VbReloaded2012\Chap04\Color Mixer Solution-Advanced folder. Add a label at the bottom of the form. Change the label's Name property to messageLabel. Remove its Text property value. (If necessary, you can use the Properties window's Object box to access the label.) Modify the View Color button's Click event procedure so that it determines whether each RGB entry is valid. A valid entry is a number from 0 through 255. If the Red entry is invalid, display the message "Invalid Red code" in the messageLabel. If the Green entry is invalid, display the message "Invalid Green code" in the messageLabel. If the Blue entry is invalid, display the message "Invalid Blue code" in the messageLabel. If more than one entry is incorrect, the messageLabel should display each message on a separate line. Change the oval shape to the appropriate color only when all three entries are correct. Save the solution and then start and test the application. Close the solution. (2-4, 8, 9)

ADVANCED

29. In this exercise, you will learn how to generate and display random real numbers, which are numbers that contain a decimal place. Open the Random Float Solution (Random Float Solution.sln) file contained in the VbReloaded2012\Chap04\Random Float Solution folder.

DISCOVERY

a. You can use the Random.NextDouble method to return a random real number that is greater than or equal to 0.0, but less than 1.0. The method's syntax is *randomObjectName*.NextDouble. Code the Display Random Number button's Click event procedure so that it displays a random real number in the numberLabel. Save the solution and then start the application. Click the Display Random Number button several times. Each time you click the button, a random number that is greater than or equal to 0.0 but less than 1.0 appears in the numberLabel. Click the Exit button to end the application.

b. You can use the following formula to generate random real numbers within a specified range: (*maxValue* – *minValue* + 1.0) * *randomObjectName*.NextDouble + *minValue*. For example, the formula (10.0 – 1.0 + 1.0) * randomGenerator.NextDouble + 1.0 generates real numbers that are greater than or equal to 1.0, but less than 11.0. Modify the Display Random Number button's Click event procedure so that it displays a random real number that is greater than or equal to 25.0 but less than 51.0. Display two decimal places in the number. Save the solution and then start the application. Click the Display Random Number button several times to verify that the code you entered is working correctly. Close the solution.

30. Open the Debug Solution (Debug Solution.sln) file contained in the VbReloaded2012\Chap04\Debug Solution folder. Read the comments in the Code Editor window. Start and then test the application. Locate and then correct any errors. When the application is working correctly, close the solution. (3, 4)

SWAT THE BUGS

Case Projects

FICA Tax Calculator

When you either work for an employer or are self-employed, you must pay payroll taxes that fund Social Security and Medicare. These taxes are called FICA taxes because they are collected under the authority of the Federal Insurance Contributions Act. The 2013 FICA tax rate is 7.65% of your gross earnings for the year. The 7.65% includes a 6.2% contribution to the Old-Age, Survivors, and Disability Insurance (OASDI) program and a 1.45% contribution to Medicare's Hospital Insurance (HI) program. The 6.2% contribution is on the first $113,700 of earnings for the year; there is no earnings limit for the 1.45%. Create an application that calculates and displays the FICA tax to deduct from the current pay period's check. Use the following names for the solution and project, respectively: FICA Solution and FICA Project. Save the application in the VbReloaded2012\Chap04 folder. Change the form file's name to Main Form.vb. The interface should allow the user to enter two values: the user's current year-to-date earnings (which do not include the current pay period) and the earnings for the current pay period. You can either create your own user interface or create the one shown in Figure 4-46. The image in the picture box is stored in the VbReloaded2012\ Chap04\FICA.png file. (1-4)

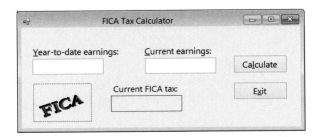

Figure 4-46   Sample interface for the FICA Tax Calculator application

Novelty Warehouse

Novelty Warehouse needs an application that allows the user to enter an item's price. When the user clicks a button in the interface, the button's Click event procedure should add the price to the total of the prices already entered; this amount represents the subtotal owed by the customer. The application should display the subtotal on the screen. It also should display a 3% sales tax, the shipping charge, and the grand total owed by the customer. The grand total is calculated by adding together the subtotal, the 3% sales tax, and a $15 shipping charge. For example, if the user enters 26.75 as the price and then clicks the button, the button's Click event procedure should display 26.75 as the subtotal, 0.80 as the sales tax, 15.00 as the shipping charge, and 42.55 as the grand total. If the user subsequently enters 30 as the price and then clicks the button, the button's Click event procedure should display 56.75 as the subtotal, 1.70 as the sales tax, 15.00 as the shipping charge, and 73.45 as the grand total. However, when the subtotal is at least $100, the shipping charge is 0 (zero). Use the following names for the solution and project, respectively: Novelty Solution and Novelty Project. Save the solution in the VbReloaded2012\ Chap04 folder. Change the form file's name to Main Form.vb. You can either create your own user interface or create the one shown in Figure 4-47. (1-4)

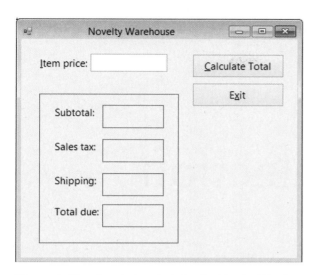

Figure 4-47   Sample interface for the Novelty Warehouse application

 ## Addition Practice

Create an application that displays two random integers from 1 through 10 in the interface. The application should allow the user to enter the sum of both numbers. It then should check whether the user's answer is correct. Display an appropriate message (or image) when the answer is correct. Also display an appropriate message (or image) when the answer is incorrect. Use the following names for the solution and project, respectively: Addition Practice Solution and Addition Practice Project. Save the solution in the VbReloaded2012\Chap04 folder. Change the form file's name to Main Form.vb. (1-4, 12)

 ## Sunflower Resort

Create a reservation application for Sunflower Resort. The application should allow the user to enter the following information: the number of rooms to reserve, the length of stay (in nights), the number of adult guests, and the number of child guests. Each room can accommodate a maximum of six guests. If the number of rooms reserved is less than the number of rooms required, the application should display the message "You have exceeded the maximum guests per room." The resort charges $284 per room per night. It also charges a 15.25% sales and lodging tax, which is based on the room charge. In addition, there is a $15 resort fee per room per night. The application should display the total room charge, the sales and lodging tax, the resort fee, and the total due. Use the following names for the solution and project, respectively: Sunflower Solution and Sunflower Project. Save the solution in the VbReloaded2012\Chap04 folder. Change the form file's name to Main Form.vb. (1-4)

CHAPTER 5

More on the Selection Structure

After studying Chapter 5, you should be able to:

1 Determine whether a solution requires a nested selection structure

2 Include a nested selection structure in pseudocode and in a flowchart

3 Code a nested selection structure

4 Determine whether a solution requires a multiple-alternative selection structure

5 Include a multiple-alternative selection structure in pseudocode and in a flowchart

6 Code a multiple-alternative selection structure

7 Include radio buttons in an interface

8 Display a message in a message box

9 Use a message box's return value

10 Prevent the entry of invalid characters in a text box

Reading and Study Guide

Before you begin reading Chapter 5, view the Ch05_ReadingStudyGuide.pdf file. You can open the file using Adobe Reader, which is available for free on the Adobe Web site at *www.adobe.com/downloads/*.

Making More than One Decision

As you learned in Chapter 4, you use the selection structure when you want the computer to evaluate a condition and then take the appropriate action based on the result. The appropriate action is contained in either the selection structure's True path or its False path. Both paths in a selection structure can include instructions that declare variables, perform calculations, and so on. In this chapter, you will learn that both paths can also include other selection structures. When either a selection structure's True path or its False path contains another selection structure, the inner selection structure is referred to as a **nested selection structure** because it is contained (nested) within the outer selection structure.

The only way to determine whether a problem's solution requires a nested selection structure is by studying the problem specification. The first problem specification you will examine in this chapter involves a basketball player named Derek. The problem specification and an illustration of the problem are shown in Figure 5-1, along with an appropriate solution. The solution requires a selection structure, but not a nested one. This is because only one decision—whether the basketball went through the hoop—is necessary. The selection structure's condition is shaded in the figure.

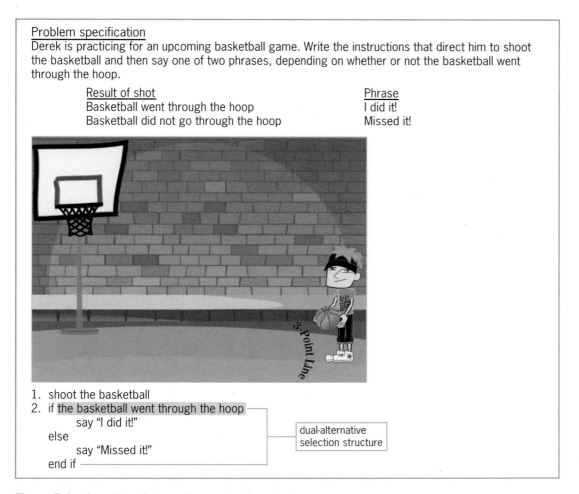

Problem specification
Derek is practicing for an upcoming basketball game. Write the instructions that direct him to shoot the basketball and then say one of two phrases, depending on whether or not the basketball went through the hoop.

Result of shot	Phrase
Basketball went through the hoop	I did it!
Basketball did not go through the hoop	Missed it!

1. shoot the basketball
2. if the basketball went through the hoop
        say "I did it!"
   else
        say "Missed it!"
   end if

dual-alternative selection structure

Figure 5-1   A problem that requires a selection structure
Image by Diane Zak; Created with Reallusion CrazyTalk Animator

Now we'll make a slight change to the problem specification. This time, Derek should say either one or two phrases, depending not only on whether or not the ball went through the hoop, but also on where he was standing when he made the basket. Figure 5-2 shows the modified problem specification and solution. The modified solution contains an outer dual-alternative selection structure and a nested dual-alternative selection structure. The conditions in both selection structures are shaded in the figure. For a nested selection structure to work correctly, it must be contained entirely within either the outer selection structure's True path or its False path. The nested selection structure in Figure 5-2 appears entirely within the outer selection structure's True path.

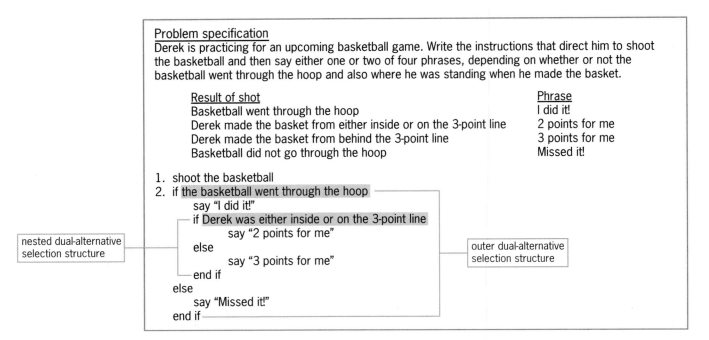

Figure 5-2   A problem that requires a nested selection structure
© 2013 Cengage Learning

Figure 5-3 shows a modified version of the previous problem specification, along with the modified solution. In this version of the problem, Derek should still say "Missed it!" when the basketball misses its target. However, if the basketball hits the rim, he should also say "So close". In addition to the nested dual-alternative selection structure from the previous solution, the modified solution also contains a nested single-alternative selection structure. The nested single-alternative selection structure is contained entirely within the outer selection structure's False path.

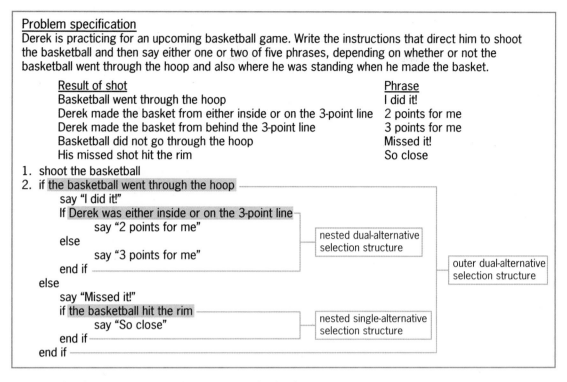

Figure 5-3 A problem that requires two nested selection structures
© 2013 Cengage Learning

The Concord Steaks Application

Figure 5-4 shows the problem specification for the Concord Steaks application, which calculates the total amount a customer owes, including shipping. The shipping charge depends on two items: the subtotal and the club membership. If the subtotal is greater than $79, the order ships for free. However, if the subtotal is not greater than $79, the shipping charge depends on whether the customer is a member of the company's Shipping Club. If the customer *is* a member, the shipping charge is $10; otherwise, it's $20. Notice that determining the club membership status is important only *after* the subtotal is determined. Because of this, the decision regarding the subtotal is considered the primary decision, while the decision regarding the club membership status is considered the secondary decision because whether it needs to be made depends on the result of the primary decision. A primary decision is always made by an outer selection structure, while a secondary decision is always made by a nested selection structure.

Also included in Figure 5-4 is a correct solution to the problem in flowchart form. The first diamond represents the outer selection structure's condition, which checks whether the subtotal is greater than $79. If the condition evaluates to True, the outer selection structure's True path assigns the number 0 as the shipping. If the outer selection structure's condition evaluates to False, on the other hand, the nested selection structure determines the customer's club membership status. The nested selection structure's condition is represented by the second diamond in the figure. If the customer is a club member, the nested selection structure's True path assigns $10 as the shipping; otherwise, its False path assigns $20. After the appropriate shipping charge is assigned, both selection structures end. Then, the total amount owed is calculated and displayed. Notice that the nested selection structure is processed only when the outer selection structure's condition evaluates to False.

244

Problem specification
The Concord Steaks company sells steaks by the box. Each box contains two steaks and costs $19.99. The company wants an application that allows the user to enter the number of boxes a customer orders. The application should calculate the subtotal, shipping, and total owed. The subtotal is calculated by multiplying the number of boxes ordered by the price per box. The total owed is calculated by adding the shipping charge (if any) to the subtotal. The shipping charges are shown here:

Shipping	Criteria
$0	subtotal is greater than $79
$10	subtotal is not greater than $79, but the customer belongs to the company's Shipping Club
$20	subtotal is not greater than $79, and the customer does not belong to the company's Shipping Club

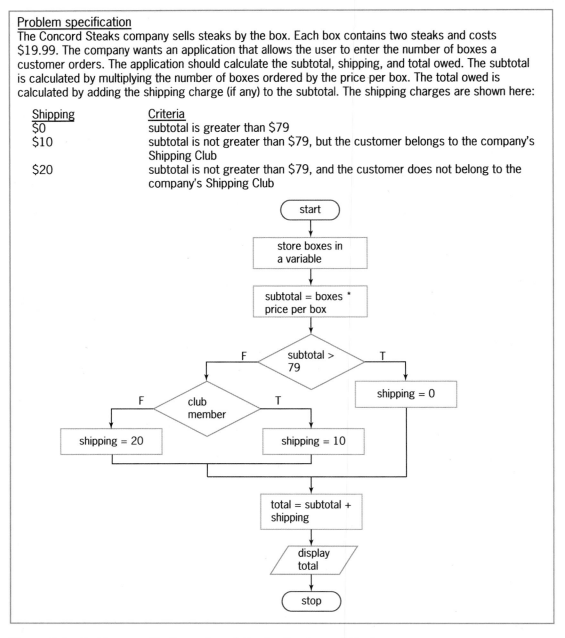

Figure 5-4   Problem specification and a solution for the Concord Steaks company
© 2013 Cengage Learning

Even small procedures can have more than one solution. Figure 5-5 shows another correct solution, also in flowchart form. As in the previous solution, the outer selection structure in this solution determines the subtotal (the primary decision), and the nested selection structure determines the club membership status (the secondary decision). In this solution, however, the outer selection structure's condition is the opposite of the one in Figure 5-4: It checks whether the subtotal is less than or equal to 79, rather than checking if it is greater than 79. (Recall that *less than or equal to* is the opposite of *greater than*.) In addition, the nested selection structure appears in the outer selection structure's True path in this solution, which means it will be processed only when the outer selection structure's condition evaluates to True. The solutions in Figures 5-4 and 5-5 produce the same result. Neither solution is better than the other; each simply represents a different way of solving the same problem.

Problem specification
The Concord Steaks company sells steaks by the box. Each box contains two steaks and costs $19.99. The company wants an application that allows the user to enter the number of boxes a customer orders. The application should calculate the subtotal, shipping, and total owed. The subtotal is calculated by multiplying the number of boxes ordered by the price per box. The total owed is calculated by adding the shipping charge (if any) to the subtotal. The shipping charges are shown here:

Shipping	Criteria
$0	subtotal is greater than $79
$10	subtotal is not greater than $79, but the customer belongs to the company's Shipping Club
$20	subtotal is not greater than $79, and the customer does not belong to the company's Shipping Club

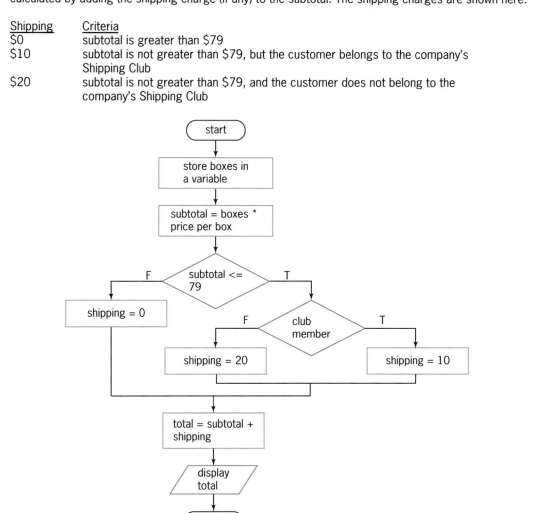

Figure 5-5   Another correct solution for the Concord Steaks company
© 2013 Cengage Learning

Figure 5-6 shows the code corresponding to the flowcharts in Figures 5-4 and 5-5. It also includes a sample run of the application.

246

Example 1 – code for the flowchart in Figure 5-4

```vb
Private Sub calcButton_Click(sender As Object,
e As EventArgs) Handles calcButton.Click
    ' calculates the total amount owed

    Const PricePerBox As Double = 19.99
    Dim boxes As Integer
    Dim subtotal As Double
    Dim shipping As Integer
    Dim total As Double

    Integer.TryParse(boxesTextBox.Text, boxes)
    subtotal = boxes * PricePerBox

    ' determine shipping
    If subtotal > 79 Then
        shipping = 0
    Else
        If clubCheckBox.Checked Then
            shipping = 10
        Else
            shipping = 20
        End If
    End If
    ' calculate and display total owed
    total = subtotal + shipping
    totalLabel.Text = total.ToString("C2")
End Sub
```

nested selection structure in the False path

Example 2 – code for the flowchart in Figure 5-5

```vb
Private Sub calcButton_Click(sender As Object,
e As EventArgs) Handles calcButton.Click
    ' calculates the total amount owed

    Const PricePerBox As Double = 19.99
    Dim boxes As Integer
    Dim subtotal As Double
    Dim shipping As Integer
    Dim total As Double

    Integer.TryParse(boxesTextBox.Text, boxes)
    subtotal = boxes * PricePerBox

    ' determine shipping
    If subtotal <= 79 Then
        If clubCheckBox.Checked Then
            shipping = 10
        Else
            shipping = 20
        End If
    Else
        shipping = 0
    End If
    ' calculate and display total owed
    total = subtotal + shipping
    totalLabel.Text = total.ToString("C2")
End Sub
```

nested selection structure in the True path

Figure 5-6   Code and sample run for the flowcharts in Figures 5-4 and 5-5 *(continues)*

(continued)

Figure 5-6 Code and sample run for the flowcharts in Figures 5-4 and 5-5
© 2013 Cengage Learning

If you want to experiment with the Concord Steaks application, open the solution contained in the Try It 1! folder.

Mini-Quiz 5-1

1. The manager of a golf club wants an application that displays the appropriate fee to charge a golfer. Club members pay a $5 fee. Non-members golfing on Monday through Thursday pay $15. Non-members golfing on Friday through Sunday pay $25. The condition in the outer selection structure should check the ——————, while the condition in its nested selection structure should check the ——————. (1)

    a. membership status, day of the week
    b. day of the week, membership status
    c. membership status, fee
    d. fee, day of the week

2. Write the pseudocode for the outer and nested selection structures from Question 1. (2)

3. Draw a flowchart for the outer and nested selection structures from Question 1. (2)

4. Write the Visual Basic code corresponding to the selection structures from Questions 2 and 3. If the memberCheckBox in the interface is selected, it means that the person is a member. The day of the week is stored in an Integer variable named **dayNum**. The **dayNum** values range from 1 (Monday) through 7 (Sunday). Display the fee in the feeLabel. (3)

The answers to Mini-Quiz questions are located in Appendix A. Each question is associated with one or more objectives listed at the beginning of the chapter.

Multiple-Alternative Selection Structures

Figure 5-7 shows the problem specification for the Yardley Theater application, which displays either the price of a ticket or an error message. The ticket price is based on a code entered by the user; the valid codes are 1, 2, 3, and 4. In order to display the appropriate output, the application will need to use a **multiple-alternative selection structure**, which is a selection structure that can choose from several alternatives—in this case, from several ticket codes. Multiple-alternative selection structures are also referred to as **extended selection structures**. Figure 5-7 also shows the pseudocode and flowchart for a procedure that will display the appropriate output.

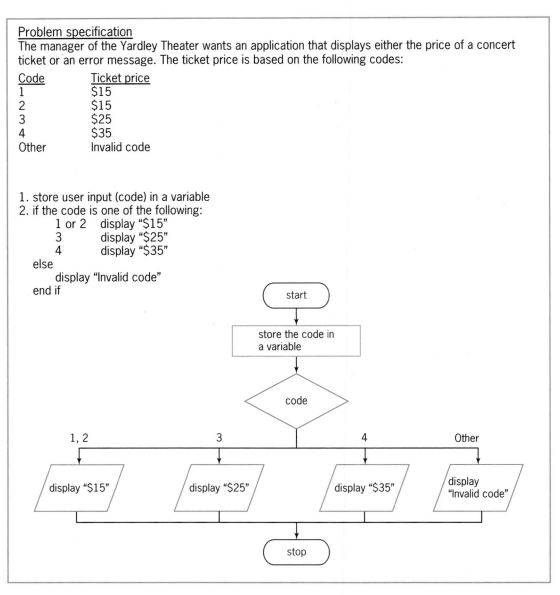

Problem specification
The manager of the Yardley Theater wants an application that displays either the price of a concert ticket or an error message. The ticket price is based on the following codes:

Code	Ticket price
1	$15
2	$15
3	$25
4	$35
Other	Invalid code

1. store user input (code) in a variable
2. if the code is one of the following:
      1 or 2   display "$15"
         3   display "$25"
         4   display "$35"
   else
      display "Invalid code"
   end if

Figure 5-7 Problem specification and a solution for the Yardley Theater application
© 2013 Cengage Learning

The diamond in the flowchart in Figure 5-7 represents the multiple-alternative selection structure's condition. As you already know, the diamond is also used to represent the condition in both the single-alternative and dual-alternative selection structures. However, unlike the diamond in both of those selection structures, the diamond in a multiple-alternative selection structure has several flowlines (rather than only two flowlines) leading out of the symbol. Each flowline represents a possible path and must be marked appropriately, indicating the value(s) necessary for the path to be chosen.

Figure 5-8 shows two ways of using the If...Then...Else statement to code the pseudocode and flowchart from Figure 5-7. Both versions of the code produce the same result. The second version is simply a more convenient and compact way of writing a multiple-alternative selection structure.

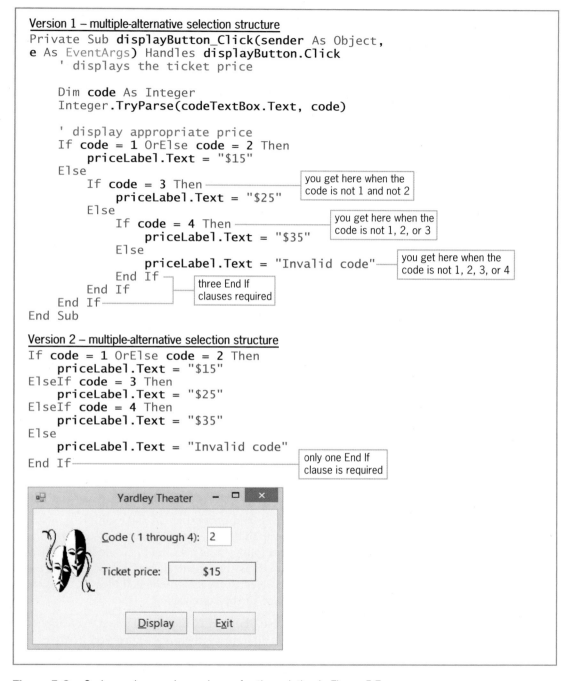

```
Version 1 – multiple-alternative selection structure
Private Sub displayButton_Click(sender As Object,
e As EventArgs) Handles displayButton.Click
    ' displays the ticket price

    Dim code As Integer
    Integer.TryParse(codeTextBox.Text, code)

    ' display appropriate price
    If code = 1 OrElse code = 2 Then
        priceLabel.Text = "$15"
    Else
        If code = 3 Then ───────────  you get here when the
            priceLabel.Text = "$25"    code is not 1 and not 2
        Else
            If code = 4 Then ───────  you get here when the
                priceLabel.Text = "$35"  code is not 1, 2, or 3
            Else
                priceLabel.Text = "Invalid code" ──  you get here when the
            End If ─┐                                 code is not 1, 2, 3, or 4
        End If      │  three End If
    End If ─────────┘  clauses required
End Sub
```

```
Version 2 – multiple-alternative selection structure
If code = 1 OrElse code = 2 Then
    priceLabel.Text = "$15"
ElseIf code = 3 Then
    priceLabel.Text = "$25"
ElseIf code = 4 Then
    priceLabel.Text = "$35"
Else
    priceLabel.Text = "Invalid code"
End If ─────────────  only one End If
                      clause is required
```

Yardley Theater

Code (1 through 4): 2

Ticket price: $15

Display   Exit

If you want to try using the If...Then...Else statement in the Yardley Theater application, open the solution contained in the Try It 2! folder.

Figure 5-8 Code versions and sample run for the solution in Figure 5-7
© 2013 Cengage Learning

The Select Case Statement

When a multiple-alternative selection structure has many paths from which to choose, it is often simpler and clearer to code the selection structure using the **Select Case statement** rather than several If...Then...Else statements. The Select Case statement's syntax is shown in Figure 5-9. The figure also shows how you can use the Select Case statement to code the multiple-alternative selection structure from Figure 5-7.

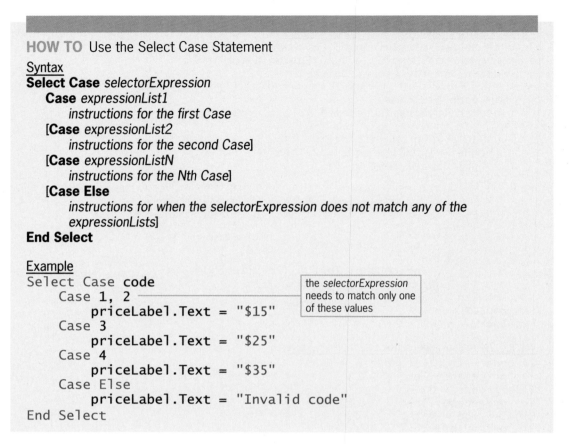

HOW TO Use the Select Case Statement

Syntax
Select Case *selectorExpression*
    Case *expressionList1*
        instructions for the first Case
    [**Case** *expressionList2*
        instructions for the second Case]
    [**Case** *expressionListN*
        instructions for the Nth Case]
    [**Case Else**
        instructions for when the selectorExpression does not match any of the
        expressionLists]
End Select

Example
```
Select Case code
    Case 1, 2                              the selectorExpression
        priceLabel.Text = "$15"            needs to match only one
    Case 3                                 of these values
        priceLabel.Text = "$25"
    Case 4
        priceLabel.Text = "$35"
    Case Else
        priceLabel.Text = "Invalid code"
End Select
```

Figure 5-9   How to use the Select Case statement
© 2013 Cengage Learning

If you want to try using the Select Case statement in the Yardley Theater application, open the solution contained in the Try It 3! folder.

The *selectorExpression* in the Select Case clause can contain any combination of variables, constants, keywords, functions, methods, operators, and properties. In the example in Figure 5-9, the selectorExpression is an Integer variable named **code**. Each Case clause represents a different path that the computer can follow. It is customary to indent each Case clause and the instructions within each Case clause, as shown in the figure. You can have as many Case clauses as necessary. However, if the Select Case statement includes a Case Else clause, the Case Else clause must be the last clause in the statement.

Each of the individual Case clauses, except the Case Else clause, must contain an *expressionList*, which can include one or more expressions. To include more than one expression in an expressionList, you separate each expression with a comma, as in the expressionList **Case 1, 2.** The selectorExpression needs to match only one of the expressions listed in an expressionList. The data type of the expressions must be compatible with the data type of the selectorExpression. If the selectorExpression is numeric, the expressions in the Case clauses should be numeric. Likewise, if the selectorExpression is a string, the expressions should be strings. In the example in Figure 5-9, the selectorExpression (**code**) is an integer, and so are the expressions 1, 2, 3, and 4.

The Select Case statement looks more complicated than it really is. When processing the statement, the computer simply compares the value of the selectorExpression with the value or values listed in each of the Case clauses, one Case clause at a time beginning with the first. If the selectorExpression matches at least one of the values listed in a Case clause, the computer processes only the instructions contained in that Case clause. After the Case clause instructions are processed, the Select Case statement ends and the computer skips to the instruction following the End Select clause. For instance, if the **code** variable in Figure 5-9 contains the number 2, the computer will display the string "$15" in the priceLabel and then skip to the instruction following the End Select clause. Similarly, if the **code** variable contains the number 3, the computer will display the string "$25" in the priceLabel before skipping to the instruction following the End Select clause. Keep in mind that if the selectorExpression matches a value in more than one Case clause, only the instructions in the first match's Case clause are processed.

Specifying a Range of Values in a Case Clause

In addition to specifying one or more discrete values in a Case clause, you can specify a range of values, such as the values 1 through 5 or values greater than 10. You do this using either the keyword **To** or the keyword **Is**. You use the **To** keyword when you know both the upper and lower values in the range. The **Is** keyword is appropriate when you know only one end of the range (either the upper or lower end). Figure 5-10 shows the syntax for using both keywords. It also contains an example of a Select Case statement that assigns a price based on the number of items ordered.

HOW TO Specify a Range of Values in a Case Clause

Syntax
Case *smallest value in the range* **To** *largest value in the range*
Case Is *comparisonOperator value*

Example
The ABC Corporation's price chart is shown here:

Quantity ordered	Price per item
1 – 5	$25
6 – 10	$23
More than 10	$20
Less than 1	$0

```
Select Case quantity
    Case 1 To 5
        price = 25
    Case 6 To 10
        price = 23
    Case Is > 10
        price = 20
    Case Else
        price = 0
End Select
```

Be sure to test the Select Case statement thoroughly because the computer will not display an error message when the value preceding To in a Case clause is greater than the value following To; instead, the statement will not give the correct results.

Figure 5-10 How to specify a range of values in a Case clause
© 2013 Cengage Learning

According to the price chart shown in Figure 5-10, the price for 1 to 5 items is $25 each. Using discrete values, the first Case clause would look like this: **Case 1, 2, 3, 4, 5**. However, the **To** keyword provides a more convenient way of writing that range of numbers, like this: **Case 1 To 5**. The expression **1 To 5** specifies the range of numbers from 1 to 5, inclusive. The expression **6 To 10** in the second Case clause in the example specifies the range of numbers from 6 through 10. Notice that both Case clauses state both the lower (1 and 6) and upper (5 and 10) values in each range.

The third Case clause, `Case Is > 10`, contains the `Is` keyword rather than the `To` keyword. Recall that you use the `Is` keyword when you know only one end of the range of values. In this case, you know only the lower end of the range: 10. The `Is` keyword is always used in combination with one of the following comparison operators: =, <, <=, >, >=, <>. The `Case Is > 10` clause specifies all numbers greater than the number 10. Because `quantity` is an Integer variable, you can also write this Case clause as `Case Is >= 11`. The Case Else clause in the example is processed only when the `quantity` variable contains a value that is not included in any of the previous Case clauses.

252

The answers to Mini-Quiz questions are located in Appendix A. Each question is associated with one or more objectives listed at the beginning of the chapter.

Mini-Quiz 5-2

1. A Select Case statement's selectorExpression is a String variable named `colorCode`. Which of the following Case clauses will process the same instructions for color codes from 1 through 4? (6)

   a. `Case 1, 2, 3, 4`

   b. `Case "1", "2", "3", "4"`

   c. `Case "4" To "1"`

   d. both b and c

2. A Select Case statement's selectorExpression is an Integer variable named `colorCode`. Which of the following Case clauses will process the same instructions for color codes from 10 through 15? (6)

   a. `Case 10, 11, 12, 13, 14, 15`

   b. `Case 15 To 10`

   c. `Case Is >= 10 AndAlso <= 15`

   d. all of the above

3. You can code a multiple-alternative selection structure using either If...Then...Else statements or the Select Case statement. (6)

   a. True

   b. False

Using Radio Buttons in an Interface

You can also use a list box, checked list box, or combo box to limit the user to only one choice from a group of related but mutually exclusive choices.

Multiple-alternative selection structures are commonly used when coding applications whose interface contains radio buttons. You create a radio button using the RadioButton tool in the toolbox. **Radio buttons** allow you to limit the user to only one choice from a group of two or more related but mutually exclusive choices. The interface shown in Figure 5-11 contains five radio buttons. Each radio button is labeled so the user knows the choice it represents. You enter the label using sentence capitalization in the radio button's Text property. Each radio button also has a unique access key that allows the user to select the button using the keyboard.

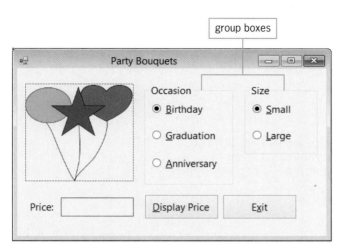

group boxes

Figure 5-11 Interface for the Party Bouquets application

Ch05-Radio
Buttons

The radio buttons in Figure 5-11 are separated into two groups: one group contains the three Occasion radio buttons and one contains the two Size radio buttons. To include two groups of radio buttons in an interface, at least one of the groups must be placed within a container, such as a group box, panel, or table layout panel. Otherwise, the radio buttons are considered to be in the same group and only one can be selected at any one time.

You add a **group box** to a form using the GroupBox tool, which is located in the Containers section of the toolbox. Placing each group of radio buttons in a separate group box allows the user to select one button from each group. Keep in mind that the minimum number of radio buttons in a group is two; this is because the only way to deselect a radio button is to select another radio button. The recommended maximum number of radio buttons in a group is seven.

It is customary in Windows applications to have one of the radio buttons in each group already selected when the interface first appears. The automatically selected button is called the **default radio button** and is either the radio button that represents the user's most likely choice or the first radio button in the group. You designate the default radio button by setting the button's Checked property to the Boolean value True. When you set the Checked property to True in the Properties window, a colored dot appears inside the button's circle to indicate that the button is selected. In Figure 5-11, the Birthday and Small radio buttons are the default buttons in the Occasion and Size groups, respectively.

When the user clicks the Display Price button, the button's Click event procedure should display the appropriate price for a bouquet of balloons. The price information is shown in Figure 5-12 along with two versions of the Display Price button's code: one using If...Then...Else statements and one using the Select Case statement. Notice that both versions of the code use the Checked property to determine the radio button selected in each group.

Party Bouquets Price Chart

Occasion	Price for a small bouquet
Birthday	$35
Graduation	$32.50
Anniversary	$30
Large bouquet	additional $10

Version 1 – If...Then...Else statements

```
Private Sub displayButton_Click(sender As Object,
e As EventArgs) Handles displayButton.Click
    ' displays the price for a bouquet of balloons

    Dim price As Double

    ' determine occasion
    If bdayRadioButton.Checked Then
        price = 35
    ElseIf gradRadioButton.Checked Then
        price = 32.5
    Else
        price = 30
    End If

    ' if necessary, add $10 for a large bouquet
    If largeRadioButton.Checked Then
        price += 10
    End If

    ' display price
    priceLabel.Text = price.ToString("C2")
End Sub
```

> you can also use If bdayRadioButton.Checked = True Then

> you can also use If largeRadioButton.Checked = True Then

Version 2 – Select Case statement

```
Private Sub displayButton_Click(sender As Object,
e As EventArgs) Handles displayButton.Click
    ' displays the price for a bouquet of balloons

    Dim price As Double

    ' determine occasion
    Select Case True
        Case bdayRadioButton.Checked
            price = 35
        Case gradRadioButton.Checked
            price = 32.5
        Case Else
            price = 30
    End Select

    ' if necessary, add $10 for a large bouquet
    If largeRadioButton.Checked Then
        price += 10
    End If

    ' display price
    priceLabel.Text = price.ToString("C2")
End Sub
```

> you can also use price = price + 10

If you want to experiment with the Party Bouquets application, open the solution contained in the Try It 4! folder.

Figure 5-12 Price chart and two versions of the displayButton_Click procedure
© 2013 Cengage Learning

The MessageBox.Show Method

At times, an application may need to communicate with the user during run time. One means of doing this is through a message box. You display a message box using the **MessageBox.Show method**. The message box contains text, one or more buttons, and an icon. Figure 5-13 shows the method's syntax and also lists the meaning of each argument. The figure also includes two examples of using the method. Figure 5-14 shows the message boxes created by the two examples. (Your message boxes will look slightly different if you are using Windows 7.)

HOW TO Use the MessageBox.Show Method

Syntax
MessageBox.Show(text, caption, buttons, icon[, defaultButton]**)**

Argument	Meaning
text	text to display in the message box; use sentence capitalization
caption	text to display in the message box's title bar; use book title capitalization
buttons	buttons to display in the message box; can be one of the following constants: MessageBoxButtons.AbortRetryIgnore MessageBoxButtons.OK (default setting) MessageBoxButtons.OKCancel MessageBoxButtons.RetryCancel MessageBoxButtons.YesNo MessageBoxButtons.YesNoCancel
icon	icon to display in the message box; typically, one of the following constants: MessageBoxIcon.Exclamation ⚠ MessageBoxIcon.Information ⓘ MessageBoxIcon.Stop ⊗
defaultButton	button automatically selected when the user presses Enter; can be one of the following constants: MessageBoxDefaultButton.Button1 (default setting) MessageBoxDefaultButton.Button2 MessageBoxDefaultButton.Button3

Example 1
```
MessageBox.Show("Record deleted.", "Payroll",
    MessageBoxButtons.OK, MessageBoxIcon.Information)
```
displays an information message box that contains the message "Record deleted."

Example 2
```
MessageBox.Show("Delete this record?", "Payroll",
    MessageBoxButtons.YesNo, MessageBoxIcon.Exclamation,
    MessageBoxDefaultButton.Button2)
```
displays a warning message box that contains the message "Delete this record?"

Figure 5-13 How to use the MessageBox.Show method
© 2013 Cengage Learning

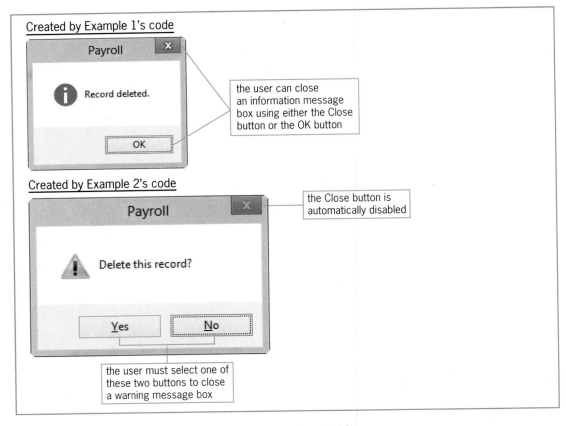

Figure 5-14   Message boxes created by the code in Figure 5-13

After displaying the message box, the MessageBox.Show method waits for the user to choose one of the buttons. It then closes the message box and returns an integer indicating the button chosen by the user. Sometimes you are not interested in the value returned by the MessageBox.Show method. This is the case when the message box is for informational purposes only, like the first message box shown in Figure 5-14. Many times, however, the button selected by the user determines the next task performed by the computer. For example, selecting the Yes button in the second message box shown in Figure 5-14 indicates that the record should be deleted; selecting the No button indicates that it should *not* be deleted.

Figure 5-15 lists the integer values returned by the MessageBox.Show method. Each value is associated with a button that can appear in a message box. The figure also lists the DialogResult values assigned to each integer, and the meaning of the integers and DialogResult values. As the figure indicates, the MessageBox.Show method returns the integer 6 when the user selects the Yes button. The integer 6 is represented by the DialogResult value, `Windows.Forms.DialogResult.Yes`. When referring to the method's return value in code, you should use the DialogResult values rather than the integers because the values make the code more self-documenting and easier to understand. Figure 5-15 also shows two examples of using the MessageBox.Show method's return value.

HOW TO Use the MessageBox.Show Method's Return Value

Integer	DialogResult value	Meaning
1	Windows.Forms.DialogResult.OK	user chose the OK button
2	Windows.Forms.DialogResult.Cancel	user chose the Cancel button
3	Windows.Forms.DialogResult.Abort	user chose the Abort button
4	Windows.Forms.DialogResult.Retry	user chose the Retry button
5	Windows.Forms.DialogResult.Ignore	user chose the Ignore button
6	Windows.Forms.DialogResult.Yes	user chose the Yes button
7	Windows.Forms.DialogResult.No	user chose the No button

Example 1
```
Dim dlgButton As DialogResult
dlgButton =
    MessageBox.Show("Delete this record?", "Payroll",
    MessageBoxButtons.YesNo, MessageBoxIcon.Exclamation,
    MessageBoxDefaultButton.Button2)
If dlgButton = Windows.Forms.DialogResult.Yes Then
    ' instructions to delete the record
End If
```

Example 2
```
If MessageBox.Show("Play another game?", "Math Monster",
    MessageBoxButtons.YesNo,
    MessageBoxIcon.Exclamation) =
    Windows.Forms.DialogResult.Yes Then
    ' instructions to start another game
Else    ' No button
    ' instructions to close the game application
End If
```

Figure 5-15   How to use the MessageBox.Show method's return value
© 2013 Cengage Learning

If you want to experiment with the MessageBox. Show method, open the solution contained in the Try It 5! folder.

In the first example in Figure 5-15, the method's return value is assigned to a DialogResult variable named **button**. The selection structure in the example compares the contents of the **button** variable with the Windows.Forms.DialogResult.Yes value. In the second example, the method's return value is not stored in a variable. Instead, the method appears in a selection structure's condition, where its return value is compared with the Windows.Forms.DialogResult.Yes value. The selection structure in Example 2 performs one set of tasks when the user selects the Yes button in the message box, but a different set of tasks when the user selects the No button. Many programmers document the Else portion of the selection structure as shown in Figure 5-15 to make it clear that the Else portion is processed only when the user selects the No button.

Using the KeyPress Event

Earlier, in Figure 5-6, you viewed a sample run of the Concord Steaks application, whose interface provides a text box for entering the number of boxes of steaks ordered. The user should enter the number of boxes as an integer. The number of boxes should not contain any letters, spaces, punctuation marks, or special characters. Unfortunately, you can't stop the user from trying to enter an inappropriate character into a text box. However, you can prevent the text box from accepting the character; you do this by coding the text box's KeyPress event procedure.

A control's **KeyPress event** occurs each time the user presses a key while the control has the focus. When the event occurs, a character corresponding to the pressed key is sent to the event's e parameter, which appears between the parentheses in the event's procedure header. For example, when the user presses the period while entering data into a text box, the text box's KeyPress event occurs and a period is sent to the event's e parameter. Similarly, when the Shift key along with a lowercase letter is pressed, the uppercase version of the letter is sent to the e parameter.

To prevent a text box from accepting an inappropriate character, you first use the e parameter's **KeyChar property** to determine the pressed key. (KeyChar stands for "key character.") You then use the e parameter's **Handled property** to cancel the pressed key if it is an inappropriate one. You cancel the key by setting the Handled property to True, like this: e.Handled = True.

In the Concord Steaks application, the boxesTextBox's KeyPress event procedure should allow the text box to accept only numbers and the Backspace key, which is used for editing. Figure 5-16 shows two versions of the procedure's code. The If clause in both versions determines whether the value stored in the KeyChar property is inappropriate for the text box. In this case, an inappropriate value is one that is either less than "0" or greater than "9" and, at the same time, is not the Backspace key. You refer to the Backspace key on your keyboard using Visual Basic's **ControlChars.Back constant**. (The KeyPress event automatically allows the use of the Delete key for editing.)

HOW TO Use the KeyPress Event to Control the Characters Accepted by a Text Box

Version 1
```
Private Sub boxesTextBox_KeyPress(sender As Object,
e As KeyPressEventArgs) Handles boxesTextBox.KeyPress
    ' accept only numbers and the Backspace key

    If (e.KeyChar < "0" OrElse e.KeyChar > "9") AndAlso
        e.KeyChar <> ControlChars.Back Then
        e.Handled = True
    End If
End Sub
```

Version 2
```
Private Sub boxesTextBox_KeyPress(sender As Object,
e As KeyPressEventArgs) Handles boxesTextBox.KeyPress
    ' accept only numbers and the Backspace key    line continuation character

    If (e.KeyChar < "0" OrElse e.KeyChar > "9") _
        AndAlso e.KeyChar <> ControlChars.Back Then
        e.Handled = True
    End If
End Sub
```

Figure 5-16   How to use the KeyPress event to control the characters accepted by a text box
© 2013 Cengage Learning

If you want to experiment with the KeyPress event, open the solution contained in the Try It 6! folder.

You can enter the entire If clause on one line in the Code Editor window. Or, you can split the clause into two lines, as shown in both versions in Figure 5-16. Depending on where you break a line of code, you may or may not need a line continuation character. The **line continuation character** is the underscore shown in Version 2. Examples of places where you can break a line of code without using the line continuation character include the following: after a comma, after an opening parenthesis, before a closing parenthesis, and after an operator (arithmetic, assignment, comparison, logical, or concatenation). If you do use the line continuation character, it must be immediately preceded by a space and appear at the end of a physical line of code in the Code Editor window.

Mini-Quiz 5-3

1. Which of the following constants represents the Backspace key? (10)

    a. `Control.Back`

    b. `Control.Backspace`

    c. `ControlKey.Back`

    d. `ControlChars.Back`

2. You designate a default radio button by setting its _____ property to True. (7)

    a. Checked

    b. Chosen

    c. Default

    d. Selected

3. The Abort button in a message box is represented by which of the following values? (8, 9)

    a. `Windows.Forms.Button.Abort`

    b. `Windows.Forms.Dialog.Abort`

    c. `Windows.Forms.DialogResult.Abort`

    d. `Windows.Forms.Result.Abort`

4. When entered in a text box's KeyPress event procedure, which of the following statements cancels the key pressed by the user? (10)

    a. `e.Cancel = True`

    b. `e.Handled = True`

    c. `e.KeyCancel = True`

    d. `e.KeyChar = True`

The answers to Mini-Quiz questions are located in Appendix A. Each question is associated with one or more objectives listed at the beginning of the chapter.

You have completed the concepts section of Chapter 5. The Programming Tutorial section is next.

PROGRAMMING TUTORIAL 1

Creating the Rock, Paper, Scissors Game Application

In this tutorial, you will create an application that simulates a game called Rock, Paper, Scissors. The game is meant to be played with two people. However, the application you create will allow one person to play against the computer. "Rock, Paper, Scissors" refers to the three choices each player can indicate using hand gestures. To play the game, the players face each other, call out "Rock, paper, scissors, shoot," and then make the hand gesture corresponding to their choice: a fist (rock), a flat hand (paper), or two fingers forming a V shape (scissors). The rules for determining a win are listed in Figure 5-17 along with the application's TOE chart. The application's MainForm is shown in Figure 5-18. The MainForm contains five picture boxes, four labels, one table layout panel, and one button.

Rules for the Rock, Paper, Scissors Game

Rock breaks scissors, so rock wins.
Paper covers rock, so paper wins.
Scissors cut paper, so scissors win.

Task	Object	Event
1. Display the appropriate image in the playerPictureBox 2. Generate a random integer from 1 through 3 to represent the computer's choice 3. Use the random integer to display the rock, paper, or scissors image in the computerPictureBox 4. Determine whether the game is tied or there is a winner, and then display an appropriate message in the winnerLabel	rockPictureBox, paperPictureBox, scissorsPictureBox	Click
End the application	exitButton	Click
Show the message that indicates either the winner or a tie game (from rockPictureBox, paperPictureBox, or scissorsPictureBox)	winnerLabel	None
Display the image corresponding to the player's choice (from rockPictureBox, paperPictureBox, or scissorsPictureBox)	playerPictureBox	None
Display the image corresponding to the computer's choice (from rockPictureBox, paperPictureBox, or scissorsPictureBox)	computerPictureBox	None

Figure 5-17   Rules and TOE chart for the Rock, Paper, Scissors Game application
© 2013 Cengage Learning

Figure 5-18   MainForm for the Rock, Paper, Scissors Game application
OpenClipArt.org/Meister

Coding the Rock, Paper, Scissors Game Application

According to the application's TOE chart, the Click event procedures for the rockPictureBox, paperPictureBox, scissorsPictureBox, and exitButton need to be coded.

To begin coding the application:

1. Start Visual Studio. Open the **RockPaperScissorsGame Solution** (**RockPaperScissorsGame Solution.sln**) file contained in the VbReloaded2012\Chap05\ RockPaperScissorsGame Solution folder. If necessary, open the designer window.

2. Open the Code Editor window. Notice that the exitButton_Click procedure has already been coded for you.

3. In the comments that appear in the General Declarations section, replace <your name> and <current date> with your name and the current date, respectively.

4. The application will use variables, so you should enter the appropriate Option statements in the General Declarations section. Click the **blank line** above the Public Class clause and then enter the following three statements:

   Option Explicit On
   Option Infer Off
   Option Strict On

Before coding the Click event procedures for the picture boxes, study closely the chart shown in Figure 5-19. The chart indicates the combinations that can occur when playing the game, and the corresponding outcome of each combination.

Player's choice	Computer's choice	Outcome
Rock	Rock	Tie
	Paper	Computer wins because paper covers rock
	Scissors	Player wins because rock breaks scissors
Paper	Rock	Player wins because paper covers rock
	Paper	Tie
	Scissors	Computer wins because scissors cut paper
Scissors	Rock	Computer wins because rock breaks scissors
	Paper	Player wins because scissors cut paper
	Scissors	Tie

Figure 5-19 Chart showing the game combinations and outcomes
© 2013 Cengage Learning

Now study the pseudocode shown in Figure 5-20. The pseudocode indicates the tasks to be performed by the rockPictureBox's Click event procedure.

---

rockPictureBox Click event procedure

1. display the rockPictureBox image, which represents the player's choice, in the playerPictureBox
2. generate a random integer from 1 through 3 to represent the computer's choice
3. if the random number is one of the following:
   1 display the rockPictureBox image in the computerPictureBox
      display the string "It's a tie." in the winnerLabel
   2 display the paperPictureBox image in the computerPictureBox
      display the string "Computer wins because paper covers rock." in the winnerLabel
   3 display the scissorsPictureBox image in the computerPictureBox
      display the string "Player wins because rock breaks scissors." in the winnerLabel
   end if

Figure 5-20   Pseudocode for the rockPictureBox_Click procedure
© 2013 Cengage Learning

To code the rockPictureBox_Click procedure and then test the procedure's code:

1. Open the code template for the rockPictureBox's Click event procedure. Type the following comment and then press **Enter** twice:

   ' determines the winner or a tie game

2. The procedure will need a Random object to represent the pseudo-random number generator. It will use an Integer variable to store the random number. Enter the following two Dim statements. Press **Enter** twice after typing the second Dim statement.

   Dim randomGenerator As New Random
   Dim computerChoice As Integer

3. The first step in the pseudocode displays the rockPictureBox image, which represents the player's choice, in the playerPictureBox. Enter the following comment and assignment statement. Press **Enter** twice after typing the assignment statement.

   ' display the player's choice
   playerPictureBox.Image = rockPictureBox.Image

4. The next step generates a random integer from 1 through 3. You will assign the random integer to the computerChoice variable. Enter the following comment and assignment statement:

   ' generate a random integer from 1 through 3
   computerChoice = randomGenerator.Next(1, 4)

5. The last step in the pseudocode uses the random integer to display the appropriate image and message in the computerPictureBox and winnerLabel, respectively. Enter the additional comment and code shown in Figure 5-21.

```
Private Sub rockPictureBox_Click(sender As Object, e As EventArgs) Handles rockP
    ' determines the winner or a tie game

    Dim randomGenerator As New Random
    Dim computerChoice As Integer

    ' display the player's choice
    playerPictureBox.Image = rockPictureBox.Image

    ' generate a random integer from 1 through 3
    computerChoice = randomGenerator.Next(1, 4)
    ' display the computer's choice and the outcome
    Select Case computerChoice
        Case 1
            computerPictureBox.Image = rockPictureBox.Image
            winnerLabel.Text = "It's a tie."
        Case 2
            computerPictureBox.Image = paperPictureBox.Image
            winnerLabel.Text = "Computer wins because paper covers rock."
        Case 3
            computerPictureBox.Image = scissorsPictureBox.Image
            winnerLabel.Text = "Player wins because rock breaks scissors."
    End Select
End Sub
```

enter this comment and the Select Case statement

Figure 5-21   rockPictureBox_Click procedure

6. Save the solution and then start the application. Click the **rockPictureBox** several times to verify that its Click event procedure is working properly. Figure 5-22 shows a sample run of the procedure. Because the procedure generates a random number for the computer's choice, a different image and message might appear in the computerPictureBox and winnerLabel controls on your screen.

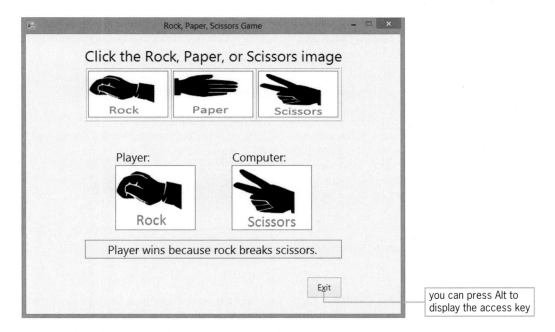

you can press Alt to display the access key

Figure 5-22   Sample run of the rockPictureBox_Click procedure
OpenClipArt.org/Meister

7. Click the **Exit** button to end the application.

Next, you will code the paperPictureBox's Click event procedure. The procedure's pseudocode is shown in Figure 5-23.

---

paperPictureBox Click event procedure

1. display the paperPictureBox image, which represents the player's choice, in the playerPictureBox
2. generate a random integer from 1 through 3 to represent the computer's choice
3. if the random number is one of the following:
    1 display the rockPictureBox image in the computerPictureBox
       display the string "Player wins because paper covers rock." in the winnerLabel
    2 display the paperPictureBox image in the computerPictureBox
       display the string "It's a tie." in the winnerLabel
    3 display the scissorsPictureBox image in the computerPictureBox
       display the string "Computer wins because scissors cut paper." in the winnerLabel
  end if

Figure 5-23   Pseudocode for the paperPictureBox_Click procedure
© 2013 Cengage Learning

To code the paperPictureBox_Click procedure and then test the procedure's code:

1. Open the code template for the paperPictureBox's Click event procedure.

2. Copy the comments and code from the rockPictureBox_Click procedure to the paperPictureBox_Click procedure. (Do not copy the procedure header or footer.)

3. Make the appropriate modifications to the paperPictureBox_Click procedure.

4. Save the solution and then start the application. Click the **paperPictureBox** several times to verify that its Click event procedure is working properly, and then click the **Exit** button.

Finally, you will code the scissorsPictureBox_Click procedure. The procedure's pseudocode is shown in Figure 5-24.

---

scissorsPictureBox Click event procedure

1. display the scissorsPictureBox image, which represents the player's choice, in the playerPictureBox
2. generate a random integer from 1 through 3 to represent the computer's choice
3. if the random number is one of the following:
    1 display the rockPictureBox image in the computerPictureBox
       display the string "Computer wins because rock breaks scissors." in the winnerLabel
    2 display the paperPictureBox image in the computerPictureBox
       display the string "Player wins because scissors cut paper." in the winnerLabel
    3 display the scissorsPictureBox image in the computerPictureBox
       display the string "It's a tie." in the winnerLabel
  end if

Figure 5-24   Pseudocode for the scissorsPictureBox_Click procedure
© 2013 Cengage Learning

To code the scissorsPictureBox_Click procedure and then test the procedure's code:

1. Open the code template for the scissorsPictureBox's Click event procedure.

2. Copy the comments and code from the rockPictureBox_Click procedure to the scissorsPictureBox_Click procedure. (Do not copy the procedure header or footer.)

3. Make the appropriate modifications to the scissorsPictureBox_Click procedure.

4. Save the solution and then start the application. Click the **scissorsPictureBox** several times to verify that its Click event procedure is working properly, and then click the **Exit** button.

5. Close the Code Editor window and then close the solution. Figure 5-25 shows the application's code.

```
 1 ' Project name:        RockPaperScissorsGame Project
 2 ' Project purpose:     Simulates the Rock, Paper, Scissors game
 3 ' Created/revised by:  <your name> on <current date>
 4
 5 Option Explicit On
 6 Option Infer Off
 7 Option Strict On
 8
 9 Public Class MainForm
10
11    Private Sub exitButton_Click(sender As Object,
      e As EventArgs) Handles exitButton.Click
12       Me.Close()
13    End Sub
14
15    Private Sub rockPictureBox_Click(sender As Object,
      e As EventArgs) Handles rockPictureBox.Click
16        ' determines the winner or a tie game
17
18       Dim randomGenerator As New Random
19       Dim computerChoice As Integer
20
21        ' display the player's choice
22       playerPictureBox.Image = rockPictureBox.Image
23
24        ' generate a random integer from 1 through 3
25       computerChoice = randomGenerator.Next(1, 4)
26        ' display the computer's choice and the outcome
27       Select Case computerChoice
28         Case 1
29           computerPictureBox.Image = rockPictureBox.Image
30           winnerLabel.Text = "It's a tie."
31         Case 2
32           computerPictureBox.Image = paperPictureBox.Image
33           winnerLabel.Text = "Computer wins because paper covers rock."
34         Case 3
35           computerPictureBox.Image = scissorsPictureBox.Image
36           winnerLabel.Text = "Player wins because rock breaks scissors."
37       End Select
38    End Sub
39
40    Private Sub paperPictureBox_Click(sender As Object,
      e As EventArgs) Handles paperPictureBox.Click
41        ' determines the winner or a tie game
42
43       Dim randomGenerator As New Random
44       Dim computerChoice As Integer
45
46        ' display the player's choice
47       playerPictureBox.Image = paperPictureBox.Image
48
49        ' generate a random integer from 1 through 3
50       computerChoice = randomGenerator.Next(1, 4)
```

Figure 5-25 Code for the Rock, Paper, Scissors Game application *(continues)*

(continued)

```
51          ' display the computer's choice and the outcome
52          Select Case computerChoice
53            Case 1
54              computerPictureBox.Image = rockPictureBox.Image
55              winnerLabel.Text = "Player wins because paper covers rock."
56            Case 2
57              computerPictureBox.Image = paperPictureBox.Image
58              winnerLabel.Text = "It's a tie."
59            Case 3
60              computerPictureBox.Image = scissorsPictureBox.Image
61              winnerLabel.Text = "Computer wins because scissors cut paper."
62          End Select
63        End Sub
64
65        Private Sub scissorsPictureBox_Click(sender As Object,
          e As EventArgs) Handles scissorsPictureBox.Click
66            ' determines the winner or a tie game
67
68          Dim randomGenerator As New Random
69          Dim computerChoice As Integer
70
71            ' display the player's choice
72          playerPictureBox.Image = scissorsPictureBox.Image
73
74            ' generate a random integer from 1 through 3
75          computerChoice = randomGenerator.Next(1, 4)
76            ' display the computer's choice and the outcome
77          Select Case computerChoice
78            Case 1
79              computerPictureBox.Image = rockPictureBox.Image
80              winnerLabel.Text = "Computer wins because rock breaks scissors."
81            Case 2
82              computerPictureBox.Image = paperPictureBox.Image
83              winnerLabel.Text = "Player wins because scissors cut paper."
84            Case 3
85              computerPictureBox.Image = scissorsPictureBox.Image
86              winnerLabel.Text = "It's a tie."
87          End Select
88        End Sub
89 End Class
```

Figure 5-25   Code for the Rock, Paper, Scissors Game application
© 2013 Cengage Learning

PROGRAMMING TUTORIAL 2

Coding the Charleston Cable Company Application

In this tutorial, you will create an application for the Charleston Cable Company. The application calculates and displays a customer's monthly cable bill, which is based on the information shown in Figure 5-26. The figure also includes the application's TOE chart. The application's MainForm is shown in Figure 5-27. The MainForm provides radio buttons and check boxes for selecting the cable package and additional features, respectively.

Packages/Additional features	Charge
Basic	39.99
Bronze	44.99
Silver	59.99
Gold	74.99
HBI movie channels	10.00
Showtimer movie channels	11.50
Cinematic movie channels	12.00
Local stations	5.00

Task	Object	Event
Specify the cable package	basicRadioButton, bronzeRadioButton, silverRadioButton, goldRadioButton	None
Specify any additional charges	hbiCheckBox, showtimerCheckBox, cinematicCheckBox, localCheckBox	None
1. Calculate the cable bill 2. Display the cable bill in a message box	calcButton	Click
End the application	exitButton	Click

Figure 5-26 Rates and TOE chart for the Charleston Cable Company application
© 2013 Cengage Learning

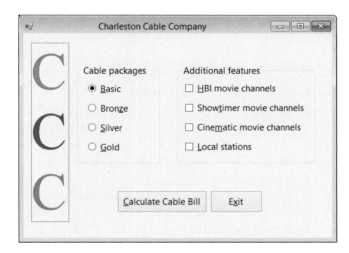

Figure 5-27 MainForm for the Charleston Cable Company application

Coding the Charleston Cable Company Application

According to the application's TOE chart, the Click event procedures for the calcButton and exitButton need to be coded.

To begin coding the application:

1. Start Visual Studio. Open the **Charleston Cable Solution (Charleston Cable Solution.sln)** file contained in the VbReloaded2012\Chap05\Charleston Cable Solution folder. If necessary, open the designer window.

2. Open the Code Editor window. Notice that the exitButton_Click procedure has already been coded for you.

3. In the comments that appear in the General Declarations section, replace <your name> and <current date> with your name and the current date, respectively.

4. Enter the appropriate Option statements in the General Declarations section.

The application's TOE chart indicates that the calcButton's Click event procedure is responsible for calculating and displaying the cable bill. The procedure's pseudocode is shown in Figure 5-28.

---

calcButton Click event procedure

1. if one of the following radio buttons is selected in the Cable packages group:

Basic	cable bill = 39.99
Bronze	cable bill = 44.99
Silver	cable bill = 59.99
Gold	cable bill = 74.99

   end if

2. if the HBI movie channels check box is selected
        add 10 to the cable bill
   end if

3. if the Showtimer movie channels check box is selected
        add 11.50 to the cable bill
   end if

4. if the Cinematic movie channels check box is selected
        add 12 to the cable bill
   end if

5. if the Local stations check box is selected
        add 5 to the cable bill
   end if

6. display the cable bill in a message box

Figure 5-28   Pseudocode for the calcButton_Click procedure
© 2013 Cengage Learning

As you know, before you begin coding a procedure, you first study the procedure's pseudocode (or flowchart) to determine any variables or named constants the procedure will require. In this case, the calcButton_Click procedure will use eight named constants to store the package prices and additional charges. It will also use a Double variable to keep track of the cable bill. The named constants and variable are listed in Figure 5-29.

Named constants	Data type	Value
Basic	Double	39.99
Bronze	Double	44.99
Silver	Double	59.99
Gold	Double	74.99
Hbi	Double	10.00
Showtimer	Double	11.50
Cinematic	Double	12.00
Local	Double	5.00

Variable	Data type	Value source
cableBill	Double	procedure calculation

Figure 5-29   Memory locations for the calcButton_Click procedure
© 2013 Cengage Learning

To code the calcButton_Click procedure and then test the procedure's code:

1. Open the code template for the calcButton's Click event procedure. Type the following comment and then press **Enter** twice:

    ' calculates a monthly cable bill

2. Enter the statements to declare the nine memory locations listed in Figure 5-29. Press **Enter** twice after typing the last declaration statement.

3. Step 1 in the pseudocode determines the radio button selected in the Cable packages group, and then assigns the appropriate charge as the cable bill. First, type **' determine package charge** and press **Enter**. Then, enter a multiple-alternative selection structure to assign the appropriate charge to the cableBill variable. Use the If…Then…Else statement.

4. The second through fifth steps in the pseudocode determine whether the customer should be charged for any additional features. Insert **two blank lines** above the End Sub clause. In the blank line immediately above the clause, type **' add any additional charges** and press **Enter**. Now enter four single-alternative selection structures to add the additional charges (if any) to the cable bill.

5. The last step in the pseudocode displays the cable bill in a message box. Insert **two blank lines** above the End Sub clause. In the blank line immediately above the clause, type **' display the cable bill** and press **Enter**. Now enter an appropriate MessageBox.Show method. The message box should contain the message "Your monthly cable bill is " followed by the contents of the cableBill variable, formatted with a dollar sign and two decimal places. The message box should also contain an OK button and the Information icon. The company's name, Charleston Cable Company, should appear in the message box's title bar.

6. Save the solution and then start the application. The Basic radio button, which is the default radio button, is already selected in the interface.

7. Click the **Silver** radio button, the **Local stations** check box, and the **Calculate Cable Bill** button. The monthly cable bill appears in a message box, as shown in Figure 5-30.

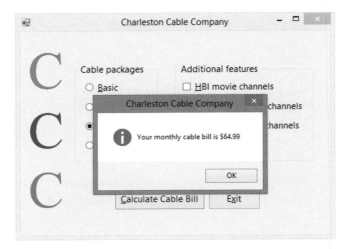

Figure 5-30   Message box showing the monthly cable bill

8. Close the message box. Click the **Local stations** check box to deselect it. Click the **Basic** radio button, the **HBI movie channels** check box, the **Showtimer movie channels** check box, and the **Calculate Cable Bill** button. The message box indicates that the monthly cable bill is $61.49.

9. Close the message box and then click the **Exit** button. Close the Code Editor window and then close the solution. Figure 5-31 shows the application's code.

```
1 ' Project name:        Charleston Cable Project
2 ' Project purpose:     Displays a customer's cable bill
3 ' Created/revised by:  <your name> on <current date>
4
5 Option Explicit On
6 Option Infer Off
7 Option Strict On
8
9 Public Class MainForm
10
11    Private Sub exitButton_Click(sender As Object,
      e As EventArgs) Handles exitButton.Click
12        Me.Close()
13    End Sub
14
15    Private Sub calcButton_Click(sender As Object,
      e As EventArgs) Handles calcButton.Click
16        ' calculates a monthly cable bill
17
18        Const Basic As Double = 39.99
19        Const Bronze As Double = 44.99
20        Const Silver As Double = 59.99
21        Const Gold As Double = 74.99
22        Const Hbi As Double = 10.0
23        Const Showtimer As Double = 11.5
24        Const Cinematic As Double = 12.0
25        Const Local As Double = 5.0
26        Dim cableBill As Double
27
```

Figure 5-31   Code for the Charleston Cable Company application *(continues)*

(continued)

```
28          ' determine package charge
29          If basicRadioButton.Checked Then
30              cableBill += Basic
31          ElseIf bronzeRadioButton.Checked Then
32              cableBill += Bronze
33          ElseIf silverRadioButton.Checked Then
34              cableBill += Silver
35          Else
36              cableBill += Gold
37          End If
38
39          ' add any additional charges
40          If hbiCheckBox.Checked Then
41              cableBill += Hbi
42          End If
43          If showtimerCheckBox.Checked Then
44              cableBill += Showtimer
45          End If
46          If cinematicCheckBox.Checked Then
47              cableBill += Cinematic
48          End If
49          If localCheckBox.Checked Then
50              cableBill += Local
51          End If
52
53          ' display the cable bill
54          MessageBox.Show("Your monthly cable bill is " &
55                          cableBill.ToString("C2"),
56                          "Charleston Cable Company",
57                          MessageBoxButtons.OK,
58                          MessageBoxIcon.Information)
59
60      End Sub
61  End Class
```

Figure 5-31 Code for the Charleston Cable Company application
© 2013 Cengage Learning

PROGRAMMING EXAMPLE

CD Warehouse Application

Each CD at CD Warehouse costs $11.99. If a customer has a CD Warehouse coupon, he or she is entitled to a 5% discount when purchasing three or fewer CDs, but a 10% discount when purchasing more than three CDs. Create an interface that provides a text box for the sales clerk to enter the number of CDs purchased. The text box should accept only numbers and the Backspace key. Use a message box to ask the sales clerk whether the customer has a coupon. Display the amount of the discount and the total price in labels on the form. Use the following names for the solution and project, respectively: CD Solution and CD Project. Save the application in the VbReloaded2012\Chap05 folder. Change the form file's name to Main Form.vb. See Figures 5-32 through 5-37. The image in the picture box is contained in the VbReloaded2012\Chap05\CDW.png file. Test the application using the data shown in Figure 5-36; the figure also shows the correct results.

Task	Object	Event
1. Determine whether the customer gets a discount 2. Calculate the discount (if necessary) 3. Calculate the total price 4. Display the discount and total price in discountLabel and totalLabel	calcButton	Click
End the application	exitButton	Click
Display the discount (from calcButton)	discountLabel	None
Display the total price (from calcButton)	totalLabel	None
Get and display the number of CDs purchased	cdsTextBox	None
Allow the text box to accept only numbers and the Backspace key		KeyPress

Figure 5-32   TOE chart
© 2013 Cengage Learning

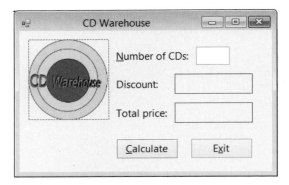 

Figure 5-33   MainForm and tab order

Object	Property	Setting
MainForm	AcceptButton Font StartPosition Text	calcButton Segoe UI, 11pt CenterScreen CD Warehouse
discountLabel	AutoSize BorderStyle Text TextAlign	False FixedSingle (empty) MiddleCenter
totalPriceLabel	AutoSize BorderStyle Text TextAlign	False FixedSingle (empty) MiddleCenter

Figure 5-34   Objects, properties, and settings
© 2013 Cengage Learning

```
exitButton Click event procedure
close the application

calcButton Click event procedure

1.  assign user input (number of CDs) to a variable
2.  total price = number of CDs * CD price
3.  use a message box to ask the user whether the customer has a coupon
4.  if the customer has a coupon
        if the number of CDs is more than 3
                discount = total price * 10%
        else
                discount = total price * 5%
        end if
        total price = total price – discount
    end if
5.  display the discount in discountLabel
6.  display the total price in totalLabel

cdsTextBox KeyPress event procedure

if the user pressed a key that is not a number from 0 through 9 or the Backspace key
        cancel the key
end if
```

Figure 5-35   Pseudocode
© 2013 Cengage Learning

Number of CDs	Coupon	Discount	Total price
2	No	$0.00	$23.98
2	Yes	$1.20	$22.78
4	No	$0.00	$47.96
4	Yes	$4.80	$43.16

Figure 5-36   Test data and results
© 2013 Cengage Learning

```
1  ' Project name:        CD Project
2  ' Project purpose:     Displays the discount and total price
3  ' Created/revised by:  <your name> on <current date>
4
5  Option Explicit On
6  Option Strict On
7  Option Infer Off
8
9  Public Class MainForm
10
11     Private Sub exitButton_Click(sender As Object,
         e As EventArgs) Handles exitButton.Click
12         Me.Close()
13     End Sub
14
```

Figure 5-37   Code (continues)

PROGRAMMING EXAMPLE

(continued)

```
15      Private Sub cdsTextBox_KeyPress(sender As Object,
        e As KeyPressEventArgs) Handles cdsTextBox.KeyPress
16          ' accept only numbers and the Backspace key
17
18          If (e.KeyChar < "0" OrElse e.KeyChar > "9") AndAlso
19              e.KeyChar <> ControlChars.Back Then
20              e.Handled = True
21          End If
22      End Sub
23
24      Private Sub calcButton_Click(sender As Object,
        e As EventArgs) Handles calcButton.Click
25          ' calculates and displays the
26          ' discount and total price
27
28          Const CdPrice As Double = 11.99
29          Const CouponQuestion As String =
30              "Does the customer have a coupon?"
31          Const RateOverThree As Double = 0.1
32          Const RateThreeOrLess As Double = 0.05
33
34          Dim numCds As Integer
35          Dim discount As Double
36          Dim totalPrice As Double
37          Dim button As DialogResult
38
39          ' convert user input to integer
40          Integer.TryParse(cdsTextBox.Text, numCds)
41
42          ' calculate the total before any discount
43          totalPrice = numCds * CdPrice
44
45          ' ask whether the customer has a coupon
46          button = MessageBox.Show(CouponQuestion,
47                                   "CD Warehouse",
48                                   MessageBoxButtons.YesNo,
49                                   MessageBoxIcon.Exclamation)
50
51          ' if the customer has a coupon, calculate the
52          ' discount and subtract it from the total price
53          If button = Windows.Forms.DialogResult.Yes Then
54              If numCds > 3 Then
55                  discount = totalPrice * RateOverThree
56              Else
57                  discount = totalPrice * RateThreeOrLess
58              End If
59              totalPrice -= discount
60          End If
61
62          ' display the discount and total price
63          discountLabel.Text = discount.ToString("C2")
64          totalLabel.Text = totalPrice.ToString("C2")
65      End Sub
66 End Class
```

Figure 5-37 Code
© 2013 Cengage Learning

Summary

- You can nest a selection structure in either the True or False path of another selection structure.

- The primary decision is always made by an outer selection structure. The secondary decision is always made by a nested selection structure.

- You can code a multiple-alternative selection structure using either If…Then…Else statements or the Select Case statement.

- In a flowchart, a diamond is used to represent the condition in a multiple-alternative selection structure. The diamond has several flowlines leading out of the symbol, with each flowline representing a possible path.

- In a Select Case statement, the data type of the expressions in the Case clauses should match the data type of the statement's selectorExpression.

- A Case clause in a Select Case statement can contain more than one expression. The selectorExpression needs to match only one of the expressions for the instructions in that Case to be processed.

- You use the keyword To in a Case clause's expressionList when you know both the upper and lower values of the range you want to specify. You use the keyword Is when you know only one end of the range.

- Radio buttons allow you to limit the user to only one choice from a group of two or more related but mutually exclusive choices.

- If you need to include two groups of radio buttons in an interface, at least one of the groups must be placed within a container, such as a group box, panel, or table layout panel.

- It is customary to have one radio button in each group of radio buttons selected when the interface first appears. The selected radio button is called the default radio button.

- If a radio button is selected, its Checked property contains the Boolean value True; otherwise, it contains the Boolean value False.

- The MessageBox.Show method allows an application to communicate with the user while the application is running.

- The MessageBox.Show method displays a message box that contains text, one or more buttons, and an icon. It returns an integer indicating the button chosen by the user. You should use the DialogResult value associated with the integer when referring to the return value in code.

- Use sentence capitalization for the text argument in the MessageBox.Show method, but book title capitalization for the caption argument.

- You can code a text box's KeyPress event procedure to prevent the text box from accepting an inappropriate character. The character is stored in the e parameter's KeyChar property. To cancel the character, you set the e parameter's Handled property to True.

Key Terms

ControlChars.Back constant—the Visual Basic constant that represents the Backspace key on your keyboard

Default radio button—a radio button that is automatically selected when an interface first appears

Extended selection structures—another name for multiple-alternative selection structures

Group box—a control that is used to contain other controls; instantiated using the GroupBox tool, which is located in the Containers section of the toolbox

Handled property—a property of the KeyPress event procedure's **e** parameter; used to cancel the key pressed by the user

KeyChar property—a property of the KeyPress event procedure's **e** parameter; stores the character associated with the key pressed by the user

KeyPress event—occurs each time the user presses a key while a text box has the focus

Line continuation character—an underscore that is immediately preceded by a space and located at the end of a physical line of code; used to split a long instruction into two or more physical lines in the Code Editor window

MessageBox.Show method—displays a message box that contains text, one or more buttons, and an icon; allows an application to communicate with the user during run time

Multiple-alternative selection structure—a selection structure that contains several alternatives; also called an extended selection structure; can be coded using either If...Then...Else statements or the Select Case statement

Nested selection structure—a selection structure that is wholly contained (nested) within either the True or False path of another selection structure

Radio buttons—used in an interface to limit the user to only one choice from a group of two or more related but mutually exclusive choices

Select Case statement—used to code a multiple-alternative selection structure

Each Review Question is associated with one or more objectives listed at the beginning of the chapter.

Review Questions

1. A nested selection structure can appear in ———————— of another selection structure. (1, 2)

    a. only the True path

    b. only the False path

    c. either the True path or the False path

2. If a Select Case statement's selectorExpression is an Integer variable named **code**, which of the following Case clauses is valid? (6)

    a. `Case Is > 7`

    b. `Case 3, 5`

    c. `Case 1 To 4`

    d. all of the above

Use the code shown in Figure 5-38 to answer Questions 3 through 5.

```
If number <= 100 Then
     number *= 2
Else
     If number > 500 Then
          number *= 3
     End If
End If
```

Figure 5-38 Code for Review Questions 3 through 5
© 2013 Cengage Learning

3. The number variable contains the number 90 before the code in Figure 5-38 is processed. What value will be in the number variable after the code is processed? (3)

   a. 0

   b. 90

   c. 180

   d. 270

4. The number variable contains the number 1000 before the code in Figure 5-38 is processed. What value will be in the number variable after the code is processed? (3)

   a. 0

   b. 1000

   c. 2000

   d. 3000

5. The number variable contains the number 200 before the code in Figure 5-38 is processed. What value will be in the number variable after the code is processed? (3)

   a. 0

   b. 200

   c. 400

   d. 600

Use the code shown in Figure 5-39 to answer Questions 6 through 9.

```
If code = "A" Then
    plan = "Standard"
ElseIf code = "C" OrElse code = "T" Then
    plan = "Deluxe"
ElseIf code = "R" Then
    plan = "Premier"
Else
    plan = "Invalid code"
End If
```

Figure 5-39 Code for Review Questions 6 through 9
© 2013 Cengage Learning

6. What will the code in Figure 5-39 assign to the `plan` variable when the `code` variable contains the letter T? (6)

   a. Deluxe

   b. Premier

   c. Standard

   d. Invalid code

7. What will the code in Figure 5-39 assign to the `plan` variable when the `code` variable contains the letter R? (6)

   a. Deluxe

   b. Premier

   c. Standard

   d. Invalid code

8. What will the code in Figure 5-39 assign to the `plan` variable when the `code` variable contains the letter C? (6)

   a. Deluxe

   b. Premier

   c. Standard

   d. Invalid code

9. What will the code in Figure 5-39 assign to the `plan` variable when the `code` variable contains the letter X? (6)

   a. Deluxe

   b. Premier

   c. Standard

   d. Invalid code

Use the code shown in Figure 5-40 to answer Questions 10 through 12.

```
Select Case id
    Case 1
        city = "Chicago"
    Case 2 To 4
        city = "San Francisco"
    Case 5, 7
        city = "Boston"
    Case Else
        city = "N/A"
End Select
```

Figure 5-40   Code for Review Questions 10 through 12
© 2013 Cengage Learning

10. What will the code in Figure 5-40 assign to the `city` variable when the `id` variable contains the number 2? (6)

    a. Boston

    b. Chicago

    c. San Francisco

    d. N/A

11. What will the code in Figure 5-40 assign to the city variable when the id variable contains the number 3? (6)

   a. Boston
   b. Chicago
   c. San Francisco
   d. N/A

12. What will the code in Figure 5-40 assign to the city variable when the id variable contains the number 6? (6)

   a. Boston
   b. Chicago
   c. San Francisco
   d. N/A

13. If the user clicks the Cancel button in a message box, the MessageBox.Show method returns the number 2, which is equivalent to which of the following values? (9)

   a. `Windows.Forms.DialogResult.Cancel`
   b. `Windows.Forms.DialogResult.CancelButton`
   c. `Windows.Forms.MessageBox.Cancel`
   d. `Windows.Forms.MessageResult.Cancel`

14. A Select Case statement's selectorExpression is an Integer variable. Which of the following Case clauses tells the computer to process the instructions when the Integer variable contains one of the following numbers: 1, 2, 3, 4, or 5? (6)

   a. `Case 1, 2, 3, 4, And 5`
   b. `Case 1 To 5`
   c. `Case Is > 1 And < 5`
   d. all of the above

15. A text box's _____ event occurs when a user presses a key while the text box has the focus. (10)

   a. Key
   b. KeyPress
   c. Press
   d. PressKey

Each Exercise, except the DISCOVERY exercise, is associated with one or more objectives listed at the beginning of the chapter.

Exercises

Pencil and Paper

INTRODUCTORY

1. Carl is at a store's checkout counter. He'd like to pay for his purchase using one of his credit cards—either his Discovery card or his Vita card, but preferably his Discovery card. However, he is not sure whether the store accepts either card. If the store doesn't accept either card, he will need to pay cash for the items. Write an appropriate solution, using only the instructions listed in Figure 5-41. (1, 2)

```
else
end if
pay for your items using your Vita card
pay for your items using your Discovery card
pay for your items using cash
if the store accepts the Vita card
if the store accepts the Discovery card
ask the store clerk whether the store accepts the Vita card
ask the store clerk whether the store accepts the Discovery card
```

Figure 5-41   Instructions for Exercise 1
© 2013 Cengage Learning

INTRODUCTORY

2. Write the code to display the message "Entry error" in the msgLabel when the value in the Integer **units** variable is less than or equal to 0. Otherwise, calculate the total owed as follows: If the value stored in the **units** variable is less than 20, multiply the value by $10; otherwise, multiply it by $5. Store the total owed in the **total** variable. Use the If…Then…Else statement. (1, 3, 4, 6)

INTRODUCTORY

3. A procedure stores sales amounts in two Integer variables named **region1Sales** and **region2Sales**. Write the code to display the message "Both regions sold the same amount." when both variables contain the same number. If the variables contain different numbers, the code should compare the numbers and then display either the message "Region 1 sold more than region 2." or the message "Region 2 sold more than region 1." Use the If…Then…Else statement. Display the appropriate message in the msgLabel. (1, 3, 4, 6)

INTRODUCTORY

4. A selection structure needs to display the name of the month associated with a number that is stored in an Integer variable named monthNum. If the monthNum variable contains the number 1, the selection structure should display the string "January" in the monthLabel. If the monthNum variable contains the number 2, the selection structure should display the string "February", and so on. If the month number is not 1 through 12, the selection structure should display the "Incorrect month number" message in the monthLabel. Write two versions of the selection structure's code. In the first version, use the If…Then…Else statement. Use the Select Case statement in the second version. (4, 6)

INTRODUCTORY

5. Write two versions of the code to compare the contents of an Integer variable named **ordered** with the number 10. When the **ordered** variable contains the number 10, display the string "Equal". When the **ordered** variable contains a number that is greater than 10, display the string "Over 10". When the **ordered** variable contains a number that is less than 10, display the string "Not over 10". Display the appropriate message in the msgLabel. In the first version, use the Select Case statement. Use the If…Then…Else statement in the second version. (1, 3, 4, 6)

INTRODUCTORY

6. Write two versions of the code to display the message "Great!" when a student's test score is at least 90. When the test score is from 70 through 89, display the message "Good job". For all other test scores, display the message "Retake the test". The test score is stored in an Integer variable named **score**. Display the appropriate message in the msgLabel. In the first version, use the If…Then…Else statement. Use the Select Case statement in the second version. (1, 3, 4, 6)

INTRODUCTORY

7. What will the solution in Figure 5-42 display if Derek was inside the 3-point line when the basketball went through the hoop? What will it display if Derek was behind the

3-point line when the basketball went through the hoop? What will it display if Derek was on the 3-point line when the basketball missed the hoop? What will it display if Derek was behind the 3-point line when the basketball missed the hoop? Does the solution in Figure 5-42 give you the same results as the solution shown in Figure 5-2 in the chapter? (2)

```
1.  shoot the basketball
2.  if the basketball went through the hoop and Derek was either inside or on the 3-point line
        say "I did it!"
        say "2 points for me"
    else
            if Derek was behind the 3-point line
                say "I did it!"
                say "3 points for me"
            else
                say "Missed it!"
            end if
    end if
```

Figure 5-42 Instructions for Exercise 7
© 2013 Cengage Learning

8. What will the solution in Figure 5-43 display if Derek was inside the 3-point line when the basketball went through the hoop? What will it display if Derek was behind the 3-point line when the basketball went through the hoop? What will it display if Derek was on the 3-point line when the basketball missed the hoop? What will it display if Derek was behind the 3-point line when the basketball missed the hoop? Does the solution in Figure 5-43 give you the same results as the solution shown in Figure 5-2 in the chapter? (2)

INTRODUCTORY

```
1.  shoot the basketball
2.  if the basketball did not go through the hoop
        say "Missed it!"
    else
            say "I did it!"
            if Derek was either inside or on the 3-point line
                say "2 points for me"
            else
                say "3 points for me"
            end if
    end if
```

Figure 5-43 Instructions for Exercise 8
© 2013 Cengage Learning

9. A procedure uses a String variable named `department` and two Double variables named `salary` and `raise`. The `department` variable contains one of the following letters (entered in either uppercase or lowercase): A, B, C, or D. Employees in departments A and B are receiving a 2% raise. Employees in department C are receiving a 1.5% raise, and employees in department D are receiving a 3% raise. Write two versions of the code to calculate the appropriate raise amount. In the first version, use the Select Case statement. Use the If...Then...Else statement in the second version. (4, 6)

INTERMEDIATE

INTERMEDIATE

10. Code the partial flowchart shown in Figure 5-44. Use an Integer variable named **code** and a Double variable named **rate**. Display the rate formatted with a percent sign and no decimal places. Use the Select Case statement to code the multiple-alternative selection structure in the figure. (4-6)

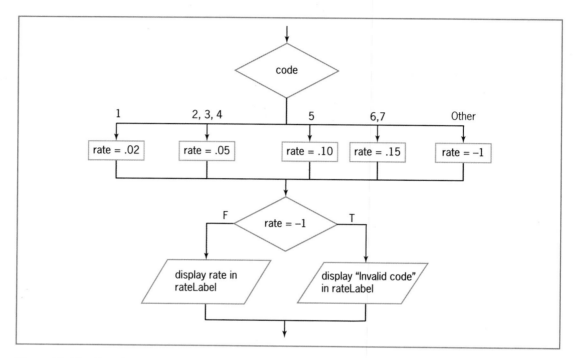

Figure 5-44 Flowchart
© 2013 Cengage Learning

ADVANCED

11. The answerTextBox should accept only the letters Y, y, N, or n, and the Backspace key. Write the appropriate selection structure for the text box's KeyPress event procedure. (10)

Computer

MODIFY THIS

12. If necessary, complete the Rock, Paper, Scissors Game application from this chapter's Programming Tutorial 1, and then close the solution. Use Windows to make a copy of the RockPaperScissorsGame Solution folder. Rename the folder RockPaperScissorsGame Solution-ModifyThis. Open the RockPaperScissorsGame Solution (RockPaperScissorsGame Solution.sln) file contained in the RockPaperScissorsGame Solution-ModifyThis folder. Change the Select Case statements to If...Then...Else statements. Save the solution and then start and test the application. Close the solution. (6)

MODIFY THIS

13. If necessary, complete the Charleston Cable Company application from this chapter's Programming Tutorial 2, and then close the solution. Use Windows to make a copy of the Charleston Cable Solution folder. Rename the folder Charleston Cable Solution-ModifyThis. Open the Charleston Cable Solution (Charleston Cable Solution.sln) file contained in the Charleston Cable Solution-ModifyThis folder. Change the multiple-alternative selection structure in the calcButton_Click procedure to a Select Case statement. Save the solution and then start and test the application. Close the solution. (6)

14. Use Windows to make a copy of the AddSub Solution folder contained in the VbReloaded2012\Chap05 folder. Rename the folder AddSub Solution-ModifyThis. Open the AddSub Solution (AddSub Solution.sln) file contained in the AddSub Solution-ModifyThis folder. (1, 3, 10)

    MODIFY THIS

    a. Set the operationTextBox's MaxLength property to 1.

    b. The operationTextBox should accept only the letters A, a, S, or s, and the Backspace key. Code the appropriate event procedure.

    c. The num1TextBox and num2TextBox controls should accept only numbers, the period, and the Backspace key. Code the appropriate event procedure.

    d. Modify the calcButton_Click procedure to display "N/A" in the answerLabel when the operationTextBox is empty.

    e. Save the solution and then start and test the application. Close the solution.

15. Use Windows to make a copy of the AddSub Solution folder contained in the VbReloaded2012\Chap05 folder. Rename the folder AddSub Solution-ModifyThis-RadioButtons. Open the AddSub Solution (AddSub Solution.sln) file contained in the AddSub Solution-ModifyThis-RadioButtons folder. (7, 10)

    MODIFY THIS

    a. Provide the user with radio buttons, rather than a text box, for entering the mathematical operation. Make the appropriate modifications to the code.

    b. The num1TextBox and num2TextBox controls should accept only numbers, the period, and the Backspace key. Code the appropriate event procedure.

    c. Save the solution and then start and test the application. Close the solution.

16. Open the Shipping Solution (Shipping Solution.sln) file contained in the VbReloaded2012\Chap05\Shipping Solution folder. The application should display a shipping charge that is based on the state selected by the user. The states and shipping charges are shown in Figure 5-45. Code the application. Save the solution and then start and test the application. Close the solution. (4, 6, 7)

    INTRODUCTORY

State	Shipping charge
Alaska	$50
California	$40
Hawaii	$80
North Dakota	$40
Oregon	$40
Texas	$35
Wyoming	$45

Figure 5-45 States and shipping charges
© 2013 Cengage Learning

17. Open the Bonus Solution (Bonus Solution.sln) file contained in the VbReloaded2012\Chap05\Bonus Solution folder. (4, 6, 8, 10)

    INTRODUCTORY

    a. The user will enter the sales amount as an integer in the salesTextBox, which should accept only numbers and the Backspace key. Code the appropriate event procedure.

    b. The calcButton_Click procedure should display the salesperson's bonus. A salesperson with sales from $0 through $3,500 receives a 1% bonus. A salesperson with sales from $3,501 through $10,000 receives a 5% bonus. A salesperson whose sales are more than $10,000 receives a 10% bonus. The procedure should display the bonus, formatted with a dollar sign and two decimal places, in the bonusLabel. The procedure should not make any calculations when the salesTextBox is empty; rather, it should display an appropriate message in a message box. Code the procedure.

c. Save the solution and then start and test the application. Close the solution.

INTRODUCTORY

18. Open the Random Solution (Random Solution.sln) file contained in the VbReloaded2012\Chap05\Random Solution folder. The generateButton_Click procedure should generate two random integers from 1 through 10. It then should display one of the following messages in the messageLabel: x is equal to y, x is greater than y, or x is less than y. In each message, x and y are the first and second random integers, respectively, generated by the procedure. Draw the flowchart for the generateButton_Click procedure and then code the application. Save the solution and then start and test the application. Close the solution. (1-6)

INTERMEDIATE

19. The JK Department Store has five departments, which are listed in Figure 5-46. The store manager wants an application that displays a department's telephone extension. Create a Windows application. Use the following names for the solution and project, respectively: JK Solution and JK Project. Save the application in the VbReloaded2012\Chap05 folder. Change the form file's name to Main Form.vb. Build an appropriate interface. Provide the user with radio buttons for selecting the department. Save the solution and then start and test the application. Close the solution. (4, 6, 7)

Department	Extension
Apparel	582
Electronics	340
Small appliances	168
Pharmacy	456
Toys	233

Figure 5-46   Departments and extensions
© 2013 Cengage Learning

INTERMEDIATE

20. The manager of the Barren Community Center wants an application that displays a seminar fee. The fee is based on a person's membership status and age. Non-members who are at least 65 years old pay $20; all other non-members pay $50. Members who are at least 65 years old pay $5; all other members pay $10. Create a Windows application. Use the following names for the solution and project, respectively: Barren Solution and Barren Project. Save the application in the VbReloaded2012\Chap05 folder. Change the form file's name to Main Form.vb. Build an appropriate interface. Provide a text box for entering the age. The text box should accept only numbers and the Backspace key. Display an appropriate message if the text box is empty. Use a message box to ask the user whether the person is a member. Code the application. Save the solution and then start and test the application. Close the solution. (1-3, 8, 9)

INTERMEDIATE

21. Create a Windows application. Use the following names for the solution and project, respectively: Currency Solution and Currency Project. Save the application in the VbReloaded2012\Chap05 folder. Change the form file's name to Main Form.vb. The application's interface should provide a text box for the user to enter the number of U.S. dollars, and radio buttons for the seven currencies listed in Figure 5-47. The text box should accept only numbers and the Backspace key. The interface should convert the U.S. dollars to the selected currency and then display the result (formatted to three

decimal places). Use the exchange rates shown in Figure 5-47. Code the application. Save the solution and then start and test the application. Close the solution. (4-7, 10)

Currency	Exchange rate
Canadian dollar	1.01
Euro	0.76
Indian rupee	53.86
Japanese yen	99.10
Mexican peso	12.07
South African rand	8.93
British pound	0.64

Figure 5-47 Currencies and exchange rates
© 2013 Cengage Learning

22. Create a Windows application for Hinsbrook Health Club. Use the following names for the solution and project, respectively: Hinsbrook Solution and Hinsbrook Project. Save the application in the VbReloaded2012\Chap05 folder. Change the form file's name to Main Form.vb. The application should display the number of daily calories needed to maintain a person's current weight. The number of calories is based on the person's gender, activity level, and weight, as shown in Figure 5-48. Create the interface using radio buttons for the gender and activity information, and using a text box for the current weight. Code the application. Save the solution and then start and test the application. Close the solution. (1-3, 7, 10)

INTERMEDIATE

Gender	Activity level	Total daily calories formula
Female	Moderately active	weight * 12 calories per pound
Female	Relatively inactive	weight * 10 calories per pound
Male	Moderately active	weight * 15 calories per pound
Male	Relatively inactive	weight * 13 calories per pound

Figure 5-48 Formulas
© 2013 Cengage Learning

23. Open the Blane Solution (Blane Solution.sln) file contained in the VbReloaded2012\ Chap05\Blane Solution folder. Blane Ltd. sells economic development software to cities around the country. The company is having its annual user's forum next month. The price per person depends on the number of people a user registers. The first 3 people a user registers are charged $150 per person. Registrants 4 through 10 are charged $100 per person. Registrants over 10 are charged $60 per person. For example, if a user registers 8 people, then the total amount owed is $950. The $950 is calculated by first multiplying 3 by 150, giving 450. You then multiply 5 by 100, giving 500. You then add the 500 to the 450, giving 950. Display the total amount owed (formatted with a dollar sign and no decimal places) in the totalLabel. The numberTextBox should accept only numbers and the Backspace key. No calculations should be made when the numberTextBox is empty; rather, display an appropriate message. Save the solution and then start and test the application. Close the solution. (4, 6, 8, 10)

ADVANCED

24. Golf Pro, a U.S. company, sells golf equipment both domestically and abroad. Each of Golf Pro's salespeople receives a commission based on the total of his or her domestic and international sales. The sales manager wants an application that allows him to enter two amounts: the salesperson's domestic sales and his or her international sales. Both amounts may contain decimal places. The application should calculate the salesperson's bonus, using the information shown in Figure 5-49. It then should display the bonus,

ADVANCED

formatted with a dollar sign and two decimal places. Create a Windows application. Use the following names for the solution and project, respectively: Golf Pro Solution and Golf Pro Project. Save the application in the VbReloaded2012\Chap05 folder. Change the form file's name to Main Form.vb. Build an appropriate interface. Code the application. Save the solution and then start and test the application. Close the solution. (4-6, 10)

Sales ($)	Commission rate
0 – 100,000	2% of sales
100,000.99 – 400,000	$2,000 + 5% * sales over $100,000
Over 400,000	$17,000 + 10% * sales over $400,000

Figure 5-49   Sales and commission rates
© 2013 Cengage Learning

ADVANCED

25. If necessary, complete the Rock, Paper, Scissors Game application from this chapter's Programming Tutorial 1, and then close the solution. Use Windows to make a copy of the RockPaperScissorsGame Solution folder. Rename the folder RockPaperScissorsGame Solution-Advanced. Open the RockPaperScissorsGame Solution (RockPaperScissorsGame Solution.sln) file contained in the RockPaperScissorsGame Solution-Advanced folder. Modify the interface to display the number of times the player wins and the number of times the computer wins. Also make the appropriate modifications to the code. Save the solution and then start and test the application. Close the solution. (6)

DISCOVERY

26. In this exercise, you will learn about the SelectAll method and a text box control's Enter event.

   a. Open the Name Solution (Name Solution.sln) file contained in the VbReloaded2012\Chap05\Name Solution folder. Start the application. Type your first name in the First text box and then press Tab. Type your last name in the Last text box and then click the Concatenate Names button. Your full name appears in the Full name label.

   b. Press Tab twice to move the focus to the First text box. Notice that the insertion point appears after your first name in the text box. It is customary in Windows applications to have a text box's existing text selected (highlighted) when the text box receives the focus. You can select a text box's existing text by entering the text box's SelectAll method in the text box's Enter event procedure. The Enter event occurs when the text box receives the focus.

   c. Click the Exit button to end the application. Open the Code Editor window. Enter the SelectAll method in the Enter event procedures for the firstTextBox and lastTextBox controls. The method's syntax is *object*.SelectAll().

   d. Save the solution and then start the application. Type your first name in the First text box and then press Tab. Type your last name in the Last text box and then click the Concatenate Names button. Your full name appears in the Full name label. Press Tab twice to move the focus to the First text box. Notice that your first name is selected in the text box. Press Tab to move the focus to the Last text box. Notice that your last name is selected in the text box. Click the Exit button and then close the solution.

SWAT THE BUGS

27. Open the Debug Solution (Debug Solution.sln) file contained in the VbReloaded2012\Chap05\Debug Solution folder. The application should display the total amount a customer owes; however, it does not always work correctly. Open the Code Editor window and review the existing code. Start and then test the application. Locate and then correct any errors. When the application is working correctly, close the solution. (6, 7)

Case Projects

 Shopper Stoppers

Shopper Stoppers wants an application that displays the number of reward points a customer earns each month. The reward points are based on the customer's membership type and total monthly purchase amount, as shown in Figure 5-50. Use the following names for the solution and project, respectively: Shopper Solution and Shopper Project. Save the solution in the VbReloaded2012\Chap05 folder. Change the form file's name to Main Form.vb. You can either create your own user interface or create the one shown in Figure 5-51. Display the reward points without any decimal places. (1-7, 10)

Membership Type	Total monthly purchase ($)	Reward points
Basic	Less than 100	5% of the total monthly purchase
	100 and over	7% of the total monthly purchase
Standard	Less than 150	6% of the total monthly purchase
	150 – 299.99	8% of the total monthly purchase
	300 and over	10% of the total monthly purchase
Premium	Less than 200	7% of the total monthly purchase
	200 and over	15% of the total monthly purchase

Figure 5-50 Reward points chart
© 2013 Cengage Learning

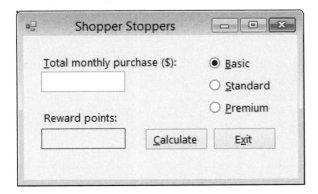

Figure 5-51 Sample interface for the Shopper Stoppers application

 Campbell Tea Shoppe

Campbell Tea Shoppe sells tea by the box, with each box containing 30 tea bags. The tea comes in the following flavors: Citrus Green, Breakfast Blend, Earl Grey, Spiced Chai, and Chamomile. The price for a box of tea depends on the number of boxes ordered, as shown in Figure 5-52. The user will need to enter the number of boxes of each flavor ordered by the customer. He or she will also need to specify whether the customer should be charged a 5% sales tax. Use a message box to get the sales tax information. Create an application that displays the total number of boxes ordered, the sales tax (if any), and the total price of the order. Use the following names for the solution and project, respectively: Campbell Tea Solution and

Campbell Tea Project. Save the application in the VbReloaded2012\Chap05 folder. Change the form file's name to Main Form.vb. You can either create your own user interface or create the one shown in Figure 5-53. The image in the picture box is stored in the VbReloaded2012\Chap05\Tea.png file. (1-10)

Number of boxes	Price per box
1 – 5	6.95
6 – 10	5.95
Over 10	4.95

Figure 5-52 Tea prices
© 2013 Cengage Learning

Figure 5-53 Sample interface for the Campbell Tea Shoppe application

Johnson Supply

The manager of Johnson Supply wants an application that displays the price of an order. The price is based on the number of units ordered and the customer's status (either wholesaler or retailer), as shown in Figure 5-54. Use the following names for the solution and project, respectively: Johnson Solution and Johnson Project. Save the solution in the VbReloaded2012\Chap05 folder. Change the form file's name to Main Form.vb. You can either create your own user interface or create the one shown in Figure 5-55. (1-7, 10)

Wholesaler		Retailer	
Number of units	Price per unit ($)	Number of units	Price per unit ($)
1 – 10	20	1 – 5	30
11 and over	15	6 – 15	28
		16 and over	25

Figure 5-54 Pricing chart
© 2013 Cengage Learning

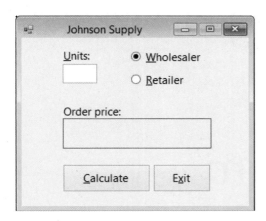

Figure 5-55   Sample interface for the Johnson Supply application

Just Tees

Just Tees sells organic cotton tee shirts for both men and women. The tees come in three sizes: S, M, and L. The women's tees are $17.75 each. The men's tees in size S are also $17.75; however, the men's tees in sizes M and L are $19.75. Each tee can be customized with a picture and/or a name. The additional charge for including a picture on a woman's tee is $5. The additional charge for including a picture on a man's tee in sizes S or M is also $5; however, the additional charge for a man's tee in size L is $6. The additional charge for including a name on a tee is $7.50. The application should allow the user to enter more than one of the same tee. Create an application that displays the total price of the tee(s), including a 2% sales tax. Use the following names for the solution and project, respectively: Just Tees Solution and Just Tees Project. Save the solution in the VbReloaded2012\Chap05 folder. Change the form file's name to Main Form.vb. (1-10)

CHAPTER 6

Repeating Program Instructions

After studying Chapter 6, you should be able to:

1 Differentiate between a looping condition and a loop exit condition

2 Differentiate between a pretest loop and a posttest loop

3 Include pretest and posttest loops in pseudocode and in a flowchart

4 Write a Do...Loop statement

5 Utilize counters and accumulators

6 Display a dialog box using the InputBox function

7 Use a text box's Multiline, ReadOnly, and ScrollBars properties

8 Include a list box in an interface

9 Enable and disable a control

10 Refresh the screen and delay program execution

11 Use the Not logical operator (Programming Tutorial 1)

Before you begin reading Chapter 6, view the Ch06_ReadingStudyGuide.pdf file. You can open the file using Adobe Reader, which is available for free on the Adobe Web site at *www.adobe.com/downloads/.*

The Repetition Structure

Recall that all of the procedures in an application are written using the sequence structure; most also contain the selection and repetition structures. You learned about the sequence and selection structures in previous chapters. This chapter provides an introduction to the repetition structure. Programmers use the **repetition structure**, referred to more simply as a **loop**, when they need the computer to repeatedly process one or more program instructions. The loop contains a condition that controls whether the instructions are repeated.

Like the condition in a selection structure, the condition in a loop must evaluate to either True or False. The condition is evaluated with each repetition (or iteration) of the loop and can be phrased in one of two ways: It can specify either the requirement for repeating the instructions or the requirement for *not* repeating them. The requirement for repeating the instructions is referred to as the **looping condition** because it indicates when the computer should continue "looping" through the instructions. The requirement for *not* repeating the instructions is referred to as the **loop exit condition** because it tells the computer when to exit (or stop) the loop. Every looping condition has an opposing loop exit condition; one is the opposite of the other.

The examples in Figure 6-1 may help illustrate the difference between the looping condition and the loop exit condition. In each example, the looping condition indicates when to continue an action, while the loop exit condition indicates when to stop the action.

Keep your car's windshield wipers on
      while it is raining. (looping condition)
      until it stops raining. (loop exit condition)

At the end of the concert, clap your hands
      while the performers are on stage. (looping condition)
      until the performers leave the stage. (loop exit condition)

When playing musical chairs, walk around the chairs
      while the music is playing. (looping condition)
      until the music stops playing. (loop exit condition)

Figure 6-1   Examples of looping and loop exit conditions
© 2013 Cengage Learning

In Chapter 5's Figure 5-1, you viewed a problem specification and solution involving a basketball player named Derek; the solution from that figure is shown in Figure 6-2. Notice that the solution contains the sequence and selection structures only. In this chapter, we will make a slight change to the original problem specification. Now, Derek should continue shooting the basketball until it goes through the hoop. Figure 6-2 shows the modified problem specification, with the modification shaded. It also shows two modified solutions: one using a looping condition and one using a loop exit condition.

292

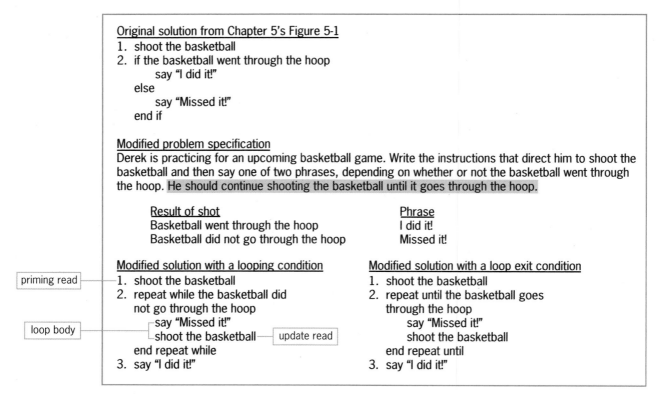

Figure 6-2 Modified problem specification and solutions
© 2013 Cengage Learning

Notice that the modified solutions contain two "shoot the basketball" instructions. One of the instructions appears above the loop, and the other appears as the last instruction in the loop body. Programmers refer to the "shoot the basketball" instruction above the loop as the **priming read** because it is used to prime (prepare or set up) the loop. The priming read initializes the loop's condition by providing its first value. In this case, the priming read gets only Derek's first shot. The first shot is important because it determines whether the two instructions in the loop body are processed at all: If Derek's first shot goes through the hoop, the two instructions will be skipped over, and Derek will say "I did it!"; otherwise, both instructions will be processed.

If the two instructions in the loop body are processed, Derek will say "Missed it!" before shooting the basketball again. The "shoot the basketball" instruction within the loop gets Derek's second and subsequent shots (if any). Programmers refer to this instruction as the **update read** because it updates the value (in this case, Derek's shot) associated with the loop's condition. If Derek's second shot goes through the hoop, the instructions in the loop body will be skipped over, and Derek will say "I did it!". If Derek's second shot does not go through the hoop, the instructions in the loop body tell him to say "Missed it!" before taking his third shot at the basket. The instructions in the loop body will be processed until Derek finally makes a basket.

Typically, the update read is an exact copy of the priming read.

The Savers Club Application

To determine whether a problem's solution requires a loop, you must study the problem specification. The first problem specification you will examine in this chapter is for the Savers Club. The problem specification is shown in Figure 6-3 along with the pseudocode and code for the calcButton's Click event procedure. The procedure requires only the sequence structure.

It does not need a selection structure or a loop because no decisions need to be made and no instructions need to be repeated to calculate and display the account balance at the end of one year. The figure also contains a sample run of the application.

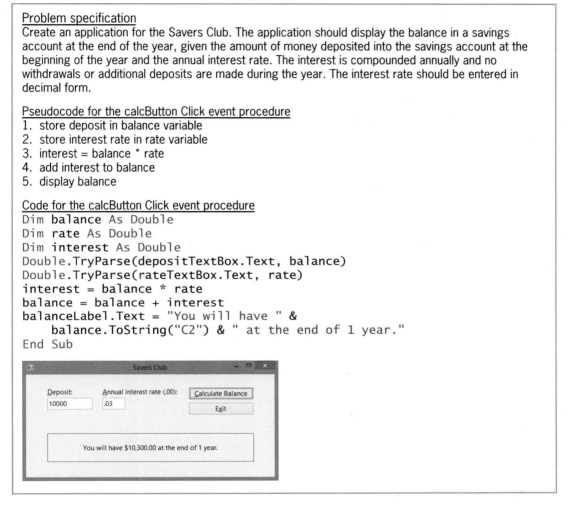

Figure 6-3　Savers Club application
© 2013 Cengage Learning

Now we'll make a slight change to the problem specification from Figure 6-3. The Savers Club application will now need to display the number of years required for the savings account to reach $100,000, and the balance in the account at that time. Consider the changes you will need to make to the calcButton's pseudocode in Figure 6-3.

The first two steps in the original pseudocode store the input items (deposit and interest rate) in variables; the modified pseudocode will still need both of these steps. Steps 3 and 4 calculate the interest and then add the interest to the savings account balance. The modified pseudocode will need to repeat both of those steps either *while* the balance is less than $100,000 (looping condition) or *until* the balance is greater than or equal to $100,000 (loop exit condition). Notice that the loop exit condition is the opposite of the looping condition. The loop in the modified pseudocode will also need to keep track of the number of times the instructions in Steps 3 and 4 are processed because each time represents a year. The last step in the original pseudocode displays the account balance. The modified pseudocode will need to display the account balance and also the number of years.

The modified problem description is shown in Figure 6-4 along with four versions of the modified pseudocode. (As mentioned in Chapter 5, even small procedures can have more than one solution.) Only the loop is different in each version. Each loop's condition is shaded in the figure.

Modified problem specification
Create an application for the Savers Club. The application should display the number of years required for the balance in a savings account to reach at least $100,000, given the amount of money deposited into the savings account at the beginning of the year and the annual interest rate. The application should also display the account balance at that time. The interest is compounded annually and no withdrawals or additional deposits are made during any of the years. The interest rate should be entered in decimal form.

Modified pseudocode for the calcButton Click event procedure

looping condition specifies when to continue

Version 1 – pretest loop
1. store deposit in balance variable
2. store interest rate in rate variable
3. repeat while balance < 100,000
        interest = balance * rate
        add interest to balance
        add 1 to number of years
    end repeat while
4. display balance and number of years

Version 2 – pretest loop
1. store deposit in balance variable
2. store interest rate in rate variable
3. repeat until balance >= 100,000
        interest = balance * rate
        add interest to balance
        add 1 to number of years
    end repeat until
4. display balance and number of years

loop exit condition specifies when to stop

Version 3 – posttest loop
1. store deposit in balance variable
2. store interest rate in rate variable
3. repeat
        interest = balance * rate
        add interest to balance
        add 1 to number of years
    end repeat while balance < 100,000
4. display balance and number of years

looping condition specifies when to continue

Version 4 – posttest loop
1. store deposit in balance variable
2. store interest rate in rate variable
3. repeat
        interest = balance * rate
        add interest to balance
        add 1 to number of years
    end repeat until balance >= 100,000
4. display balance and number of years

loop exit condition specifies when to stop

Figure 6-4   Modified problem specification and pseudocode
© 2013 Cengage Learning

The loops in Versions 1 and 2 in Figures 6-4 are pretest loops. In a **pretest loop**, the condition appears at the beginning of the loop, indicating that it is evaluated *before* the instructions within the loop are processed. The condition in Version 1 is a looping condition because it tells the computer when to *continue* repeating the loop instructions. Version 2's condition, on the other hand, is a loop exit condition because it tells the computer when to *stop* repeating the instructions. Depending on the result of the evaluation, the instructions in a pretest loop may never be processed. For example, if the user enters $102,000 as the deposit, the "while balance < 100,000" looping condition in Version 1 will evaluate to False and the loop instructions will be skipped over. Similarly, the "until balance >= 100,000" loop exit condition in Version 2 will evaluate to True, causing the loop instructions to be bypassed.

The loops in Versions 3 and 4 in Figure 6-4, on the other hand, are posttest loops. In a **posttest loop**, the condition appears at the end of the loop, indicating that it is evaluated *after* the instructions within the loop are processed. The condition in Version 3 is a looping condition, whereas the condition in Version 4 is a loop exit condition. Unlike the instructions in a pretest loop, the instructions in a posttest loop will always be processed at least once. In this case, if the user enters $102,000 as the deposit, the instructions in the two posttest loops will be processed once before the loop ends. Posttest loops should be used only when you are certain that the loop instructions should be processed at least once.

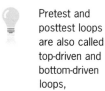

Pretest and posttest loops are also called top-driven and bottom-driven loops, respectively.

The answers to Mini-Quiz questions are located in Appendix A. Each question is associated with one or more objectives listed at the beginning of the chapter.

295

Mini-Quiz 6-1

1. It's possible that the instructions in this type of loop may never be processed. (2)

    a. posttest

    b. pretest

2. The "repeat until your hair is clean" instruction is an example of which type of condition? (1)

    a. looping

    b. loop exit

3. Which condition indicates when the loop instructions should be repeated? (1)

    a. looping

    b. loop exit

The Visual Basic language provides three different statements for coding loops: Do...Loop, For... Next, and For Each...Next. The Do...Loop statement can be used to code both pretest and posttest loops, whereas the For...Next and For Each...Next statements are used only for pretest loops. You will learn about the Do...Loop statement in this chapter. The For...Next and For Each...Next statements are covered in Chapters 7 and 9, respectively.

The Do...Loop Statement

Figure 6-5 shows two versions of the syntax for the **Do...Loop statement**: one for coding a pretest loop and the other for coding a posttest loop. The {While | Until} portion in each syntax indicates that you can select only one of the keywords appearing within the braces. You follow the keyword with a *condition*, which can contain variables, constants, properties, methods, keywords, and operators. Notice that the keyword and the condition appear in the Do clause in a pretest loop, but they appear in the Loop clause in a posttest loop. The examples in Figure 6-5 show how you could use both syntax versions to display the numbers 1, 2, and 3 in a label control. The figure also includes a sample run of an application that contains either example.

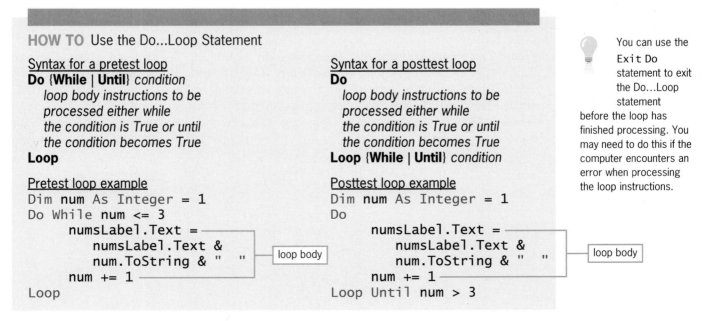

HOW TO Use the Do...Loop Statement

Syntax for a pretest loop
Do {While | Until} *condition*
    loop body instructions to be
    processed either while
    the condition is True or until
    the condition becomes True
Loop

Pretest loop example
```
Dim num As Integer = 1
Do While num <= 3
    numsLabel.Text =
        numsLabel.Text &
        num.ToString & "  "
    num += 1
Loop
```

Syntax for a posttest loop
Do
    loop body instructions to be
    processed either while
    the condition is True or until
    the condition becomes True
Loop {While | Until} *condition*

Posttest loop example
```
Dim num As Integer = 1
Do
    numsLabel.Text =
        numsLabel.Text &
        num.ToString & "  "
    num += 1
Loop Until num > 3
```

loop body

loop body

You can use the `Exit Do` statement to exit the Do...Loop statement before the loop has finished processing. You may need to do this if the computer encounters an error when processing the loop instructions.

Figure 6-5 How to use the Do...Loop statement *(continues)*

296

(continued)

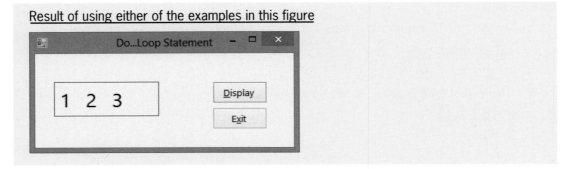

Figure 6-5   How to use the Do…Loop statement
© 2013 Cengage Learning

A loop's condition must evaluate to a Boolean value, either True or False. The condition can be phrased either as a looping condition or as a loop exit condition. You use the `While` keyword in a looping condition to specify that the loop body should be processed *while* (in other words, as long as) the condition evaluates to True. You use the `Until` keyword in a loop exit condition to specify that the loop body should be processed *until* the condition becomes True, at which time the loop should stop. The condition is evaluated with each repetition of the loop and determines whether the computer processes the loop body.

Although both examples in Figure 6-5 produce the same results, pretest and posttest loops are not always interchangeable. For instance, if the `num` variable in the pretest loop in Figure 6-5 is initialized to 10 rather than to 1, the instructions in the pretest loop will not be processed because the `num <= 3` condition (which is evaluated before the instructions are processed) evaluates to False. However, if the `num` variable in the posttest loop is initialized to 10 rather than to 1, the instructions in the posttest loop will be processed one time because the `num > 3` condition is evaluated after (rather than before) the loop instructions are processed.

Ch06-Do
Loop

Flowcharting a Loop

It's often easier to understand loops when viewed in flowchart form. Figure 6-6 shows the flowcharts associated with the loop examples from Figure 6-5. The diamond in each flowchart indicates the beginning of a repetition structure (loop). Like the diamond in a selection structure, the diamond in a repetition structure contains a condition that evaluates to either True or False only. The condition determines whether the instructions within the loop are processed. Also like the diamond in a selection structure, the diamond in a repetition structure has one flowline entering the symbol and two flowlines leaving the symbol. The two flowlines leading out of the diamond should be marked so that anyone reading the flowchart can distinguish the True path from the False path.

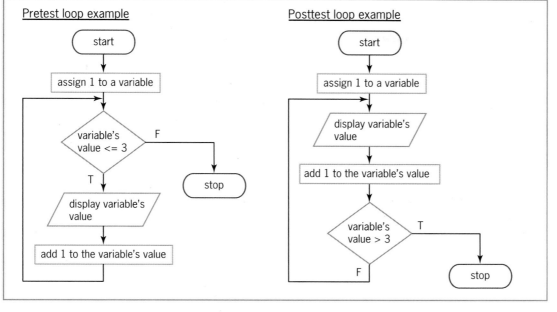

Figure 6-6 Flowcharts for the loop examples from Figure 6-5
© 2013 Cengage Learning

Rather than using T and F, you can use Y and N (for yes and no).

In the pretest loop's flowchart in Figure 6-6, a circle or loop is formed by the flowline entering the diamond combined with the diamond and the symbols and flowlines within the True path. In the posttest loop's flowchart, the loop (circle) is formed by all of the symbols and flowlines in the False path. It is this loop (circle) that distinguishes the repetition structure from the selection structure in a flowchart.

Coding the Savers Club Application

Earlier, in Figure 6-4, you viewed four versions of the modified pseudocode for the Savers Club application. Figure 6-7 shows the pseudocode from Version 1. It also shows the corresponding Visual Basic code. The looping condition in the Do...Loop statement tells the computer to repeat the loop body as long as (or while) the number in the `balance` variable is less than 100,000. Rather than using a looping condition in the Do clause, you can use a loop exit condition, like this: `Do Until balance >= 100000`. (Recall that >= is the opposite of <.) Figure 6-7 also shows a sample run of the application.

Version 1 pseudocode from Figure 6-4
1. store deposit in balance variable
2. store interest rate in rate variable
3. repeat while balance < 100,000
       interest = balance * rate
       add interest to balance
       add 1 to number of years
   end repeat while
4. display balance and number of years

Figure 6-7 Savers Club application using a loop *(continues)*

(continued)

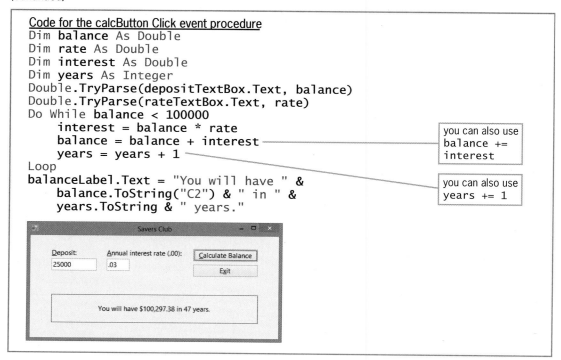

Figure 6-7 Savers Club application using a loop
© 2013 Cengage Learning

As you learned in previous chapters, it's important to test your code thoroughly, using both valid and invalid data. In this case, invalid data for both text boxes would include a letter, a space, or a special character. However, a text box that contains only the number 0, as well as one that contains no data at all, would also be inappropriate. You can use each text box's KeyPress event procedure to prevent the text box from accepting letters, spaces, and special characters. However, you can't use it to prevent the user either from entering only the number 0 or from leaving the text box empty. If the user clicks the Calculate Balance button without entering the deposit and/or rate, or entering only the number 0 in either or both text boxes, a run time error will occur. As a result, one of the error message boxes shown in Figure 6-8 will appear.

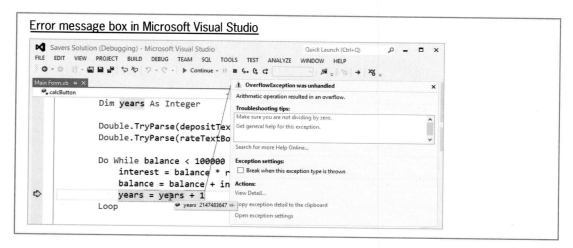

Figure 6-8 Error message boxes *(continues)*

(continued)

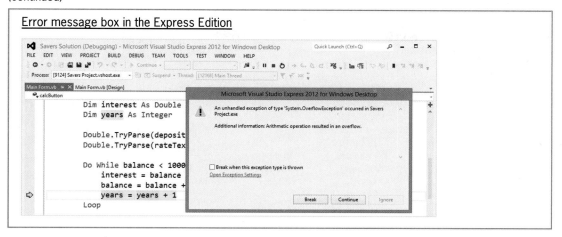

Figure 6-8   Error message boxes

Both error messages in Figure 6-8 indicate that an arithmetic operation—in this case, adding 1 to the `years` variable—resulted in an overflow. An **overflow error** occurs when the value assigned to a memory location is too large for the location's data type. (An overflow error is similar to trying to fill an 8-ounce glass with 10 ounces of water.) In this case, the `years` variable already contains the highest value that can be stored in an Integer variable (2,147,483,647 according to Figure 3-3 in Chapter 3). Therefore, when the `years = years + 1` statement attempts to increase the variable's value by 1, an overflow error occurs.

But why does the `years` variable contain 2,147,483,647 when one or both text boxes are either empty or contain only the number 0? When you don't provide a valid amount for the initial deposit and/or interest rate, the loop's condition (`balance < 100000`) will always evaluate to True; it will never evaluate to False, which is required for stopping the loop. A loop that has no way to end is called an **infinite loop** or an **endless loop**. You can stop a program that has an infinite loop by clicking DEBUG on the menu bar and then clicking Stop Debugging. (If you are using the Express Edition, you will need to click the Break button in the error message box before clicking the DEBUG menu.)

You can use a selection structure to prevent the overflow error. The structure's condition will determine whether the `balance` and `rate` variables contain values that are greater than 0. The final pseudocode and code for the calcButton's Click event procedure are shown in Figure 6-9. The figure also shows the result of clicking the Calculate Balance button when both text boxes are empty.

Selection structure added to the pseudocode from Figure 6-7
1. store deposit in balance variable
2. store interest rate in rate variable
3. if balance and rate are greater than 0
        repeat while balance < 100,000
            interest = balance * rate
            add interest to balance
            add 1 to number of years
        end repeat while
    end if
4. display balance and number of years

Figure 6-9   Final pseudocode and code for the calcButton Click event procedure *(continues)*

(continued)

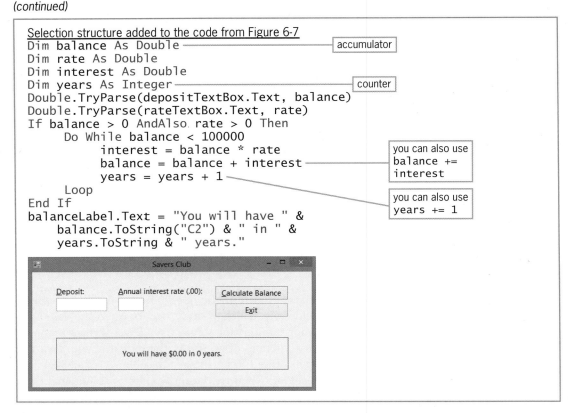

Figure 6-9   Final pseudocode and code for the calcButton Click event procedure
© 2013 Cengage Learning

If you want to experiment with the Savers Club application, open the solution contained in the Try It 1! folder.

The Click event procedure in Figure 6-9 uses a counter to keep track of the number of years. It also uses an accumulator to keep track of the account balance. Counters and accumulators are covered in the next section.

Counters and Accumulators

Some procedures require you to calculate a subtotal, a total, or an average. You make these calculations using a loop that includes a counter, an accumulator, or both. A **counter** is a numeric variable used for counting something, such as the number of employees paid in a week. An **accumulator** is a numeric variable used for accumulating (adding together) something, such as the total dollar amount of a week's payroll. The `years` variable in the code shown earlier in Figure 6-9 is a counter because it keeps track of the number of years required for the account balance to reach 100,000. The `balance` variable in the code is an accumulator because it adds each annual interest amount to the current account balance.

Two tasks are associated with counters and accumulators: initializing and updating. **Initializing** means to assign a beginning value to the counter or accumulator. The initialization task is performed before the loop is processed because it needs to be performed only once. In most cases, counters and accumulators are initialized to the number 0. However, they can be initialized to any number, depending on the value required by the procedure's code. The procedure shown earlier in Figure 6-9, for example, needs to start counting the years at 0, but start accumulating the interest amounts beginning with the user's initial deposit. The `years` variable in the code is initialized to 0 in its declaration statement. The `balance` variable is initialized to the initial deposit in the first TryParse method.

Updating refers to the process of either adding a number to (called **incrementing**) or subtracting a number from (called **decrementing**) the value stored in the counter or accumulator. The number can be either positive or negative, integer or non-integer. A counter is always updated by a constant amount, which is usually the number 1. An accumulator, on the other hand, is updated by an amount that varies, and it is usually updated by incrementing rather than by decrementing. The assignment statement that updates a counter or an accumulator is placed within the loop body. This is because the update task must be performed each time the loop instructions are processed. In the code shown earlier in Figure 6-9, the last two assignment statements in the loop body update the `years` counter and `balance` accumulator: The counter is incremented by 1, and the accumulator is incremented by the annual interest amount.

Figure 6-10 shows the syntax used for updating counters and accumulators, and it includes examples of using the syntax. The syntax for counters tells the computer to add (or subtract) the *constantValue* to (from) the *counterVariable* first, and then place the result back in the *counterVariable*. If the `years` variable contains the number 1, then the update statement `years = years + 1` will change the variable's contents to 2. You can also write the update statement as `years += 1`. The syntax for accumulators tells the computer to add the *value* to (or subtract the *value* from) the *accumulatorVariable* first, and then place the result back in the *accumulatorVariable*. If the `balance` and `interest` variables contain the numbers 2015.41 and 10.15, respectively, then the update statement `balance = balance + interest` will change the `balance` variable's contents to 2025.56. You can also write the update statement as `balance += interest`.

HOW TO Update Counters and Accumulators

Syntax for counters
counterVariable = *counterVariable* {**+** | **−**} *constantValue*
counterVariable {**+=** | **−=**} *constantValue*

Counter examples
```
years = years + 1
years += 1
students = students – 1
evenNum = evenNum + 2
```

Syntax for accumulators
accumulatorVariable = *accumulatorVariable* {**+** | **−**} *value*
accumulatorVariable {**+=** | **−=**} *value*

Accumulator examples
```
balance = balance + interest
balance += interest
sum = sum + num
totalSales += sales
```

Figure 6-10   How to update counters and accumulators
© 2013 Cengage Learning

Mini-Quiz 6-2

1. Which of the following clauses will stop the loop when the `age` variable contains a number that is greater than 21? (1, 4)

    a.   Do While age <= 21

    b.   Do Until age > 21

    c.   Loop Until age > 21

    d.   all of the above

2. Write an assignment statement that updates an accumulator named `sum` by the value in the `score` variable. Both variables have the Double data type. (5)

3. Write an assignment statement that updates a counter named `numValues` by 5. (5)

4. Write an assignment statement that updates a counter named `numItems` by −1 (a negative 1). (5)

The answers to Mini-Quiz questions are located in Appendix A.
Each question is associated with one or more objectives listed at the beginning of the chapter.

The InputBox Function

At times, you may want to prompt the user to enter some specific information while an application is running; you can do this using the **InputBox function**. The function displays an input dialog box, which is one of the standard dialog boxes available in Visual Basic. An example of an input dialog box is shown in Figure 6-11. The message in the dialog box should prompt the user to enter the appropriate information in the input area. The user closes the dialog box by clicking the OK button, the Cancel button, or the Close button. The value returned by the InputBox function depends on the button the user chooses. If the user clicks the OK button, the function returns the value contained in the input area of the dialog box; the return value is always treated as a string. If the user clicks either the Cancel button in the dialog box or the Close button on the dialog box's title bar, the function returns an empty (or zero-length) string.

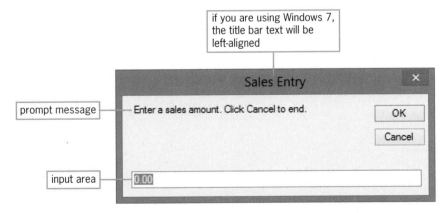

Figure 6-11   Example of an input dialog box

Figure 6-12 shows the basic syntax of the InputBox function. The *prompt* argument contains the message to display inside the dialog box. The optional *title* and *defaultResponse* arguments control the text that appears in the dialog box's title bar and input area, respectively. If you omit the *title* argument, the project name appears in the title bar. If you omit the *defaultResponse* argument, a blank input area appears when the dialog box opens.

The *prompt, title,* and *defaultResponse* arguments must be enclosed in quotation marks, unless that information is stored in a String named constant or a String variable. The Windows standard is to use sentence capitalization for the prompt, but book title capitalization for the title. The capitalization (if any) you use for the defaultResponse depends on the text itself. In most cases, you assign the value returned by the InputBox function to a String variable, as shown in the first three examples in Figure 6-12. However, you can also store the value in a numeric variable by first converting the value to the appropriate numeric data type, as shown in Example 4 in the figure. You will use the InputBox function to code the Average Stock Price application in the next section.

HOW TO Use the InputBox Function

Syntax
InputBox(*prompt*[*, title*][*, defaultResponse*]**)**

Example 1
```
Dim inputSales As String
inputSales =
    InputBox("Enter a sales amount. Click Cancel to end.",
    "Sales Entry", "0.00")
```
Displays the input dialog box shown in Figure 6-11. When the user closes the dialog box, the assignment statement assigns the function's return value to the `inputSales` variable.

Example 2
```
Dim city As String
city = InputBox("City name:", "City Entry")
```
Displays an input dialog box that shows City name: as the prompt, City Entry in the title bar, and an empty input area. When the user closes the dialog box, the assignment statement assigns the function's return value to the `city` variable.

Example 3
```
Const Prompt As String = "Hours worked:"
Const Title As String = "Hours"
Dim hours As String
hours = InputBox(Prompt, Title, "40.0")
```
Displays an input dialog box that shows Hours worked: as the prompt, Hours in the title bar, and 40.0 in the input area. When the user closes the dialog box, the assignment statement assigns the function's return value to the `hours` variable.

Example 4
```
Dim age As Integer
Integer.TryParse(InputBox("How old are you?",
                "Discount Verification"), age)
```
Displays an input dialog box that shows How old are you? as the prompt, Discount Verification in the title bar, and an empty input area. When the user closes the dialog box, the TryParse method converts the function's return value from String to Integer and then stores the result in the `age` variable.

The InputBox function's syntax also includes optional *XPos* and *YPos* arguments for specifying the dialog box's horizontal and vertical positions, respectively. If both arguments are omitted, the dialog box appears centered on the screen.

Figure 6-12 How to use the InputBox function
© 2013 Cengage Learning

Average Stock Price Application

Figure 6-13 shows the problem specification for the Average Stock Price application, which uses a loop, a counter, and an accumulator to calculate the average stock price entered by the user. The figure also includes the pseudocode and flowchart for the calcButton's Click event procedure. The priming and update reads are shaded in the pseudocode and flowchart. As you learned earlier, the priming read appears above the loop, while the update read appears within the loop.

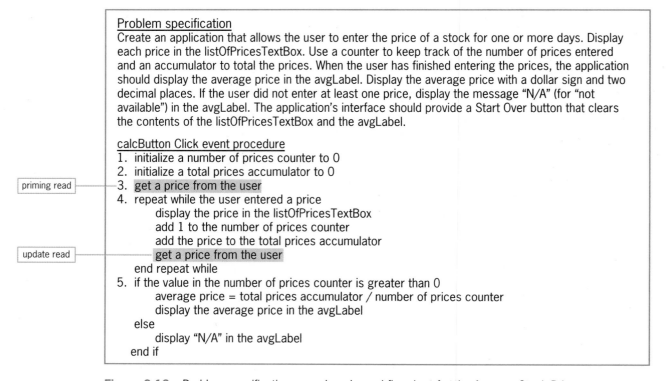

Problem specification
Create an application that allows the user to enter the price of a stock for one or more days. Display each price in the listOfPricesTextBox. Use a counter to keep track of the number of prices entered and an accumulator to total the prices. When the user has finished entering the prices, the application should display the average price in the avgLabel. Display the average price with a dollar sign and two decimal places. If the user did not enter at least one price, display the message "N/A" (for "not available") in the avgLabel. The application's interface should provide a Start Over button that clears the contents of the listOfPricesTextBox and the avgLabel.

calcButton Click event procedure
1. initialize a number of prices counter to 0
2. initialize a total prices accumulator to 0
3. get a price from the user ← priming read
4. repeat while the user entered a price
        display the price in the listOfPricesTextBox
        add 1 to the number of prices counter
        add the price to the total prices accumulator
        get a price from the user ← update read
   end repeat while
5. if the value in the number of prices counter is greater than 0
        average price = total prices accumulator / number of prices counter
        display the average price in the avgLabel
   else
        display "N/A" in the avgLabel
   end if

Figure 6-13   Problem specification, pseudocode, and flowchart for the Average Stock Price application *(continues)*

(continued)

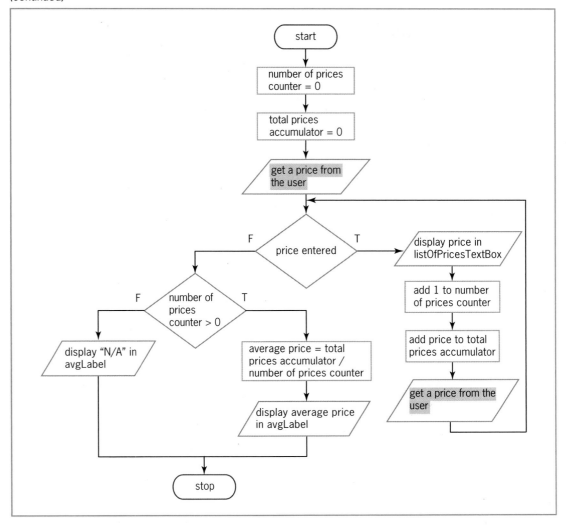

Figure 6-13 Problem specification, pseudocode, and flowchart for the Average Stock Price application
© 2013 Cengage Learning

Figure 6-14 shows the code corresponding to the pseudocode and flowchart from Figure 6-13; it also includes a sample run of the application. The listOfPricesTextBox in the interface has its Multiline and ReadOnly properties set to True, and its ScrollBars property set to Vertical. When a text box's **Multiline property** is set to True, the text box can both accept and display multiple lines of text; otherwise, only one line of text can be entered in the text box. Changing a text box's **ReadOnly property** from its default value (False) to True prevents the user from changing the contents of the text box during run time. A text box's **ScrollBars property** specifies whether the text box has no scroll bars (the default), a horizontal scroll bar, a vertical scroll bar, or both horizontal and vertical scroll bars. The listOfPricesTextBox also has its TextAlign property set to Right.

```
Private Sub calcButton_Click(sender As Object,
e As EventArgs) Handles calcButton.Click
    ' calculates the average stock price

    Const Prompt As String = "Enter a stock price. " &
        ControlChars.NewLine &
        "Click Cancel or leave blank to end."
    Const Title As String = "Stock Price Entry"
    Dim inputPrice As String
    Dim price As Decimal
    Dim numPrices As Integer
    Dim totalPrices As Decimal
    Dim avgPrice As Decimal

    ' get first stock price
    inputPrice = InputBox(Prompt, Title)

    ' repeat as long as the user enters a price
    Do While inputPrice <> String.Empty
        ' convert the price to a number
        Decimal.TryParse(inputPrice, price)

        ' update the counter and accumulator
        numPrices += 1
        totalPrices += price

        ' display the price in the text box
        listOfPricesTextBox.Text =
            listOfPricesTextBox.Text &
            price.ToString("N2") & ControlChars.NewLine

        ' get the next price
        inputPrice = InputBox(Prompt, Title)
    Loop

    ' verify that the counter is greater than 0
    If numPrices > 0 Then
        avgPrice = totalPrices / numPrices
        avgLabel.Text = avgPrice.ToString("C2")
    Else
        avgLabel.Text = "N/A"
    End If
End Sub
```

priming read → inputPrice = InputBox(Prompt, Title)

update read → inputPrice = InputBox(Prompt, Title)

If you want to experiment with the Average Stock Price application, open the solution contained in the Try It 2! folder.

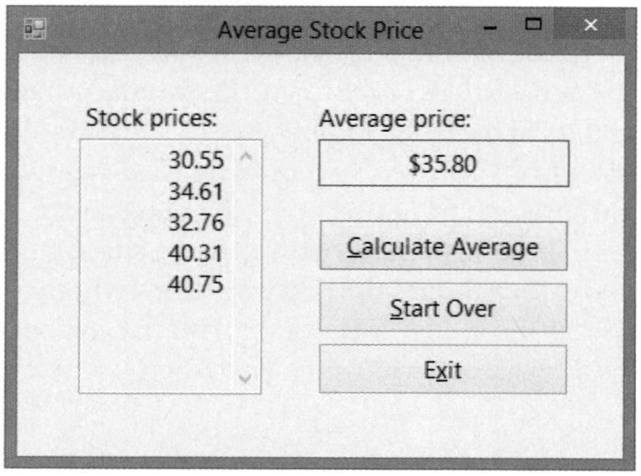

Figure 6-14   Code and a sample run of the Average Stock Price application
© 2013 Cengage Learning

Notice that the InputBox function is used for both the priming read and the update read. The importance of the update read cannot be stressed enough. If you don't include the update read in the loop body, there will be no way to enter a value that will stop the loop after it has been processed the first time. This is because the priming read is processed only once and gets only the first stock price from the user. Without the update read, the loop will have no way of stopping on its own. As you learned earlier, a loop that has no way to end is called an infinite (or endless) loop.

Mini-Quiz 6-3

The answers to Mini-Quiz questions are located in Appendix A. Each question is associated with one or more objectives listed at the beginning of the chapter.

1. Which of the following properties allows a text box to accept and display multiple lines of text? (7)

   a. Multiline

   b. MultipleLine

   c. MultipleLines

   d. none of the above

2. The update read appears ——————— the loop. (4)

   a. above

   b. within

3. Which of the following statements prompts the user to enter a ZIP code and then assigns the user's response to a String variable named `zip`? (6)

   a. `InputBox("ZIP code:", "ZIP", zip)`

   b. `Input("ZIP code:", "ZIP", zip)`

   c. `zip = Input("ZIP code:", "ZIP")`

   d. `zip = InputBox("ZIP code:", "ZIP")`

Note: You have learned a lot so far in this chapter. You may want to take a break at this point before continuing.

Including a List Box in an Interface

The Do...Loop statement is often used to assign values to a list box. You add a list box to an interface using the ListBox tool in the toolbox. A **list box** displays a list of items from which the user can select zero items, one item, or multiple items. The number of items the user can select is controlled by the list box's **SelectionMode property**. The default value for the property, One, allows the user to select only one item at a time.

You can learn more about list boxes in Computer Exercises 33 and 34 at the end of this chapter.

In most cases, a list box should be sized so that it displays at least three items but no more than eight items at a time. If you have more items than can fit into the list box, the control automatically displays a scroll bar for viewing the complete list of items. You should use a label control to provide keyboard access to the list box. For the access key to work correctly, you must set the label's TabIndex property to a value that is one number less than the list box's TabIndex value.

If you have only two items to offer the user, use two radio buttons rather than a list box.

Adding Items to a List Box

The items in a list box belong to a collection called the **Items collection**. A **collection** is a group of individual objects treated as one unit. The first item in the Items collection appears as the first item in the list box. The second item in the collection appears as the second item in the list box, and so on. You can use the String Collection Editor window, which is shown in Figure 6-15, to specify the list box items during design time. You can open the window by clicking the ellipsis button in the list box's Items property in the Properties list. Or you can click Edit Items on the list box's task list.

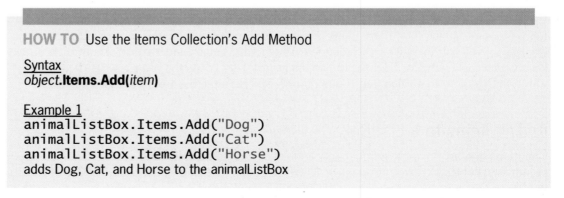

If you want to experiment with the Cities application, open the solution contained in the Try It 3! folder.

Figure 6-15   String Collection Editor window

Rather than using the String Collection Editor window to add items to a list box, you can use the Items collection's **Add method**. Figure 6-16 shows the method's syntax, and includes examples and the results of using the method. In the syntax, *object* is the name of the list box control, and the *item* argument is the text you want to add to the control's list. The three Add methods in Example 1 will add the strings "Dog", "Cat", and "Horse" to the animalListBox. In Example 2, the Add method appears in the body of a pretest loop that repeats its instructions for **code** values of 100 through 105. As a result, the Add method will add the values 100, 101, 102, 103, 104, and 105 (each converted to the String data type) to the codeListBox. You can also write the Add method in Example 2 as follows: `codeListBox.Items.Add(Convert.ToString(code))`.

HOW TO Use the Items Collection's Add Method

Syntax
object.**Items.Add(***item***)**

Example 1
```
animalListBox.Items.Add("Dog")
animalListBox.Items.Add("Cat")
animalListBox.Items.Add("Horse")
```
adds Dog, Cat, and Horse to the animalListBox

Figure 6-16   How to use the Items Collection's Add Method *(continues)*

(continued)

Example 2
```
Dim code As Integer = 100
Do While code <= 105
      codeListBox.Items.Add(code.ToString)
      code += 1
Loop
```
adds 100, 101, 102, 103, 104, and 105 to the codeListBox

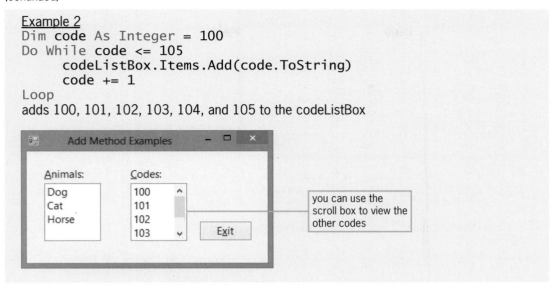

Figure 6-16 How to use the Items Collection's Add Method
© 2013 Cengage Learning

In most cases, you enter the Add methods in the Load event procedure of a form, as shown in Figure 6-17. To open the Load event procedure, you click the Class Name list arrow in the Code Editor window and then click (*formName* Events) in the list, where *formName* is the name of your form. You then click the Method Name list arrow and click Load. A form's **Load event** occurs when an application is started and the form is about to be displayed for the first time. Any code contained in the Load event procedure is processed before the form is displayed on the screen. In this case, the Add methods in Figure 6-17 ensure that the list boxes display their values when the interface comes into view.

```
Main Form.vb ⇒ ✕ Main Form.vb [Design]
⨍ (MainForm Events)                                          ⨍ Load

        Private Sub MainForm_Load(sender As Object, e As EventArgs) Handles Me.Load

            ' add items to the animalListBox
            animalListBox.Items.Add("Dog")
            animalListBox.Items.Add("Cat")
            animalListBox.Items.Add("Horse")

            ' add items to the codeListBox
            Dim code As Integer = 100
            Do While code <= 105
                codeListBox.Items.Add(code.ToString)
                code += 1
            Loop
        End Sub
```

Figure 6-17 Add methods entered in the MainForm's Load event procedure

If you want to experiment with the Add Method Examples application, open the solution contained in the Try It 4! folder.

At times, you may want to allow the user to add items to a list box during run time. The Jasper's Food Hut application accomplishes this by providing a text box for entering an item, and a button for adding the item to the list box. Figure 6-18 shows a sample run of the application. It also shows the addButton_Click procedure, which uses the Add method to add the contents of the nameTextBox to the workerListBox.

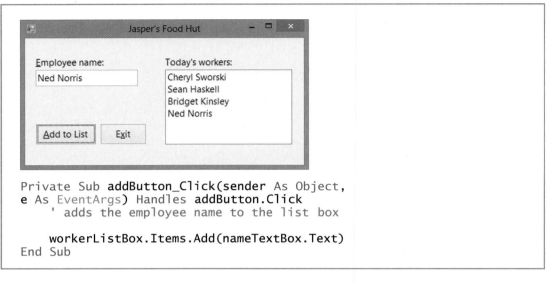

If you want to experiment with the Jasper's Food Hut application, open the solution contained in the Try It 5! folder.

```
Private Sub addButton_Click(sender As Object,
e As EventArgs) Handles addButton.Click
    ' adds the employee name to the list box

    workerListBox.Items.Add(nameTextBox.Text)
End Sub
```

Figure 6-18   Sample run and code for the Jasper's Food Hut application
© 2013 Cengage Learning

The Clark's Chicken application uses a different approach to allow the user to add items to a list box during run time. Figure 6-19 shows a sample run of the application. It also shows the enterButton_Click procedure, which uses the Add method, a pretest loop, and the InputBox function to add employee names to the list box.

If you want to experiment with the Clark's Chicken application, open the solution contained in the Try It 6! folder.

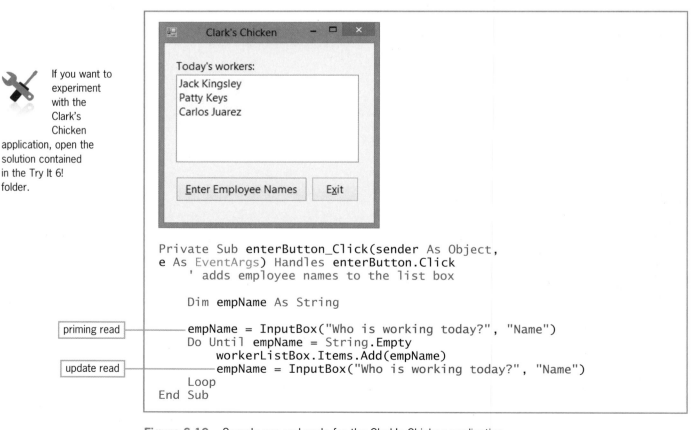

```
Private Sub enterButton_Click(sender As Object,
e As EventArgs) Handles enterButton.Click
    ' adds employee names to the list box

    Dim empName As String

    empName = InputBox("Who is working today?", "Name")
    Do Until empName = String.Empty
        workerListBox.Items.Add(empName)
        empName = InputBox("Who is working today?", "Name")
    Loop
End Sub
```

priming read

update read

Figure 6-19   Sample run and code for the Clark's Chicken application
© 2013 Cengage Learning

Clearing the Items from a List Box

You can use the Items collection's **Clear method** to clear the items from a list box. The method's syntax and an example of using the method are shown in Figure 6-20.

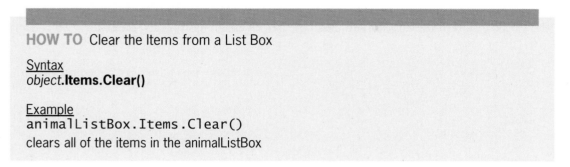

HOW TO Clear the Items from a List Box

Syntax
object.**Items.Clear()**

Example
```
animalListBox.Items.Clear()
```
clears all of the items in the animalListBox

Figure 6-20 How to clear the items from a list box
© 2013 Cengage Learning

The Sorted Property

The position of an item in a list box depends on the value stored in the list box's **Sorted property**. When the Sorted property is set to False (the default value), the item is added at the end of the list. When the Sorted property is set to True, the item is sorted along with the existing items and then placed in its proper position in the list. Visual Basic sorts the list box items in dictionary order, which means that numbers are sorted before letters, and a lowercase letter is sorted before its uppercase equivalent. The items in a list box are sorted based on the leftmost characters in each item. As a result, the items "Personnel", "Inventory", and "Payroll" will appear in the following order when the deptListBox's Sorted property is set to True: Inventory, Payroll, and Personnel. Likewise, the items 1, 2, 3, and 10 will appear in the following order when the numListBox's Sorted property is set to True: 1, 10, 2, and 3. Both list boxes are shown in Figure 6-21.

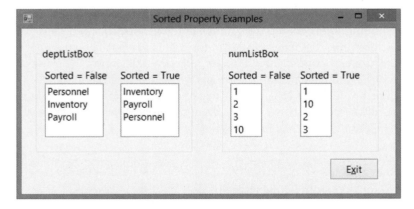

Figure 6-21 Examples of the list box's Sorted property

The requirements of the application you are creating determine whether you display the list box items in either sorted order or the order in which they are added to the list box. If several list items are selected much more frequently than other items, you typically leave the list box's Sorted property set to False and then add the frequently used items first to ensure that they appear at the beginning of the list. However, if the list box items are selected fairly equally, you typically set the list box's Sorted property to True because it is easier to locate items when they appear in a sorted order.

Accessing Items in a List Box

Each item in the Items collection is identified by a unique number, which is called an **index**. The first item in the collection (which also is the first item in the list box) has an index of 0. The second item's index is 1, and so on. The index allows you to access a specific item in the list box, as shown in the syntax and examples in Figure 6-22. Notice that you need to convert the list box item to the appropriate data type before assigning it to a variable.

HOW TO Access an Item in a List Box

Syntax
object.**Items**(*index*)

Example 1
```
Dim animalType As String
animalType = Convert.ToString(animalListBox.Items(0))
```
or
```
animalType = animalListBox.Items(0).ToString
```
assigns the first item in the animalListBox to the animalType variable

Example 2
```
Dim myCode As Integer
myCode = Convert.ToInt32(codeListBox.Items(2))
```
or
```
Integer.TryParse(codeListBox.Items(2).ToString, myCode)
```
assigns the third item in the codeListBox to the myCode variable

Figure 6-22 How to access an item in a list box
© 2013 Cengage Learning

Determining the Number of Items in a List Box

The number of items in a list box is stored in the Items collection's **Count property**. The property's value is always one number more than the last index in the list box; this is because the first index in a list box is 0. For example, the highest index in the animalListBox shown earlier in Figure 6-16 is 2, but the Count property contains the number 3. Figure 6-23 shows the syntax of the Count property and includes examples of using the property. Notice that the loop instructions in Example 2 will be processed as long as the index variable contains a value that is less than the number of items in the codeListBox. This is because the codeListBox's highest index is 4, but the value in its Count property is 5.

HOW TO Determine the Number of Items in a List Box

Syntax
object.**Items.Count**

Example 1
```
Dim numAnimals As Integer
numAnimals = animalListBox.Items.Count
```
assigns the number 3, which is the number of items contained in the animalListBox (shown earlier in Figure 6-16) to the **numAnimals** variable

Figure 6-23 How to determine the number of items in a list box *(continues)*

(continued)

```
Example 2
Dim numCodes As Integer
Dim index As Integer
numCodes = codeListBox.Items.Count
Do While index < numCodes
    MessageBox.Show(codeListBox.Items(index).ToString)
    index += 1
Loop
```
displays the codeListBox items (100, 101, 102, 103, 104, and 105) in message boxes
(You can also use the Convert.ToString method rather than the ToString method.)

Figure 6-23 How to determine the number of items in a list box
© 2013 Cengage Learning

The SelectedItem and SelectedIndex Properties

You can use either the **SelectedItem property** or the **SelectedIndex property** to determine whether an item is selected in a list box. When no item is selected, the SelectedItem property contains the empty string, and the SelectedIndex property contains the number −1 (negative 1). Otherwise, the SelectedItem and SelectedIndex properties contain the value of the selected item and the item's index, respectively. Figure 6-24 shows examples of using the SelectedItem and SelectedIndex properties. The examples refer to the list boxes shown earlier in Figure 6-16.

HOW TO Use the SelectedItem and SelectedIndex Properties

Example 1 (SelectedItem property)
```
animalLabel.Text = Convert.ToString(animalListBox.SelectedItem)
```
converts the item selected in the animalListBox to String and then assigns the result to the animalLabel

Example 2 (SelectedItem property)
```
If Convert.ToInt32(codeListBox.SelectedItem) = 103 Then
```
converts the item selected in the codeListBox to Integer and then compares the result to the integer 103

Example 3 (SelectedItem property)
```
If Convert.ToString(codeListBox.SelectedItem) = "103" Then
```
converts the item selected in the codeListBox to String and then compares the result to the string "103"

Example 4 (SelectedItem property)
```
If Convert.ToString(codeListBox.SelectedItem) <> String.Empty Then
```
converts the item selected in the codeListBox to String and then compares the result to the empty string

Figure 6-24 How to use the SelectedItem and SelectedIndex properties *(continues)*

(continued)

Example 5 (SelectedIndex property)
```
MessageBox.Show(animalListBox.SelectedIndex.ToString)
```
converts the index of the item selected in the animalListBox to String and then displays the result in a message box (You also can use the Convert.ToString method rather than the ToString method.)

Example 6 (SelectedIndex property)
```
If codeListBox.SelectedIndex = 0 Then
```
compares the index of the item selected in the codeListBox with the number 0

Figure 6-24 How to use the SelectedItem and SelectedIndex properties
© 2013 Cengage Learning

If a list box allows the user to make only one selection, it is customary in Windows applications to have one of the list box items already selected when the interface appears. The selected item, called the **default list box item**, should be either the item selected most frequently or the first item in the list. You can use either the SelectedItem property or the SelectedIndex property to select the default list box item from code, as shown in the examples in Figure 6-25. The examples refer to the list boxes shown earlier in Figure 6-16. In most cases, you enter the appropriate code in the form's Load event procedure.

HOW TO Select the Default List Box Item

Example 1 (SelectedItem property)
```
animalListBox.SelectedItem = "Cat"
```
selects the Cat item in the animalListBox

Example 2 (SelectedItem property)
```
codeListBox.SelectedItem = "101"
```
selects the 101 item in the codeListBox

Example 3 (SelectedIndex property)
```
codeListBox.SelectedIndex = 2
```
selects the third item in the codeListBox

Figure 6-25 How to select the default list box item
© 2013 Cengage Learning

The SelectedValueChanged and SelectedIndexChanged Events

Each time either the user or a statement selects an item in a list box, the list box's **SelectedValueChanged event** occurs followed by its **SelectedIndexChanged event**. You can use the procedures associated with these events to perform one or more tasks when the selected item has changed.

Figure 6-26 shows the SelectedValueChanged and SelectedIndexChanged procedures for the animalListBox and codeListBox, respectively, in the ListBox Events application. It also shows the form's Load event procedure, which fills the list boxes with items and then selects the default item in each list box. Selecting the default item will invoke the list box's SelectedValueChanged and SelectedIndexChanged events, causing the computer to process any code contained in the corresponding event procedures. The figure also contains a sample run of the application.

314

```
Private Sub MainForm_Load(sender As Object,
e As EventArgs) Handles Me.Load

    ' add items to the animalListBox
    animalListBox.Items.Add("Dog")
    animalListBox.Items.Add("Cat")
    animalListBox.Items.Add("Horse")

    ' add items to the codeListBox
    Dim code As Integer = 100
    Do While code <= 105
        codeListBox.Items.Add(code.ToString)
        code += 1
    Loop

    ' select the default list box item
        animalListBox.SelectedIndex = 0 ────────┐ selects the
        codeListBox.SelectedItem = "100"─────────┘ default item
End Sub

Private Sub animalListBox_SelectedValueChanged( ──── SelectedValueChanged
sender As Object, e As EventArgs                     procedure
) Handles animalListBox.SelectedValueChanged
    ' displays the animal's name

    Dim animal As String
    animal = Convert.ToString(animalListBox.SelectedItem)

    Select Case animal
        Case "Dog"
            animalLabel.Text = "Rover"
        Case "Cat"
            animalLabel.Text = "Fluffy"
        Case Else
            animalLabel.Text = "Poco"
    End Select
End Sub

Private Sub codeListBox_SelectedIndexChanged( ──── SelectedIndexChanged
sender As Object, e As EventArgs                   procedure
) Handles codeListBox.SelectedIndexChanged
    ' displays the department name

    Select Case codeListBox.SelectedIndex
        Case 0
            deptLabel.Text = "Personnel"
        Case 1
            deptLabel.Text = "Payroll"
        Case 2
            deptLabel.Text = "Budget"
        Case 3
            deptLabel.Text = "Inventory"
        Case 4
            deptLabel.Text = "Security"
        Case Else
            deptLabel.Text = "Accounting"
    End Select
End Sub
```

Figure 6-26 Code and a sample run for the ListBox Events application *(continues)*

(continued)

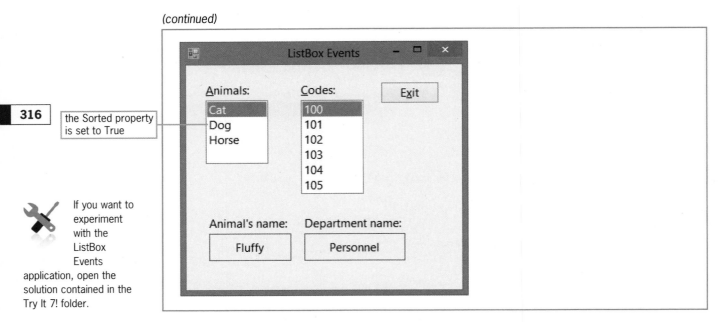

the Sorted property is set to True

If you want to experiment with the ListBox Events application, open the solution contained in the Try It 7! folder.

Figure 6-26   Code and a sample run for the ListBox Events application
© 2013 Cengage Learning

The SelectedValueChanged procedure in Figure 6-26 uses the SelectedItem property to determine the item selected in the animalListBox. It then uses that information to display the name of the animal associated with the selected item. You also could have entered this code in the animalListBox's SelectedIndexChanged procedure.

The SelectedIndexChanged procedure in Figure 6-26 uses the SelectedIndex property to determine the index of the code selected in the list box. It then uses that information to display the name of the department associated with the selected code. You also could have entered this code in the codeListBox's SelectedValueChanged procedure.

When coding a list box's SelectedValueChanged procedure, you can use either the SelectedItem property (as shown in Figure 6-26) or the SelectedIndex property to determine the selected item. Similarly, you can use either the SelectedIndex property (as shown in Figure 6-26) or the SelectedItem property in the list box's SelectedIndexChanged procedure.

The Product Finder Application

The Product Finder application demonstrates most of what you learned about list boxes. It also provides another example of using a repetition structure. The problem specification and pseudocode are shown in Figure 6-27.

Problem specification

Create an application that searches a list box for the product ID entered by the user. If the product ID is included in the list box, highlight (select) the ID in the list. Otherwise, ensure that no ID is highlighted in the list box, and then display a message indicating that the ID was not found.

findButton Click event procedure
1. assign the product ID entered by the user to a variable
2. assign the number of list box items to a variable
3. repeat while the list box item's index is less than the number of items in the list and the product ID has not been found
      if the product ID entered by the user is the same as the current item in the list box
          indicate that the product ID was found by assigning True to a Boolean variable
      else
          continue the search by adding 1 to the list box index
      end if
   end repeat while

4. if the product ID was found (indicated by a True value in the Boolean variable)
      select the product ID in the list box
   else
      clear any selection in the list box
      display the "Not found" message in a message box
   end if

Figure 6-27 Problem specification and pseudocode for the Product Finder application
© 2013 Cengage Learning

Figure 6-28 shows most of the application's code and includes two sample runs of the application.

```
Private Sub MainForm_Load(sender As Object,
e As EventArgs) Handles Me.Load
    ' fills the list box with IDs

    idListBox.Items.Add("FX123")
    idListBox.Items.Add("AB654")
    idListBox.Items.Add("JH733")
    idListBox.Items.Add("FX457")
    idListBox.Items.Add("NK111")
    idListBox.Items.Add("KYT897")
    idListBox.Items.Add("KVB419")
    idListBox.Items.Add("PQR333")
    idListBox.Items.Add("UVP492")
End Sub
```

Figure 6-28 Code and sample runs for the Product Finder application *(continues)*

(continued)

```vb
Private Sub findButton_Click(sender As Object,
e As EventArgs) Handles findButton.Click
    ' searches a list box for a specific ID

    Dim isFound As Boolean
    Dim index As Integer
    Dim numItems As Integer
    Dim id As String

    ' assign ID and number of list box
    ' items to variables
    id = idTextBox.Text.ToUpper
    numItems = idListBox.Items.Count

    ' search the list box, stopping either after the
    ' last item or when the item is found
    Do While index < numItems AndAlso isFound = False
        If id = idListBox.Items(index).ToString.ToUpper Then
            isFound = True
        Else
            index += 1
        End If
    Loop

    If isFound = True Then
        idListBox.SelectedIndex = index
    Else
        idListBox.SelectedIndex = -1
        MessageBox.Show("Not found", "Product Finder",
            MessageBoxButtons.OK, MessageBoxIcon.Information)
    End If
End Sub
```

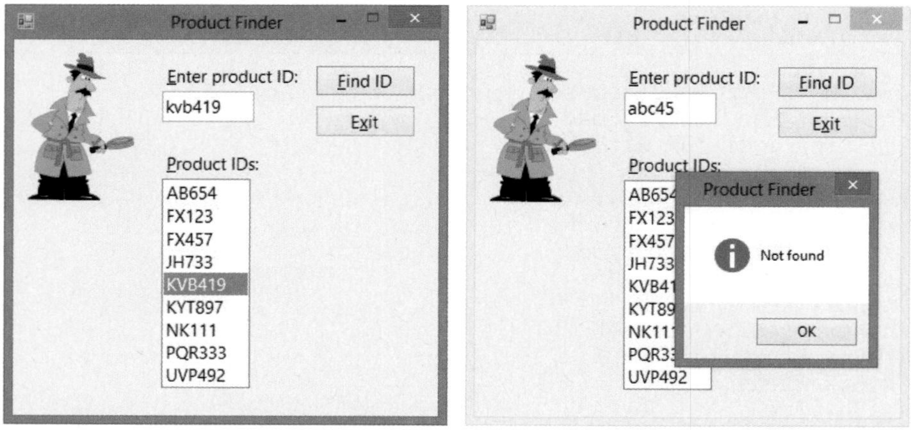

If you want to experiment with the Product Finder application, open the solution contained in the Try It 8! folder.

Figure 6-28 Code and sample runs for the Product Finder application
OpenClipArt.org/sammo/sammo241; © 2013 Cengage Learning

The last concepts covered in this chapter involve enabling and disabling a control, refreshing the screen, and pausing program execution. You will use these concepts in the Color Viewer application coded in the next section. You will also use the concepts in the game application coded in Programming Tutorial 1.

The Color Viewer Application

Figure 6-29 shows the MainForm in the Color Viewer application. When the user clicks the View Colors button, the viewButton_Click procedure should disable the button and then change the color of the colorOvalShape to blue, then to yellow, and then to red. You disable a control by changing its Enabled property from its default value (True) to False. When a control's **Enabled property** is set to False, the control appears dimmed (grayed out) during run time, indicating that it is not currently available to the user. The button will remain unavailable until the procedure enables it, which will occur immediately before the procedure ends.

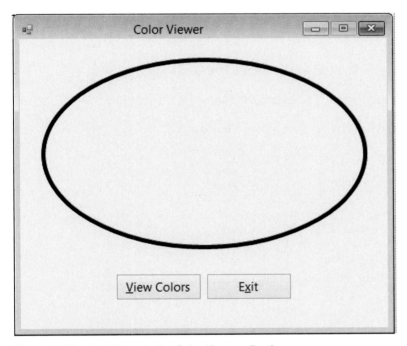

Figure 6-29 MainForm in the Color View application

You can change the oval shape's color to blue using the statement colorOvalShape.FillColor = Color.Blue. Similarly, you can change its color to yellow and red using the statements colorOvalShape.FillColor = Color.Yellow and colorOvalShape.FillColor = Color.Red, respectively. However, because the computer will process the color change instructions so rapidly, you will see only the last color (red) when you click the View Colors button. You can solve this problem by refreshing the interface and then delaying program execution each time the FillColor property is changed. You refresh the interface using the **Refresh method**, which tells the computer to process any previous lines of code that affect the interface's appearance. You delay program execution using the **Sleep method**. Figure 6-30 shows each method's syntax. In the Refresh method, Me refers to the current form. The Sleep method's *milliseconds* argument is the number of milliseconds to suspend the program. A millisecond is 1/1000 of a second; in other words, there are 1000 milliseconds in a second. Figure 6-30 also shows the viewButton_Click procedure.

320

HOW TO Use the Refresh and Sleep Methods

Syntax
Me.Refresh()
System.Threading.Thread.Sleep(_milliseconds_**)**

```
Private Sub viewButton_Click(sender As Object,
e As EventArgs) Handles viewButton.Click
    ' changes the fill color of the colorOvalShape

    ' disable the View Colors button
    viewButton.Enabled = False

    ' change the color
    colorOvalShape.FillColor = Color.Blue
    Me.Refresh()
    System.Threading.Thread.Sleep(1000)

    colorOvalShape.FillColor = Color.Yellow
    Me.Refresh()
    System.Threading.Thread.Sleep(1000)

    colorOvalShape.FillColor = Color.Red

    ' enable the View Colors button
    viewButton.Enabled = True
End Sub
```

If you want to experiment with the Color Viewer application, open the solution contained in the Try It 9! folder.

Figure 6-30 How to use the Refresh and Sleep methods
© 2013 Cengage Learning

The answers to Mini-Quiz questions are located in Appendix A. Each question is associated with one or more objectives listed at the beginning of the chapter.

Mini-Quiz 6-4

1. Items are added to a list box using the _____ method. (8)
    a. Add
    b. AddList
    c. Item
    d. ItemAdd

2. The items in a list box belong to the _____ collection. (8)
    a. ItemList
    b. Items
    c. List
    d. ListItems

3. When an item is selected in a list box, the computer stores the item's index in the _____ property. (8)
    a. Index
    b. ItemIndex
    c. SelectedIndex
    d. SelectedItem

4. Which of the following will delay program execution for two seconds? (10)

    a. `System.Threading.Thread.Sleep(2)`

    b. `System.Threading.Thread.Sleep(200)`

    c. `System.Threading.Thread.Sleep(2000)`

    d. `System.Threading.Thread.Sleep(20000)`

You have completed the concepts section of Chapter 6. The Programming Tutorial section is next.

PROGRAMMING TUTORIAL 1

Creating the Roll 'Em Game Application

In this tutorial, you will create an application that simulates a dice game called Roll 'Em. The game is played using two dice. Each player takes a turn at rolling the dice. The first player who rolls the same number on both dice wins the game. Figures 6-31 and 6-32 show the application's TOE chart and MainForm, respectively. The images at the bottom of the MainForm represent the six sides of a die. The application will use random numbers to display the appropriate image in the firstDiePictureBox and secondDiePictureBox controls. For example, if the random numbers are 6 and 3, the application will display the image containing six dots in the firstDiePictureBox, and display the image containing three dots in the secondDiePictureBox. The images in the firstDiePictureBox and secondDiePictureBox controls will correspond to a roll of the dice.

Task	Object	Event
1. Keep track of the current player 2. Display the current player's number in the msgLabel 3. Generate two random integers from 1 through 6 4. Use the random integers to display the appropriate images in the firstDiePictureBox and secondDiePictureBox 5. Determine whether the current player won, and display an appropriate message in the msgLabel	rollButton	Click
End the application	exitButton	Click
Display a message indicating either the current player or the winner (from rollButton)	msgLabel	None
Display the image corresponding to the first die (from rollButton)	firstDiePictureBox	None
Display the image corresponding to the second die (from rollButton)	secondDiePictureBox	None

Figure 6-31   TOE chart for the Roll 'Em Game application
© 2013 Cengage Learning

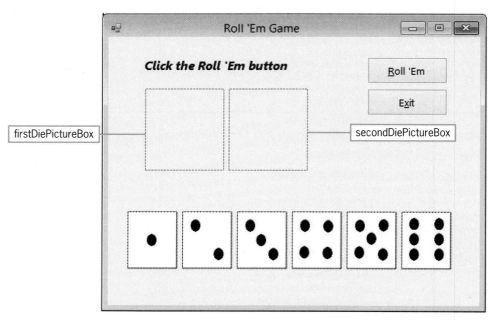

Figure 6-32   MainForm for the Roll 'Em Game application

Coding the Roll 'Em Game Application

According to the application's TOE chart, only the Click event procedures for the rollButton and the exitButton need to be coded.

To begin coding the application:

1. Start Visual Studio. Open the **Roll Em Game Solution** (**Roll Em Game Solution.sln**) file contained in the VbReloaded2012\Chap06\Roll Em Game Solution folder. If necessary, open the designer window.

2. Open the Code Editor window. Notice that the exitButton's Click event procedure has already been coded for you. In the comments that appear in the General Declarations section, replace <your name> and <current date> with your name and the current date, respectively.

Figure 6-33 shows the pseudocode for the rollButton's Click event procedure. As the pseudocode indicates, the procedure will use a static variable to keep track of the player number (either 1 or 2). In addition, it will use two random integers to display the appropriate images in the firstDiePictureBox and secondDiePictureBox.

---

rollButton Click event procedure
1. player 1 rolls first, so initialize a static variable to 1
2. remove any existing images from firstDiePictureBox and secondDiePictureBox
3. display a message (in the msgLabel) indicating the current player
4. generate two random integers from 1 through 6
5. if the first random integer is one of the following:
    1 display dot1PictureBox image in firstDiePictureBox
    2 display dot2PictureBox image in firstDiePictureBox
    3 display dot3PictureBox image in firstDiePictureBox
    4 display dot4PictureBox image in firstDiePictureBox
    5 display dot5PictureBox image in firstDiePictureBox
    6 display dot6PictureBox image in firstDiePictureBox
    end if

Figure 6-33   Pseudocode for the rollButton_Click procedure *(continues)*

(continued)

6. if the second random integer is one of the following:
    1 display dot1PictureBox image in secondDiePictureBox
    2 display dot2PictureBox image in secondDiePictureBox
    3 display dot3PictureBox image in secondDiePictureBox
    4 display dot4PictureBox image in secondDiePictureBox
    5 display dot5PictureBox image in secondDiePictureBox
    6 display dot6PictureBox image in secondDiePictureBox
end if

7. if both random integers are equal
    display a message (in the msgLabel) indicating the winning player
end if

8. if the static variable contains the number 1
    assign the number 2 to the static variable because it's player 2's turn next
else
    assign the number 1 to the static variable because it's player 1's turn next
end if

Figure 6-33 Pseudocode for the rollButton_Click procedure
© 2013 Cengage Learning

To code the rollButton's Click event procedure and then test the procedure's code:

1. Open the code template for the rollButton's Click event procedure. Type the following comment and then press **Enter** twice:

  ' simulates the Roll 'Em game

2. The procedure will need a Random object to represent the pseudo-random number generator, and two Integer variables to store the two random integers. Enter the following three Dim statements:

  Dim randGen As New Random
  Dim random1 As Integer
  Dim random2 As Integer

3. The first step in the pseudocode initializes a static variable to 1. Type the following declaration statement and then press **Enter** twice:

  Static player As Integer = 1

4. Next, the pseudocode removes any existing images from the firstDiePictureBox and secondDiePictureBox controls and then displays a message indicating the current player. You can remove an image from a picture box by assigning the keyword Nothing to the control's Image property. Enter the following comment and assignment statements. Press **Enter** twice after typing the last assignment statement.

  ' clear images and display message
  firstDiePictureBox.Image = Nothing
  secondDiePictureBox.Image = Nothing
  msgLabel.Text = "Player " &
    player.ToString & " rolled:"

5. The next step in the pseudocode generates two random integers from 1 through 6. Enter the following comment and assignment statements. Press **Enter** twice after typing the last assignment statement.

  ' generate two random integers from 1 through 6
  random1 = randGen.Next(1, 7)
  random2 = randGen.Next(1, 7)

6.　The fifth step in the pseudocode contains a multiple-alternative selection structure. The structure uses the first random integer to display the appropriate image in the firstDiePictureBox. Enter the additional comment and code shown in Figure 6-34, and then position the insertion point as indicated in the figure.

```
random2 = randGen.Next(1, 7)

' display appropriate image in firstDiePictureBox
Select Case random1
    Case 1
        firstDiePictureBox.Image = dot1PictureBox.Image
    Case 2
        firstDiePictureBox.Image = dot2PictureBox.Image
    Case 3
        firstDiePictureBox.Image = dot3PictureBox.Image
    Case 4
        firstDiePictureBox.Image = dot4PictureBox.Image
    Case 5
        firstDiePictureBox.Image = dot5PictureBox.Image
    Case Else
        firstDiePictureBox.Image = dot6PictureBox.Image
End Select

End Sub
```

enter this comment and the Select Case statement

position the insertion point here

Figure 6-34　First selection structure entered in the procedure

7.　The sixth step in the pseudocode also contains a multiple-alternative selection structure. This structure uses the second random number to display the appropriate image in the secondDiePictureBox. Enter the additional comment and code shown in Figure 6-35, and then position the insertion point as indicated in the figure.

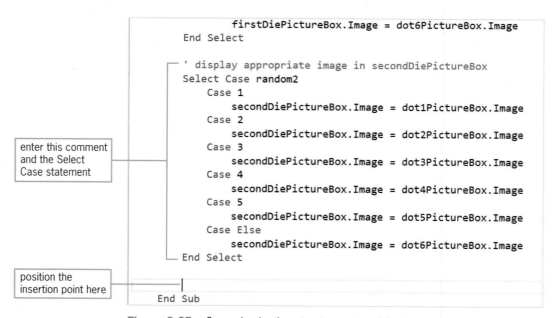

```
        firstDiePictureBox.Image = dot6PictureBox.Image
    End Select

' display appropriate image in secondDiePictureBox
Select Case random2
    Case 1
        secondDiePictureBox.Image = dot1PictureBox.Image
    Case 2
        secondDiePictureBox.Image = dot2PictureBox.Image
    Case 3
        secondDiePictureBox.Image = dot3PictureBox.Image
    Case 4
        secondDiePictureBox.Image = dot4PictureBox.Image
    Case 5
        secondDiePictureBox.Image = dot5PictureBox.Image
    Case Else
        secondDiePictureBox.Image = dot6PictureBox.Image
End Select

End Sub
```

enter this comment and the Select Case statement

position the insertion point here

Figure 6-35　Second selection structure entered in the procedure

8. The seventh step in the pseudocode is a single-alternative selection structure that compares both random integers for equality. If both integers are equal, the selection structure's True path displays a message indicating the winning player. Enter the additional comment and code shown in Figure 6-36, and then position the insertion point as indicated in the figure.

Figure 6-36   Third selection structure entered in the procedure

9. The last step in the pseudocode is a dual-alternative selection structure that uses the static variable to determine the current player, and then resets the variable's value accordingly. If the static variable contains the number 1, it indicates that the first player rolled the dice. Therefore, the selection structure's True path assigns the number 2 to the variable to indicate that it's the second player's turn. Otherwise, the selection structure's False path assigns the number 1 to the static variable to indicate that it's the first player's turn. Enter the following comment and selection structure:

```
' reset the current player
If player = 1 Then
    player = 2
Else
    player = 1
End If
```

10. Save the solution and then start the application. Click the **Roll 'Em** button. Figure 6-37 shows the result of player 1 rolling the dice. Because random integers determine the images assigned to the firstDiePictureBox and secondDiePictureBox controls, your application might display different images than those shown in the figure. In addition, the "Congratulations, player 1!" message, rather than the "Player 1 rolled:" message, may appear on your screen.

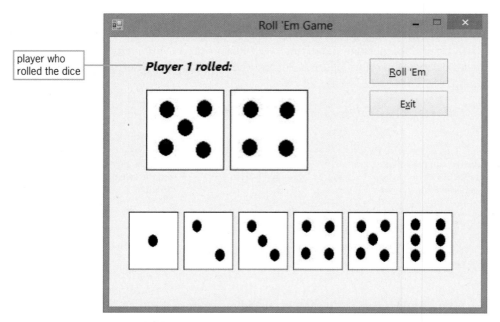

Figure 6-37   Player 1's roll of the dice

11.   Click the **Roll 'Em** button again. Notice that the message (either "Player 2 rolled:" or "Congratulations, player 2!") refers to player 2.

12.   Click the **Roll 'Em** button several times until there is a winner. Figure 6-38 shows a sample of the interface when player 2 wins.

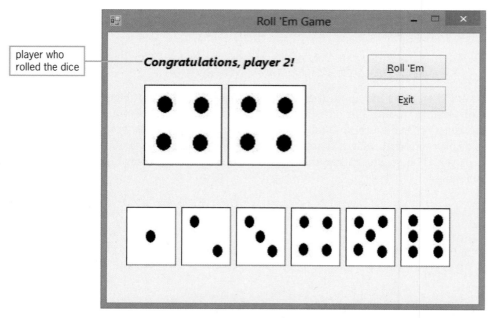

Figure 6-38   Result of player 2 winning

13.   Click the **Exit** button to end the application.

14.   There is no need to show the six images at the bottom of the form during run time. Make the Designer window the active window, and then unlock the controls on the form. Drag the form's bottom border until it hides the six images, and then lock the controls again.

15.   Save the solution.

Modifying the Application

In this section, you will modify the rollButton_Click procedure to make the application a bit more exciting. First, you will have the procedure delay program execution after displaying the "Player *x* rolled:" message, but before displaying the dice images. The delay will give the player a short time to anticipate the roll. You will delay the execution for one second, which is 1000 milliseconds.

To modify the rollButton's code and then test the code:

1. Make the Code Editor window the active window. Click the **blank line** above the `' generate two random integers from 1 through 6` comment, and then press **Enter** to insert a new blank line. Enter the following comment and statements:

   ' refresh form and then delay execution
   Me.Refresh()
   System.Threading.Thread.Sleep(1000)

2. Save the solution and then start the application. Click the **Roll 'Em** button. Notice that there is a slight delay from when the message appears to when the dice images appear. Click the **Exit** button to end the application.

3. The disadvantage of the delay between the message and the dice images is that it might cause the user to click the Roll 'Em button before the dice images appear. You can fix this problem by disabling the Roll 'Em button after it has been clicked, and then enabling it after all of the code in its Click event procedure is processed. Click the **blank line** above the `' refresh form and then delay execution` comment, and then press **Enter** to insert a new blank line. Enter the following comment and assignment statement:

   ' disable Roll 'Em button
   rollButton.Enabled = False

4. Click immediately after the letter **f** in the last End If clause in the procedure and then press **Enter** twice. Enter the following comment and assignment statement:

   ' enable Roll 'Em button
   rollButton.Enabled = True

5. Save the solution and then start the application. Click the **Roll 'Em** button. Notice that the Roll 'Em button is disabled until after the dice images appear. Click the **Exit** button to end the application.

Finally, you will use a loop to make the Congratulations message blink several times when a player wins the game. You can make a control blink by switching its Visible property from True to False and then back again several times. However, because the computer will process the switching instructions so rapidly, you won't notice that the control is blinking unless you refresh the form and then delay program execution each time you switch the Visible property's setting.

Figure 6-39 shows two versions of the modifications you will make to the rollButton_Click procedure in the next set of steps. Version 2 uses the **Not logical operator**, which reverses the truth value of the msgLabel's Visible property. If the Visible property contains True when the `msgLabel.Visible = Not msgLabel.Visible` statement is processed, the `Not msgLabel.Visible` expression evaluates to False; as a result, the statement assigns False to the Visible property. On the other hand, if the Visible property contains False when the statement is processed, the `Not msgLabel.Visible` expression evaluates to True and the statement assigns True to the Visible property.

HOW TO Make a Control Blink

Version 1
```
Dim count As Integer = 1
Do While count <= 10
    If msgLabel.Visible = True Then
        msgLabel.Visible = False
    Else
        msgLabel.Visible = True
    End If
    Me.Refresh()
    System.Threading.Thread.Sleep(100)
    count += 1
Loop
```

Version 2
```
Dim count As Integer = 1
Do While count <= 10
    msgLabel.Visible = Not msgLabel.Visible
    Me.Refresh()
    System.Threading.Thread.Sleep(100)
    count += 1
Loop
```

Figure 6-39   How to make a control blink
© 2013 Cengage Learning

To finish coding the rollButton_Click procedure and then test it:

1. Locate the single-alternative selection structure in the procedure, and then insert a **blank line** above the End If clause.

2. Enter either version of the code shown in Figure 6-39. (If you find the Not operator confusing, enter Version 1 of the code.)

3. Save the solution and then start the application. Click the **Roll 'Em** button several times until one player wins, which causes the msgLabel to blink.

4. Click the **Exit** button to end the application. Close the Code Editor window and then close the solution. Figure 6-40 shows the application's code. (The figure contains Version 2 of the code shown in Figure 6-39. Your code may contain Version 1.)

```
1  ' Project name:        Roll Em Game Project
2  ' Project purpose:      Simulates the Roll 'Em game
3  ' Created/revised by:   <your name> on <current date>
4
5  Option Explicit On
6  Option Strict On
7  Option Infer Off
8
9  Public Class MainForm
10
11     Private Sub exitButton_Click(sender As Object,
       e As EventArgs) Handles exitButton.Click
12         Me.Close()
13     End Sub
14
15     Private Sub rollButton_Click(sender As Object,
       e As EventArgs) Handles rollButton.Click
16         ' simulates the Roll 'Em game
17
18         Dim randGen As New Random
19         Dim random1 As Integer
20         Dim random2 As Integer
21         Static player As Integer = 1
22
23         ' clear images and display message
24         firstDiePictureBox.Image = Nothing
25         secondDiePictureBox.Image = Nothing
26         msgLabel.Text = "Player " &
27             player.ToString & " rolled:"
28
29         ' disable Roll 'Em button
30         rollButton.Enabled = False
31
32         ' refresh form and then delay execution
33         Me.Refresh()
34         System.Threading.Thread.Sleep(1000)
35
36         ' generate two random integers from 1 through 6
37         random1 = randGen.Next(1, 7)
38         random2 = randGen.Next(1, 7)
39
40         ' display appropriate image in firstDiePictureBox
41         Select Case random1
42             Case 1
43                 firstDiePictureBox.Image = dot1PictureBox.Image
44             Case 2
45                 firstDiePictureBox.Image = dot2PictureBox.Image
46             Case 3
47                 firstDiePictureBox.Image = dot3PictureBox.Image
48             Case 4
49                 firstDiePictureBox.Image = dot4PictureBox.Image
50             Case 5
51                 firstDiePictureBox.Image = dot5PictureBox.Image
52             Case Else
53                 firstDiePictureBox.Image = dot6PictureBox.Image
54         End Select
55
56         ' display appropriate image in secondDiePictureBox
57         Select Case random2
58             Case 1
59                 secondDiePictureBox.Image = dot1PictureBox.Image
60             Case 2
61                 secondDiePictureBox.Image = dot2PictureBox.Image
```

Figure 6-40 Code for the Roll 'Em Game application *(continues)*

(continued)

```
62              Case 3
63                  secondDiePictureBox.Image = dot3PictureBox.Image
64              Case 4
65                  secondDiePictureBox.Image = dot4PictureBox.Image
66              Case 5
67                  secondDiePictureBox.Image = dot5PictureBox.Image
68              Case Else
69                  secondDiePictureBox.Image = dot6PictureBox.Image
70          End Select
71
72          ' check if there is a winner
73          If random1 = random2 Then
74              msgLabel.Text = "Congratulations, player " &
75                  player.ToString & "!"
76              Dim count As Integer = 1
77              Do While count <= 10
78                  msgLabel.Visible = Not msgLabel.Visible
79                  Me.Refresh()
80                  System.Threading.Thread.Sleep(100)
81                  count += 1
82              Loop
83          End If
84
85          ' reset the current player
86          If player = 1 Then
87              player = 2
88          Else
89              player = 1
90          End If
91
92          ' enable Roll 'Em button
93          rollButton.Enabled = True
94
95      End Sub
96 End Class
```

Figure 6-40 Code for the Roll 'Em Game application
© 2013 Cengage Learning

PROGRAMMING TUTORIAL 2

Coding the Just Birthdays Application

In this tutorial, you will create an application for the Just Birthdays store, which sells unique supplies for birthday parties. The store's price list is shown in Figure 6-41. The application calculates and displays a customer's total charge, which is based on the type of birthday party and the number of guests. The application will also generate a set of test data that can be used when testing the application's code. The application's TOE chart and MainForm are shown in Figures 6-42 and 6-43, respectively.

Type of birthday party	Charge per guest ($)
Kid's	11
21st	20
40th	25
Other	15

Figure 6-41 Just Birthdays price list
© 2013 Cengage Learning

Task	Object	Event
Get and display the number of guests	guestsTextBox	None
Allow the text box to accept only numbers and the Backspace key		KeyPress
Specify the birthday type	typeListBox	None
Display the birthday types in the typeListBox	MainForm	Load
1. Calculate the total charge 2. Display the total charge in totalLabel	calcButton	Click
Display the total charge (from calcButton)	totalLabel	None
End the application	exitButton	Click
Generate test data	testDataButton	Click
Display test data	testDataLabel	None

Figure 6-42 TOE chart for the Just Birthdays application
© 2013 Cengage Learning

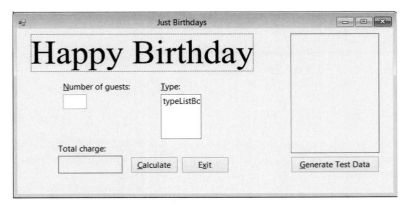

Figure 6-43 MainForm for the Just Birthdays application

Coding the Just Birthdays Application

According to the application's TOE chart, the guestsTextBox's KeyPress event procedure, the MainForm's Load event procedure, and the Click event procedures for the three buttons need to be coded.

To begin coding the application:

1. Start Visual Studio. Open the **Just Birthdays Solution (Just Birthdays Solution.sln)** file contained in the VbReloaded2012\Chap06\Just Birthdays Solution folder. If necessary, open the designer window.

2. Open the Code Editor window. Notice that the exitButton_Click and the guestsTextBox_KeyPress procedures have already been coded for you. In the comments that appear in the General Declarations section, replace <your name> and <current date> with your name and the current date, respectively.

3. The MainForm's Load event procedure is responsible for displaying the birthday types in the typeListBox. Open the code template for the MainForm's Load event procedure. Recall that you do this by selecting (MainForm Events) in the Class Name list box, and then selecting Load in the Method Name list box. Type the following comment and then press **Enter** twice:

   ' fills the list box and selects the first item

4. Enter the following four Add methods:

typeListBox.Items.Add("Kid's")
typeListBox.Items.Add("21st")
typeListBox.Items.Add("40th")
typeListBox.Items.Add("Other")

5. Next, enter a statement that uses the SelectedIndex property to select the first item in the typeListBox.

6. Save the solution and then start the application. Four items appear in the Type list box. The first item is selected (highlighted), as shown in Figure 6-44.

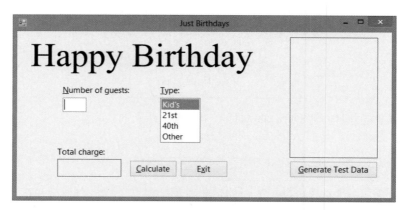

Figure 6-44 Result of processing the MainForm_Load procedure

7. Click the **Exit** button to end the application.

According to the application's TOE chart, the Calculate button's Click event procedure should calculate and display the total charge. The procedure's pseudocode is shown in Figure 6-45 along with the variables it requires.

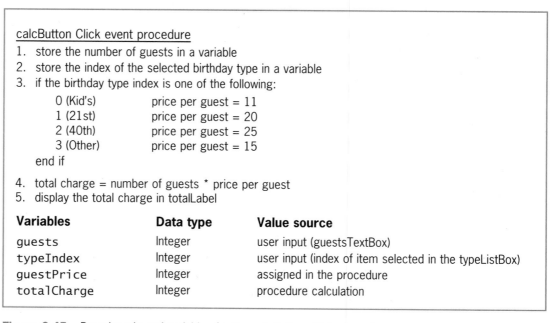

Figure 6-45 Pseudocode and variables for the calcButton_Click procedure
© 2013 Cengage Learning

To code the calcButton_Click procedure and then test it:

1. Open the code template for the calcButton's Click event procedure. Type the following comment and then press **Enter** twice:

   ' displays the total charge

2. Enter the statements to declare the four variables listed in Figure 6-45. Press **Enter** twice after typing the last declaration statement.

3. The first step in the pseudocode stores the number of guests in a variable. Enter a TryParse method that will store the contents of the guestsTextBox in the `guests` variable.

4. The second step in the pseudocode stores the index of the selected birthday type in a variable. Enter the appropriate assignment statement to accomplish this task. Store the index in the `typeIndex` variable. Press **Enter** twice after typing the assignment statement.

5. The third step in the pseudocode contains a multiple-alternative selection structure that uses the birthday type index to determine the price per guest. Enter the following comment:

   ' determine the price per guest

6. Now, enter the appropriate Select Case statement. Assign the price per guest to the `guestPrice` variable. Use comments to make the Select Case statement more self-documenting. For example, enter `Case 0 ' Kid's` for the first Case clause.

7. The fourth step in the pseudocode calculates the total charge by multiplying the number of guests by the price per guest. If necessary, insert **two blank lines** between the End Select clause and the End Sub clause. In the blank line above the End Sub clause, enter the following comment:

   ' calculate and display the total charge

8. Now, enter the assignment statement to calculate the total charge. Assign the total charge to the `totalCharge` variable.

9. The last step in the pseudocode displays the total charge in the totalLabel. Enter the appropriate assignment statement. Display the total charge with a dollar sign and no decimal places.

10. Save the solution and then start the application. Type **10** as the number of guests and then click **40th** in the list box. Click the **Calculate** button. $250 appears in the interface, as shown in Figure 6-46.

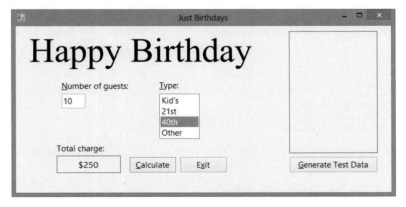

Figure 6-46   Total charge shown in the interface

11. On your own, test the application using different values for the number of guests and birthday types. When you are finished, click the **Exit** button to end the application.

Generating Test Data for the Just Birthdays Application

As you know, you should test an application as thoroughly as possible because you don't want to give the user an application that either produces incorrect output or ends abruptly with an error. For all of the applications you have created so far, you were either given the test data or expected to create your own test data. However, it's also possible to have the computer create a set of test data for you. As you will learn in the next set of steps, you do this using a loop and the random number generator. The Generate Test Data button's Click event procedure will be responsible for generating 10 sets of random test data. The procedure's pseudocode is shown in Figure 6-47.

---

testDataButton Click event procedure

1. initialize a counter variable to 1
2. clear the contents of the testDataLabel
3. repeat

 generate a random integer from 1 through 50 to represent the number of guests
 generate a random integer from 0 through 3 to represent the birthday type index
 if the birthday type index is one of the following:

0 (Kid's)	price per guest = 11
1 (21st)	price per guest = 20
2 (40th)	price per guest = 25
3 (Other)	price per guest = 15

 end if
 total charge = number of guests * price per guest
 display the birthday type index, number of guests, and total charge in the testDataLabel
 add 1 to the counter variable
end repeat until the counter variable is greater than 10

Figure 6-47 Pseudocode for the testDataButton_Click procedure
© 2013 Cengage Learning

To code the testDataButton_Click procedure and then test it:

1. Highlight the comments and code contained in the calcButton_Click procedure, beginning with the `Dim guests As Integer` statement and ending with the blank line above the End Sub clause. Click **EDIT** on the menu bar and then click **Copy**.

2. Open the testDataButton's Click event procedure. Click **EDIT** on the menu bar and then click **Paste**.

3. The testDataButton_Click procedure will need a Random object to represent the random number generator. Click the **blank line** below the last Dim statement and then enter the following declaration statement:

 Dim randGen As New Random

4. The first step in the pseudocode initializes a counter variable to 1. Type the following declaration statement and then press **Enter** twice:

 Dim setsOfDataCounter As Integer = 1

5. The second step in the pseudocode clears the contents of the testDataLabel. Type the following statement and then press **Enter** twice:

 testDataLabel.Text = String.Empty

6. The third step in the pseudocode contains a posttest loop. Type **Do** and press **Enter**. Now, change the Loop clause to **Loop Until setsOfDataCounter > 10**.

7. Delete the statement containing the TryParse method. Also delete the statement that assigns the SelectedIndex value to the `typeIndex` variable, as well as the blank line that follows that statement.

8. Now you can start coding the loop body. According to the pseudocode, the first instruction in the loop body should generate a random integer from 1 through 50 to represent the number of guests. Click the **blank line** between the Do and Loop clauses, and then enter the following statement:

   guests = randGen.Next(1, 51)

9. The next instruction in the loop body should generate a random integer from 0 through 3 to represent the birthday type index. Type the following statement and then press **Enter** twice:

   typeIndex = randGen.Next(0, 4)

10. The procedure already contains the code corresponding to the selection structure and calculation task shown in the pseudocode. You just need to move that code into the loop. Highlight all of the comments and code, beginning with the `' determine the price per guest` comment and ending with the blank line below the last assignment statement. Click **EDIT** on the menu bar and then click **Cut**.

11. Click the **blank line** above the Loop clause. Click **EDIT** on the menu bar and then click **Paste**.

12. After calculating the total charge, the procedure will need to display the birthday type index, number of guests, and total charge in the testDataLabel. Change the `totalLabel.Text = totalCharge.ToString("C0")` statement in the loop body to the following (There are six spaces within the first two sets of quotation marks.):

    testDataLabel.Text = testDataLabel.Text &
       typeIndex.ToString & "   " &
       guests.ToString & "   " &
       totalCharge.ToString("C0") &
       ControlChars.NewLine

13. The last instruction in the loop body should update the counter variable by 1. Enter the following statement in the blank line above the Loop clause:

    setsOfDataCounter += 1

14. Save the solution and then start the application. Click the **Generate Test Data** button. The test data appears in the testDataLabel. See Figure 6-48.

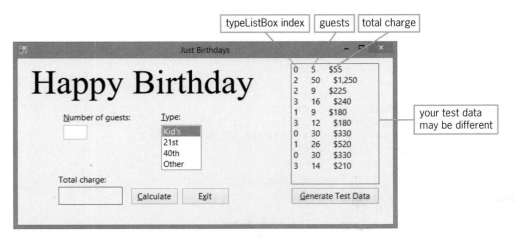

Figure 6-48   Test data generated by the testDataButton_Click procedure

15. Now, manually calculate the total charges using the values shown in the first two columns of the testDataLabel, and then compare your answers with the values in the third column. For example, in the first set of test data shown in Figure 6-48, the 0 and 5 indicate a Kid's birthday with 5 guests, respectively. The price per guest for a Kid's birthday is $11. If you multiply 5 by 11, the result is 55, which agrees with the value shown in the third column for this set of test data.

16. Click the **Exit** button. Close the Code Editor window and then close the solution. Figure 6-49 shows the code for the Just Birthdays application.

```
1 ' Project name:        Just Birthdays Project
2 ' Project purpose:     Displays the total charge
3 ' Created/revised by:  <your name> on <current date>
4
5 Option Explicit On
6 Option Strict On
7 Option Infer Off
8
9 Public Class MainForm
10
11     Private Sub exitButton_Click(sender As Object,
        e As EventArgs) Handles exitButton.Click
12         Me.Close()
13     End Sub
14
15     Private Sub guestsTextBox_KeyPress(sender As Object,
        e As KeyPressEventArgs) Handles guestsTextBox.KeyPress
16         ' allows only numbers and the Backspace key
17
18         If (e.KeyChar < "0" OrElse e.KeyChar > "9") AndAlso
19             e.KeyChar <> ControlChars.Back Then
20             e.Handled = True
21         End If
22     End Sub
23
24     Private Sub MainForm_Load(sender As Object,
        e As EventArgs) Handles Me.Load
25         ' fills the list box and selects the first item
26
27         typeListBox.Items.Add("Kid's")
28         typeListBox.Items.Add("21st")
29         typeListBox.Items.Add("40th")
30         typeListBox.Items.Add("Other")
31         typeListBox.SelectedIndex = 0
32
33     End Sub
34
35     Private Sub calcButton_Click(sender As Object,
        e As EventArgs) Handles calcButton.Click
36         ' displays the total charge
37
38         Dim guests As Integer
39         Dim typeIndex As Integer
40         Dim guestPrice As Integer
41         Dim totalCharge As Integer
42
```

Figure 6-49   Code for the Just Birthdays application (*continues*)

(continued)

```
43          Integer.TryParse(guestsTextBox.Text, guests)
44          typeIndex = typeListBox.SelectedIndex
45
46          ' determine the price per guest
47          Select Case typeIndex
48              Case 0   ' Kid's
49                  guestPrice = 11
50              Case 1   ' 21st
51                  guestPrice = 20
52              Case 2   ' 40th
53                  guestPrice = 25
54              Case Else   ' other
55                  guestPrice = 15
56          End Select
57
58          ' calculate and display the total charge
59          totalCharge = guests * guestPrice
60          totalLabel.Text = totalCharge.ToString("C0")
61
62      End Sub
63
64      Private Sub testDataButton_Click(sender As Object,
        e As EventArgs) Handles testDataButton.Click
65          Dim guests As Integer
66          Dim typeIndex As Integer
67          Dim guestPrice As Integer
68          Dim totalCharge As Integer
69          Dim randGen As New Random
70          Dim setsOfDataCounter As Integer = 1
71
72          testDataLabel.Text = String.Empty
73
74          Do
75              guests = randGen.Next(1, 51)
76              typeIndex = randGen.Next(0, 4)
77
78              ' determine the price per guest
79              Select Case typeIndex
80                  Case 0   ' Kid's
81                      guestPrice = 11
82                  Case 1   ' 21st
83                      guestPrice = 20
84                  Case 2   ' 40th
85                      guestPrice = 25
86                  Case Else   ' other
87                      guestPrice = 15
88              End Select
89
90              ' calculate and display the total charge
91              totalCharge = guests * guestPrice
92              testDataLabel.Text = testDataLabel.Text &
93                  typeIndex.ToString & "        " &
94                  guests.ToString & "        " &
95                  totalCharge.ToString("C0") &
96                  ControlChars.NewLine
97              setsOfDataCounter += 1
98
99          Loop Until setsOfDataCounter > 10
100
101     End Sub
102 End Class
```

Figure 6-49 Code for the Just Birthdays application

PROGRAMMING EXAMPLE

Lockett Sales Application

Create an application that allows the sales manager to enter each salesperson's annual sales amount. When the sales manager has finished entering the sales amounts, the application should calculate and display the average sales amount. Use the following names for the solution and project, respectively: Lockett Project and Lockett Solution. Save the application in the VbReloaded2012\ Chap06 folder. Change the form file's name to Main Form.vb. See Figures 6-50 through 6-54.

Task	Object	Event
1. Get the sales amounts 2. Display the sales amounts in salesListBox 3. Calculate the average sales amount 4. Display either the average sales amount or "N/A" (if the user didn't enter any sales amounts) in avgLabel	calcButton	Click
End the application	exitButton	Click
Display the sales amounts (from calcButton)	salesListBox	None
Display either the average sales amount or "N/A" (from calcButton)	avgLabel	None
Clear the salesListBox and avgLabel	startOverButton	Click

Figure 6-50 TOE chart
© 2013 Cengage Learning

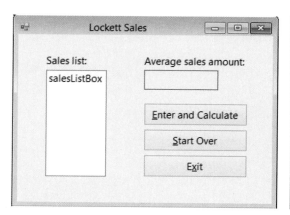
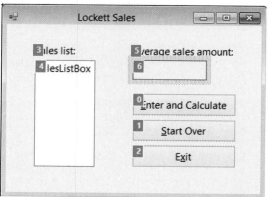

Figure 6-51 MainForm and tab order

Object	Property	Setting
MainForm	Font StartPosition Text	Segoe UI, 11pt CenterScreen Lockett Sales
salesListBox	Enabled	False
avgLabel	AutoSize BorderStyle Text TextAlign	False FixedSingle (empty) MiddleCenter

Figure 6-52 Objects, properties, and settings
© 2013 Cengage Learning

PROGRAMMING EXAMPLE

exitButton Click event procedure
close the application

calcButton Click event procedure

1. initialize a number of sales counter to 0
2. initialize a total sales accumulator to 0
3. get a sales amount from the user
4. repeat while the user enters a sales amount
        display the sales amount in the salesListBox
        add 1 to the number of sales counter
        add the sales amount to the total sales accumulator
        get a sales amount from the user
    end repeat while
5. if the value in the number of sales counter is greater than 0
        average sales amount = total sales accumulator / number of sales counter
        display the average sales amount in the avgLabel
    else
        display "N/A" in the avgLabel
    end if

startOverButton Click event procedure
1. clear the salesListBox
2. clear the avgLabel

Figure 6-53   Pseudocode
© 2013 Cengage Learning

```
1 ' Project name:          Lockett Sales Project
2 ' Project purpose:       Displays the average sales amount
3 ' Created/revised by:    <your name> on <current date>
4
5 Option Explicit On
6 Option Strict On
7 Option Infer Off
8
9 Public Class MainForm
10
11    Private Sub exitButton_Click(sender As Object,
      e As EventArgs) Handles exitButton.Click
12        Me.Close()
13    End Sub
14
15    Private Sub calcButton_Click(sender As Object,
      e As EventArgs) Handles calcButton.Click
16        ' calculates the average sales amount
17
18        Const Prompt As String =
19            "Enter a sales amount. " &
20            ControlChars.NewLine &
21            "Click Cancel or leave blank to end."
22        Const Title As String = "Sales Entry"
23        Dim inputSales As String
24        Dim decSales As Decimal
25        Dim numSales As Integer      ' counter
26        Dim totalSales As Decimal    ' accumulator
27        Dim avgSales As Decimal
28
```

Figure 6-54   Code *(continues)*

(continued)

```
29          inputSales = InputBox(Prompt, Title, "0")
30          ' repeat as long as the user enters a sales amount
31          Do While inputSales <> String.Empty
32              Decimal.TryParse(inputSales, decSales)
33              salesListBox.Items.Add(decSales.ToString("N2"))
34              numSales += 1
35              totalSales += decSales
36              inputSales = InputBox(Prompt, Title)
37          Loop
38
39          ' verify that the counter is greater than 0
40          If numSales > 0 Then
41              avgSales = totalSales / numSales
42              avgLabel.Text = avgSales.ToString("C2")
43          Else
44              avgLabel.Text = "N/A"
45          End If
46      End Sub
47
48      Private Sub startOverButton_Click(sender As Object,
        e As EventArgs) Handles startOverButton.Click
49          ' clear screen
50
51          salesListBox.Items.Clear()
52          avgLabel.Text = String.Empty
53      End Sub
54 End Class
```

Figure 6-54   Code
© 2013 Cengage Learning

Summary

- The three basic control structures are sequence, selection, and repetition.

- You use the repetition structure, also called a loop, to repeatedly process one or more program instructions either while the looping condition is true or until the loop exit condition has been met. A loop's condition must evaluate to either True or False only.

- A repetition structure can be either a pretest loop or a posttest loop. Depending on the loop's condition, the instructions in a pretest loop may never be processed. The instructions in a posttest loop, on the other hand, are always processed at least once.

- You can use the Do...Loop statement to code both pretest loops and posttest loops. The condition used in the Do...Loop statement must evaluate to a Boolean value.

- When used in the Do...Loop statement, the keyword While indicates that the loop instructions should be processed *while* (as long as) the condition evaluates to True. The keyword Until indicates that the loop instructions should be processed *until* the condition evaluates to True.

- In a flowchart, the loop's condition is represented by the decision symbol, which is a diamond.

- An overflow error occurs when the value assigned to a memory location is too large for the location's data type.

- A loop that has no way to end is called an infinite loop or an endless loop.

- You use a counter and/or an accumulator to calculate subtotals, totals, and averages.

- All counters and accumulators must be initialized and updated. The initialization is done outside of the loop that uses the counter or accumulator, and the updating is done within the loop. Counters are updated by a constant value, whereas accumulators are usually updated by an amount that varies.

- The input instruction located above a loop's condition is referred to as the priming read. The input instruction within the loop body is referred to as the update read. The priming read gets only the first value from the user. The update read gets the remaining values (if any).

- The InputBox function displays an input dialog box that can be used to prompt the user to enter some specific information. The function's return value is always treated as a string.

- In the InputBox function, you should use sentence capitalization for the prompt, but book title capitalization for the title.

- Before using a variable as the divisor in an expression, you should verify that the variable does not contain the number 0. Dividing by 0 is mathematically impossible and will cause the application to end abruptly with an error.

- You can use a text box's Multiline property to control whether the text box accepts and displays either one line of text or multiple lines of text. The value in a text box's ReadOnly property determines whether the user can edit the contents of the text box during run time. The value in a text box's ScrollBars property determines whether scroll bars appear on the text box.

- A list box displays a list of items from which the user can select zero items, one item (the default), or multiple items, depending on the value of its SelectionMode property.

- Use a label control to provide keyboard access to a list box. Set the label's TabIndex property to a value that is one number less than the list box's TabIndex value.

- You can use the String Collection Editor window to add items to a list box during design time. You can add items to a list box during run time using the Items collection's Add method. You can clear a list box using the Item collection's Clear method.

- The code contained in a form's Load event procedure will be processed before the form appears on the screen.

- List box items are either arranged by use, with the most used entries appearing first in the list, or sorted in ascending order.

- You use a list box item's index to access the item. The index of the first item in a list box is 0.

- The number of items in a list box is contained in the Items collection's Count property. The value in the Count property is always one number more than the list box's highest index.

- When an item is selected in a list box, the item appears highlighted in the list. The item's value is stored in the list box's SelectedItem property, and the item's index is stored in the list box's SelectedIndex property.

341

- If a list box allows the user to make only one selection at a time, then a default item should be selected in the list box when the interface first appears. The default item should be either the item selected most frequently or the first item in the list.

- A list box's SelectedItem property and its SelectedIndex property can be used both to determine the item selected in the list box and to select a list box item from code.

- When you select an item in a list box, the list box's SelectedValueChanged and SelectedIndexChanged events occur.

- You use a control's Enabled property to enable or disable the control.

- You can use the Sleep method to delay program execution, and use the Refresh method to refresh (redraw) the form.

Key Terms

Accumulator—a numeric variable used for accumulating (adding together) something

Add method—the Items collection's method used to add items to a list box

Clear method—the Items collection's method used to clear the items from a list box

Collection—a group of individual objects treated as one unit

Count property—a property of the Items collection; stores an integer that represents the number of items contained in a list box

Counter—a numeric variable used for counting something

Decrementing—decreasing a value

Default list box item—the item automatically selected in a list box when the interface appears on the screen

Do...Loop statement—a Visual Basic statement that can be used to code both pretest loops and posttest loops

Enabled property—used to enable and display a control

Endless loop—a loop whose instructions are processed indefinitely; also called an infinite loop

Incrementing—increasing a value

Index—the unique number that identifies each item in a collection; used to access an item in a list box; the first index in a list box is 0

Infinite loop—another name for an endless loop

Initializing—the process of assigning a beginning value to a memory location, such as a counter variable or an accumulator variable

InputBox function—a Visual Basic function that displays an input dialog box containing a message, OK and Cancel buttons, and an input area

Items collection—the collection composed of the items in a list box

List box—a control used to display a list of items from which the user can select zero items, one item, or multiple items

Load event—the event that occurs when an application is started and the form is displayed the first time

Loop—another name for the repetition structure

Loop exit condition—the requirement that must be met for the computer to *stop* processing the loop body instructions

Looping condition—the requirement that must be met for the computer to *continue* processing the loop body instructions

Multiline property—determines whether a text box can accept and display only one line of text or multiple lines of text

Not logical operator—reverses the truth value of a condition

Overflow error—occurs when the value assigned to a memory location is too large for the location's data type

Posttest loop—a loop whose condition is evaluated *after* the instructions in its loop body are processed

Pretest loop—a loop whose condition is evaluated *before* the instructions in its loop body are processed

Priming read—the input instruction that appears above the loop that it controls; used to get the first input item from the user

ReadOnly property—determines whether the user is allowed to change the contents of a text box during run time

Refresh method—refreshes (redraws) a form

Repetition structure—the control structure used to repeatedly process one or more program instructions; also called a loop

ScrollBars property—a property of a text box; specifies whether the text box has scroll bars

SelectedIndex property—stores the index of the item selected in a list box

SelectedIndexChanged event—occurs when an item is selected in a list box

SelectedItem property—stores the value of the item selected in a list box

SelectedValueChanged event—occurs when an item is selected in a list box

SelectionMode property—determines the number of items that can be selected in a list box

Sleep method—used to delay program execution

Sorted property—specifies whether the list box items should appear in the order they are entered or in sorted order

Update read—the input instruction that appears within a loop and is associated with the priming read

Updating—the process of either adding a number to or subtracting a number from the value stored in a counter or accumulator variable

Review Questions

1. Which of the following clauses will stop the loop when the value in the order variable is less than the number 0? (1, 4)

    a. Do While order >= 0

    b. Do Until order < 0

    c. Loop While order >= 0

    d. all of the above

Each Review Question is associated with one or more objectives listed at the beginning of the chapter.

2. How many times will the MessageBox.Show method in the following code be processed?
    (1, 2, 4, 5)

```
Dim counter As Integer
Do While counter > 3
   MessageBox.Show("Hello")
   counter += 1
Loop
```

    a. 0
    b. 1
    c. 3
    d. 4

3. How many times will the MessageBox.Show method in the following code be processed?
    (1, 2, 4, 5)

```
Dim counter As Integer
Do
   MessageBox.Show("Hello")
   counter += 1
Loop While counter > 3
```

    a. 0
    b. 1
    c. 3
    d. 4

Refer to Figure 6-55 to answer Review Questions 4 through 7.

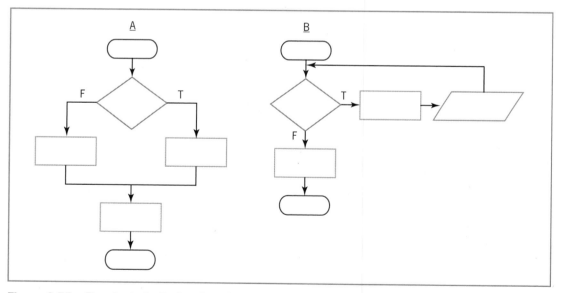

Figure 6-55   Flowcharts for Review Questions 4 through 7 *(continues)*

(continued)

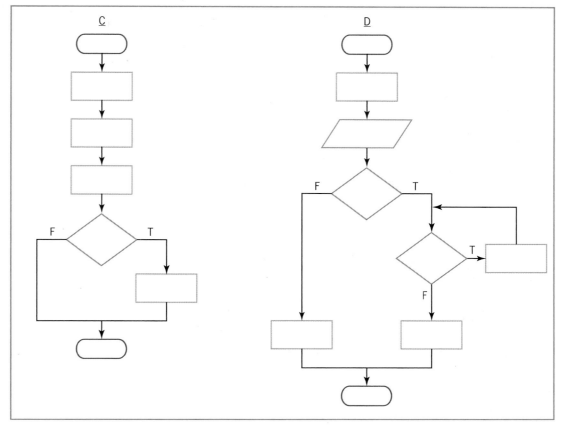

Figure 6-55   Flowcharts for Review Questions 4 through 7

4. In addition to the sequence structure, which of the following control structures are used in flowchart A in Figure 6-55? (3)

   a. selection

   b. repetition

   c. both selection and repetition

5. In addition to the sequence structure, which of the following control structures are used in flowchart B in Figure 6-55? (3)

   a. selection

   b. repetition

   c. both selection and repetition

6. In addition to the sequence structure, which of the following control structures are used in flowchart C in Figure 6-55? (3)

   a. selection

   b. repetition

   c. both selection and repetition

7. In addition to the sequence structure, which of the following control structures are used in flowchart D in Figure 6-55? (3)

    a.   selection

    b.   repetition

    c.   both selection and repetition

8. What does the InputBox function return when the user clicks the Cancel button in its dialog box? (6)

    a.   the number 0

    b.   the empty string

    c.   an error message

    d.   none of the above

9. Which property stores the index of the item selected in a list box? (8)

    a.   Index

    b.   SelectedIndex

    c.   Selection

    d.   SelectionIndex

10. Which of the following selects the third item in the animalListBox? (8)

    a.   `animalListBox.SelectedIndex = 2`

    b.   `animalListBox.SelectedIndex = 3`

    c.   `animalListBox.SelectedItem = 2`

    d.   `animalListBox.SelectedItem = 3`

11. Which event occurs when the user selects an item in a list box? (8)

    a.   SelectionChanged

    b.   SelectedItemChanged

    c.   SelectedValueChanged

    d.   none of the above

Each Exercise, except the DISCOVERY exercises, is associated with one or more objectives listed at the beginning of the chapter.

Exercises

Pencil and Paper

INTRODUCTORY

1. Write a Visual Basic Do clause that processes the loop instructions as long as the value in the **quantity** variable is greater than the number 0. Use the `While` keyword. Then rewrite the Do clause using the `Until` keyword. (1, 4)

INTRODUCTORY

2. Write a Visual Basic Do clause that stops the loop when the value in the **quantity** variable is less than or equal to the value in the **ordered** variable. Use the `Until` keyword. Then rewrite the Do clause using the `While` keyword. (1, 4)

INTRODUCTORY

3. Write an assignment statement that updates the **quantity** variable by 2. (5)

INTRODUCTORY

4. Write an assignment statement that updates the **total** variable by −3. (5)

INTRODUCTORY

5. Write an assignment statement that updates the **totalPurchases** variable by the value stored in the **purchases** variable. (5)

6. Write an assignment statement that updates the `salesReturns` variable by subtracting the contents of the `sales` variable. (5)

7. Write a Visual Basic Loop clause that processes the loop instructions as long as the value in the `letter` variable is either Y or y. Use the `While` keyword. Then rewrite the Loop clause using the `Until` keyword. (1, 4)

8. Write a Visual Basic Do clause that processes the loop instructions as long as the value in the `empName` variable is not "Done" (in any case). Use the `Until` keyword. Then rewrite the Do clause using the `While` keyword. (1, 4)

9. What will the following code display in message boxes? (1, 2, 4, 5)

```
Dim x As Integer
Do While x < 5
  MessageBox.Show(x.ToString)
  x += 1
Loop
```

10. What will the following code display in message boxes? (1, 2, 4, 5)

```
Dim x As Integer
Do
  MessageBox.Show(x.ToString)
  x += 1
Loop Until x > 5
```

11. What will the following code display in message boxes? (1, 2, 4, 5)

```
Dim totalEmp As Integer
Do While totalEmp <= 5
  MessageBox.Show(totalEmp.ToString)
  totalEmp += 2
Loop
```

12. What will the following code display in message boxes? (1, 2, 4, 5)

```
Dim totalEmp As Integer = 1
Do
  MessageBox.Show(totalEmp.ToString)
  totalEmp += 2
Loop Until totalEmp >= 3
```

13. Write two different statements that you can use to select the fifth item in the deptListBox. The fifth item is Security. (8)

14. Write the Visual Basic code that corresponds to the flowchart shown in Figure 6-56. Display the calculated results in the numberListBox. (1-5)

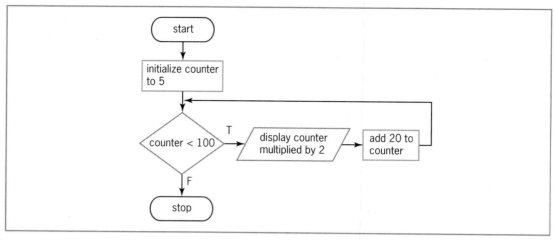

Figure 6-56   Flowchart for Exercise 14
© 2013 Cengage Learning

SWAT THE BUGS

15. The following code should display the numbers 1 through 4, but it is not working correctly. Correct the code. (1, 2, 4, 5)

```
Dim number As Integer = 1
Do While number < 5
    MessageBox.Show(number.ToString)
Loop
```

SWAT THE BUGS

16. The following code should display the numbers 10 through 1, but it is not working correctly. Correct the code. (1, 2, 4, 5)

```
Dim number As Integer = 10
Do
    MessageBox.Show(number.ToString)
Loop Until number = 0
```

Computer

MODIFY THIS

17. If necessary, complete the Roll 'Em Game application from this chapter's Programming Tutorial 1, and then close the solution. Use Windows to make a copy of the Roll Em Game Solution folder. Rename the folder Roll Em Game Solution-ModifyThis. Open the Roll Em Game Solution (Roll Em Game Solution.sln) file contained in the Roll Em Game Solution-ModifyThis folder. First, change the Do clause to use a loop exit condition rather than a looping condition. Then, modify the code to allow three people to play the game. Save the solution and then start and test the application. Close the solution. (1, 4)

MODIFY THIS

18. If necessary, complete the Just Birthdays application from this chapter's Programming Tutorial 2, and then close the solution. Use Windows to make a copy of the Just Birthdays Solution folder. Rename the folder Just Birthdays Solution-ModifyThis. Open the Just Birthdays Solution (Just Birthdays Solution.sln) file contained in the Just Birthdays Solution-ModifyThis folder. Modify the testDataButton_Click procedure so that it displays the type of birthday, rather than the type's index, in the testDataLabel. (In other words, display "Kid's" rather than 0.) Save the solution and then start and test the application. Close the solution. (8)

19. If necessary, complete the Lockett Sales application from this chapter's Programming Example, and then close the solution. Use Windows to make a copy of the Lockett Solution folder. Rename the folder Lockett Solution-ModifyThis. Open the Lockett Solution (Lockett Solution.sln) file contained in the Lockett Solution-ModifyThis folder. Currently, the Do clause contains a looping condition. Change the Do clause to a loop exit condition. Save the solution and then start and test the application. Close the solution. (1, 4)

20. Open the Savers Solution (Savers Solution.sln) file contained in the Savers Solution-ModifyThis folder. Currently, the Do clause contains a looping condition. Change the Do clause to a loop exit condition. Also, rather than using $100,000 as the savings goal, the user should be able to enter any savings goal. Provide a text box for the user to enter the savings goal. Save the solution and then start and test the application. Close the solution. (1, 2, 4, 5)

21. Open the Go Team Solution (Go Team Solution.sln) file contained in the Go Team Solution folder. The Click Here button should disable itself and then blink the "Go Team!" message 10 times. Each time the message blinks, its font color should change from black to red and then back to black. After the message blinks 10 times, the button should enable itself. Code the button's Click event procedure. Save the solution and then start and test the application. Close the solution. (1, 2, 4, 5, 9, 10)

22. Open the Even Odd Solution (Even Odd Solution.sln) file contained in the VbReloaded2012\Chap06\Even Odd Solution folder. The pretestButton_Click procedure should clear the contents of the pretestListBox and then use a pretest loop to display the even integers from 2 through 10 in the list box. The posttestButton_Click procedure should clear the contents of the posttestListBox and then use a posttest loop to display the odd integers from 21 through 39 in the list box. Code both procedures. Save the solution and then start and test the application. Close the solution. (1, 2, 4, 5, 8)

23. Open the Even Squares Solution (Even Squares Solution.sln) file contained in the VbReloaded2012\Chap06\Even Squares Solution folder. The displayButton_Click procedure should use a pretest loop to display the squares of the even integers from 2 through 12. Display each square on a separate line in the squaresLabel. Code the procedure. Save the solution and then start and test the application. Close the solution. (1, 2, 4, 5)

24. Open the Woodson Solution (Woodson Solution.sln) file contained in the VbReloaded2012\Chap06\Woodson Solution folder. The calcButton_Click procedure should allow the user to enter zero or more sales amounts. Use the InputBox function to get the sales amounts. Display the sales amounts in the salesListBox. When the user has completed entering the sales amounts, the procedure should display the total sales in the totalSalesLabel. It should also display a 10% bonus in the bonusLabel. Code the procedure. Save the solution and then start and test the application. Close the solution. (1, 2, 4-6, 8)

25. Open the Calculator Solution (Calculator Solution.sln) file contained in the VbReloaded2012\Chap06\Calculator Solution folder. The addButton_Click procedure should perform the following three tasks: add the integer entered in the numTextBox to an accumulator, display the integer on a separate line in the numsTextBox, and display the accumulator's value in the sumLabel. The startOverButton_Click procedure should clear the contents of both text boxes and the sumLabel. It should also start the accumulator at 0. Code the procedures. Save the solution and then start and test the application. Close the solution. (5, 7)

26. Open the Average Solution (Average Solution.sln) file contained in the VbReloaded2012\Chap06\Average Solution folder. The calcButton_Click procedure should get from zero to five test scores from the user. Display the test scores in the scoresListBox. When the user has finished entering the scores, the procedure should calculate and display the average test score. Code the procedure. Save the solution and then start and test the application. Close the solution. (1, 2, 4-6, 8)

INTERMEDIATE

27. Create an application for Premium Paper. Use the following names for the solution and project, respectively: Premium Solution and Premium Project. Save the solution in the VbReloaded2012\Chap06 folder. Change the form file's name to Main Form.vb. The application should allow the sales manager to enter the company's income and expense amounts. The number of income and expense amounts may vary each time the application is started. For example, the user may enter five income amounts and three expense amounts. Or, he or she may enter 20 income amounts and 30 expense amounts. The application should calculate and display the company's total income, total expenses, and profit (or loss). Use the InputBox function to get the individual income and expense amounts. (1-6)

a. Design an appropriate interface. Use label controls to display the total income, total expenses, and profit (loss). Display the calculated amounts with a dollar sign and two decimal places. If the company experienced a loss, display the amount of the loss using a red font; otherwise, display the profit using a black font.

b. Code the application. Keep in mind that the income and expense amounts may contain decimal places.

c. Save the solution and then start the application. Test the application twice. For the first test, use 750.75 and 935.67 as the income amounts, and use 1995.65 as the expense amount. For the second test, use income amounts of 5000, 6000, 35000, and 78000, and use expense amounts of 1000, 2000, and 600. Close the solution.

INTERMEDIATE

28. Create an application that displays the ZIP code (or codes) corresponding to the city name selected in a list box. The city names and ZIP codes are shown in Figure 6-57. Use the following names for the solution and project, respectively: Zip Solution and Zip Project. Save the application in the VbReloaded2012\Chap06 folder. Change the form file's name to Main Form.vb. (8)

a. Create the interface shown in Figure 6-58. The items in the list box should be sorted; set the appropriate property.

b. The form's Load event procedure should add the city names shown in Figure 6-57 to the list box and then select the first name in the list. Code the procedure.

c. The citiesListBox_SelectedValueChanged procedure should assign the item selected in the list box to a variable, and then use the Select Case statement to display the city's ZIP code(s). Code the procedure.

d. Save the solution and then start and test the application.

e. Change the code you entered in the citiesListBox_SelectedValueChanged procedure to comments. Now, enter the code to assign the index of the selected item to a variable, and then use a Select Case statement to display the city's ZIP code(s).

f. Save the solution and then start and test the application. Close the solution.

City	ZIP code(s)
Park Ridge	60068
Barrington	60010, 60011
Glen Ellyn	60137, 60138
Algonquin	60102
Crystal Lake	60012

Figure 6-57 Cities and ZIP codes
© 2013 Cengage Learning

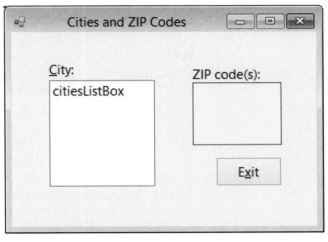

Figure 6-58   Interface for Exercise 28

29. In this exercise, you will create a Windows application that displays a multiplication table. Use the following names for the solution and project, respectively: Multiplication Solution and Multiplication Project. Save the solution in the VbReloaded2012\Chap06 folder. Change the form file's name to Main Form.vb. Create the interface shown in Figure 6-59. The Number box should accept only numbers and the Backspace key. Code the application. Save the solution and then start and test the application. Close the solution. (1, 2, 4, 5, 7)

INTERMEDIATE

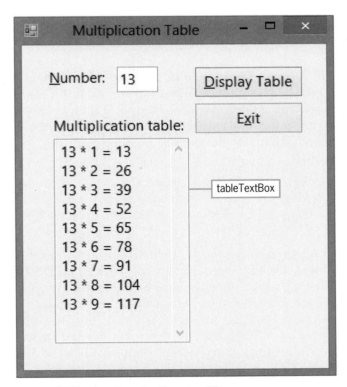

Figure 6-59   Interface for Exercise 29

ADVANCED

30. Open the Fibonacci Solution (Fibonacci Solution.sln) file contained in the VbReloaded2012\Chap06\Fibonacci Solution folder. The application should display the first 10 Fibonacci numbers (1, 1, 2, 3, 5, 8, 13, 21, 34, and 55). Notice that beginning with the third number in the series, each Fibonacci number is the sum of the prior two numbers. In other words, 2 is the sum of 1 plus 1, 3 is the sum of 1 plus 2, 5 is the sum of 2 plus 3, and so on. Code the application. Save the solution and then start and test the application. Close the solution. (1, 2, 4, 5)

ADVANCED

31. Create a Windows application. Use the following names for the solution and project, respectively: GPA Solution and GPA Project. Save the solution in the VbReloaded2012\ Chap06 folder. Change the form file's name to Main Form.vb. Create an interface that uses list boxes for entering the gender (either F or M) and GPA (0.0 through 4.0) for any number of students. The application should calculate the average GPA for all students, the average GPA for male students, and the average GPA for female students. Code the application. Save the solution and then start and test the application. Close the solution. (1-5, 8)

ADVANCED

32. If necessary, complete the Roll 'Em Game application from this chapter's Programming Tutorial 1, and then close the solution. Use Windows to make a copy of the Roll Em Game Solution folder. Rename the folder Roll Em Game Solution-Advanced. Open the Roll Em Game Solution (Roll Em Game Solution.sln) file contained in the Roll Em Game Solution-Advanced folder. Modify the interface and code so the application rolls three dice rather than two. In addition, include labels on the form to keep track of the number of times each player has won. To win the game, the player must roll the same number on all three dice. Save the solution and then start and test the application. Close the solution. (4, 5, 9-11)

DISCOVERY

33. In this exercise, you learn how to create a list box that allows the user to select more than one item at a time. Open the Multi Solution (Multi Solution.sln) file contained in the VbReloaded2012\Chap06\Multi Solution folder. The interface contains a list box named namesListBox. The list box's Sorted and SelectionMode properties are set to True and One, respectively.

a. Open the Code Editor window. The MainForm_Load procedure adds five names to the namesListBox. Code the singleButton_Click procedure so that it displays, in the resultLabel, the item selected in the list box. For example, if the user clicks Debbie in the list box and then clicks the Single Selection button, the name Debbie should appear in the resultLabel. (Hint: Use the Convert.ToString method.)

b. Save the solution and then start the application. Click Debbie in the list box, click Ahmad, and then click Bill. Notice that when the list box's SelectionMode property is set to One, you can select only one item at a time in the list. Click the Single Selection button. The name Bill appears in the resultLabel. Click the Exit button to end the application.

c. Change the list box's SelectionMode property to MultiSimple. Save the solution and then start the application. Click Debbie in the list box, click Ahmad, click Bill, and then click Ahmad. Notice that when the list box's SelectionMode property is set to MultiSimple, you can select more than one item at a time in the list. Also notice that you click to both select and deselect an item. (You can also use Ctrl+click and Shift+click, as well as press the Spacebar, to select and deselect items when the list box's SelectionMode property is set to MultiSimple.) Click the Exit button.

d. Change the list box's SelectionMode property to MultiExtended. Save the solution and then start the application. Click Debbie in the list, and then click Jim. Notice that in this case, clicking Jim deselects Debbie. When a list box's SelectionMode property is set to MultiExtended, you use Ctrl+click to select multiple items in the list. You also use Ctrl+click to deselect items in the list. Click Debbie in the list, Ctrl+click Ahmad, and then Ctrl+click Debbie.

e. Next, click Bill in the list, and then Shift+click Jim; this selects all of the names from Bill through Jim. Click the Exit button.

f. As you know, when a list box's SelectionMode property is set to One, the item selected in the list box is stored in the SelectedItem property, and the item's index is stored in the SelectedIndex property. However, when a list box's SelectionMode property is set to either MultiSimple or MultiExtended, the items selected in the list box are stored (as strings) in the SelectedItems property, and the indices of the items are stored (as integers) in the SelectedIndices property. Code the multiButton_Click procedure so that it first clears the contents of the resultLabel. The procedure should then display the selected names (which are stored in the SelectedItems property) on separate lines in the resultLabel.

g. Save the solution and then start the application. Click Ahmad in the list box, and then Shift+click Jim. Click the Multi-Selection button. The five names should appear on separate lines in the resultLabel. Close the solution.

DISCOVERY

34. In this exercise, you learn how to use the Items collection's Insert, Remove, and RemoveAt methods. Open the Items Solution (Items Solution.sln) file contained in the VbReloaded2012\Chap06\Items Solution folder.

a. You can use the Items collection's Insert method to add an item at a desired position in a list box during run time. The Insert method's syntax is *object*.`Items.Insert` (*position, item*), where *position* is the index of the item. Code the insertButton_Click procedure so it adds your name as the fourth item in the list box.

b. You can use the Items collection's Remove method to remove an item from a list box during run time. The Remove method's syntax is *object*.`Items.Remove`(*item*), where *item* is the item's value. Code the removeButton_Click procedure so it removes your name from the list box.

c. Like the Remove method, the Items collection's RemoveAt method also allows you to remove an item from a list box while an application is running. However, in the RemoveAt method, you specify the item's index rather than its value. The RemoveAt method's syntax is *object*.`Items.RemoveAt`(*index*), where *index* is the item's index. Code the removeAtButton_Click procedure so it removes the second name from the list box.

d. Save the solution and then start and test the application. Close the solution.

SWAT THE BUGS

35. Open the Debug Solution (Debug Solution.sln) file contained in the VbReloaded2012\ Chap06\Debug Solution folder. Open the Code Editor window and review the existing code. Start and then test the application. Locate and then correct any errors. When the application is working correctly, close the solution. (5, 6)

Case Projects

Martin Company

Create an application that the Martin Company's accountant can use to calculate an asset's annual depreciation. Use the following names for the solution and project, respectively: Martin Solution and Martin Project. Save the solution in the VbReloaded2012\Chap06 folder. Change the form file's name to Main Form.vb. You can either create your own interface or create the one shown in Figure 6-60. The figure shows a sample depreciation schedule for an asset with a cost of $100,000, a useful life of four years, and a salvage value of $15,000. The accountant will enter the asset's cost, useful life (in years), and salvage value (which is the value of the asset at the end of its useful life). Use a list box to allow the user to select the useful life. Display the numbers from 3 through 20 in the list box. The application should calculate the annual straight-line depreciation amounts using the Financial.SLN method. ("SLN" stands for "straight-line".) The method's syntax is `Financial.SLN (cost, salvage, life)`, in which *cost*, *salvage*, and *life* are the asset's cost, salvage value, and useful life, respectively. The method returns the depreciation amount as a Double number. The Asset cost and Salvage value text boxes shown in Figure 6-60 should accept only numbers, the period, and the Backspace key. The Depreciation Schedule image in the picture box is stored in the VbReloaded2012\Chap06\Martin.png file. (1-5, 7, 8)

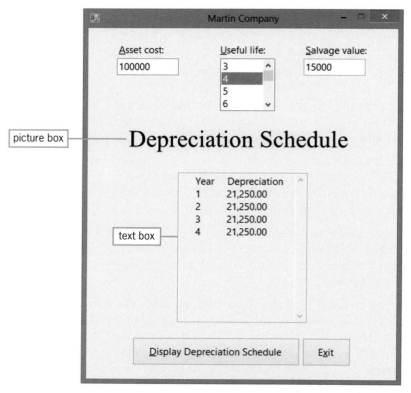

Figure 6-60   Sample interface for the Martin Company application

 ## Cook College

Create an application that displays the total credit hours and GPA for a Cook College student during one semester. Use the following names for the solution and project, respectively: Cook Solution and Cook Project. Save the solution in the VbReloaded2012\Chap06 folder. Change the form file's name to Main Form.vb. You can either create your own interface or create the one shown in Figure 6-61. The figure, which shows a sample run of the application, uses three labels for the output: one for the total credit hours, one for the GPA, and one for the number of grades entered. When the user clicks the Enter Data button, two input boxes should appear in succession: one for the number of credit hours (such as 3) and the next for the corresponding letter grade (such as A). One credit hour of A is worth 4 grade points, an hour of B is worth 3 grade points, and so on. The Enter Data button's Click event procedure should allow the user to enter as many sets of credit hours and grades as desired. The labels on the form should be updated after the user enters the letter grade. The sample output shown in Figure 6-61 is a result of entering 3 as the credit hours, A as the grade, 5 as the credit hours, B as the grade, 3 as the credit hours, and B as the grade. (1-6)

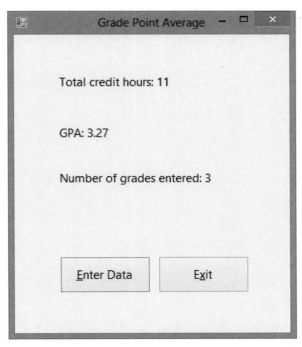

Figure 6-61 Sample interface for the Cook College application

 Zena Manufacturing

Zena Manufacturing has two warehouses, which the company refers to as warehouse A and warehouse B. Create an application that uses two list boxes to display the IDs of the company's products: one for products stored in warehouse A and one for products stored in warehouse B. Use the following names for the solution and project, respectively: Zena Solution and Zena Project. Save the solution in the VbReloaded2012\Chap06 folder. Change the form file's name to Main Form.vb. You can either create your own interface or create the one shown in Figure 6-62. The application should allow the user to enter a product ID, which will contain only letters and numbers. It then should search for the ID in the first list box. If it finds the ID in the first list box, the application should display the letter A in the Location box. If the ID is not in the first list box, the application should search the second list box. If it finds the ID in the second list box, the application should display the letter B in the Location box. If the ID is not included in either list box, the application should display an appropriate message. Use the following IDs for the first list box: AB11, HY16, JK56, MM12, PY63, PY64, AB21, and AB14. Use the following IDs for the second list box: AB20, JM17, PJ23, JK52, and TR16. (1-6, 8)

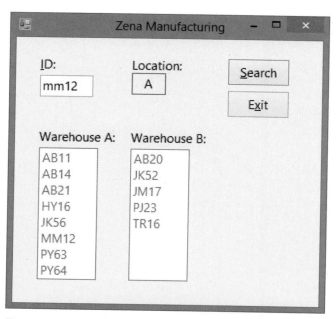

Figure 6-62   Sample interface for the Zena Manufacturing application

Powder Skating Rink

Powder Skating Rink holds a weekly ice-skating competition. Competing skaters must perform a two-minute program in front of a panel of six judges. At the end of a skater's program, each judge assigns a score of 0 through 10 to the skater. The manager of the ice rink wants an application that calculates and displays a skater's average score. Use list boxes to allow the manager to select the names of the judges. (You will need to make up your own names to use.) Also use a list box to allow the manager to select the score. After a judge's score has been recorded, remove his/her name from the list box. Doing this will prevent the user from entering a judge's score more than once. (Hint: Complete Computer Exercise 34 before coding this application.) After displaying the skater's average, display each judge's name in the list box for the next skater's scores. Use the following names for the solution and project, respectively: Powder Solution and Powder Project. Save the solution in the VbReloaded2012\Chap06 folder. Change the form file's name to Main Form.vb. (1-5, 8)

CHAPTER 7

More on the Repetition Structure

After studying Chapter 7, you should be able to:

1 Code a counter-controlled loop

2 Nest repetition structures

3 Calculate a periodic payment using the Financial.Pmt method

4 Select the existing text in a text box

5 Code the Enter and TextChanged event procedures for a text box

6 Include a combo box in an interface

7 Code the TextChanged event procedure for a combo box

8 Store images in an image list control

9 Display an image stored in an image list control

10 Calculate the future value of an investment using the Financial.FV method (Programming Tutorial 2)

Reading and Study Guide

Before you begin reading Chapter 7, view the Ch07_ReadingStudyGuide.pdf file. You can open the file using Adobe Reader, which is available for free on the Adobe Web site at *www.adobe.com/downloads/*.

Counter-Controlled Loops

In Chapter 6, you learned about counters, which are numeric variables used for counting something, such as the number of items purchased by a customer. Programmers also use counters to control loops whose instructions must be processed a precise number of times; such loops are referred to as **counter-controlled loops**. The partial game program shown in Figure 7-1, for example, uses a counter-controlled loop to process the loop instructions three times. As the figure indicates, a counter-controlled loop can be either a pretest loop or a posttest loop.

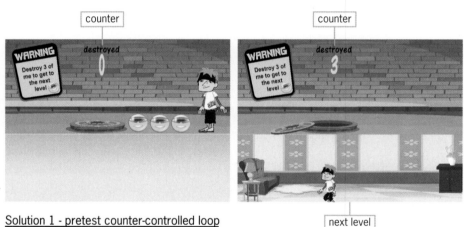

To advance to the next level in the game, Eddie must destroy the three smiley faces by jumping on each one. He then must jump through the manhole.

Solution 1 - pretest counter-controlled loop
1. initialize destroyed counter to 0
2. repeat while destroyed counter is less than 3
     jump on smiley face to destroy it
     add 1 to destroyed counter
  end repeat
3. jump into manhole to advance to the next level

Solution 2 - posttest counter-controlled loop
1. initialize destroyed counter to 0
2. repeat
     jump on smiley face to destroy it
     add 1 to destroyed counter
  end repeat until destroyed counter is 3
3. jump into manhole to advance to the next level

Ch07-Counter-Controlled Loops

Figure 7-1 Example of a partial game program that uses a counter-controlled loop
Image by Diane Zak; Created with Reallusion CrazyTalk Animator

The For...Next Statement

In Visual Basic, you code a posttest counter-controlled loop using the Do...Loop statement. A pretest counter-controlled loop, on the other hand, can be coded using either the Do...Loop statement or the For...Next statement. However, the **For...Next statement** provides a more convenient way to code that type of loop because it takes care of initializing and updating the counter, as well as evaluating the loop condition.

The For...Next statement's syntax is shown in Figure 7-2. The *counterVariableName* that appears in the For and Next clauses is the name of a numeric variable. The computer will use the variable to keep track of (in other words, count) the number of times the loop body instructions are processed. Although, technically, you do not need to specify the name of the counter variable in the Next clause, doing so is highly recommended because it makes your code more self-documenting. The figure also includes examples of using the For...Next statement, as well as the tasks the computer performs when processing the statement.

HOW TO Use the For...Next Statement

Syntax
For *counterVariableName* [**As** *dataType*] = *startValue* **To** *endValue* [**Step** *stepValue*]
      loop body instructions
Next *counterVariableName*

stepValue	Loop body processed when	Loop ends when
positive number	counter's value <= *endValue*	counter's value > *endValue*
negative number	counter's value >= *endValue*	counter's value < *endValue*

Example 1
```
For price As Integer = 10 To 13
    priceListBox.Items.Add(price.ToString)
Next price
```
adds 10, 11, 12, and 13 to the priceListBox

Example 2
```
Dim city As String
For x As Integer = 5 To 1 Step -1
    city = InputBox("City:", "City Entry")
    cityListBox.Items.Add(city)
Next x
```
adds the five city names entered by the user to the cityListBox

Example 3
```
Dim rate As Double
For rate = 0.05 To 0.1 Step 0.01
    rateListBox.Items.Add(rate.ToString("P0"))
Next rate
```
adds 5 %, 6 %, 7 %, 8 %, 9 %, and 10 % to the rateListBox

Figure 7-2 How to use the For...Next statement *(continues)*

(continued)

> Processing tasks
> 1. If the counter variable is declared in the For clause, the variable is created and then initialized to the *startValue*; otherwise, it is just initialized to the *startValue*. The initialization is done only once, at the beginning of the loop.
> 2. The counter's value is compared with the *endValue* to determine whether the loop should end. If the *stepValue* is a positive number, the comparison determines whether the counter's value is greater than the *endValue*. If the *stepValue* is a negative number, the comparison determines whether the counter's value is less than the *endValue*. Notice that the computer evaluates the loop condition before processing the instructions within the loop.
> 3. If the comparison from task 2 evaluates to True, the loop ends and processing continues with the statement following the Next clause. Otherwise, the loop body instructions are processed and then task 4 is performed.
> 4. Task 4 is performed only when the comparison from task 2 evaluates to False. In this task, the *stepValue* is added to the counter's value, and then tasks 2, 3, and 4 are repeated until the loop condition evaluates to True.

Figure 7-2   How to use the For...Next statement
© 2013 Cengage Learning

You can use the `Exit For` statement to exit the loop before it has finished processing. You may need to do this if the computer encounters an error when processing the loop instructions.

You can use the **As** *dataType* portion of the For clause to declare the counter variable, as shown in the first two examples in Figure 7-2. When you declare a variable in the For clause, the variable has block scope and can be used only within the For...Next loop. Alternatively, you can declare the counter variable in a Dim statement, as shown in Example 3. As you know, a variable declared in a Dim statement at the beginning of a procedure has procedure scope and can be used within the entire procedure. When deciding where to declare the counter variable, keep in mind that if the variable is needed only by the For...Next loop, then you should declare the variable in the For clause. As mentioned in Chapter 3, fewer unintentional errors occur in applications when the variables are declared using the minimum scope needed. Block-level variables have the smallest scope, followed by procedure-level variables and then class-level variables. You should declare the counter variable in a Dim statement only when its value is required by statements outside the For...Next loop in the procedure.

The *startValue*, *endValue*, and *stepValue* items in the For clause control the number of times the loop body is processed. The startValue and endValue tell the computer where to begin and end counting, respectively. The stepValue tells the computer how much to count by—in other words, how much to add to the counter variable each time the loop body is processed. If you omit the stepValue, a stepValue of positive 1 is used. In Example 1 in Figure 7-2, the startValue is 10, the endValue is 13, and the stepValue (which is omitted) is 1. Those values tell the computer to start counting at 10 and, counting by 1s, stop at 13—in other words, count 10, 11, 12, and 13. The computer will process the instructions in Example 1's loop body four times.

The startValue, endValue, and stepValue items must be numeric and can be either positive or negative, integer or non-integer. As indicated in Figure 7-2, if the stepValue is a positive number, the startValue must be less than or equal to the endValue for the loop instructions to be processed. If, on the other hand, the stepValue is a negative number, then the startValue must be greater than or equal to the endValue for the loop instructions to be processed.

Figure 7-3 describes the steps the computer follows when processing the loop shown in Example 1 in Figure 7-2. As Step 2 indicates, the loop's condition is evaluated before the loop body is processed. This is because the loop created by the For...Next statement is a pretest loop. Notice that the `price` variable contains the number 14 when the For...Next statement ends. The number 14 is the first integer that is greater than the loop's endValue of 13.

Processing steps for Example 1
1. The For clause creates the `price` variable and initializes it to 10.
2. The For clause compares the `price` value (10) with the endValue (13) to determine whether the loop should end. 10 is not greater than 13, so the computer adds 10 to the priceListBox, and then the For clause increments `price` by 1, giving 11.
3. The For clause compares the `price` value (11) with the endValue (13) to determine whether the loop should end. 11 is not greater than 13, so the computer adds 11 to the priceListBox, and then the For clause increments `price` by 1, giving 12.
4. The For clause compares the `price` value (12) with the endValue (13) to determine whether the loop should end. 12 is not greater than 13, so the computer adds 12 to the priceListBox, and then the For clause increments `price` by 1, giving 13.
5. The For clause compares the `price` value (13) with the endValue (13) to determine whether the loop should end. 13 is not greater than 13, so the computer adds 13 to the priceListBox, and then the For clause increments `price` by 1, giving 14.
6. The For clause compares the `price` value (14) with the endValue (13) to determine whether the loop should end. 14 is greater than 13, so the loop ends. Processing will continue with the statement following the Next clause.

Figure 7-3 Processing steps for Example 1 in Figure 7-2
© 2013 Cengage Learning

The New Salary Calculator Application

Figure 7-4 shows the problem specification for the New Salary Calculator application. It also shows the pseudocode and flowchart for the calcButton's Click event procedure. The procedure uses a counter-controlled loop to repeat the loop body instructions five times. Many programmers use a hexagon, which is a six-sided figure, to represent the For clause in a flowchart. Within the hexagon, you record the four items contained in the clause: *counterVariableName*, *startValue*, *endValue*, and *stepValue*. The counterVariableName and stepValue are placed at the top and bottom, respectively, of the hexagon. The startValue and endValue are placed on the left and right sides, respectively. The hexagon in Figure 7-4 indicates that the counterVariableName is `year`, the startValue is 1, the endValue is 5, and the stepValue is 1. The <= sign that precedes the endValue indicates that the loop body will be processed as long as the counter variable's value is less than or equal to 5.

Problem specification
Create an application that displays an employee's new salary for the next five years, assuming the employee receives a 2% raise each year. Display the new salary amounts in a list box.

Pseudocode and flowchart for the calcButton Click event procedure
1. store beginning salary in salary variable
2. clear the list box
3. repeat for year from 1 through 5 in increments of 1
    raise = salary * .02
    add raise to salary
    display year and salary in the list box
    end repeat for

Figure 7-4 Problem specification, pseudocode, and flowchart for the New Salary Calculator application
(continues)

(continued)

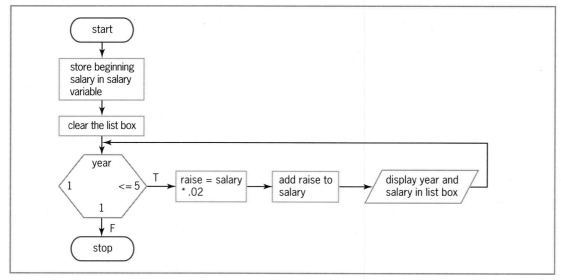

Figure 7-4 Problem specification, pseudocode, and flowchart for the New Salary Calculator application
© 2013 Cengage Learning

Figure 7-5 shows the code corresponding to the pseudocode and flowchart shown in Figure 7-4. It also includes a sample run of the New Salary Calculator application.

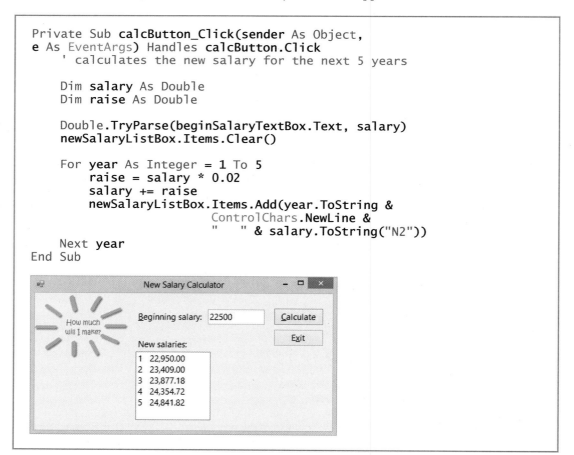

```
Private Sub calcButton_Click(sender As Object,
e As EventArgs) Handles calcButton.Click
    ' calculates the new salary for the next 5 years

    Dim salary As Double
    Dim raise As Double

    Double.TryParse(beginSalaryTextBox.Text, salary)
    newSalaryListBox.Items.Clear()

    For year As Integer = 1 To 5
        raise = salary * 0.02
        salary += raise
        newSalaryListBox.Items.Add(year.ToString &
                        ControlChars.NewLine &
                    "    " & salary.ToString("N2"))
    Next year
End Sub
```

If you want to experiment with the New Salary Calculator application, open the solution contained in the Try It 1! folder.

Figure 7-5 Code and sample run for the New Salary Calculator application
© 2013 Cengage Learning

As mentioned earlier, you can code a counter-controlled pretest loop using either the For...Next statement or the Do...Loop statement. To understand why the For...Next statement is more convenient to use for that type of loop, compare the For...Next statement in Figure 7-6 with the Do...Loop statement shown in the figure. Notice that when using the Do...Loop statement, your code must also include statements to declare, initialize, and update the counter variable. You also must be sure to include the appropriate comparison in the Do clause. In the For...Next statement, the For clause handles the declaration, initialization, comparison, and update tasks.

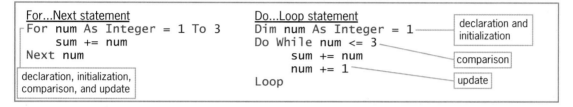

Figure 7-6   Comparison of the For...Next and Do...Loop statements
© 2013 Cengage Learning

Mini-Quiz 7-1

The answers to Mini-Quiz questions are located in Appendix A. Each question is associated with one or more objectives listed at the beginning of the chapter.

1. Which of the following For clauses processes the loop body as long as the x variable's value is less than or equal to the number 100? (1)

    a.   For x As Integer = 10 To 100 Step 10

    b.   For x As Integer = 1 To 100

    c.   For x As Integer = 3 To 100 Step 2

    d.   all of the above

2. A For...Next statement contains the following For clause: For x As Integer = 5 To 11 Step 2. The computer will stop processing the loop body when the x variable contains the number ———————. (1)

    a.   11

    b.   12

    c.   13

    d.   none of the above

3. Write a For...Next statement that displays the integers 6, 5, 4, 3, 2, and 1 in the numListBox. Use num as the counter variable's name. (1)

Nested Repetition Structures

Like selection structures, repetition structures can be nested, which means you can place one loop (called the nested or inner loop) within another loop (called the outer loop). Both loops can be pretest loops, or both can be posttest loops. Or, one can be a pretest loop and the other a posttest loop.

A clock uses nested loops to keep track of the time. For simplicity, consider a clock's minute and second hands only. The second hand on a clock moves one position, clockwise, for every second that has elapsed. After the second hand moves 60 positions, the minute hand moves one position, also clockwise. The second hand then begins its journey around the clock again. Figure 7-7 shows three versions of the logic used by a clock's minute and second hands. In each version, an outer loop controls the minute hand, while an inner (nested) loop controls the second hand. Notice that the entire nested loop is contained within the outer loop in each version. This must be true for the loop to be nested and for it to work correctly. The next iteration of the outer loop (which controls the minute hand) occurs only after the nested loop (which controls the second hand) has finished processing.

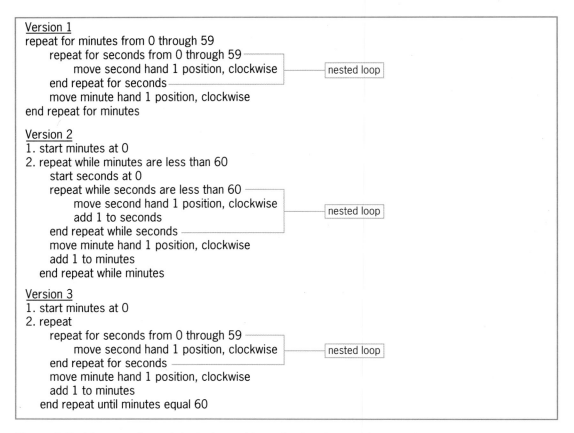

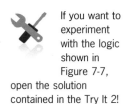
If you want to experiment with the logic shown in Figure 7-7, open the solution contained in the Try It 2! folder.

Figure 7-7   Three versions of the logic used by a clock's minute and second hands
© 2013 Cengage Learning

You will use a nested loop to code a modified version of the New Salary Calculator application from the previous section. In the original version, the application displays the new salary amounts for five years, assuming the employee receives a 2% annual raise. The modified application will also display the new salary amounts for five years; however, it will do so using annual raise rates of 2%, 3%, and 4%. The modified problem specification and pseudocode are shown in Figure 7-8. The modifications are shaded in the figure. Notice that the outer loop keeps track of the raise rates, and the nested loop keeps track of the years.

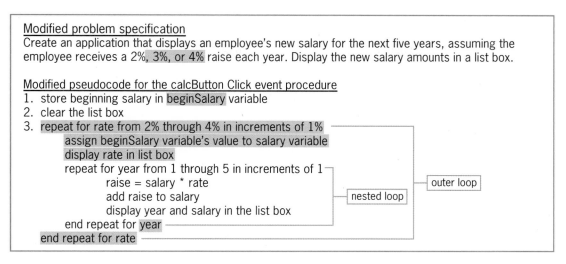

Modified problem specification
Create an application that displays an employee's new salary for the next five years, assuming the employee receives a 2%, 3%, or 4% raise each year. Display the new salary amounts in a list box.

Modified pseudocode for the calcButton Click event procedure
1. store beginning salary in beginSalary variable
2. clear the list box
3. repeat for rate from 2% through 4% in increments of 1%
    assign beginSalary variable's value to salary variable
    display rate in list box
    repeat for year from 1 through 5 in increments of 1
        raise = salary * rate
        add raise to salary
        display year and salary in the list box
    end repeat for year
end repeat for rate

(labels: nested loop, outer loop)

Figure 7-8 New Salary Calculator application's modified problem specification and pseudocode
© 2013 Cengage Learning

Figure 7-9 shows two ways of coding the pseudocode shown in Figure 7-8. Version 1 uses two For...Next statements. Version 2 uses a Do...Loop statement in the outer loop and uses a For...Next statement in the nested loop. Figure 7-9 also includes a sample run of the modified application.

```
Version 1 – For...Next statements
Private Sub calcButton_Click(sender As Object,
e As EventArgs) Handles calcButton.Click
    ' calculates the new salary for the next 5 years

    Dim beginSalary As Double
    Dim salary As Double
    Dim raise As Double

    Double.TryParse(beginSalaryTextBox.Text, beginSalary)
    newSalaryListBox.Items.Clear()

    For rate As Double = 0.02 To 0.04 Step 0.01
        salary = beginSalary
        newSalaryListBox.Items.Add(rate.ToString("P0") &
                        ControlChars.NewLine)
        For year As Integer = 1 To 5
            raise = salary * rate
            salary += raise
            newSalaryListBox.Items.Add(year.ToString &
                        ControlChars.NewLine &
                        "    " & salary.ToString("N2"))
        Next year
        newSalaryListBox.Items.Add(ControlChars.NewLine)
    Next rate
End Sub
```

declares, initializes, compares, and updates the rate variable

declares, initializes, compares, and updates the year variable

Figure 7-9 Modified code and a sample run of the modified application *(continues)*

(continued)

366

declares and initializes the rate variable

compares the rate variable

declares, initializes, compares, and updates the year variable

updates the rate variable

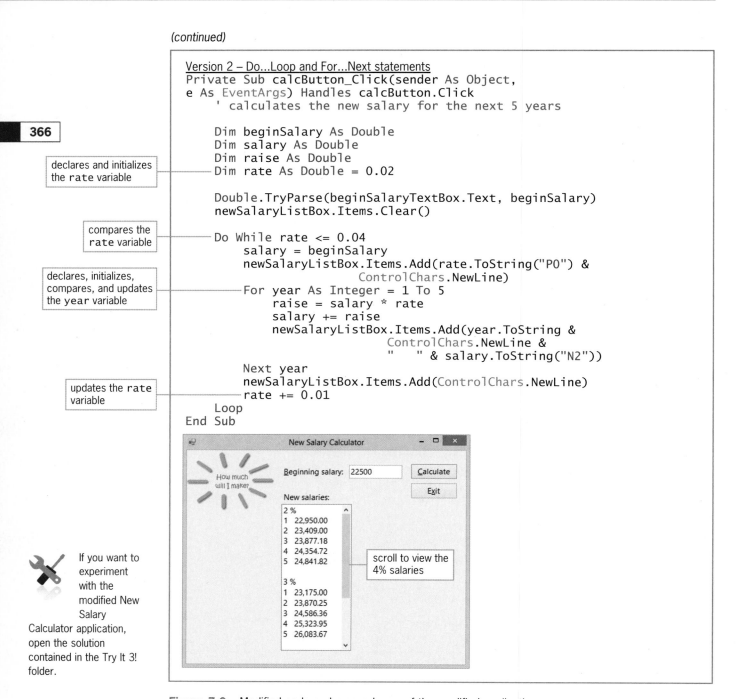

```
Version 2 – Do...Loop and For...Next statements
Private Sub calcButton_Click(sender As Object,
e As EventArgs) Handles calcButton.Click
    ' calculates the new salary for the next 5 years

    Dim beginSalary As Double
    Dim salary As Double
    Dim raise As Double
    Dim rate As Double = 0.02

    Double.TryParse(beginSalaryTextBox.Text, beginSalary)
    newSalaryListBox.Items.Clear()

    Do While rate <= 0.04
        salary = beginSalary
        newSalaryListBox.Items.Add(rate.ToString("P0") &
                        ControlChars.NewLine)
        For year As Integer = 1 To 5
            raise = salary * rate
            salary += raise
            newSalaryListBox.Items.Add(year.ToString &
                        ControlChars.NewLine &
                        "    " & salary.ToString("N2"))
        Next year
        newSalaryListBox.Items.Add(ControlChars.NewLine)
        rate += 0.01
    Loop
End Sub
```

New Salary Calculator

How much will I make?

Beginning salary: 22500   Calculate

Exit

New salaries:

```
2 %
1  22,950.00
2  23,409.00
3  23,877.18
4  24,354.72
5  24,841.82

3 %
1  23,175.00
2  23,870.25
3  24,586.36
4  25,323.95
5  26,083.67
```

scroll to view the 4% salaries

If you want to experiment with the modified New Salary Calculator application, open the solution contained in the Try It 3! folder.

Figure 7-9   Modified code and a sample run of the modified application
© 2013 Cengage Learning

Mini-Quiz 7-2

1. A nested loop can be _____ . (2)

    a. a pretest loop only

    b. a posttest loop only

    c. either a pretest loop or a posttest loop

2. For _____ loop to work correctly, it must be contained entirely within the _____ loop. (2)

    a. a nested, outer

    b. an outer, nested

3. A clock's hour hand is controlled by a(n) _____ loop, while its minute hand is controlled by a(n) _____ loop. (2)

    a. nested, outer

    b. outer, nested

The answers to Mini-Quiz questions are located in Appendix A. Each question is associated with one or more objectives listed at the beginning of the chapter.

367

The Financial.Pmt Method

Visual Basic's Financial class contains many methods that your applications can use to perform financial calculations. Figure 7-10 lists some of the more commonly used methods defined in the class. All of the methods return the result of their calculation as a Double number.

Method	Purpose
Financial.DDB	calculate the depreciation of an asset for a specific time period using the double-declining balance method
Financial.FV	calculate the future value of an annuity based on periodic, fixed payments and a fixed interest rate
Financial.IPmt	calculate the interest payment for a given period of an annuity based on periodic, fixed payments and a fixed interest rate
Financial.IRR	calculate the internal rate of return for a series of periodic cash flows (payments and receipts)
Financial.Pmt	calculate the payment for an annuity based on periodic, fixed payments and a fixed interest rate
Financial.PPmt	calculate the principal payment for a given period of an annuity based on periodic fixed payments and a fixed interest rate
Financial.PV	calculate the present value of an annuity based on periodic, fixed payments to be paid in the future and a fixed interest rate
Financial.SLN	calculate the straight-line depreciation of an asset for a single period
Financial.SYD	calculate the sum-of-years digits depreciation of an asset for a specified period

Figure 7-10 Some of the methods defined in the Financial class
© 2013 Cengage Learning

In the next section, you will use the **Financial.Pmt method** to calculate the monthly payment on a loan. ("Pmt" stands for "payment".) Figure 7-11 shows the method's basic syntax and lists the meaning of each argument. The *Rate* and *NPer* (number of periods) arguments must be expressed using the same units. If Rate is a monthly interest rate, then NPer must specify the number of monthly payments. Likewise, if Rate is an annual interest rate, then NPer must specify the number of annual payments. Figure 7-11 also includes examples of using the Financial.Pmt method.

HOW TO Use the Financial.Pmt Method

Syntax
Financial.Pmt(Rate, NPer, PV)

Argument	Meaning
Rate	interest rate per period
NPer	total number of payment periods (the term)
PV	present value of the loan (the loan amount)

Example 1
```
Financial.Pmt(.05, 3, 9000)
```
Calculates the annual payment for a loan of $9,000 for 3 years at 5% interest. Rate is .05, NPer is 3, and PV is 9000. The annual payment returned by the method (rounded to the nearest cent) is −3304.88.

Example 2
```
-Financial.Pmt(.06 / 12, 5 * 12, 12000)
```
Calculates the monthly payment for a loan of $12,000 for 5 years at 6% interest. Rate is .06 / 12, NPer is 5 * 12, and PV is 12000. The monthly payment returned by the method (rounded to the nearest cent and expressed as a positive number) is 231.99.

Figure 7-11 How to use the Financial.Pmt method
© 2013 Cengage Learning

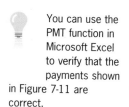

You can use the PMT function in Microsoft Excel to verify that the payments shown in Figure 7-11 are correct.

Example 1 in Figure 7-11 calculates the annual payment for a loan of $9,000 for 3 years at 5% interest. As the example indicates, the annual payment returned by the method (rounded to the nearest cent) is −3304.88. This means that if you borrow $9,000 for 3 years at 5% interest, you will need to make three annual payments of $3,304.88 to pay off the loan. Notice that the Financial.Pmt method returns a negative number. You can change the negative number to a positive number by preceding the method with the negation operator, like this: −Financial.Pmt(.05, 3, 9000). As you learned in Chapter 3, the negation operator reverses the sign of a number: A negative number preceded by the negation operator becomes a positive number, and vice versa.

The Financial.Pmt method shown in Example 2 in Figure 7-11 calculates the monthly payment for a loan of $12,000 for 5 years at 6% interest. In this example, the Rate and NPer arguments are expressed in monthly terms rather than in annual terms. You change an annual rate to a monthly rate by dividing the annual rate by 12. You change the term from years to months by multiplying the number of years by 12. The monthly payment for the loan in Example 2, rounded to the nearest cent and expressed as a positive number, is 231.99.

The Payment Calculator Application

Figure 7-12 shows the problem specification for the Payment Calculator application, which requires a loop and the Financial.Pmt method. The figure also contains the pseudocode and code for the calcButton's Click event procedure, as well as a sample run of the application.

Problem specification
Create an application that calculates the monthly payments on a car loan, using annual interest rates of 3%, 3.5%, 4%, 4.5%, 5%, 5.5%, and 6%. The user will enter the loan amount and the term (in years). The term, which is the number of years the user has to pay off the loan, can be 2 years, 3 years, 4 years, or 5 years only.

Pseudocode for the calcButton Click event procedure
1. store user input (loan and term) in variables
2. clear the paymentsLabel
3. repeat for rate from .03 through .06 in increments of .005
      calculate the monthly payment (using the loan, rate, term, and Financial.Pmt method)
      display rate and monthly payment amount in paymentsLabel
   end repeat for
4. send the focus to the loanTextBox

```
Private Sub calcButton_Click(sender As Object,
e As EventArgs) Handles calcButton.Click
    ' calculates the monthly payments on a loan
    ' using interest rates of 3% through 6% in
    ' increments of .5%

    Dim loan As Double
    Dim term As Integer
    Dim monthlyPayment As Double

    ' assign input to variables
    Double.TryParse(loanTextBox.Text, loan)
    term = Convert.ToInt32(termListBox.SelectedItem)

    ' clear contents of the paymentsLabel
    paymentsLabel.Text = String.Empty

    ' calculate and display monthly payments
    For rate As Double = 0.03 To 0.06 Step 0.005
        monthlyPayment =
            -Financial.Pmt(rate / 12, term * 12, loan)
        paymentsLabel.Text = paymentsLabel.Text &
            rate.ToString("P1") & ":   " &
            monthlyPayment.ToString("C2") &
            ControlChars.NewLine
    Next rate
    loanTextBox.Focus()
End Sub
```

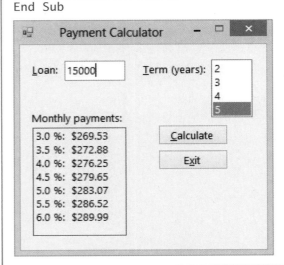

Figure 7-12 Problem specification, pseudocode, code, and sample run for the Payment Calculator application
© 2013 Cengage Learning

Before the calcButton_Click procedure ends, it sends the focus to the loanTextBox. Doing this places the cursor after the existing text in the text box, as shown in Figure 7-12. However, it is customary in Windows applications to select (highlight) the existing text when a text box receives the focus.

Selecting the Existing Text in a Text Box

Visual Basic provides the **SelectAll method** for selecting a text box's existing text. The method's syntax is shown in Figure 7-13 along with an example of using the method.

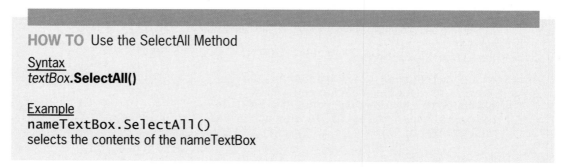

HOW TO Use the SelectAll Method

Syntax
*textBox.***SelectAll()**

Example
```
nameTextBox.SelectAll()
```
selects the contents of the nameTextBox

Figure 7-13 How to use the SelectAll method
© 2013 Cengage Learning

In the Payment Calculator application, you can use the SelectAll method to select the contents of the Loan text box when the text box receives the focus. You do this by entering the SelectAll method in the text box's Enter event procedure. A text box's **Enter event** occurs when the text box receives the focus, which can happen as a result of the user either tabbing to the control or using the control's access key. It also occurs when the Focus method is used to send the focus to the control. Figure 7-14 shows the Loan text box's Enter event procedure. It also shows the result of the computer processing the procedure's code.

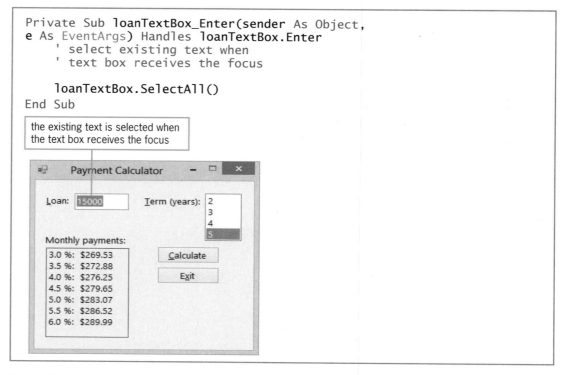

```
Private Sub loanTextBox_Enter(sender As Object,
e As EventArgs) Handles loanTextBox.Enter
    ' select existing text when
    ' text box receives the focus

    loanTextBox.SelectAll()
End Sub
```

the existing text is selected when the text box receives the focus

Payment Calculator

Loan: 15000   Term (years): 2
                             3
                             4
                             5

Monthly payments:

3.0 %: $269.53
3.5 %: $272.88
4.0 %: $276.25
4.5 %: $279.65
5.0 %: $283.07
5.5 %: $286.52
6.0 %: $289.99

Calculate

Exit

Figure 7-14 Code and result of processing the loanTextBox_Enter procedure
© 2013 Cengage Learning

Now consider what happens when the user enters the number 25000 in the Loan text box, as shown in Figure 7-15. Even though the loan amount has changed, the Monthly payments box still lists the monthly payments for a $15,000 loan. The monthly payments for a $25,000 loan will not appear until the user clicks the Calculate button. To prevent any confusion, it would be better to clear the contents of the Monthly payments box when the user enters a different value in the Loan text box. You can do this by coding the Loan text box's TextChanged event procedure.

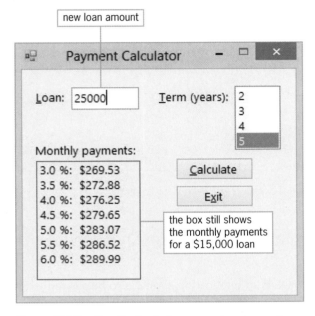

Figure 7-15   Result of entering a new loan amount

Coding the TextChanged Event Procedure

A control's **TextChanged event** occurs when a change is made to the contents of the control's Text property. This can happen as a result of either the user entering data into the control or the application's code assigning data to the control's Text property. In the Payment Calculator application, the loanTextBox_TextChanged procedure will remove the monthly payments from the Monthly payments box when the user changes the loan amount. Figure 7-16 shows the procedure's code and includes a sample run of the application. In the sample run, the user enters the number 2 in the Loan text box after calculating the monthly payments for a $15,000 loan. Notice that the monthly payments no longer appear in the Monthly payments box.

```
Private Sub loanTextBox_TextChanged(sender As Object,
e As EventArgs) Handles loanTextBox.TextChanged
    ' clears the paymentsLabel when the
    ' contents of the text box changes

    paymentsLabel.Text = String.Empty
End Sub
```

Figure 7-16   Code and result of processing the loanTextBox_TextChanged procedure *(continues)*

(continued)

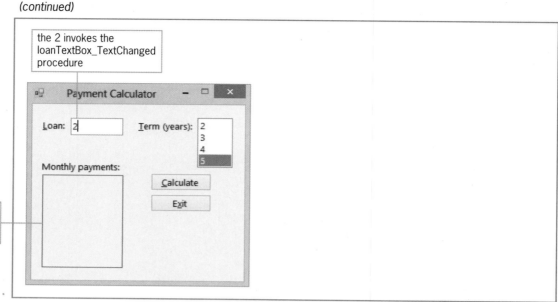

the 2 invokes the loanTextBox_TextChanged procedure

the box is cleared when the user enters a value in the text box

Figure 7-16 Code and result of processing the loanTextBox_TextChanged procedure
© 2013 Cengage Learning

Coding the SelectedValueChanged and SelectedIndexChanged Event Procedures

The Monthly payments box in the Payment Calculator application should also be cleared when the user selects a different term in the termListBox. You can accomplish this by entering the `paymentsLabel.Text = String.Empty` statement in either the termListBox's SelectedValueChanged procedure or its SelectedIndexChanged procedure. Both procedures are shown in Figure 7-17; however, you need to enter the statement in only one of the procedures.

If you want to experiment with the Payment Calculator application, open the solution contained in the Try It 4! folder.

you need to code only one of these procedures

```
termListBox SelectedIndexChanged event procedure
Private Sub termListBox_SelectedIndexChanged(
sender As Object, e As EventArgs
) Handles termListBox.SelectedIndexChanged
    ' clears the paymentsLabel when the term changes

    paymentsLabel.Text = String.Empty
End Sub

termListBox SelectedValueChanged event procedure
Private Sub termListBox_SelectedValueChanged(
sender As Object, e As EventArgs
) Handles termListBox.SelectedValueChanged
    ' clears the paymentsLabel when the term changes

    paymentsLabel.Text = String.Empty
End Sub
```

Figure 7-17 termListBox's SelectedIndexChanged and SelectedValueChanged procedures
© 2013 Cengage Learning

Mini-Quiz 7-3

1. Which of the following calculates the monthly payment on a $5000 loan for 2 years using an annual interest rate of 4%? Payments should be expressed as a positive number. (3)

   a. `-Financial.Pmt(5000, .04 / 12, 24)`

   b. `-Financial.Pmt(24, .04 / 12, 5000)`

   c. `-Financial.Pmt(.04 / 12, 24, 5000)`

   d. `-Financial.Pmt(5000, 24, .04 / 12)`

2. Write the statement to select the contents of the cityTextBox. (4)

3. Which of the following will invoke the nameTextBox's Enter event? (5)

   a. the user tabbing to the nameTextBox

   b. the user employing the nameTextBox's access key

   c. the computer processing the statement `nameTextBox.Focus()`

   d. all of the above

The answers to Mini-Quiz questions are located in Appendix A. Each question is associated with one or more objectives listed at the beginning of the chapter.

373

Note: You have learned a lot so far in this chapter. You may want to take a break at this point before continuing.

Including a Combo Box in an Interface

In many interfaces, combo boxes are used in place of list boxes. You use the ComboBox tool in the toolbox to add a combo box to an interface. A **combo box** is similar to a list box in that it allows the user to select from a list of choices. However, unlike a list box, the full list of choices in a combo box can be hidden, allowing you to save space on the form. Also unlike a list box, a combo box contains a text field. Depending on the style of the combo box, the text field may or may not be editable by the user, as indicated in Figure 7-18. The style is controlled by the combo box's **DropDownStyle property**, which can be set to Simple, DropDown (the default), or DropDownList. Figure 7-18 also shows an example of each combo box style.

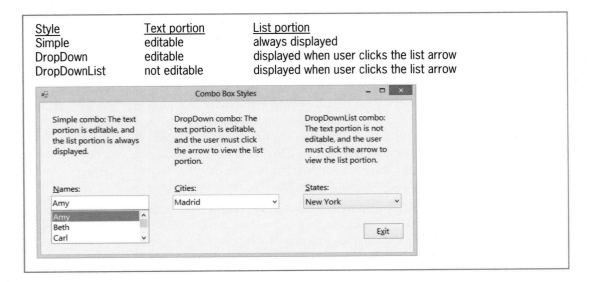

Style	Text portion	List portion
Simple	editable	always displayed
DropDown	editable	displayed when user clicks the list arrow
DropDownList	not editable	displayed when user clicks the list arrow

Figure 7-18 Combo box styles
© 2013 Cengage Learning

374

You should use a label control to provide keyboard access to the combo box, as shown in Figure 7-18. For the access key to work correctly, the value in the label's TabIndex property must be one number less than the value in the combo box's TabIndex property. Like the items in a list box, the items in the list portion of a combo box are either arranged by use, with the most frequently used entries listed first, or sorted in ascending order. To sort the items in the list portion of a combo box, you set the combo box's **Sorted property** to True in the Properties window.

As you can with a list box, you can use the String Collection Editor window to specify the combo box items during design time. You can open the window by clicking Edit Items on the combo box's task list. Or, you can click the ellipsis button in the Items property in the Properties list. During run time, you use the Items collection's **Add method** to add an item to a combo box, as shown in the code in Figure 7-19. Like the first item in a list box, the first item in a combo box has an index of 0. You can use any of the following properties to select a default item, which will appear in the text portion of the combo box: SelectedIndex, SelectedItem, or Text. If no item is selected, the SelectedItem and Text properties contain the empty string, and the SelectedIndex property contains −1 (negative one).

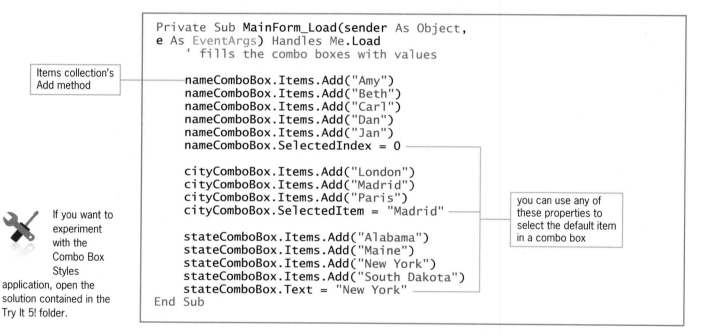

Items collection's
Add method

```
Private Sub MainForm_Load(sender As Object,
e As EventArgs) Handles Me.Load
    ' fills the combo boxes with values

    nameComboBox.Items.Add("Amy")
    nameComboBox.Items.Add("Beth")
    nameComboBox.Items.Add("Carl")
    nameComboBox.Items.Add("Dan")
    nameComboBox.Items.Add("Jan")
    nameComboBox.SelectedIndex = 0

    cityComboBox.Items.Add("London")
    cityComboBox.Items.Add("Madrid")
    cityComboBox.Items.Add("Paris")
    cityComboBox.SelectedItem = "Madrid"

    stateComboBox.Items.Add("Alabama")
    stateComboBox.Items.Add("Maine")
    stateComboBox.Items.Add("New York")
    stateComboBox.Items.Add("South Dakota")
    stateComboBox.Text = "New York"
End Sub
```

you can use any of these properties to select the default item in a combo box

If you want to experiment with the Combo Box Styles application, open the solution contained in the Try It 5! folder.

Figure 7-19   Code for the combo boxes in Figure 7-18
© 2013 Cengage Learning

It is easy to confuse a combo box's SelectedItem property with its Text property. The **SelectedItem property** contains the value of the item selected in the list portion of the combo box, whereas the **Text property** contains the value that appears in the text portion. A value can appear in the text portion as a result of the user either selecting an item in the list portion of the control or typing an entry in the text portion itself. It also can appear in the text portion as a result of a statement that assigns a value to the control's SelectedIndex, SelectedItem, or Text property.

If the combo box is a DropDownList style, where the text portion is not editable, you can use the SelectedItem and Text properties interchangeably. However, if the combo box is either a Simple or DropDown style, where the user can type an entry in the text portion, you should use the Text property because it contains the value either selected or entered by the user. When the value in the Text property changes, either as a result of the user selecting a different item in the list portion of the combo box or entering a value in the text portion, the combo box's TextChanged event occurs.

You can use the Items collection's **Count property** to determine the number of items in the list portion of a combo box, like this: nameComboBox.Items.Count. The property's value will always be one number more than the combo box's highest index. You can use the Items collection's **Clear method** to clear the items from the list portion of the combo box, like this: `nameComboBox.Items.Clear()`.

Figure 7-20 shows a sample run of the Payment Calculator application using a DropDown combo box rather than a list box. It also includes most of the application's code. Notice that the paymentsLabel is cleared when the combo box's TextChanged event occurs. (The figure does not show the exitButton_Click and loanTextBox_KeyPress procedures.)

```vb
Private Sub MainForm_Load(sender As Object,
e As EventArgs) Handles Me.Load
    ' fills the termComboBox

    For term As Integer = 2 To 5
        termComboBox.Items.Add(term.ToString)
    Next term
    termComboBox.SelectedItem = "4"
End Sub

Private Sub calcButton_Click(sender As Object,
e As EventArgs) Handles calcButton.Click
    ' calculates the monthly payments on a loan
    ' using interest rates of 3% through 6% in
    ' increments of .5%

    Dim loan As Double
    Dim term As Integer
    Dim monthlyPayment As Double

    ' assign input to variables
    Double.TryParse(loanTextBox.Text, loan)
    term = Convert.ToInt32(termComboBox.Text)    ⟵ uses the combo box's
                                                   Text property to determine
                                                   the term
    ' clear contents of the paymentsLabel
    paymentsLabel.Text = String.Empty

    ' calculate and display monthly payments
    For rate As Double = 0.03 To 0.06 Step 0.005
        monthlyPayment =
            -Financial.Pmt(rate / 12, term * 12, loan)
        paymentsLabel.Text = paymentsLabel.Text &
            rate.ToString("P1") & ":   " &
            monthlyPayment.ToString("C2") &
            ControlChars.NewLine
    Next rate

    loanTextBox.Focus()
End Sub

Private Sub loanTextBox_Enter(sender As Object,
e As EventArgs) Handles loanTextBox.Enter
    ' select existing text when
    ' text box receives the focus

    loanTextBox.SelectAll()
End Sub

Private Sub loanTextBox_TextChanged(sender As Object,
e As EventArgs) Handles loanTextBox.TextChanged
    ' clears the paymentsLabel when the
    ' contents of the text box changes

    paymentsLabel.Text = String.Empty
End Sub
```

Figure 7-20 Code and a sample run of the application using a combo box (continues)

(continued)

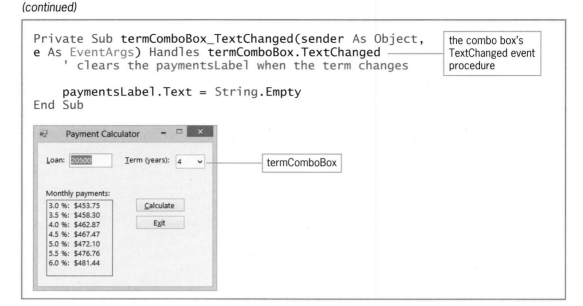

```
Private Sub termComboBox_TextChanged(sender As Object,
e As EventArgs) Handles termComboBox.TextChanged
    ' clears the paymentsLabel when the term changes

    paymentsLabel.Text = String.Empty
End Sub
```

the combo box's TextChanged event procedure

376

If you want to experiment with this version of the Payment Calculator application, open the solution contained in the Try It 6! folder.

termComboBox

Figure 7-20   Code and a sample run of the application using a combo box
© 2013 Cengage Learning

The last concept covered in this chapter is how to use an image list control. You will use the control in the Slot Machine application coded in Programming Tutorial 1.

Using an Image List Control

You can use an **image list control** to store a collection of images. You instantiate an image list control using the ImageList tool, which is located in the Components section of the toolbox. An image list control does not appear on the form. Instead, it appears in the component tray, as shown in the Image Viewer application in Figure 7-21.

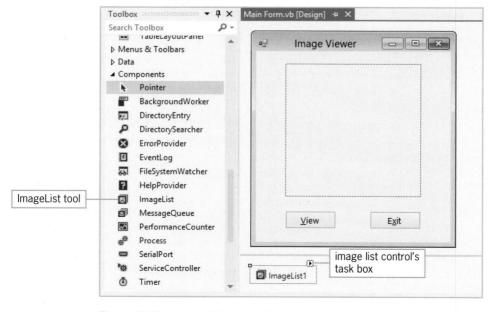

Figure 7-21   Image Viewer application

The collection of images stored in an image list control is called the **Images collection**. You add images to the collection using the Images Collection Editor window. The steps for doing this are listed in Figure 7-22, which also shows the completed Images Collection Editor window in the Image Viewer application.

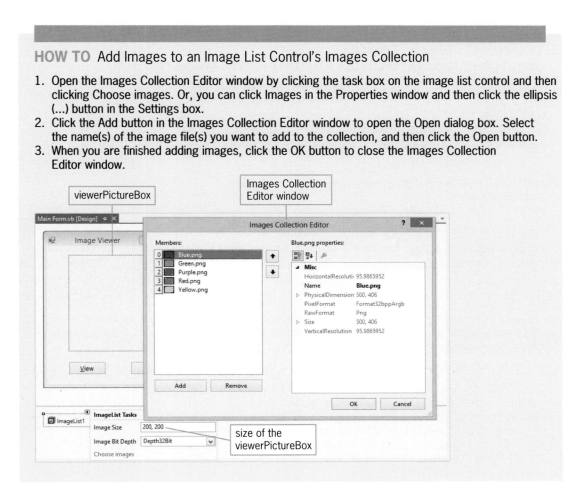

HOW TO Add Images to an Image List Control's Images Collection

1. Open the Images Collection Editor window by clicking the task box on the image list control and then clicking Choose images. Or, you can click Images in the Properties window and then click the ellipsis (...) button in the Settings box.
2. Click the Add button in the Images Collection Editor window to open the Open dialog box. Select the name(s) of the image file(s) you want to add to the collection, and then click the Open button.
3. When you are finished adding images, click the OK button to close the Images Collection Editor window.

Figure 7-22 How to add images to an image list control's Images collection
© 2013 Cengage Learning

Each image in the Images collection has a unique index. The first image's index is 0; the second image's index is 1, and so on. You refer to an image in the Images collection using the Images collection's Item property, as shown in the syntax in Figure 7-23. In the syntax, *object* is the name of the image list control, and *index* is the index of the image you want to access. Figure 7-23 also includes examples of using the syntax.

378

HOW TO Refer to an Image in the Images Collection

<u>Syntax</u>
object.**Images.Item**(*index*)

<u>Example 1</u>
`ImageList1.Images.Item(0)`
refers to the first image stored in the ImageList1 control's Images collection

> determines the number of images
> contained in the Images collection

<u>Example 2</u>
`ImageList1.Images.Item(ImageList1.Images.Count - 1)`
refers to the last image stored in the ImageList1 control's Images collection

Figure 7-23   How to refer to an image in the Images collection
© 2013 Cengage Learning

Example 1 in Figure 7-23 shows how you refer to the first image stored in the ImageList1 control's Images collection. Example 2 shows how you refer to the last image stored in the ImageList1 control's Images collection. The code in Example 2 uses the Images collection's Count property to determine the number of images stored in the collection. The index of the last image in the collection will always be one number less than the value in the collection's Count property.

An image list control merely stores images; it does not display them. To display the images, you need to use another control, such as a picture box. In the Image Viewer application, the viewButton_Click procedure will display the images stored in the ImageList1 control, one at a time, in the viewerPictureBox. Figure 7-24 shows the procedure's code along with a sample run of the application.

```
Private Sub viewButton_Click(sender As Object,
e As EventArgs) Handles viewButton.Click
    ' view images, one at a time

    Dim numImages As Integer = ImageList1.Images.Count

    For index As Integer = 0 To numImages - 1
        viewerPictureBox.Image =
            ImageList1.Images.Item(index)
        Me.Refresh()
        System.Threading.Thread.Sleep(1000)
    Next index
End Sub
```

Figure 7-24   Code and a sample run of the Image Viewer application *(continues)*

(continued)

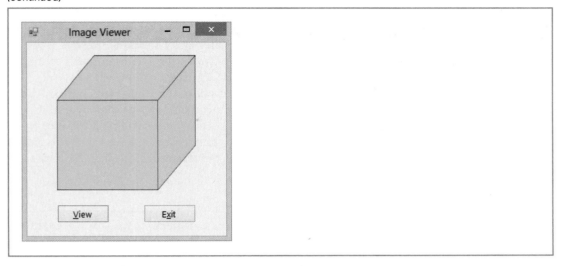

Figure 7-24 Code and a sample run of the Image Viewer application
© 2013 Cengage Learning

If you want to experiment with the Image Viewer application, open the solution contained in the Try It 7! folder.

The answers to Mini-Quiz questions are located in Appendix A. Each question is associated with one or more objectives listed at the beginning of the chapter.

Mini-Quiz 7-4

1. Which method is used to add items to a combo box? (6)

    a. Add

    b. AddItem

    c. AddList

    d. ItemAdd

2. The text portion of a combo box is always editable. (6)

    a. True

    b. False

3. Which of the following stores an integer that represents the number of items in the list portion of the stateComboBox? (6)

    a. `stateComboBox.Count`

    b. `stateComboBox.Count.Items`

    c. `stateComboBox.Items.Count`

    d. none of the above

4. Write the statement to refer to the second image stored in the ImageList1 control's Images collection. (8, 9)

You have completed the concepts section of Chapter 7. The Programming Tutorial section is next.

PROGRAMMING TUTORIAL 1

Creating the Slot Machine Application

In this tutorial, you will create an application that simulates a slot machine. Figures 7-25 and 7-26 show the application's TOE chart and MainForm, respectively. The MainForm contains a table layout panel, three picture boxes, and two buttons. The application will store six different images in an image list control. When the user clicks the Click Here button, the button's Click event procedure will generate 10 sets of three random integers, which will be used to select images from the image list control. The selected images will be displayed, one at a time, in the three picture boxes. If the final three random numbers are the same, the picture boxes will contain the same image, and the Click event procedure will display the message "Congratulations!" in a message box.

Task	Object	Event
1. Display 10 random images from the ImageList1 control, one at a time, in the leftPictureBox, centerPictureBox, and rightPictureBox 2. Display "Congratulations!" in a message box when the leftPictureBox, centerPictureBox, and rightPictureBox contain the same image	clickHereButton	Click
End the application	exitButton	Click
Store 6 different images	ImageList1	None
Display random images stored in ImageList1 (from clickHereButton)	leftPictureBox, centerPictureBox, rightPictureBox	None

Figure 7-25   TOE chart for the Slot Machine application
© 2013 Cengage Learning

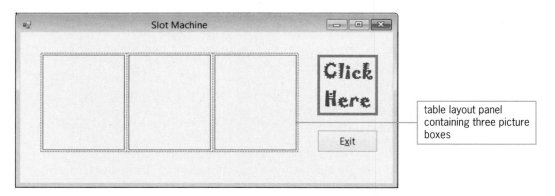

Figure 7-26   MainForm for the Slot Machine application

Instantiating the ImageList1 Control

Before you begin coding the Slot Machine application, you will need to instantiate the ImageList1 control and then store the six images in its Images collection. (The six images are from the Open Clip Art Library at *http://openclipart.org.*)

To instantiate the ImageList1 control and then store images in its Images collection:

1. Start Visual Studio. Open the **Slot Machine Solution** (**Slot Machine Solution.sln**) file contained in the VbReloaded2012\Chap07\Slot Machine Solution folder. If necessary, open the designer window.

2. If necessary, open the Toolbox window and expand the Components section. Click **ImageList** and then drag an image list control to the form. Release the mouse button. The ImageList1 control appears in the component tray.

3. Click the ImageList1 control's **task box** and then click **Choose images** to open the Images Collection Editor window. Click the **Add** button. Open the VbReloaded2012\ Chap07 folder. Click **Apple.png** in the list of filenames, and then Ctrl+click the following filenames: **Banana.png**, **Cherries.png**, **Lemon.png**, **Pineapple.png**, and **Strawberry.png**. Click the **Open** button. The filenames and small images appear in the Members list section of the Images Collection Editor window, as shown in Figure 7-27.

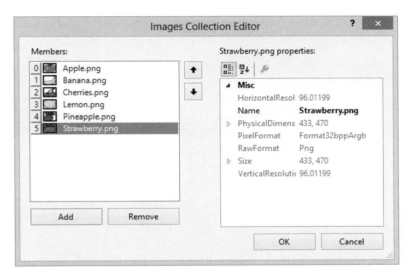

Figure 7-27 Completed Images Collection Editor window
OpenClipArt.org/nicubunu

4. Click the **OK** button to add the six images to the ImageList1 control's Images collection.

5. Change the Image Size in the ImageList Tasks box to **126, 150** (which is the size of the picture boxes on the form), and change the Image Bit Depth to **Depth32Bit**.

6. Click the **form** to close the ImageList Tasks box. Close the Toolbox window and then save the solution.

Coding the Slot Machine Application

According to the application's TOE chart, only the Click event procedures for the two buttons need to be coded.

To begin coding the application:

1. Open the Code Editor window. Notice that the exitButton_Click procedure has already been coded for you.

2. In the comments that appear in the General Declarations section, replace <your name> and <current date> with your name and the current date, respectively.

Figure 7-28 shows the pseudocode for the clickHereButton's Click event procedure. As the pseudocode indicates, the procedure will use random integers to display the appropriate images in the three picture boxes. It then will compare the random integers to determine whether the "Congratulations!" message should be displayed.

---

clickHereButton Click event procedure
1. disable the clickHereButton
2. repeat for spins from 1 through 10 in increments of 1
     generate a random integer from 0 through 5 and store it in a variable named leftIndex
     use the leftIndex variable to display the appropriate ImageList1 image in the leftPictureBox
     refresh the screen and pause the application

     generate a random integer from 0 through 5 and store it in a variable named centerIndex
     use the centerIndex variable to display the appropriate ImageList1 image in the centerPictureBox
     refresh the screen and pause the application

     generate a random integer from 0 through 5 and store it in a variable named rightIndex
     use the rightIndex variable to display the appropriate ImageList1 image in the rightPictureBox
     refresh the screen and pause the application
   end repeat for
3. if the leftIndex, centerIndex, and rightIndex variables contain the same integer
     display "Congratulations!" in a message box
   end if
4. enable the clickHereButton
5. send the focus to the clickHereButton

Figure 7-28   Pseudocode for the clickHereButton_Click procedure
© 2013 Cengage Learning

To code the clickHereButton_Click procedure and then test the code:

1. Locate the clickHereButton_Click procedure. The procedure will need a Random object to represent the pseudo-random number generator, and three Integer variables to store the random integers. Click the **blank line** above the End Sub clause and then enter the following four Dim statements. Press **Enter** twice after typing the last Dim statement.

    Dim randGen As New Random
    Dim leftIndex As Integer
    Dim centerIndex As Integer
    Dim rightIndex As Integer

2. The first step in the pseudocode disables the clickHereButton. Enter the following assignment statement:

    clickHereButton.Enabled = False

3. The second step in the pseudocode is a counter-controlled loop that repeats the loop body 10 times. Enter the following For clause:

    For spins As Integer = 1 To 10

4. Notice that the Code Editor enters the Next clause for you. Change the Next clause to **Next spins** and press **Enter**.

5. The first instruction in the loop body generates a random integer from 0 through 5 and stores it in the leftIndex variable. Click the **blank line** between the For and Next clauses, and then enter the following assignment statement:

leftIndex = randGen.Next(0, 6)

6. The second instruction in the loop body uses the value in the leftIndex variable to display the appropriate image in the leftPictureBox. Enter the following assignment statement:

leftPictureBox.Image =
    ImageList1.Images.Item(leftIndex)

7. Next, you need to refresh the screen and then pause the application. Enter the following two statements. Press **Enter** twice after typing the second statement.

Me.Refresh()
System.Threading.Thread.Sleep(50)

8. The next three instructions in the pseudocode generate a random number and store it in the centerIndex variable, then use the variable's value to display the appropriate image in the centerPictureBox, and then refresh the screen and pause the application. Enter the following statements. Press **Enter** twice after typing the last statement.

centerIndex = randGen.Next(0, 6)
centerPictureBox.Image =
        ImageList1.Images.Item(centerIndex)
  Me.Refresh()
  System.Threading.Thread.Sleep(50)

9. The last three instructions in the loop body generate a random number and store it in the rightIndex variable, then use the variable's value to display the appropriate image in the rightPictureBox, and then refresh the screen and pause the application. Enter the following statements:

   rightIndex = randGen.Next(0, 6)
   rightPictureBox.Image =
        ImageList1.Images.Item(rightIndex)
   Me.Refresh()
   System.Threading.Thread.Sleep(50)

10. The third step in the pseudocode is a single-alternative selection structure that determines whether the "Congratulations!" message should be displayed. Click the **blank line** below the Next spins clause and then press **Enter** to insert another blank line. Enter the following selection structure:

If leftIndex = centerIndex AndAlso
    leftIndex = rightIndex Then
    MessageBox.Show("Congratulations!", "Winner",
                MessageBoxButtons.OK,
                MessageBoxIcon.Information)
End If

11. The last two steps in the pseudocode enable the clickHereButton and then send the focus to the button. Click immediately after the letter **f** in the End If clause and then press **Enter**. Enter the following statements:

clickHereButton.Enabled = True
clickHereButton.Focus()

12. Save the solution and then start the application. Click the **Click Here** button. See Figure 7-29. Because random integers determine the images assigned to the three picture boxes, your application might display different images than those shown in the figure. In addition, the "Congratulations!" message may appear in a message box on your screen. If necessary, click the **OK** button to close the message box.

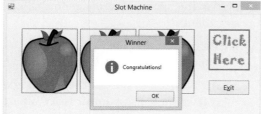

Figure 7-29   Sample runs of the application

OpenClipArt.org/nicubunu

13. If necessary, click the **Click Here** button until there is a winner. (You may need to click the button many times.) Then click the **OK** button to close the message box.

14. Click the **Exit** button to end the application. Close the Code Editor window and then close the solution. Figure 7-30 shows the application's code.

```
1 ' Project name:          Slot Machine Project
2 ' Project purpose:       Simulates a slot machine
3 ' Created/revised by:    <your name> on <current date>
4
5 Option Explicit On
6 Option Infer Off
7 Option Strict On
8
9 Public Class MainForm
10
11     Private Sub exitButton_Click(sender As Object,
        e As EventArgs) Handles exitButton.Click
12        Me.Close()
13     End Sub
14
15     Private Sub clickHereButton_Click(sender As Object,
        e As EventArgs) Handles clickHereButton.Click
16        ' simulates a slot machine
17
18        Dim randGen As New Random
19        Dim leftIndex As Integer
20        Dim centerIndex As Integer
21        Dim rightIndex As Integer
22
23        clickHereButton.Enabled = False
24        For spins As Integer = 1 To 10
25            leftIndex = randGen.Next(0, 6)
26            leftPictureBox.Image =
27                ImageList1.Images.Item(leftIndex)
28            Me.Refresh()
29            System.Threading.Thread.Sleep(50)
30
```

Figure 7-30   Code for the Slot Machine application *(continues)*

(continued)

```
31              centerIndex = randGen.Next(0, 6)
32              centerPictureBox.Image =
33                  ImageList1.Images.Item(centerIndex)
34              Me.Refresh()
35              System.Threading.Thread.Sleep(50)
36
37              rightIndex = randGen.Next(0, 6)
38              rightPictureBox.Image =
39                  ImageList1.Images.Item(rightIndex)
40              Me.Refresh()
41              System.Threading.Thread.Sleep(50)
42
43          Next spins
44
45          If leftIndex = centerIndex AndAlso
46              leftIndex = rightIndex Then
47              MessageBox.Show("Congratulations!", "Winner",
48                          MessageBoxButtons.OK,
49                          MessageBoxIcon.Information)
50          End If
51          clickHereButton.Enabled = True
52          clickHereButton.Focus()
53
54      End Sub
55 End Class
```

Figure 7-30 Code for the Slot Machine application
© 2013 Cengage Learning

PROGRAMMING TUTORIAL 2

Creating the College Savings Application

In this tutorial, you will create the College Savings application. The application displays the balance in a savings account at the end of 18 years, assuming the amount saved per month is $100, $150, or $200, and the annual interest rate is 2%, 3%, 4%, or 5%. The application's TOE chart and MainForm are shown in Figures 7-31 and 7-32, respectively.

Task	Object	Event
1. Calculate the account balance at the end of 18 years, using fixed monthly deposits and fixed annual interest rates 2. Display the account balance in balanceListBox	calcButton	Click
Display the account balance (from calcButton)	balanceListBox	None
End the application	exitButton	Click

Figure 7-31 TOE chart for the College Savings application
© 2013 Cengage Learning

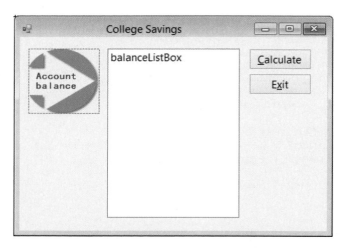

Figure 7-32   MainForm for the College Savings application

Coding the College Savings Application

According to the application's TOE chart, only the Click event procedures for the calcButton and exitButton need to be coded. The pseudocode for the calcButton's Click event procedure is shown in Figure 7-33, along with the memory locations the procedure will use.

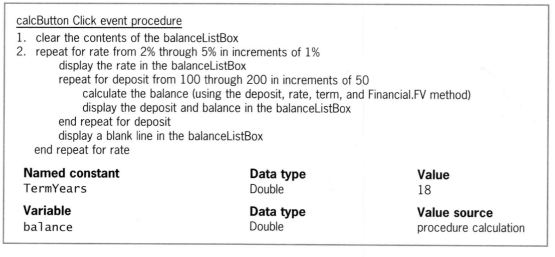

calcButton Click event procedure
1. clear the contents of the balanceListBox
2. repeat for rate from 2% through 5% in increments of 1%
        display the rate in the balanceListBox
        repeat for deposit from 100 through 200 in increments of 50
            calculate the balance (using the deposit, rate, term, and Financial.FV method)
            display the deposit and balance in the balanceListBox
        end repeat for deposit
        display a blank line in the balanceListBox
    end repeat for rate

Named constant	Data type	Value
TermYears	Double	18

Variable	Data type	Value source
balance	Double	procedure calculation

Figure 7-33   Pseudocode and memory locations for the calcButton_Click procedure
© 2013 Cengage Learning

To begin coding the application:

1. Start Visual Studio. Open the **College Savings Solution (College Savings Solution.sln)** file contained in the VbReloaded2012\Chap07\College Savings Solution folder. If necessary, open the designer window.

2. Open the Code Editor window. Notice that the exitButton's Click event procedure has already been coded for you. In the comments that appear in the General Declarations section, replace <your name> and <current date> with your name and the current date, respectively.

3. Locate the calcButton_Click procedure. Click the **blank line** above the End Sub clause and then enter the statements to declare the named constant and variable listed in Figure 7-33. Press **Enter** twice after typing the second declaration statement.

4. The first step in the pseudocode clears the contents of the balanceListBox. Type the appropriate statement and then press **Enter** twice.

5. The second step in the pseudocode begins with a counter-controlled loop that repeats its loop body four times—once for each of the four rates. Enter an appropriate For clause. Use `rates` as the counter variable's name, and use Double as its data type. Be sure to change the Next clause to **Next rates**, and then press **Enter**.

6. The first instruction in the loop body displays the rate in the balanceListBox. Click the **blank line** below the For clause. Type the following statement and then press **Enter**:

   balanceListBox.Items.Add(rates.ToString("P0"))

7. The second instruction in the loop body is a nested counter-controlled loop that repeats its loop body three times—once for each of the three deposit amounts. Enter an appropriate For clause. Use `deposits` and Double as the counter variable's name and data type, respectively. Be sure to change the Next clause to **Next deposits**, and then press **Enter**.

The first instruction in the nested loop calculates the savings account balance. To make the calculation, the procedure needs to use the current deposit amount, the current interest rate, the term, and the **Financial.FV method**. The Financial.FV method's syntax is shown in Figure 7-34 along with examples of using the method. The FV stands for "future value."

HOW TO Use the Financial.FV Method

Syntax
Financial.FV(Rate, NPer, Pmt**)**

Argument	Meaning
Rate	interest rate per period
NPer	total number of payment periods (the term)
Pmt	periodic payment

Example 1
`Financial.FV(.05, 3, 9000)`
Calculates the future value of an investment of $9,000 per year for 3 years at 5% interest. Rate is .05, NPer is 3, and Pmt is 9000. The future returned by the method is −28372.50.

Example 2
`-Financial.FV(.03 / 12, 18 * 12, 100)`
Calculates the future value of an investment of $100 per month for 18 years at 3% interest. Rate is .03 / 12, NPer is 18 * 12, and Pmt is 100. The future value returned by the method (rounded to the nearest cent and expressed as a positive number) is 28594.03.

Figure 7-34   How to use the Financial.FV method
© 2013 Cengage Learning

To finish coding the application:

1. Click the **blank line** below the nested For clause. The deposit amounts will be made monthly, so you will need to convert the annual interest rate to a monthly rate by dividing it by 12. You will also need to convert the 18-year term to months by multiplying it by 12. Type the following statement (be sure to include the negation operator) and then press **Enter**:

   balance =
      −Financial.FV(rates / 12, TermYears * 12, deposits)

2. The last instruction in the nested loop displays the deposit and balance in the balanceListBox. Type the following statement (include three spaces between the second set of quotes) and then click the **blank line** below the Next deposits clause:

   balanceListBox.Items.Add(deposits.ToString("C0") &
                          " " & balance.ToString("C2"))

3. The last instruction in the outer loop displays a blank line in the balanceListBox. Type the appropriate statement and then click the **blank line** below the Next rates clause.

4. Save the solution and then start the application. Click the **Calculate** button. The savings account balances appear in the balanceListBox, as shown in Figure 7-35.

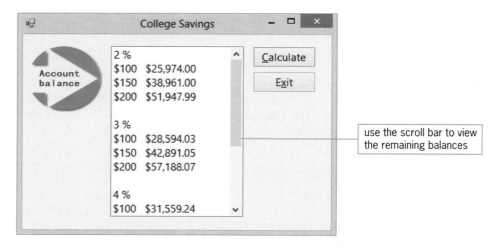

Figure 7-35   Savings account balances shown in the interface

5. Use the scroll bar to view the remaining account balances, then click the **Exit** button to end the application. Close the Code Editor window and then close the solution. Figure 7-36 shows the application's code.

```
1 ' Project name:       College Savings Project
2 ' Project purpose:    Displays the balance in a savings account
3 ' Created/revised by: <your name> on <current date>

4 Option Explicit On
5 Option Strict On
6 Option Infer Off
7
8 Public Class MainForm
9
10   Private Sub exitButton_Click(sender As Object,
     e As EventArgs) Handles exitButton.Click
11       Me.Close()
12   End Sub
13
14   Private Sub calcButton_Click(sender As Object,
     e As EventArgs) Handles calcButton.Click
15       ' calculate the savings account balance
16       ' at the end of 18 years, using a fixed
17       ' monthly savings amount and a fixed
18       ' annual interest rate
19
```

Figure 7-36   Code for the College Savings application *(continues)*

(continued)

```
20      Const TermYears As Double = 18
21      Dim balance As Double
22
23      balanceListBox.Items.Clear()
24
25      For rates As Double = 0.02 To 0.05 Step 0.01
26          balanceListBox.Items.Add(rates.ToString("P0"))
27          For deposits As Double = 100 To 200 Step 50
28              balance =
29                  -Financial.FV(rates / 12, TermYears * 12, deposits)
30              balanceListBox.Items.Add(deposits.ToString("C0") &
31                                      "    " & balance.ToString("C2"))
32          Next deposits
33          balanceListBox.Items.Add(ControlChars.NewLine)
34      Next rates
35
36  End Sub
37 End Class
```

Figure 7-36   Code for the College Savings application
© 2013 Cengage Learning

PROGRAMMING EXAMPLE

Discount Calculator Application

Create an application that allows the user to enter the original price of an item and a discount rate. The application should calculate the discount and the new price and then display both amounts in the interface. Provide a text box for entering the original price, and a combo box for entering the discount rate, which should be 5%, 6%, 7%, 8%, 9%, or 10%. Use the following names for the solution and project, respectively: Discount Solution and Discount Project. Save the application in the VbReloaded2012\Chap07 folder. Change the form file's name to Main Form.vb. See Figures 7-37 through 7-41.

Task	Object	Event
1. Fill the combo box with rates 2. Select the first rate in the combo box	MainForm	Load
1. Calculate the discount 2. Calculate the new price 3. Display the discount in discountLabel 4. Display the new price in newPriceLabel	calcButton	Click
End the application	exitButton	Click
Display the discount (from calcButton)	discountLabel	None
Display the new price (from calcButton)	newPriceLabel	None
Get the original price Select the existing text Accept numbers, period, and Backspace Clear discountLabel and newPriceLabel	originalTextBox	None Enter KeyPress TextChanged
Get the discount rate Clear discountLabel and newPriceLabel	discountRateComboBox	None TextChanged

Figure 7-37   TOE chart
© 2013 Cengage Learning

 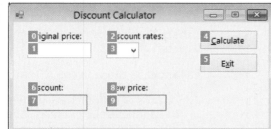

Figure 7-38   MainForm and tab order

Object	Property	Setting
MainForm	Font	Segoe UI, 10pt
	StartPosition	CenterScreen
	Text	Discount Calculator
discountLabel	AutoSize	False
	BorderStyle	FixedSingle
	Text	(empty)
	TextAlign	MiddleCenter
newPriceLabel	AutoSize	False
	BorderStyle	FixedSingle
	Text	(empty)
	TextAlign	MiddleCenter

Figure 7-39   Objects, properties, and settings
© 2013 Cengage Learning

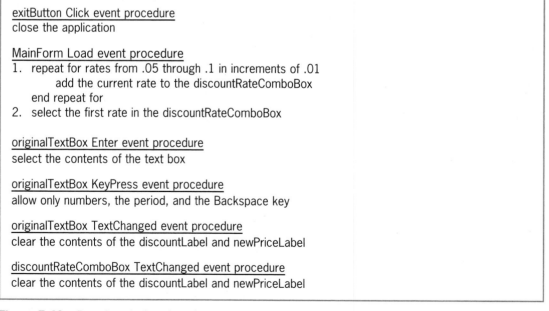

exitButton Click event procedure
close the application

MainForm Load event procedure
1. repeat for rates from .05 through .1 in increments of .01
        add the current rate to the discountRateComboBox
   end repeat for
2. select the first rate in the discountRateComboBox

originalTextBox Enter event procedure
select the contents of the text box

originalTextBox KeyPress event procedure
allow only numbers, the period, and the Backspace key

originalTextBox TextChanged event procedure
clear the contents of the discountLabel and newPriceLabel

discountRateComboBox TextChanged event procedure
clear the contents of the discountLabel and newPriceLabel

Figure 7-40   Pseudocode *(continues)*

(continued)

> <u>calcButton Click event procedure</u>
> 1. store user input (original price and discount rate) in variables
> 2. calculate the discount by multiplying the original price by the discount rate
> 3. calculate the new price by subtracting the discount from the original price
> 4. display the discount in discountLabel
> 5. display the new price in newPriceLabel
> 6. send the focus to the originalTextBox

Figure 7-40 Pseudocode
© 2013 Cengage Learning

```vbnet
1 ' Project name:         Discount Project
2 ' Project purpose:      Display the discount and new price
3 ' Created/revised by:   <your name> on <current date>
4
5 Option Explicit On
6 Option Strict On
7 Option Infer Off
8
9 Public Class MainForm
10
11    Private Sub exitButton_Click(sender As Object,
      e As EventArgs) Handles exitButton.Click
12        Me.Close()
13    End Sub
14
15    Private Sub MainForm_Load(sender As Object,
      e As EventArgs) Handles Me.Load
16        ' fill combo box with discount rates
17
18        For rates As Decimal = 0.05D To 0.1D Step 0.01D
19            discountRateComboBox.Items.Add(rates.ToString)
20        Next rates
21        ' select first discount rate
22        discountRateComboBox.SelectedIndex = 0
23    End Sub
24
25    Private Sub originalTextBox_Enter(sender As Object,
      e As EventArgs) Handles originalTextBox.Enter
26        ' select existing text
27
28        originalTextBox.SelectAll()
29    End Sub
30
31    Private Sub originalTextBox_KeyPress(sender As Object,
      e As KeyPressEventArgs) Handles originalTextBox.KeyPress
32        ' accept only numbers, the period, and the Backspace
33
34        If (e.KeyChar < "0" OrElse e.KeyChar > "9") AndAlso
35            e.KeyChar <> "." AndAlso
36            e.KeyChar <> ControlChars.Back Then
37            e.Handled = True
38        End If
39    End Sub
40
```

Figure 7-41 Code *(continues)*

(continued)

```
41    Private Sub originalTextBox_TextChanged(
      sender As Object, e As EventArgs
      ) Handles originalTextBox.TextChanged
42        ' clear calculated amounts from labels
43
44        discountLabel.Text = String.Empty
45        newPriceLabel.Text = String.Empty
46    End Sub
47
48    Private Sub discountRateComboBox_TextChanged(
      sender As Object, e As EventArgs
      ) Handles discountRateComboBox.TextChanged
49        ' clear calculated amounts from labels
50
51        discountLabel.Text = String.Empty
52        newPriceLabel.Text = String.Empty
53    End Sub
54
55    Private Sub calcButton_Click(sender As Object,
      e As EventArgs) Handles calcButton.Click
56        ' calculate the discount and new price
57
58        Dim origlPrice As Decimal
59        Dim discRate As Decimal
60        Dim discount As Decimal
61        Dim newPrice As Decimal
62
63        Decimal.TryParse(originalTextBox.Text, origlPrice)
64        Decimal.TryParse(discountRateComboBox.Text, discRate)
65
66        discount = origlPrice * discRate
67        newPrice = origlPrice - discount
68
69        discountLabel.Text = discount.ToString("N2")
70        newPriceLabel.Text = newPrice.ToString("N2")
71
72        originalTextBox.Focus()
73    End Sub
74  End Class
```

Figure 7-41   Code
© 2013 Cengage Learning

Summary

- You can use either the For...Next statement or the Do...Loop statement to code a pretest counter-controlled loop.

- A variable declared in a For clause has block scope and can be used only within the body of the For...Next statement.

- The For clause's startValue, stepValue, and endValue items can be positive or negative numbers, integer or non-integer.

- Many programmers use a hexagon to represent the For clause in a flowchart. The hexagon indicates the counter variable's name and its startValue, stepValue, and endValue.

- For a nested loop to work correctly, it must be contained entirely within an outer loop.

- You can use the Financial.Pmt method to calculate a periodic payment on a loan. You can use the Financial.FV method to calculate the future value of an investment.

- It is customary in Windows applications to highlight (select) the existing text in a text box when the text box receives the focus. You can do this by entering the SelectAll method in the text box's Enter event procedure.

- A control's TextChanged event occurs when either the user or the application's code changes the contents of the control's Text property.

- A list box's SelectedValueChanged and SelectedIndexChanged events occur when either the user or the application's code selects a different item in the list box.

- Combo boxes are similar to list boxes in that they allow the user to select from a list of choices. However, combo boxes also have a text field that may or may not be editable.

- Three styles of combo boxes are available. The style is specified in a combo box's DropDownStyle property. You can use a combo box to save space in an interface.

- You should use a label control to provide keyboard access to a combo box. Set the label's TabIndex property to a value that is one number less than the combo box's TabIndex value.

- You use the Items collection's Add method to add an item to a combo box during run time. You can use the String Collection Editor window to add an item to a combo box during design time.

- You can use the SelectedIndex, SelectedItem, or Text property to select the default item in a combo box.

- The number of items in the list portion of a combo box is stored in the Items collection's Count property.

- You can use the Sorted property to sort the items listed in a combo box.

- You can use the Items collection's Clear method to clear the items from the list portion of a combo box.

- A combo box's SelectedItem property contains the value of the item selected in the list portion of the combo box. A combo box's Text property contains the value that appears in the text portion of the combo box.

- A combo box's TextChanged event occurs when the user either selects an item in the list portion or types a value in the text portion.

- The images stored in an image list control belong to the Images collection. Each image in the collection has a unique index; the index of the first image is 0.

- You access an image in the Images collection using the collection's Item property along with the index of the image you want to access.

- You use the Images collection's Count property to determine the number of images in the collection.

- You need to use another control, such as a picture box, to display an image contained in an image list control.

Key Terms

Add method—the Items collection's method used to add items to a combo box

Clear method—the Items collection's method used to clear the items from a combo box

Combo box—a control that allows the user to select from a list of choices and also has a text field that may or may not be editable

Count property—a property of both the Items collection and the Images collection; stores an integer that represents the number of items contained in the list portion of a combo box, or the number of images contained in an image list control

Counter-controlled loops—loops whose processing is controlled by a counter; the loop body will be processed a precise number of times

DropDownStyle property—determines the style of a combo box

Enter event—occurs when a control receives the focus, which can happen as a result of the user either tabbing to the control or using the control's access key; also occurs when the Focus method sends the focus to the control

Financial.FV method—calculates the future value of an investment

Financial.Pmt method—calculates a periodic payment on either a loan or an investment

For...Next statement—used to code a pretest counter-controlled loop

Image list control—instantiated with the ImageList tool located in the Components section of the toolbox; stores the Images collection

Images collection—a collection composed of images

SelectAll method—used to select the contents of a text box

SelectedItem property—stores the value of the item selected in the list portion of a combo box

Sorted property—specifies whether the combo box items should appear in the order they are entered or in sorted order

Text property—stores the value of the item that appears in the text portion of a combo box

TextChanged event—occurs when a change is made to the contents of a control's Text property

Each Review Question is associated with one or more objectives listed at the beginning of the chapter.

Review Questions

1. How many times will the computer process the MessageBox.Show method in the following code? (1)

    ```
    For counter As Integer = 4 To 11 Step 2
            MessageBox.Show("Hello")
    Next counter
    ```

    a. 3
    b. 4
    c. 5
    d. 8

2. What `counter` variable value will cause the loop in Review Question 1 to stop? (1)

    a. 10
    b. 11
    c. 12
    d. 13

Use the code in Figure 7-42 to answer Review Questions 3 through 5.

```
For x As Integer = 1 To 2
    For y As Integer = 1 To 3
        msgLabel.Text = msgLabel.Text & "*"
    Next y
    msgLabel.Text = msgLabel.Text & ControlChars.NewLine
Next x
```

Figure 7-42 Code for Review Questions 3 through 5
© 2013 Cengage Learning

3. What will the code in Figure 7-42 display in the msgLabel? (1, 2)

   a.
   ```
   ***
   ***
   ```
   b.
   ```
   ***
   ***
   ***
   ```
   c.
   ```
   **
   **
   **
   ```
   d.
   ```
   ****
   ****
   ****
   ****
   ```

4. What x variable value will terminate the outer loop in Figure 7-42? (1, 2)

   a. 2

   b. 3

   c. 4

   d. none of the above

5. What y variable value will terminate the nested loop in Figure 7-42? (1, 2)

   a. 2

   b. 3

   c. 4

   d. none of the above

Use the code in Figure 7-43 to answer Review Question 6.

```
Dim sum As Integer
Dim y As Integer
Do While y < 3
    For x As Integer = 1 To 4
        sum += x
    Next x
    y += 1
Loop
msgLabel.Text = sum.ToString
```

Figure 7-43   Code for Review Question 6
© 2013 Cengage Learning

6. What number will the code in Figure 7-43 display in the msgLabel? (1, 2)

   a. 5

   b. 8

   c. 15

   d. 30

7. Which of the following calculates an annual payment on a $50,000 loan? The term is 10 years and the annual interest rate is 3%. (3)

   a. –Financial.Pmt(.03 / 12, 10, 50000)

   b. –Financial.Pmt(.03 / 12, 10 * 12, 50000)

   c. –Financial.Pmt(.03, 10, 50000)

   d. –Financial.Pmt(.03, 10 * 12, 50000)

8. Which of the following selects the "Cat" item, which is the third item in the animalComboBox? (6)

   a. `animalComboBox.SelectedIndex = 2`

   b. `animalComboBox.SelectedItem = "Cat"`

   c. `animalComboBox.Text = "Cat"`

   d. all of the above

9. The item entered by the user in the text field of a combo box is stored in which property? (6)

   a. SelectedItem

   b. SelectedValue

   c. Text

   d. TextItem

10. Which of the following refers to the third item in the ImageList1 control? (8, 9)

    a. `ImageList1.Images.Item(2)`

    b. `ImageList1.Images.Item(3)`

    c. `ImageList1.Item.Images(2)`

    d. `ImageList1.ItemImages(3)`

Each Exercise, except the DISCOVERY exercise, is associated with one or more objectives listed at the beginning of the chapter.

Exercises

Pencil and Paper

INTRODUCTORY

1. Put the For...Next statement's tasks in their proper order by placing the numbers 1 through 3 on the line to the left of the task. (1)

   _____ Adds the stepValue to the counter variable

   _____ Initializes the counter variable to the startValue

   _____ Checks whether the counter variable's value is greater (less) than the endValue

INTRODUCTORY

2. Create a chart (similar to the one shown earlier in Figure 7-3) that lists the processing steps for the code shown in Example 2 in Figure 7-2. (1)

INTRODUCTORY

3. Create a chart (similar to the one shown earlier in Figure 7-3) that lists the processing steps for the code shown in Example 3 in Figure 7-2. (1)

INTRODUCTORY

4. Write the code to calculate the annual payment on a loan of $6,000 for 3 years at 9% interest. Payments should be expressed as a negative number. (3)

INTRODUCTORY

5. Write the statement to select the existing text in the itemTextBox. (4)

INTERMEDIATE

6. Write three different statements that you can use to select the first item in the deptComboBox. The first item is Accounting. (6)

INTERMEDIATE

7. Write the code to calculate the quarterly payment on a loan of $6,000 for 3 years at 9% interest. Payments should be expressed as a positive number. (3)

INTERMEDIATE

8. Write the code for a pretest loop that lists the even integers from 2 through 10 in the numbersListBox. First, use the For...Next statement and an Integer variable named evenNum. Then rewrite the code using the Do...Loop statement. (1)

9. Write an assignment statement that displays (in the msgLabel) the number of images contained in the ImageList1 control. (8)

INTERMEDIATE

10. Write a For...Next statement that displays the images stored in the ImageList1 control. Display the images, one at a time, in the imagePictureBox. Display the images in reverse order; in other words, display the last image first. Refresh the screen and pause the application for 100 milliseconds between images. (1, 8, 9)

INTERMEDIATE

11. Write the code to display the following pattern of asterisks in the asterisksLabel. Use two For...Next statements. (1, 2)

INTERMEDIATE

```
*****
*****
*****
```

12. Rewrite the code from Exercise 11 using two Do...Loop statements. Both loops should be pretest loops. (1, 2)

INTERMEDIATE

13. Rewrite the code from Exercise 11 using two Do...Loop statements. Both loops should be posttest loops. (1, 2)

ADVANCED

14. Rewrite the code from Exercise 11 using a For...Next statement for the outer loop, and a Do...Loop statement for the nested loop. The nested loop should be a posttest loop. (1, 2)

ADVANCED

15. The following code should display three rows of percent signs in the msgLabel. The first row should contain one percent sign, the second row should contain two percent signs, and the third row should contain three percent signs. However, the code is not working correctly. Correct the code. (1, 2)

SWAT THE BUGS

```
For row As Integer = 1 To 3
    For percent As Integer = 1 To 3
        msgLabel.Text = msgLabel.Text & "%"
    Next percent
Next row
```

Computer

16. Use Windows to make a copy of the New Salary Solution-Nested folder. Rename the folder New Salary Solution-PretestDoLoop. Open the New Salary Solution (New Salary Solution.sln) file contained in the New Salary Solution-PretestDoLoop folder. Change both For...Next statements to Do...Loop statements. Both loops should be pretest loops. Save the solution and then start and test the application. Close the solution. (1, 2)

MODIFY THIS

17. Use Windows to make a copy of the New Salary Solution-Nested folder. Rename the folder New Salary Solution-PosttestDoLoop. Open the New Salary Solution (New Salary Solution.sln) file contained in the New Salary Solution-PosttestDoLoop folder. Change both For...Next statements to Do...Loop statements. Both loops should be posttest loops. Save the solution and then start and test the application. Close the solution. (1, 2)

MODIFY THIS

18. If necessary, complete the Slot Machine application from this chapter's Programming Tutorial 1, and then close the solution. Use Windows to make a copy of the Slot Machine Solution folder. Rename the folder Slot Machine Solution-ModifyThis. Open the Slot Machine Solution (Slot Machine Solution.sln) file contained in the Slot Machine Solution-ModifyThis folder. Modify the code so that it uses a counter to keep track of the number of times the user clicked the Click Here button before the "Congratulations!" message appeared. Display the counter's value in a label on the

MODIFY THIS

form. Be sure to reset the counter after the user wins. Save the solution and then start and test the application. Close the solution. (1)

MODIFY THIS

19. If necessary, complete the College Savings application from this chapter's Programming Tutorial 2, and then close the solution. Use Windows to make a copy of the College Savings Solution folder. Rename the folder College Savings Solution-ModifyThis. Open the College Savings Solution (College Savings Solution.sln) file contained in the College Savings Solution-ModifyThis folder. Change the two For...Next statements to two pretest Do...Loop statements. Save the solution and then start and test the application. Close the solution. (1, 2)

MODIFY THIS

20. Use Windows to make a copy of the Savers Solution folder contained in the VbReloaded2012\Chap07 folder. Rename the folder Savers Solution-ComboBox. Open the Savers Solution (Savers Solution.sln) file contained in the Savers Solution-ComboBox folder. (4-7)

   a. Replace the rateTextBox with a combo box named rateComboBox. Be sure to reset the tab order. The combo box should list annual interest rates from .03 to .1 in increments of .01. However, the user should also be allowed to enter an interest rate that is not on the list.

   b. Before ending, the Calculate Balance button's Click event procedure should send the focus to the depositTextBox.

   c. Clear the balanceLabel when a change is made to either the text box or the combo box.

   d. The text box's existing text should be selected when the text box receives the focus.

   e. Remove the rateTextBox's KeyPress event procedure, and code the rateComboBox's KeyPress event procedure.

   f. Save the solution and then start and test the application. Close the solution.

MODIFY THIS

21. Use Windows to make a copy of the Savers Solution-Nested folder contained in the VbReloaded2012\Chap07 folder. Rename the folder Savers Solution-Formula. Open the Savers Solution (Savers Solution.sln) file contained in the Savers Solution-Formula folder. Replace the interest and balance calculations with the following formula: $balance = deposit * (1 + rate)^{numPeriods}$. Save the solution and then start and test the application. Close the solution. (2)

MODIFY THIS

22. If necessary, complete the Discount Calculator application from this chapter's Programming Example, and then close the solution. Use Windows to make a copy of the Discount Solution folder. Rename the folder Discount Solution-ModifyThis. Open the Discount Solution (Discount Solution.sln) file contained in the Discount Solution-ModifyThis folder. Change the For...Next statement in the Load event procedure to a posttest Do...Loop statement. Save the solution and then start and test the application. Close the solution. (1)

MODIFY THIS

23. To complete this exercise, you need to have completed the Roll 'Em Game application from Chapter 6's Programming Tutorial 1. Use Windows to copy the Roll Em Game Solution folder from the VbReloaded2012\Chap06 folder to the VbReloaded2012\Chap07 folder. Open the Roll Em Game Solution (Roll Em Game Solution.sln) file contained in the Roll Em Game Solution folder. Change the Do...Loop statement in the rollButton_Click procedure to a For...Next statement. Save the solution and then start and test the application. Close the solution. (1)

MODIFY THIS

24. To complete this exercise, you need to have completed the Just Birthdays application from Chapter 6's Programming Tutorial 2. Use Windows to copy the Just Birthdays Solution folder from the VbReloaded2012\Chap06 folder to the VbReloaded2012\Chap07 folder.

Open the Just Birthdays Solution (Just Birthdays Solution.sln) file contained in the Just Birthdays Solution folder. Change the Do...Loop statement in the testDataButton_Click procedure to a For...Next statement. Save the solution and then start and test the application. Close the solution. (1)

25. Open the Car Solution (Car Solution.sln) file contained in the VbReloaded2012\Chap07\ Car Solution folder. When the user clicks the Click Me button, the "I WANT THIS CAR!" message should blink 10 times. In other words, it should disappear and then reappear, disappear and then reappear, and so on, 10 times. Code the button's Click event procedure using the For...Next statement. Save the solution and then start and test the application. Close the solution. (1)

INTRODUCTORY

26. Open the Odd Squares Solution (Odd Squares Solution.sln) file contained in the VbReloaded2012\Chap07\Odd Squares Solution folder. Code the Display button's Click event procedure so that it displays the squares of the odd integers from 1 through 9 in the squaresLabel. Display each square on a separate line in the control. Use the For...Next statement. Save the solution and then start and test the application. Close the solution. (1, 2)

INTERMEDIATE

27. In this exercise, you will create a Windows application that displays a multiplication table. Use the following names for the solution and project, respectively: Multiplication Solution and Multiplication Project. Save the solution in the VbReloaded2012\Chap07 folder. Change the form file's name to Main Form.vb. Create the interface shown in Figure 7-44. The Number box should accept only numbers and the Backspace key, and its contents should be selected when it receives the focus. Code the application. Save the solution and then start and test the application. Close the solution. (1, 2, 4, 5)

INTERMEDIATE

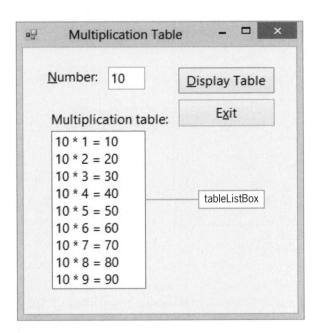

Figure 7-44 Interface for Exercise 27

28. Open the Gentry Supplies Solution (Gentry Supplies Solution.sln) file contained in the VbReloaded2012\Chap07\Gentry Supplies Solution folder. Add the four state names listed in Figure 7-45 to the combo box. The combo box's TextChanged event procedure should display the message "The shipping charge for *state* is *charge*." in the msgLabel. In the message, *state* is the name of the state either selected or entered in the combo box, and *charge* is the shipping charge. The shipping charges are listed in Figure 7-45. Save the solution and then start and test the application. Close the solution. (6, 7)

INTERMEDIATE

State	Shipping charge
Alabama	$20
Georgia	$35
Louisiana	$30
North Carolina	$28
All other entries	$15

Figure 7-45   Shipping information for Exercise 28
© 2013 Cengage Learning

INTERMEDIATE

29.   Create a Visual Basic Windows application. Use the following names for the solution and project, respectively: Planets Solution and Planets Project. Save the application in the VbReloaded2012\Chap07 folder. Change the form file's name to Main Form.vb. Create the interface shown in Figure 7-46. The combo box should have the DropDownList style and contain the following planet names: Mercury, Venus, Mars, Jupiter, Saturn, Uranus, Neptune, and Pluto. The application should convert the earth weight to the weight on the planet selected in the combo box, and then display the converted weight in the label control. Use the Internet to research the formula for making the conversions. Save the solution and then start and test the application. Close the Code Editor window and then close the solution. (4-7)

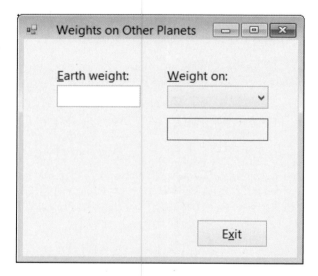

Figure 7-46   Interface for Exercise 29

ADVANCED

30.   In this exercise, you code an application that allows the user to enter two integers. The application then displays all of the odd numbers between both integers and all of the even numbers between both integers. Open the OddEven Solution (OddEven Solution.sln) file contained in the VbReloaded2012\Chap07\OddEven Solution folder. Code the application using the For...Next statement. Save the solution and then start the application. Test the application using the following integers: 6 and 25. The application should display the following odd numbers: 7, 9, 11, 13, 15, 17, 19, 21, and 23. It should also display the following even numbers: 8, 10, 12, 14, 16, 18, 20, 22, and 24. Now test it again using the following integers: 10 and 3. The application should display the following odd numbers: 5, 7, and 9. It should also display the following even numbers: 4, 6, and 8. Close the solution. (1, 2, 4, 5)

31. Open the Numbers Table Solution (Numbers Table Solution.sln) file contained in the VbReloaded2012\Chap07\Numbers Table Solution folder. Code the application so that it displays a table consisting of four rows and six columns. The first column should contain the numbers 1 through 4. The second and subsequent columns should contain the result of multiplying the number in the first column by the numbers 0 through 4. The table will look similar to the one shown in Figure 7-47. However, don't be concerned about the alignment of the numbers within each column. Use two For...Next statements. Save the solution and then start and test the application. Close the solution. (1, 2)   **ADVANCED**

1	0	1	2	3	4
2	0	2	4	6	8
3	0	3	6	9	12
4	0	4	8	12	16

Figure 7-47 Sample output for Exercise 31
© 2013 Cengage Learning

32. If necessary, complete the Slot Machine application from this chapter's Programming Tutorial 1, and then close the solution. Use Windows to make a copy of the Slot Machine Solution folder. Rename the folder Slot Machine Solution-Discovery. Open the Slot Machine Solution (Slot Machine Solution.sln) file contained in the Slot Machine Solution-Discovery folder. Open the Code Editor window and locate the clickHereButton_Click procedure. The procedure disables the button at the beginning of the procedure and then enables it at the end of the procedure. Start the application and then click the Click Here button; the button appears dimmed (grayed out) while its Click event procedure is running. If necessary, close the message box. Now, click the button, quickly, three times. Notice that even though the button appears dimmed, its Click procedure is still invoked each time you click the button. You can fix this problem using the Application.DoEvents method. Research the method and then use it in the clickHereButton_Click procedure. Save the solution and then start and test the application. Close the solution.   **DISCOVERY**

33. Open the Debug Solution (Debug Solution.sln) file contained in the VbReloaded2012\Chap07\Debug Solution folder. Open the Code Editor window and review the existing code. Start and then test the application. Locate and then correct any errors. When the application is working correctly, close the solution. (1, 2)   **SWAT THE BUGS**

Case Projects

 Loan Calculator

Create an application that displays a monthly payment on a loan. The application should also display the amount applied to the loan's principal each month and the amount that represents interest. Use the following names for the solution and project, respectively: Loan Solution and Loan Project. Save the solution in the VbReloaded2012\Chap07 folder. Change the form file's name to Main Form.vb. The application should use annual interest rates from 2% through 10% in increments of 1%, and terms from 1 through 30 years. You can use the Financial.PPmt method to calculate the portion of the payment applied to the principal each month. The method's syntax is `Financial.PPmt(Rate, Per, NPer, PV)`. In the syntax, *Rate* is the interest rate, *NPer* is the number of payment periods, and *PV* is the present value of the loan. The *Per* argument is the payment period for which you want to calculate the portion applied to the principal. The *Per* argument must be a number from 1 through *NPer*. The method returns the calculated value as a Double number. You can either create your own interface or create the one shown in Figure 7-48; the figure shows a sample run of the application. The combo box that gets the interest rate is the DropDown style. The combo box that gets the term is the DropDownList style. The text box that displays the output has its Multiline and ReadOnly properties set to True, and its ScrollBars property set to Vertical. (1, 2, 4-7)

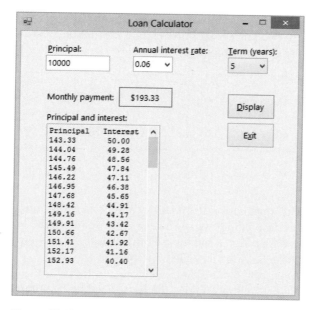

Figure 7-48   Sample interface for the Loan Calculator application

 Kenton Incorporated

The payroll manager at Kenton Incorporated wants an application that allows her to enter five payroll amounts for each of three stores: Store 1, Store 2, and Store 3. Use the InputBox function. The application should calculate and display each store's total payroll and the total company payroll. Display the payroll amounts with a dollar sign and two decimal places. Use the following names for the solution and project, respectively: Kenton Solution and Kenton Project. Save the solution in the VbReloaded2012\Chap07 folder. Change the form file's name to Main Form.vb. You can either create your own interface or create the one shown in Figure 7-49. (1, 2)

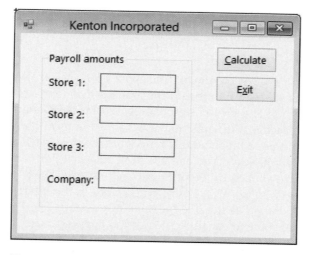

Figure 7-49   Sample interface for the Kenton Incorporated application

Happy Temps

Happy Temps has hired you as a temporary worker for 10 days. The company offers you two pay options. Option 1 doubles your pay each day; however, the first day's pay is only $1. In other words, you would earn $1 the first day, $2 the second day, $4 the third day, $8 the fourth day, and so on. Option 2 is to be paid $100 per day. Create an application that calculates and displays your daily pay under each pay plan. Also display the total amount you would earn under each pay plan. Use the following names for the solution and project, respectively: Happy Temps Solution and Happy Temps Project. Save the solution in the VbReloaded2012\Chap07 folder. Change the form file's name to Main Form.vb. You can either create your own interface or create the one shown in Figure 7-50. (1, 2)

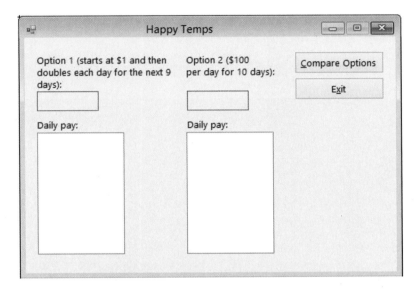

Figure 7-50 Sample interface for the Happy Temps application

 South Central Investments

South Central Investments wants an application that calculates and displays the amount a customer needs to save each month to accumulate a specific amount. The user will enter three items of information: the amount he or she wants to accumulate, the term (in years), and the annual interest rate. The interface should provide a text box for entering the desired ending amount. It should also provide combo boxes for the term and annual interest rate. The term combo box should display terms from 1 through 50, and it should not allow the user to enter a different term. The interest rate combo box should allow the user to select an annual interest rate from 2% through 11% in increments of 1%; however, it should allow the user to enter a different interest rate. Research the full syntax of the Financial.Pmt method. Display the monthly amount as a positive number. Use the following names for the solution and project, respectively: South Central Solution and South Central Project. Save the solution in the VbReloaded2012\ Chap07 folder. Change the form file's name to Main Form.vb. (1-7)

CHAPTER 8

Sub and Function Procedures

After studying Chapter 8, you should be able to:

1 Create and call an independent Sub procedure

2 Pass data to a procedure

3 Explain the difference between passing data *by value* and passing data *by reference*

4 Code the CheckedChanged event procedure

5 Desk-check an application's code

6 Associate a procedure with more than one object and event

7 Explain the purpose of the `sender` and e parameters

8 Explain the difference between Sub and Function procedures

9 Create and invoke a Function procedure

10 Convert an Object variable to a different type using the TryCast operator

11 Utilize a timer control

Reading and Study Guide

Before you begin reading Chapter 8, view the Ch08_ReadingStudyGuide.pdf file. You can open the file using Adobe Reader, which is available for free on the Adobe Web site at *www.adobe.com/downloads/.*

Sub Procedures

There are two types of Sub procedures in Visual Basic: event procedures and independent Sub procedures. All of the procedures coded in the previous chapters were event procedures. As you already know, an event procedure is a Sub procedure that is associated with a specific object and event, such as a button's Click event or a text box's TextChanged event. The computer automatically processes an event procedure's code when the event occurs. An **independent Sub procedure**, on the other hand, is a procedure that is independent of any object and event. An independent Sub procedure is processed only when called (invoked) from code. In Visual Basic, you invoke an independent Sub procedure using the **Call statement**.

Programmers use independent Sub procedures for several reasons. First, they allow the programmer to avoid duplicating code when different sections of a program need to perform the same task. Rather than entering the same code in each of those sections, the programmer can enter the code in a procedure and then have each section call the procedure to perform its task when needed. Second, consider an event procedure that must perform many tasks. To keep the event procedure's code from getting unwieldy and difficult to understand, the programmer can assign some of the tasks to one or more independent Sub procedures. Doing this makes the event procedure easier to code because it allows the programmer to concentrate on one small piece of the code at a time. And finally, independent Sub procedures are used extensively in large and complex programs, which typically are written by a team of programmers. The programming team will break up the program into small and manageable tasks, and then assign some of the tasks to different team members to be coded as independent Sub procedures. Doing this allows more than one programmer to work on the program at the same time, decreasing the time it takes to write the program.

Figure 8-1 shows the syntax of both an independent Sub procedure and the Call statement in Visual Basic. An independent Sub procedure can be entered anywhere between the Public Class and End Class clauses in the Code Editor window; however, it must be outside of any other procedure.

HOW TO Create and Call an Independent Sub Procedure

<u>Syntax of an independent Sub procedure</u>
Private Sub *procedureName*(**[***parameterList***]**)
    statements
End Sub

<u>Syntax of the Call statement</u>
Call *procedureName*(**[***argumentList***]**)

<u>Example</u>
```
Private Sub ClearLabels()
    regularLabel.Text = String.Empty
    overtimeLabel.Text = String.Empty
    grossLabel.Text = String.Empty
End Sub

Call ClearLabels()
```

calls the ClearLabels procedure

Figure 8-1   How to create and call an independent Sub procedure
© 2013 Cengage Learning

You can also call the ClearLabels procedure using the statement ClearLabels(). This is because the Call keyword is optional when invoking a Sub procedure.

Like event procedures, independent Sub procedures have a procedure header and procedure footer. In most cases, the procedure header begins with the Private keyword, which indicates that the procedure can be used only within the Code Editor window in which it is defined. After the Private keyword is the Sub keyword, which identifies the procedure as a Sub procedure, followed by the procedure name. The rules for naming an independent Sub procedure are the same as those for naming variables; however, procedure names are usually entered using Pascal case. The Sub procedure's name should indicate the task the procedure performs. It is a common practice to begin the name with a verb. For example, a good name for a Sub procedure that clears the contents of the label controls in an interface is ClearLabels.

Following the procedure name in the procedure header is a set of parentheses that contains an optional *parameterList*. If the procedure header does not contain a parameterList, then an empty set of parentheses follows the procedure name in both the procedure header and the Call statement, as shown in the example in Figure 8-1. You will learn much more about a procedure header's parameterList and also the Call statement's argumentList later in this chapter. The ClearLabels procedure from Figure 8-1 is used in the Lanza Trinkets application, which you view in the next section.

The Lanza Trinkets Application

Figure 8-2 shows the problem specification for the Lanza Trinkets application, which calculates and displays an employee's regular pay, overtime pay, and gross pay. The figure also shows most of the application's code and includes a sample run of the application. The code uses an independent Sub procedure named ClearLabels to clear the contents of the label controls in the interface. The procedure is called from three different event procedures: clearButton_Click, hoursComboBox_TextChanged, and rateComboBox_TextChanged.

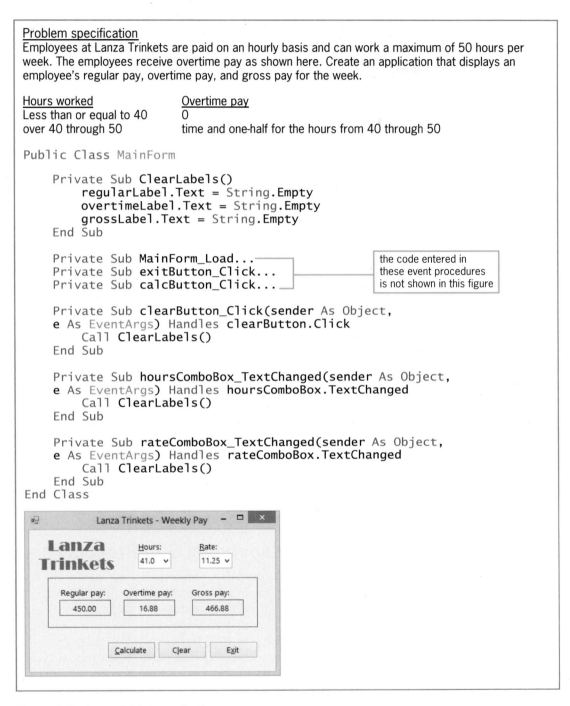

Problem specification

Employees at Lanza Trinkets are paid on an hourly basis and can work a maximum of 50 hours per week. The employees receive overtime pay as shown here. Create an application that displays an employee's regular pay, overtime pay, and gross pay for the week.

Hours worked	Overtime pay
Less than or equal to 40	0
over 40 through 50	time and one-half for the hours from 40 through 50

```
Public Class MainForm

    Private Sub ClearLabels()
        regularLabel.Text = String.Empty
        overtimeLabel.Text = String.Empty
        grossLabel.Text = String.Empty
    End Sub

    Private Sub MainForm_Load...
    Private Sub exitButton_Click...          the code entered in
    Private Sub calcButton_Click...          these event procedures
                                             is not shown in this figure

    Private Sub clearButton_Click(sender As Object,
    e As EventArgs) Handles clearButton.Click
        Call ClearLabels()
    End Sub

    Private Sub hoursComboBox_TextChanged(sender As Object,
    e As EventArgs) Handles hoursComboBox.TextChanged
        Call ClearLabels()
    End Sub

    Private Sub rateComboBox_TextChanged(sender As Object,
    e As EventArgs) Handles rateComboBox.TextChanged
        Call ClearLabels()
    End Sub
End Class
```

Figure 8-2 Lanza Trinkets application
© 2013 Cengage Learning

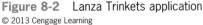 If you want to experiment with the Lanza Trinkets application, open the solution contained in the Try It 1! folder.

Rather than entering the instructions to clear the labels in the ClearLabels procedure, you also can enter them in each of the three event procedures. However, entering the code in an independent Sub procedure saves you from having to enter the same statements more than once. In addition, if you subsequently need to assign the string "0.00" rather than the empty string to the labels, you will need to make the change in only one place in the code.

When the computer processes the `Call ClearLabels()` statement in the clearButton_Click procedure, it temporarily leaves the procedure to process the code in the ClearLabels procedure.

The assignment statements in the ClearLabels procedure remove the contents of the regularLabel, overtimeLabel, and grossLabel controls. After processing the assignment statements, the computer processes the ClearLabels procedure's End Sub clause, which ends the procedure. The computer then returns to the clearButton_Click procedure and processes the line of code located immediately below the Call statement—in this case, the event procedure's End Sub clause. A similar process is followed when either combo box's TextChanged event occurs: The computer temporarily leaves the event procedure to process the code contained in the ClearLabels procedure. When the ClearLabels procedure ends, the computer returns to the event procedure and processes the code immediately below the Call statement.

The answers to Mini-Quiz questions are located in Appendix A. Each question is associated with one or more objectives listed at the beginning of the chapter.

Mini-Quiz 8-1

1. An event procedure is a Sub procedure that is associated with a specific object and event. (1)

   a. True

   b. False

2. Which of the following is the correct way to write a procedure header that does not require a parameterList? (1)

   a. `Private Sub DisplayMessage`

   b. `Private Sub DisplayMessage()`

   c. `Private Sub DisplayMessage(none)`

   d. `Private Sub DisplayMessage[]`

3. Which of the following invokes the DisplayMessage procedure from Question 2? (1)

   a. `Call DisplayMessage`

   b. `Call Sub DisplayMessage()`

   c. `Call DisplayMessage(none)`

   d. `Call DisplayMessage()`

Including Parameters in an Independent Sub Procedure

As shown earlier in Figure 8-1, an independent Sub procedure can contain a parameterList. The parameterList lists the data type and name of one or more parameters. A **parameter** is a memory location that stores an item of data passed to the procedure when the procedure is invoked. Each parameter in the parameterList has procedure scope, which means it can be used only within the procedure. The data is passed to the procedure through the Call statement's *argumentList*, which is a comma-separated list of arguments you want passed to the procedure. The number of arguments should agree with the number of parameters. If the parameterList contains one parameter, then the argumentList should have one argument. Similarly, a procedure that contains three parameters in its procedure header requires three arguments in the Call statement that invokes it. (Refer to the Tip on the bottom of this page for an exception to this general rule.)

In addition to having the same number of arguments as parameters, the data type and order (or position) of each argument should agree with the data type and order (position) of its corresponding parameter. If the first parameter has a data type of String and the second a data type of Double, then the first argument in the Call statement should have the String data type and the second should have the Double data type. This is because when the procedure is called, the computer associates the first argument with the first parameter, the second argument with the second parameter, and so on.

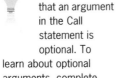
You can specify that an argument in the Call statement is optional. To learn about optional arguments, complete Computer Exercise 35 at the end of this chapter.

You can pass a literal constant, a named constant, a keyword, or a variable to a procedure. However, in most cases, you will pass a variable.

Passing Variables

Each variable declared in a program has both a value and a unique address that represents the variable's location in the computer's internal memory. Visual Basic allows you to pass either a copy of the variable's value or its address to the receiving procedure. Passing a copy of the variable's value is referred to as **passing by value**, whereas passing its address is referred to as **passing by reference**. The method you choose—*by value* or *by reference*—depends on whether you want the receiving procedure to have access to the variable in memory. In other words, it depends on whether you want to allow the receiving procedure to change the variable's contents.

Although the idea of passing information *by value* and *by reference* may sound confusing at first, it is a concept with which you are already familiar. We'll use the illustrations shown in Figure 8-3 to demonstrate this fact. Assume you have a savings account at a local bank. (Think of the savings account as a variable.) During a conversation with your friend Joan, you mention the amount of money you have in the account, as shown in Illustration A. Sharing this information with Joan is similar to passing a variable *by value*. Knowing the balance in your savings account does not give Joan access to the account. It merely provides information that she can use to compare with the amount of money she has saved.

Now, we'll use the savings account example to demonstrate passing information *by reference*. (Here again, think of your savings account as a variable.) To either deposit money in your account or withdraw money from your account, you must provide the bank teller with your account number, as shown in Illustration B in Figure 8-3. The account number represents the location of your account at the bank and allows the teller to change the account balance. Giving the teller your bank account number is similar to passing a variable *by reference*. The account number allows the teller to change the contents of your bank account, similar to the way a variable's address allows the receiving procedure to change the contents of the variable.

409

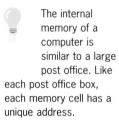 The internal memory of a computer is similar to a large post office. Like each post office box, each memory cell has a unique address.

 Ch08-Passing Data

Figure 8-3 Illustrations of passing *by value* and passing *by reference*
Image by Diane Zak; Created with Reallusion CrazyTalk Animator

Passing Variables by Value

To pass a variable *by value*, you include the keyword `ByVal` before the name of its corresponding parameter in the receiving procedure's parameterList. When you pass a variable *by value*, the computer passes a copy of the variable's contents to the receiving procedure. When only a copy of the contents is passed, the receiving procedure is not given access to the variable in memory. Therefore, it cannot change the value stored inside the variable. It is appropriate to pass a variable *by value* when the receiving procedure needs to *know* the variable's contents, but it does not need to *change* the contents.

The Actor/Actress application provides an example of passing variables *by value*. Figure 8-4 shows the problem specification and most of the application's code. The code contains an independent Sub procedure named DisplayMsg, whose task is to display a message that includes the type of performer (either actor or actress), as well as the name entered by the user. Also included in Figure 8-4 is a sample run of the application.

410

Problem specification
Create an application that prompts the user to enter the name of his or her favorite actor or actress. The application should then display either the message "Your favorite actor is *name*." or the message "Your favorite actress is *name*." In both messages, *name* is the name entered by the user.

```
Public Class MainForm

    Private Sub DisplayMsg(ByVal type As String,
                        ByVal performer As String)         parameterList

        msgLabel.Text = "Your favorite " & type &
            " is " & performer & "."
    End Sub

    Private Sub displayButton_Click(sender As Object,
    e As EventArgs) Handles displayButton.Click

        Dim category As String
        Dim name As String

        If actorRadioButton.Checked = True Then
            category = "actor"
            name = InputBox("Your favorite actor?", "Actor")
        Else
            category = "actress"
            name = InputBox("Your favorite actress?", "Actress")
        End If                          argumentList

        Call DisplayMsg(category, name)
    End Sub

    Private Sub exitButton_Click...

    Private Sub actorRadioButton_CheckedChanged(
    sender As Object, e As EventArgs
    ) Handles actorRadioButton.CheckedChanged
        msgLabel.Text = String.Empty
    End Sub

    Private Sub actressRadioButton_CheckedChanged(
    sender As Object, e As EventArgs
    ) Handles actressRadioButton.CheckedChanged
        msgLabel.Text = String.Empty
    End Sub
End Class
```

the code entered in this event procedure is not shown in this figure

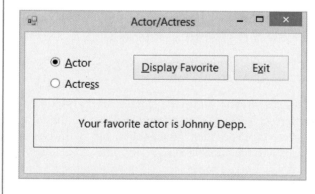

If you want to experiment with the Actor/Actress application, open the solution contained in the Try It 2! folder.

Figure 8-4 Actor/Actress application
© 2013 Cengage Learning

Depending on which radio button is selected, the displayButton_Click procedure prompts the user to enter the name of either an actor or an actress. Before the event procedure ends, it calls the DisplayMsg procedure, passing it a copy of the values stored in the `category` and `name` variables. The variables are passed *by value* because the DisplayMsg procedure does not need to change the values stored in the variables. You can tell that the variables are passed *by value* because the keyword `ByVal` appears before each variable's corresponding parameter in the DisplayMsg procedure header.

Notice that the number, data type, and position of the arguments in the Call statement match the number, data type, and position of the corresponding parameters in the DisplayMsg procedure header. Also notice that the names of the arguments do not need to be identical to the names of the corresponding parameters. In fact, to avoid confusion, you should use different names for the arguments and their corresponding parameters.

When the DisplayMsg procedure receives the two values from the Call statement, it stores them in its parameters. The first value is stored in the first parameter (`type`), and the second value is stored in the second parameter (`performer`). Next, the DisplayMsg procedure displays the appropriate message in the msgLabel, and then the procedure ends. Processing continues with the instruction immediately below the Call statement in the displayButton_Click procedure. That instruction is the End Sub clause, which ends the event procedure.

The code in Figure 8-4 also contains two CheckedChanged event procedures. The **CheckedChanged event** occurs when the value in the Checked property of either a radio button or a check box changes. When you select a check box, for example, its Checked property changes from False to True; this change invokes its CheckedChanged event. Likewise, when you deselect a check box, its Checked property changes from True to False, thereby invoking its CheckedChanged event. When you select a radio button, its Checked property changes from False to True and its CheckedChanged event occurs. In addition, the Checked property of the previously selected radio button in the same group changes from True to False, thereby invoking that radio button's CheckedChanged event. The CheckedChanged event procedures in Figure 8-4 will clear the contents of the msgLabel each time the user selects a different radio button.

Passing Variables by Reference

Instead of passing a copy of a variable's value to a procedure, you can pass its address in the computer's internal memory. As you learned earlier, passing a variable's address is referred to as passing *by reference*, and it gives the receiving procedure access to the variable being passed. It's appropriate to pass a variable *by reference* when you want the receiving procedure to change the contents of the variable. To pass a variable *by reference* in Visual Basic, you include the keyword `ByRef` before the name of the corresponding parameter in the receiving procedure's header. The `ByRef` keyword tells the computer to pass the variable's address rather than a copy of its contents.

We'll modify the Lanza Trinkets application shown earlier in Figure 8-2 to demonstrate passing a variable *by reference*. The modified problem specification is shown in Figure 8-5 along with the code entered in the CalcOvertime and calcButton_Click procedures. The Call statement in the calcButton_Click procedure invokes the CalcOvertime procedure, passing it three items of data. The parameterList indicates that the first two items are passed to the procedure *by value*, whereas the third item is passed *by reference*. Here, too, notice that the number, data type, and position of the arguments in the Call statement match the number, data type, and position of the corresponding parameters in the CalcOvertime procedure header. Also notice that the names of the arguments are not identical to the names of their corresponding parameters. Figure 8-5 also includes a sample run of the modified application.

411

The Call statement does not indicate whether a variable is being passed *by value* or *by reference*. To make that determination, you need to look at the receiving procedure's header.

<u>Modified problem specification</u>
Employees at Lanza Trinkets are paid on an hourly basis and can work a maximum of 50 hours per week. The employees receive overtime pay as shown here. Create an application that displays an employee's regular pay, overtime pay, and gross pay for the week.

<u>Hours worked</u>	<u>Overtime pay</u>
Less than or equal to 40	0
over 40 through 50	time and one-half for the hours from 40 through 45
	double time for the hours from 45 through 50

```vb
Private Sub CalcOvertime(ByVal hoursWkd As Double,
                         ByVal rateOfPay As Double,
                         ByRef extraPay As Double)
    ' calculates the overtime pay

    extraPay = (hoursWkd - 40) * rateOfPay * 1.5
    If hoursWkd > 45 Then
        ' add extra half-time for double time hours
        extraPay = extraPay +
            (hoursWkd - 45) * rateOfPay * 0.5
    End If
End Sub
```

> the parameterList indicates whether the variables are passed *by value* or *by reference*

```vb
Private Sub calcButton_Click(sender As Object,
e As EventArgs) Handles calcButton.Click
    ' calculates regular pay, overtime pay,
    ' and gross pay

    Dim hours As Double
    Dim rate As Double
    Dim regular As Double
    Dim overtime As Double
    Dim gross As Double

    Double.TryParse(hoursComboBox.Text, hours)
    Double.TryParse(rateComboBox.Text, rate)

    If hours <= 40 Then
        regular = hours * rate
    Else
        regular = 40 * rate
        ' call procedure to calculate overtime pay
        Call CalcOvertime(hours, rate, overtime)
    End If
```

> *passed by value*   *passed by reference*

```vb
    ' calculate gross pay
    gross = regular + overtime

    ' display calculated results
    regularLabel.Text = regular.ToString("N2")
    overtimeLabel.Text = overtime.ToString("N2")
    grossLabel.Text = gross.ToString("N2")
End Sub
```

Figure 8-5 Modified Lanza Trinkets application *(continues)*

(continued)

413

If you want to experiment with this version of the Lanza Trinkets application, open the solution contained in the Try It 3! folder.

Figure 8-5 Modified Lanza Trinkets application
© 2013 Cengage Learning

Desk-checking the procedures shown in Figure 8-5 will help clarify the difference between passing *by value* and passing *by reference*. **Desk-checking** refers to the process of reviewing the program instructions while seated at your desk rather than in front of the computer. Desk-checking is also called **hand-tracing** because you use a pencil and paper to follow each of the instructions by hand.

Before you begin the desk-check, you first choose a set of sample data for the input values, which you then use to manually compute the expected output values. You will desk-check Figure 8-5's procedures using 47 and $10 as the hours worked and pay rate, respectively. Figure 8-6 shows how the expected pay amounts are calculated.

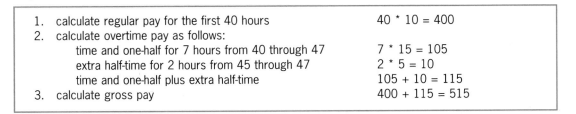

1.	calculate regular pay for the first 40 hours	40 * 10 = 400
2.	calculate overtime pay as follows:	
	time and one-half for 7 hours from 40 through 47	7 * 15 = 105
	extra half-time for 2 hours from 45 through 47	2 * 5 = 10
	time and one-half plus extra half-time	105 + 10 = 115
3.	calculate gross pay	400 + 115 = 515

Figure 8-6 Pay calculations using sample input values
© 2013 Cengage Learning

When the user clicks the Calculate button after selecting 47.0 and 10.00 in the hoursComboBox and rateComboBox, respectively, the Dim statements in the button's Click event procedure create and initialize five Double variables. Next, the two TryParse methods convert the items selected in the combo boxes to Double, storing the results in the hours and rate variables. The selection structure's condition is evaluated next. The condition evaluates to False because the value in the hours variable is not less than or equal to 40. As a result, the selection structure's False path is processed. The first instruction in the False path calculates the regular pay by multiplying the value in the rate variable (10.0) by the number 40; it assigns the result (400.0) to the regular variable. The second instruction in the False path is a Call statement. Figure 8-7 shows the contents of the variables before the Call statement is processed.

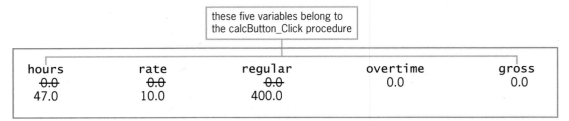

Figure 8-7   Desk-check table before the Call statement is processed
© 2013 Cengage Learning

The computer processes the Call statement next. The Call statement invokes the CalcOvertime procedure, passing it three arguments. At this point, the computer temporarily leaves the Click event procedure to process the code contained in the CalcOvertime procedure, beginning with the procedure header. The `ByVal` keyword indicates that the first two parameters are receiving values from the Call statement—in this case, copies of the numbers stored in the `hours` and `rate` variables. As a result, the computer creates the `hoursWkd` and `rateOfPay` variables listed in the parameterList, and stores the numbers 47.0 and 10.0, respectively, in the variables.

The `ByRef` keyword indicates that the third parameter is receiving the address of a variable. When you pass a variable's address to a procedure, the computer uses the address to locate the variable in its internal memory. It then assigns the parameter name to the memory location. In this case, the computer locates the `overtime` variable in memory and assigns the name `extraPay` to it. As indicated in the desk-check table shown in Figure 8-8, the memory location now has two names: one assigned by the calcButton_Click procedure and one assigned by the CalcOvertime procedure. Although both procedures can access the memory location, each procedure uses a different name to do so: The calcButton_Click procedure uses the name `overtime`, whereas the CalcOvertime procedure uses the name `extraPay`.

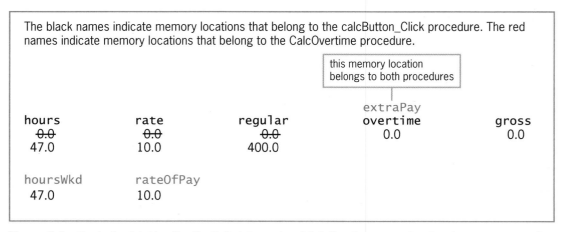

Figure 8-8   Desk-check table after the Call statement and CalcOvertime procedure header are processed
© 2013 Cengage Learning

After processing the CalcOvertime procedure header, the computer processes the code contained in the procedure. The first statement calculates time and one-half for the seven overtime hours; it assigns the result (105.0) to the `extraPay` variable, as shown in Figure 8-9. Notice that when the value in the `extraPay` variable changes, the value in the `overtime` variable also changes. This happens because the names `extraPay` and `overtime` refer to the same location in the computer's internal memory.

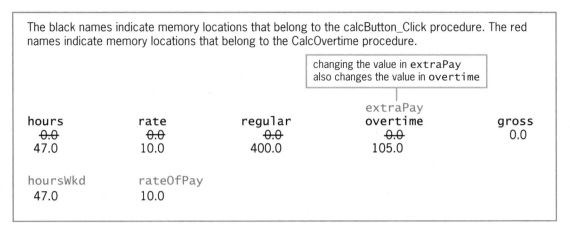

Figure 8-9 Desk-check table after the first statement in the CalcOvertime procedure is processed
© 2013 Cengage Learning

The selection structure in the CalcOvertime procedure is processed next. The structure's condition evaluates to True because the value in the **hoursWkd** variable is greater than 45. As a result, the statement in the structure's True path calculates the additional half-time for the two hours that are over 45 and then adds the result (10.0) to the contents of the **extraPay** variable, giving 115.0. Figure 8-10 shows the desk-check table after the statement is processed.

The black names indicate memory locations that belong to the calcButton_Click procedure. The red names indicate memory locations that belong to the CalcOvertime procedure.

hours	rate	regular	extraPay overtime	gross
0.0	0.0	0.0	0.0	0.0
47.0	10.0	400.0	105.0	
			115.0	

hoursWkd	rateOfPay
47.0	10.0

Figure 8-10 Desk-check table after the True path in the CalcOvertime procedure is processed
© 2013 Cengage Learning

The CalcOvertime procedure's End Sub clause is processed next and ends the procedure. At this point, the computer removes the **hoursWkd** and **rateOfPay** variables from its internal memory. It also removes the **extraPay** name from the appropriate location in memory, as indicated in Figure 8-11. Notice that the **overtime** memory location now has only one name: the name assigned to it by the calcButton_Click procedure.

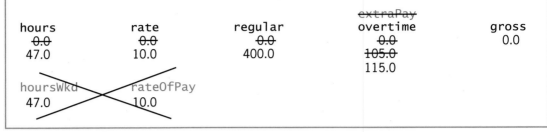

The black names indicate memory locations that belong to the calcButton_Click procedure. The red names indicate memory locations that belong to the CalcOvertime procedure.

hours	rate	regular	~~extraPay~~ overtime	gross
~~0.0~~	~~0.0~~	~~0.0~~	~~0.0~~	0.0
47.0	10.0	400.0	~~105.0~~	
			115.0	

~~hoursWkd~~	~~rateOfPay~~
47.0	10.0

Figure 8-11   Desk-check table after the CalcOvertime procedure ends
© 2013 Cengage Learning

After the CalcOvertime procedure ends, the computer returns to the calcButton_Click procedure to finish processing the event procedure's code. More specifically, it returns to the End If clause, which ends the selection structure. The assignment statement that calculates the gross pay is processed next. The statement adds together the contents of the `regular` and `overtime` variables and assigns the result (515.0) to the `gross` variable, as shown in Figure 8-12.

The black names indicate memory locations that belong to the calcButton_Click procedure. The red names indicate memory locations that belong to the CalcOvertime procedure.

hours	rate	regular	~~extraPay~~ overtime	gross
~~0.0~~	~~0.0~~	~~0.0~~	~~0.0~~	~~0.0~~
47.0	10.0	400.0	~~105.0~~	515.0
			115.0	

~~hoursWkd~~	~~rateOfPay~~
47.0	10.0

Figure 8-12   Desk-check table after the gross pay is calculated
© 2013 Cengage Learning

The last three assignment statements in the calcButton_Click procedure display the regular, overtime, and gross pay amounts in the interface. These amounts agree with the manual calculations shown earlier in Figure 8-6. They also agree with the sample run shown earlier in Figure 8-5.

Finally, the computer processes the Click event procedure's End Sub clause. When the Click event procedure ends, the computer removes the procedure's variables (`hours`, `rate`, `regular`, `overtime`, and `gross`) from memory.

The answers to Mini-Quiz questions are located in Appendix A. Each question is associated with one or more objectives listed at the beginning of the chapter.

Mini-Quiz 8-2

1. Which of the following indicates that the procedure receives a copy of the values stored in two String variables? (2, 3)

    a. `Private Sub Display(ByRef x As String, ByRef y As String)`

    b. `Private Sub Display(ByVal x As String, ByVal y As String)`

    c. `Private Sub Display(ByValue x As String, ByValue y As String)`

    d. `Private Sub Display(ByCopy x As String, ByCopy y As String)`

2. Which of the following indicates that the procedure will receive two items of data: an integer and the address of a Double variable? (2, 3)

    a. `Private Sub Calc(ByVal x As Integer, ByRef y As Double)`

    b. `Private Sub Calc(Value x As Integer, Address y As Double)`

    c. `Private Sub Calc(ByInt x As Integer, ByAdd y As Double)`

    d. `Private Sub Calc(ByCopy x As Integer, ByAdd y As Double)`

3. Which of the following invokes the Calc procedure from Question 2, passing it an Integer variable named **sales** and a Double variable named **bonus**? (2, 3)

    a. `Call Calc(ByVal sales, ByRef bonus)`

    b. `Call Calc(sales, bonus)`

    c. `Call Calc(bonus, sales)`

    d. both b and c

Associating a Procedure with Different Objects and Events

As you learned in Chapter 1, the Handles clause in an event procedure's header indicates the object and event associated with the procedure. The Handles clause in Figure 8-13, for example, indicates that the procedure is associated with the Click event of the exitButton. As a result, the procedure will be processed when the exitButton's Click event occurs.

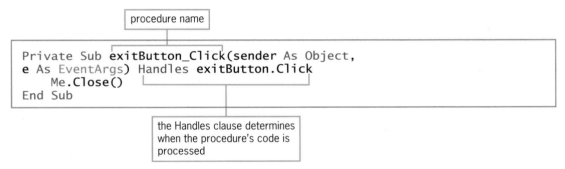

procedure name

```
Private Sub exitButton_Click(sender As Object,
e As EventArgs) Handles exitButton.Click
    Me.Close()
End Sub
```

the Handles clause determines when the procedure's code is processed

Figure 8-13 Click event procedure for the exitButton
© 2013 Cengage Learning

Although an event procedure's name contains the names of its associated object and event, separated by an underscore, that is not a requirement. You can change the name of an event procedure to any name that follows the naming rules for procedures. For example, you can change the name exitButton_Click to EndApp and the procedure will still work correctly. This is because the Handles clause, rather than the event procedure's name, determines when the procedure is invoked.

Figure 8-14 shows the steps for associating a procedure with more than one object and event. It also includes an example of a procedure that is associated with the clearButton.Click, midtermTextBox.TextChanged, and finalTextBox.TextChanged events. The ClearResults procedure will be processed when any of these events occurs.

> **HOW TO** Associate a Procedure with Different Objects and Events
> 1. Open the code template for one of the events with which you want to associate a procedure.
> 2. Change the event procedure's name to one that describes the procedure's task.
> 3. Verify that the parameterList in each event you want to associate is the same as the parameterList in the code template opened in Step 1. (If necessary, you can open the code templates for the other events to view their parameterLists.)
> 4. In the procedure's Handles clause, list each object and event that you want to associate. Separate the object and event with a period, like this: *object.event*. Use a comma to separate each *object.event* from the next *object.event*.
>
> Example
> ```
> Private Sub ClearResults(sender As Object, e As EventArgs
>                          ) Handles clearButton.Click,
>                          midtermTextBox.TextChanged,
>                          finalTextBox.TextChanged
>     avgLabel.Text = String.Empty
>     gradeLabel.Text = String.Empty
> End Sub
> ```

Figure 8-14 How to associate a procedure with different objects and events
© 2013 Cengage Learning

Associating a procedure with more than one object and event allows the programmer to avoid duplicating code in different parts of the program. However, as indicated in Figure 8-14, all of the associated events must have the same parameters in their procedure header. The Click and TextChanged events associated with the ClearResults procedure in Figure 8-14 have the same parameters: `sender` and `e`. You may have noticed that all event procedures contain these two parameters. The **sender parameter** contains a copy of the object that raised the event (in other words, caused the event to occur). For example, when the clearButton's Click event occurs, a copy of the button is stored in the `sender` parameter. Similarly, when the TextChanged event occurs for either of the text boxes, a copy of the corresponding text box is stored in the `sender` parameter.

The **e parameter** in an event procedure's header contains additional information provided by the object that raised the event. The e parameter in the KeyPress event procedure's header, for instance, contains a character that corresponds to the key pressed by the user. You can determine the items of information contained in an event procedure's e parameter by viewing its properties. You do this by displaying the event procedure's code template in the Code Editor window, and then typing the letter e followed by a period. The Code Editor displays a list that includes the **e** parameter's properties.

To see the advantage of associating a procedure with more than one object and event, compare both versions of code shown in Figure 8-15. Version 1's code, which was shown earlier in Figure 8-2, contains four procedures: an independent Sub procedure named ClearLabels and three event procedures that call the ClearLabels procedure. You can replace all of Version 1's code with the code shown in Version 2. Version 2's code contains only one procedure, but the procedure is associated with three objects and events.

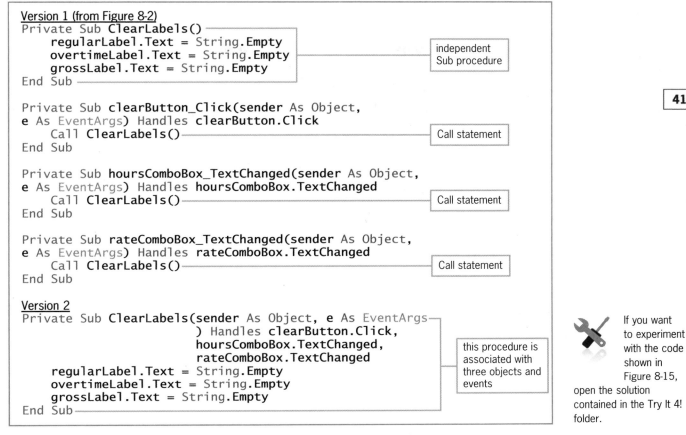

```
Version 1 (from Figure 8-2)
Private Sub ClearLabels()
    regularLabel.Text = String.Empty
    overtimeLabel.Text = String.Empty
    grossLabel.Text = String.Empty
End Sub

Private Sub clearButton_Click(sender As Object,
e As EventArgs) Handles clearButton.Click
    Call ClearLabels()
End Sub

Private Sub hoursComboBox_TextChanged(sender As Object,
e As EventArgs) Handles hoursComboBox.TextChanged
    Call ClearLabels()
End Sub

Private Sub rateComboBox_TextChanged(sender As Object,
e As EventArgs) Handles rateComboBox.TextChanged
    Call ClearLabels()
End Sub

Version 2
Private Sub ClearLabels(sender As Object, e As EventArgs
                       ) Handles clearButton.Click,
                       hoursComboBox.TextChanged,
                       rateComboBox.TextChanged
    regularLabel.Text = String.Empty
    overtimeLabel.Text = String.Empty
    grossLabel.Text = String.Empty
End Sub
```

— independent Sub procedure

— Call statement

— Call statement

— Call statement

— this procedure is associated with three objects and events

Figure 8-15 Two versions of some of the code in the Lanza Trinkets application
© 2013 Cengage Learning

If you want to experiment with the code shown in Figure 8-15, open the solution contained in the Try It 4! folder.

Function Procedures

In addition to creating Sub procedures in Visual Basic, you also can create Function procedures. The difference between both types of procedures is that a **Function procedure** returns a value after performing its assigned task, whereas a Sub procedure does not return a value. Function procedures are referred to more simply as **functions**. The illustration shown in Figure 8-16 may help clarify the difference between Sub procedures and functions. Sarah and her two siblings are planning a surprise birthday party for their mother. Being the oldest of the three children, Sarah will handle most of the party plans herself. However, she does need to delegate some tasks to her brother (Jacob) and sister (Sonja). She delegates the task of putting up the decorations (streamers, balloons, and so on) to Jacob, and delegates the task of getting the birthday present (a bottle of perfume) to Sonja. Like a Sub procedure, Jacob will perform his task but won't need to return anything to Sarah after doing so. However, like a function, Sonja will perform her task and then return a value (the bottle of perfume) to Sarah for wrapping.

Figure 8-16   Illustration of a Sub procedure and a function
Image by Diane Zak; Created with Reallusion CrazyTalk Animator

Figure 8-17 provides another example of the difference between a Sub procedure and a function. In Illustration A, Helen is at the ticket counter in her local movie theater, requesting a ticket for the current movie. Helen gives the ticket agent a $5 bill and expects a ticket in return. The ticket agent is similar to a function in that he performs his task (fulfilling Helen's request for a ticket) and then returns a value (a ticket) to Helen. Compare that with Illustration B, where Helen and her granddaughter, Penelope, are at the Blast Off Games arcade. Helen wants Penelope to have fun, so she gives Penelope a $5 bill to play some games. But, unlike with the ticket agent, Helen expects nothing from Penelope in return. This is similar to the way a Sub procedure works. Penelope performs her task (having fun by playing games), but doesn't need to return any value to her grandmother.

Illustration A

Helen:
1. ask ticket agent for a senior ticket
2. give ticket agent $5
3. receive senior ticket from ticket agent

Ticket agent (function):
1. take $5 from Helen
2. give Helen a senior ticket

Illustration B

Helen:
1. tell Penelope to have fun playing games
2. give Penelope $5

Penelope (Sub procedure):
1. take $5 from Helen
2. buy game tickets with the $5
3. play games and have fun

Figure 8-17   Another example of the difference between a Sub procedure and a function
Image by Diane Zak; Created with Reallusion CrazyTalk Animator

Figure 8-18 shows the syntax and examples of functions in Visual Basic. Unlike a Sub procedure, a function's header and footer contain the Function keyword rather than the Sub keyword. A function's header also includes the As *dataType* section, which specifies the data type of the value the function will return. The value is returned by the **Return statement**, which typically is the last statement within a function. The Return statement's syntax is Return *expression*, where *expression* represents the one and only value that will be returned to the statement that invoked the function. The data type of the *expression* must agree with the data type specified in the As *dataType* section of the header. Like a Sub procedure, a function can receive information either *by value* or *by reference*. The information it receives is listed in its parameterList.

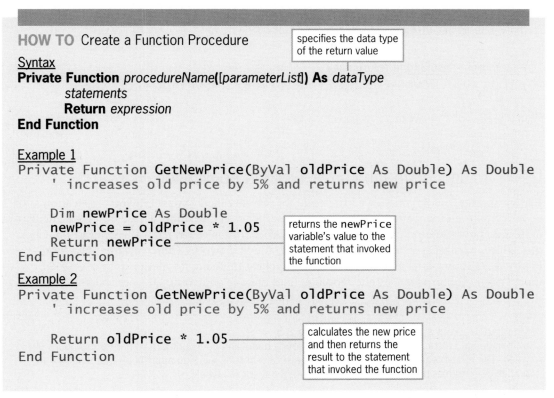

HOW TO Create a Function Procedure

specifies the data type of the return value

Syntax
Private Function *procedureName*([*parameterList*]) **As** *dataType*
    statements
      Return *expression*
End Function

Example 1
```
Private Function GetNewPrice(ByVal oldPrice As Double) As Double
    ' increases old price by 5% and returns new price

    Dim newPrice As Double
    newPrice = oldPrice * 1.05
    Return newPrice
End Function
```
returns the newPrice variable's value to the statement that invoked the function

Example 2
```
Private Function GetNewPrice(ByVal oldPrice As Double) As Double
    ' increases old price by 5% and returns new price

    Return oldPrice * 1.05
End Function
```
calculates the new price and then returns the result to the statement that invoked the function

Figure 8-18 How to create a Function procedure
© 2013 Cengage Learning

As with Sub procedures, you can enter your functions anywhere in the Code Editor window, as long as you enter them between the Public Class and End Class clauses and outside of any other procedure. Like Sub procedure names, function names are entered using Pascal case and typically begin with a verb. The name should indicate the task the function performs. The GetNewPrice name used in the examples in Figure 8-18 indicates that each function returns a new price.

You can invoke a function from one or more places in an application's code. You invoke a function that you create in exactly the same way as you invoke one of Visual Basic's built-in functions, such as the InputBox function. You do this by including the function's name and arguments (if any) in a statement. The number, data type, and position of the arguments should agree with the number, data type, and position of the function's parameters. In most cases, the statement that invokes a function assigns the function's return value to a variable. However, it also may use the return value in a calculation or simply display the return value. Figure 8-19 shows examples of invoking the GetNewPrice function from Figure 8-18. The GetNewPrice(price) entry in each example invokes the function, passing it the value stored in the price variable.

HOW TO Invoke a Function Procedure

Example 1 – assign the return value to a variable
```
updatedPrice = GetNewPrice(price)
               or
price = GetNewPrice(price)
```

Example 2 – use the return value in a calculation
```
totalDue = quantity * GetNewPrice(price)
```
multiplies the value in the `quantity` variable by the function's return value and then assigns the result to the `totalDue` variable

Example 3 – display the return value
```
priceLabel.Text = GetNewPrice(price).ToString("C2")
```

Figure 8-19 How to invoke a Function procedure
© 2013 Cengage Learning

Using a Function in the Lanza Trinkets Application

Earlier, in Figure 8-5, you viewed the code for the modified Lanza Trinkets application. The code contains an independent Sub procedure named CalcOvertime, whose task is to calculate an employee's overtime pay. The CalcOvertime procedure is called from the calcButton_Click procedure, which passes it three items of data: the first two *by value* and the third *by reference*. Figure 8-20 shows how you could code the application using a function rather than an independent Sub procedure. The modified lines of code and comments are shaded in the figure.

Modified problem specification (from Figure 8-5)
Employees at Lanza Trinkets are paid on an hourly basis and can work a maximum of 50 hours per week. The employees receive overtime pay as shown here. Create an application that displays an employee's regular pay, overtime pay, and gross pay for the week.

Hours worked	Overtime pay
Less than or equal to 40	0
over 40 through 50	time and one-half for the hours from 40 through 45
	double time for the hours from 45 through 50

```
Private Function CalcOvertime(ByVal hoursWkd As Double,
                              ByVal rateOfPay As Double) As Double
    ' calculates the overtime pay

    Dim extraPay As Double

    extraPay = (hoursWkd - 40) * rateOfPay * 1.5
    If hoursWkd > 45 Then
        ' add extra half-time for double time hours
        extraPay = extraPay +
            (hoursWkd - 45) * rateOfPay * 0.5
    End If
    Return extraPay
End Function
```

Figure 8-20 Lanza Trinkets application using a function *(continues)*

(continued)

```vb
Private Sub calcButton_Click(sender As Object,
e As EventArgs) Handles calcButton.Click
    ' calculates regular pay, overtime pay,
    ' and gross pay

    Dim hours As Double
    Dim rate As Double
    Dim regular As Double
    Dim overtime As Double
    Dim gross As Double

    Double.TryParse(hoursComboBox.Text, hours)
    Double.TryParse(rateComboBox.Text, rate)

    If hours <= 40 Then
        regular = hours * rate
    Else
        regular = 40 * rate
        ' call function to calculate
        ' and return overtime pay
        overtime = CalcOvertime(hours, rate)
    End If

    ' calculate gross pay
    gross = regular + overtime

    ' display calculated results
    regularLabel.Text = regular.ToString("N2")
    overtimeLabel.Text = overtime.ToString("N2")
    grossLabel.Text = gross.ToString("N2")
End Sub
```

423

> invokes the function and assigns the return value to the `overtime` variable

> passed *by value*

Lanza Trinkets - Weekly Pay

Lanza Trinkets

Hours: `47.0 ▾` Rate: `10.00 ▾`

Regular pay: `400.00` Overtime pay: `115.00` Gross pay: `515.00`

[Calculate] [Clear] [Exit]

Figure 8-20   Lanza Trinkets application using a function
© 2013 Cengage Learning

If you want to experiment with this version of the Lanza Trinkets application, open the solution contained in the Try It 5! folder.

We'll desk-check the procedures shown in Figure 8-20 using 47 and $10 as the hours worked and pay rate, respectively. This is the same data used to desk-check the procedures from Figure 8-5. The expected results are as follows: 400 for the regular pay, 115 for the overtime pay, and 515 for the gross pay.

When the user clicks the Calculate button after selecting 47.0 and 10.00 in the hoursComboBox and rateComboBox, respectively, the Dim statements in the button's Click event procedure create and initialize five Double variables. Next, the two TryParse methods convert the items selected in the combo boxes to Double, storing the results in the hours and rate variables. The selection structure's condition is evaluated next. The condition evaluates to False because the value in the **hours** variable is not less than or equal to 40. As a result, the selection structure's False path is processed. The first instruction in the False path calculates the regular pay by multiplying the value in the **rate** variable (10.0) by the number 40; it assigns the result (400.0) to the **regular** variable. Figure 8-21 shows the contents of the variables after the first statement in the False path is processed.

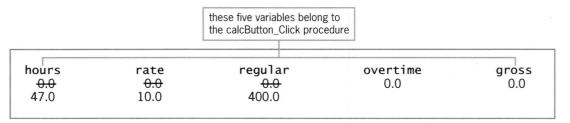

		these five variables belong to the calcButton_Click procedure		
hours	rate	regular	overtime	gross
~~0.0~~	~~0.0~~	~~0.0~~	0.0	0.0
47.0	10.0	400.0		

Figure 8-21   Desk-check table after the first statement in the False path is processed
© 2013 Cengage Learning

The computer processes the second statement in the False path next. That statement invokes the CalcOvertime function, passing it two arguments. At this point, the computer temporarily leaves the Click event procedure to process the code contained in the CalcOvertime function, beginning with the function header. The **ByVal** keyword before each parameter indicates that the function is receiving values from the statement that invoked it—in this case, copies of the numbers stored in the **hours** and **rate** variables. As a result, the computer creates the **hoursWkd** and **rateOfPay** variables listed in the parameterList, and stores the numbers 47.0 and 10.0, respectively, in the variables.

After processing the CalcOvertime function header, the computer processes the code contained in the function. The Dim statement creates a variable named **extraPay** and initializes it to 0.0. The next statement calculates time and one-half for the seven overtime hours, and then assigns the result (105.0) to the **extraPay** variable. The selection structure in the CalcOvertime function is processed next. The structure's condition evaluates to True because the value in the **hoursWkd** variable is greater than 45. As a result, the statement in the structure's True path calculates the additional half-time for the two hours that are over 45 and then adds the result (10.0) to the contents of the **extraPay** variable, giving 115.0. Figure 8-22 shows the desk-check table before the next statement, **Return extraPay**, is processed.

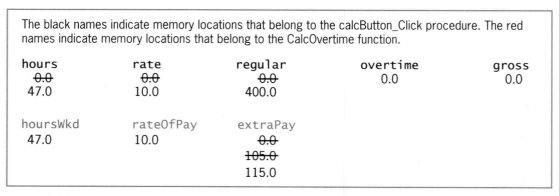

The black names indicate memory locations that belong to the calcButton_Click procedure. The red names indicate memory locations that belong to the CalcOvertime function.

hours	rate	regular	overtime	gross
~~0.0~~	~~0.0~~	~~0.0~~	0.0	0.0
47.0	10.0	400.0		
hoursWkd	rateOfPay	extraPay		
47.0	10.0	~~0.0~~		
		~~105.0~~		
		115.0		

Figure 8-22   Desk-check table before the Return statement is processed
© 2013 Cengage Learning

The Return extraPay statement returns the contents of the extraPay variable to the statement that invoked the function. That statement is the overtime = CalcOvertime(hours, rate) statement in the calcButton_Click procedure. The statement assigns the function's return value to the overtime variable. The End Function clause is processed next and ends the CalcOvertime function. At this point, the computer removes the hoursWkd, rateOfPay, and extraPay variables from its internal memory. Figure 8-23 shows the desk-check table after the CalcOvertime function ends. Notice that the overtime variable now contains the overtime pay amount.

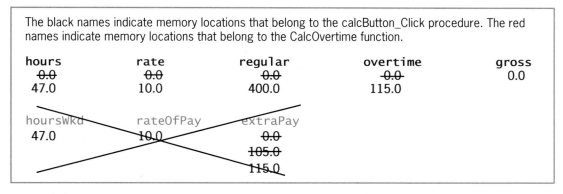

Figure 8-23 Desk-check table after the CalcOvertime function ends
© 2013 Cengage Learning

After the CalcOvertime function ends, the computer returns to the calcButton_Click procedure to finish processing the event procedure's code. More specifically, it returns to the End If clause, which ends the selection structure. The assignment statement that calculates the gross pay is processed next. The statement adds together the contents of the regular and overtime variables and assigns the result (515.0) to the gross variable, as shown in Figure 8-24.

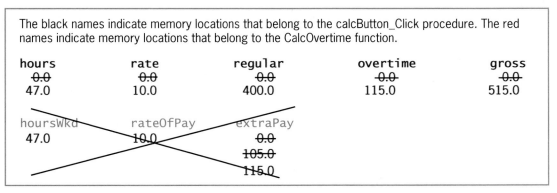

Figure 8-24 Desk-check table after the gross pay is calculated
© 2013 Cengage Learning

The last three assignment statements in the calcButton_Click procedure display the regular, overtime, and gross pay amounts in the interface. The amounts agree with the manual calculations shown earlier in Figure 8-6. They also agree with the sample run shown earlier in Figure 8-20.

Finally, the computer processes the Click event procedure's End Sub clause. When the Click event procedure ends, the computer removes the procedure's variables (hours, rate, regular, overtime, and gross) from memory.

The last concepts covered in this chapter are how to convert Object variables to a different data type and how to use a timer control. You will use one more both of these concepts in this chapter's programming tutorials.

Converting Object Variables

Every event procedure contains the sender As Object code in its procedure header. The code creates a variable named sender and assigns the Object data type to it. As you learned in Chapter 3, an Object variable can store any type of data. In this case, the sender variable contains a copy of the object that raised the event.

Unlike variables declared using the String and numeric data types, variables declared using the Object data type do not have a set of properties. This is because there are no common attributes for all of the different types of data that can be stored in an Object variable. If you need to access the properties of the object stored in the sender variable, you must convert the variable to the appropriate data type. The process of converting a variable from one data type to another is sometimes referred to as **type casting** or, more simply, as **casting**.

You can cast a variable from the Object data type to a different data type using the **TryCast operator**. The operator's syntax is shown in Figure 8-25, along with examples of using the operator.

HOW TO Use the TryCast Operator

<u>Syntax</u>
TryCast(*object, dataType***)**

<u>Example 1</u>
```
Dim thisTextBox As TextBox
thisTextBox = TryCast(sender, TextBox)
thisTextBox.SelectAll()
```
The TryCast operator casts (converts) the sender variable to the TextBox data type, and then the assignment statement assigns the result to a TextBox variable named thisTextBox. The SelectAll method selects (highlights) the contents of the text box stored in the thisTextBox variable.

<u>Example 2</u>
```
Dim clickedButton As Button
clickedButton = TryCast(sender, Button)
MessageBox.Show(clickedButton.Text)
```
The TryCast operator casts (converts) the sender variable to the Button data type, and then the assignment statement assigns the result to a Button variable named clickedButton. The MessageBox.Show method displays the Text property of the button stored in the clickedButton variable.

Figure 8-25 How to use the TryCast operator
© 2013 Cengage Learning

The Full Name Application

The Full Name application's interface provides text boxes for entering a first name and a last name. When one of the text boxes receives the focus, its Enter event procedure should select its existing text; Figure 8-26 shows two ways of accomplishing this task. In Version 1's code, the SelectAll method appears in each text box's Enter event procedure. In Version 2's code, each text box's Enter event is associated with a procedure named SelectText. The SelectText procedure converts the sender parameter to the appropriate text box. It then uses the text box's SelectAll method to select the existing text. Figure 8-26 also shows a sample run of the application.

```
Version 1
Private Sub firstTextBox_Enter(sender As Object,
e As EventArgs) Handles firstTextBox.Enter
    firstTextBox.SelectAll()
End Sub

Private Sub lastTextBox_Enter(sender As Object,
e As EventArgs) Handles lastTextBox.Enter
    lastTextBox.SelectAll()
End Sub

Version 2
Private Sub SelectText(sender As Object, e As EventArgs
            ) Handles firstTextBox.Enter, lastTextBox.Enter
    ' selects the existing text

    Dim thisTextBox As TextBox
    thisTextBox = TryCast(sender, TextBox)
    thisTextBox.SelectAll()
End Sub
```

the text is selected when the text box receives the focus

Full Name

First name: Jasper   Concatenate

Last name: Hendricks   Exit

Full name:

Figure 8-26 Two ways of coding each text box's Enter event
© 2013 Cengage Learning

If you want to experiment with the Full Name application, open the solution contained in the Try It 6! folder.

Using a Timer Control

The game application in Programming Tutorial 2 requires you to use a timer control. You instantiate a timer control using the Timer tool, which is located in the Components section of the toolbox. When you drag the Timer tool to the form and then release the mouse button, the timer control will be placed in the component tray rather than on the form. Recall that the component tray stores controls that do not appear in the user interface during run time.

The purpose of a **timer control** is to process code at one or more regular intervals. The length of each interval is specified in milliseconds and entered in the timer's **Interval property**. As you learned in Chapter 6, a millisecond is 1/1000 of a second; in other words, there are 1000 milliseconds in a second. The timer's state—either running or stopped—is determined by its Enabled property, which can be set to either True or False. When the property is set to True, the timer is running; when it is set to False, the timer is stopped.

If the timer is running, its **Tick event** occurs each time an interval has elapsed. Each time the Tick event occurs, the computer processes any code contained in the Tick event procedure. If the timer is stopped, the Tick event does not occur and, therefore, any code entered in the Tick event procedure is not processed.

The Timer Example Application

The Timer Example application uses a timer to blink a label 10 times. The application's interface is shown in Figure 8-27, along with the code entered in the blinkButton_Click and blinkTimer_Tick procedures.

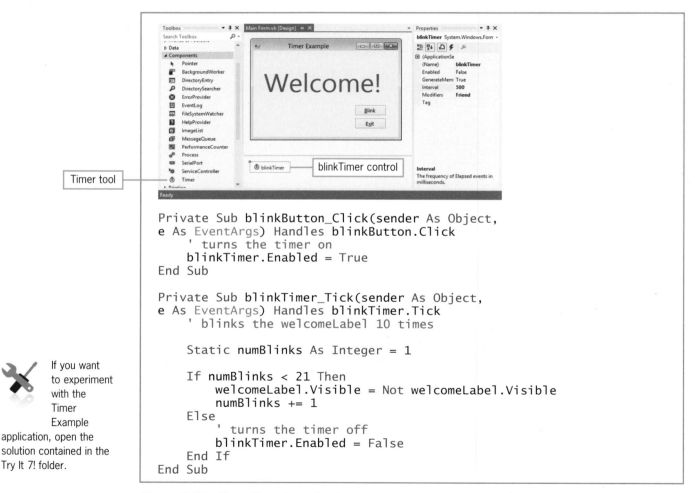

```vb
Private Sub blinkButton_Click(sender As Object,
e As EventArgs) Handles blinkButton.Click
    ' turns the timer on
    blinkTimer.Enabled = True
End Sub

Private Sub blinkTimer_Tick(sender As Object,
e As EventArgs) Handles blinkTimer.Tick
    ' blinks the welcomeLabel 10 times

    Static numBlinks As Integer = 1

    If numBlinks < 21 Then
        welcomeLabel.Visible = Not welcomeLabel.Visible
        numBlinks += 1
    Else
        ' turns the timer off
        blinkTimer.Enabled = False
    End If
End Sub
```

If you want to experiment with the Timer Example application, open the solution contained in the Try It 7! folder.

Figure 8-27   Timer Example application
© 2013 Cengage Learning

Mini-Quiz 8-3

1. Which of the following associates a procedure with the TextChanged events of the nameTextBox and salesTextBox? (6)

   a. `Handles nameTextBox_TextChanged,`
      `    salesTextBox_TextChanged`

   b. `Handles nameTextBox.TextChanged AndAlso`
      `    salesTextBox.TextChanged`

   c. `Handles nameTextBox-TextChanged,`
      `    salesTextBox-TextChanged`

   d. `Handles nameTextBox.TextChanged,`
      `    salesTextBox.TextChanged`

2. Which of the following headers indicates that the procedure returns a Decimal number? (8, 9)

   a. `Private Function Calc() As Decimal`

   b. `Private Sub Calc() As Decimal`

   c. `Private Function Calc(Decimal)`

   d. both a and b

3. A function can return _____. (8, 9)

   a. zero or more values

   b. one or more values

   c. one value only

4. Which of the following converts the **sender** parameter to the Label data type, assigning the result to a Label variable named **currentLabel**? (7, 10)

   a. `TryCast(sender, Label, currentLabel)`

   b. `currentLabel = TryCast(sender, Label)`

   c. `currentLabel = TryCast(Label, sender)`

   d. `sender = TryCast(currentLabel, Label)`

5. To turn on a timer, you set its _____ property to True. (11)

   a. Enabled

   b. Running

   c. Start

   d. none of the above

The answers to Mini-Quiz questions are located in Appendix A. Each question is associated with one or more objectives listed at the beginning of the chapter.

You have completed the concepts section of Chapter 8. The Programming Tutorial section is next.

PROGRAMMING TUTORIAL 1

Coding the Tri-County Electricity Application

In this tutorial, you will code an application for the Tri-County Electricity Company. Figures 8-28 and 8-29 show the application's TOE chart and MainForm, respectively. The interface allows the user to enter three items of data: the rate code, previous meter reading, and current meter reading. When the user clicks the Calculate button, the button's Click event procedure should verify that the current meter reading is greater than or equal to the previous meter reading. If it is, the application should calculate and display the number of electrical units used during the month and also the total charge. The total charge is based on the number of units used and the rate code. Residential customers are charged $0.09 per unit, with a minimum charge of $17.65. Commercial customers are charged $0.12 per unit, with a minimum charge of $21.75. If the current meter reading is less than the previous meter reading, the application should display an appropriate message.

Task	Object	Event
End the application	exitButton	Click
Get the rate code	residentialRadioButton, commercialRadioButton	None
Get and display the current meter reading and previous meter reading	currentTextBox, previousTextBox	None
Select the existing text	currentTextBox, previousTextBox	Enter
Allow only numbers and the Backspace key	currentTextBox, previousTextBox	KeyPress
Clear usageLabel and totalLabel	currentTextBox, previousTextBox	TextChanged
	residentialRadioButton, commercialRadioButton	CheckedChanged
1. Determine whether the current meter reading is greater than or equal to the previous meter reading 2. If necessary, calculate the monthly usage and total charge and then display the results in usageLabel and totalLabel 3. If necessary, display "The current reading must be greater than or equal to the previous reading." message in a message box	calcButton	Click
Display monthly usage (from calcButton)	usageLabel	None
Display total charge (from calcButton)	totalLabel	None

Figure 8-28   TOE chart for the Tri-County Electricity application

© 2013 Cengage Learning

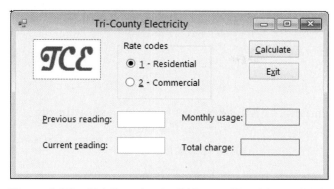

Figure 8-29 MainForm for the Tri-County Electricity application

Coding the Application

According to the application's TOE chart, each button's Click event procedure and each radio button's CheckedChanged event procedure need to be coded. Each text box's Enter, KeyPress, and TextChanged event procedures also need to be coded.

To open the Tri-County Electricity application:

1. Start Visual Studio. Open the **Tri-County Solution (Tri-County Solution.sln)** file contained in the VbReloaded2012\Chap08\Tri-County Solution folder. If necessary, open the designer window.

2. Open the Code Editor window. Notice that the exitButton_Click procedure has already been coded for you.

3. In the comments that appear in the General Declarations section, replace <your name> and <current date> with your name and the current date, respectively.

First, you will code the Enter event procedures for both text boxes. The procedures should select the text box's existing text when the text box receives the focus. You can code each text box's Enter event procedure individually. Or, you can enter the code in a Sub procedure and then associate both Enter events with the procedure; this is the method you will use.

To code each text box's Enter event:

1. Open the code template for the currentTextBox's Enter event procedure. In the procedure header, change currentTextBox_Enter to **SelectText**.

2. Change the Handles clause in the procedure header to the following:

   Handles currentTextBox.Enter, previousTextBox.Enter

3. In the blank line below the procedure header, type **' select existing text** and then press **Enter** twice.

4. Now, enter the following code:

   Dim thisTextBox As TextBox
   thisTextBox = TryCast(sender, TextBox)
   thisTextBox.SelectAll()

5. Save the solution and then start the application. Type **12** in the Previous reading box, press **Tab**, and then type **200** in the Current reading box. Press **Tab** four times to move the focus to the Previous reading box; doing this selects the text entered in the box. Press **Tab** again to move the focus to the Current reading box, which selects that box's text.

6. Click the **Exit** button.

Next, you will code the KeyPress event procedures for both text boxes. Each procedure should allow its text box to accept only numbers and the Backspace key. Here again, you can code each KeyPress event procedure separately. Or, you can enter the code in a Sub procedure that is associated with both KeyPress events.

To code each text box's KeyPress event:

1. Open the code template for the currentTextBox's KeyPress event procedure. In the procedure header, change `currentTextBox_KeyPress` to **CancelKeys**.

2. Change the Handles clause in the procedure header to the following:

    Handles currentTextBox.KeyPress, previousTextBox.KeyPress

3. In the blank line below the procedure header, type the following comment and then press **Enter** twice:

    ' allow only numbers and the Backspace

4. Now, enter the following code:

    **If (e.KeyChar < "0" OrElse e.KeyChar > "9") AndAlso
        e.KeyChar <> ControlChars.Back Then
        e.Handled = True
    End If**

5. Save the solution and then start the application. On your own, test the KeyPress event procedures. You can do this by trying to enter characters other than numbers into each text box. Also be sure to verify that the text boxes accept numbers and the Backspace key.

6. Click the **Exit** button.

Next, you will code the TextChanged event procedures for both text boxes and also the CheckedChanged event procedures for both radio buttons. The procedures should clear the contents of the usageLabel and totalLabel. Here, too, you can code each event procedure individually. Or, you can enter the code in a Sub procedure that is associated with the events.

To code the TextChanged and CheckedChanged event procedures:

1. Open the code template for the currentTextBox's TextChanged event procedure. In the procedure header, change `currentTextBox_TextChanged` to **ClearLabels**.

2. Change the Handles clause in the procedure header to the following:

    **Handles currentTextBox.TextChanged, previousTextBox.TextChanged,
    residentialRadioButton.CheckedChanged, commercialRadioButton.CheckedChanged**

3. In the blank line below the procedure header, type the following comment and then press **Enter** twice:

    ' clear calculated value

4. Now, enter the following code:

    **usageLabel.Text = String.Empty
    totalLabel.Text = String.Empty**

5. Save the solution. You won't be able to test the ClearLabels procedure until the calcButton_Click procedure is coded.

Completing the Application's Code

Figure 8-30 shows the pseudocode for the calcButton's Click event procedure. The procedure will use an independent Sub procedure to calculate the total charge for residential customers. It will use a function to calculate the total charge for commercial customers. A Sub procedure and function were chosen, rather than two Sub procedures or two Function procedures, simply to allow you to practice with both types of procedures. The pseudocode for both procedures is included in Figure 8-30.

---

calcButton Click event procedure
1. assign user input (previous reading and current reading) to variables
2. if current reading is greater than or equal to previous reading
        usage = current reading − previous reading

        if the residentialRadioButton is selected
            call CalcResidentialTotal Sub procedure to calculate the total charge; pass the
            procedure the usage value and a variable in which to store the total charge
        else
            total charge = invoke the GetCommercialTotal function; pass the function the
            usage value
        end if
        display the usage and total charge in usageLabel and totalLabel
    else
        display message in a message box
    end if

CalcResidentialTotal Sub procedure (receives the usage value and the address of a variable in which to store the total charge)
1. declare constants to store the unit charge (0.09) and the minimum fee (17.65)
2. total charge = usage value * unit charge
3. if total charge is less than the minimum fee
        total charge = minimum fee
    end if

GetCommercialTotal function (receives the usage value)
1. declare constants to store the unit charge (0.12) and the minimum fee (21.75)
2. declare a variable to store the total charge
3. total charge = usage value * unit charge
4. if total charge is less than the minimum fee
        total charge = minimum fee
    end if
5. return total charge

Figure 8-30 Pseudocode for three procedures in the application
© 2013 Cengage Learning

The CalcResidentialTotal Sub procedure will be coded first. According to its pseudocode, the procedure will receive two items of data from the statement that calls it: the usage value and the address of a variable where it can place the total charge after it has been calculated. The procedure will store the data it receives in two parameters named `units` and `charge`.

To code the CalcResidentialTotal Sub procedure:

1. Scroll to the top of the Code Editor window. Click the **blank line** below the Public Class clause and then press **Enter** to insert a new blank line. Type the following procedure header and then press **Enter**. When you press Enter, the Code Editor automatically enters the End Sub clause for you.

    Private Sub CalcResidentialTotal(ByVal units As Integer,
    ByRef charge As Double)

2. Type the following comment and then press **Enter** twice:

   ' calculates the total charge for a residential customer

3. The first step in the procedure's pseudocode declares constants to store the unit charge and minimum fee. Enter the following declaration statements. Press **Enter** twice after typing the second declaration statement.

   Const UnitCharge As Double = .09
   Const MinFee As Double = 17.65

4. The second step in the pseudocode calculates the total charge. Enter the following assignment statement:

   charge = units * UnitCharge

5. The third step in the pseudocode is a single-alternative selection structure whose condition compares the total charge with the minimum fee. If the total charge is less than the minimum fee, the selection structure's True path assigns the minimum fee as the total charge. Enter the following code:

   If charge < MinFee Then
       charge = MinFee
   End If

6. Save the solution.

Next, you will code the GetCommercialTotal function. According to its pseudocode, the function will receive one item of data from the statement that calls it: the usage value. The function will store the usage value in a parameter named `units`.

To code the GetCommercialTotal function:

1. Click **immediately after the letter b** in the CalcResidentialTotal procedure's End Sub clause, and then press **Enter** twice.

2. Type the following function header and then press **Enter**. When you press Enter, the Code Editor automatically enters the End Function clause for you. Don't be concerned about the jagged line that appears below the clause; it will disappear when you enter the Return statement.

   Private Function GetCommercialTotal(ByVal units As Integer) As Double

3. Type the following comment and then press **Enter** twice:

   ' calculates the total charge for a commercial customer

4. The first step in the pseudocode declares constants to store the unit charge and minimum fee. Enter the following declaration statements:

   Const UnitCharge As Double = .12
   Const MinFee As Double = 21.75

5. The second step in the pseudocode declares a variable to store the total charge. Type the following declaration statement and then press **Enter** twice:

   Dim charge As Double

6. The third step in the pseudocode calculates the total charge. Enter the following assignment statement:

   charge = units * UnitCharge

7. The fourth step in the pseudocode is a single-alternative selection structure whose condition compares the total charge with the minimum fee. If the total charge is less than

the minimum fee, the selection structure's True path assigns the minimum fee as the total charge. Enter the following code:

If charge < MinFee Then
    charge = MinFee
End If

8. The final step in the pseudocode returns the total charge. Click immediately after the letter **f** in the End If clause and then press **Enter** twice. Enter the following statement:

Return charge

9. Insert a **blank line** below the End Function clause, and then save the solution.

The last procedure you need to code is the calcButton's Click event procedure.

To code the calcButton's Click event procedure and then test the code:

1. Open the code template for the calcButton's Click event procedure. Type the following comment and then press **Enter** twice:

' displays the monthly usage and total charge

2. The procedure will use three Integer variables to store the previous reading, current reading, and usage amount. It will also use a Double variable to store the total charge. Enter the following declaration statements. Press **Enter** twice after typing the last declaration statement.

Dim previous As Integer
Dim current As Integer
Dim usage As Integer
Dim total As Double

3. The first step in the pseudocode assigns the user input to variables. Enter the following TryParse methods. Press **Enter** twice after typing the last TryParse method.

Integer.TryParse(previousTextBox.Text, previous)
Integer.TryParse(currentTextBox.Text, current)

4. The second step in the pseudocode is a dual-alternative selection structure whose condition determines whether the current reading is greater than or equal to the previous reading. If the selection structure's condition evaluates to True, the first instruction in the True path calculates the usage amount. Enter the additional code shown in Figure 8-31, and then position the insertion point as shown in the figure.

```
        Integer.TryParse(previousTextBox.Text, previous)
        Integer.TryParse(currentTextBox.Text, current)

        If current >= previous Then ──────┐
            usage = current - previous    ┌──────────────┐
            │─────────────┐               │enter these lines
                    insertion point       │of code       │
        End If ───────────────────────────└──────────────┘
    End Sub
```

Figure 8-31   Additional code entered in the calcButton_Click procedure

5. The next instruction in the True path is a nested dual-alternative selection structure whose condition determines whether the residentialRadioButton is selected. If the condition evaluates to True, the nested structure's True path calls the CalcResidentialTotal Sub procedure, passing it the **usage** variable *by value* and the **total** variable *by reference*. If the condition evaluates to False, on the other hand, the nested structure's False path invokes the GetCommercialTotal function, passing it the **usage** variable *by value*; it then assigns the function's return value to the **total** variable. Enter the nested selection structure shown in Figure 8-32, and then position the insertion point as shown in the figure.

```
If current >= previous Then
    usage = current - previous
    If residentialRadioButton.Checked Then
        Call CalcResidentialTotal(usage, total)
    Else
        total = GetCommercialTotal(usage)
    End If
```

enter the nested selection structure

position the insertion point here

```
    End If
End Sub
```

Figure 8-32   Nested selection structure entered in the calcButton_Click procedure

6. The last instruction in the outer selection structure's True path displays the usage and total charge in the usageLabel and totalLabel, respectively. Enter the following two assignment statements:

usageLabel.Text = usage.ToString("N0")
totalLabel.Text = total.ToString("C2")

7. According to the pseudocode, the outer selection structure's False path should display a message in a message box. Enter the additional code shown in Figure 8-33.

```
        usageLabel.Text = usage.ToString("N0")
        totalLabel.Text = total.ToString("C2")
    Else
        MessageBox.Show("The current reading must " &
                        "be greater than or equal to the " &
                        "previous reading.",
                        "Tri-County Electricity",
                        MessageBoxButtons.OK,
                        MessageBoxIcon.Information)
    End If
End Sub
```

enter these lines of code

Figure 8-33   Outer selection structure's False path entered in the calcButton_Click procedure

8. Save the solution and then start the application. Type **2500** in the Previous reading box, and then type **3500** in the Current reading box. Click the **Calculate** button. The monthly usage and total charge appear in the interface, as shown in Figure 8-34.

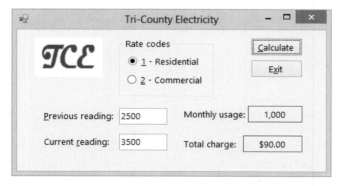

Figure 8-34   Interface showing the monthly usage and total charge

9. Click the **2 - Commercial** radio button. The radio button's Click event procedure clears the contents of the Monthly usage and Total charge boxes. Click the **Calculate** button. The interface shows that the monthly usage and total charge are 1,000 and $120.00, respectively.

10. Press **Tab** three times to place the focus in the Previous reading box. Type **4**. The previousTextBox's TextChanged event procedure clears the contents of the Monthly usage and Total charge boxes. Click the **Calculate** button.

11. Press **Tab** four times to place the focus in the Current reading box. Type **2**. The currentTextBox's TextChanged event procedure clears the contents of the Monthly usage and Total charge boxes. Click the **Calculate** button.

12. The message "The current reading must be greater than or equal to the previous reading." appears in a message box. Close the message box.

13. Click the **Exit** button to end the application. Close the Code Editor window, and then close the solution. Figure 8-35 shows the application's code.

```
 1 ' Project name:         Tri-County Project
 2 ' Project purpose:      Displays a monthly electric bill
 3 ' Created/revised by:   <your name> on <current date>
 4
 5 Option Explicit On
 6 Option Strict On
 7 Option Infer Off
 8
 9 Public Class MainForm
10
11     Private Sub CalcResidentialTotal(ByVal units As Integer,
12                                      ByRef charge As Double)
13         ' calculates the total charge for a residential customer
14
15         Const UnitCharge As Double = 0.09
16         Const MinFee As Double = 17.65
17
18         charge = units * UnitCharge
19         If charge < MinFee Then
20             charge = MinFee
21         End If
22     End Sub
23
24     Private Function GetCommercialTotal(ByVal units As Integer)
        As Double
25         ' calculates the total charge for a commercial customer
26
27         Const UnitCharge As Double = 0.12
28         Const MinFee As Double = 21.75
29         Dim charge As Double
30
31         charge = units * UnitCharge
32         If charge < MinFee Then
33             charge = MinFee
34         End If
35
36         Return charge
37
38     End Function
39
40     Private Sub exitButton_Click(sender As Object,
        e As EventArgs) Handles exitButton.Click
41         Me.Close()
42     End Sub
43
44     Private Sub SelectText(sender As Object,
        e As EventArgs) Handles currentTextBox.Enter,
        previousTextBox.Enter
```

Figure 8-35 Code for the Tri-County Electricity application (*continues*)

(continued)

```
45            ' select existing text
46
47            Dim thisTextBox As TextBox
48            thisTextBox = TryCast(sender, TextBox)
49            thisTextBox.SelectAll()
50
51        End Sub
52
53        Private Sub CancelKeys(sender As Object,
          e As KeyPressEventArgs) Handles currentTextBox.KeyPress,
          previousTextBox.KeyPress
54            ' allow only numbers and the Backspace
55
56            If (e.KeyChar < "0" OrElse e.KeyChar > "9") AndAlso
57                e.KeyChar <> ControlChars.Back Then
58                e.Handled = True
59            End If
60        End Sub
61
62        Private Sub ClearLabels(sender As Object,
          e As EventArgs) Handles currentTextBox.TextChanged,
          previousTextBox.TextChanged,
63        residentialRadioButton.CheckedChanged,
          commercialRadioButton.CheckedChanged
64            ' clear calculated value
65
66            usageLabel.Text = String.Empty
67            totalLabel.Text = String.Empty
68
69        End Sub
70
71        Private Sub calcButton_Click(sender As Object,
          e As EventArgs) Handles calcButton.Click
72            ' displays the monthly usage and total charge
73
74            Dim previous As Integer
75            Dim current As Integer
76            Dim usage As Integer
77            Dim total As Double
78
79            Integer.TryParse(previousTextBox.Text, previous)
80            Integer.TryParse(currentTextBox.Text, current)
81
82            If current >= previous Then
83                usage = current - previous
84                If residentialRadioButton.Checked Then
85                    Call CalcResidentialTotal(usage, total)
86                Else
87                    total = GetCommercialTotal(usage)
88                End If
89
90                usageLabel.Text = usage.ToString("N0")
91                totalLabel.Text = total.ToString("C2")
92            Else
93                MessageBox.Show("The current reading must " &
94                               "be greater than or equal to the " &
95                               "previous reading.",
96                               "Tri-County Electricity",
97                               MessageBoxButtons.OK,
98                               MessageBoxIcon.Information)
99            End If
100       End Sub
101   End Class
```

Figure 8-35 Code for the Tri-County Electricity application

PROGRAMMING TUTORIAL 2

Coding the Concentration Game Application

In this tutorial, you will code an application that simulates a game called Concentration. The game board contains 16 labels. Scattered among the labels are eight pairs of matching words that are hidden from view. The user begins by clicking one of the labels to reveal a word. He or she then clicks another label to reveal another word. If the two words match, the words remain on the screen. If the words do not match, they are hidden once again. The game is over when all of the matching words are revealed. The user can start a new game by clicking the New Game button in the interface. In each game, the words will appear in different locations on the game board. This is accomplished using an independent Sub procedure that generates random numbers and then uses the random numbers to shuffle the words. The application's TOE chart and MainForm are shown in Figures 8-36 and 8-37, respectively.

Task	Object	Event
1. Fill the list box with 8 pairs of matching words 2. Call a procedure to shuffle the words in the wordListBox	MainForm	Load
End the application	exitButton	Click
1. Clear the label controls and then enable them 2. Reset the counter, which is used by the 16 labels, to 0 3. Call a procedure to shuffle the words in the wordListBox	newButton	Click
1. Enable the boardTableLayoutPanel 2. Disable the matchTimer	matchTimer	Tick
1. Clear the words from the chosen labels 2. Enable the boardTableLayoutPanel 3. Disable the noMatchTimer	noMatchTimer	Tick
1. Use a counter to keep track of whether this is the first or second label clicked 2. If this is the first label clicked, display a word from the wordListBox in the label 3. If this is the second label clicked, disable the boardTableLayoutPanel, display a word from the wordListBox in the label, and then compare both words 4. If both words match, disable both labels and then turn on the matchTimer 5. If both words do not match, turn on the noMatchTimer 6. Reset the counter, which is used by the 16 labels, to 0	16 labels	Click
Store the 16 words	wordListBox	None
Display the game board	boardTableLayoutPanel	None

Figure 8-36 TOE chart for the Concentration Game application
© 2013 Cengage Learning

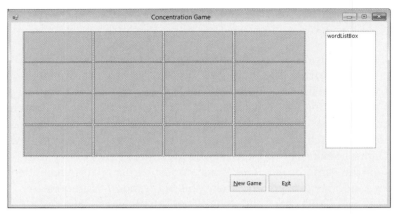

Figure 8-37 MainForm for the Concentration Game application

Coding the Application

According to the application's TOE chart, the MainForm's Load event procedure and the Click event procedures for the exitButton, newButton, and 16 labels need to be coded. You also need to code the Tick event procedures for the two timers. (If you need help while coding the application, you can look ahead to Figure 8-48.)

To open the Concentration Game application:

1. Start Visual Studio. Open the **Concentration Solution (Concentration Solution.sln)** file contained in the VbReloaded2012\Chap08\Concentration Solution folder. If necessary, open the designer window. The MainForm contains a table layout panel, 16 labels, two buttons, and a list box. The component tray contains two timers.

2. If necessary, permanently display the Properties window. On your own, click **each of the labels** in the table layout panel, one at a time. Notice that the TabIndex values in the Properties window range from 0 through 15. The TabIndex values will be used to access the appropriate word in the wordListBox, whose indexes also range from 0 through 15. Auto-hide the Properties window.

3. Open the Code Editor window, which already contains some of the application's code. In the comments that appear in the General Declarations section, replace <your name> and <current date> with your name and the current date, respectively.

First, you will complete the MainForm's Load event procedure, which is responsible for filling the wordListBox with eight pairs of matching words and then reordering the words. The procedure's pseudocode is shown in Figure 8-38.

MainForm Load event procedure
1. fill the wordListBox with 8 pairs of matching words
2. call the ShuffleWords procedure to reorder the words in the wordListBox

---

Figure 8-38 Pseudocode for the MainForm_Load procedure
© 2013 Cengage Learning

To complete the MainForm_Load procedure:

1. Scroll down the Code Editor window (if necessary) to view the code already entered in the MainForm_Load procedure. Notice that the first eight statements in the procedure add eight unique words to the wordListBox control, and the last eight statements duplicate the words in the control.

2. Save the solution and then start the application. The MainForm_Load procedure adds the 16 words to the list box, as shown in Figure 8-39. The words appear in the order in which they are added to the list box.

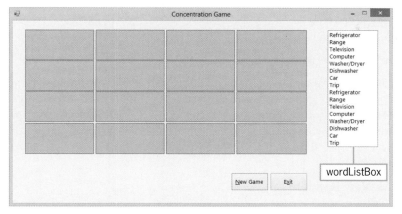

Figure 8-39   Sixteen words added to the wordListBox

3. Click the **Exit** button to end the application.

4. To complete the MainForm_Load procedure, you just need to enter a statement to call the ShuffleWords procedure, which will reorder (or shuffle) the words in the wordListBox. If you do not shuffle the words, they will appear in the exact same location on the game board each time the application is started. Shuffling the words makes the game more challenging because the user will never be sure exactly where each word will appear on the game board. The ShuffleWords procedure will be a Sub procedure because it will not need to return a value. The procedure will not be passed any data when it is invoked. Click the **blank line** above the End Sub clause in the MainForm_Load procedure, and then enter the appropriate Call statement. (Do not be concerned about the jagged line that appears below ShuffleWords in the Call statement. The line will disappear when you create the procedure in the next section.)

Coding the ShuffleWords Procedure

The ShuffleWords procedure is responsible for reordering the words in the wordListBox. Reordering the words will ensure that most of the words appear in different locations in each game. An easy way to reorder a list of words is to swap one word with another word. For example, you can swap the word that appears at the top of the list with the word that appears in the middle of the list. In this application, you will use random integers to select the positions of the two words to be swapped. You will perform the swap 40 times to ensure that the words are sufficiently reordered. The procedure's pseudocode is shown in Figure 8-40.

```
ShuffleWords procedure
repeat 40 times
     generate two random integers from 0 through 15
     use the random integers to swap words in the wordListBox
end repeat
```

Figure 8-40   Pseudocode for the ShuffleWords procedure
© 2013 Cengage Learning

To code the ShuffleWords procedure and then test the procedure:

1. Click the **blank line** immediately below the Public Class clause and then press **Enter** to insert another blank line. Type **Private Sub ShuffleWords()** and press **Enter**. The Code Editor enters the procedure footer for you. Notice that the jagged line no longer appears below the ShuffleWords name in the Load event procedure.

2. Type the following comment and then press **Enter** twice:

   ' shuffles the words in the wordListBox

3. The ShuffleWords procedure will use four variables. The `randGen` variable will represent the pseudo-random number generator in the procedure. The `index1` and `index2` variables will store two random integers from 0 through 15. Each integer corresponds to the index of a word in the wordListBox. The `temp` variable will be used during the swapping process. Enter the following Dim statements. Press **Enter** twice after typing the last Dim statement.

   Dim randGen As New Random
   Dim index1 As Integer
   Dim index2 As Integer
   Dim temp As String

4. The first step in the pseudocode is a loop that repeats its instructions 40 times. Enter the following For clause:

   For counter As Integer = 1 To 40

5. Change the Next clause to **Next counter**.

6. The first instruction in the loop will generate two random integers from 0 through 15. Click the **blank line** below the For clause, and then enter the following comment and assignment statements:

   ' generate two random numbers
   index1 = randGen.Next(0, 16)
   index2 = randGen.Next(0, 16)

7. The second instruction in the loop will use the random integers to swap the words in the wordListBox. You learned how to swap the contents of two variables in Chapter 4. You can use a similar process to swap two words in the wordListBox. The `index1` variable contains the index of the first word you want to swap. You begin by storing that word in the `temp` variable. Enter the following comment and assignment statement:

   ' swap two words
   temp = wordListBox.Items(index1).ToString

8. Next, you will replace the word located in the `index1` position in the wordListBox with the word located in the `index2` position. Enter the following assignment statement:

   wordListBox.Items(index1) =
   **   wordListBox.Items(index2)**

9. Finally, you will replace the word located in the `index2` position in the wordListBox with the word stored in the `temp` variable. On your own, enter the appropriate assignment statement.

10. If necessary, delete the blank line above the `Next counter` clause.

11. Save the solution and then start the application. The 16 words appear in the wordListBox. This time, however, they do not appear in the order in which they are entered in the Load event procedure. Instead, they appear in a random order. Click the **Exit** button to end the application.

Coding the Labels' Click Event Procedures

Next, you will code the Click event procedures for the 16 labels in the interface. Each label is associated with a word in the list box. The first label is associated with the first word, the second label with the second word, and so on.

When the user clicks a label, the label's Click event procedure will access the appropriate word in the wordListBox and then display the word in the label. For example, if the user clicks the first label on the game board, the Click event procedure will assign the first word in the list box to the label's Text property. After the user selects two labels, the procedure will determine whether the labels contain matching words. If the words match, they will remain visible in their respective labels. If the words do not match, the user will be given a short amount of time to memorize the location of the words before the words are hidden again. The pseudocode for the labels' Click event procedures is shown in Figure 8-41.

---

16 Labels' Click event procedure

1. add 1 to the selection counter, which keeps track of whether this is the first or second label selected on the game board
2. if this is the first label selected
     assign the current label's TabIndex property to an Integer variable named index1

     use the index1 variable to access the appropriate word in the wordListBox, and then display the word in the current label

  else (which means it is the second label selected)
     disable the game board to prevent the user from making another selection

     assign the current label's TabIndex property to an Integer variable named index2

     use the index2 variable to access the appropriate word in the wordListBox, and then display the word in the current label

     if the first label and second label contain the same word
          disable both labels on the game board
          turn the matchTimer on

     else
          turn the noMatchTimer on
     end if
     reset the selection counter to 0
  end if

Figure 8-41 Pseudocode for the 16 labels' Click event procedures
© 2013 Cengage Learning

To code the Click event procedures for the 16 labels:

1. Locate the TestForMatch procedure in the Code Editor window. The Handles clause indicates that the procedure will be processed when the Click event occurs for any of the 16 labels.

2. The TestForMatch procedure will use two Integer variables named `index1` and `index2`. The variables will store the TabIndex values associated with the two labels clicked by the user. The procedure will use the values to access the corresponding words in the wordListBox. For example, if the user clicks the Label1 control, which is located in the upper-left corner of the game board, the procedure will assign the control's TabIndex value—in this case, 0—to the `index1` variable. It then will use the value in the `index1` variable to access the appropriate word in the list box. The appropriate word is the one

whose index value matches the TabIndex value. Click the **blank line** above the End Sub clause in the TestForMatch procedure, and then enter the following Dim statements. Press **Enter** twice after typing the last Dim statement.

> **Dim index1 As Integer**
> **Dim index2 As Integer**

3. The procedure will also use three class-level variables named `selectionCounter`, `firstLabel`, and `secondLabel`. The variables need to be class-level variables because they will be used by more than one procedure in the application. The `selectionCounter` variable will keep track of whether the user has clicked one or two labels. The `firstLabel` and `secondLabel` variables will keep track of the labels the user clicked. Click the **blank line** below the Public Class clause and then press **Enter** to insert another blank line. Enter the following Private statements:

> **Private selectionCounter As Integer**
> **Private firstLabel As Label**
> **Private secondLabel As Label**

4. Click the **blank line** above the End Sub clause in the TestForMatch procedure. The first step in the pseudocode shown in Figure 8-41 adds the number 1 to the selection counter. Enter the following comment and assignment statement. Press **Enter** twice after typing the assignment statement.

> **' update the selection counter**
> **selectionCounter += 1**

5. The next step in the pseudocode is a dual-alternative selection structure whose condition determines whether this is the first label control selected by the user. Enter the following comment and If clause:

> **' determine whether this is the first or second selection**
> **If selectionCounter = 1 Then**

6. If this is the first of two labels selected on the game board, the selection structure's True path should assign the label's TabIndex value to the `index1` variable. First, however, you will need to use the `sender` parameter to determine the label that was clicked. Recall that the parameter contains a copy of the object that raised the event. Enter an assignment statement that uses the TryCast method to convert the `sender` parameter to the Label data type, assigning the result to the `firstLabel` variable. (Remember that if you need help, you can look ahead to Figure 8-48.)

7. Now, enter a statement that assigns the label's TabIndex property value to the `index1` variable.

8. Next, enter a statement that uses the `index1` variable to access the appropriate word in the wordListBox. The appropriate word is the one whose index matches the value contained in the `index1` variable. Assign the word to the label's Text property.

9. You have finished coding the selection structure's True path; you will code its False path next. Type **Else** and press **Tab** twice. Type **' second label selected** and press **Enter**.

10. If this is the second of two labels selected on the game board, the procedure will need to compare the contents of both labels before the user makes the next selection. Therefore, you will disable the game board, temporarily. Enter an assignment statement that changes the boardTableLayoutPanel control's Enabled property to **False**.

11. Next, enter an assignment statement that uses the TryCast method to convert the `sender` parameter to the Label data type, and then assigns the result to the `secondLabel` variable.

12. Now, enter a statement that assigns the label's TabIndex property value to the `index2` variable.

13. Next, enter a statement that uses the `index2` variable to access the appropriate word in the wordListBox. The appropriate word is the one whose index matches the value contained in the `index2` variable. Assign the word to the label's Text property.

14. The next instruction in the False path is a nested dual-alternative selection structure whose condition compares the contents of both labels. If both labels contain the same word, the nested structure's True path will disable the labels to prevent them from responding if the user inadvertently clicks them again; it will also turn on the matchTimer. If the labels do not contain the same word, the nested structure's False path will turn on the noMatchTimer. Enter the additional comment and selection structure shown in Figure 8-42, and then position the insertion point as shown in the figure.

```
Else      ' second label selected
    boardTableLayoutPanel.Enabled = False
    secondLabel = TryCast(sender, Label)
    index2 = secondLabel.TabIndex
    secondLabel.Text = wordListBox.Items(index2).ToString
    ' compare words in both labels
    If firstLabel.Text = secondLabel.Text Then       ← enter this comment and
        firstLabel.Enabled = False                      nested selection structure
        secondLabel.Enabled = False
        matchTimer.Enabled = True
    Else
        noMatchTimer.Enabled = True
    End If
    |                                       ← position the insertion
End If                                        point here
```

Figure 8-42   Nested selection structure entered in the TestForMatch procedure

15. The last instruction in the pseudocode (shown earlier in Figure 8-41) resets the selection counter to 0. Recall that the selection counter keeps track of whether the user has clicked one or two labels. Type ' **reset the selection counter** and press **Enter**. Then, enter an assignment statement to assign the number 0 to the `selectionCounter` variable.

16. Save the solution.

Coding Each Timer's Tick Event Procedure

Figure 8-43 shows the pseudocode for the matchTimer_Tick procedure, which performs two tasks. First, it enables the game board so the user can make another selection. Second, it turns off the matchTimer. Turning off the timer stops the timer's Tick event and prevents its code from being processed again. The matchTimer_Tick procedure will not be processed again until the timer is turned back on, which happens when the user locates a matching pair of words on the game board.

```
matchTimer Tick event procedure
1.  enable the game board
2.  turn the matchTimer off
```

Figure 8-43   Pseudocode for the matchTimer_Tick procedure
© 2013 Cengage Learning

To code the matchTimer's Tick event procedure:

1. Locate the matchTimer_Tick procedure in the Code Editor window.

2. Click the **blank line** above the procedure's End Sub clause. Enter an assignment statement to enable the boardTableLayoutPanel.

3. Next, enter an assignment statement to disable the matchTimer.

Figure 8-44 shows the pseudocode for the noMatchTimer_Tick procedure, which performs three tasks. The first task clears the contents of the label controls associated with the firstLabel and secondLabel variables. The second task enables the game board so the user can make another selection. The third task turns off the noMatchTimer to prevent the timer's Tick event from occurring and, therefore, prevent its code from being processed. The noMatchTimer_Tick procedure will not be processed again until the timer is turned back on, which happens when the two labels selected by the user contain different words.

---

noMatchTimer Tick event procedure
1. clear the contents of the labels associated with the firstLabel and secondLabel variables
2. enable the game board
3. turn the noMatchTimer off

Figure 8-44   Pseudocode for the noMatchTimer_Tick procedure
© 2013 Cengage Learning

To code the noMatchTimer_Tick procedure:

1. Locate the noMatchTimer_Tick procedure in the Code Editor window, and then click the **blank line** above the procedure's End Sub clause.

2. Enter two assignment statements to clear the Text properties of the labels associated with the firstLabel and secondLabel variables.

3. Now, enter an assignment statement to enable the boardTableLayoutPanel.

4. Next, enter an assignment statement to disable the noMatchTimer.

5. Save the solution.

Coding the New Game Button's Click Event Procedure

The last procedure you need to code is the newButton's Click event procedure. The procedure's pseudocode is shown in Figure 8-45. The first two steps have already been coded for you in the Code Editor window.

---

newButton Click event procedure
1. clear the contents of the 16 labels
2. enable the 16 labels
3. reset the selection counter to 0
4. call the ShuffleWords procedure to reorder the words in the wordsListBox

---

Figure 8-45   Pseudocode for the newButton_Click procedure
© 2013 Cengage Learning

To complete the newButton_Click procedure:

1. Locate the newButton_Click procedure in the Code Editor window, and then click the **blank line** above the procedure's End Sub clause.

2. Enter an assignment statement to assign the number 0 to the `selectionCounter` variable.

3. Now, enter a statement to call the ShuffleWords procedure.

Testing the Concentration Game Application

In this section, you will test the application to verify that it is working correctly.

To test the Concentration Game application:

1. Save the solution and then start the application. Click the **label in the upper-left corner of the game board**. The TestForMatch procedure (which is associated with the label's Click event) assigns the first word in the wordListBox to the label's Text property. See Figure 8-46. Recall that the ShuffleWords procedure uses random integers to reorder the list of words in the list box. Therefore, the first word in your list box, as well as the word in the Label1 control, might be different from the one shown in the figure.

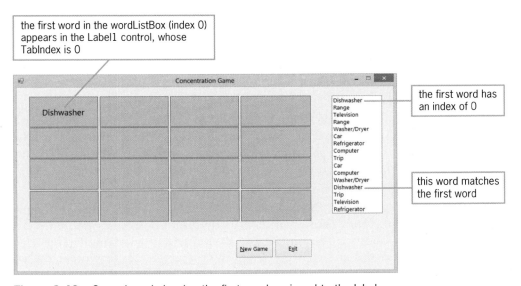

the first word in the wordListBox (index 0) appears in the Label1 control, whose TabIndex is 0

the first word has an index of 0

this word matches the first word

Figure 8-46 Game board showing the first word assigned to the label

2. First, you will test the code that handles two matching words. To do this, you will need to find the word in the list box that matches the first word, and then click its associated label on the game board. Count down the list of words in the list box on your screen, stopping when you reach the word that matches the first word in your list box. In Figure 8-46, the word that matches the first word (Dishwasher) is the thirteenth word in the list box.

3. Now count each label, from left to right, beginning with the first row on the game board. Stop counting when you reach the label whose number is the same as in the previous step. In Figure 8-46, for example, you would stop counting when you reached the thirteenth label, which is located in the first column of the fourth row. Click the **label associated with the matching word**. See Figure 8-47.

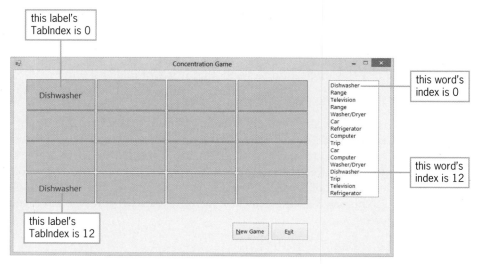

Figure 8-47 Game board showing that both labels contain the same word

4. Click the **Label1 control** again. Nothing happens because the TestForMatch procedure disables the label when its matching word is found.

5. Now, you will test the code that handles two words that do not match. First, click any **blank label control on the game board**. Now, click **another blank label control**; however, be sure that the second label's word is not the same as the first label's word. Because both words are not the same, they are hidden after a short time.

6. Finally, you will verify that the code entered in the newButton_Click procedure works correctly. Click the **New Game** button. The button's Click event procedure clears the contents of the label controls and also enables them. In addition, it resets the selection counter to 0 and calls the ShuffleWords procedure to reorder the words in the list box.

7. On your own, test the application several more times. When you are finished, click the **Exit** button to end the application.

8. Now that you know that the application works correctly, you can resize the form to hide the list box. Close the Code Editor window. Unlock the controls on the form and then drag the form's right border until the list box is no longer visible. Lock the controls on the form.

9. Save the solution and then close it. Figure 8-48 shows the application's code.

```
 1  ' Project name:        Concentration Project
 2  ' Project purpose:     Simulates the Concentration game,
 3  '                      where a player tries to find
 4  '                      matching pairs of words
 5  ' Created/revised by:  <your name> on <current date>
 6
 7  Option Explicit On
 8  Option Strict On
 9  Option Infer Off
10
11  Public Class MainForm
12
13      Private selectionCounter As Integer
14      Private firstLabel As Label
15      Private secondLabel As Label
16
17      Private Sub ShuffleWords()
18          ' shuffles the words in the wordListBox
19
20          Dim randGen As New Random
21          Dim index1 As Integer
22          Dim index2 As Integer
23          Dim temp As String
24
25          For counter As Integer = 1 To 40
26              ' generate two random numbers
27              index1 = randGen.Next(0, 16)
28              index2 = randGen.Next(0, 16)
29              ' swap two words
30              temp = wordListBox.Items(index1).ToString
31              wordListBox.Items(index1) =
32                  wordListBox.Items(index2)
33              wordListBox.Items(index2) = temp
34          Next counter
35      End Sub
36
37      Private Sub MainForm_Load(sender As Object,
        e As EventArgs) Handles Me.Load
38          ' fills the list box with 8 pairs of matching
39          ' words, then calls a procedure to shuffle
40          ' the words
41
42          wordListBox.Items.Add("Refrigerator")
43          wordListBox.Items.Add("Range")
44          wordListBox.Items.Add("Television")
45          wordListBox.Items.Add("Computer")
46          wordListBox.Items.Add("Washer/Dryer")
47          wordListBox.Items.Add("Dishwasher")
48          wordListBox.Items.Add("Car")
49          wordListBox.Items.Add("Trip")
50          wordListBox.Items.Add("Refrigerator")
51          wordListBox.Items.Add("Range")
52          wordListBox.Items.Add("Television")
53          wordListBox.Items.Add("Computer")
54          wordListBox.Items.Add("Washer/Dryer")
55          wordListBox.Items.Add("Dishwasher")
56          wordListBox.Items.Add("Car")
57          wordListBox.Items.Add("Trip")
58
59          Call ShuffleWords()
60
61      End Sub
```

Figure 8-48 Code for the Concentration Game application *(continues)*

(continued)

```
62
63      Private Sub exitButton_Click(sender As Object,
        e As EventArgs) Handles exitButton.Click
64          Me.Close()
65      End Sub
66
67      Private Sub newButton_Click(sender As Object,
        e As EventArgs) Handles newButton.Click
68          ' removes any words from the label controls, then
69          ' enables the label controls, then resets the
70          ' selection counter, and then calls a procedure
71          ' to shuffle the words
72
73          Label1.Text = String.Empty
74          Label2.Text = String.Empty
75          Label3.Text = String.Empty
76          Label4.Text = String.Empty
77          Label5.Text = String.Empty
78          Label6.Text = String.Empty
79          Label7.Text = String.Empty
80          Label8.Text = String.Empty
81          Label9.Text = String.Empty
82          Label10.Text = String.Empty
83          Label11.Text = String.Empty
84          Label12.Text = String.Empty
85          Label13.Text = String.Empty
86          Label14.Text = String.Empty
87          Label15.Text = String.Empty
88          Label16.Text = String.Empty
89
90          Label1.Enabled = True
91          Label2.Enabled = True
92          Label3.Enabled = True
93          Label4.Enabled = True
94          Label5.Enabled = True
95          Label6.Enabled = True
96          Label7.Enabled = True
97          Label8.Enabled = True
98          Label9.Enabled = True
99          Label10.Enabled = True
100         Label11.Enabled = True
101         Label12.Enabled = True
102         Label13.Enabled = True
103         Label14.Enabled = True
104         Label15.Enabled = True
105         Label16.Enabled = True
106
107         selectionCounter = 0
108         Call ShuffleWords()
109
110     End Sub
111
112     Private Sub TestForMatch(sender As Object,
        e As EventArgs) Handles Label1.Click,
113     Label2.Click, Label3.Click, Label4.Click, Label5.Click,
        Label6.Click, Label7.Click,
114     Label8.Click, Label9.Click, Label10.Click, Label11.Click,
        Label12.Click, Label13.Click,
115     Label14.Click, Label15.Click, Label16.Click
116         ' displays the appropriate words and determines
117         ' whether the user selected a matching pair
118
```

Figure 8-48 Code for the Concentration Game application *(continues)*

(continued)

```
119         Dim index1 As Integer
120         Dim index2 As Integer
121
122         ' update the selection counter
123         selectionCounter += 1
124
125         ' determine whether this is the first or second selection
126         If selectionCounter = 1 Then
127             firstLabel = TryCast(sender, Label)
128             index1 = firstLabel.TabIndex
129             firstLabel.Text = wordListBox.Items(index1).ToString
130         Else    ' second label selected
131             boardTableLayoutPanel.Enabled = False
132             secondLabel = TryCast(sender, Label)
133             index2 = secondLabel.TabIndex
134             secondLabel.Text = wordListBox.Items(index2).ToString
135             ' compare words in both labels
136             If firstLabel.Text = secondLabel.Text Then
137                 firstLabel.Enabled = False
138                 secondLabel.Enabled = False
139                 matchTimer.Enabled = True
140             Else
141                 noMatchTimer.Enabled = True
142             End If
143
144             ' reset the selection counter
145             selectionCounter = 0
146
147         End If
148     End Sub
149
150     Private Sub matchTimer_Tick(sender As Object,
        e As EventArgs) Handles matchTimer.Tick
151         ' when the two words match, the game board is
152         ' enabled and the timer is turned off
153
154         boardTableLayoutPanel.Enabled = True
155         matchTimer.Enabled = False
156
157     End Sub
158
159     Private Sub noMatchTimer_Tick(sender As Object,
        e As EventArgs) Handles noMatchTimer.Tick
160         ' when the words do not match, the words are
161         ' removed from the labels, the game board is
162         ' enabled, and the timer is turned off
163
164         firstLabel.Text = String.Empty
165         secondLabel.Text = String.Empty
166         boardTableLayoutPanel.Enabled = True
167         noMatchTimer.Enabled = False
168
169     End Sub
170 End Class
```

Figure 8-48   Code for the Concentration Game application

© 2013 Cengage Learning

PROGRAMMING EXAMPLE

Rainfall Calculator Application

Create an application that allows the user to enter monthly rainfall amounts in a text box. The application should calculate and display two amounts: the total rainfall and the average rainfall. Use the following names for the solution and project, respectively: Rainfall Solution and Rainfall Project. Save the application in the VbReloaded2012\Chap08 folder. Change the form file's name to Main Form.vb. See Figures 8-49 through 8-53.

Task	Object	Event
1. Use a counter and an accumulator to keep track of the number of rainfall amounts entered and the total rainfall	calcButton	Click
2. Call a procedure to calculate the average rainfall		
3. Display the total rainfall and average rainfall in totalLabel and averageLabel		
4. Send the focus to the monthTextBox		
5. Select the monthTextBox's existing text		
End the application	exitButton	Click
Display the total rainfall amount (from calcButton)	totalLabel	None
Display the average rainfall amount (from calcButton)	averageLabel	None
Get and display the monthly rainfall amounts	monthTextBox	None
Select the existing text		Enter
Allow numbers, the period, and the Backspace key		KeyPress
Clear totalLabel and averageLabel		TextChanged

Figure 8-49 TOE chart

© 2013 Cengage Learning

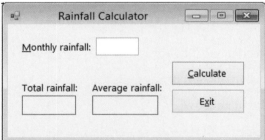
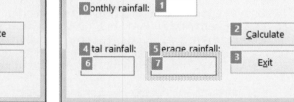

Figure 8-50 MainForm and tab order

Object	Property	Setting
MainForm	AcceptButton	calcButton
	Font	Segoe UI, 10pt
	MaximizeBox	False
	StartPosition	CenterScreen
	Text	Rainfall Calculator
totalLabel	AutoSize	False
	BorderStyle	FixedSingle
	Text	(empty)
	TextAlign	MiddleCenter
averageLabel	AutoSize	False
	BorderStyle	FixedSingle
	Text	(empty)
	TextAlign	MiddleCenter

Figure 8-51 Objects, properties, and settings
© 2013 Cengage Learning

exitButton Click event procedure
close the application

monthTextBox Enter event procedure
select the existing text

monthTextBox KeyPress event procedure
allow only numbers, the period, and the Backspace key

monthTextBox TextChanged event procedure
clear the contents of totalLabel and averageLabel

calcButton Click event procedure
1. if the monthTextBox is not empty
        add the monthly rainfall to the total rainfall accumulator
        add 1 to the rainfall counter
    end if
2. Call the CalcAverage procedure to calculate the average rainfall; pass the procedure the rainfall
    counter and rainfall accumulator values, and also the address of a variable in which to store the
    average rainfall
3. send the focus to the monthTextBox
4. select the existing text in the monthTextBox

CalcAverage procedure (receives the rainfall counter and rainfall accumulator values and the address of a
variable in which to store the average rainfall)
if the rainfall counter > 0
        average rainfall = rainfall accumulator / rainfall counter
else
        average rainfall = 0
end if

Figure 8-52 Pseudocode
© 2013 Cengage Learning

454

```
1 ' Project name:        Rainfall Project
2 ' Project purpose:     Displays the total and average
3 '                      rainfall amounts
4 ' Created/revised by:  <your name> on <current date>
5
6 Option Explicit On
7 Option Strict On
8 Option Infer Off
9
10 Public Class MainForm
11
12     Private Sub CalcAverage(ByVal counter As Integer,
13                             ByVal accumulator As Decimal,
14                             ByRef avg As Decimal)
15         ' calculates the average rainfall amount
16
17         If counter > 0 Then
18             avg = accumulator / counter
19         Else
20             avg = 0
21         End If
22     End Sub
23
24     Private Sub exitButton_Click(sender As Object,
    e As EventArgs) Handles exitButton.Click
25         Me.Close()
26     End Sub
27
28     Private Sub calcButton_Click(sender As Object,
    e As EventArgs) Handles calcButton.Click
29         ' displays the total and average rainfall amount
30
31         Static rainCounter As Integer
32         Static rainAccum As Decimal
33         Dim monthRain As Decimal
34         Dim avgRain As Decimal
35
36         If monthTextBox.Text <> String.Empty Then
37             Decimal.TryParse(monthTextBox.Text, monthRain)
38             ' update the accumulator and counter
39             rainAccum += monthRain
40             rainCounter += 1
41         End If
42
43         ' calculate the average
44         Call CalcAverage(rainCounter, rainAccum, avgRain)
45
46         totalLabel.Text = rainAccum.ToString("N2")
47         averageLabel.Text = avgRain.ToString("N2")
48         monthTextBox.Focus()
49         monthTextBox.SelectAll()
50     End Sub
51
52     Private Sub monthTextBox_Enter(sender As Object,
    e As EventArgs) Handles monthTextBox.Enter
53         monthTextBox.SelectAll()
54     End Sub
55
56     Private Sub monthTextBox_KeyPress(sender As Object,
    e As KeyPressEventArgs) Handles monthTextBox.KeyPress
57         ' allow numbers, period, and Backspace
58
```

Figure 8-53 Code (continues)

(continued)

```
59          If (e.KeyChar < "0" OrElse e.KeyChar > "9") AndAlso
60          e.KeyChar <> "." AndAlso e.KeyChar <> ControlChars.Back Then
61              e.Handled = True
62          End If
63      End Sub
64
65      Private Sub monthTextBox_TextChanged(sender As Object,
          e As EventArgs) Handles monthTextBox.TextChanged
66          totalLabel.Text = String.Empty
67          averageLabel.Text = String.Empty
68      End Sub
69 End Class
```

Figure 8-53   Code
© 2013 Cengage Learning

Summary

- An event procedure is a Sub procedure that is associated with one or more objects and events.

- Independent Sub procedures and Function procedures are not associated with any specific object or event. The names of independent Sub procedures and Function procedures typically begin with a verb.

- The difference between a Sub procedure and a Function procedure is that a Function procedure returns a value, whereas a Sub procedure does not return a value.

- Procedures allow programmers to avoid duplicating code in different parts of a program. They also allow the programmer to concentrate on one small piece of a program at a time. In addition, they allow a team of programmers to work on large and complex programs.

- You can use the Call statement to invoke an independent Sub procedure. The Call statement allows you to pass arguments to the Sub procedure.

- When calling a procedure, the number of arguments listed in the argumentList should agree with the number of parameters listed in the parameterList in the procedure header. Also, the data type and position of each argument in the argumentList should agree with the data type and position of its corresponding parameter in the parameterList.

- You can pass information to a Sub or Function procedure either *by value* or *by reference*. To pass a variable *by value*, you precede the variable's corresponding parameter with the keyword ByVal. To pass a variable *by reference*, you precede the variable's corresponding parameter with the keyword ByRef. The procedure header indicates whether a variable is being passed *by value* or *by reference*.

- When you pass a variable *by value*, only a copy of the variable's contents is passed. When you pass a variable *by reference*, the variable's address is passed.

- Variables that appear in the parameterList in a procedure header have procedure scope, which means they can be used only by the procedure.

- You can use an event procedure's Handles clause to associate the procedure with more than one object and event.

- You invoke a Function procedure, also called a function, by including its name and any arguments in a statement. Usually the statement assigns the function's return value to a variable. However, it also may use the return value in a calculation or display the return value.

- You can use the TryCast operator to convert an Object variable to a different data type.

- The purpose of a timer control is to process code at one or more specified intervals. You start a timer by setting its Enabled property to True. You stop a timer by setting its Enabled property to False. You use a timer's Interval property to specify the number of milliseconds that must elapse before the timer's Tick event occurs.

Key Terms

Call statement—the statement used to invoke an independent Sub procedure in a Visual Basic program

Casting—another term for type casting

CheckedChanged event—occurs when the value in the Checked property of either a radio button or a check box changes

Desk-checking—the process of manually walking through your code, using sample data; also called hand-tracing

e parameter—one of the parameters in an event procedure's header; contains additional information provided by the object that raised the event

Function procedure—a procedure that returns a value after performing its assigned task; also called a function

Functions—another term for Function procedures

Hand-tracing—another term for desk-checking

Independent Sub procedure—a procedure that is not associated with any specific object or event and is processed only when invoked (called) from code

Interval property—a property of a timer control; stores the length of each interval

Parameter—a memory location listed in a procedure header; stores an item of data passed to the procedure when it is invoked

Passing by reference—refers to the process of passing a variable's address to a procedure so that the value in the variable can be changed

Passing by value—refers to the process of passing a copy of a variable's value to a procedure

Return statement—returns a function's value to the statement that invoked the function

sender parameter—one of the parameters in an event procedure's header; contains a copy of the object that raised the event

Tick event—one of the events of a timer control; occurs each time an interval has elapsed

Timer control—used to process code at one or more regular intervals

TryCast operator—used to convert an Object variable to a different data type

Type casting—the process of converting a variable from one data type to another; also called casting

Each Review Question is associated with one or more objectives listed at the beginning of the chapter.

Review Questions

1. To determine whether a variable is being passed to a procedure *by value* or *by reference*, you will need to examine _____ . (2, 3)

    a. the Call statement

    b. the procedure header

    c. the statements entered in the procedure

    d. either a or b

2. Which of the following invokes the CalcArea Sub procedure, passing it two variables *by value*? (1-3)

   a. `Call CalcArea(length, width)`

   b. `Call CalcArea(ByVal length, ByVal width)`

   c. `Invoke CalcArea ByVal(length, width)`

   d. `CalcArea(length, width) As Double`

3. Which of the following is a valid header for a procedure that receives an integer followed by a number with a decimal place? (1-3)

   a. `Private Sub CalcFee(base As Integer, rate As Number)`

   b. `Private Sub CalcFee(ByRef base As Integer, ByRef rate As Decimal)`

   c. `Private Sub CalcFee(ByVal base As Integer, ByVal rate As Decimal)`

   d. none of the above

4. Which of the following indicates that the procedure should be processed when the user clicks either the firstCheckBox or the secondCheckBox? (6)

   a. `Private Sub Clear(sender As Object, e As EventArgs)`
      `Handles firstCheckBox.Click, secondCheckBox.Click`

   b. `Private Sub Clear(sender As Object, e As EventArgs)`
      `Handles firstCheckBox_Click, secondCheckBox_Click`

   c. `Private Sub Clear_Click(sender As Object, e As EventArgs)`
      `Handles firstCheckBox, secondCheckBox`

   d. `Private Sub Clear(sender As Object, e As EventArgs)`
      `Handles firstCheckBox.Click AndAlso secondCheckBox.Click`

5. Which of the following is false? (1-3)

   a. The position of the arguments listed in the Call statement should agree with the position of the parameters listed in the receiving procedure's parameterList.

   b. The data type of each argument in the Call statement should match the data type of its corresponding parameter in the receiving procedure's parameterList.

   c. The name of each argument in the Call statement should be identical to the name of its corresponding parameter in the receiving procedure's parameterList.

   d. When you pass items of data to a procedure *by value*, the procedure stores the value of each item it receives in a separate memory location.

6. Which of the following instructs a function to return the contents of the `stateTax` variable? (9)

   a. `Return stateTax`

   b. `Return stateTax ByVal`

   c. `Return ByVal stateTax`

   d. `Return ByRef stateTax`

7. Which of the following is a valid header for a procedure that receives the value stored in an Integer variable first, and the address of a Decimal variable second? (1-3)

   a. `Private Sub CalcFee(ByVal base As Integer,`
                `ByAdd rate As Decimal)`

   b. `Private Sub CalcFee(base As Integer,`
                `rate As Decimal)`

   c. `Private Sub CalcFee(ByVal base As Integer,`
                `ByRef rate As Decimal)`

   d. none of the above

458

8. Which of the following is false? (2, 3, 5)

    a. When you pass a variable *by reference*, the receiving procedure can change its contents.

    b. To pass a variable *by reference* in Visual Basic, you include the keyword `ByRef` before the variable's name in the Call statement.

    c. When you pass a variable *by value*, the receiving procedure creates a procedure-level variable that it uses to store the value passed to it.

    d. At times, a computer memory location may have more than one name.

9. A Sub procedure named CalcEnd is passed four Integer variables named `begin`, `sales`, `purchases`, and `ending`. The procedure should calculate the ending inventory using the beginning inventory, sales, and purchase amounts passed to the procedure. The result should be stored in the `ending` variable. Which of the following procedure headers is correct? (1-3)

    a. `Private Sub CalcEnd(ByVal b As Integer, ByVal s As Integer, ByVal p As Integer, ByRef final As Integer)`

    b. `Private Sub CalcEnd(ByVal b As Integer, ByVal s As Integer, ByVal p As Integer, ByVal final As Integer)`

    c. `Private Sub CalcEnd(ByRef b As Integer, ByRef s As Integer, ByRef p As Integer, ByVal final As Integer)`

    d. `Private Sub CalcEnd(ByRef b As Integer, ByRef s As Integer, ByRef p As Integer, ByRef final As Integer)`

10. Which of the following statements should you use to call the CalcEnd procedure described in Review Question 9? (1-3)

    a. `Call CalcEnd(begin, sales, purchases, ending)`

    b. `Call CalcEnd(ByVal begin, ByVal sales, ByVal purchases, ByRef ending)`

    c. `Call CalcEnd(ByRef begin, ByRef sales, ByRef purchases, ByRef ending)`

    d. `Call CalcEnd(ByVal begin, ByVal sales, ByVal purchases, ByVal ending)`

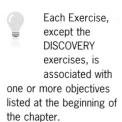

Each Exercise, except the DISCOVERY exercises, is associated with one or more objectives listed at the beginning of the chapter.

Exercises

Pencil and Paper

INTRODUCTORY

1. Explain the difference between a Sub procedure and a function. (8)

INTRODUCTORY

2. Explain the difference between passing a variable *by value* and passing it *by reference*. (3)

INTRODUCTORY

3. Explain the difference between invoking a Sub procedure and invoking a function. (1, 8, 9)

INTRODUCTORY

4. Write the code for a Sub procedure that receives a Double number passed to it. The procedure should divide the number by 2 and then display the result in the numLabel. Name the procedure DivideByTwo. Then write a statement to invoke the procedure, passing it the number 120. (1-3)

INTRODUCTORY

5. Write the code for a Sub procedure named GetCountry. The procedure should prompt the user to enter the name of a country. It should store the user's response in its String parameter, which is named `countryName`. Then write a statement to invoke the procedure, passing it the `country` variable. (1-3)

6. Write the code for a function named GetCountry. The function should prompt the user to enter the name of a country and then return the user's response. Then write a statement to invoke the function. Display the function's return value in a message box. (2, 3, 9)

INTRODUCTORY

7. Write the code for a Sub procedure that receives three Double variables: the first two *by value* and the last one *by reference*. The procedure should divide the first variable by the second variable and then store the result in the third variable. Name the procedure CalcQuotient. (1-3)

INTRODUCTORY

8. Write the code for a function that receives a copy of the value stored in an Integer variable. The procedure should divide the value by 2 and then return the result, which may contain a decimal place. Name the function GetQuotient. Then write an appropriate statement to invoke the function, passing it the `number` variable. Assign the function's return value to the `answer` variable. (2, 3, 9)

INTRODUCTORY

9. Write the code for a function that receives a copy of the contents of four Integer variables. The function should calculate the average of the four integers and then return the result, which may contain a decimal place. Name the function GetAverage. Then write a statement to invoke the function, passing it the `num1`, `num2`, `num3`, and `num4` variables. Assign the function's return value to a Double variable named `average`. (2, 3, 9)

INTERMEDIATE

10. Write the code for a Sub procedure that receives four Integer variables: the first two *by value* and the last two *by reference*. The procedure should calculate both the sum of and the difference between the two variables passed *by value*, and then store the results in the variables passed *by reference*. When calculating the difference, subtract the contents of the second variable from the contents of the first variable. Name the procedure GetSumAndDiff. Then write an appropriate statement to invoke the procedure, passing it the `first`, `second`, `sum`, and `difference` variables. (1-3)

INTERMEDIATE

11. Write the procedure header for a Sub procedure named CalculateTax. The procedure should be invoked when any of the following occurs: the rate1Button's Click event, the rate2Button's Click event, and the salesListBox's SelectedValueChanged event. (6)

INTERMEDIATE

12. Write the statement to convert the `sender` parameter to a radio button. Assign the result to a RadioButton variable named `currentRadioButton`. (7, 10)

INTERMEDIATE

Computer

13. In this exercise, you experiment with passing variables *by value* and *by reference*. (1-3)

MODIFY THIS

a. Open the Passing Solution (Passing Solution.sln) file contained in the VbReloaded2012\Chap08\Passing Solution folder. Open the Code Editor window and review the existing code. Notice that the `myName` variable is passed *by value* to the GetName procedure. Start the application. Click the Display Name button. When prompted to enter a name, type your name and press Enter. Explain why the displayButton_Click procedure does not display your name in the nameLabel. Stop the application.

b. Modify the code so that it passes the `myName` variable *by reference* to the GetName procedure. Save the solution and then start the application. Click the Display Name button. When prompted to enter a name, type your name and press Enter. This time, your name appears in the nameLabel. Explain why the displayButton_Click procedure now works correctly. Stop the application and close the solution.

MODIFY THIS ▸   14.   Open the Actor Actress Solution (Actor Actress Solution.sln) file contained in the VbReloaded2012\Chap08\Actor Actress Solution folder. Modify the interface and code to allow the user to also enter the title of his or her favorite movie. Save the solution and then start and test the application. Close the solution. (1-4)

MODIFY THIS ▸   15.   If necessary, complete the Tri-County Electricity application from this chapter's Programming Tutorial 1, and then close the solution. Use Windows to make a copy of the Tri-County Solution folder. Rename the folder Tri-County Solution-ModifyThis. Open the Tri-County Solution (Tri-County Solution.sln) file contained in the Tri-County Solution-ModifyThis folder. Modify the code so that it uses a function named GetResidentialTotal (rather than the CalcResidentialTotal Sub procedure) to calculate the charge for residential customers. Also modify the code so that it uses a Sub procedure named CalcCommercialTotal (rather than the GetCommercialTotal function) to calculate the charge for commercial customers. Save the solution and then start and test the application. Close the solution. (1-3, 8, 9)

MODIFY THIS ▸   16.   If necessary, complete the Concentration Game application from this chapter's Programming Tutorial 2, and then close the solution. Use Windows to make a copy of the Concentration Solution folder. Rename the folder Concentration Solution-ModifyThis. Open the Concentration Solution (Concentration Solution.sln) file contained in the Concentration Solution-ModifyThis folder. When the user finds a matching pair of words, change the BackColor property of the corresponding labels to a different color. Be sure to return the labels to their original color when the user clicks the New Game button. Also modify the application so that it displays the message "Game Over" when the user has located all of the matching pairs. In addition, modify the code so that it doesn't allow the user to click the same label for both the first and second selection. Save the solution and then start and test the application. Close the solution. (6, 7, 10)

MODIFY THIS ▸   17.   If necessary, complete the Rainfall Calculator application from this chapter's Programming Example, and then close the solution. Use Windows to make a copy of the Rainfall Solution folder. Rename the folder Rainfall Solution-ModifyThis. Open the Rainfall Solution (Rainfall Solution.sln) file contained in the Rainfall Solution-ModifyThis folder. Replace the CalcAverage procedure with a function named GetAverage. Save the solution and then start and test the application. Close the solution. (2, 3, 8, 9)

INTRODUCTORY ▸   18.   Open the Bonus Calculator Solution (Bonus Calculator Solution.sln) file contained in the VbReloaded2012\Chap08\Bonus Calculator Solution folder. Code the application, using a Sub procedure to both calculate and display a 10% bonus. Also use a Sub procedure named ClearLabel to clear the contents of the bonusLabel when the TextChanged event occurs for either text box. In addition, associate each text box's Enter event with a procedure that selects the contents of the text box. Save the solution and then start and test the application. Close the solution. (1-3, 6, 7, 10)

INTRODUCTORY ▸   19.   Open the Car Solution (Car Solution.sln) file contained in the VbReloaded2012\Chap08\Car Solution folder. When the Click Me button is clicked, the "I WANT THIS CAR!" message should blink 14 times. Add a timer control to the application. Code the control's Tick event procedure. Save the solution and then start and test the application. Close the solution. (11)

INTRODUCTORY ▸   20.   Open the Gross Pay Solution (Gross Pay Solution.sln) file contained in the VbReloaded2012\Chap08\Gross Pay Solution-Sub folder. The application should display an employee's gross pay. Employees receive time and one-half for the hours worked over 40. Use a Sub procedure to calculate the gross pay. Display the gross pay with a dollar sign and two decimal places. Save the solution and then start and test the application. Close the solution. (1-3)

21. Open the Gross Pay Solution (Gross Pay Solution.sln) file contained in the VbReloaded2012\Chap08\Gross Pay Solution-Function folder. The application should display an employee's gross pay. Employees receive time and one-half for the hours worked over 40. Use a function to calculate and return the gross pay. Display the gross pay with a dollar sign and two decimal places. Save the solution and then start and test the application. Close the solution. (2, 3, 9)

INTRODUCTORY

22. Open the Circle Area Solution (Circle Area Solution.sln) file contained in the VbReloaded2012\Chap08\Circle Area Solution-Sub folder. The application should display the area of a circle. Use 3.141593 as the value of pi. Use a Sub procedure to calculate the area. Display the area with two decimal places. Create a desk-check table for the application; use 10 as the radius. Save the solution and then start and test the application. Close the solution. (1-3, 5)

INTRODUCTORY

23. Open the Circle Area Solution (Circle Area Solution.sln) file contained in the VbReloaded2012\Chap08\Circle Area Solution-Function folder. The application should display the area of a circle. Use 3.141593 as the value of pi. Use a function to calculate and return the area. Display the area with two decimal places. Create a desk-check table for the application; use 10 as the radius. Save the solution and then start and test the application. Close the solution. (2, 3, 5, 9)

INTRODUCTORY

24. If necessary, complete the Rainfall Calculator application from this chapter's Programming Example, and then close the solution. Use Windows to make a copy of the Rainfall Solution folder. Rename the folder Rainfall Solution-Intermediate. Open the Rainfall Solution (Rainfall Solution.sln) file contained in the Rainfall Solution-Intermediate folder. Modify the code so that it uses two functions rather than the CalcAverage procedure. One of the functions should calculate and return the total rainfall; the other should calculate and return the average rainfall. Save the solution and then start and test the application. Close the solution. (2, 3, 9)

INTERMEDIATE

25. Use Windows to make a copy of the Temperature Solution folder contained in the VbReloaded2012\Chap08 folder. Rename the folder Temperature Solution-Subs. Open the Temperature Solution (Temperature Solution.sln) file contained in the Temperature Solution-Subs folder. Code the application so that it uses two independent Sub procedures: one to convert a temperature from Fahrenheit to Celsius, and the other to convert a temperature from Celsius to Fahrenheit. Save the solution and then start and test the application. Close the solution. (1-3)

INTERMEDIATE

26. Use Windows to make a copy of the Temperature Solution folder contained in the VbReloaded2012\Chap08 folder. Rename the folder Temperature Solution-Functions. Open the Temperature Solution (Temperature Solution.sln) file contained in the Temperature Solution-Functions folder. Code the application so that it uses two functions: one to convert a temperature from Fahrenheit to Celsius, and the other to convert a temperature from Celsius to Fahrenheit. Save the solution and then start and test the application. Close the solution. (2, 3, 9)

INTERMEDIATE

27. Open the Translator Solution (Translator Solution.sln) file contained in the VbReloaded2012\Chap08\Translator Solution-Functions folder. Code the application so that it uses three functions to translate the English words into French, Spanish, or Italian. (Hint: If the Code Editor indicates that a String variable is being passed before it has been assigned a value, assign the String.Empty constant to the variable in its Dim statement.) Clear the label when a different radio button is selected. Save the solution and then start and test the application. Close the solution. (2-4, 9)

INTERMEDIATE

28. Open the Translator Solution (Translator Solution.sln) file contained in the VbReloaded2012\Chap08\Translator Solution-Subs folder. Code the application so that it uses three independent Sub procedures to translate the English words into French, Spanish, or Italian. (Hint: If the Code Editor indicates that a String variable is being

INTERMEDIATE

passed before it has been assigned a value, assign the String.Empty constant to the variable in its Dim statement.) Clear the label when a different radio button is selected. Save the solution and then start and test the application. Close the solution. (1-4, 9)

INTERMEDIATE   29.   Create an application that displays the subtotal, discount, and total due for concert tickets purchased from Concert-Mania Inc. Use the following names for the solution and project, respectively: Concert Solution and Concert Project. Save the solution in the VbReloaded2012\Chap08 folder. Change the form file's name to Main Form.vb. The company's ticket prices are shown in Figure 8-54. Use a text box to get the number of tickets purchased, and use radio buttons to determine whether the tickets are Standard or VIP tickets. The text box should accept only integers and the Backspace key. Use a function to get the appropriate discount rate. Be sure to clear the calculated results when a change is made to the number of tickets. Also clear the calculated results when the user selects a different radio button. Create the interface and then code the application. Save the solution and then start and test the application. Close the solution. (2-4, 6, 9)

Type	Price
Standard	$32
VIP	$75

Number of tickets purchased	Discount rate
3 or less	None
4 or 5	3%
6 or more	10%

Figure 8-54   Ticket information for Exercise 29
© 2013 Cengage Learning

ADVANCED   30.   If necessary, complete the Concentration Game application from this chapter's Programming Tutorial 2, and then close the solution. Use Windows to make a copy of the Concentration Solution folder. Rename the folder Concentration Solution-Advanced. Open the Concentration Solution (Concentration Solution.sln) file contained in the Concentration Solution-Advanced folder. Replace the Washer/Dryer values in the list box with two Wild Card values. A Wild Card value matches any other value on the game board. Display the "Game Over" message when the game is over, which happens either when all of the words are revealed or when two unmatched words remain on the game board. Make the appropriate modifications to the code. Save the solution and then start and test the application. Close the solution. (1-3)

ADVANCED   31.   If necessary, complete the Tri-County Electricity application from this chapter's Programming Tutorial 1, and then close the solution. Use Windows to make a copy of the Tri-County Solution folder. Rename the folder Tri-County Solution-Sub. Open the Tri-County Solution (Tri-County Solution.sln) file contained in the Tri-County Solution-Sub folder. Replace the CalcResidentialTotal Sub procedure and the GetCommercialTotal function with a Sub procedure named CalcTotal. Modify the Calculate button's Click event procedure so that it uses the CalcTotal procedure for both residential and commercial customers. Save the solution and then start and test the application. Close the solution. (1-3)

ADVANCED   32.   If necessary, complete the Tri-County Electricity application from this chapter's Programming Tutorial 1, and then close the solution. Use Windows to make a copy of the Tri-County Solution folder. Rename the folder Tri-County Solution-Function. Open the Tri-County Solution (Tri-County Solution.sln) file contained in the Tri-County Solution-Function folder. Replace the CalcResidentialTotal Sub procedure and the

GetCommercialTotal function with a function named GetTotal. Modify the Calculate button's Click event procedure so that it uses the GetTotal function for both residential and commercial customers. Save the solution and then start and test the application. Close the solution. (2, 3, 9)

33. If necessary, complete the Concentration Game application from this chapter's Programming Tutorial 2, and then close the solution. Use Windows to make a copy of the Concentration Solution folder. Rename the folder Concentration Solution-Counters. Open the Concentration Game Solution (Concentration Game Solution.sln) file contained in the Concentration Solution-Counters folder. Modify the application so that it displays (in two labels) the number of times the user selects a matching pair of words, and the number of times the user does not select a matching pair of words. Also modify the code so that it doesn't allow the user to click the same label for both the first and second selections. Save the solution and then start and test the application. Close the solution. (6)

34. If necessary, complete the Concentration Game application from this chapter's Programming Tutorial 2, and then close the solution. Use Windows to make a copy of the Concentration Solution folder. Rename the folder Concentration Solution-Discovery. Open the Concentration Solution (Concentration Solution.sln) file contained in the Concentration Solution-Discovery folder.

   a. Replace each Washer/Dryer entry in the wordListBox with the word Wild; this word will now match any word contained in the wordListBox.

   b. Open the Code Editor window and locate the TestForMatch procedure. Now, locate the nested selection structure in the procedure. The condition should also evaluate to True when at least one of the labels contains the word Wild. However, if only one of the labels contains Wild, the TestForMatch procedure should search the wordListBox for the word that matches the one in the other label; it should then display that word in its corresponding label. For example, if the firstLabel contains Car, and the secondLabel contains Wild, the TestForMatch procedure should locate the other Car entry in the wordListBox and then display the word in its proper location on the game board. Make the appropriate modifications to the code. Save the solution and then start and test the application. Close the solution.

35. In this exercise, you will learn how to specify that one or more arguments are optional in a Call statement. Open the Optional Solution (Optional Solution.sln) file contained in the VbReloaded2012\Chap08\Optional Solution folder.

   a. Open the Code Editor window and review the existing code. The calcButton_Click procedure contains two Call statements. The first Call statement passes three variables to the CalcBonus procedure. The second call statement, however, passes only two variables to the procedure. (Do not be concerned about the jagged line that appears below the second Call statement.) Notice that the `rate` variable is omitted from the second Call statement. You indicate that the `rate` variable is optional in the Call statement by including the keyword `Optional` before the variable's corresponding parameter in the procedure header. You enter the `Optional` keyword before the `ByVal` keyword. You also assign a default value that the procedure will use for the missing parameter when the procedure is called. You assign the default value by entering the assignment operator and the default value after the parameter. In this case, you will assign the number 0.1 as the default value for the `rate` variable. (Optional parameters must be listed at the end of the procedure header.)

   b. Change `ByVal bonusRate As Double` in the procedure header appropriately. Save the solution and then start the application. Enter a and 1000 in the Code and Sales boxes, respectively. Click the Calculate button. Type .05 and press Enter. The `Call CalcBonus` (sales, bonus, rate) statement calls the CalcBonus procedure, passing it the number 1000, the address of the **bonus** variable, and the number .05. The CalcBonus procedure stores the number 1000 in the **totalSales** variable. It also assigns the name **bonusAmount** to the **bonus** variable and stores the number .05 in the **bonusRate** variable. The procedure then multiplies the contents of the **totalSales** variable (1000) by the contents of the **bonusRate** variable (.05), assigning the result (50) to the **bonusAmount** variable. The **bonusLabel.Text = bonus.ToString("C2")** statement then displays $50.00 in the bonusLabel.

c. Now enter b and 2000 in the Code and Sales boxes, respectively. Click the Calculate button. The **Call CalcBonus(sales, bonus)** statement calls the CalcBonus procedure, passing it the number 2000 and the address of the **bonus** variable. The CalcBonus procedure stores the number 2000 in the **totalSales** variable and assigns the name **bonusAmount** to the **bonus** variable. Because the Call statement did not supply a value for the **bonusRate** parameter, the default value (0.1) is assigned to the variable. The procedure then multiplies the contents of the **totalSales** variable (2000) by the contents of the **bonusRate** variable (0.1), assigning the result (200) to the **bonusAmount** variable. The **bonusLabel.Text = bonus.ToString("C2")** statement then displays $200.00 in the bonusLabel. Close the solution.

SWAT THE BUGS   36. Open the Debug Solution (Debug Solution.sln) file contained in the VbReloaded2012\ Chap08\Debug Solution folder. Open the Code Editor window and review the existing code. Start and then test the application. Locate and then correct any errors. When the application is working correctly, close the solution. (2)

Case Projects

 Car Shoppers Inc.

In an effort to boost sales, Car Shoppers Inc. is offering buyers a choice of either a large cash rebate or an extremely low financing rate, much lower than the rate most buyers would pay by financing the car through their local bank. Jake Miller, the manager of Car Shoppers Inc., wants you to create an application that helps buyers decide whether to take the lower financing rate from his dealership, or take the rebate and then finance the car through their local bank. Be sure to use one or more independent Sub or Function procedures in the application. (Hint: Use the Financial.Pmt method to calculate the payments.) Use the following names for the solution and project, respectively: Car Shoppers Solution and Car Shoppers Project. Save the solution in the VbReloaded2012\Chap08 folder. Change the form file's name to Main Form.vb. You can either create your own interface or create the one shown in Figure 8-55. (1-3, 6-9)

Figure 8-55   Sample interface for the Car Shoppers Inc. application

Wallpaper Warehouse

Last year, Johanna Liu opened a new wallpaper store named Wallpaper Warehouse. Johanna would like you to create an application that the salesclerks can use to quickly calculate and display the number of single rolls of wallpaper required to cover a room. Be sure to use one or more independent Sub or Function procedures in the application. Use the following names for the solution and project, respectively: Wallpaper Solution and Wallpaper Project. Save the solution in the VbReloaded2012\Chap08 folder. Change the form file's name to Main Form.vb. You can either create your own interface or create the one shown in Figure 8-56. (1-3, 6-9)

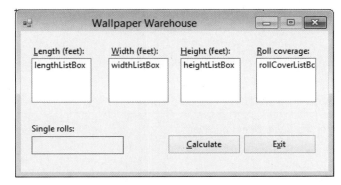

Figure 8-56 Sample interface for the Wallpaper Warehouse application

 ## Cable Direct

Sharon Barrow, the billing supervisor at Cable Direct (a local cable company), has asked you to create an application that calculates and displays a customer's bill. The cable rates are shown in Figure 8-57. Business customers must have at least one connection. Be sure to use one or more independent Sub or Function procedures in the application. Use the following names for the solution and project, respectively: Cable Solution and Cable Project. Save the solution in the VbReloaded2012\Chap08 folder. Change the form file's name to Main Form.vb. You can either create your own interface or create the one shown in Figure 8-57. (1-3, 6-9)

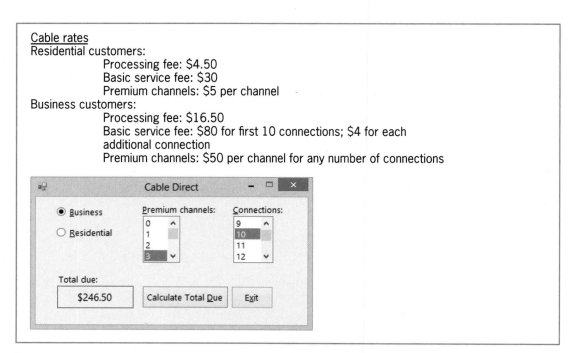

Cable rates

Residential customers:
  Processing fee: $4.50
  Basic service fee: $30
  Premium channels: $5 per channel

Business customers:
  Processing fee: $16.50
  Basic service fee: $80 for first 10 connections; $4 for each
  additional connection
  Premium channels: $50 per channel for any number of connections

Figure 8-57 Cable rates and a sample run of the Cable Direct application
© 2013 Cengage Learning

Harvey Industries

Khalid Patel, the payroll manager at Harvey Industries, has asked you to create an application that displays an employee's weekly gross pay, Social Security and Medicare (FICA) tax, federal withholding tax (FWT), and net pay. Use the following names for the solution and project, respectively: Harvey Industries Solution and Harvey Industries Project. Save the solution in the VbReloaded2012\ Chap08 folder. Change the form file's name to Main Form.vb. Create an appropriate interface. Employees at Harvey Industries are paid every Friday. All employees are paid on an hourly basis, with time and one-half paid for the hours worked over 40. The amount of FICA tax to deduct from an employee's weekly gross pay is calculated by multiplying the gross pay amount by 7.65%. The amount of FWT to deduct from an employee's weekly gross pay is based on the employee's filing status—either single (including head of household) or married—and his or her weekly taxable wages. You calculate the weekly taxable wages by first multiplying the number of withholding allowances by $75 (the value of a withholding allowance), and then subtracting the result from the weekly gross pay. For example, if your weekly gross pay is $400 and you have two withholding allowances, your weekly taxable wages are $250. You use the weekly taxable wages, along with the filing status and the appropriate weekly Federal Withholding Tax table, to determine the amount of FWT to withhold. The weekly tax tables for the year 2013 are shown in Figure 8-58. Be sure to use one or more independent Sub or Function procedures in the application. (1-4, 6, 9)

FWT Tables – Weekly Payroll Period

Single person (including head of household)

If the taxable
wages are: The amount of income tax to withhold is:

Over	But not over	Base amount	Percentage	Of excess over
	$ 42	0		
$ 42	$ 214	0	10%	$ 42
$ 214	$ 739	$ 17.20 plus	15%	$ 214
$ 739	$1,732	$ 95.95 plus	25%	$ 739
$1,732	$3,566	$ 344.20 plus	28%	$1,732
$3,566	$7,703	$ 857.72 plus	33%	$3,566
$7,703	$7,735	$2,222.93 plus	35%	$7,703
$7,735		$2,234.13 plus	39.6%	$7,735

Married person

If the taxable
wages are: The amount of income tax to withhold is:

Over	But not over	Base amount	Percentage	Of excess over
	$ 160	0		
$ 160	$ 503	0	10%	$ 160
$ 503	$1,554	$ 34.30 plus	15%	$ 503
$1,554	$2,975	$ 191.90 plus	25%	$1,554
$2,975	$4,449	$ 547.20 plus	28%	$2,975
$4,449	$7,820	$ 959.92 plus	33%	$4,449
$7,820	$8,813	$2,072.35 plus	35%	$7,820
$8,813		$2,419.90 plus	39.6%	$8,813

Figure 8-58   Weekly FWT tables

© 2013 Cengage Learning

CHAPTER 9

Arrays

After studying Chapter 9, you should be able to:

1 Declare and initialize one-dimensional and two-dimensional arrays

2 Store and access data in an array

3 Determine the number of array elements and the highest subscript

4 Traverse an array

5 Code a loop using the For Each...Next statement

6 Compute the total and average of an array's contents

7 Find the highest value in an array

8 Associate a list box with a one-dimensional array

9 Use a one-dimensional array as an accumulator or a counter

10 Sort a one-dimensional array

11 Search an array

Reading and Study Guide

Before you begin reading Chapter 9, view the Ch09_ReadingStudyGuide.pdf file. You can open the file using Adobe Reader, which is available for free on the Adobe Web site at *www.adobe.com/downloads/*.

Arrays

All of the variables you have used so far have been simple variables. A **simple variable**, also called a **scalar variable**, is one that is unrelated to any other variable in memory. At times, however, you will encounter situations in which some of the variables in a program *are* related to each other. In those cases, it is easier and more efficient to treat the related variables as a group.

You already are familiar with the concept of grouping. The clothes in your closet are probably separated into groups, such as coats, sweaters, shirts, and so on. Grouping your clothes in this manner allows you to easily locate your favorite sweater because you just need to look through the sweater group rather than through the entire closet. You also probably have your CD (compact disc) collection grouped by either music type or artist. If your collection is grouped by artist, it will take only a few seconds to find all of your Beatles CDs and, depending on the number of Beatles CDs you own, only a short time after that to locate a particular CD.

When you group together related variables, the group is referred to as an array of variables or, more simply, an **array**. You might use an array of 50 variables to store the population of each U.S. state. Or, you might use an array of four variables to store the sales made in each of your company's four sales regions. Storing data in an array increases the efficiency of a program because data can be both stored in and retrieved from the computer's internal memory much faster than it can be written to and read from a file on a disk. In addition, after the data is entered into an array, which typically is done at the beginning of a program, the program can use the data as many times as necessary without having to enter the data again. Your company's sales program, for example, can use the sales amounts stored in an array to calculate the total company sales and the percentage that each region contributed to the total sales. It also can use the sales amounts in the array either to calculate the average sales amount or to simply display the sales made in a specific region. As you will learn in this chapter, the variables in an array can be used just like any other variables. You can assign values to them, use them in calculations, display their contents, and so on.

The most commonly used arrays in business applications are one-dimensional and two-dimensional. You will learn about one-dimensional and two-dimensional arrays in this chapter. Arrays having more than two dimensions are beyond the scope of this book.

At this point, it's important to point out that arrays are one of the more challenging topics for beginning programmers. Therefore, it is important for you to read and study each section in this chapter thoroughly before moving on to the next section. If you still feel overwhelmed by the end of the chapter, try reading the chapter again, paying particular attention to the examples and procedures shown in the figures.

One-Dimensional Arrays

The variables in an array are stored in consecutive locations in the computer's internal memory. Each variable in an array is referred to as an **element**, and each has the same name and data type. You distinguish one element in a **one-dimensional array** from another element in the same array using a unique number. The unique number, which is always an integer, is called a subscript. The **subscript** indicates the element's position in the array and is assigned by the computer when the array is created in internal memory. The first element in a one-dimensional array is assigned a subscript of 0, the second a subscript of 1, and so on.

You refer to each element in an array by the array's name and the element's subscript, which is specified in a set of parentheses immediately following the array name. Figure 9-1 illustrates a one-dimensional array named `beatles` that contains three elements. You use `beatles(0)`—read "`beatles` sub zero"—to refer to the first element. You use `beatles(1)` to refer to the second element, and use `beatles(2)` to refer to the third (and last) element. The last subscript in an array is always one number less than the total number of elements in the array. This is because array subscripts in Visual Basic (and in many other programming languages) start at 0.

Figure 9-1   Illustration of the one-dimensional `beatles` array
Image by Diane Zak; created with Reallusion CrazyTalk Animator

Declaring a One-Dimensional Array

Before you can use an array in a program, you first must declare (create) it. Figure 9-2 shows two versions of the syntax for declaring a one-dimensional array in Visual Basic. The {Dim | Private | Static} portion in each version indicates that you can select only one of the keywords appearing within the braces. The appropriate keyword depends on whether you are creating a procedure-level array or a class-level array. *ArrayName* is the name of the array, and *dataType* is the type of data the array elements will store. In syntax Version 1, *highestSubscript* is an integer that specifies the highest subscript in the array. Because the first element in a one-dimensional array has a subscript of 0, the array will contain one element more than the number specified in the highestSubscript argument. In other words, an array whose highest subscript is 2 will contain three elements. In syntax Version 2, *initialValues* is a comma-separated list of values you want assigned to the array elements. Also included in Figure 9-2 are examples of using both versions of the syntax.

HOW TO Declare a One-Dimensional Array

Syntax – Version 1
{**Dim** | **Private** | **Static**} *arrayName*(*highestSubscript*) **As** *dataType*

Syntax – Version 2
{**Dim** | **Private** | **Static**} *arrayName*() **As** *dataType* = {*initialValues*}

Example 1
`Dim beatles(2) As String`
declares a three-element procedure-level array named `beatles`; each element is automatically initialized using the keyword `Nothing`

Figure 9-2   How to declare a one-dimensional array *(continues)*

(continued)

Example 2
```
Static numbers(4) As Integer
```
declares a static, five-element procedure-level array named `numbers`; each element is automatically initialized to 0

Example 3
```
Dim states() As String = {"Alaska", "Florida", "Iowa", "Ohio"}
```
declares and initializes a four-element procedure-level array named `states`

Example 4
```
Private pays() As Double = {12.25, 11.23, 15.67, 75.0, 7.75}
```
declares and initializes a five-element class-level array named `pays` (Note: Like class-level variables, class-level arrays are declared in the form's Declarations section.)

Figure 9-2   How to declare a one-dimensional array
© 2013 Cengage Learning

When you use syntax Version 1, the computer automatically initializes each element when the array is created. If the array's data type is String, each element is initialized using the keyword `Nothing`. As you learned in Chapter 3, variables initialized to `Nothing` do not actually contain the word "Nothing"; rather, they contain no data at all. Elements in a numeric array are initialized to the number 0, and elements in a Boolean array are initialized using the Boolean keyword `False`. Date array elements are initialized to 12:00 AM January 1, 0001.

Rather than having the computer use a default value to initialize each array element, you can use syntax Version 2 to specify each element's initial value when the array is declared. Assigning initial values to an array is often referred to as **populating the array**. You list the initial values in the initialValues section of the syntax, using commas to separate the values, and you enclose the list of values in braces ({}).

Notice that syntax Version 2 does not include the highestSubscript argument; instead, an empty set of parentheses follows the array name. The computer automatically calculates the highest subscript based on the number of values listed in the initialValues section. Because the first subscript in a one-dimensional array is the number 0, the highest subscript is always one number less than the number of values listed in the initialValues section. The Dim statement in Example 3 in Figure 9-2, for instance, creates a four-element array with subscripts of 0, 1, 2, and 3. Similarly, the Private statement in Example 4 creates a five-element array with subscripts of 0, 1, 2, 3, and 4. The arrays are initialized as shown in Figure 9-3.

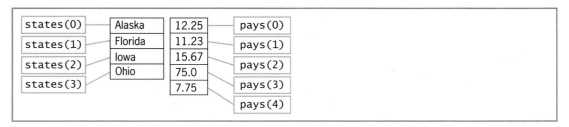

Figure 9-3   Illustration of the `states` and `pays` arrays
© 2013 Cengage Learning

Storing Data in a One-Dimensional Array

After an array is declared, you can use another statement to store a different value in an array element. Examples of such statements include assignment statements and statements that contain the TryParse method. Figure 9-4 shows examples of both types of statements.

HOW TO Store Data in a One-Dimensional Array

Example 1
```
states(0) = "New Mexico"
```
assigns the string "New Mexico" to the first element in the **states** array

Example 2
```
For x As Integer = 1 To 5
    numbers(x - 1) = x ^ 2
Next x
```
assigns the squares of the numbers from 1 through 5 to the **numbers** array

Example 3
```
Dim subscript As Integer
Do While subscript < 5
    numbers(subscript) = 100
    subscript += 1
Loop
```
assigns the number 100 to each element in the **numbers** array

Example 4
```
pays(1) *= .1
```
multiplies the contents of the second element in the **pays** array by .1 and then assigns the result to the element; you can also write this statement as `pays(1) = pays(1) * .1`

Example 5
```
Double.TryParse(payTextBox.Text, pays(2))
```
assigns either the value entered in the payTextBox (converted to Double) or the number 0 to the third element in the **pays** array

Figure 9-4   How to store data in a one-dimensional array
© 2013 Cengage Learning

Determining the Number of Elements in an Array

The number of elements in an array is stored, as an integer, in the array's **Length property**. Figure 9-5 shows the property's syntax and includes an example of using the property. The Length property is shaded in the example.

HOW TO Determine the Number of Elements in an Array

Syntax
arrayName.**Length**

Example
```
Dim cities(12) As String
Dim numElements As Integer
numElements = cities.Length
```
assigns the number 13 to the `numElements` variable

Figure 9-5   How to determine the number of elements in an array
© 2013 Cengage Learning

Determining the Highest Subscript in a One-Dimensional Array

As you learned earlier, the highest subscript in a one-dimensional array is always one number less than the number of array elements. Therefore, one way to determine the highest subscript is by subtracting the number 1 from the array's Length property, like this: `cities.Length – 1`. However, you can also use the array's GetUpperBound method. Figure 9-6 shows the method's syntax and includes an example of using the method. The **GetUpperBound method**, which is shaded in the example, returns an integer that represents the highest subscript in the specified dimension in the array. When used with a one-dimensional array, the specified dimension (which appears between the parentheses after the method's name) is always 0.

HOW TO Determine the Highest Subscript in a One-Dimensional Array

Syntax
arrayName.**GetUpperBound(0)**

> the specified dimension for a one-dimensional array is always 0

Example
```
Dim cities(12) As String
Dim highestSub As Integer
highestSub = cities.GetUpperBound(0)
```
assigns the number 12 to the `highestSub` variable

Figure 9-6   How to determine the highest subscript in a one-dimensional array
© 2013 Cengage Learning

Mini-Quiz 9-1

1. Which of the following declares a four-element, one-dimensional String array named `letters`? (1)

   a. `Dim letters(3) As String`

   b. `Dim letters() As String = "A", "B", "C", "D"`

   c. `Dim letters(3) As String = {"A", "B", "C", "D"}`

   d. all of the above

The answers to Mini-Quiz questions are located in Appendix A. Each question is associated with one or more objectives listed at the beginning of the chapter.

2. Which of the following assigns the number of elements contained in a one-dimensional array named `items` to the `numElements` variable? (3)

    a. `numElements = items.Length`

    b. `numElements = items.GetUpperBound(0) + 1`

    c. `numElements = items.GetNumItems(0)`

    d. both a and b

3. Which of the following assigns the string "Scottsburg" to the fifth element in a one-dimensional array named `cities`? (2)

    a. `cities(4) = "Scottsburg"`

    b. `cities(5) = "Scottsburg"`

    c. `cities[4] = "Scottsburg"`

    d. `cities[5] = "Scottsburg"`

Traversing a One-Dimensional Array

At times, you may need to traverse an array, which means to look at each array element, one by one, beginning with the first element and ending with the last element. You traverse an array using a loop. Figure 9-7 shows two examples of loops that traverse the `states` array, displaying each element's value in the statesListBox, as shown in the figure. The loop in Example 1 is coded using the For...Next statement; Example 2's loop uses the Do...Loop statement.

HOW TO Traverse a One-Dimensional Array

```
Dim states() As String = {"Alaska", "Florida", "Iowa", "Ohio"}
```
you can also use the Length property, as shown in Example 2

```
Example 1 – For...Next
Dim highestSub As Integer = states.GetUpperBound(0)
For subscript As Integer = 0 To highestSub
    statesListBox.Items.Add(states(subscript))
Next subscript
```
you can also use the GetUpperBound method, as shown in Example 1

```
Example 2 – Do...Loop
Dim highestSub As Integer = states.Length - 1
Dim subscript As Integer
Do While subscript <= highestSub
    statesListBox.Items.Add(states(subscript))
    subscript += 1
Loop
```

Figure 9-7 How to traverse a one-dimensional array *(continues)*

474

(continued)

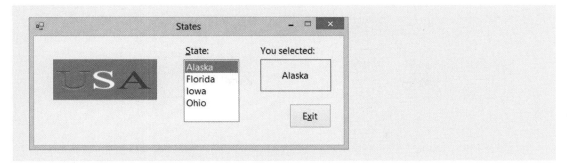

Figure 9-7 How to traverse a one-dimensional array
© 2013 Cengage Learning

If you want to experiment with the States application, open the solution contained in the Try It 1! folder.

As you learned in Chapter 6, in addition to using the Do...Loop and For...Next statements to code a loop, you can also use the For Each...Next statement.

The For Each...Next Statement

Visual Basic's **For Each...Next statement** provides a convenient way of coding a loop whose instructions you want processed for each element in a group, such as for each element in an array. An advantage of using the For Each...Next statement to process an array is that your code does not need to keep track of the array subscripts or even know the number of array elements. However, unlike the loop instructions in a Do...Loop or For...Next statement, the instructions in a For Each...Next statement can only read the array values; they cannot permanently modify the values.

Figure 9-8 shows the For Each...Next statement's syntax. The *elementVariableName* that appears in the For Each and Next clauses is the name of a variable that the computer can use to keep track of each element in the *group*. Although, technically, you do not need to specify the elementVariableName in the Next clause, doing so is highly recommended because it makes your code more self-documenting. The variable's data type is specified in the As *dataType* portion of the For Each clause and must be the same as the group's data type. A variable declared in the For Each clause has block scope and is recognized only by the instructions within the For Each...Next loop. The example in Figure 9-8 shows how to write the loops from Figure 9-7 using the For Each...Next statement.

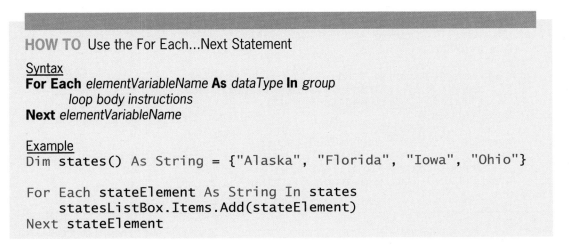

HOW TO Use the For Each...Next Statement

Syntax
For Each elementVariableName **As** dataType **In** group
      loop body instructions
Next elementVariableName

Example
```
Dim states() As String = {"Alaska", "Florida", "Iowa", "Ohio"}

For Each stateElement As String In states
    statesListBox.Items.Add(stateElement)
Next stateElement
```

If you want to experiment with this version of the States application, open the solution contained in the Try It 2! folder.

Figure 9-8 How to use the For Each...Next statement (*continues*)

(continued)

Figure 9-8   How to use the For Each...Next statement
© 2013 Cengage Learning

Calculating the Total and Average Values

Figure 9-9 shows the problem specification for the Starward Coffee application, which displays the total number of pounds of coffee used during a 12-month period and the average number of pounds used each month. It also shows most of the application's code and includes a sample run of the application.

If you want to experiment with the Starward Coffee application, open the solution contained in the Try It 3! folder.

Problem specification
The store manager at Starward Coffee wants an application that displays two items: the total number of pounds of coffee used during a 12-month period, and the average number of pounds used each month. Last year, the monthly usage amounts were as follows: 400.5, 450, 475.5, 336.5, 457, 325, 220.5, 276, 300, 320.5, 400.5, and 415. The application should store the monthly amounts in a 12-element one-dimensional array. It then should calculate and display the two output items. The total usage is calculated by accumulating the array values. The average monthly usage is calculated by dividing the total usage by the number of array elements.

```vbnet
Private poundsUsed() As Double = {400.5, 450, 475.5,    ← class-level array
                                  336.5, 457, 325,          declared in the form's
                                  220.5, 276, 300,          Declarations section
                                  320.5, 400.5, 415}

Private Sub forNextButton_Click(sender As Object,
e As EventArgs) Handles forNextButton.Click
    ' displays the total and average pounds used

    Dim highSub As Integer = poundsUsed.GetUpperBound(0)
    Dim total As Double
    Dim average As Double

    ' accumulate pounds used
    For subscript As Integer = 0 To highSub
        total += poundsUsed(subscript)
    Next subscript
    ' calculate average
    average = total / poundsUsed.Length

    totalLabel.Text = total.ToString("N1")
    averageLabel.Text = average.ToString("N2")
End Sub
```

Figure 9-9   Problem specification, code, and sample run for the Starward Coffee application *(continues)*

(continued)

```
Private Sub doLoopButton_Click(sender As Object,
e As EventArgs) Handles doLoopButton.Click
    ' displays the total and average pounds used

    Dim highSub As Integer = poundsUsed.GetUpperBound(0)
    Dim total As Double
    Dim average As Double
    Dim subscript As Integer

    ' accumulate pounds used
    Do While subscript <= highSub
        total += poundsUsed(subscript)
        subscript += 1
    Loop
    ' calculate average
    average = total / poundsUsed.Length

    totalLabel.Text = total.ToString("N1")
    averageLabel.Text = average.ToString("N2")
End Sub

Private Sub forEachNextButton_Click(sender As Object,
e As EventArgs) Handles forEachNextButton.Click
    ' displays the total and average pounds used

    Dim total As Double
    Dim average As Double

    ' accumulate pounds used
    For Each pound As Double In poundsUsed
        total += pound
    Next pound
    ' calculate average
    average = total / poundsUsed.Length

    totalLabel.Text = total.ToString("N1")
    averageLabel.Text = average.ToString("N2")
End Sub
```

Figure 9-9 Problem specification, code, and sample run for the Starward Coffee application
OpenClipArt.org/momoko; © 2013 Cengage Learning

The Private statement in the MainForm's Declarations section declares and initializes a class-level Double array named poundsUsed. Each button's Click event procedure uses a loop to traverse the 12-element poundsUsed array, adding each array element's value to the total variable. The code pertaining to each loop is shaded in Figure 9-9. Notice that you need to specify the highest array subscript in the For...Next and Do...Loop statements, but not in the For Each...Next statement. The For...Next and Do...Loop statements must also keep track of the array subscripts; this task is not necessary in the For Each...Next statement, thereby making it easier to use.

After accumulating the array values, each button's Click event procedure calculates the average monthly usage by dividing the value stored in the **total** variable by the number of elements in the array. Each procedure then displays the total and average amounts on the form.

Finding the Highest Value

Figure 9-10 shows the problem specification for the Car-Mart application, which displays the highest commission amount earned during the month and the number of salespeople who earned that amount. It also shows most of the application's code and includes a sample run of the application.

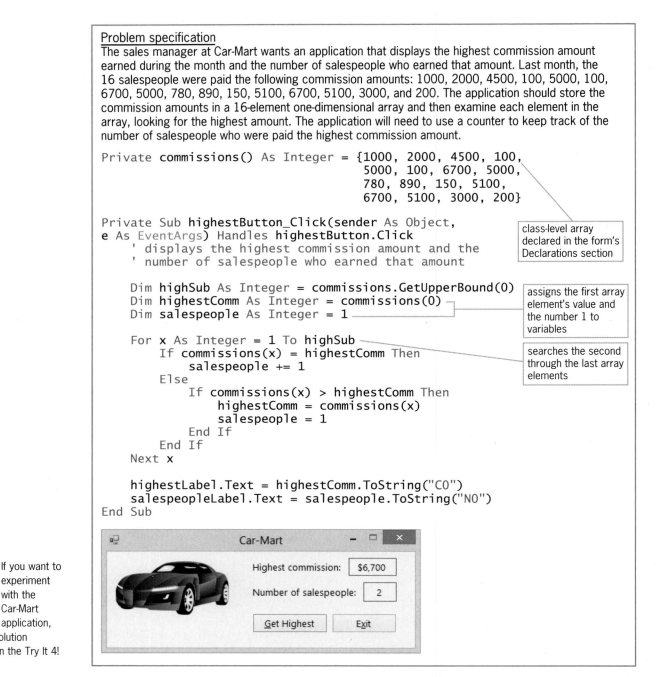

Problem specification
The sales manager at Car-Mart wants an application that displays the highest commission amount earned during the month and the number of salespeople who earned that amount. Last month, the 16 salespeople were paid the following commission amounts: 1000, 2000, 4500, 100, 5000, 100, 6700, 5000, 780, 890, 150, 5100, 6700, 5100, 3000, and 200. The application should store the commission amounts in a 16-element one-dimensional array and then examine each element in the array, looking for the highest amount. The application will need to use a counter to keep track of the number of salespeople who were paid the highest commission amount.

```
Private commissions() As Integer = {1000, 2000, 4500, 100,
                                    5000, 100, 6700, 5000,
                                    780, 890, 150, 5100,
                                    6700, 5100, 3000, 200}
```
class-level array declared in the form's Declarations section

```
Private Sub highestButton_Click(sender As Object,
e As EventArgs) Handles highestButton.Click
    ' displays the highest commission amount and the
    ' number of salespeople who earned that amount

    Dim highSub As Integer = commissions.GetUpperBound(0)
    Dim highestComm As Integer = commissions(0)
    Dim salespeople As Integer = 1
```
assigns the first array element's value and the number 1 to variables

```
    For x As Integer = 1 To highSub
        If commissions(x) = highestComm Then
            salespeople += 1
        Else
            If commissions(x) > highestComm Then
                highestComm = commissions(x)
                salespeople = 1
            End If
        End If
    Next x
```
searches the second through the last array elements

```
    highestLabel.Text = highestComm.ToString("C0")
    salespeopleLabel.Text = salespeople.ToString("N0")
End Sub
```

Car-Mart

Highest commission: $6,700

Number of salespeople: 2

Get Highest   Exit

If you want to experiment with the Car-Mart application, open the solution contained in the Try It 4! folder.

Figure 9-10 Problem specification, code, and sample run for the Car-Mart application
OpenClipArt.org/LiquidSnake; © 2013 Cengage Learning

The Private statement declares and initializes a 16-element, class-level Integer array named commissions. The first Dim statement in the highestButton_Click procedure declares an Integer variable named highSub and initializes it to the highest subscript in the commissions array (15). The second Dim statement declares an Integer variable named highestComm and initializes it to the value stored in the first array element. The procedure will use the highestComm variable to keep track of the highest value in the array. The salespeople variable declared in the third Dim statement will be used as a counter to keep track of the number of salespeople whose commission matches the amount stored in the highestComm variable. The salespeople variable is initialized to 1 because, at this point, one salesperson (the first one) has earned the amount currently stored in the highestComm variable.

Notice that the loop in Figure 9-10 searches the second through the last element in the commissions array. The first element is not included in the search because its value is already contained in the highestComm variable. The loop body contains an outer selection structure and a nested selection structure. The outer selection structure's condition compares the value stored in the current array element with the value stored in the highestComm variable. If both values are equal, the outer selection structure's True path adds 1 to the salespeople counter; otherwise, the nested selection structure in its False path is processed.

The nested selection structure's condition determines whether the value stored in the current array element is greater than the value stored in the highestComm variable. If it is, the nested selection structure's True path assigns the current array element's value to the highestComm variable. It also assigns the number 1 to the salespeople counter because, at this point, only one salesperson has earned that commission amount.

After both selection structures end, the loop proceeds to the next element in the array. When the loop has finished processing, the last two assignment statements in the procedure display the highest commission amount ($6,700) and the number of people earning that amount (2) in the interface.

You may be wondering why the commissions array in Figure 9-10 is declared as a class-level array in the form's Declarations section rather than as a procedure-level array in the highestButton_Click procedure. If you declare the array in the procedure, it will remain in the computer's internal memory only while the procedure is being processed; it will be removed from memory when the procedure ends. As a result, it will need to be recreated each time the user selects the Get Highest button. Using a procedure-level array is fine when the array contains only a few elements. However, having the computer recreate a large array every time a button is clicked is very inefficient. Since most arrays used in business applications are large, a better approach is to use a class-level array. Like class-level variables, class-level arrays remain in memory until the application ends.

Arrays and Collections

It's not uncommon for programmers to associate the values in an array with the items in a list box. This is because the items in a list box belong to a collection (more specifically, the Items collection), and collections and arrays have several things in common. First, each is a group of individual objects treated as one unit. Second, each individual object in the group is identified by a unique number. The unique number is called an index when referring to a collection, but a subscript when referring to an array. Third, both the first index in a collection and the first subscript in an array are 0. These commonalities allow you to associate the list box items and array elements by their positions within their respective groups. In other words, you can associate the first item in a list box with the first element in an array, the second item with the second element, and so on.

To associate a list box with an array, you first add the appropriate items to the list box. You then store each item's related value in its corresponding position in the array. You will use a list box and a one-dimensional array in the Rose Performing Arts Center application, whose problem specification is shown in Figure 9-11. The figure also shows most of the application's code and includes a sample run of the application.

Problem specification

The manager at Rose Performing Arts Center wants an application that displays the total amount a customer owes for tickets. The ticket price is based on the seating section, as shown here. The application's interface should provide a text box for entering the number of tickets purchased, and a list box from which the user can select the seating section. The application should store the ticket prices in a four-element one-dimensional array, and then use the index of the selected list box item to access the appropriate price from the array.

Section	Price ($)
A	103.00
B	95.00
C	75.50
D	32.50

```
Private prices() As Double = {103, 95, 75.5, 32.5}
```
— class-level array declared in the form's Declarations section

```
Private Sub MainForm_Load(sender As Object,
e As EventArgs) Handles Me.Load
    ' fills list box

    sectionListBox.Items.Add("A")
    sectionListBox.Items.Add("B")
    sectionListBox.Items.Add("C")
    sectionListBox.Items.Add("D")
    sectionListBox.SelectedIndex = 0
End Sub

Private Sub calcButton_Click(sender As Object,
e As EventArgs) Handles calcButton.Click
    ' calculates the total due for tickets

    Dim numTickets As Integer
    Dim subscript As Integer
    Dim ticketPrice As Double
    Dim totalDue As Double

    Integer.TryParse(ticketsTextBox.Text, numTickets)
    subscript = sectionListBox.SelectedIndex
    ticketPrice = prices(subscript)
    totalDue = ticketPrice * numTickets

    totalPriceLabel.Text = totalDue.ToString("C2")
End Sub
```
— uses the selected item's index as the array subscript

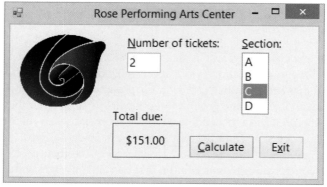

If you want to experiment with the Rose Performing Arts Center application, open the solution contained in the Try It 5! folder.

Figure 9-11 Problem specification, code, and sample run for the Rose Performing Arts Center application
OpenClipArt.org/Merlin2525; © 2013 Cengage Learning

The MainForm's Load event procedure adds the four seating sections to the sectionListBox and then selects the first item in the list. The Private statement in the form's Declarations section initializes the first element in the `prices` array to 103, which is the price associated with the first item in the Section list box (A). The remaining array elements are initialized to the prices corresponding to their list box items. The relationship between the sectionListBox and the `prices` array is illustrated in Figure 9-12.

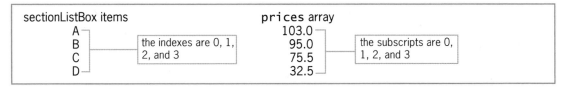

Figure 9-12 Illustration of the relationship between the list box and the array
© 2013 Cengage Learning

The `subscript = sectionListBox.SelectedIndex` statement in the calcButton_Click procedure assigns the index of the item selected in the list box to the `subscript` variable. The `ticketPrice = prices(subscript)` statement uses the value in the `subscript` variable to access the appropriate element in the `prices` array.

Accumulator and Counter Arrays

One-dimensional arrays are often used to either accumulate or count related values; such arrays are commonly referred to as accumulator arrays and counter arrays, respectively. You will use an accumulator array in the Allen School application, whose problem specification is shown in Figure 9-13. The figure also shows most of the application's code and includes a sample run of the application.

Problem specification
Allen School is having its annual Cookie Fund Raiser event. Students sell boxes of the following five types of cookies: Chunky Chocolate, Macadamia, Peanut Butter, Snickerdoodle, and Sugar. The school principal wants an application that allows him to enter the number of boxes of each cookie type sold by each student. The application's interface should provide a list box for selecting the cookie type, and a text box for entering the number of boxes sold. The application should use a five-element one-dimensional array to accumulate the number of boxes sold for each cookie type, and then display that information in label controls in the interface.

```
Private Sub MainForm_Load(sender As Object,
e As EventArgs) Handles Me.Load
    ' fill the list box with values

    cookieListBox.Items.Add("Chunky Chocolate")
    cookieListBox.Items.Add("Macadamia")
    cookieListBox.Items.Add("Peanut Butter")
    cookieListBox.Items.Add("Snickerdoodle")
    cookieListBox.Items.Add("Sugar")
    cookieListBox.SelectedIndex = 0
End Sub

Private Sub addButton_Click(sender As Object,
e As EventArgs) Handles addButton.Click
    ' add amount sold to the appropriate total

    ' declare array and variables
    Static totalBoxesSold(4) As Integer ——— static procedure-level array
    Dim sold As Integer
    Dim subscript As Integer
```

Figure 9-13 Problem specification, code, and sample run for the Allen School application *(continues)*

482

(continued)

```
        Integer.TryParse(soldTextBox.Text, sold)
        subscript = cookieListBox.SelectedIndex

        ' update array value
        totalBoxesSold(subscript) += sold

        ' display array values
        chunkyChocLabel.Text = totalBoxesSold(0).ToString
        macadamiaLabel.Text = totalBoxesSold(1).ToString
        peanutButLabel.Text = totalBoxesSold(2).ToString
        snickerLabel.Text = totalBoxesSold(3).ToString
        sugarLabel.Text = totalBoxesSold(4).ToString

        soldTextBox.Focus()
    End Sub
```

> uses the selected item's index as the array subscript

Figure 9-13   Problem specification, code, and sample run for the Allen School application
© 2013 Cengage Learning

 If you want to experiment with the Allen School application, open the solution contained in the Try It 6! folder.

The MainForm's Load event procedure adds the five cookie types to the cookieListBox and then selects the first type in the list. The Static statement in the addButton_Click procedure declares a procedure-level Integer array named `totalBoxesSold`. The array has five elements, each corresponding to an item listed in the cookieListBox. Each array element will be used to accumulate the sales of its corresponding list box item. Like static variables, which you learned about in Chapter 3, static arrays remain in memory and retain their values until the application ends.

The two Dim statements in the addButton_Click procedure in Figure 9-13 declare and initialize two Integer variables named `sold` and `subscript`. The TryParse method stores the contents of the soldTextBox, converted to Integer, in the `sold` variable. The first assignment statement in the procedure assigns the index of the item selected in the list box to the `subscript` variable. The `totalBoxesSold(subscript) += sold` statement uses the number stored in the `subscript` variable to locate the appropriate element in the `totalBoxesSold` array; it then adds the contents of the `sold` variable to the element's contents. The last five assignment statements in the procedure display the contents of the array in the interface. The last statement in the procedure sends the focus to the soldTextBox.

Rather than using a static array, you can use a class-level array.

Sorting a One-Dimensional Array

In some applications, you might need to arrange the contents of a one-dimensional array in either ascending or descending order. Arranging data in a specific order is called **sorting**. You can use the **Array.Sort method** to sort the elements in ascending order. To sort a one-dimensional array in descending order, you first use the Array.Sort method to sort the array in ascending order, and then use the **Array.Reverse method** to reverse the array elements. Figure 9-14 shows the syntax of both methods. In each syntax, *arrayName* is the name of a one-dimensional array.

HOW TO Use the Array.Sort and Array.Reverse Methods

Syntax
Array.Sort(arrayName**)**
Array.Reverse(arrayName**)**

Example 1
```
Dim pays() As Double = {9.75, 12.5, 10.75, 8.35}
Array.Sort(pays)
```
sorts the contents of the array in ascending order, as follows: 8.35, 9.75, 10.75, and 12.5

Example 2
```
Dim pays() As Double = {9.75, 12.5, 10.75, 8.35}
Array.Reverse(pays)
```
reverses the contents of the array, placing the values in the following order: 8.35, 10.75, 12.5, and 9.75

Example 3
```
Dim pays() As Double = {9.75, 12.5, 10.75, 8.35}
Array.Sort(pays)
Array.Reverse(pays)
```
sorts the contents of the array in ascending order and then reverses the contents, placing the values in descending order as follows: 12.5, 10.75, 9.75, and 8.35

If you want to experiment with the code shown in Figure 9-14, open the solution contained in the Try It 7! folder.

Figure 9-14 How to use the Array.Sort and Array.Reverse methods
© 2013 Cengage Learning

Mini-Quiz 9-2

The answers to Mini-Quiz questions are located in Appendix A. Each question is associated with one or more objectives listed at the beginning of the chapter.

1. The **scores** array is a five-element Integer array. Which of the following will total the array values? (4-6)

   a. ```
      For Each scoreElement As Integer In scores
          total += scores(scoreElement)
      Next scoreElement
      ```

   b. ```
      For Each scoreElement As Integer In scores
          total += scoreElement
      Next scoreElement
      ```

   c. ```
      For Each score As Integer In scores
          total = scores(score) + score
      Next score
      ```

   d. ```
      For Each element As Array In scores
          total = total + scores(element)
      Next element
      ```

2. Rewrite the code from Question 1 using a For...Next statement. Use **subscript** as the counterVariableName in the For clause. (3, 4, 6)

3. Rewrite the code from Question 2 using a Do...Loop statement. (3, 4, 6)

4. Write the code to sort the **scores** array in ascending order. (10)

Note: You have learned a lot so far in this chapter. You may want to take a break at this point before continuing.

Ch09-One-Dimensional Arrays

484

Two-Dimensional Arrays

As you learned earlier, the most commonly used arrays in business applications are one-dimensional and two-dimensional. You can visualize a one-dimensional array as a column of variables in memory. A **two-dimensional array**, on the other hand, resembles a table in that the variables (elements) are in rows and columns. You can determine the number of elements in a two-dimensional array by multiplying the number of its rows by the number of its columns. An array that has four rows and three columns, for example, contains 12 elements. You can also use the array's Length property.

Each element in a two-dimensional array is identified by a unique combination of two subscripts that the computer assigns to the element when the array is created. The subscripts specify the element's row and column positions in the array. Elements located in the first row in a two-dimensional array are assigned a row subscript of 0, elements in the second row are assigned a row subscript of 1, and so on. Similarly, elements located in the first column in a two-dimensional array are assigned a column subscript of 0, elements in the second column are assigned a column subscript of 1, and so on.

You refer to each element in a two-dimensional array by the array's name and the element's row and column subscripts, with the row subscript listed first and the column subscript listed second. The subscripts are separated by a comma and specified in a set of parentheses immediately following the array name. For example, to refer to the element located in the first row, first column in a two-dimensional array named cds, you use cds(0, 0)—read "cds sub zero comma zero." Similarly, to refer to the element located in the second row, third column, you use cds(1, 2). Notice that the subscripts are one number less than the row and column in which the element is located. This is because the row and column subscripts start at 0 rather than at 1. You will find that the last row subscript in a two-dimensional array is always one number less than the number of rows in the array. Likewise, the last column subscript is always one number less than the number of columns in the array. Figure 9-15 illustrates the elements contained in the two-dimensional cds array.

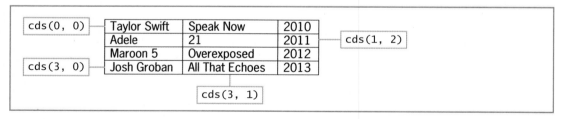

Figure 9-15 Names of some of the elements in the cds array
© 2013 Cengage Learning

Figure 9-16 shows two versions of the syntax for declaring a two-dimensional array in Visual Basic. The figure also includes examples of using both syntax versions. In each version, *arrayName* is the name of the array, and *dataType* is the type of data the array variables will store.

HOW TO Declare a Two-Dimensional Array

<u>Syntax – Version 1</u>
{**Dim** | **Private** | **Static**} *arrayName*(*highestRowSubscript*, *highestColumnSubscript*) **As** *dataType*

<u>Syntax – Version 2</u>
{**Dim** | **Private** | **Static**} *arrayName*(,) **As** *dataType* = {{*initialValues*},...{*initialValues*}}

<u>Example 1</u>
```
Dim states(49, 3) As String
```
declares a 50-row, four-column procedure-level array named `states`; each element is automatically initialized using the keyword `Nothing`

<u>Example 2</u>
```
Static totals(4, 2) As Integer
```
declares a static, five-row, three-column procedure-level array named `totals`; each element is automatically initialized to 0

<u>Example 3</u>
```
Private cds(,) As String =
              {{"Taylor Swift", "Speak Now", "2010"},
               {"Adele", "21", "2011"},
               {"Maroon 5", "Overexposed", "2012"},
               {"Josh Groban", "All That Echoes", "2013"}}
```
declares and initializes a four-row, three-column class-level array named `cds` (the array is illustrated in Figure 9-15)

<u>Example 4</u>
```
Private prices(,) As Double = {{100.5, 83.67},
                               {45.8, 90.4},
                               {54.3, 22.9}}
```
declares and initializes a three-row, two-column class-level array named `prices`

Figure 9-16 How to declare a two-dimensional array
© 2013 Cengage Learning

In Version 1's syntax, *highestRowSubscript* and *highestColumnSubscript* are integers that specify the highest row and column subscripts, respectively, in the array. When the array is created, it will contain one row more than the number specified in the highestRowSubscript argument and one column more than the number specified in the highestColumnSubscript argument. This is because the first row and column subscripts in a two-dimensional array are 0. When you declare a two-dimensional array using the syntax shown in Version 1, the computer automatically initializes each element in the array when the array is created.

You would use Version 2's syntax when you want to specify each variable's initial value. You do this by including a separate *initialValues* section, enclosed in braces, for each row in the array. If the array has six rows, then the statement that declares and initializes the array should have six initialValues sections. Within the individual initialValues sections, you enter one or more values separated by commas. The number of values to enter corresponds to the number of columns in the array. If the array contains 10 columns, then each individual initialValues section should contain 10 values. In addition to the set of braces enclosing each individual initialValues section, Version 2's syntax also requires all of the initialValues sections to be enclosed in a set of braces.

When using Version 2's syntax, be sure to include a comma within the parentheses that follow the array's name. The comma indicates that the array is a two-dimensional array. (Recall that a comma is used to separate the row subscript from the column subscript in a two-dimensional array.)

After a two-dimensional array is declared, you can use another statement to store a different value in an array element. Examples of such statements include assignment statements and statements that contain the TryParse method. Figure 9-17 shows examples of both types of statements, using three of the arrays from Figure 9-16.

HOW TO Store Data in a Two-Dimensional Array

Example 1
```
states(0, 1) = "Montgomery"
```
assigns the string "Montgomery" to the element located in the first row, second column in the **states** array

Example 2
```
For row As Integer = 0 To 4
    For column As Integer = 0 To 2
        totals(row, column) += 1
    Next column
Next row
```
adds the number 1 to the contents of each element in the **totals** array

Example 3
```
Dim row As Integer
Dim column As Integer
Do While row < 3
    column = 0
    Do While column < 2
        prices(row, column) *= 1.05
        column += 1
    Loop
    row += 1
Loop
```
increases the contents of each element in the **prices** array by 5%; you can also write the calculation statement as `prices(row, column) = prices(row, column) * 1.05`

Example 4
```
prices(2, 1) += 2.25
```
adds 2.25 to the value stored in the third row, second column in the **prices** array and then assigns the result to the element; you can also write this statement as `prices(2, 1) = prices(2, 1) + 2.25`

Example 5
```
Double.TryParse(priceTextBox.Text, prices(0, 0))
```
assigns either the value entered in the priceTextBox (converted to Double) or the number 0 to the element located in the first row, first column in the **prices** array

Figure 9-17 How to store data in a two-dimensional array

486

Earlier, you learned how to use the GetUpperBound method to determine the highest subscript in a one-dimensional array. You can also use the GetUpperBound method to determine the highest row and column subscripts in a two-dimensional array, as shown in Figure 9-18. The GetUpperBound methods are shaded in the example shown in the figure.

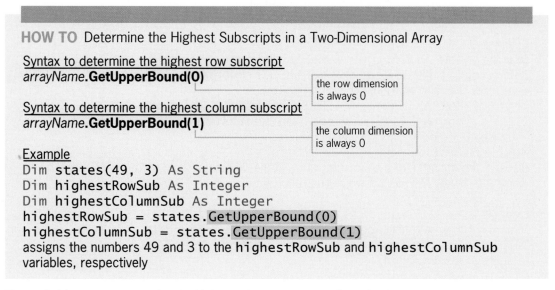

HOW TO Determine the Highest Subscripts in a Two-Dimensional Array

Syntax to determine the highest row subscript
arrayName.**GetUpperBound(0)**   the row dimension is always 0

Syntax to determine the highest column subscript
arrayName.**GetUpperBound(1)**   the column dimension is always 0

Example
```
Dim states(49, 3) As String
Dim highestRowSub As Integer
Dim highestColumnSub As Integer
highestRowSub = states.GetUpperBound(0)
highestColumnSub = states.GetUpperBound(1)
```
assigns the numbers 49 and 3 to the `highestRowSub` and `highestColumnSub` variables, respectively

Figure 9-18 How to determine the highest subscripts in a two-dimensional array
© 2013 Cengage Learning

Traversing a Two-Dimensional Array

Recall that you use a loop to traverse a one-dimensional array. To traverse a two-dimensional array, you typically use two loops: an outer loop and a nested loop. One of the loops keeps track of the row subscript and the other keeps track of the column subscript. You can code the loops using either the For...Next statement or the Do...Loop statement. Rather than using two loops to traverse a two-dimensional array, you can also use one For Each...Next loop. However, recall that the instructions in a For Each...Next loop can only read the array values; they cannot permanently modify the values.

Figure 9-19 shows examples of loops that traverse the `months` array, displaying each element's value in the monthsListBox. Both loops in Example 1 are coded using the For...Next statement. However, either one of the loops could be coded using the Do...Loop statement instead. Or, both loops could be coded using the Do...Loop statement, as shown in Example 2. The loop in Example 3 is coded using the For Each...Next statement.

HOW TO Traverse a Two-Dimensional Array

```
Private months(,) As String = {{"Jan", "31"},
                               {"Feb", "28"},
                               {"Mar", "31"},
                               {"Apr", "30"}}
```

Example 1
```
Dim highRow As Integer = months.GetUpperBound(0)
Dim highCol As Integer = months.GetUpperBound(1)
For row As Integer = 0 To highRow
    For col As Integer = 0 To highCol
        monthsListBox.Items.Add(months(row, col))
    Next col
Next row
```
displays the contents of the **months** array in the monthsListBox; the contents are displayed row by row, as shown in Illustration A

Example 2
```
Dim highRow As Integer = months.GetUpperBound(0)
Dim highCol As Integer = months.GetUpperBound(1)
Dim row As Integer
Dim col As Integer
Do While col <= highCol
    row = 0
    Do While row <= highRow
        monthsListBox.Items.Add(months(row, col))
        row += 1
    Loop
    col += 1
Loop
```
displays the contents of the **months** array in the monthsListBox; the contents are displayed column by column, as shown in Illustration B

Example 3
```
For Each monthElement As String In months
    monthsListBox.Items.Add(monthElement)
Next monthElement
```
displays the contents of the **months** array in the monthsListBox; the contents are displayed as shown in Illustration A

Illustration A   Illustration B

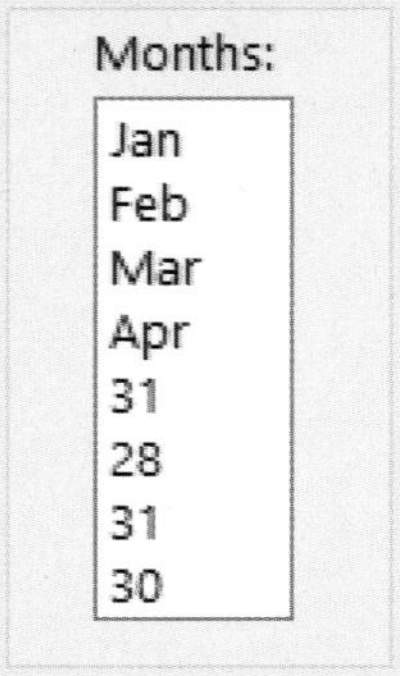

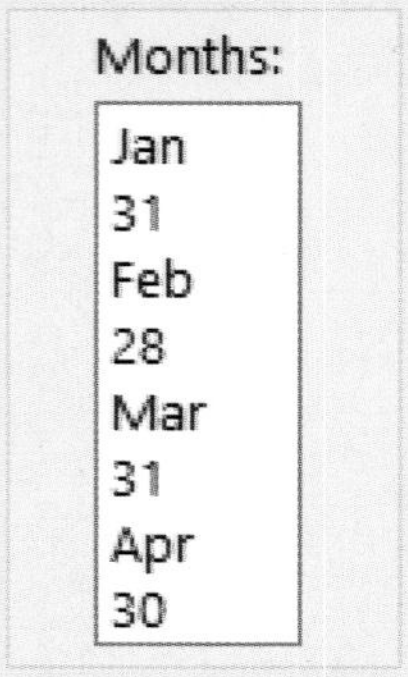 Months:
Jan
31
Feb
28
Mar
31
Apr
30

Months:
Jan
Feb
Mar
Apr
31
28
31
30

If you want to experiment with the code shown in Figure 9-19, open the solution contained in the Try It 8! folder.

Figure 9-19 How to traverse a two-dimensional array
© 2013 Cengage Learning

Totaling the Values Stored in a Two-Dimensional Array

Figure 9-20 shows the problem specification for the Tyler Motors application, which displays the total number of new cars sold, the total number of used cars sold, and the total number of cars sold. The figure also shows most of the application's code and includes a sample run of the application.

Problem specification
Tyler Motors sells new and used cars in each of its three dealerships. The sales manager wants an application that displays the total number of new cars sold, the total number of used cars sold, and the total number of cars sold in the previous month. The numbers sold for the previous month are shown here. The application will store the numbers sold in a two-dimensional array that has three rows and two columns. Each row will contain the data pertaining to one of the three dealerships. The first column in each row will contain the number of new cars sold at the dealership, and the second column will contain the number of used cars sold. The application will calculate the total number of new cars sold by accumulating the values stored in the array's first column. It will calculate the total number of used cars sold by accumulating the values stored in the array's second column. To calculate the total number of cars sold, the application will need to accumulate the values stored in the entire array.

	New cars sold	Used cars sold
Dealership 1	100	50
Dealership 2	84	35
Dealership 3	87	22

```
Private carsSold(,) As Integer = {{100, 50},        ┌─ class-level array declared
                                  {84, 35},          in the form's Declarations
                                  {87, 22}}          section

Private Sub newButton_Click(sender As Object,
e As EventArgs) Handles newButton.Click
    ' calculates the number of new cars sold

    Dim highRow As Integer = carsSold.GetUpperBound(0)
    Dim totalNew As Integer

    For row As Integer = 0 To highRow ┐
        totalNew += carsSold(row, 0)   ├── accumulates the first
    Next row ──────────────────────────┘    column's values
    newLabel.Text = totalNew.ToString
End Sub

Private Sub usedButton_Click(sender As Object,
e As EventArgs) Handles usedButton.Click
    ' calculates the number of used cars sold

    Dim highRow As Integer = carsSold.GetUpperBound(0)
    Dim totalUsed As Integer

    For row As Integer = 0 To highRow ┐
        totalUsed += carsSold(row, 1)  ├── accumulates the
    Next row ──────────────────────────┘    second column's values
    usedLabel.Text = totalUsed.ToString
End Sub

Private Sub totalButton_Click(sender As Object,
e As EventArgs) Handles totalButton.Click
    ' calculates the total number of cars sold

    Dim highRow As Integer = carsSold.GetUpperBound(0)
    Dim totalCars As Integer
```

If you want to experiment with the Tyler Motors application, open the solution contained in the Try It 9! folder.

Figure 9-20 Problem specification, code, and sample run for the Tyler Motors application (*continues*)

(continued)

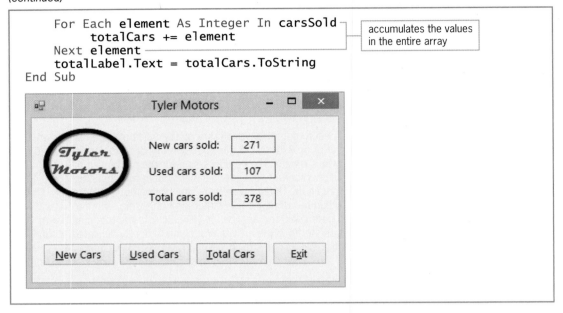

```
        For Each element As Integer In carsSold
            totalCars += element
        Next element
        totalLabel.Text = totalCars.ToString
    End Sub
```

accumulates the values in the entire array

Figure 9-20   Problem specification, code, and sample run for the Tyler Motors application
© 2013 Cengage Learning

The newButton_Click and usedButton_Click procedures in Figure 9-20 use the For...Next statement to accumulate the values in the first and second columns, respectively. The totalButton_Click procedure uses the For Each...Next statement to accumulate all of the array values.

Searching a Two-Dimensional Array

Figure 9-21 shows the problem specification for the O'Reilly Studios application, which displays the amount a customer owes for artwork. The figure also shows most of the application's code and includes a sample run of the application.

<u>Problem specification</u>
O'Reilly Studios sells paintings for local artists. The studio manager wants an application that allows him to enter the number of paintings a customer orders. The application should display the total cost of the order. The price per painting depends on the number of paintings ordered, as shown in the chart below. Notice that each price in the chart is associated with a range of values. The minimum value in the first range is 1, and the maximum value is 5. The minimum and maximum values in the second range are 6 and 10, respectively. The third range has only a minimum value, 11. The application should store each range's minimum value and price in a two-dimensional array that has three rows and two columns. The first column will contain the minimum values for the three ranges, entered in descending order: 11, 6, and 1. The second column will contain the prices associated with the minimum values: 75, 90, and 100. The application should search the first column in the array, row by row, looking for the first minimum value that is less than or equal to the quantity ordered. The appropriate price can be found in the same row as that minimum value, but in the second column.

Minimum order	Maximum order	Price per painting ($)
1	5	100
6	10	90
11		75

Figure 9-21   Problem specification, code, and sample run for the O'Reilly Studios application *(continues)*

(continued)

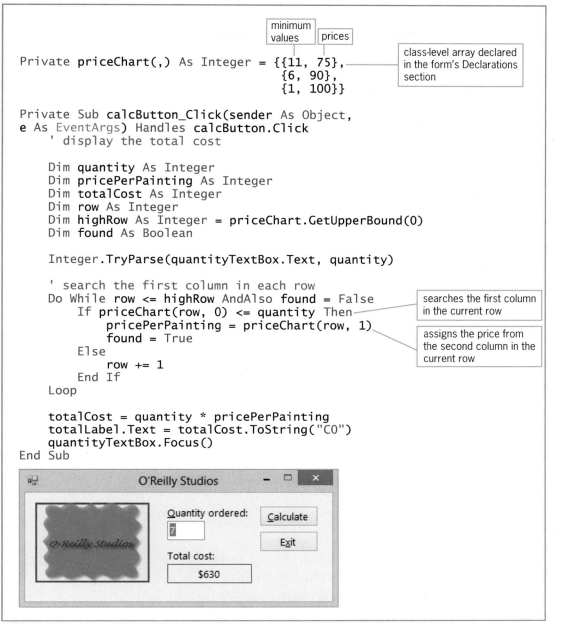

```vb
                                    minimum    prices
                                    values

Private priceChart(,) As Integer = {{11, 75},          class-level array declared
                                    {6, 90},           in the form's Declarations
                                    {1, 100}}          section

Private Sub calcButton_Click(sender As Object,
e As EventArgs) Handles calcButton.Click
    ' display the total cost

    Dim quantity As Integer
    Dim pricePerPainting As Integer
    Dim totalCost As Integer
    Dim row As Integer
    Dim highRow As Integer = priceChart.GetUpperBound(0)
    Dim found As Boolean

    Integer.TryParse(quantityTextBox.Text, quantity)

    ' search the first column in each row
    Do While row <= highRow AndAlso found = False        searches the first column
        If priceChart(row, 0) <= quantity Then            in the current row
            pricePerPainting = priceChart(row, 1)
            found = True                                  assigns the price from
        Else                                              the second column in the
            row += 1                                      current row
        End If
    Loop

    totalCost = quantity * pricePerPainting
    totalLabel.Text = totalCost.ToString("C0")
    quantityTextBox.Focus()
End Sub
```

O'Reilly Studios

Quantity ordered: **7**   [Calculate]

[Exit]

Total cost: **$630**

Figure 9-21 Problem specification, code, and sample run for the O'Reilly Studios application
© 2013 Cengage Learning

 If you want to experiment with the O'Reilly Studios application, open the solution contained in the Try It 10! folder.

The Private statement in the form's Declarations section declares and initializes the three-row, two-column priceChart array. Notice that the minimum values, which appear in ascending order in the chart shown in Figure 9-21, are entered in the array in descending order. The first three Dim statements in the calcButton_Click procedure declare and initialize variables to store the quantity ordered, price per painting, and total cost. The next three Dim statements declare the variables that will be used to search the array. The row variable will keep track of the row subscripts in the array, and the highRow variable will store the highest row subscript in the array. The Boolean found variable, which is automatically initialized to False, will keep track of whether the appropriate minimum value is located in the first column in the array.

After the variables are declared, the TryParse method converts the contents of the quantityTextBox to Integer and stores the result in the **quantity** variable. The Do clause then tells the computer to repeat the loop body while the current row subscript is less than or equal to the highest row subscript and, at the same time, the **found** variable contains False.

Within the loop body is a dual-alternative selection structure whose condition compares the value stored in the first column in the current row of the array with the quantity ordered. If the array value is less than or equal to the quantity ordered, the selection structure's True path assigns the price from the second column in the current row to the **pricePerPainting** variable. It also assigns the Boolean value True to the **found** variable to indicate that the appropriate range was located. On the other hand, if the array value is greater than the quantity ordered, the instruction in the selection structure's False path updates the row subscript by 1, allowing the loop to search the next row in the array. When the loop ends, the procedure calculates the total price and then displays the result in the interface. As shown earlier in Figure 9-21, the procedure displays $630 when the user enters 7 in the Quantity ordered box.

The answers to Mini-Quiz questions are located in Appendix A. Each question is associated with one or more objectives listed at the beginning of the chapter.

Mini-Quiz 9-3

1. Which of the following declares a four-row, two-column String array named **letters**? (1)

   a. `Dim letters(3, 1) As String`

   b. `Private letters(3, 1) As String`

   c. `Dim letters(,) As String = {{"A", "B"}, {"C", "D"}, {"E", "F"}, {"G", "H"}}`

   d. all of the above

2. Which of the following assigns the Boolean value True to the element located in the third row, first column of a two-dimensional Boolean array named **testAnswers**? (2)

   a. `testAnswers(0, 2) = True`

   b. `testAnswers(2, 0) = True`

   c. `testAnswers(3, 1) = True`

   d. `testAnswers(1, 3) = True`

3. An application uses a two-dimensional array named **population**. Which of the following assigns the array's highest column subscript to the **highCol** variable? (3)

   a. `highCol = population.GetUpperBound(0)`

   b. `highCol = population.GetUpperBound(1)`

   c. `highCol = population.GetUpperColumn(0)`

   d. `highCol = population.UpperColumn(1)`

You have completed the concepts section of Chapter 9. The Programming Tutorial section is next.

492

PROGRAMMING TUTORIAL 1

Coding the Lottery Game Application

In this tutorial, you will code the Lottery Game application. Figures 9-22 and 9-23 show the application's TOE chart and MainForm, respectively. When the user clicks the Get Numbers button, the button's Click event procedure should generate and display six unique random numbers. Each number can range from 1 through 54 only.

Task	Object	Event
1. Generate random numbers from 1 through 54	getButton	Click
2. Store six unique random numbers in a one-dimensional array		
3. Display the contents of the array in the numbersLabel		
End the application	exitButton	Click
Display the six unique random numbers (from getButton)	numbersLabel	None

Figure 9-22 TOE chart for the Lottery Game application
© 2013 Cengage Learning

Figure 9-23 MainForm for the Lottery Game application

Coding the Application

According to the application's TOE chart, only the Click event procedures for the two buttons need to be coded.

To open the Lottery Game application:

1. Start Visual Studio. Open the **Lottery Game Solution** (**Lottery Game Solution.sln**) file contained in the VbReloaded2012\Chap09\Lottery Game Solution folder. If necessary, open the designer window.

2. Open the Code Editor window. Notice that the exitButton_Click procedure has already been coded for you. In the comments that appear in the General Declarations section, replace <your name> and <current date> with your name and the current date, respectively.

Figure 9-24 shows the pseudocode for the getButton_Click procedure, which is responsible for generating and displaying six unique lottery numbers.

---

getButton Click event procedure
1. declare a six-element Integer array named numbers
2. generate a random number from 1 through 54 and then store it in the first array element
3. repeat until all of the remaining array elements contain a unique random number
        generate a random number from 1 through 54

        search the array elements that already contain numbers

        if the random number is not already in the array
                store the random number in the current array element and
                then continue with the next array element
        end if
    end repeat

4. display the contents of the array in the numbersLabel

Figure 9-24   Pseudocode for the getButton_Click procedure
© 2013 Cengage Learning

To begin coding the getButton_Click procedure:

1. Locate the getButton's Click event procedure. The procedure will store the six unique lottery numbers in a one-dimensional Integer array that has six elements. Click the **blank line** above the End Sub clause and then enter the following Dim statement:

    Dim numbers(5) As Integer

2. Next, you need to declare a Random object to represent the pseudo-random number generator in the procedure. Enter the following Dim statement:

    Dim randGen As New Random

3. The procedure will store the random numbers generated by the pseudo-random number generator in an Integer variable named randomNum. Enter the following Dim statement:

    Dim randomNum As Integer

4. While the procedure's loop is filling the array with values, it will use an Integer variable to keep track of the array subscripts. Enter the following Dim statement:

    Dim subscript As Integer

5. The procedure's loop will use another Integer variable to keep track of the array subscripts while the array is being searched. Enter the following Dim statement:

    Dim searchSubscript As Integer

6. The procedure will use a Boolean variable to indicate whether the current random number is already contained in the array. Enter the following Dim statement:

    Dim found As Boolean

7. The last variable you need to declare will store the highest subscript in the numbers array. Type the following statement and then press **Enter** twice:

    Dim highestSub As Integer = numbers.GetUpperBound(0)

8. The first step in the procedure's pseudocode (shown earlier in Figure 9-24) is to declare the numbers array; that step has already been coded. The second step is to generate a random number from 1 through 54 and then store it in the first array element. Enter the following comments and assignment statement. Press **Enter** twice after typing the assignment statement.

   ' generate the first random number and
   ' store it in the first array element
   numbers(0) = randGen.Next(1, 55)

9. Next, the procedure should fill the remaining array elements, which have subscripts of 1 through 5, with unique random numbers. Enter the following comments and lines of code. (The Code Editor will automatically enter the Loop clause for you.) Press **Enter** twice after typing the last assignment statement.

   ' fill remaining array elements with
   ' unique random numbers
   subscript = 1
   Do While subscript <= highestSub
   **   randomNum = randGen.Next(1, 55)**

10. Save the solution.

Now, the procedure needs to search the array to verify that it does not contain the newly generated random number, which is stored in the randomNum variable. Only the array elements that already contain numbers need to be searched. Those elements have subscripts starting with 0 and ending with the subscript that is one less than the current subscript. In other words, if the current subscript is 1, you need to search only the numbers(0) element because that is the only element that contains a number. Similarly, if the current subscript is 4, you need to search only the numbers(0), numbers(1), numbers(2), and numbers(3) elements.

To finish coding the getButton_Click procedure and then test the code:

1. Enter the following comments:

   ' search the array for the random number
   ' stop the search when there are no more
   ' elements or when the random number is found

2. The search should begin with the first array element. Enter the following statement:

   searchSubscript = 0

3. Before the search begins, the procedure will assume that the newly generated random number is not already in the array. Enter the following statement:

   found = False

4. The procedure should continue searching as long as there are array elements to search and, at the same time, the random number has not been found in the array. Enter the following code. (The Code Editor will automatically enter the Loop clause for you.)

   Do While searchSubscript < subscript AndAlso found = False

5. Now, enter the following comments and code:

   ' if the random number is in the current
   ' array element, assign True to found
   ' otherwise, examine the next element
   If numbers(searchSubscript) = randomNum Then
   **   found = True**
   Else
   **   searchSubscript += 1**
   End If

6. If the newly generated random number is *not* in the array, the procedure should assign the random number to the current array element and then prepare to fill the next element. Insert **two blank lines** between the two Loop clauses, and then position the insertion point in the second blank line. Enter the following comments and selection structure:

```
' if the random number is not in the array
' assign the random number to the current array
' element and then move to the next element
If found = False Then
    numbers(subscript) = randomNum
    subscript += 1
End If
```

7. The last step in the procedure's pseudocode displays the contents of the `numbers` array, which now contains the six unique lottery numbers. Insert **two blank lines** between the outer Loop clause and the End Sub clause. In the blank line above the End Sub clause, enter the following comment and code. Be sure to include two spaces between the quotation marks. Also be sure to change the Next clause to `Next num`.

```
' display the contents of the array
numbersLabel.Text = String.Empty
For Each num As Integer In numbers
    numbersLabel.Text = numbersLabel.Text &
    " " & num.ToString
Next num
```

8. Save the solution and then start the application. Click the **Get Numbers** button. Six unique numbers appear in the Lottery numbers box. See Figure 9-25.

Figure 9-25 Sample run of the Lottery Game application

9. Click the **Get Numbers** button several times to continue testing the code. When you are finished, click the **Exit** button. Close the Code Editor window and then close the solution. Figure 9-26 shows the application's code.

```vbnet
1  ' Project name:          Lottery Game Project
2  ' Project purpose:       Displays six unique random
3  '                        numbers from 1 through 54
4  ' Created/revised by:    <your name> on <current date>
5
6  Option Explicit On
7  Option Strict On
8  Option Infer Off
9
10 Public Class MainForm
11
12     Private Sub exitButton_Click(sender As Object,
       e As EventArgs) Handles exitButton.Click
13         Me.Close()
14     End Sub
15
16     Private Sub getButton_Click(sender As Object,
       e As EventArgs) Handles getButton.Click
17         ' generates and displays six unique random
18         ' numbers from 1 through 54
19
20         Dim numbers(5) As Integer
21         Dim randGen As New Random
22         Dim randomNum As Integer
23         Dim subscript As Integer
24         Dim searchSubscript As Integer
25         Dim found As Boolean
26         Dim highestSub As Integer = numbers.GetUpperBound(0)
27
28         ' generate the first random number and
29         ' store it in the first array element
30         numbers(0) = randGen.Next(1, 55)
31
32         ' fill remaining array elements with
33         ' unique random numbers
34         subscript = 1
35         Do While subscript <= highestSub
36             randomNum = randGen.Next(1, 55)
37
38             ' search the array for the random number
39             ' stop the search when there are no more
40             ' elements or when the random number is found
41             searchSubscript = 0
42             found = False
43             Do While searchSubscript < subscript AndAlso found = False
44                 ' if the random number is in the current
45                 ' array element, assign True to found
46                 ' otherwise, examine the next element
47                 If numbers(searchSubscript) = randomNum Then
48                     found = True
49                 Else
50                     searchSubscript += 1
51                 End If
52             Loop
53
54             ' if the random number is not in the array
55             ' assign the random number to the current array
56             ' element and then move to the next element
57             If found = False Then
58                 numbers(subscript) = randomNum
59                 subscript += 1
60             End If
61         Loop
62
```

Figure 9-26   Code for the Lottery Game application *(continues)*

(continued)

```
63          ' display the contents of the array
64          numbersLabel.Text = String.Empty
65          For Each num As Integer In numbers
66              numbersLabel.Text = numbersLabel.Text &
67              "    " & num.ToString
68          Next num
69      End Sub
70 End Class
```

Figure 9-26 Code for the Lottery Game application
© 2013 Cengage Learning

PROGRAMMING TUTORIAL 2

Coding the Patterson Museum Application

In this tutorial, you will code an application for the Patterson Museum. The application displays the annual fees for three different membership levels: Gold, Silver, and Bronze. The annual fees are based on the membership type, which can be Individual, Family, or Patron. The appropriate fees are listed in Figure 9-27. The application's TOE chart and MainForm are shown in Figures 9-28 and 9-29, respectively.

Membership type	Membership level	Fee ($)
Individual	Gold	300
	Silver	200
	Bronze	100
Family	Gold	500
	Silver	425
	Bronze	350
Patron	Gold	900
	Silver	775
	Bronze	600

Figure 9-27 Patterson Museum's annual membership fees
© 2013 Cengage Learning

Task	Object	Event
Declare and initialize a class-level array named feeTable that has three rows and three columns	MainForm	Declarations section
1. Fill the membershipListBox with the membership types 2. Select the first membership type in the membershipListBox		Load
End the application	exitButton	Click
Specify the membership type Use the index of the item selected in the membershipListBox to display the fees for the three membership levels in the goldLabel, silverLabel, and bronzeLabel	membershipListBox	None SelectedIndexChanged
Display the fees for the three membership levels (from membershipListBox)	goldLabel, silverLabel, bronzeLabel	None

Figure 9-28 TOE chart for the Patterson Museum application
© 2013 Cengage Learning

Figure 9-29 MainForm for the Patterson Museum application

Coding the Application

According to the application's TOE chart, three procedures need to be coded: the MainForm's Load event procedure, the exitButton's Click event procedure, and the membershipListBox's SelectedIndexChanged event procedure. You also need to declare and initialize a two-dimensional array in the MainForm's Declarations section.

To begin coding the application:

1. Start Visual Studio. Open the **Patterson Solution (Patterson Solution.sln)** file contained in the VbReloaded2012\Chap09\Patterson Solution folder. If necessary, open the designer window.

2. Open the Code Editor window. Notice that the exitButton's Click event procedure has already been coded for you. In the comments that appear in the General Declarations section, replace <your name> and <current date> with your name and the current date, respectively.

3. First, you will complete the MainForm's Load event procedure, which is responsible for filling the membershipListBox with the three membership types and then selecting the first type. Open the code template for the MainForm's Load event procedure. Type the following comment and then press **Enter** twice:

   ' fills the list box

4. Enter the statements to add the following three membership types to the membershipListBox: Individual, Family, and Patron.

5. Now, enter the statement to select the first type in the membershipListBox.

6. Save the solution and then start the application. The three membership types appear in the membershipListBox, with the first type selected in the list.

7. Click the **Exit** button to end the application.

Next, you will declare the `feeTable` array in the MainForm's Declarations section. The array should have three rows and three columns. Each row represents a membership type (Individual, Family, and Patron), and each column represents a membership level (Gold, Silver, and Bronze).

To declare and initialize the array:

1. Click the **blank line** below the `' class-level array` comment, and then enter the statement to declare a three-row, three-column Integer array named `feeTable`. Initialize the array using the fees shown earlier in Figure 9-27.

2. Save the solution.

The last procedure you need to code is the list box's SelectedIndexChanged event procedure.

To code the membershipListBox_SelectedIndexChanged procedure, and then test the code:

1. Open the code template for the membershipListBox's SelectedIndexChanged event procedure. Type the following comment and then press **Enter** twice:

   ' display annual membership fees

2. Next, enter the statement to declare an Integer variable named **row**. The statement should initialize the variable to the index of the item selected in the list box.

3. Now, enter three assignment statements. Each assignment statement should assign the appropriate fees to the goldLabel, silverLabel, and bronzeLabel controls, respectively, in the interface. Format the fees with a dollar sign and no decimal places.

4. Save the solution and then start the application. The fees for an Individual membership appear in the interface, as shown in Figure 9-30.

Figure 9-30   Sample run of the Patterson Museum application

5. Click **Family** in the list box. The fees for a Family membership ($500, $425, and $350) appear in the interface.

6. Click **Patron** in the list box. The fees for a Patron membership ($900, $775, and $600) appear in the interface.

7. Click the **Exit** button. Close the Code Editor window and then close the solution. Figure 9-31 shows the code for the Patterson Museum application.

```
1 ' Project name:       Patterson Project
2 ' Project purpose:    Display the annual membership fees
3 ' Created/revised by: <your name> on <current date>
4
5 Option Explicit On
6 Option Strict On
7 Option Infer Off
8
9 Public Class MainForm
10
11     ' class-level array
12     Private feeTable(,) As Integer = {{300, 200, 100},
13                                       {500, 425, 350},
14                                       {900, 775, 600}}
15
16     Private Sub exitButton_Click(sender As Object,
        e As EventArgs) Handles exitButton.Click
17         Me.Close()
18     End Sub
19
```

Figure 9-31   Code for the Patterson Museum application *(continues)*

(continued)

```
20      Private Sub MainForm_Load(sender As Object,
        e As EventArgs) Handles Me.Load
21          ' fills the list box
22
23          membershipListBox.Items.Add("Individual")
24          membershipListBox.Items.Add("Family")
25          membershipListBox.Items.Add("Patron")
26          membershipListBox.SelectedIndex = 0
27
28      End Sub
29
30      Private Sub membershipListBox_SelectedIndexChanged(
        sender As Object, e As EventArgs
        ) Handles membershipListBox.SelectedIndexChanged
31          ' display annual membership fees
32
33          Dim row As Integer = membershipListBox.SelectedIndex
34          goldLabel.Text = feeTable(row, 0).ToString("C0")
35          silverLabel.Text = feeTable(row, 1).ToString("C0")
36          bronzeLabel.Text = feeTable(row, 2).ToString("C0")
37
38      End Sub
39 End Class
```

Figure 9-31 Code for the Patterson Museum application
© 2013 Cengage Learning

PROGRAMMING EXAMPLE

Professor Coleman Application

Create an interface that allows Professor Coleman to select one of the following letter grades from a list box: A, B, C, D, or F. The application should display the names of the students who earned the selected letter grade. The application should store each student's name and letter grade in a two-dimensional array that has 11 rows and two columns. The first column should contain the student names, and the second column should contain the grades. Use the following names for the solution and project, respectively: Coleman Solution and Coleman Project. Save the application in the VbReloaded2012\Chap09 folder. Change the form file's name to Main Form.vb. See Figures 9-32 through 9-36.

Task	Object	Event
Declare and initialize a class-level array named studentInfo that has 11 rows and two columns	MainForm	Declarations section
1. Fill the gradeListBox with the letter grades 2. Select the first letter grade in the gradeListBox		Load
End the application	exitButton	Click
Specify the letter grade Clear the namesListBox	gradeListBox	None SelectedIndexChanged
1. Search the studentInfo array for the letter grade selected in the gradeListBox 2. Display the names of students who earned the selected letter grade in the namesListBox	findButton	Click
Display the names of students who earned the grade selected in the gradeListBox (from findButton)	namesListBox	None

Figure 9-32 TOE chart
© 2013 Cengage Learning

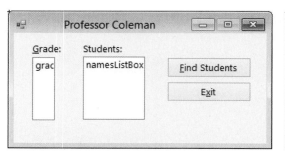

Figure 9-33 MainForm and tab order

Object	Property	Setting
MainForm	Font	Segoe UI, 10 point
	MaximizeBox	False
	StartPosition	CenterScreen
	Text	Professor Coleman
namesListBox	SelectionMode	None

Figure 9-34 Objects, properties, and settings
© 2013 Cengage Learning

---

exitButton Click event procedure
close the application

MainForm Load event procedure
1. fill the gradeListBox with the following letter grades: A, B, C, D, and F
2. select the first letter grade in the gradeListBox

gradeListBox SelectedIndexChanged event procedure
clear the namesListBox

Figure 9-35 Pseudocode *(continues)*

502

(continued)

findButton Click event procedure
1. assign the grade selected in the gradeListBox to a variable named searchGrade
2. repeat for array rows from 0 through the highest row subscript
        if the grade stored in the second column in the current row matches
        the grade stored in the searchGrade variable
                add the student name, which is stored in the first column in
                the current row, to the namesListBox
        end if
    end repeat for

3. if the namesListBox does not contain any names
        display "NONE" in the namesListBox
    end if

Figure 9-35 Pseudocode
© 2013 Cengage Learning

```
1  ' Project name:         Coleman Project
2  ' Project purpose:      Display the names of students
3  '                       who earned a specific grade
4  ' Created/revised by:   <your name> on <current date>
5
6  Option Explicit On
7  Option Strict On
8  Option Infer Off
9
10 Public Class MainForm
11
12     Private studentInfo(,) As String = {{"Carol", "A"},
13                         {"Toby", "C"}, {"George", "A"},
14                         {"Elaine", "B"}, {"Francisco", "C"},
15                         {"Khalid", "B"}, {"Jack", "C"},
16                         {"Carl", "F"}, {"Susan", "B"},
17                         {"Mark", "A"}, {"Monica", "B"}}
18
19     Private Sub exitButton_Click(sender As Object,
       e As EventArgs) Handles exitButton.Click
20         Me.Close()
21     End Sub
22
23     Private Sub gradeListBox_SelectedIndexChanged(
       sender As Object, e As EventArgs
       ) Handles gradeListBox.SelectedIndexChanged
24         namesListBox.Items.Clear()
25     End Sub
26
27     Private Sub MainForm_Load(sender As Object,
       e As EventArgs) Handles Me.Load
28         gradeListBox.Items.Add("A")
29         gradeListBox.Items.Add("B")
30         gradeListBox.Items.Add("C")
31         gradeListBox.Items.Add("D")
32         gradeListBox.Items.Add("F")
33         gradeListBox.SelectedIndex = 0
34     End Sub
35
```

Figure 9-36 Code (continues)

```
36    Private Sub findButton_Click(sender As Object,
      e As EventArgs) Handles findButton.Click
37        ' displays the names of students who earned the
38        ' grade selected in the gradeListBox
39
40        Dim highRowSub As Integer =
41            studentInfo.GetUpperBound(0)
42        Dim searchGrade As String
43
44        searchGrade = gradeListBox.SelectedItem.ToString
45        For row As Integer = 0 To highRowSub
46            If studentInfo(row, 1) = searchGrade Then
47                namesListBox.Items.Add(studentInfo(row, 0))
48            End If
49        Next row
50
51        If namesListBox.Items.Count = 0 Then
52            namesListBox.Items.Add("NONE")
53        End If
54    End Sub
55 End Class
```

Figure 9-36 Code
© 2013 Cengage Learning

Summary

- Programmers use arrays to temporarily store related data in the internal memory of the computer.

- All of the elements in an array have the same name and data type. However, each has a different subscript (one-dimensional array) or subscripts (two-dimensional array).

- When declaring a one-dimensional array, you provide either the highest subscript or the initial values.

- Each element in a one-dimensional array is identified by a unique subscript that appears in parentheses after the array's name. The first subscript in a one-dimensional array is 0.

- You refer to an element in a one-dimensional array using the array's name followed by the element's subscript, which is enclosed in parentheses.

- Examples of statements that you can use to change the data stored in an array include assignment statements and statements that contain the TryParse method.

- A one-dimensional array's Length property contains an integer that represents the number of elements in the array. The number of elements is always one more than the array's highest subscript.

- A one-dimensional array's GetUpperBound method returns an integer that represents the highest subscript in the array. The highest subscript is always one number less than the number of array elements.

- You use a loop to traverse a one-dimensional array. You can code the loop using the For...Next, Do...Loop, or For Each...Next statements. However, keep in mind that the instructions within a For Each...Next loop can only read the array values; the instructions cannot permanently change the values.

- You can associate the items in a list box with the elements in an array. You do this using the list box's index and the array's subscript, both of which start at 0.

- You can use the elements in an array as accumulators or counters.

- The Array.Sort method sorts the elements in a one-dimensional array in ascending order. The Array.Reverse method reverses the order of the elements in a one-dimensional array.

- A two-dimensional array resembles a table in that the elements are in rows and columns.

- When declaring a two-dimensional array, you provide either the highest row and column subscripts or the initial values.

- The number of rows in a two-dimensional array is one number more than its highest row subscript. Likewise, the number of columns is one number more than its highest column subscript.

- You can determine the number of elements in a two-dimensional array by multiplying the number of its rows by the number of its columns. You can also use the array's Length property.

- Each element in a two-dimensional array is identified by a unique combination of two subscripts: a row subscript and a column subscript. The subscripts appear in parentheses after the array's name. You list the row subscript first, followed by a comma and the column subscript. The first row subscript in a two-dimensional array is 0. Likewise, the first column subscript also is 0.

- You can use a two-dimensional array's GetUpperBound method to determine the highest row subscript and highest column subscript in the array.

- You can traverse a two-dimensional array using either two loops (coded with the For...Next or Do...Loop statements) or one loop (coded with the For Each...Next statement). However, recall that the instructions in a For Each...Next loop can only read the array values; they cannot permanently change the values.

Key Terms

Array—a group of related variables that have the same name and data type and are distinguished by one or more subscripts

Array.Reverse method—reverses the order of the elements in a one-dimensional array

Array.Sort method—sorts the elements in a one-dimensional array in ascending order

Element—a variable in an array

For Each...Next statement—used to code a loop whose instructions you want processed for each element in a group

GetUpperBound method—returns an integer that represents the highest subscript in a specified dimension; the dimension is 0 for a one-dimensional array; for a two-dimensional array, the dimension is 0 for the row subscript, but 1 for the column subscript

Length property—one of the properties of an array; stores an integer that represents the number of array elements

One-dimensional array—an array whose elements are identified by a unique subscript

Populating the array—refers to the process of initializing the elements in an array

Scalar variable—another term for a simple variable

Simple variable—a variable that is unrelated to any other variable in the computer's internal memory; also called a scalar variable

Sorting—the process of arranging data in a specific order

Subscript—a unique number that identifies the position of an element in an array

Two-dimensional array—an array made up of rows and columns; each element has the same name and data type and is identified by a unique combination of two subscripts: a row subscript and a column subscript

Review Questions

1. Which of the following declares a five-element array named **prices**? (1)

    a. `Dim prices(4) As Decimal`

    b. `Dim prices(5) As Decimal`

    c. `Dim prices() As Decimal = {3.55D, 6.7D, 8D, 4D, 2.34D}`

    d. both a and c

Each Review Question is associated with one or more objectives listed at the beginning of the chapter.

2. The **items** array is declared using the `Dim items(20) As String` statement. The **x** variable keeps track of the array subscripts and is initialized to 0. Which of the following Do clauses will process the loop instructions for each element in the array? (3, 4)

    a. `Do While x > items.GetUpperBound(0)`

    b. `Do While x < items.GetUpperBound(0)`

    c. `Do While x >= items.GetUpperBound(0)`

    d. `Do While x <= items.GetUpperBound(0)`

Use the information shown in Figure 9-37 to answer Review Questions 3 through 7.

```
Dim sales() As Integer = {10000, 12000, 900, 500, 20000}
```

Figure 9-37 Code for Review Questions 3 through 7

© 2013 Cengage Learning

3. The `sales(3) += 10` statement will replace the number _____. (2)

    a. 500 with 10

    b. 500 with 510

    c. 900 with 10

    d. 900 with 910

4. The `sales(4) = sales(4 - 2)` statement will replace the number _____. (2)

    a. 20000 with 900

    b. 20000 with 19998

    c. 500 with 12000

    d. 500 with 498

5. Which of the following If clauses verifies that the array subscript stored in the **x** variable is valid for the **sales** array? (3)

    a. `If sales(x) >= 0 AndAlso sales(x) < 4 Then`

    b. `If sales(x) >= 0 OrElse sales(x) <= 4 Then`

    c. `If x >= 0 AndAlso`
        `x <= sales.GetUpperBound(0) Then`

    d. `If x >= 0 AndAlso`
        `x < sales.GetUpperBound(0) Then`

6. Which of the following will correctly add 100 to each element in the `sales` array? The `x` variable was declared using the `Dim x As Integer` statement. (2-4, 9)

a.
```
Do While x <= sales.GetUpperBound(0)
    x += 100
Loop
```

b.
```
Do While x <= sales.GetUpperBound(0)
    sales += 100
Loop
```

c.
```
Do While sales < sales.Length
    sales(x) += 100
Loop
```

d.
```
Do While x < sales.Length
    sales(x) += 100
    x += 1
Loop
```

7. Which of the following statements sorts the `sales` array in ascending order? (10)

a. `Array.Sort(sales)`

b. `sales.Sort()`

c. `Sort(sales)`

d. `SortArray(sales)`

Use the information shown in Figure 9-38 to answer Review Question 8.

```
Dim numbers() As Double = {10, 5, 7, 2}
Dim x As Integer
Dim total As Double
Dim avg As Double
```

Figure 9-38 Code for Review Question 8
© 2013 Cengage Learning

8. Which of the following will correctly calculate the average of the elements included in the `numbers` array? (2-4, 6)

a.
```
Do While x < numbers.Length
    numbers(x) = total + total
    x += 1
Loop
avg = total / x
```

b.
```
Do While x < numbers.Length
    total += numbers(x)
    x += 1
Loop
avg = total / x
```

c. ```
Do While x < numbers.Length
    total += numbers(x)
    x += 1
Loop
avg = total / x - 1
```

d. ```
Do While x < numbers.Length
    total += numbers(x)
    x += 1
Loop
avg = total / (x - 1)
```

9. Which of the following statements creates an array that contains three rows and four columns? (1)

a. `Dim temps(2, 3) As Decimal`
b. `Dim temps(3, 4) As Decimal`
c. `Dim temps(3, 2) As Decimal`
d. `Dim temps(4, 3) As Decimal`

Use the information shown in Figure 9-39 to answer Review Questions 10 and 11.

```
Dim sales(,) As Decimal = {{1000, 1200, 900, 500, 2000},
                          {350, 600, 700, 800, 100}}
```

Figure 9-39 Code for Review Questions 10 and 11
© 2013 Cengage Learning

10. The `sales(1, 3) += 10` statement will replace the number ——————. (2)

a. 900 with 910
b. 500 with 510
c. 700 with 710
d. 800 with 810

11. Which of the following If clauses verifies that the array subscripts stored in the r and c variables are valid for the `sales` array? (3)

a. ```
If sales(r, c) >= 0 AndAlso
    sales(r, c) <= sales.UpperBound(0) Then
```

b. ```
If sales(r, c) >= 0 AndAlso
    sales(r, c) < sales.Length Then
```

c. ```
If r >= 0 AndAlso r < sales.Length AndAlso
    c >= 0 AndAlso c < sales.Length Then
```

d. ```
If r >= 0 AndAlso r <= sales.GetUpperBound(0) AndAlso
    c >= 0 AndAlso c <= sales.GetUpperBound(1) Then
```

12. Which of the following assigns the string "California" to the variable located in the third column, fifth row of the **states** array? (2)

    a. `states(3, 5) = "California"`

    b. `states(5, 3) = "California"`

    c. `states(4, 2) = "California"`

    d. `states(2, 4) = "California"`

Each Exercise, except the DISCOVERY exercise, is associated with one or more objectives listed at the beginning of the chapter.

Exercises

Pencil and Paper

1. Write a Dim statement that declares a 10-element, one-dimensional Integer array named **population**. Then write the statement to store the number 7800 in the second element in the array. (1, 2)

   INTRODUCTORY

2. Write the code to display the contents of the **population** array from Pencil and Paper Exercise 1 in the popListBox. Use the For Each...Next statement. Then rewrite the code using the For...Next statement. (3-5)

   INTRODUCTORY

3. Write a Private statement that declares and initializes a five-element, one-dimensional Double array named **rates**. Use the following numbers to initialize the array: 6.5, 8.3, 4.0, 2.0, and 10.5. (1)

   INTRODUCTORY

4. Write the code to display the contents of the **rates** array from Pencil and Paper Exercise 3 in the ratesListBox. Use the Do...Loop statement. Then rewrite the code using the For Each...Next statement. (3-5)

   INTRODUCTORY

5. Write a statement that assigns the number of elements in the one-dimensional **flowerTypes** array to an Integer variable named **numTypes**. (3)

   INTRODUCTORY

6. Write a statement that assigns the highest subscript in the one-dimensional **flowerTypes** array to an Integer variable named **highSub**. (3)

   INTRODUCTORY

7. The **nums** array is a one-dimensional Integer array. Write the code to multiply the value stored in the array's first element by 2. Assign the result to the **numDoubled** variable. (2)

   INTRODUCTORY

8. Write the code to add together the numbers stored in the first and second elements in a one-dimensional Integer array named **nums**. Display the sum in the sumLabel. (2)

   INTRODUCTORY

9. Write a Private statement that declares a four-row, six-column Double array named **balances**. (1)

   INTRODUCTORY

10. Write the code to display the contents of a two-dimensional String array named **parts** in the partsListBox. Use the For Each...Next statement. Then rewrite the code using two For...Next statements to display the array, row by row. (2-5)

    INTERMEDIATE

11. The **dogTypes** array is a two-dimensional String array. Write the statements that assign the highest row subscript and the highest column subscript to Integer variables named **highRow** and **highColumn**, respectively. (3)

    INTERMEDIATE

12. The **dogTypes** array is a two-dimensional String array. Write the statement that assigns the number of array elements to an Integer variable named **numTypes**. (3)

    INTERMEDIATE

13. Write the code to subtract the number 1 from each element in a one-dimensional Integer array named **quantities**. Use the Do...Loop statement. (2-4, 9)

    INTERMEDIATE

INTERMEDIATE

14. The `sales` array is a two-dimensional Double array. Write the statement to total the numbers stored in the following three array elements: the first row, first column; the second row, third column; and the third row, fourth column. Assign the sum to the `total` variable. (2)

INTERMEDIATE

15. The `quantities` array is a two-dimensional Integer array. Write the code to subtract the number 1 from each array element. Use two For...Next statements. (2-4, 9)

ADVANCED

16. The `orders` array is a two-dimensional Integer array. Write the code to determine the largest number stored in the first column of the array. Use the For...Next statement. (2-4, 7)

 Computer

MODIFY THIS

17. Open the Starward Coffee Solution (Starward Coffee Solution.sln) file contained in the VbReloaded2012\Chap09\Starward Coffee Solution folder. Modify the interface and code so that each button (except the Exit button) also displays the lowest and highest values stored in the `poundsUsed` array. Save the solution and then start and test the application. Close the solution. (2-5, 7)

MODIFY THIS

18. Open the Car-Mart Solution (Car-Mart Solution.sln) file contained in the VbReloaded2012\Chap09\Car-Mart Solution folder. Replace the For...Next statement in the code with the For Each...Next statement. Save the solution and then start and test the application. Close the solution. (2, 4, 5, 7)

MODIFY THIS

19. If necessary, complete the Patterson Museum application from this chapter's Programming Tutorial 2, and then close the solution. Use Windows to make a copy of the Patterson Solution folder. Rename the folder Patterson Solution-ModifyThis. Open the Patterson Solution (Patterson Solution.sln) file contained in the Patterson Solution-ModifyThis folder. The museum has just announced a new membership type: Military. The fees for the Gold, Silver, and Bronze levels are $250, $200, and $150, respectively. Modify the interface and code to accommodate the new membership type. Save the solution and then start and test the application. Close the solution. (2, 8)

INTRODUCTORY

20. In this exercise, you code an application that sums the values contained in a two-dimensional array. Open the Inventory Solution (Inventory Solution.sln) file contained in the VbReloaded2012\Chap09\Inventory Solution folder. Code the displayButton_Click procedure so that it adds together the values stored in the `inventory` array. Display the sum in the totalLabel. (2-6)

INTRODUCTORY

21. Open the Update Prices Solution (Update Prices Solution.sln) file contained in the VbReloaded2012\Chap09\Update Prices Solution folder. Declare a class-level, one-dimensional Double array named `prices`. Initialize the array using the following 10 prices: 6.75, 12.50, 33.50, 10.00, 9.50, 25.50, 7.65, 8.35, 9.75, and 3.50. Open the code template for the increaseButton_Click procedure. The procedure should ask the user for a percentage amount by which each price in the array should be increased. It then should increase each price by that amount, displaying each increased price (with two decimal places) in the list box. Save the solution and then start the application. Click the Increase button. Increase each price by 5%. Close the solution. (1-5, 8)

22. Open the Tips Solution (Tips Solution.sln) file contained in the VbReloaded2012\ Chap09\Tips Solution folder. (The image in the picture box was downloaded from the Open Clip Art Library at *http://openclipart.org.*) Declare a class-level, one-dimensional array containing the following tip amounts: 101.5, 95, 67.75, and 83. The forNextButton_Click procedure should use the For...Next statement to calculate the average tip. The doLoopButton_Click procedure should use the Do...Loop statement to calculate the average tip. The forEachNextButton_Click procedure should use the For Each...Next statement to calculate the average tip. Code the procedures, which should display the average tip (with two decimal places) in the avgLabel. Save the solution and then start and test the application. Close the solution. (1-6) **INTRODUCTORY**

23. In this exercise, you modify the application from Computer Exercise 21. The modified application will allow the user to update a specific price. (1-5, 8) **INTERMEDIATE**

    a. Use Windows to make a copy of the Update Prices Solution folder. Rename the folder Update Prices Solution-Specific.

    b. Open the Update Prices Solution (Update Prices Solution.sln) file contained in the Update Prices Solution-Specific folder.

    c. Modify the increaseButton_Click procedure so that it also asks the user to enter a number from 1 through 10. If the user enters the number 1, the procedure should update the first price in the array. If the user enters the number 2, the procedure should update the second price in the array, and so on.

    d. Save the solution and then start the application. Click the Increase button. Increase the second price by 10%. Click the Increase button again. This time, increase the tenth price by 2%. (The second price in the list box should still reflect the 10% increase.) Close the solution.

24. In this exercise, you code an application that allows Professor Carver to display a student's grade based on the number of points the student enters. The grading scale is shown in Figure 9-40. Open the Carver Solution (Carver Solution.sln) file contained in the VbReloaded2012\Chap09\Carver Solution folder. Declare two class-level arrays: a one-dimensional Integer array named `points` and a one-dimensional String array named `grades`. Store the minimum points in the `points` array, and the corresponding grades in the `grades` array. The displayButton_Click procedure should search the `points` array and then display the corresponding grade from the `grades` array. Code the procedure. Save the solution and then start the application. Enter 455 in the Points box and then click the Display Grade button. The letter A appears in the Grade box. Enter 210 in the Points box and then click the Display Grade button. The letter F appears in the Grade box. Close the solution. (2-4, 11) **INTERMEDIATE**

Minimum points	Maximum points	Grade
0	299	F
300	349	D
350	399	C
400	449	B
450	500	A

Figure 9-40   Grading scale for Exercise 24
© 2013 Cengage Learning

INTERMEDIATE

25. In this exercise, you code an application that displays the highest score earned on the midterm exam and the highest score earned on the final exam. Open the Highest Solution (Highest Solution.sln) file contained in the VbReloaded2012\Chap09\Highest Solution folder. Code the displayButton_Click procedure so that it displays (in the appropriate label controls) the highest score earned on the midterm exam and the highest score earned on the final exam. Save the solution and then start and test the application. Close the solution. (2-4, 7, 11)

INTERMEDIATE

26. In this exercise, you code an application that allows Ms. Laury to display a shipping charge based on the number of items ordered by a customer. The shipping charges are shown in Figure 9-41. Open the Laury Solution (Laury Solution.sln) file contained in the VbReloaded2012\Chap09\Laury Solution folder. Declare a class-level, two-dimensional Integer array to store the minimum order amounts and shipping charges. Code the displayButton_Click procedure so that it displays the appropriate shipping charge with a dollar sign and two decimal places. Save the solution and then start and test the application. Close the solution. (1-4, 11)

Minimum order	Maximum order	Shipping
1	10	15
11	50	10
51	100	5
101	No maximum	0

Figure 9-41   Shipping charges for Exercise 26
© 2013 Cengage Learning

INTERMEDIATE

27. Open the Sales Solution (Sales Solution.sln) file contained in the VbReloaded2012\Chap09\Sales Solution folder. The interface allows the user to enter a sales amount. Code the searchButton_Click procedure so that it displays the number of salespeople selling at least that amount. The sales amounts are stored in the **sales** array. Save the solution and then start and test the application. Close the solution. (2-5, 11)

ADVANCED

28. Open the Tyler Solution (Tyler Solution.sln) file contained in the VbReloaded2012\Chap09\Tyler Solution folder. Modify the newButton_Click procedure so that it also displays, in a message box, the dealership that sold the most new cars and the dealership that sold the fewest new cars. Modify the usedButton_Click procedure so that it also displays, in a message box, the dealership that sold the most used cars and the dealership that sold the fewest used cars. Modify the totalButton_Click procedure so that it also displays, in a message box, the dealership that sold the most cars and the dealership that sold the fewest cars. Save the solution and then start and test the application. Close the solution. (2-4, 7, 11)

ADVANCED

29. In this exercise, you code an application that displays the number of students earning a specific score. (1-5, 11)

a. Open the Scores Solution (Scores Solution.sln) file contained in the VbReloaded2012\Chap09\Scores Solution folder. Declare a class-level, one-dimensional Integer array named **scores**. Initialize the array using the following 20 numbers: 88, 72, 99, 20, 66, 95, 99, 100, 72, 88, 78, 45, 57, 89, 85, 78, 75, 88, 72, and 88.

b. Open the code template for the displayButton_Click procedure. The procedure should prompt the user to enter a score from 0 through 100. It should then display (in a message box) the number of students who earned that score. Code the procedure.

c. Save the solution and then start the application. Use the application to answer the following questions: How many students earned a score of 72? How many students earned a score of 88? How many students earned a score of 20? How many students earned a score of 99? Close the solution.

30. In this exercise, you modify the application from Computer Exercise 29. The modified application will allow the user to display the number of students earning a score within a specific range. (1-5, 11)

    ADVANCED

  a. Use Windows to make a copy of the Scores Solution folder contained in the VbReloaded2012\Chap09 folder. Rename the folder Scores Solution-Range.

  b. Open the Scores Solution (Scores Solution.sln) file contained in the Scores Solution-Range folder. The displayButton_Click procedure should prompt the user to enter a minimum score and a maximum score. It should then display (in a message box) the number of students who earned a score within that range. Modify the procedure.

  c. Save the solution and then start the application. Use the application to answer the following questions: How many students earned a score from 70 through 79? How many students earned a score from 65 through 85? How many students earned a score from 0 through 50? Close the solution.

31. In this exercise, you code an application that displays the number of times a value appears in a two-dimensional array. Open the Count Solution (Count Solution.sln) file contained in the VbReloaded2012\Chap09\Count Solution folder. Code the Display button's Click event procedure so that it displays the number of times each of the numbers from 1 through 9 appears in the **numbers** array. (Hint: Store the counts in a one-dimensional array.) Save the solution and then start and test the application. Close the solution. (1-4, 9, 11)

    ADVANCED

32. In this exercise, you will learn about the ReDim statement.

    DISCOVERY

  a. Research the Visual Basic ReDim statement. What is the purpose of the statement? What is the purpose of the **Preserve** keyword?

  b. Open the ReDim Solution (ReDim Solution.sln) file contained in the VbReloaded2012\Chap09\ReDim Solution folder. Open the Code Editor window. Notice that the array contains only one element. Modify the displayButton_Click procedure to allow it to store any number of sales amounts in the array.

  c. Save the solution and then start the application. Click the Display Sales button and then enter the following sales amounts, one at a time: 700, 550, and 800. Click the Cancel button in the input box. The three sales amounts should appear in the list box.

  d. Click the Display Sales button again and then enter the following sales amounts, one at a time: 5, 9, 45, 67, 8, and 0. Click the Cancel button in the input box. This time, six sales amounts should appear in the list box. Close the solution.

33. Open the Debug Solution (Debug Solution.sln) file contained in the VbReloaded2012\Chap09\Debug Solution folder. Open the Code Editor window and review the existing code. Correct the syntax errors. When the application is working correctly, close the solution. (1-4)

    SWAT THE BUGS

Case Projects

 JM Sales

JM Sales employs five salespeople. The sales manager wants an application that allows him to enter any number of sales amounts for each of the five salespeople. The application should accumulate the sales amounts in a one-dimensional array. The application should also display a report similar to the one shown in Figure 9-42. The report contains each salesperson's ID and total sales. It also contains the total company sales. Use the following names for the solution and project, respectively: JM Sales Solution and JM Sales Project. Save the application in the VbReloaded2012\Chap09 folder. Change the form file's name to Main Form.vb. You can either create your own interface or create the one shown in Figure 9-42. The text box that displays the report has its BorderStyle property set to Fixed3D, its Font property set to Courier New 10pt, its MultiLine and ReadOnly properties set to True, and its ScrollBars property set to Vertical. (1-4, 6, 8, 9)

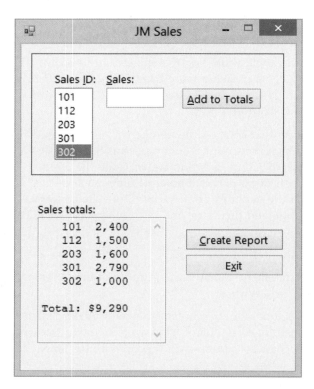

Figure 9-42   Sample run of the JM Sales application

 Waterglen Horse Farms

Each year, Sabrina Cantrell, the owner of Waterglen Horse Farms, enters four of her horses in five local horse races. She uses the table shown in Figure 9-43 to keep track of her horses' performances in each race. In the table, a 1 indicates that the horse won the race, a 2 indicates second place, and a 3 indicates third place. A 0 indicates that the horse did not finish in the top three places. Sabrina wants an application that displays a summary of each horse's individual performance, as well as the performances of all the horses. For example, according to the table shown in Figure 9-43, horse 1 won one race, finished second in one race, finished third in one race, and didn't finish in the top three in two races. Overall, Sabrina's horses won four races, finished second in three races, finished third in three races, and didn't finish in the top three in 10 races. Be sure to use one or more arrays in the application. Use the following names for the solution and project, respectively: Waterglen Solution and Waterglen Project. Save the application in the VbReloaded2012\Chap09 folder. Change the form file's name to Main Form.vb. You can either create your own interface or create the one shown in Figure 9-44. The horse image is stored in the VbReloaded2012\Chap09 folder. (1-4, 6)

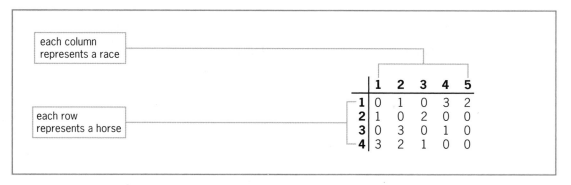

Figure 9-43 Horse race results for Waterglen Horse Farms
© 2013 Cengage Learning

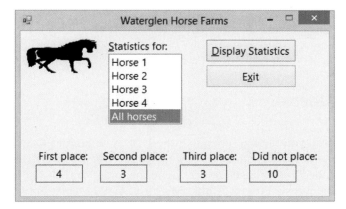

Figure 9-44 Sample run of the Waterglen Horse Farms application
OpenClipArt.org/johnny_automatic

 Conway Enterprises

Conway Enterprises has both domestic and international sales operations. The company's sales manager wants an application that she can use to display the total domestic, total international, and total company sales made during a six-month period. The sales amounts are listed in Figure 9-45. Be sure to use one or more arrays in the application. Use the following names for the solution and project, respectively: Conway Solution and Conway Project. Save the application in the VbReloaded2012\Chap09 folder. Change the form file's name to Main Form.vb. You can either create your own interface or create the one shown in Figure 9-46. (1-4, 6)

Month	Domestic	International
1	100,000	150,000
2	90,000	120,000
3	75,000	210,000
4	88,000	50,000
5	125,000	220,000
6	63,000	80,000

Figure 9-45 Sales amounts for Conway Enterprises
© 2013 Cengage Learning

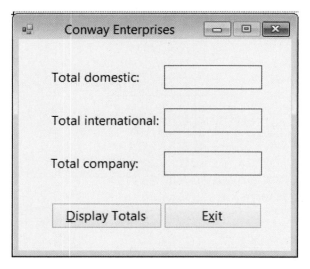

Figure 9-46　Sample interface for Conway Enterprises

 ## Modified Harvey Industries

Before you can complete this Case Project, you need to complete the Harvey Industries Case Project from Chapter 8. After doing so, use Windows to make a copy of the Harvey Industries Solution folder contained in the VbReloaded2012\Chap08 folder. Copy the folder to the VbReloaded2012\Chap09 folder. Store the weekly Federal Withholding Tax (FWT) tables in two two-dimensional arrays, and then make the appropriate modifications to the code. The FWT tables are shown in Figure 8-58 in Chapter 8. (1-4, 11)

 ## Tic-Tac-Toe

Create an application that simulates the Tic-Tac-Toe game, which requires two players. Be sure to use one or more arrays in the application. Use the following names for the solution and project, respectively: TicTacToe Solution and TicTacToe Project. Save the application in the VbReloaded2012\Chap09 folder. Change the form file's name to Main Form.vb. (Hint: You may find it helpful to create an array of Label controls.) (1-5)

CHAPTER 10

String Manipulation and Menus

After studying Chapter 10, you should be able to:

1 Determine the number of characters in a string
2 Remove characters from a string
3 Insert characters in a string
4 Align the characters in a string
5 Search a string
6 Access the characters in a string
7 Compare strings using pattern matching
8 Add a menu to a form
9 Code a menu item's Click event procedure

Reading and Study Guide

Before you begin reading Chapter 10, view the Ch10_ReadingStudyGuide.pdf file. You can open the file using Adobe Reader, which is available for free on the Adobe Web site at *www.adobe.com/downloads/*.

Working with Strings

Many times, an application will need to manipulate (process) string data in some way. For example, it may need to look at the first character in an inventory part number to determine the part's location in the warehouse. Or, it may need to search an address to determine the street name. In this chapter, you will learn several ways to manipulate strings in Visual Basic. You will begin by learning how to determine the number of characters in a string.

Determining the Number of Characters in a String

If an application expects the user to enter a seven-digit phone number or a five-digit ZIP code, you should verify that the user's entry contains the required number of characters. The number of characters contained in a string is stored as an integer in the string's **Length property**. Figure 10-1 shows the syntax of the Length property and includes examples of using the property. In the syntax, *string* can be a String variable, a String named constant, or the Text property of a control.

HOW TO Determine the Number of Characters in a String

Syntax
string.**Length**

Example 1
```
Dim custName As String = "Inez Espinoza"
Dim numChars As Integer = custName.Length
```
assigns the number 13 to the numChars variable

Example 2
```
Dim numChars As Integer
numChars = phoneTextBox.Text.Length
```
assigns the number of characters in the phoneTextBox's Text property to the numChars variable

Example 3
```
Dim zip As String
Do
    zip = InputBox("5-digit ZIP code", "ZIP")
Loop Until zip.Length = 5
```
continues prompting the user for a ZIP code until the user enters exactly five characters

---

Figure 10-1 How to determine the number of characters in a string
© 2013 Cengage Learning

Removing Characters from a String

Visual Basic provides the Trim and Remove methods for removing characters from a string. The **Trim method** removes (trims) any space characters from both the beginning and end of a string. The **Remove method**, on the other hand, removes a specified number of characters located anywhere in a string. Figure 10-2 shows the syntax of both methods and includes examples of using the methods. In each syntax, *string* can be a String variable, a String named constant, or the Text property of a control. When processing the Trim and Remove methods, the computer first makes a temporary copy of the *string* in memory. It then performs the specified removal on the copy only. In other words, neither method removes any characters from the original *string*. Both methods return a string with the appropriate characters removed.

The Trim method can also be used to remove other characters. To learn more about the Trim method, as well as its companion TrimStart and TrimEnd methods, complete Computer Exercise 34 at the end of this chapter.

519

HOW TO Remove Characters from a String

<u>Syntax</u>
string.**Trim**
string.**Remove**(*startIndex*[, *numCharsToRemove*])

<u>Example 1</u>
```
Dim customer As String
customer = customerTextBox.Text.Trim
```
assigns the contents of the customerTextBox's Text property, excluding any leading and trailing spaces, to the `customer` variable

<u>Example 2</u>
```
Dim fullName As String = "Martha Moranski"
lastTextBox.Text = fullName.Remove(0, 7)
```
assigns the string "Moranski" to the lastTextBox's Text property

<u>Example 3</u>
```
Dim fullName As String = "Martha Moranski"
firstTextBox.Text = fullName.Remove(6)
```
assigns the string "Martha" to the firstTextBox's Text property; you can also write the assignment statement as `firstTextBox.Text = fullName.Remove(6, 9)`

<u>Example 4</u>
```
Dim firstName As String = "Jose"
firstName = firstName.Remove(2, 1)
```
assigns the string "Joe" to the `firstName` variable

Figure 10-2 How to remove characters from a string
© 2013 Cengage Learning

The *startIndex* argument in the Remove method is the index of the first character you want removed from the copy of the *string*. A character's index is an integer that indicates the character's position in the string. The first character in a string has an index of 0; the second character has an index of 1; and so on. The optional *numCharsToRemove* argument is the number of characters you want removed. To remove only the first character from a string, you use 0 as the startIndex and 1 as the numCharsToRemove. To remove the fourth through eighth characters, you use 3 as the startIndex and 5 as the numCharsToRemove. If the numCharsToRemove argument is omitted, the Remove method removes all of the characters from the startIndex position through the end of the string, as indicated in Example 3 in Figure 10-2.

Inserting Characters in a String

Visual Basic's **Insert method** allows you to insert characters anywhere in a string. Possible uses for the method include inserting an employee's middle initial within his or her name and inserting parentheses around the area code in a phone number. The method's syntax is shown in

Figure 10-3 along with examples of using the method. In the syntax, *string* can be a String variable, a String named constant, or the Text property of a control. When processing the Insert method, the computer first makes a temporary copy of the *string* in memory. It then performs the specified insertion on the copy only. The Insert method does not affect the original *string*. The method's *startIndex* argument is an integer that specifies where in the string's copy you want the *value* inserted. The integer represents the character's index (position in the string). To insert the value at the beginning of a string, you use a startIndex of 0, as shown in Example 1 in Figure 10-3. To insert the value beginning with the sixth character in the string, you use a startIndex of 5, as shown in Example 2. The Insert method returns a string with the appropriate characters inserted.

HOW TO Insert Characters in a String

Syntax
string.**Insert**(*startIndex, value*)

Example 1
```
Dim phone As String = "111-2222"
phone = phone.Insert(0, "(877) ")
```
assigns the string "(877) 111-2222" to the **phone** variable

Example 2
```
Dim fullName As String = "Rita Prebus"
fullName = fullName.Insert(5, "G. ")
```
assigns the string "Rita G. Prebus" to the **fullName** variable

Figure 10-3   How to insert characters in a string
© 2013 Cengage Learning

If you want to experiment with the Length property and the Trim, Remove, and Insert methods, open the solution contained in the Try It 1! folder.

Mini-Quiz 10-1

The answers to Mini-Quiz questions are located in Appendix A. Each question is associated with one or more objectives listed at the beginning of the chapter.

1. Which of the following assigns the number of characters stored in the msgLabel to the numChars variable? (1)

    a.   numChars = Len(msgLabel.Text)

    b.   numChars = Length(msgLabel.Text)

    c.   numChars = msgLabel.Length.Text

    d.   numChars = msgLabel.Text.Length

2. Which of the following changes the contents of the **state** variable from Kentucky to Ky? (2)

    a.   state = state.Remove(1, 5)

    b.   state = state.Remove(1, 6)

    c.   state = state.Remove(0, 6)

    d.   state = state.Remove(2, 6)

3. Which of the following changes the contents of the **state** variable from Dakota to South Dakota? (3)

    a.   state = state.Insert(0, "South ")

    b.   state = state.Insert(1, "South ")

    c.   state = state.Insert("South ", 0)

    d.   state = state.Insert("South", 1)

Aligning the Characters in a String

You can use Visual Basic's PadLeft and PadRight methods to align the characters in a string. The methods do this by inserting (padding) the string with zero or more characters until the string is a specified length; each method then returns the padded string. The **PadLeft method** pads the string on the left, which means it inserts the padded characters at the beginning of the string; doing this right-aligns the characters within the string. The **PadRight method**, on the other hand, pads the string on the right, which means it inserts the padded characters at the end of the string and left-aligns the characters within the string.

Figure 10-4 shows the syntax of both methods and includes examples of using them. In each syntax, *string* can be a String variable, a String named constant, or the Text property of a control. When processing the methods, the computer first makes a temporary copy of the *string* in memory; it then pads the copy only. The *totalChars* argument in each syntax is an integer that represents the total number of characters you want the string's copy to contain. The optional *padCharacter* argument is the character that each method uses to pad the string until the desired number of characters is reached. If the padCharacter argument is omitted, the default padding character is the space character.

HOW TO Align the Characters in a String

<u>Syntax</u>
string.**PadLeft**(*totalChars*[, *padCharacter*])
string.**PadRight**(*totalChars*[, *padCharacter*])

<u>Example 1</u>
```
Dim num As String = "100"
numLabel.Text = num.PadLeft(5)
```
assigns the string "⎵⎵100" to the numLabel control's Text property

[two spaces]

<u>Example 2</u>
```
Dim first As String = "Pat"
first = first.PadRight(10)
```
assigns the string "Pat⎵⎵⎵⎵⎵⎵⎵" to the **first** variable

[seven spaces]

<u>Example 3</u>
```
Dim netPay As Double = 325.75
Dim formattedPay As String
formattedPay = netPay.ToString("C2").PadLeft(10, "*"c)
```
assigns the string "***$325.75" to the **formattedPay** variable (Many companies use this type of formatting on their employee paychecks because it makes it more difficult for someone to change the amount.)

Figure 10-4 How to align the characters in a string
© 2013 Cengage Learning

If you want to experiment with the PadLeft and PadRight methods, open the solution contained in the Try It 2! folder.

The expression in Example 3 in Figure 10-4 contains two methods: ToString and PadLeft. When an expression contains more than one method, the computer processes the methods from left to right. In this case, the computer will process the ToString method before processing the PadLeft method. Notice the letter c that appears at the end of the padCharacter argument in Example 3. The letter c is one of the literal type characters in Visual Basic. As you learned in Chapter 3, a literal type character forces a literal constant to assume a data type other than the one its form indicates. In this case, the letter c forces the "*" string in the padCharacter argument to assume the Char (character) data type.

Searching a String

If you need to determine whether a string contains a specific sequence of characters, you can use either the Contains method or the IndexOf method. Possible uses for these methods include determining whether a specific area code appears in a phone number, and whether a specific street name appears in an address. Figure 10-5 shows the syntax of both methods. In each syntax, *string* can be a String variable, a String named constant, or the Text property of a control. The *subString* argument in each syntax represents the sequence of characters for which you are searching. Both methods perform a case-sensitive search, which means the case of the subString must match the case of the string in order for both to be considered equal.

HOW TO Search a String

Syntax
string.**Contains(***subString***)**
string.**IndexOf(***substring*[, *startIndex*]**)**

Example 1
```
Dim cityState As String = "Boston, MA"
Dim isContained As Boolean
isContained = cityState.Contains("MA")
```
assigns True to the isContained variable because the string "MA" appears in the cityState variable

Example 2
```
Dim cityState As String = "Boston, MA"
Dim isContained As Boolean
isContained = cityState.Contains("Ma")
```
assigns False to the isContained variable because the string "Ma" does not appear in the cityState variable

> the Contains method performs a case-sensitive search

Example 3
```
Dim address As String = "12 Dover St."
If address.ToUpper.Contains("DOVER") Then
```
the condition evaluates to True because the string "DOVER" appears in the address variable when the variable's contents are temporarily converted to uppercase

> the ToUpper method is evaluated before the Contains method

> character index 8

Example 4
```
Dim cityState As String = "Boston, MA"
Dim charIndex As Integer
charIndex = cityState.IndexOf("MA")
```
assigns the number 8 to the charIndex variable because the string "MA" appears in the cityState variable, beginning with the character whose index is 8

Figure 10-5 How to search a string *(continues)*

(continued)

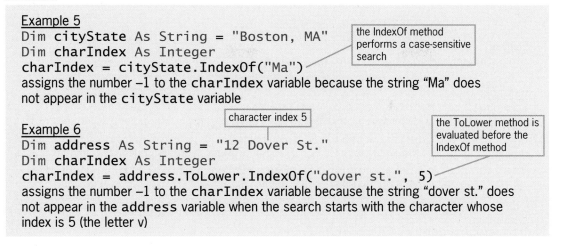

Example 5
```
Dim cityState As String = "Boston, MA"
Dim charIndex As Integer
charIndex = cityState.IndexOf("Ma")
```
the IndexOf method performs a case-sensitive search

assigns the number –1 to the `charIndex` variable because the string "Ma" does not appear in the `cityState` variable

character index 5

Example 6
```
Dim address As String = "12 Dover St."
Dim charIndex As Integer
charIndex = address.ToLower.IndexOf("dover st.", 5)
```
the ToLower method is evaluated before the IndexOf method

assigns the number –1 to the `charIndex` variable because the string "dover st." does not appear in the `address` variable when the search starts with the character whose index is 5 (the letter v)

Figure 10-5 How to search a string
© 2013 Cengage Learning

The **Contains method**, which appears in Examples 1 through 3 in Figure 10-5, returns the Boolean value True when the subString is contained anywhere in the string; otherwise, it returns the Boolean value False. The Contains method always begins the search with the first character in the string.

The **IndexOf method**, on the other hand, returns an integer: either –1 or a number that is greater than or equal to 0. The –1 indicates that the subString is not contained in the string. A number other than –1 is the character index of the subString's starting position in the string. Unless you specify otherwise, the IndexOf method starts the search with the first character in the string. To specify a different starting location, you use the optional *startIndex* argument. The IndexOf method appears in Examples 4 through 6 in Figure 10-5.

Notice that the expressions in Examples 3 and 6 in Figure 10-5 contain two methods. Recall that when an expression contains more than one method, the computer processes the methods from left to right. In this case, the computer will process the ToUpper method before the Contains method in Example 3, and process the ToLower method before the IndexOf method in Example 6.

Accessing the Characters in a String

In some applications, it is necessary to access one or more characters contained in a string. For instance, you may need to display only the string's first five characters because they identify an item's location in the warehouse. Visual Basic provides the **Substring method** for accessing any number of characters in a string. Figure 10-6 shows the method's syntax and includes examples of using the method. In the syntax, *string* can be a String variable, a String named constant, or the Text property of a control. The *startIndex* argument is the index of the first character you want to access in the string. As you already know, the first character in a string has an index of 0. The optional *numCharsToAccess* argument specifies the number of characters you want to access. The Substring method returns a string that contains the number of characters specified in the numCharsToAccess argument, beginning with the character whose index is startIndex. If you omit the numCharsToAccess argument, the Substring method returns all characters from the startIndex position through the end of the string.

HOW TO Access Characters in a String

Syntax
string.**Substring(***startIndex*[**,** *numCharsToAccess*]**)**

character index 0   character index 7

Example 1
Dim full As String = "Khalid Patel"
Dim first As String = full.Substring(0, 6)
Dim last As String = full.Substring(7)
assigns the string "Khalid" to the **first** variable and the string "Patel" to the **last** variable; you can also write the last Dim statement as Dim last
As String = full.Substring (7, 5)

character index 2

Example 2
Dim employeeNum As String = "38F45"
Dim status As String
status = employeeNum.Substring(2, 1)
assigns the string "F" to the **status** variable

Figure 10-6   How to access characters in a string
© 2013 Cengage Learning

If you want to experiment with the Contains, IndexOf, and Substring methods, open the solution contained in the Try It 3! folder.

The answers to Mini-Quiz questions are located in Appendix A. Each question is associated with one or more objectives listed at the beginning of the chapter.

Mini-Quiz 10-2

1. If the **restaurant** variable contains the string "The Bistro", what will the restaurant.ToUpper.Contains("BISTRO") method return? (5)

   a. 4

   b. 5

   c. True

   d. False

2. If the **restaurant** variable contains the string "The Bistro", what will the restaurant.ToUpper.IndexOf("BISTRO") method return? (5)

   a. 4

   b. 5

   c. True

   d. False

3. If the **restaurant** variable contains the string "Maria's Italian Deli", which of the following assigns the string "Italian" to the **foodType** variable? (6)

   a. foodType = restaurant.Substring(8)

   b. foodType = restaurant.Substring(8, 7)

   c. foodType = restaurant.Substring(9, 7)

   d. both a and b

4. Which of the following changes the contents of the **grade** variable from A to A++++? (3, 4)

   a. grade = grade.Insert(1, "++").PadRight(5, "+"c)

   b. grade = grade.PadRight(5, "+"c)

   c. grade = grade.Insert(1, "++++")

   d. all of the above

Using Pattern Matching to Compare Strings

The **Like operator** allows you to use pattern-matching characters to determine whether one string is equal to another string. Figure 10-7 shows the operator's syntax and includes examples of using the operator. In the syntax, *string* can be a String variable, a String named constant, or the Text property of a control. *Pattern* is a String expression containing one or more of the pattern-matching characters listed in the figure.

HOW TO Use Pattern Matching to Compare Strings

Syntax
string **Like** *pattern*

Pattern-matching characters	Matches in *string*
?	any single character
*	zero or more characters
#	any single digit (0-9)
[*characterList*]	any single character in the characterList (for example, "[A9M]" matches A, 9, or M, whereas "[a-z]" matches any lowercase letter)
[!*characterList*]	any single character *not* in the characterList (for example, "[!A9M]" matches any character other than A, 9, or M, whereas "[!a-z]" matches any character that is not a lowercase letter)

Example 1
```
If firstName.ToUpper Like "B?LL" Then
```
The condition evaluates to True when the string stored in the `firstName` variable (converted to uppercase) begins with the letter B followed by one character and then the two letters LL; otherwise, it evaluates to False. Examples of strings that would make the condition evaluate to True include "Bill", "Ball", "bell", and "bull". Examples of strings for which the condition would evaluate to False include "BPL", "BLL", and "billy".

Example 2
```
If stateTextBox.Text Like "K*" Then
```
The condition evaluates to True when the string stored in the stateTextBox's Text property begins with the letter K followed by zero or more characters; otherwise, it evaluates to False. Examples of strings that would make the condition evaluate to True include "KANSAS", "Ky", and "Kentucky". Examples of strings for which the condition would evaluate to False include "kansas" and "ky".

Example 3
```
Do While id Like "###*"
```
The condition evaluates to True when the string stored in the `id` variable begins with three digits followed by zero or more characters; otherwise, it evaluates to False. Examples of strings that would make the condition evaluate to True include "178" and "983Ab". Examples of strings for which the condition would evaluate to False include "X34" and "34Z5".

Figure 10-7   How to use pattern matching to compare strings *(continues)*

(continued)

Example 4
```
If firstName.ToUpper Like "T[OI]M" Then
```
The condition evaluates to True when the string stored in the `firstName` variable (converted to uppercase) is either "TOM" or "TIM". When the variable does not contain "TOM" or "TIM"—for example, when it contains "Tam" or "Tommy"—the condition evaluates to False.

Example 5
```
If letter Like "[a-z]" Then
```
The condition evaluates to True when the string stored in the `letter` variable is one lowercase letter; otherwise, it evaluates to False.

Example 6
```
Dim fullName As String
Dim currentChar As String
Dim nonLetter As Integer
fullName = nameTextBox.Text
For index As Integer = 0 To fullName.Length - 1
    currentChar = fullName.Substring(index, 1)
    If currentChar Like "[!a-zA-Z]" Then
        nonLetter += 1
    End If
Next index
```
The loop compares each character contained in the `fullName` variable with the lowercase and uppercase letters of the alphabet, and counts the number of characters that are not letters.

Example 7
```
If rateTextBox.Text Like "*.*" Then
```
The condition evaluates to True when a period appears anywhere in the rateTextBox's Text property; otherwise, it evaluates to False.

Example 8
```
If partNum.ToUpper Like "[A-Z][A-Z]##" Then
```
The condition evaluates to True when the string stored in the `partNum` variable (converted to uppercase) consists of two letters followed by two numbers; otherwise, it evaluates to False.

Figure 10-7   How to use pattern matching to compare strings
© 2013 Cengage Learning

If you want to experiment with the Like operator, open the solution contained in the Try It 4! folder.

As Figure 10-7 indicates, the question mark (?) character in a pattern represents one character only, whereas the asterisk (*) character represents zero or more characters. To represent a single digit in a pattern, you use the number (or hash) sign (#). The last two pattern-matching characters listed in the figure contain a *characterList*, which is simply a listing of characters. "[A9M]" is a characterList that contains three characters: A, 9, and M. You can also include a range of values in a characterList. You do this by using a hyphen to separate the lowest value in the range from the highest value in the range. For example, to include all lowercase letters in a characterList, you use "[a-z]". To include both lowercase and uppercase letters in a characterList, you use "[a-zA-Z]".

The Like operator compares the string to the pattern; the comparison is case sensitive. If the string matches the pattern, the Like operator returns the Boolean value True; otherwise, it returns the Boolean value False.

Mini-Quiz 10-3

1. Which of the following evaluates to True when the `partNum` variable contains the string "123X45"? (7)

   a. `partNum Like "999[A-Z]99"`

   b. `partNum Like "######"`

   c. `partNum Like "###[A-Z]##"`

   d. `partNum Like "*[A-Z]"`

2. Which of the following determines whether a comma appears anywhere in the salesTextBox's Text property? (7)

   a. `salesTextBox.Text Like ","`

   b. `salesTextBox.Text Like "*,*"`

   c. `salesTextBox.Text Like "[*,*]"`

   d. none of the above

3. Which of the following determines whether a percent sign (%) appears as the last character in the rateTextBox's Text property? (7)

   a. `rateTextBox.Text Like "%"`

   b. `rateTextBox.Text Like "*%*"`

   c. `rateTextBox.Text Like "*%"`

   d. none of the above

The answers to Mini-Quiz questions are located in Appendix A. Each question is associated with one or more objectives listed at the beginning of the chapter.

527

Adding a Menu to a Form

The Menus & Toolbars section of the toolbox contains a MenuStrip tool for instantiating a menu strip control. You use a **menu strip control** to include one or more menus on a Windows form. Each menu contains a menu title, which appears on the menu bar at the top of the form. When you click a menu title, its corresponding menu opens and displays a list of options, called menu items. The menu items can be commands (such as Open or Exit), separator bars, or submenu titles. As in all Windows applications, clicking a command on a menu executes the command, and clicking a submenu title opens an additional menu of options. Each of the options on a submenu is referred to as a submenu item. You can use a separator bar to visually group together related items on a menu or submenu. Figure 10-8 identifies the location of these menu elements. Although you can create many levels of submenus, it is best to use only one level because too many layers of submenus can be confusing to the user.

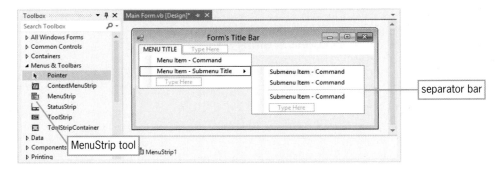

Figure 10-8 Location of menu elements

Ch10-Menus

Each menu element is considered an object; therefore, each has a set of properties associated with it. The most commonly used properties for a menu element are the Name and Text properties. The programmer uses the Name property to refer to the menu element in code. The Text property stores the menu element's caption, which is the text that the user sees when he or she is working with the menu. The caption indicates the purpose of the menu element. Examples of familiar captions for menu elements include Edit, Save As, Copy, and Exit.

Menu title captions should be one word only and entered using either uppercase letters (like the Visual Studio menu titles) or with only the first letter capitalized. Each menu title should have a unique access key. The access key allows the user to open the menu by pressing the Alt key in combination with the access key. Unlike the captions for menu titles, the captions for menu items typically consist of one to three words. The Windows standard is to use book title capitalization for the menu item captions. Each menu item should have an access key that is unique within its menu. The access key allows the user to select the item by pressing the access key when the menu is open. If a menu item requires additional information from the user, the Windows standard is to place an ellipsis (...) at the end of the caption. The ellipsis alerts the user that the menu item requires more information before it can perform its task.

Commonly used menu items should be assigned shortcut keys. The **shortcut keys** appear to the right of a menu item and allow the user to select the item without opening the menu. Examples of familiar shortcut keys include Ctrl+X and Ctrl+V. In Windows applications that have an Edit menu, Ctrl+X and Ctrl+V can be used to select the Cut and Paste commands, respectively, when the Edit menu is closed. You specify a menu item's shortcut keys in its ShortcutKeys property in the Properties window.

Figure 10-9 shows the FILE menu you will create in Programming Tutorial 1. The menu contains two menu items: New Game and Exit. The menu title and both menu items have access keys. In addition, shortcut keys are provided for the New Game menu item.

 A menu item's access key can be used only when the menu is open, and its shortcut keys can be used only when the menu is closed.

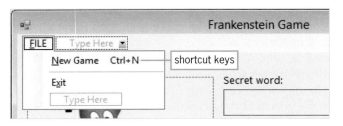

Figure 10-9 FILE menu
OpenClipArt.org/Merlin2525

If an item on a menu or submenu is a command, you enter the appropriate instructions in the item's Click event procedure. Figure 10-10 shows the Click event procedure for the Exit command from Figure 10-9.

```
Private Sub fileExitMenuItem_Click(sender As Object,
e As EventArgs) Handles fileExitMenuItem.Click
    Me.Close()
End Sub
```

Figure 10-10 Exit command's Click event procedure
© 2013 Cengage Learning

You have completed the concepts section of Chapter 10. The Programming Tutorial section is next.

PROGRAMMING TUTORIAL 1

Coding the Frankenstein Game Application

In this tutorial, you will code the application for the Frankenstein Game, which is played by two people. Figures 10-11 and 10-12 show the application's TOE chart and MainForm, respectively. The MainForm contains five labels, six picture boxes (only one is visible in the figure), one text box, and one button. It also contains a FILE menu that has two options: New Game and Exit. When the user clicks the New Game option, the option's Click event procedure will prompt player 1 to enter a five-letter word. Player 2 will then be given six chances to guess the word, letter by letter. If player 2's letter does not appear in the word, the application will begin drawing a Frankenstein image that contains six parts: a head, a torso, a right arm, a left arm, a right leg, and a left leg. The game is over when player 2 either guesses all of the letters in the word or makes six incorrect guesses, whichever comes first. If player 2 guesses the word, the application will display the "Great guessing!" message. If player 2 does not guess the word, the application will display the message "Sorry, the word is" followed by the word.

Task	Object	Event
1. Get a five-letter word from player 1, trim spaces, and convert to uppercase 2. Determine whether the word contains 5 letters 3. If the word contains 5 letters, hide the 6 picture boxes, display 5 dashes in wordLabel, clear incorrectLabel, set incorrect guesses counter to 0, clear letterTextBox, enable checkButton, and send focus to letterTextBox 4. If the word doesn't contain 5 letters, display "5 letters are required" in a message box	fileNewMenuItem	Click
1. Search the word for the letter entered by player 2 2. If the letter is contained in the word, replace the appropriate dashes in wordLabel; if there aren't any other dashes in the word, the game is over because player 2 guessed the word, so display "Great guessing!" in a message box, disable checkButton, and set incorrect guesses counter to 0 3. If the letter is not contained in the word, display the letter in incorrectLabel, add 1 to the incorrect guesses counter, and show the appropriate picture box; if player 2 made 6 incorrect guesses, the game is over, so display "Sorry, the word is *word*." in a message box, disable checkButton, and set incorrect guesses counter to 0 4. Clear letterTextBox and send focus to it	checkButton	Click
End the application	fileExitMenuItem	Click
Display the Frankenstein images	headPictureBox, torsoPictureBox, rightArmPictureBox, leftArmPictureBox, rightLegPictureBox, leftLegPictureBox	None
Accept only letters and the Backspace key	letterTextBox	KeyPress
Display dashes and letters (from fileNewMenuItem and checkButton)	wordLabel	None
Display the incorrect letters (from checkButton)	incorrectLabel	None

Figure 10-11   TOE chart for the Frankenstein Game application

© 2013 Cengage Learning

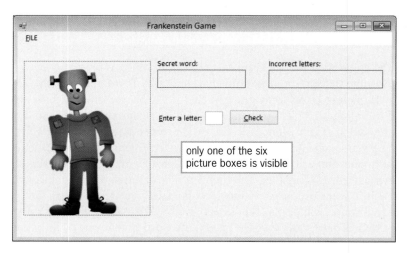

Figure 10-12 MainForm for the Frankenstein Game application
OpenClipArt.org/Merlin2525

Completing the Interface

Before you can code the application, you need to complete its interface.

To complete the application's interface:

1. Start Visual Studio. Open the **Frankenstein Solution (Frankenstein Solution.sln)** file contained in the VbReloaded2012\Chap10\Frankenstein Solution folder. If necessary, open the designer window. See Figure 10-13.

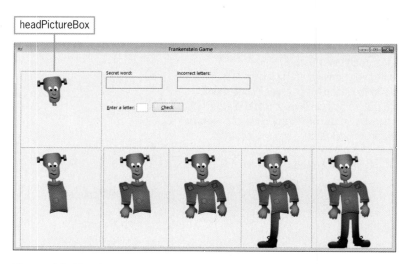

Figure 10-13 Partially completed interface
OpenClipArt.org/Merlin2525

2. Click the **headPictureBox** control to select it as the reference control. Then Ctrl+Click the other **five picture boxes**. Use the FORMAT menu to align the controls by their left and top margins.

3. Click the **form** and then size the form, using either its sizing handles or its Size property, to match Figure 10-14. (The form in the figure has its Size property set to 695, 425.)

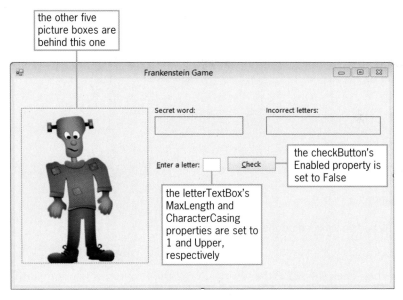

the other five picture boxes are behind this one

the checkButton's Enabled property is set to False

the letterTextBox's MaxLength and CharacterCasing properties are set to 1 and Upper, respectively

Figure 10-14 Current status of the form
OpenClipArt.org/Merlin2525

4. Lock the controls on the form.

5. Open the Toolbox window (if necessary), and then click **MenuStrip** in the Menus & Toolbars section. Drag the mouse pointer to the form and then release the mouse button. A MenuStrip control named MenuStrip1 appears in the component tray, and the words "Type Here" appear in a box below the form's title bar. See Figure 10-15.

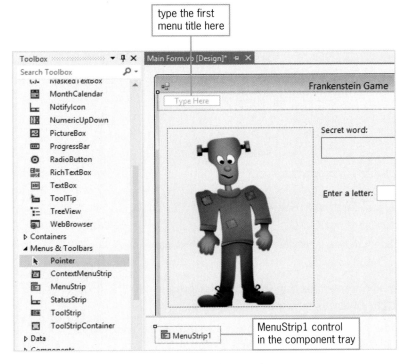

type the first menu title here

MenuStrip1 control in the component tray

Figure 10-15 MenuStrip control added to the form
OpenClipArt.org/Merlin2525

6. Auto-hide the toolbox and then display the Properties window (if necessary). Click the **Type Here** box on the menu bar and then type **&FILE**. See Figure 10-16. You use the Type Here box that appears below the menu title to add a menu item to the FILE menu. You use the Type Here box that appears to the right of the menu title to add another menu title to the menu bar.

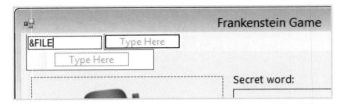

Figure 10-16   Menu title included on the form

7. Press **Enter** and then click the **FILE** menu title. Scroll the Properties window until you see the Text property, which contains &FILE. Now, scroll to the top of the Properties window and then click **(Name)**. Type **fileMenuTitle** and then press **Enter**.

8. Click the **Type Here** box that appears below the FILE menu title. Type **&New Game** and then press **Enter**. Click the **New Game** menu item. Change the menu item's name to **fileNewMenuItem**.

9. Next, you will assign Ctrl+N as the shortcut keys for the New Game menu item. Click **ShortcutKeys** in the Properties window and then click the **list arrow** in the Settings box. A box opens and allows you to specify a modifier and a key. In this case, the modifier and the key will be Ctrl and N, respectively. Click the **Ctrl** check box to select it, and then click the **list arrow** that appears in the Key combo box. An alphabetical list of keys appears. Scroll the list until you see the letter N, and then click **N** in the list. See Figure 10-17.

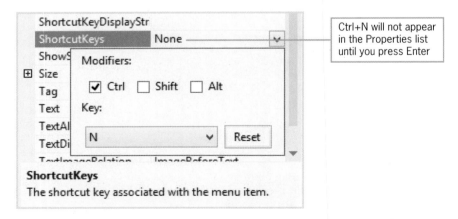

Figure 10-17   Shortcut keys specified in the ShortcutKeys box

10. Press **Enter**. Ctrl+N appears in the ShortcutKeys property in the Properties list. It also appears to the right of the New Game menu item.

11. Next, you will add a separator bar to the FILE menu. Place your mouse pointer on the Type Here box that appears below the New Game menu item, but don't click the box. Instead, click the **list arrow** that appears inside the box. See Figure 10-18.

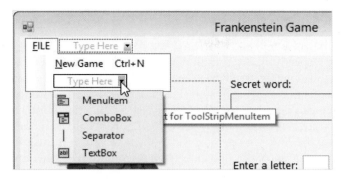

Figure 10-18   Drop-down list

12. Click **Separator** in the list. A horizontal line, called a separator bar, appears below the New Game menu item.

13. Click the **Type Here** box that appears below the separator bar. Type **E&xit** and then press **Enter**. Click the **Exit** menu item. Change the menu item's name to **fileExitMenuItem**.

14. Save the solution and then start the application. Click **FILE** on the menu bar. The FILE menu opens and offers two options separated by a separator bar. See Figure 10-19.

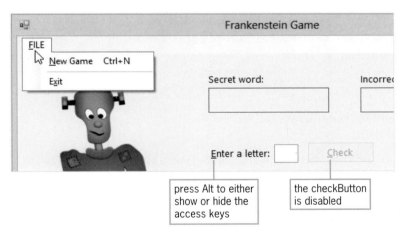

press Alt to either show or hide the access keys

the checkButton is disabled

Figure 10-19   FILE menu opened during run time
OpenClipArt.org/Merlin2525

15. Click the **Close** button on the form's title bar.

Coding the FILE Menu's Exit Option

According to the application's TOE chart, the Click event procedures for the two menu items and the checkButton need to be coded. The KeyPress event procedure for the letterTextBox also needs to be coded. You'll begin by coding the fileExitMenuItem_Click procedure.

To code the fileExitMenuItem_Click procedure:

1. Open the Code Editor window, which already contains some of the application's code. In the comments that appear in the General Declarations section, replace <your name> and <current date> with your name and the current date, respectively.

2. Open the code template for the fileExitMenuItem's Click event procedure. Type **Me.Close()** and press **Enter**.

Coding the letterTextBox's KeyPress Event

As indicated earlier in Figure 10-14, the letterTextBox's MaxLength and CharacterCasing properties are set to 1 and Upper, respectively. As a result, the text box will accept one character only. If the character is a letter of the alphabet, it will be converted to uppercase. In the next set of steps, you will prevent the text box from accepting a character that is not either a letter of the alphabet or the Backspace key. You can do this using an If...Then...Else statement with the following condition: `e.KeyChar Like "[!A-Za-z]" AndAlso e.KeyChar <> ControlChars.Back`. The sub-condition on the left side of the AndAlso operator will evaluate to True if the user's entry is not one of the uppercase or lowercase letters of the alphabet. The sub-condition on the right side of the AndAlso operator will evaluate to True if the user's entry is not the Backspace key. If both sub-conditions evaluate to True, the compound condition evaluates to True and the text box should not accept the user's entry.

To code and then test the letterTextBox_KeyPress procedure:

1. Open the code template for the letterTextBox's KeyPress event procedure. Type the comment and selection structure shown in Figure 10-20.

```
Private Sub letterTextBox_KeyPress(sender As Obj
        ' accept only letters and the Backspace key

    If e.KeyChar Like "[!A-Za-z]" AndAlso
        e.KeyChar <> ControlChars.Back Then
        e.Handled = True
    End If
End Sub
```

enter this comment and selection structure

Figure 10-20   letterTextBox_KeyPress procedure

2. Save the solution and then start the application. Type **a** in the text box. Notice that the letter is changed to its uppercase equivalent, A. Press the **Backspace** key to delete the letter A.

3. Now, try entering a character other than a letter of the alphabet or the Backspace key; you won't be able to do so. Also try entering more than one letter; here, too, you won't be able to do so.

4. Click **FILE** on the Frankenstein Game application's menu bar and then click **Exit** to end the application. Close the Code Editor window and then close the solution.

Coding the FILE Menu's New Game Option

The fileNewMenuItem_Click procedure is invoked when the user either clicks the New Game option on the FILE menu or presses Ctrl+N (the option's shortcut keys). The procedure should get a five-letter word from player 1 and then verify that the word contains five letters. The procedure's pseudocode is shown in Figure 10-21.

---

fileNewMenuItem Click event procedure

1. get a 5-letter word from player 1, trim leading and trailing spaces, and convert to uppercase
2. if the word contains 5 letters
     hide the 6 picture boxes
     display 5 dashes in wordLabel
     clear contents of incorrectLabel
     assign 0 to the incorrect counter variable
     clear contents of letterTextBox
     enable checkButton
     send focus to letterTextBox
  else
     display "5 letters are required" message in a message box
  end if

Figure 10-21 Pseudocode for the fileNewMenuItem_Click procedure
© 2013 Cengage Learning

To begin coding the fileNewMenuItem_Click procedure:

1. First, scroll to the top of the Code Editor window. The form's Declarations section declares two class-level variables. The `word` variable will store the word entered by player 1. The `incorrect` variable will keep track of the number of incorrect letters entered by player 2.

2. Now, open the code template for the fileNewMenuItem_Click procedure. Type the following comment and then press **Enter** twice:

   ' start a new game

3. According to its pseudocode, the procedure should begin by getting a five-letter word from player 1. It should trim any leading and trailing spaces from the word and also convert the word to uppercase. Enter the following comment and lines of code. Press **Enter** twice after typing the last line.

   ' get a 5-letter word from player 1
   ' and then trim and convert to uppercase
   word = InputBox("Enter a 5-letter word:",
          "Frankenstein Game").Trim.ToUpper

Next, the procedure should verify that player 1's word contains exactly five letters. Figure 10-22 shows two ways of accomplishing this task. Example 1 uses the Length property and the Substring method; both are shaded in the figure. Example 2 uses the Like operator, which is also shaded in the figure. Although the code in both examples produces the same result, Example 2's code is much more concise and easier to understand.

```
Example 1
Dim validWord As Boolean

' determine whether the word contains 5 letters
validWord = True   ' assume word is valid
If word.Length <> 5 Then
    validWord = False
Else
    Dim index As Integer
    Do While index < 5 AndAlso validWord = True
        If word.Substring(index, 1) Like "[!A-Z]" Then
            validWord = False
        End If
        index += 1
    Loop
End If

If validWord = True Then
    instructions to be processed when the word is valid
Else
    instructions to be processed when the word is not valid
End If

Example 2
If word Like "[A-Z][A-Z][A-Z][A-Z][A-Z]" Then
    instructions to be processed when the word is valid
Else
    instructions to be processed when the word is not valid
End If
```

Figure 10-22   Two ways of determining whether the word contains five letters
© 2013 Cengage Learning

To complete and then test the fileNewMenuItem_Click procedure:

1. Enter the following comment and If clause:

    ' determine whether the word contains 5 letters
    If word Like "[A-Z][A-Z][A-Z][A-Z][A-Z]" Then

2. If player 1's word contains five letters, the selection structure's True path should hide the six picture boxes. Enter the following comment and six assignment statements. Press **Enter** twice after typing the last assignment statement.

    ' hide the picture boxes
    headPictureBox.Visible = False
    torsoPictureBox.Visible = False
    rightArmPictureBox.Visible = False
    leftArmPictureBox.Visible = False
    rightLegPictureBox.Visible = False
    leftLegPictureBox.Visible = False

3. Next, the True path should display five dashes (one for each letter in the word) in the wordLabel. It then should clear the contents of the incorrectLabel, which displays the incorrect letters entered by the user. It also should assign the number 0 to the incorrect variable, which is the class-level variable that keeps track of the number of incorrect letters entered by the user. Enter the following comments and assignment statements. Press **Enter** twice after typing the last statement.

    ' display 5 dashes in wordLabel, clear
    ' incorrectLabel, and assign 0 to incorrect

> **wordLabel.Text = "-----"**
> **incorrectLabel.Text = String.Empty**
> **incorrect = 0**

4. The final three tasks in the selection structure's True path clear the contents of the letterTextBox, enable the checkButton, and send the focus to the letterTextBox. Enter the following comments and assignment statements:

> **' clear the text box, enable the**
> **' button, set the focus**
> **letterTextBox.Text = String.Empty**
> **checkButton.Enabled = True**
> **letterTextBox.Focus()**

5. Now you need to code the selection structure's False path. According to the pseudocode, the False path should display the "5 letters are required" message when player 1's word does not contain five letters. Enter the following lines of code:

> **Else**
>   **MessageBox.Show("5 letters are required",**
>   **"Frankenstein Game",**
>   **MessageBoxButtons.OK,**
>   **MessageBoxIcon.Information)**

6. If necessary, delete the blank line above the End If clause.

7. Save the solution and then run the application. Click **FILE** on the menu bar and then click **New Game**. A dialog box opens and prompts you to enter a five-letter word. First, you will enter a valid word. Type **house** in the dialog box and then press **Enter**. The picture boxes are hidden from view and five dashes appear in the Secret word box. In addition, the Check button is enabled for the user. See Figure 10-23.

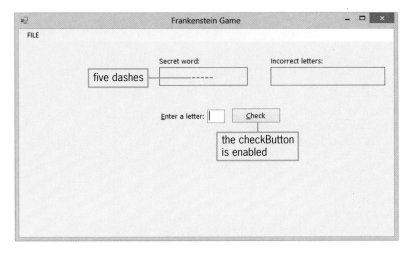

Figure 10-23   Result of entering a valid word

8. Next, you will enter a word that does not contain five letters. Press **Ctrl+n**, which are the shortcut keys for the New Game option. Type **hous3** in the dialog box and then press **Enter**. The message "5 letters are required" appears in a message box. Close the message box.

9. On your own, test the procedure using a word that has less than five letters. Also test it using a word that has more than five letters. In both cases, the message "5 letters are required" should appear in a message box. When you are finished testing the procedure, click the **Exit** option on the game's FILE menu to end the application.

Completing the checkButton's Click Event Procedure

Figure 10-24 shows the pseudocode for the checkButton's Click event procedure. It also shows the pseudocode for two independent Sub procedures named DisplayPicture and DetermineGameOver. Both independent Sub procedures are used by the checkButton_Click procedure.

---

checkButton Click event procedure

1. repeat for each letter in player 1's word
    if the current letter is the same as the letter entered by player 2
        replace the corresponding dash in wordLabel
        assign True to the dashReplaced variable
    end if
  end repeat
2. if the dashReplaced variable contains True
    call the DetermineGameOver procedure to determine whether player 2 guessed
    the word; pass the dashReplaced variable
  else
    display player 2's letter in incorrectLabel
    add 1 to the incorrect counter variable
    call DisplayPicture procedure to display the appropriate picture box
    call the DetermineGameOver procedure to determine whether player 2 made
    6 incorrect guesses; pass the dashReplaced variable
  end if

DisplayPicture procedure

use the incorrect counter variable's value to display the appropriate picture box
    if incorrect counter variable contains:

      1   display headPictureBox
      2   display torsoPictureBox
      3   display rightArmPictureBox
      4   display leftArmPictureBox
      5   display rightLegPictureBox
      6   display leftLegPictureBox

DetermineGameOver procedure

if a dash was replaced in player 1's word
    if there aren't any other dashes in the word
        display "Great guessing!" in a message box
        disable checkButton
        assign 0 to the incorrect counter variable
    end if
  else
    if the user entered 6 incorrect letters
        display "Sorry, the word is *word*." in a message box
        disable checkButton
        assign 0 to the incorrect counter variable
    end if
  end if

Figure 10-24 Pseudocode for the checkButton_Click, DisplayPicture, and DetermineGameOver procedures
© 2013 Cengage Learning

The DisplayPicture and DetermineGameOver procedures have already been coded for you. The Code Editor window also contains most of the code for the checkButton_Click procedure. You will complete the procedure in the next set of steps.

To complete the checkButton_Click procedure and then test it:

1. Locate the checkButton_Click procedure. The first step in the procedure's pseudocode is a loop that performs its instructions for each letter in player 1's word. The word, which is stored in the word variable, contains five letters whose indexes are 0, 1, 2, 3, and 4. Click the **blank line** below the ' `look at each letter in the word` comment and then enter the following For clause:

   For index As Integer = 0 To 4

2. Change the Next clause to **Next index** and then click the **blank line** below the For clause.

3. According to the pseudocode, the first instruction in the loop is a selection structure that compares the current letter in the word variable with the letter entered by player 2. You can use the Substring method to access an individual character in a string. The method's *startIndex* argument is the index of the first character you want to access, and its optional *numCharsToAccess* argument specifies the number of characters you want to access. Enter the following comment and If clause:

   ' if the letter appears in the word, replace the letter
   If word.Substring(index, 1) = letter Then

4. If the current letter in the word variable matches player 2's letter, the selection structure's True path should replace the corresponding dash in the wordLabel with player 2's letter. You can use the Remove and Insert methods to make the replacement. Enter the following assignment statements:

   wordLabel.Text = wordLabel.Text.Remove(index, 1)
   wordLabel.Text = wordLabel.Text.Insert(index, letter)

5. Finally, the selection structure's True path should assign the Boolean value True to the dashReplaced variable to indicate that a replacement was made. Type the additional assignment statement shown in Figure 10-25 and then click the **blank line** below the Next clause.

```
' look at each letter in the word
For index As Integer = 0 To 4
    ' if the letter appears in the word, replace the letter
    If word.Substring(index, 1) = letter Then
        wordLabel.Text = wordLabel.Text.Remove(index, 1)
        wordLabel.Text = wordLabel.Text.Insert(index, letter)
        dashReplaced = True          type this assignment
    End If                           statement
Next index
```

Figure 10-25   Additional code entered in the checkButton_Click procedure

6. Before testing the checkButton_Click procedure, review the code contained in the DisplayPicture and DetermineGameOver procedures. Notice that the DetermineGameOver procedure uses the Contains method to determine whether there are any dashes in the wordLabel.

7. Now, save the solution and then start the application. Click **FILE** on the application's menu bar and then click **New Game**. Type **dress** in the input dialog box and then press **Enter**.

8. Type **s** in the Enter a letter text box and then press **Enter**. The letter S replaces two of the dashes in the Secret word box.

9. Type **a** in the text box and then press **Enter**. The letter A appears in the Incorrect letters box. In addition, the headPictureBox, which shows an image of Frankenstein's head, is now visible.

10. Type the following letters in the text box, pressing **Enter** after typing each one: **r, c, t, d**, and **e**. See Figure 10-26.

Figure 10-26   Result of guessing the secret word
OpenClipArt.org/Merlin2525

11. Close the message box. Now, press **Ctrl+n** and then type **chair** in the input dialog box. Type the following letters in the text box, pressing **Enter** after typing each one: **c, e, t, y, a, b, x**, and **z**. See Figure 10-27.

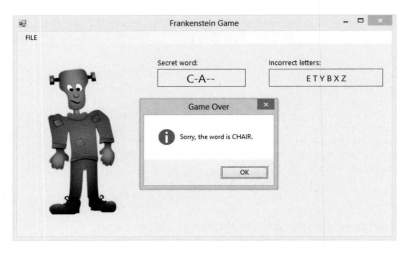

Figure 10-27   Result of not guessing the secret word
OpenClipArt.org/Merlin2525

12. Close the message box. Click **FILE** on the Frankenstein Game application's menu bar and then click **Exit**. Close the Code Editor window and then close the solution. Figure 10-28 shows the application's code.

```vbnet
1  ' Project name:           Frankenstein Project
2  ' Project purpose:        Allows the user to guess a
3  '                         word letter-by-letter
4  ' Created/revised by:     <your name> on <current date>
5
6  Option Explicit On
7  Option Strict On
8  Option Infer Off
9
10 Public Class MainForm
11
12     Private word As String
13     Private incorrect As Integer
14
15     Private Sub DisplayPicture()
16         ' display appropriate picture
17
18         Select Case incorrect
19             Case 1
20                 headPictureBox.Visible = True
21             Case 2
22                 torsoPictureBox.Visible = True
23             Case 3
24                 rightArmPictureBox.Visible = True
25             Case 4
26                 leftArmPictureBox.Visible = True
27             Case 5
28                 rightLegPictureBox.Visible = True
29             Case 6
30                 leftLegPictureBox.Visible = True
31         End Select
32     End Sub
33
34     Private Sub DetermineGameOver(ByVal dashReplaced As Boolean)
35         ' determine whether the game is over and
36         ' take the appropriate action
37
38         If dashReplaced = True Then
39             ' if the word does not contain any dashes,
40             ' the game is over because player 2
41             ' guessed the word
42             If wordLabel.Text.Contains("-") = False Then
43                 MessageBox.Show("Great guessing!", "Game Over",
44                         MessageBoxButtons.OK,
45                         MessageBoxIcon.Information)
46                 checkButton.Enabled = False
47                 incorrect = 0
48             End If
49         Else
50             ' if the user made 6 incorrect guesses,
51             ' the game is over
52             If incorrect = 6 Then
53                 MessageBox.Show("Sorry, the word is " &
54                         word & ".", "Game Over",
55                         MessageBoxButtons.OK,
56                         MessageBoxIcon.Information)
57                 checkButton.Enabled = False
58                 incorrect = 0
59             End If
60         End If
61     End Sub
```

Figure 10-28   Code for the Frankenstein Game application *(continues)*

(continued)

```
62
63      Private Sub checkButton_Click(sender As Object,
        e As EventArgs) Handles checkButton.Click
64          ' check if the letter appears in the word
65
66          Dim letter As String
67          Dim dashReplaced As Boolean
68
69          letter = letterTextBox.Text
70
71          ' look at each letter in the word
72          For index As Integer = 0 To 4
73              ' if the letter appears in the word, replace the letter
74              If word.Substring(index, 1) = letter Then
75                  wordLabel.Text = wordLabel.Text.Remove(index, 1)
76                  wordLabel.Text = wordLabel.Text.Insert(index, letter)
77                  dashReplaced = True
78              End If
79          Next index
80
81          If dashReplaced = True Then
82              Call DetermineGameOver(dashReplaced)
83          Else  ' no dash was replaced
84              incorrectLabel.Text =
85                  incorrectLabel.Text & " " & letter
86              incorrect += 1
87              Call DisplayPicture()
88              Call DetermineGameOver(dashReplaced)
89          End If
90
91          ' clear text box and set focus
92          letterTextBox.Text = String.Empty
93          letterTextBox.Focus()
94      End Sub
95
96      Private Sub fileExitMenuItem_Click(sender As Object,
        e As EventArgs) Handles fileExitMenuItem.Click
97          Me.Close()
98
99      End Sub
100
101     Private Sub letterTextBox_KeyPress(sender As Object,
        e As KeyPressEventArgs) Handles letterTextBox.KeyPress
102         ' accept only letters and the Backspace key
103
104         If e.KeyChar Like "[!A-Za-z]" AndAlso
105             e.KeyChar <> ControlChars.Back Then
106             e.Handled = True
107         End If
108     End Sub
109
110     Private Sub fileNewMenuItem_Click(sender As Object,
        e As EventArgs) Handles fileNewMenuItem.Click
111         ' start a new game
112
113         ' get a 5-letter word from player 1
114         ' and then trim and convert to uppercase
115         word = InputBox("Enter a 5-letter word:",
116             "Frankenstein Game").Trim.ToUpper
117
```

Figure 10-28   Code for the Frankenstein Game application (continues)

(continued)

```
118            ' determine whether the word contains 5 letters
119          If word Like "[A-Z][A-Z][A-Z][A-Z][A-Z]" Then
120              ' hide the picture boxes
121              headPictureBox.Visible = False
122              torsoPictureBox.Visible = False
123              rightArmPictureBox.Visible = False
124              leftArmPictureBox.Visible = False
125              rightLegPictureBox.Visible = False
126              leftLegPictureBox.Visible = False
127
128              ' display 5 dashes in wordLabel, clear
129              ' incorrectLabel, and assign 0 to incorrect
130              wordLabel.Text = "-----"
131              incorrectLabel.Text = String.Empty
132              incorrect = 0
133
134              ' clear the text box, enable the
135              ' button, set the focus
136              letterTextBox.Text = String.Empty
137              checkButton.Enabled = True
138              letterTextBox.Focus()
139          Else
140              MessageBox.Show("5 letters are required",
141                      "Frankenstein Game",
142                      MessageBoxButtons.OK,
143                      MessageBoxIcon.Information)
144          End If
145      End Sub
146 End Class
```

Figure 10-28 Code for the Frankenstein Game application
© 2013 Cengage Learning

PROGRAMMING TUTORIAL 2

Creating the Bucky Burgers Application

In this tutorial, you will code an application for the manager of the Bucky Burgers restaurant. The application's interface provides a text box for entering the names of employees who worked the previous day. Each name is added, using proper case, to a list box. Proper case means that the first and last names begin with an uppercase letter, while the remaining letters in the names are lowercase. The application allows the manager to print the interface. The application's TOE chart and MainForm are shown in Figures 10-29 and 10-30, respectively.

Task	Object	Event
Display the FILE menu	MenuStrip1	None
End the application	fileExitMenuItem	Click
Print the interface (use a print form control)	filePrintMenuItem	Click
Get the employee's name Select the text box's existing text	nameTextBox	None Enter
Display the employee names (from addButton)	namesListBox	None
1. change the employee name to proper case 2. add the employee name to the namesListBox 3. send the focus to the nameTextBox 4. select the nameTextBox's existing text	addButton	Click

Figure 10-29   TOE chart for the Bucky Burgers application
© 2013 Cengage Learning

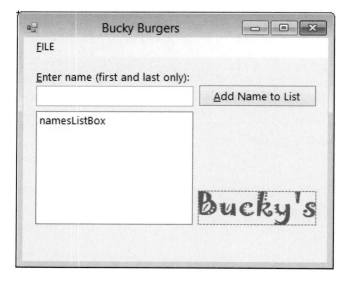

Figure 10-30   MainForm for the Bucky Burgers application

Completing the Interface

Before you can code the application, you need to add the FILE menu to the form.

To add the FILE menu to the form:

1. Start Visual Studio. Open the **Bucky Burgers Solution** (**Bucky Burgers Solution.sln**) file contained in the VbReloaded2012\Chap10\Bucky Burgers Solution folder. If necessary, open the designer window.

2. Open the Toolbox window (if necessary), and then click **MenuStrip** in the Menus & Toolbars section. Drag the mouse pointer to the form and then release the mouse button. The MenuStrip1 control will appear in the component tray.

3. Auto-hide the Toolbox window and then display the Properties window (if necessary). Create the menu shown in Figure 10-31. Use the following names for the menu title and menu items: fileMenuTitle, filePrintMenuItem, and fileExitMenuItem.

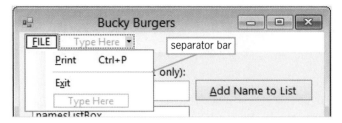

Figure 10-31 FILE menu

4. Save the solution and then start the application. Click **FILE** on the menu bar. The FILE menu opens and offers two options separated by a separator bar.

5. Click the **Close** button on the form's title bar.

Coding the Application

According to the application's TOE chart, four event procedures need to be coded: the Click event procedures for the two menu items, the text box's Enter event procedure, and the addButton's Click event procedure. You will begin by coding the Click event procedures for the two menu items.

To code the two menu items and then test the code:

1. Open the Code Editor window. The nameTextBox_Enter procedure has already been coded for you. In the comments that appear in the General Declarations section, replace <your name> and <current date> with your name and the current date, respectively.

2. Open the code template for the fileExitMenuItem's Click event procedure. Enter the following statement:

   Me.Close()

3. Open the code template for the filePrintMenuItem's Click event procedure. Type the following statement and then press **Enter** twice:

   ' sends the printout to the Print preview window

4. Now, enter the following statements:

   **PrintForm1.PrintAction =
       Printing.PrintAction.PrintToPreview
   PrintForm1.Print()**

5. Save the solution and then start the application. Click **FILE** on the application's menu bar and then click **Print**. An image of the interface appears in the Print preview window. Close the Print preview window.

6. Click **FILE** on the menu bar and then click **Exit** to end the application.

Next, you will code the addButton's Click event procedure. The procedure's pseudocode is shown in Figure 10-32.

---

addButton Click event procedure

1. assign user input (full name), excluding any leading or trailing spaces, to a variable
2. if the variable is empty
      display the "Please enter a name" message in a message box
   else
      use the IndexOf method to search for the space in the full name; assign the space's index to the index variable

      if the full name contains a space
            use the location of the space to separate the first and last names; assign the first and last names to separate variables

            change the first name to proper case
            change the last name to proper case
            concatenate the first name, a space, and the last name
      else
            change the full name to proper case
      end if
      add the full name to the namesListBox
   end if
3. send the focus to the nameTextBox
4. select the nameTextBox's existing text

Figure 10-32   Pseudocode for the addButton_Click procedure
© 2013 Cengage Learning

To code the addButton_Click procedure and then test the code:

1. Open the code template for the addButton's Click procedure. Type the following comment and then press **Enter** twice:

   ' adds names in proper case to the list box

2. The procedure will use three String variables to store the full name, first name, and last name. Enter the appropriate Dim statements, using the names `fullName`, `firstName`, and `lastName`.

3. The pseudocode indicates that the procedure will search for a space in the full name. The procedure will use an Integer variable named `index` to store the index of the space. Type the appropriate Dim statement and then press **Enter** twice.

4. The first step in the pseudocode assigns the user input, excluding any leading and trailing spaces, to a variable. Enter a statement that assigns the contents of the nameTextBox, excluding any leading and trailing spaces, to the `fullName` variable.

5. The second step in the pseudocode is a dual-alternative selection structure whose condition determines whether the `fullName` variable is empty. If it is empty, the selection structure's True path should display the "Please enter a name" message in a message box. Enter an appropriate If clause and MessageBox.Show method.

6. Type **Else** and press **Enter**. If the `fullName` variable is not empty, the selection structure's False path should use the IndexOf method to search for the space in the `fullName` variable. The space's index should be assigned to the `index` variable. Type **' locate the space** and then press **Enter**. Now, enter the appropriate assignment statement.

7. The next instruction in the False path is a nested dual-alternative selection structure whose condition determines whether the `fullName` variable contains a space. Type the following If clause and then press **Enter**:

   If index > −1 Then

8. If the `fullName` variable contains a space, the nested structure's True path should use the location of the space to separate the first and last names. Type **' separate first and last names** and then press **Enter**. Now, enter a statement that uses the Substring method to assign the first name to the `firstName` variable. (Hint: The first name starts with index 0 in the `fullName` variable, and it contains the number of characters stored in the `index` variable.)

9. Next, enter a statement that uses the Substring method to assign the last name to the `lastName` variable. (Hint: The last name starts with the character immediately after the space in the `fullName` variable.)

10. The next two instructions in the nested structure's True path should change the first and last names to proper case, which means the first letter in each name should be uppercase and the remaining letters should be lowercase. Press **Enter**. Type **' change first name to proper case** and then press **Enter**. Now, enter the appropriate code to change the first name to proper case. (Hint: You will need to use the Substring, ToUpper, and ToLower methods.)

11. Next, type **' change last name to proper case** and then press **Enter**. Now, enter the appropriate code to change the last name to proper case.

12. The last instruction in the nested structure's True path concatenates the first name, a space, and the last name. Type **' concatenate first, space, and last** and then press **Enter**. Enter a statement that performs the concatenation and assigns the result to the `fullName` variable.

13. It's possible that the user may enter only an employee's first or last name in the nameTextBox. In that case, the `fullName` variable will not contain a space, and the nested structure's False path should simply change the variable's contents to proper case. Type **Else** and press **Tab** twice. Type **' no space in name** and press **Enter**. Now, enter the code to change the contents of the `fullName` variable to proper case.

14. If necessary, delete the blank line above the nested End If clause.

15. The last instruction in the outer selection structure's False path adds the full name to the namesListBox. Insert a **blank line** between the two End If clauses. Type **' add full name to list box** and then press **Enter**. Now, enter the appropriate statement.

16. If necessary, delete the blank line above the outer End If clause.

17. The last two instructions in the pseudocode send the focus to the nameTextBox and also select the text box's existing text. Insert a **blank line** above the End Sub clause and then enter the appropriate statements.

18. If necessary, delete the blank line above the End Sub clause.

19. Save the solution and then start the application. Click the **Add Name to List** button. The "Please enter a name" message appears in a message box. Close the message box.

20. Type **lee howard** in the text box and then press **Enter** to select the Add Name to List button, which is the form's default button. The name "Lee Howard" appears in the list box.

21. Type **cher** in the text box and then press **Enter**. The name "Cher" appears in the list box. See Figure 10-33.

Figure 10-33 Sample run of the Bucky Burgers application

22. Click **FILE** on the menu bar and then click **Exit** to end the application. Close the Code Editor window and then close the solution. Figure 10-34 shows the application's code.

```
1 ' Project name:        Bucky Burgers Project
2 ' Project purpose:     Add names in proper case
3 '                      to a list box and print
4 '                      the interface
5 ' Created/revised by:  <your name> on <current date>
6
7 Option Explicit On
8 Option Strict On
9 Option Infer Off
10
11 Public Class MainForm
12
13    Private Sub nameTextBox_Enter(sender As Object,
      e As EventArgs) Handles nameTextBox.Enter
14        nameTextBox.SelectAll()
15    End Sub
16
17    Private Sub fileExitMenuItem_Click(sender As Object,
      e As EventArgs) Handles fileExitMenuItem.Click
18        Me.Close()
19
20    End Sub
21
22    Private Sub filePrintMenuItem_Click(sender As Object,
      e As EventArgs) Handles filePrintMenuItem.Click
23        ' sends the printout to the Print preview window
24
25        PrintForm1.PrintAction =
26            Printing.PrintAction.PrintToPreview
27        PrintForm1.Print()
28
29    End Sub
30
```

Figure 10-34 Code for the Bucky Burgers application *(continues)*

(continued)

```
31      Private Sub addButton_Click(sender As Object,
        e As EventArgs) Handles addButton.Click
32          ' adds names in proper case to the list box
33
34          Dim fullName As String
35          Dim firstName As String
36          Dim lastName As String
37          Dim index As Integer
38
39          fullName = nameTextBox.Text.Trim
40          If fullName = String.Empty Then
41              MessageBox.Show("Please enter a name",
42                      "Bucky Burgers",
43                      MessageBoxButtons.OK,
44                      MessageBoxIcon.Information)
45          Else
46              ' locate the space
47              index = fullName.IndexOf(" ")
48              If index > -1 Then
49                  ' separate first and last names
50                  firstName = fullName.Substring(0, index)
51                  lastName = fullName.Substring(index + 1)
52
53                  ' change first name to proper case
54                  firstName =
55                      firstName.Substring(0, 1).ToUpper &
56                      firstName.Substring(1).ToLower
57                  ' change last name to proper case
58                  lastName =
59                      lastName.Substring(0, 1).ToUpper &
60                      lastName.Substring(1).ToLower
61                  ' concatenate first, space, and last
62                  fullName = firstName & " " & lastName
63              Else    ' no space in name
64                  fullName =
65                      fullName.Substring(0, 1).ToUpper &
66                      fullName.Substring(1).ToLower
67              End If
68              ' add full name to list box
69              namesListBox.Items.Add(fullName)
70          End If
71          nameTextBox.Focus()
72          nameTextBox.SelectAll()
73      End Sub
74  End Class
```

Figure 10-34 Code for the Bucky Burgers application
© 2013 Cengage Learning

PROGRAMMING EXAMPLE

Yolanda Drapery Application

Create an interface that allows the user to display a report in a list box, but only if the user enters the appropriate password. The password must begin with a lowercase letter, followed by two digits, either the uppercase letter E or the uppercase letter M, the number 3, a lowercase letter from a through d, and a digit. Examples of valid passwords include a34E3b9 and z61M3c2. Examples of invalid passwords include A34E3b9 and z61T3c4. The report should list the names of the Yolanda Drapery salespeople in the first column, and each salesperson's bonus amount in the second column. The names and bonus amounts are shown in Figure 10-35. Store the names in a class-level one-dimensional array named `salespeople`. Store the bonus amounts in a class-level one-dimensional array named `bonuses`. Use the following names for the solution and project, respectively: Yolanda Solution and Yolanda Project. Save the application in the VbReloaded2012\Chap10 folder. Change the form file's name to Main Form.vb. See Figures 10-35 through 10-40.

Salesperson	Bonus
Carol Jackson	3,450
Jeremiah Jeffers	500
Pat Kowalski	1,200
Jose Gutierrez	2,900
Coulter Smith	450

Figure 10-35   Salespeople and bonus amounts
© 2013 Cengage Learning

Task	Object	Event
1. Declare and initialize a class-level, 5-element String array named salespeople 2. Declare and initialize a class-level, 5-element Integer array named bonuses	MainForm	Declarations section
End the application	exitButton	Click
1. Get the password from the user 2. Determine whether the password is valid 3. If the password is valid, display the report in reportListBox; otherwise, display "Invalid password" message in a message box	reportButton	Click
Display the report (from reportButton)	reportListBox	None

Figure 10-36   TOE chart
© 2013 Cengage Learning

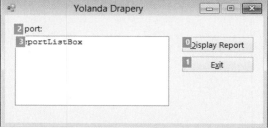

Figure 10-37   MainForm and tab order

Object	Property	Setting
MainForm	Font	Segoe UI, 10pt
	MaximizeBox	False
	StartPosition	CenterScreen
	Text	Yolanda Drapery
reportListBox	Font	Courier New, 10pt
	SelectionMode	None
	TabStop	False

Figure 10-38   Objects, properties, and settings
© 2013 Cengage Learning

exitButton Click event procedure
close the application

reportButton Click event procedure
1.   declare a variable to store the password entered by the user
2.   clear the reportListBox
3.   get a password from the user
4.   if the password is valid
       display the "Name" and "Bonus ($)" column headers
       repeat for each element in the salespeople and bonuses arrays
           concatenate the current element in both arrays
           and then add the result to the reportListBox
       end repeat for
   else
       display the "Invalid password" message in a message box
   end if

Figure 10-39   Pseudocode
© 2013 Cengage Learning

```
 1 ' Project name:        Yolanda Drapery Project
 2 ' Project purpose:     Displays a report, but only
 3 '                      if the user enters a valid
 4 '                      password
 5 ' Created/revised by:  <your name> on <current date>
 6
 7 Option Explicit On
 8 Option Strict On
 9 Option Infer Off
10
11 Public Class MainForm
12
13     Private salespeople() As String = {"Carol Jackson",
14                                        "Jeremiah Jeffers",
15                                        "Pat Kowalski",
16                                        "Jose Gutierrez",
17                                        "Coulter Smith"}
18     Private bonuses() As Integer = {3450, 500, 1200, 2900, 450}
19
20     Private Sub exitButton_Click(sender As Object,
        e As EventArgs) Handles exitButton.Click
21         Me.Close()
22     End Sub
23
```

Figure 10-40   Code (continues)

552

(continued)

```
24    Private Sub reportButton_Click(sender As Object,
      e As EventArgs) Handles reportButton.Click
25        ' display the name and bonus
26
27        Dim passWord As String
28
29        ' clear list box
30        reportListBox.Items.Clear()
31
32        ' get password
33        passWord = InputBox("Password:", "Password Entry")
34
35        ' determine whether password is valid
36        If passWord Like "[a-z]##[EM]3[a-d]#" Then
37            Const NameHead As String = "Name"
38            Const BonusHead As String = "Bonus ($)"
39            Dim line As String
40
41            ' display column headers
42            reportListBox.Items.Add(NameHead.PadRight(20) &
43                BonusHead.PadLeft(8))
44            ' display report
45            For x As Integer = 0 To salespeople.GetUpperBound(0)
46                line = salespeople(x).PadRight(20) &
47                    bonuses(x).ToString("N0").PadLeft(8)
48                reportListBox.Items.Add(line)
49            Next x
50        Else
51            MessageBox.Show("Invalid password",
52                "Password Error",
53                MessageBoxButtons.OK,
54                MessageBoxIcon.Information)
55        End If
56    End Sub
57 End Class
```

Figure 10-40   Code
© 2013 Cengage Learning

Summary

- You use a menu strip control to add one or more menus to a form.

- Each menu title and menu item should have an access key. Commonly used menu items should be assigned shortcut keys.

- Figure 10-41 contains a summary of the string manipulation techniques covered in the chapter.

Technique	Syntax	Purpose
Length property	*string*.**Length**	stores an integer that represents the number of characters contained in a string
Trim method	*string*.**Trim**	removes any spaces from both the beginning and end of a string
Remove method	*string*.**Remove(***startIndex*[, *numCharsToRemove*]**)**	removes characters from a string
Insert method	*string*.**Insert(***startIndex*, *value***)**	inserts characters in a string
Contains method	*string*.**Contains(***subString***)**	determines whether a string contains a specific sequence of characters; returns a Boolean value
IndexOf method	*string*.**IndexOf(***subString*[, *startIndex*]**)**	determines whether a string contains a specific sequence of characters; returns either –1 or an integer that indicates the starting position of the characters in the string
Substring method	*string*.**Substring(***startIndex*[, *numCharsToAccess*]**)**	accesses one or more characters in a string
PadLeft method	*string*.**PadLeft(***totalChars*[, *padCharacter*]**)**	pads the beginning of a string with a character until the string has the specified number of characters; right-aligns the string
PadRight method	*string*.**PadRight(***totalChars*[, *padCharacter*]**)**	pads the end of a string with a character until the string has the specified number of characters; left-aligns the string
Like operator	*string* **Like** *pattern*	uses pattern matching to compare strings

Figure 10-41 String manipulation techniques covered in the chapter
© 2013 Cengage Learning

553

Key Terms

Contains method—determines whether a string contains a specific sequence of characters; returns a Boolean value

IndexOf method—determines whether a string contains a specific sequence of characters; returns either –1 (if the string does not contain the sequence of characters) or an integer that represents the starting position of the sequence of characters

Insert method—inserts characters anywhere in a string

Length property—stores an integer that represents the number of characters contained in a string

Like operator—uses pattern-matching characters to determine whether one string is equal to another string

Menu strip control—located in the Menus & Toolbars section of the toolbox; used to include one or more menus on a form

PadLeft method—right-aligns a string by inserting characters at the beginning of the string

PadRight method—left-aligns a string by inserting characters at the end of the string

Remove method—removes a specified number of characters located anywhere in a string

Shortcut keys—appear to the right of a menu item and allow the user to select the item without opening the menu

Substring method—used to access any number of characters contained in a string

Trim method—removes spaces from both the beginning and end of a string

Review Questions

1. The `state` variable contains the letters K and Y followed by two spaces. Which of the following assigns only the letters K and Y to the variable? (2)

   a. state = state.Trim

   b. state = Trim(state)

   c. state = Trim(state, " ")

   d. state = Trim(2, 2)

 Each Review Question is associated with one or more objectives listed at the beginning of the chapter.

2. Which of the following assigns the first three characters in the `partNum` variable to the `code` variable? (6)

   a. code = partNum.Assign(0, 3)

   b. code = partNum.Sub(0, 3)

   c. code = partNum.Substring(0, 3)

   d. code = partNum.Substring(1, 3)

3. Which of the following changes the contents of the `product` variable from Shirts to Shirt? (2)

   a. product = product.Remove(5, "s")

   b. product = product.Remove(5)

   c. product = product.Remove(6, "s")

   d. product = product.Remove("s")

4. Which of the following changes the contents of the `zip` variable from 60121 to 60321? (2, 3)

   a. zip = zip.Remove(2, 1)
      zip = zip.Insert(2, "3")

   b. zip = zip.Insert(2, "3")
      zip = zip.Remove(3, 1)

   c. zip = zip.Remove(2, 1).Insert(2, "3")

   d. all of the above

5. If the `msg` variable contains the string "Happy New Year", what value will the `msg.IndexOf("Year")` method return? (5)

   a. −1

   b. True

   c. 10

   d. 11

6. Which of the following assigns the sixth character in the `word` variable to the `letter` variable? (6)

   a. letter = word.Substring(4, 1)

   b. letter = word.Substring(5, 1)

   c. letter = word.Substring(5)

   d. none of the above

7. Which of the following expressions evaluates to True when the `partNum` variable contains ABC73? (7)

   a. partNum Like "[A-Z]99"

   b. partNum Like "[A-Z]##"

   c. partNum Like "[A-Z][A-Z][A-Z]##"

   d. none of the above

8. If the `msg` variable contains the string "Tomorrow is Friday", which of the following returns the number 12? (5)

   a. `msg.Substring(0, "F")`

   c. `msg.IndexOf("F")`

   b. `msg.Contains("F")`

   d. `msg.IndexOf(0, "F")`

9. Which of the following changes the contents of the `amount` variable from 76.89 to 76.89!!!! (the number 76.89 followed by four exclamation points)? (3, 4)

   a. `amount = amount.PadRight(4, "!"c)`

   b. `amount = amount.PadRight(9, "!"c)`

   c. `amount = amount.PadLeft(4, "!"c)`

   d. none of the above

10. Which of the following determines whether the `userEntry` variable contains a dollar sign? (5)

    a. `userEntry.Contains("$")`

    b. `userEntry.IndexOf("$")`

    c. `userEntry.IndexOf("$", 0)`

    d. all of the above

11. Which of the following allows you to access a menu item without opening the menu? (8)

    a. an access key

    c. shortcut keys

    b. a menu key

    d. none of the above

12. Which of the following is false? (8)

    a. Menu titles should be one word only.

    b. Each menu title should have a unique access key.

    c. You should assign shortcut keys to commonly used menu titles.

    d. Menu items should be entered using book title capitalization.

Exercises

 Pencil and Paper

Each Exercise, except the DISCOVERY exercises, is associated with one or more objectives listed at the beginning of the chapter.

1. Write a statement that uses the Trim method to remove the leading and trailing spaces from the cityTextBox. (2)

   INTRODUCTORY

2. Write a statement that uses the Insert method to change the contents of the `firstName` variable from Carl to Carol. (3)

   INTRODUCTORY

3. The `productId` variable contains ABCD34G. Write a statement that assigns only the CD34 portion of the `productId` variable's contents to the `code` variable. (6)

   INTRODUCTORY

4. Write a statement that assigns the number of characters contained in the `msg` variable to the sizeLabel control. (1)

   INTRODUCTORY

5. Write a statement that uses the Insert method to change the string stored in the `word` variable from "in" to "spin". (3)

   INTRODUCTORY

6. Write a statement that uses the PadLeft method to change the string stored in the `pay` variable from "235.67" to "****235.67". (3, 4)

   INTRODUCTORY

INTRODUCTORY

7. Write the code that uses the Remove method to change the string stored in the **amount** variable from "3,123,560" to "3123560". (2)

INTRODUCTORY

8. Write a statement that determines whether the **address** variable contains the street name "Maple Street" (entered in uppercase, lowercase, or a combination of uppercase and lowercase). Use the Contains method and assign the method's return value to a Boolean variable named **isContained**. (5)

INTRODUCTORY

9. Write a statement that determines whether the **address** variable contains the street name "Elm Street" (entered in uppercase, lowercase, or a combination of uppercase and lowercase). Use the IndexOf method and assign the method's return value to an Integer variable named **indexNum**. (5)

INTERMEDIATE

10. Write the code to change the contents of the **pet** variable from dog to frog. (2, 3)

INTERMEDIATE

11. Write the code to change the contents of the **word** variable from mouse to mouth. (2, 3)

INTERMEDIATE

12. Write the code to change the string stored in the **amount** variable from "3123560" to "$3,123,560". (3)

INTERMEDIATE

13. Write an If clause that determines whether the state name stored in the **state** variable is one of the following (entered using any case): New York, New Jersey, or New Mexico. Use the Like operator. (7)

INTERMEDIATE

14. Write a Do clause that processes the loop body when the **userEntry** variable begins with the two letters J and E (entered using any case) followed by one character. Use the Like operator. (7)

INTERMEDIATE

15. Write an If clause that determines whether the name stored in the **lastName** variable is either Smith or Smyth (entered using any case). Use the Like operator. (7)

ADVANCED

16. Write the code to determine the number of lowercase letters stored in the **msg** variable. Assign the result to an Integer variable named **numLower**. (6, 7)

ADVANCED

17. Write an If clause that determines whether the last character in the rateTextBox's Text property is a percent sign (%). (7)

ADVANCED

18. Write the code to determine the number of commas in the salesTextBox's Text property. Assign the result to an Integer variable named **numCommas**. (6)

 Computer

MODIFY THIS

19. If necessary, complete the Frankenstein Game application from this chapter's Programming Tutorial 1, and then close the solution. Use Windows to make a copy of the Frankenstein Solution folder. Rename the folder Frankenstein Solution-ModifyThis. Open the Frankenstein Solution (Frankenstein Solution.sln) file contained in the Frankenstein Solution-ModifyThis folder. Modify the code to allow player 1 to enter a word that contains any number of letters, up to a maximum of 10 letters. Save the solution and then start and test the application. Close the solution. (1, 5-7)

MODIFY THIS

20. If necessary, complete the Bucky Burgers application from this chapter's Programming Tutorial 2, and then close the solution. Use Windows to make a copy of the Bucky Burgers Solution folder. Rename the folder Bucky Burgers Solution-ModifyThis. Open the Bucky Burgers Solution (Bucky Burgers Solution.sln) file contained in the Bucky Burgers Solution-ModifyThis folder. The modified application should allow the user to enter the employee's first, middle, and last names. First, remove the "(first and last only)" text from the Label1 control's Text property. Next, modify the code to display the names using proper case. Save the solution and then start and test the application. Close the solution. (5, 6)

21. If necessary, complete the Yolanda Drapery application from this chapter's Programming Example, and then close the solution. Use Windows to make a copy of the Yolanda Solution folder. Rename the folder Yolanda Solution-ModifyThis. Open the Yolanda Solution (Yolanda Solution.sln) file contained in the Yolanda Solution-ModifyThis folder. Passwords should now begin with either an uppercase or a lowercase letter, followed by three digits, any two uppercase letters, the @ symbol, and a digit. Modify the application's code. Save the solution and then start and test the application. Close the solution. (7)

MODIFY THIS

22. Open the Item Prices Solution (Item Prices Solution.sln) file contained in the VbReloaded2012\Chap10\Item Prices Solution folder. Modify the form's Load event procedure so that it right-aligns the prices listed in the rightComboBox and then selects the first price. Save the solution and then start the application. Close the solution. (4)

INTRODUCTORY

23. Open the Zip Solution (Zip Solution.sln) file contained in the VbReloaded2012\Chap10\Zip Solution folder. The Display Shipping Charge button's Click event procedure should display the appropriate shipping charge based on the ZIP code entered by the user. To be valid, the ZIP code must contain exactly five digits, and the first three digits must be either "605" or "606". The shipping charge for "605" ZIP codes is $25. The shipping charge for "606" ZIP codes is $30. Display an appropriate message if the ZIP code is invalid. Code the procedure. Save the solution and then start the application. Test the application using the following ZIP codes: 60677, 60511, 60344, and 7130. Close the solution. (7)

INTRODUCTORY

24. Open the Bonus Solution (Bonus Solution.sln) file contained in the VbReloaded2012\Chap10\Bonus Solution folder. Add a FILE menu to the form. The FILE menu should contain an Exit menu item that ends the application. Enter the appropriate code in the menu item's Click event procedure. Save the solution and then start and test the application. Close the solution. (8, 9)

INTRODUCTORY

25. Open the Commission Solution (Commission Solution.sln) file contained in the VbReloaded2012\Chap10\Commission Solution folder. Add a FILE menu and a CALCULATE menu to the form. Include an Exit menu item on the FILE menu. Include two menu items on the CALCULATE menu: 2% Commission and 5% Commission. Assign shortcut keys to the items on the CALCULATE menu. When the user clicks the Exit menu item, the application should end. When the user clicks the 2% menu item, the application should calculate and display a 2% commission on the sales entered by the user. When the user clicks the 5% menu item, the application should calculate and display a 5% commission on the sales entered by the user. Code the appropriate procedures. Save the solution and then start and test the application. Close the solution. (8, 9)

INTRODUCTORY

26. Open the Color Solution (Color Solution.sln) file contained in the VbReloaded2012\Chap10\Color Solution folder. The Display Color button's Click event procedure should display the color of the item whose item number is entered by the user. All item numbers contain exactly six characters. All items are available in four colors: blue, green, red, and purple. The fourth character in the item number indicates the item's color, as follows: a b or B indicates Blue, a g or G indicates green, an r or R indicates Red, and a p or P indicates purple. If the item number does not contain exactly six characters, or if the fourth character is not one of the valid color characters, the procedure should change the colorLabel to white and display "Invalid item number" in the colorLabel. However, if the item number contains exactly six characters and the fourth character is valid, the procedure should change the colorLabel's background to the appropriate color and also remove any message from the colorLabel. Code the procedure. Save the solution and then start the application. Test the application using the following item numbers: 12x, 123b45, 67b555, 993G44, abcr55, 78tp99, and 235abc. Close the solution. (1, 6, 7)

INTERMEDIATE

INTERMEDIATE

27. Open the Reverse Name Solution (Reverse Name Solution.sln) file contained in the VbReloaded2012\Chap10\Reverse Name Solution folder. The interface provides a text box for entering a person's first name followed by a space and the person's last name. Code the Reverse Name button's Click event procedure to display the name as follows: the last name followed by a comma, a space, and the first name. Save the solution and then start and test the application. Close the solutionan. (5, 6)

INTERMEDIATE

28. Open the Phone Solution (Phone Solution.sln) file contained in the VbReloaded2012\Chap10\Phone Solution folder. The interface provides a text box for entering a phone number. Code the Display button's Click event procedure to display the phone number, excluding any hyphens and parentheses, in the numberLabel. Save the solution and then start the application. Test the application using the following phone numbers: (555)111-1111, 555-5555, and 123-456-1111. Close the solution. (1, 2, 6, 7)

ADVANCED

29. Open the Search Name Solution (Search Name Solution.sln) file contained in the VbReloaded2012\Chap10\Search Name Solution folder. The interface provides text boxes for entering a name (first name followed by a space and the last name) and the search text. If the last name (entered in any case) begins with the search text (entered in any case), the Display Message button's Click event procedure should display the message "The last name begins with" followed by a space and the search text. If the characters in the last name come before the search text, display the message "The last name comes before" followed by a space and the search text. Finally, if the characters in the last name come after the search text, display the message "The last name comes after" followed by a space and the search text. Code the procedure. Save the solution and then start the application. To test the application, enter Helga Swanson as the name and then use the following strings for the search text: g, ab, he, s, SY, sw, swan, and wan. Close the solution. (1, 5, 6)

ADVANCED

30. Open the Sales Tax Solution (Sales Tax Solution.sln) file contained in the VbReloaded2012\Chap10\Sales Tax Solution folder. The interface provides text boxes for entering a sales amount and a tax rate. The Calculate button's Click event procedure should remove any dollar signs, spaces, and commas from the sales amount. It should also verify that the tax rate begins with a period. Code the procedure. Save the solution and then start and test the application. Close the solution. (1, 2, 6, 7)

ADVANCED

31. Open the Sales Bonus Solution (Sales Bonus Solution.sln) file contained in the VbReloaded2012\Chap10\Sales Bonus Solution folder. The interface provides a text box for entering a sales amount. The text box's KeyPress event procedure allows the text box to accept only numbers, the period, and the Backspace key. The Calculate button's Click event procedure should verify that the sales amount contains either no periods or one period. If the sales amount contains more than one period, the procedure should display an appropriate message; otherwise, it should display a 10% bonus. Code the procedure. Save the solution and then start and test the application. Close the solution. (1, 6)

ADVANCED

32. Open the Delivery Solution (Delivery Solution.sln) file contained in the VbReloaded2012\Chap10\Delivery Solution folder. The interface provides a text box for entering a product ID, which should consist of two numbers followed by either one or two letters. The letter(s) represent the delivery method, as follows: SM represents Standard Mail, PM represents Priority Mail, FS represents FedEx Standard, FO represents FedEx Overnight, and U represents UPS. Code the Select Delivery button's Click event procedure so that it selects the appropriate delivery method in the list box; use the Like operator. Display an appropriate message when the product ID does not contain two numbers followed by one or two letters, or when the letter(s) do not represent a valid delivery method. Save the solution and then start the application. Test the application using the following product IDs: 73pm, 34fs, 12u, 78h, 9FO, and 34sm. Close the solution. (7)

33. If necessary, complete the Frankenstein Game application from this chapter's Programming Tutorial 1, and then close the solution. Use Windows to make a copy of the Frankenstein Solution folder. Rename the folder Frankenstein Solution-Advanced. Open the Frankenstein Solution (Frankenstein Solution.sln) file contained in the Frankenstein Solution-Advanced folder. Replace the Contains method in the DetermineGameOver procedure with the Like operator. Save the solution and then start and test the application. Close the solution. (7)

34. Research Visual Basic's Trim, TrimStart, and TrimEnd methods, and then open the Trim Methods Solution (Trim Methods Solution.sln) file contained in the VbReloaded2012\Chap10\Trim Methods Solution folder. Code the Trim, TrimStart, and TrimEnd buttons' Click event procedures. Save the solution and then start and test the application. Close the solution.

35. Research Visual Basic's Replace method, and then open the Replace Method Solution (Replace Method Solution.sln) file contained in the VbReloaded2012\Chap10\Replace Method Solution folder. Code the Replace button's Click event procedure. Save the solution and then start and test the application. Close the solution.

36. Research Visual Basic's StartsWith and EndsWith methods, and then open the StartsWith EndsWith Solution (StartsWith EndsWith Solution.sln) file contained in the VbReloaded2012\Chap10\StartsWith EndsWith Solution folder. Code the StartsWith and EndsWith buttons' Click event procedures. Save the solution and then start and test the application. Close the solution.

37. Open the Debug Solution (Debug Solution.sln) file contained in the VbReloaded2012\Chap10\Debug Solution 1 folder. Open the Code Editor window and review the existing code. Start and then test the application. Locate and then correct any errors. When the application is working correctly, close the solution. (5, 6)

38. Open the Debug Solution (Debug Solution.sln) file contained in the VbReloaded2012\Chap10\Debug Solution 2 folder. Open the Code Editor window and review the existing code. Start and then test the application. Locate and then correct any errors. When the application is working correctly, close the solution. (2)

39. Open the Debug Solution (Debug Solution.sln) file contained in the VbReloaded2012\Chap10\Debug Solution 3 folder. Open the Code Editor window and review the existing code. Start and then test the application. Locate and then correct any errors. When the application is working correctly, close the solution. (1, 6)

Case Projects

 Vita Credit

Each credit card number issued by Vita Credit contains five digits. The last digit is determined by multiplying the second and fourth digits by 2 and then adding the products to the first and third digits. The last digit in the sum is then appended to the first four digits in the credit card number, as illustrated in Figure 10-42. Create an application that allows the credit manager to enter four digits. The application should calculate the fifth digit and then display the credit card number. Use the following names for the solution and project, respectively: Vita Solution and Vita Project. Save the application in the VbReloaded2012\Chap10 folder. Change the form file's name to Main Form.vb. You can either create your own interface or create the one shown in Figure 10-43. (1, 6, 7)

Check Digit Algorithm

First four digits in credit card number:	1	3	5	7
Step 1: Multiply the second and fourth digits by 2:		*2		*2
Result─────────────────────────►	1	6	5	14
Step 2: Add the numbers together:	1 + 6 + 5 + 14 = 26
Step 3: Take the last digit in the sum and append it to the first four digits, resulting in the final credit card number:	13576

Figure 10-42 Illustration of a check digit algorithm
© 2013 Cengage Learning

Vita Credit

Enter first four digits: [   ]

Credit card number: [   ]

[Credit Card Number]   [Exit]

Figure 10-43 Sample interface for the Vita Credit application

Holterback Finance

Create an application that allows the user to enter a password containing from five to seven characters, which must be letters and/or numbers. The application should create and display a new password using the rules specified in Figure 10-44. Use the following names for the solution and project, respectively: Holterback Solution and Holterback Project. Save the application in the VbReloaded2012\Chap10 folder. Change the form file's name to Main Form.vb. You can either create your own interface or create the one shown in Figure 10-45. (1-3, 6, 7)

1. Replace all of the vowels (A, E, I, O, or U) in the original password with a number, as follows:
   Replace the first vowel with the number 1.
   Replace the second vowel with the number 2.
   Replace all other vowels with the number 9.
2. Replace all of the numbers from 0 through 5 in the original password with the letter Z.
3. Replace all of the numbers from 6 through 9 in the original password with the asterisk (*).
4. Reverse all of the characters in the original password.

Figure 10-44 Rules for creating a new password
© 2013 Cengage Learning

Figure 10-45 Sample interface for the Holterback Finance application

 Huntington Motors

Each salesperson at Huntington Motors is assigned an ID number that consists of four characters. The first character is either the number 1 or the number 2. A 1 indicates that the salesperson sells new cars, and a 2 indicates that the salesperson sells used cars. The middle two characters are the salesperson's initials, and the last character is either the letter F or the letter P. The letter F indicates that the salesperson is a full-time employee; the letter P indicates that he or she is a part-time employee. Create an application that allows the sales manager to enter a salesperson's ID and the number of cars the salesperson sold during the month. The application should allow the sales manager to enter this information for as many salespeople as needed. The application should calculate and display the total number of cars sold by each of the following four categories of employees: full-time employees, part-time employees, employees selling new cars, and employees selling used cars. Use the following names for the solution and project, respectively: Huntington Solution and Huntington Project. Save the application in the VbReloaded2012\Chap10 folder. Change the form file's name to Main Form.vb. You can either create your own interface or create the one shown in Figure 10-46. The car image in the picture box is contained in the VbReloaded2012\Chap10\Car.png file. (1, 6, 7)

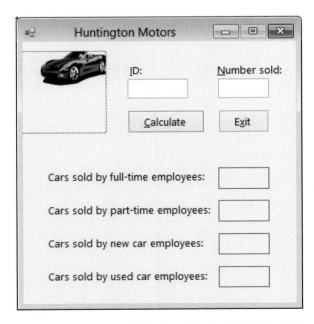

Figure 10-46 Sample interface for the Huntington Motors application

561

Pig Latin

Create an application that allows the user to enter a word. The application should display the word in pig latin form. The rules for converting a word into pig latin form are shown in Figure 10-47. Use the following names for the solution and project, respectively: Pig Latin Solution and Pig Latin Project. Save the application in the VbReloaded2012\Chap10 folder. Change the form file's name to Main Form.vb. (1-3, 6, 7)

---

1. If the word begins with a vowel (A, E, I, O, or U), add the string "-way" (a dash followed by the letters w, a, and y) to the end of the word. For example, the pig latin form of the word "ant" is "ant-way".

2. If the word does not begin with a vowel, first add a dash to the end of the word. Then continue moving the first character in the word to the end of the word until the first character is the letter A, E, I, O, U, or Y. Then add the string "ay" to the end of the word. For example, the pig latin form of the word "chair" is "air-chay".

3. If the word does not contain the letter A, E, I, O, U, or Y, then add the string "-way" to the end of the word. For example, the pig latin form of "bc" is "bc-way".

Figure 10-47 Pig latin rules

© 2013 Cengage Learning

11

Structures and Sequential Files

After studying Chapter 11, you should be able to:

1 Define a structure

2 Declare and use a structure variable

3 Pass a structure variable to a procedure

4 Create an array of structure variables

5 Write data to a sequential access file

6 Close a sequential access file

7 Read data from a sequential access file

8 Use the Exists and Peek methods

9 Code the FormClosing event procedure

10 Remove an item from a list box

11 Align columns of information

12 Use the Strings.Space method

13 Write and read records

14 Use the Split function

Reading and Study Guide

Before you begin reading Chapter 11, view the Ch11_ReadingStudyGuide.pdf file. You can open the file using Adobe Reader, which is available for free on the Adobe Web site at *www.adobe.com/downloads/*.

564

Structures

The data types used in previous chapters, such as the Integer and Double data types, are built into the Visual Basic language. You can also create your own data types in Visual Basic using the **Structure statement**; such data types are referred to as **user-defined data types** or **structures**. Similar to an array, a structure allows the programmer to group related items into a single unit. However, unlike the items in an array, the items in a structure can have different data types.

Figure 11-1 shows the Structure statement's syntax and includes an example of using the statement. The structure's name is typically entered using Pascal case, which means you capitalize the first letter in the name and the first letter of each subsequent word in the name. Between the Structure and End Structure clauses, you define the members included in the structure. The members can be variables, constants, or procedures. However, in most cases the members will be variables. This is because most programmers use the Class statement (rather than the Structure statement) to create data types that contain procedures. (You will learn about the Class statement in Chapter 12.) In most applications, you enter the Structure statement in the form's Declarations section, which begins with the Public Class clause and ends with the End Class clause.

HOW TO Define a Structure

Syntax
Structure *structureName*
    Public *memberVariableName1* **As** *dataType*
    [**Public** *memberVariableNameN* **As** *dataType*]
End Structure

Example
```
Structure Employee
    Public id As String
    Public firstName As String
    Public lastName As String
    Public pay As Double
End Structure
```

You can also include an array in a structure. This topic is explored in Computer Exercises 31 and 32 at the end of the chapter.

Figure 11-1 How to define a structure
© 2013 Cengage Learning

The variables defined in a structure are referred to as **member variables**. Each member variable's definition contains the keyword `Public` followed by the variable's name, which typically is entered using camel case. Following the variable's name is the keyword `As` and the variable's *dataType*. The dataType identifies the type of data the member variable will store and can be any of the standard data types available in Visual Basic; it can also be another structure (user-defined data type). The Employee structure shown in the example in Figure 11-1 contains four member variables: three String variables and one Double variable. The variables are related in that each is an attribute of an employee.

The Structure statement does not reserve any memory locations inside the computer. Rather, it merely provides a pattern for a data type that can be used when declaring a memory location. Variables declared using a structure as their data type are often referred to as **structure variables**. The syntax for creating a structure variable is shown in Figure 11-2. You use the `Dim` keyword to declare a procedure-level structure variable, but the `Private` keyword to declare a class-level structure variable. (Recall that class-level memory locations are declared in the form's Declarations section.) Figure 11-2 also includes examples of declaring structure variables using the Employee structure from Figure 11-1.

HOW TO Declare a Structure Variable

<u>Syntax</u>
{**Dim** | **Private**} *structureVariableName* **As** *structureName*

<u>Example 1</u>
`Dim hourly As Employee`
declares a procedure-level Employee structure variable named `hourly`

<u>Example 2</u>
`Private salaried As Employee`
declares a class-level Employee structure variable named `salaried`

Figure 11-2 How to declare a structure variable
© 2013 Cengage Learning

Similar to the way the `Dim taxRate As Double` instruction declares a Double variable named `taxRate`, the `Dim hourly As Employee` instruction in Example 1 in Figure 11-2 declares an Employee variable named `hourly`. However, unlike the `taxRate` variable, the `hourly` variable contains four member variables. In code, you refer to the entire structure variable by its name—in this case, `hourly`. You refer to a member variable by preceding its name with the name of the structure variable in which it is defined, using the dot member access operator (a period) to separate both names, like this: `hourly.id`, `hourly.firstName`, `hourly.lastName`, and `hourly.pay`. (You learned about the dot member access operator in Chapter 1.) Example 2 in Figure 11-2 declares a class-level structure variable named `salaried`. The names of the member variables within the `salaried` variable are `salaried.id`, `salaried.firstName`, `salaried.lastName`, and `salaried.pay`. Figure 11-3 illustrates the Employee structure and the `hourly` and `salaried` structure variables.

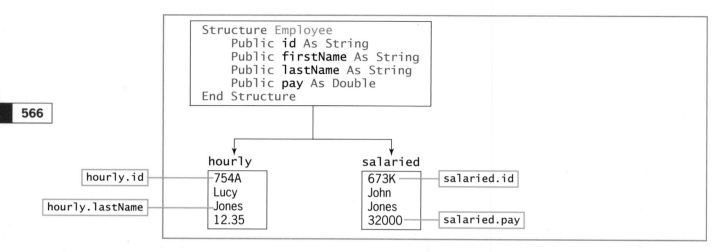

Figure 11-3   Illustration of the structure and structure variables
© Cengage Learning 2013

The member variables in a structure variable can be used just like any other variables. You can assign values to them, use them in calculations, display their contents, and so on. Figure 11-4 shows examples of statements that perform these tasks using the member variables contained in the `hourly` and `salaried` structure variables.

HOW TO Use a Member Variable

Example 1
`hourly.lastName = "Oberland"`
assigns the string "Oberland" to the `hourly.lastName` member variable

Example 2
`hourly.pay = hourly.pay * 1.03`
multiplies the contents of the `hourly.pay` member variable by 1.03 and then assigns the result to the member variable; you can also write the statement as `hourly.pay *= 1.03`

Example 3
`salaryLabel.Text = salaried.pay.ToString("C2")`
formats the value contained in the `salaried.pay` member variable and then displays the result in the salaryLabel

Figure 11-4   How to use a member variable
© 2013 Cengage Learning

Programmers use structure variables when they need to pass a group of related items to a procedure for further processing. This is because it's easier to pass one structure variable rather than many individual variables. Programmers also use structure variables to store related items in an array, even when the members have different data types. In the next two sections, you will learn how to pass a structure variable to a procedure and also store a structure variable in an array.

Passing a Structure Variable to a Procedure

Figure 11-5 shows the problem specification for Painters Paradise. It also shows most of the application's code, which does not use a structure. Notice that the calcButton_Click procedure calls the GetCostOfGoodsSold function, passing it three variables *by value*. The function uses the values to calculate the cost of goods sold. It then returns the result as a Double number to the calcButton_Click procedure, which assigns the value to the costGoodsSold variable.

Problem specification
Create an application that displays the Painters Paradise company's gross profit, which is its revenue minus its cost of goods sold. Use the following formula to calculate the cost of goods sold: beginning inventory cost + purchases cost – ending inventory cost.

```
Private Function GetCostOfGoodsSold(ByVal beginVal As Double,
                        ByVal purchVal As Double,
                        ByVal endVal As Double) As Double

    Return beginVal + purchVal - endVal
End Function

Private Sub calcButton_Click(sender As Object,
e As EventArgs) Handles calcButton.Click
    ' calculate the gross profit

    Dim revenue As Double
    Dim costBegin As Double
    Dim costPurch As Double
    Dim costEnd As Double
    Dim costGoodsSold As Double
    Dim grossProfit As Double

    Double.TryParse(revenueTextBox.Text, revenue)
    Double.TryParse(beginTextBox.Text, costBegin)
    Double.TryParse(purchasesTextBox.Text, costPurch)
    Double.TryParse(endingTextBox.Text, costEnd)

    ' calculate cost of goods sold
    costGoodsSold =
        GetCostOfGoodsSold(costBegin, costPurch, costEnd)

    ' calculate gross profit
    grossProfit = revenue - costGoodsSold

    costGoodsSoldLabel.Text = costGoodsSold.ToString("N2")
    grossProfitLabel.Text = grossProfit.ToString("C2")
End Sub
```

- receives three variables *by value*
- returns the cost of goods sold
- declares three variables to store the input data pertaining to the cost of goods sold
- stores data in the three variables
- passes three variables to the GetCostOfGoodsSold function

Painters Paradise

Revenue: `10500`
Beginning inventory ($): `1000`
Gross profit: `$6,800.00`

Purchases ($): `3500`
[Calculate]
[Exit]

Ending inventory ($): `800`

Cost of goods sold: `3,700.00`

If you want to experiment with the Painters Paradise application shown in Figure 11-5, open the solution contained in the Try It 1! folder.

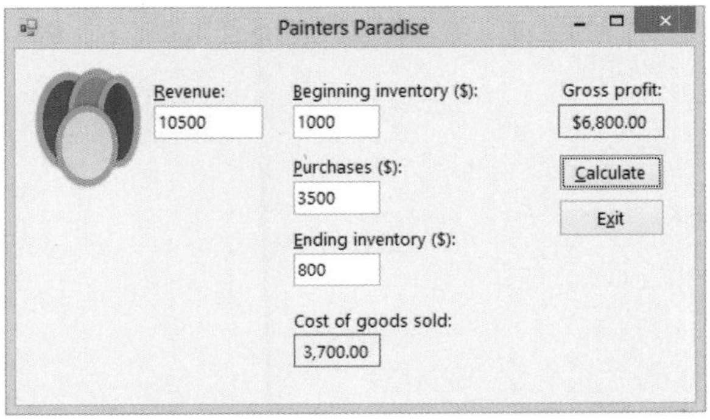

Figure 11-5 Paradise Painters application (without a structure)

568

Figure 11-6 shows a different way of writing the code for the Painters Paradise application. This version of the code contains a structure named CostOfGoodsSold. The structure groups together the three input items used to calculate the cost of goods sold. The Structure statement that defines the structure is entered in the MainForm's Declarations section and contains three member variables: beginVal, purchVal, and endVal. The code pertaining to the structure is shaded in the figure.

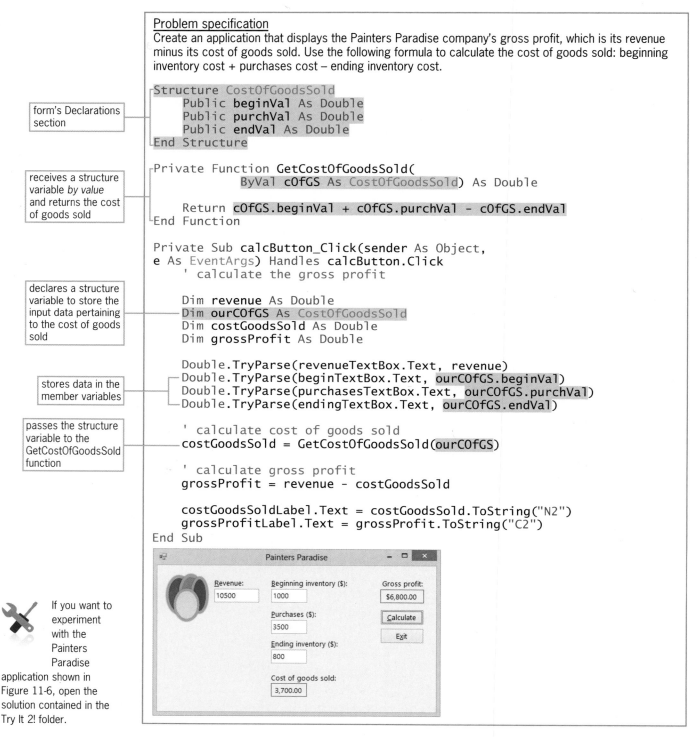

form's Declarations section

receives a structure variable *by value* and returns the cost of goods sold

declares a structure variable to store the input data pertaining to the cost of goods sold

stores data in the member variables

passes the structure variable to the GetCostOfGoodsSold function

Problem specification
Create an application that displays the Painters Paradise company's gross profit, which is its revenue minus its cost of goods sold. Use the following formula to calculate the cost of goods sold: beginning inventory cost + purchases cost − ending inventory cost.

```
Structure CostOfGoodsSold
    Public beginVal As Double
    Public purchVal As Double
    Public endVal As Double
End Structure

Private Function GetCostOfGoodsSold(
            ByVal cOfGS As CostOfGoodsSold) As Double
    Return cOfGS.beginVal + cOfGS.purchVal - cOfGS.endVal
End Function

Private Sub calcButton_Click(sender As Object,
e As EventArgs) Handles calcButton.Click
    ' calculate the gross profit

    Dim revenue As Double
    Dim ourCOfGS As CostOfGoodsSold
    Dim costGoodsSold As Double
    Dim grossProfit As Double

    Double.TryParse(revenueTextBox.Text, revenue)
    Double.TryParse(beginTextBox.Text, ourCOfGS.beginVal)
    Double.TryParse(purchasesTextBox.Text, ourCOfGS.purchVal)
    Double.TryParse(endingTextBox.Text, ourCOfGS.endVal)

    ' calculate cost of goods sold
    costGoodsSold = GetCostOfGoodsSold(ourCOfGS)

    ' calculate gross profit
    grossProfit = revenue - costGoodsSold

    costGoodsSoldLabel.Text = costGoodsSold.ToString("N2")
    grossProfitLabel.Text = grossProfit.ToString("C2")
End Sub
```

If you want to experiment with the Painters Paradise application shown in Figure 11-6, open the solution contained in the Try It 2! folder.

Figure 11-6   Paradise Painters application (with a structure)

The second Dim statement in the calcButton_Click procedure declares a CostOfGoodsSold structure variable named **ourCOfGS**, and the last three TryParse methods fill the member variables with values. The `costGoodsSold = GetCostOfGoodsSold(ourCOfGS)` statement calls the GetCostOfGoodsSold function, passing it the **ourCOfGS** structure variable *by value*. When you pass a structure variable, all of the member variables are automatically passed. The GetCostOfGoodsSold function uses the values stored in the member variables to calculate the cost of goods sold, which it returns as a Double number. The calcButton_Click procedure assigns the function's return value to the **costGoodsSold** variable.

Compare the calcButton_Click procedure in Figure 11-5 with the same procedure shown in Figure 11-6. Notice that the procedure in Figure 11-5 uses three scalar variables to store the input data, while the procedure in Figure 11-6 uses only one structure variable for this purpose. The procedure in Figure 11-5 also passes three scalar variables (rather than one structure variable) to the GetCostOfGoodsSold function, which uses three scalar variables (rather than one structure variable) to accept the data. If the data to be passed consisted of 20 items rather than just three items, consider how much easier it would be to pass one structure variable rather than 20 scalar variables.

Creating an Array of Structure Variables

As mentioned earlier, another advantage of using a structure is that a structure variable can be stored in an array, even when its members have different data types. The West Coast Emporium application can be used to illustrate this concept. The application's problem specification is shown in Figure 11-7, along with most of the application's code. The figure also includes a sample run of the application.

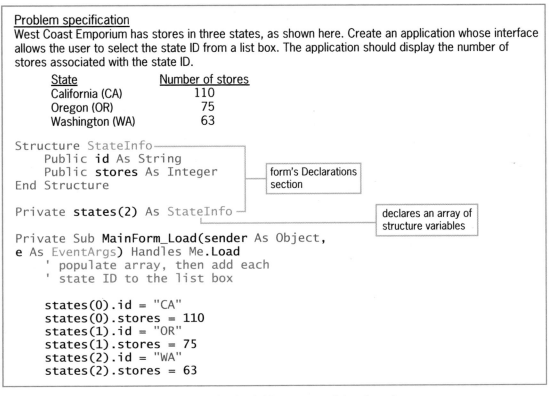

Problem specification
West Coast Emporium has stores in three states, as shown here. Create an application whose interface allows the user to select the state ID from a list box. The application should display the number of stores associated with the state ID.

State	Number of stores
California (CA)	110
Oregon (OR)	75
Washington (WA)	63

```
Structure StateInfo
    Public id As String                    form's Declarations
    Public stores As Integer               section
End Structure

Private states(2) As StateInfo            declares an array of
                                           structure variables

Private Sub MainForm_Load(sender As Object,
e As EventArgs) Handles Me.Load
    ' populate array, then add each
    ' state ID to the list box

    states(0).id = "CA"
    states(0).stores = 110
    states(1).id = "OR"
    states(1).stores = 75
    states(2).id = "WA"
    states(2).stores = 63
```

Figure 11-7 West Coast Emporium application (with a structure) *(continues)*

(continued)

displays the value stored in each array element's id member

```
   For index As Integer = 0 To 2
       idListBox.Items.Add(states(index).id)
   Next index

       idListBox.SelectedIndex = 0
End Sub

Private Sub numStoresButton_Click(sender As Object,
e As EventArgs) Handles numStoresButton.Click
    ' displays the number of stores associated
    ' with the state ID selected in the list box

       Dim index As Integer

       index = idListBox.SelectedIndex
       storesLabel.Text = states(index).stores.ToString
End Sub
```

displays the value stored in the array element's stores member

If you want to experiment with the West Coast Emporium application, open the solution contained in the Try It 3! folder.

West Coast Emporium

West Coast Emporium

State ID:
Stores:
Number of Stores

CA
OR
WA

75

Exit

Figure 11-7 West Coast Emporium application (with a structure)
© 2013 Cengage Learning

The MainForm's Declarations section defines a structure named StateInfo and then uses the structure to declare a three-element one-dimensional array named **states**. Each element in the **states** array is a structure variable that contains two member variables: a String variable named **id** and an Integer variable named **stores**. You refer to a member variable in an array element using the syntax shown in Figure 11-8.

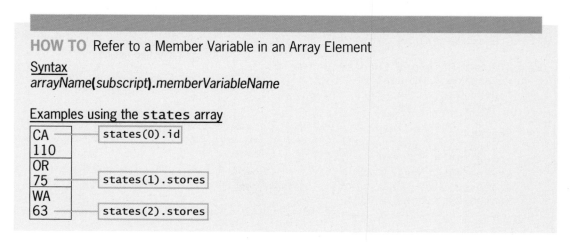

HOW TO Refer to a Member Variable in an Array Element
Syntax
arrayName(subscript).memberVariableName

Examples using the **states** array

CA	states(0).id
110	
OR	
75	states(1).stores
WA	
63	states(2).stores

Figure 11-8 How to refer to a member variable in an array element
© 2013 Cengage Learning

After the array is declared, the MainForm_Load procedure in Figure 11-7 populates the array with the appropriate IDs and numbers of stores. The procedure also adds each state ID stored in the array to the idListBox. The numStoresButton_Click procedure displays the number of stores associated with the ID selected in the list box.

Mini-Quiz 11-1

1. In most applications, the Structure statement is entered in the form's ——————. (1)

    a.   Declarations section

    b.   Definition section

    c.   Load event procedure

    d.   User-defined section

2. Which of the following assigns the string "Maple" to the `street` member variable within a structure variable named `address`? (2)

    a.   `address&street = "Maple"`

    b.   `address.street = "Maple"`

    c.   `street.address = "Maple"`

    d.   none of the above

3. An array is declared using the statement `Dim inventory(4) As Product`. Which of the following assigns the number 100 to the `quantity` member variable contained in the last array element? (4)

    a.   `inventory.quantity(4) = 100`

    b.   `inventory(4).Product.quantity = 100`

    c.   `inventory(3).quantity = 100`

    d.   `inventory(4).quantity = 100`

The answers to Mini-Quiz questions are located in Appendix A. Each question is associated with one or more objectives listed at the beginning of the chapter.

The values stored in an array usually come from a file on the computer's disk and are assigned to the array after it is declared. In most cases, the file is a sequential access file. You will learn about sequential access files in the next several sections.

Sequential Access Files

In addition to getting data from the keyboard and sending data to the computer screen, an application also can get data from and send data to a file on a disk. Getting data from a file is referred to as "reading the file," and sending data to a file is referred to as "writing to the file." Files to which data is written are called **output files** because the files store the output produced by an application. Files that are read by the computer are called **input files** because an application uses the data in these files as input.

Most input and output files are composed of lines of text that are both read and written sequentially. In other words, they are read and written in consecutive order, one line at a time, beginning with the first line in the file and ending with the last line in the file. Such files are referred to as **sequential access files** because of the manner in which the lines of text are accessed. They are also called **text files** because they are composed of lines of text. Examples of text stored in sequential access files include an employee list, a memo, and a sales report.

Writing Data to a Sequential Access File

An item of data—such as the string "Jacob"—is viewed differently by a human being and a computer. To a human being, the string represents a person's name; to a computer, it is merely a sequence of characters. Programmers refer to a sequence of characters as a **stream of characters**.

In Visual Basic, you use a **StreamWriter object** to write a stream of characters to a sequential access file. Before you create the StreamWriter object, you first declare a variable to store the object in the computer's internal memory. Figure 11-9 shows the syntax and an example of declaring a StreamWriter variable. The IO in the syntax stands for Input/Output.

HOW TO Declare a StreamWriter Variable

<u>Syntax</u>
{Dim | Private} *streamWriterVariableName* **As IO.StreamWriter**

<u>Example</u>
Dim outFile As IO.StreamWriter
declares a StreamWriter variable named outFile

Figure 11-9 How to declare a StreamWriter variable
© 2013 Cengage Learning

After declaring a StreamWriter variable, you can use the syntax shown in Figure 11-10 to create a StreamWriter object. As the figure indicates, creating a StreamWriter object involves opening a sequential access file using either the CreateText method or the AppendText method. You use the **CreateText method** to open a sequential access file for output. When you open a file for output, the computer creates a new, empty file to which data can be written. If the file already exists, the computer erases the contents of the file before writing any data to it. You use the **AppendText method** to open a sequential access file for append. When a file is opened for append, new data is written after any existing data in the file. If the file does not exist, the computer creates the file for you. In addition to opening the file, both methods automatically create a StreamWriter object to represent the file in the application. You assign the StreamWriter object to a StreamWriter variable, which you use to refer to the file in code. Figure 11-10 also includes examples of using both methods.

HOW TO Create a StreamWriter Object

<u>Syntax</u>
IO.File.*method*(*fileName*)

method	Description
CreateText	opens a sequential access file for output
AppendText	opens a sequential access file for append

<u>Example 1</u>
```
outFile = IO.File.CreateText("memo.txt")
```
opens the memo.txt file for output; creates a StreamWriter object and assigns it to the `outFile` variable

<u>Example 2</u>
```
outFile = IO.File.AppendText("F:\Chap11\pay.txt")
```
opens the pay.txt file for append; creates a StreamWriter object and assigns it to the `outFile` variable

Figure 11-10 How to create a StreamWriter object
© 2013 Cengage Learning

Because sequential access files contain text, programmers typically name them using the filename extension "txt", which is short for "text".

When processing the statement in Example 1, the computer searches for the memo.txt file in the default folder, which is the current project's bin\Debug folder. If the file exists, its contents are erased and the file is opened for output; otherwise, a new, empty file is created and opened for output. The statement then creates a StreamWriter object and assigns it to the `outFile` variable.

Unlike the *fileName* argument in Example 1, the *fileName* argument in Example 2 contains a folder path. When processing the statement in Example 2, the computer searches for the pay.txt file in the Chap11 folder on the F drive. If the computer locates the file, it opens the file for append. If it does not find the file, it creates a new, empty file and then opens the file for append. Like the statement in Example 1, the statement in Example 2 creates a StreamWriter object and assigns it to the `outFile` variable. When deciding whether to include the folder path in the fileName argument, keep in mind that a USB drive may have a different letter designation on another computer. Therefore, you should specify the folder path only when you are sure that it will not change.

After opening a file for either output or append, you can begin writing data to it using either the **Write method** or the **WriteLine method**. The difference between both methods is that the WriteLine method writes a newline character after the data. Figure 11-11 shows the syntax and an example of both methods. As the figure indicates, when using the Write method, the next character written to the file will appear immediately after the letter o in the string "Hello". When using the WriteLine method, however, the next character written to the file will appear on the line immediately below the string. You do not need to include the file's name in either method's syntax because the data will be written to the file associated with the StreamWriter variable.

574

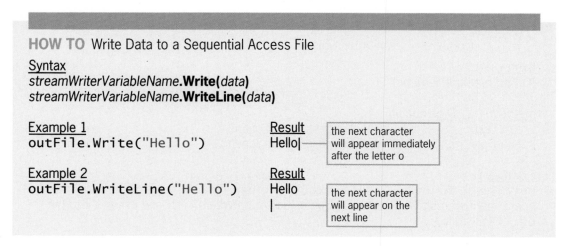

Figure 11-11   How to write data to a sequential access file
© 2013 Cengage Learning

Closing an Output Sequential Access File

You should use the **Close method** to close an output sequential access file as soon as you are finished using it. This ensures that the data is saved and it makes the file available for use elsewhere in the application. The syntax to close an output sequential access file is shown in Figure 11-12 along with an example of using the method. Here again, notice that you use the StreamWriter variable to refer to the file in code.

HOW TO Close an Output Sequential Access File

Syntax
streamWriterVariableName.**Close()**

Example
`outFile.Close()`
closes the file associated with the `outFile` variable

Figure 11-12   How to close an output sequential access file
© 2013 Cengage Learning

The answers to Mini-Quiz questions are located in Appendix A. Each question is associated with one or more objectives listed at the beginning of the chapter.

Mini-Quiz 11-2

1. A procedure needs to write information to a sequential access file. Which of the following methods can be used to open the file? (5)

    a. AppendText

    b. CreateText

    c. OpenText

    d. both a and b

2. Which of the following writes the contents of the cityTextBox's Text property, followed by the newline character, to the sequential access file associated with the outFile variable? (5)

   a. outFile.Write(cityTextBox.Text)

   b. outFile.WriteLine(cityTextBox.Text)

   c. outFile.WriteNext(cityTextBox.Text)

   d. none of the above

3. Write the statement to close the sequential access file associated with the outFile variable. (6)

Reading Data from a Sequential Access File

In Visual Basic, you use a **StreamReader object** to read data from a sequential access file. Before creating the object, you first declare a variable to store the object in the computer's internal memory. Figure 11-13 shows the syntax and an example of declaring a StreamReader variable. As mentioned earlier, the IO in the syntax stands for Input/Output.

HOW TO Declare a StreamReader Variable

Syntax
{**Dim | Private**} *streamReaderVariableName* **As IO.StreamReader**

Example
Dim inFile As IO.StreamReader
declares a StreamReader variable named inFile

Figure 11-13   How to declare a StreamReader variable
© 2013 Cengage Learning

After declaring a StreamReader variable, you can use the **OpenText method** to open a sequential access file for input, which will automatically create a StreamReader object. When a file is opened for input, the computer can read the lines of text stored in the file. Figure 11-14 shows the OpenText method's syntax along with an example of using the method. The *fileName* argument in the example does not include a folder path, so the computer will search for the memo.txt file in the current project's bin\Debug folder. If the computer finds the file, it opens the file for input. If the computer does not find the file, a runtime error occurs. You assign the StreamReader object created by the OpenText method to a StreamReader variable, which you use to refer to the file in code.

HOW TO Create a StreamReader Object

Syntax
IO.File.OpenText(*fileName***)**

Example
```
inFile = IO.File.OpenText("memo.txt")
```
opens the memo.txt file for input; creates a StreamReader object and assigns it to the
`inFile` variable

Figure 11-14 How to create a StreamReader object
© 2013 Cengage Learning

The run time error that occurs when the computer cannot locate an input file will cause
the application to end abruptly. You can use the Exists method to avoid this run time error.
Figure 11-15 shows the method's syntax and includes an example of using the method. If the
fileName argument does not include a folder path, the computer searches for the file in the
current project's bin\Debug folder. The **Exists method** returns the Boolean value True if the
file exists; otherwise, it returns the Boolean value False.

HOW TO Determine Whether a File Exists

Syntax
IO.File.Exists(*fileName***)**

Example
```
If IO.File.Exists("memo.txt") Then
```
determines whether the memo.txt file exists in the current project's bin\Debug folder; you
can also write the If clause as `If IO.File.Exists("memo.txt") = True Then`

Figure 11-15 How to determine whether a file exists
© 2013 Cengage Learning

After opening a file for input, you can use the **ReadLine method** to read the file's contents, one
line at a time. A **line** is defined as a sequence (stream) of characters followed by the newline
character. The ReadLine method returns a string that contains only the sequence of characters
in the current line. The returned string does not include the newline character at the end of the
line. In most cases, you assign the string returned by the ReadLine method to a String variable.
Figure 11-16 shows the ReadLine method's syntax and includes an example of using the method.
The ReadLine method does not require you to provide the file's name because it uses the file
associated with the StreamReader variable.

HOW TO Read Data from a Sequential Access File

Syntax
streamReaderVariableName.**ReadLine**

Example
```
If IO.File.Exists("memo.txt") Then
```
determines whether the memo.txt file exists in the current project's bin\Debug folder; you
can also write the If clause as `If IO.File.Exists("memo.txt") = True Then`

Figure 11-16 How to read data from a sequential access file
© 2013 Cengage Learning

In most cases, an application will need to read each line of text contained in a sequential access
file, one line at a time. You can do this using a loop along with the **Peek method**, which "peeks"
into the file to determine whether it contains another character to read. If it does contain
another character, the Peek method returns the character; otherwise, it returns the number –1
(a negative 1). The Peek method's syntax is shown in Figure 11-17 along with an example of
using the method. The Do clause in the example tells the computer to process the loop
instructions until the Peek method returns the number –1, which indicates that there are no
more characters to read. In other words, the Do clause tells the computer to process the loop
instructions until it reaches the end of the file.

HOW TO Use the Peek Method

Syntax
streamReaderVariableName.**Peek**

Example
```
Dim lineOfText As String
Do Until inFile.Peek = -1
    lineOfText = inFile.ReadLine
    MessageBox.Show(lineOfText)
Loop
```
reads each line of text from the sequential access file associated with the `inFile` variable,
line by line; each line (excluding the newline character) is assigned to the `lineOfText`
variable and is then displayed in a message box

Figure 11-17 How to use the Peek method
© 2013 Cengage Learning

Closing an Input Sequential Access File

Just as you do with an output sequential access file, you should use the Close method to close an
input sequential access file as soon as you are finished using it. Doing this makes the file available
for use elsewhere in the application. The syntax to close an input sequential access file is shown
in Figure 11-18 along with an example of using the method. Notice that you use the
StreamReader variable to refer to the file in code.

HOW TO Close an Input Sequential Access File

<u>Syntax</u>
streamReaderVariableName.**Close()**

<u>Example</u>
`inFile.Close()`
closes the file associated with the `inFile` variable

Figure 11-18 How to close an input sequential access file
© 2013 Cengage Learning

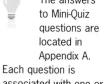

The answers to Mini-Quiz questions are located in Appendix A. Each question is associated with one or more objectives listed at the beginning of the chapter.

Mini-Quiz 11-3

1. A procedure needs to read information from a sequential access file. Which of the following methods can be used to open the file? (7)

    a. AppendText

    b. CreateText

    c. OpenText

    d. both b and c

2. Which of the following reads a line of text from the sequential access file associated with the `inFile` variable and assigns the line of text (excluding the newline character) to the `msg` variable? (7)

    a. `msg = inFile.Read`

    b. `msg = inFile.ReadLine`

    c. `inFile.ReadLine(msg)`

    d. none of the above

3. Write the statement to close the sequential access file associated with the `inFile` variable. (6)

4. What does the Peek method return when a sequential access file contains another character to read? (8)

The FormClosing Event

As you already know, you can close a form using either the `Me.Close()` statement or the Close button on the form's title bar. When a form is about to be closed, its **FormClosing event** occurs. Figure 11-19 shows examples of code you might enter in the FormClosing event procedure. Example 1 writes the contents of the membersListBox to a sequential access file named members.txt. Example 2 displays the "Do you want to exit?" message in a message box, along with the Yes and No buttons. If the user clicks the No button, it indicates that he or she does not want to exit the application. In that case, the MainForm_FormClosing procedure stops the computer from closing the MainForm by setting the **Cancel property** of the procedure's e parameter to True.

HOW TO Use the FormClosing Event Procedure

Example 1 – writes information to a sequential access file
```
Private Sub MainForm_FormClosing(sender As Object,
e As FormClosingEventArgs) Handles Me.FormClosing

    Dim outFile As IO.StreamWriter
    outFile = IO.File.CreateText("members.txt")
    For Each member As String In membersListBox.Items
        outFile.WriteLine(member)
    Next member
    outFile.Close()
End Sub
```

Example 2 – verifies that the user wants to exit the application
```
Private Sub MainForm_FormClosing(sender As Object,
e As FormClosingEventArgs) Handles Me.FormClosing

    Dim button As DialogResult
    button = MessageBox.Show("Do you want to exit?",
                            "Exit Verification",
                            MessageBoxButtons.YesNo,
                            MessageBoxIcon.Exclamation,
                            MessageBoxDefaultButton.Button2)

    If button = Windows.Forms.DialogResult.No Then
        e.Cancel = True
    End If
End Sub
```

If you want to experiment with the code shown in Figure 11-19, open the solution contained in the Try It 4! folder.

Figure 11-19 How to use the FormClosing event procedure
© 2013 Cengage Learning

The Kettleson Club Application

The Kettleson Club application uses what you have learned so far about sequential access files and the FormClosing event. The application's problem specification is shown in Figure 11-20 along with most of the application's code. The code pertaining to the sequential access file is shaded in the figure. The figure also includes a sample run of the application, as well as the contents of the members.txt file. To open a sequential access file in the IDE, you click FILE on the menu bar and then click Open File. When the Open File dialog box opens, you click the name of the file you want to open and then click the Open button. (Recall that unless you specify otherwise, the sequential access file is saved in the project's bin\Debug folder.)

Problem specification
Create an application for the Kettleson Club. When the application is started, it should display the contents of the members.txt sequential access file in a list box. The application should allow the user to add names to the list box and also delete names from the list box. When the user exits the application, it should save the contents of the list box in the members.txt file.

reads the file ────

```
Private Sub MainForm_Load(sender As Object,
e As EventArgs) Handles Me.Load
    ' reads names from a sequential access file
    ' and displays them in the list box

    Dim inFile As IO.StreamReader
    Dim name As String

    ' clear previous names from the list box
    membersListBox.Items.Clear()

    ' determine whether the file exists
    If IO.File.Exists("members.txt") Then
        ' open the file for input
        inFile = IO.File.OpenText("members.txt")
        ' process loop instructions until end of file
        Do Until inFile.Peek = -1
            ' read a name
            name = inFile.ReadLine
            ' add name to list box
            membersListBox.Items.Add(name)
        Loop
        ' close the file
        inFile.Close()
    End If
End Sub
```

writes to the file ────

```
Private Sub MainForm_FormClosing(sender As Object,
e As FormClosingEventArgs) Handles Me.FormClosing
    ' saves the contents of the list box
    ' to a sequential access file

    ' declare a StreamWriter variable
    Dim outFile As IO.StreamWriter
    ' open the file for output
    outFile = IO.File.CreateText("members.txt")
    ' write each name on a separate line in the file
    For Each member As String In membersListBox.Items
        outFile.WriteLine(member)
    Next member
    ' close the file
    outFile.Close()
End Sub
```

If you want to experiment with the Kettleson Club application shown in Figure 11-20, open the solution contained in the Try It 5! folder.

Figure 11-20   Kettleson Club application *(continues)*

(continued)

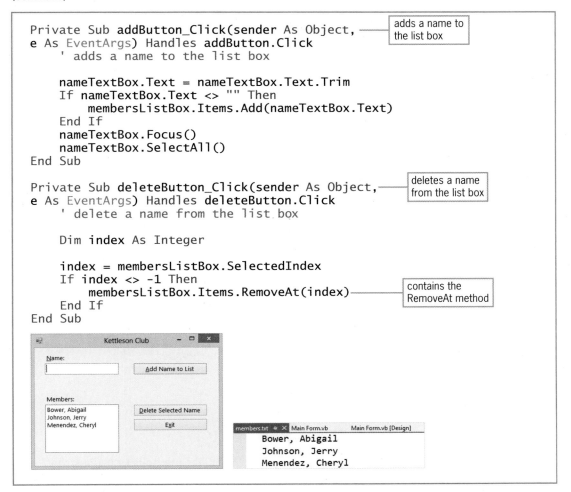

```
Private Sub addButton_Click(sender As Object,        ← adds a name to
e As EventArgs) Handles addButton.Click                 the list box
    ' adds a name to the list box

    nameTextBox.Text = nameTextBox.Text.Trim
    If nameTextBox.Text <> "" Then
        membersListBox.Items.Add(nameTextBox.Text)
    End If
    nameTextBox.Focus()
    nameTextBox.SelectAll()
End Sub

Private Sub deleteButton_Click(sender As Object,     ← deletes a name
e As EventArgs) Handles deleteButton.Click              from the list box
    ' delete a name from the list box

    Dim index As Integer

    index = membersListBox.SelectedIndex
    If index <> -1 Then
        membersListBox.Items.RemoveAt(index)         ← contains the
    End If                                               RemoveAt method
End Sub
```

Figure 11-20 Kettleson Club application
© 2013 Cengage Learning

When the application is started, the MainForm_Load procedure reads the names contained in the members.txt file and displays them in the membersListBox. The addButton_Click procedure adds the name entered in the Name box to the list box. The deleteButton_Click procedure deletes the selected name from the list box. When the user clicks either the Exit button or the Close button on the form's title bar, the MainForm_FormClosing procedure saves the contents of the list box to the members.txt file.

Notice the `membersListBox.Items.RemoveAt(index)` statement in the deleteButton_Click procedure. The statement uses the Items collection's **RemoveAt method** to remove the selected item from the membersListBox. The method's syntax is shown in Figure 11-21 along with the syntax of the Items collection's **Remove method**, which also can be used to remove the selected item. In the RemoveAt method's syntax, *index* is the item's index. In the Remove method's syntax, *item* is the item's value.

HOW TO Remove an Item from a List Box or Combo Box

Syntax
object.**Items.RemoveAt(***index***)**
object.**Items.Remove(***item***)**

Example 1 – RemoveAt
```
index = membersListBox.SelectedIndex
membersListBox.Items.RemoveAt(index)
```
uses the selected item's index to remove the item from the membersList box

Example 2 – RemoveAt
```
membersListBox.Items.RemoveAt(0)
```
removes the first item from the membersList box

Example 3 – Remove
```
membersListBox.Items.Remove("Johnson, Jerry")
```
removes the "Johnson, Jerry" item from the membersListBox

Example 4 – Remove
```
name = membersListBox.SelectedItem
membersListBox.Items.Remove(name)
```
uses the selected item's value to remove the item from the membersListBox

Figure 11-21   How to remove an item from a list box or combo box
© 2013 Cengage Learning

Aligning Columns of Information

In Chapter 10, you learned how to use the PadLeft and PadRight methods to pad a string with a character until the string is a specified length. Figure 11-22 shows the syntax of each method, along with examples of using the methods to align columns of information.

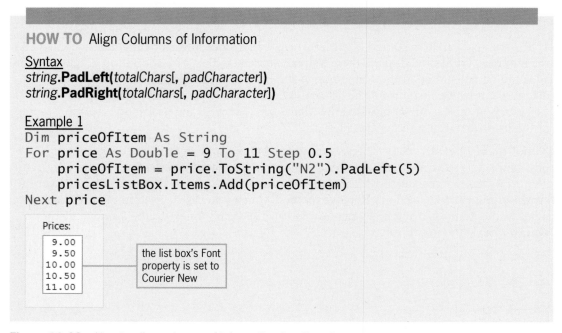

HOW TO Align Columns of Information

Syntax
string.**PadLeft(***totalChars***[, *padCharacter*])**
string.**PadRight(***totalChars***[, *padCharacter*])**

Example 1
```
Dim priceOfItem As String
For price As Double = 9 To 11 Step 0.5
    priceOfItem = price.ToString("N2").PadLeft(5)
    pricesListBox.Items.Add(priceOfItem)
Next price
```

Prices:

9.00
9.50
10.00
10.50
11.00

the list box's Font property is set to Courier New

Figure 11-22   How to align columns of information *(continues)*

(continued)

Example 2
```
Dim outFile As IO.StreamWriter
Dim heading As String =
    "Name" & Strings.Space(11) & "City"          contains the
Dim name As String                                Strings.Space
Dim city As String                                method

outFile = IO.File.CreateText("friends.txt")
outFile.WriteLine(heading)

name = InputBox("Enter name:", "Name")
Do While name <> String.Empty
    city = InputBox("Enter city:", "City")
    outFile.WriteLine(name.PadRight(15) & city)
    name = InputBox("Enter name:", "Name")
Loop
outFile.Close()
```

friends.txt ⊣ ✕

Name	City
Sarah	Westmoreland
Maryanne	Nashville
Jon	Portland

Figure 11-22   How to align columns of information
© 2013 Cengage Learning

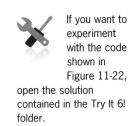

If you want to experiment with the code shown in Figure 11-22, open the solution contained in the Try It 6! folder.

Example 1 in Figure 11-22 aligns a column of numbers in a list box by the decimal point. Notice that you first format each number in the column to ensure that each has the same number of digits to the right of the decimal point. You then use the PadLeft method to insert spaces at the beginning of the number (if necessary); this right-aligns the number within the column. Because each number has the same number of digits to the right of the decimal point, aligning each number on the right will align each by its decimal point. (You also need to set the list box's Font property to a fixed-spaced font, such as Courier New. A fixed-spaced font uses the same amount of space to display each character.)

Example 2 in Figure 11-22 shows how you can align the second column of information when the first column contains strings with varying lengths. First, you use either the PadRight or PadLeft method to ensure that each string in the first column contains the same number of characters. You then concatenate the padded string to the information in the second column. The code in Example 2, for instance, uses the PadRight method to ensure that each name in the first column contains exactly 15 characters. It then concatenates the 15 characters with the string stored in the `city` variable before writing the concatenated string to a sequential access file. Because each name has 15 characters, each city entry will automatically appear beginning in character position 16 in the file. Example 2 also shows how you can use the **Strings.Space method** to include a specific number of space characters in a string. The method's syntax is `Strings.Space(number)`, in which *number* is an integer that represents the number of spaces to include.

Writing and Reading Records

In some applications, a sequential access file is used to store fields and records. A **field** is a single item of information about a person, place, or thing. Examples of fields include a name, a salary, a Social Security number, and a price. A **record** is a group of related fields that contain all of the necessary data about a specific person, place, or thing.

When writing records to a sequential access file, programmers typically write each record on a separate line in the file. They use a special character, called a **delimiter character**, to separate each field. Commonly used delimiter characters include the comma and the number (or hash) sign (#). Figure 11-23 shows examples of writing records to a sequential access file. The WriteLine method in Example 1 writes a record that contains two fields separated by a comma. The WriteLine method in Example 2 writes a record that contains three fields, with each field separated by a number sign.

HOW TO Write Records to a Sequential Access File

Example 1
```
Dim city As String = "Raleigh"
Dim state As String = "North Carolina"
outFile.WriteLine(city & "," & state)
```
writes the following record on a separate line in the file associated with the
`outFile` variable: Raleigh,North Carolina

Example 2
```
Dim salesperson As String = "Jason Kricky"
Dim sales As Integer = 5000
Dim bonus As Integer = 250
outSalesFile.WriteLine(salesperson & "#" &
    sales.ToString & "#" & bonus.ToString)
```
writes the following record on a separate line in the file associated with the
`outSalesFile` variable: Jason Kricky#5000#250

Figure 11-23   How to write records to a sequential access file
© 2013 Cengage Learning

You can use the **Split function** to read records from a sequential access file. The function's syntax is shown in Figure 11-24. In the syntax, *arrayName* is the name of a one-dimensional String array, and *streamReaderVariableName* is the name of the StreamReader variable associated with the sequential access file. The *delimiterChar* argument specifies the delimiter character that separates the fields in each record. Figure 11-24 also includes examples of using the Split function to read the records from Figure 11-23.

HOW TO Read Records from a Sequential Access File

Syntax
arrayName = *streamReaderVariableName*.**ReadLine.Split(***delimiterChar***)**

Example 1
```
Dim cityState(1) As String
cityState = inFile.ReadLine.Split(",",c)
```
reads a record from the file associated with the `inFile` variable and assigns each field to an element in the `cityState` array

Result (using the record written in Example 1 in Figure 11-23)

Raleigh	cityState(0)
North Carolina	cityState(1)

Example 2
```
Dim salesInfo(2) As String
salesInfo = inSalesFile.ReadLine.Split("#"c)
```
reads a record from the file associated with the `inSalesFile` variable and assigns each field to an element in the `salesInfo` array

Result (using the record written in Example 2 in Figure 11-23)

Jason Kricky	salesInfo(0)
5000	salesInfo(1)
250	salesInfo(2)

If you want to experiment with the code shown in Figures 11-23 and 11-24, open the solution contained in the Try It 7! folder.

Figure 11-24 How to read records from a sequential access file
© 2013 Cengage Learning

In Example 1, the ReadLine method reads a line of text from the file associated with the `inFile` variable. Then, using the delimiter character as a guide, the Split function splits the line of text into two fields and assigns each field to an element in the `cityState` array. In Example 2, the ReadLine method reads a line of text associated with the `inSalesFile` variable. The Split function then uses the number (hash) sign as a guide when dividing the line of text. In this case, the Split function divides the line of text into three fields and assigns each field to an element in the `salesInfo` array. Notice the letter c that appears after the delimiterChar argument in each example. As you learned in Chapter 10, the letter c is one of the literal type characters in Visual Basic. Recall that a literal type character forces a literal constant to assume a data type other than the one its form indicates. In this case, the letter c forces the "," and "#" delimiter characters, which are strings, to assume the Char (character) data type.

Mini-Quiz 11-4

The answers to Mini-Quiz questions are located in Appendix A. Each question is associated with one or more objectives listed at the beginning of the chapter.

1. Which of the following concatenates the contents of the `city` variable, 10 spaces, and the contents of the `state` variable, and then assigns the result to the `address` variable? (12)

   a. `address = city & Space(10) & state`

   b. `address = city & Spaces(10) & state`

   c. `address = city & Strings.Space(10) & state`

   d. `address = city & String.Space(10) & state`

2. When entered in the FormClosing event procedure, which of the following prevents the computer from closing the form? (9)

    a.   `e.Cancel = True`

    b.   `e.Close = False`

    c.   `e.Closing = False`

    d.   `e.Open = True`

3. A sequential access file contains records whose fields are separated by a dollar sign. Which of the following reads a record from the file and assigns the fields to the `customer` array? (13, 14)

    a.   `customer = inFile.ReadLine.Split($)`

    b.   `customer = inFile.ReadLine.Split("$"c)`

    c.   `customer = inFile.Split("$")`

    d.   `customer = inFile.Split.ReadLine("$"c)`

You have completed the concepts section of Chapter 11. The Programming Tutorial section is next.

PROGRAMMING TUTORIAL 1

Modifying the Concentration Game Application

In this tutorial, you will modify the Concentration Game application from Chapter 8's Programming Tutorial 2. The modified application will use the words contained in one of four different sequential access files, which will be chosen randomly when the application is started. Three of the files are contained in the Concentration Game project's bin\Debug folder. The three files are named words1.txt, words2.txt, and words3.txt. Figure 11-25 shows the contents of these files. You will create the fourth file, named words4.txt, in this tutorial.

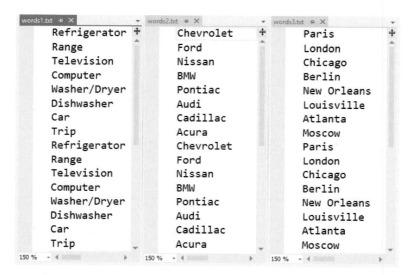

Figure 11-25   Contents of three of the four sequential access files

Creating the words4.txt File

Before modifying the application, you will create the words4.txt file.

To open the Concentration Game application and then create the words4.txt file:

1. Start Visual Studio. Open the **Concentration Solution (Concentration Solution.sln)** file contained in the VbReloaded2012\Chap11\Concentration Solution folder. If necessary, open the designer window.

2. Rather than using a StreamWriter object and the WriteLine method to create the words4.txt file, you also can use the Add New Item option on the PROJECT menu. Click **PROJECT** on the menu bar, and then click **Add New Item** to open the Add New Item dialog box. If necessary, click **Common Items** in the Installed list and then click **Text File** in the middle column of the dialog box. Click the **Add** button. The TextFile1.txt window opens in the IDE.

3. Click **FILE** and then click **Save TextFile1.txt As** to open the Save File As dialog box. Open the project's bin\Debug folder. Change the name in the File name box to **words4** and then click the **Save** button.

4. Enter the following 16 words:

   Apple
   Banana
   Kiwi
   Orange
   Watermelon
   Peach
   Pear
   Strawberry
   Apple
   Banana
   Kiwi
   Orange
   Watermelon
   Peach
   Pear
   Strawberry

5. Save the words4.txt file and then close the words4.txt window.

Modifying the MainForm_Load Procedure

Figure 11-26 shows the code entered in the MainForm_Load procedure in Chapter 8. (The complete code is shown in Figure 8-48 in Chapter 8.) First, you will modify the code so that it uses the words4.txt file to fill the list box with values.

```
Private Sub MainForm_Load(sender As Object,
e As EventArgs) Handles Me.Load
    ' fills the list box with 8 pairs of matching
    ' words, then calls a procedure to shuffle
    ' the words

    wordListBox.Items.Add("Refrigerator")
    wordListBox.Items.Add("Range")
    wordListBox.Items.Add("Television")
    wordListBox.Items.Add("Computer")
    wordListBox.Items.Add("Washer/Dryer")
    wordListBox.Items.Add("Dishwasher")
    wordListBox.Items.Add("Car")
    wordListBox.Items.Add("Trip")
    wordListBox.Items.Add("Refrigerator")
    wordListBox.Items.Add("Range")
    wordListBox.Items.Add("Television")
    wordListBox.Items.Add("Computer")
    wordListBox.Items.Add("Washer/Dryer")
    wordListBox.Items.Add("Dishwasher")
    wordListBox.Items.Add("Car")
    wordListBox.Items.Add("Trip")

    Call ShuffleWords()

End Sub
```

Figure 11-26 MainForm_Load procedure from Chapter 8
© 2013 Cengage Learning

To begin modifying the MainForm_Load procedure:

1. Open the Code Editor window. In the comments that appear in the General Declarations section, replace <your name> and <current date> with your name and the current date, respectively.

2. Locate the MainForm_Load procedure. The procedure will use a String variable to store the name of one of the four sequential access files. For now, you will initialize the variable to "words4.txt". Click the **blank line above the first Add method** and then press **Enter** to insert another blank line. Enter the following Dim statement:

    Dim fileName As String = "words4.txt"

3. The procedure will need a StreamReader variable to read the contents of the words4.txt file, line by line. Enter the following Dim statement:

    Dim inFile As IO.StreamReader

4. While reading the words4.txt file, the procedure will store each line in a String variable named word. Type the following Dim statement and then press **Enter** twice:

    Dim word As String

5. Next, you will use the Exists method to determine whether the words4.txt file exists. Enter the following If clause. (The Code Editor will automatically enter the End If clause for you.)

    If IO.File.Exists(fileName) Then

6. If the file exists, the selection structure's True path should open the file for input. Enter the following statement:

    inFile = IO.File.OpenText(fileName)

7. Now, you will use a loop to read each line in the file, assigning each line to the wordListBox. Enter the following lines of code. (The Code Editor will automatically enter the Loop clause for you.)

Do Until inFile.Peek = –1
    word = inFile.ReadLine
    wordListBox.Items.Add(word)

8. If necessary, delete the blank line above the Loop clause.

9. Next, you will close the words4.txt file. Insert a **blank line** between the Loop and End If clauses, and then enter the following statement:

inFile.Close()

10. If the words4.txt file does not exist, the selection structure's False path will display an appropriate message. Enter the following lines of code:

Else
    MessageBox.Show("Can't find " & fileName,
            "Missing File",
            MessageBoxButtons.OK,
            MessageBoxIcon.Information)

11. If necessary, delete the blank line above the End If clause.

12. After displaying the message, the False path will use the 16 existing Add methods to fill the list box with words. Cut the **End If** clause from its current location and paste it in the blank line above the `Call ShuffleWords()` statement, and then press **Enter**.

13. Save the solution and then start the application. Play the game until all of the words appear on the game board, and then click the **Exit** button.

14. Now, you will test the application using a filename that does not exist. In the MainForm_Load procedure, change "words4.txt" in the first Dim statement to **"words5.txt"**.

15. Save the solution and then start the application. The "Can't find words5.txt" message appears in a message box. Close the message box. The MainForm_Load procedure uses the 16 Add methods to fill the list box with words. Play the game until all of the words appear on the game board, and then click the **Exit** button.

As mentioned earlier, the Concentration Game application will use the words contained in one of the four sequential access files. The file to use will be chosen randomly when the application is started. The MainForm_Load procedure will accomplish this task by assigning the four filenames to an array. It then will use the random number generator to generate a random number from 0 through 3. The random number will be used to select one of the filenames stored in the array.

To complete the MainForm_Load procedure and then test the code:

1. Click the **blank line** above the first Dim statement in the MainForm_Load procedure, and then press **Enter** to insert a new blank line. Enter the following Dim statements:

Dim fileList() As String = {"words1.txt",
                       "words2.txt",
                       "words3.txt",
                       "words4.txt"}
Dim randGen As New Random

2. Change the `Dim fileName As String = "words5.txt"` statement to the following:

Dim fileName As String = fileList(randGen.Next(0, 4))

3. Save the solution and then start the application. Click **any two of the labels** on the game board and then click the **Exit** button.

4. Start the application again. Continue testing the application until each of the four files has been chosen. When you are finished testing the application, close the Code Editor window and then close the solution. Figure 11-27 shows the modified MainForm_Load procedure.

```
Private Sub MainForm_Load(sender As Object,
e As EventArgs) Handles Me.Load
    ' fills the list box with 8 pairs of matching
    ' words, then calls a procedure to shuffle
    ' the words

    Dim fileList() As String = {"words1.txt",
                                "words2.txt",
                                "words3.txt",
                                "words4.txt"}
    Dim randGen As New Random

    Dim fileName As String = fileList(randGen.Next(0, 4))
    Dim inFile As IO.StreamReader
    Dim word As String

    If IO.File.Exists(fileName) Then
        inFile = IO.File.OpenText(fileName)
        Do Until inFile.Peek = -1
            word = inFile.ReadLine
            wordListBox.Items.Add(word)
        Loop
        inFile.Close()
    Else
        MessageBox.Show("Can't find " & fileName,
                        "Missing File",
                        MessageBoxButtons.OK,
                        MessageBoxIcon.Information)

        wordListBox.Items.Add("Refrigerator")
        wordListBox.Items.Add("Range")
        wordListBox.Items.Add("Television")
        wordListBox.Items.Add("Computer")
        wordListBox.Items.Add("Washer/Dryer")
        wordListBox.Items.Add("Dishwasher")
        wordListBox.Items.Add("Car")
        wordListBox.Items.Add("Trip")
        wordListBox.Items.Add("Refrigerator")
        wordListBox.Items.Add("Range")
        wordListBox.Items.Add("Television")
        wordListBox.Items.Add("Computer")
        wordListBox.Items.Add("Washer/Dryer")
        wordListBox.Items.Add("Dishwasher")
        wordListBox.Items.Add("Car")
        wordListBox.Items.Add("Trip")
    End If

    Call ShuffleWords()

End Sub
```

Figure 11-27   Modified MainForm_Load procedure
© 2013 Cengage Learning

PROGRAMMING TUTORIAL 2

Coding the CD Collection Application

In this tutorial, you will code an application that keeps track of a person's CD collection. The application will save each CD's name, as well as the artist's name and the CD price, in a sequential access file named cds.txt. The application will allow the user to add information to the file and also remove information from the file. The application's TOE chart and MainForm are shown in Figures 11-28 and 11-29, respectively. Figure 11-30 shows the contents of the cds.txt file, which is contained in the CD Collection project's bin\debug folder.

Task	Object	Event
Read the cds.txt file and assign its contents to cdsListBox Save the contents of the cdsListBox in the cds.txt file	MainForm	Load FormClosing
End the application	exitButton	Click
1. Get CD name, artist name, and CD price 2. Add CD name, artist name, and CD price to cdsListBox	addButton	Click
Remove the selected CD from cdsListbox	removeButton	Click
Display the CD name, artist name, and CD price	cdsListBox	None

Figure 11-28   TOE chart for the CD Collection application
© 2013 Cengage Learning

Figure 11-29   MainForm for the CD Collection application

the list box's Sorted and Font properties are set to True and Courier New, respectively

```
cds.txt
    A Little Bit Longer                  Jonas Brothers        12.50
    At Folsom Prison                     Johnny Cash           11.99
    Covers                               James Taylor          11.99
    Funhouse                             Pink                   8.99
    High School Musical 3: Senior Year   Original Soundtrack   12.99
    Jennifer Hudson                      Jennifer Hudson       12.99
    Lucky Old Sun                        Kenny Chesney          9.99
    Soul                                 Seal                  10.99
```

Figure 11-30   Contents of the cds.txt file

Coding the MainForm_Load Procedure

According to the application's TOE chart, five event procedures need to be coded: the Click event procedures for the three buttons, and the MainForm's Load and FormClosing event procedures. You will code the MainForm_Load procedure first. The procedure's pseudocode is shown in Figure 11-31.

```
MainForm Load event procedure
if the cds.txt file exists
     open the file for input
     repeat until the end of the file
          read a line from the file
          add the line to the cdsListBox
     end repeat
     close the file
     select the first line in the cdsListBox
else
     display the "Can't find the cds.txt file" message in a message box
end if
```

Figure 11-31 Pseudocode for the MainForm_Load procedure
© 2013 Cengage Learning

To code the MainForm_Load procedure and then test the code:

1. Start Visual Studio. Open the **CD Collection Solution (CD Collection Solution.sln)** file contained in the VbReloaded2012\Chap11\CD Collection Solution folder. If necessary, open the designer window.

2. Open the Code Editor window. The exitButton_Click procedure has already been coded for you. In the comments that appear in the General Declarations section, replace <your name> and <current date> with your name and the current date, respectively.

3. Open the code template for the MainForm's Load event procedure. Enter the following comments. Press **Enter** twice after typing the second comment.

   ' fills the list box with data
   ' stored in a sequential access file

4. The procedure will use a StreamReader variable named `inFile`. Enter the appropriate Dim statement.

5. The procedure will store the cds.txt filename in a String variable named `fileName`. Enter the appropriate Dim statement. Initialize the `fileName` variable to **"cds.txt"**.

6. While reading the cds.txt file, the procedure will use a String variable named `cdInfo` to store each line of text. Type the appropriate Dim statement and then press **Enter** twice.

7. According to its pseudocode, the procedure should verify that the cds.txt file exists. Type **' verify that the file exists** and then press **Enter**. Then, enter the appropriate If clause, using the Exists method. (Recall that the filename is stored in the `fileName` variable.)

8. If the cds.txt file exists, the selection structure's True path should open the file for input. Type **' open the file for input** and then press **Enter**. Now, enter the appropriate statement to open the file.

9. The next instruction in the selection structure's True path is a loop that repeats its instructions until the end of the file is reached. Type **' process loop body until end of file** and then press **Enter**. Now, enter the appropriate Do clause, using the `Until` keyword and the Peek method.

10. The first instruction in the loop body reads a line from the file. Type **' read a line from the file** and then press **Enter**. Now, enter a statement that reads the line and assigns it to the `cdInfo` variable.

11. The next instruction in the loop body adds the line to the cdsListBox. Type ' **add the line to the list box** and then press **Enter**. Then, enter the appropriate statement.

12. Next, the procedure needs to close the file. Insert a **blank line** between the Loop clause and the End If clause, and then enter the appropriate statement.

13. Next, type ' **select the first line in the list box** and then press **Enter**, and then enter the appropriate statement.

14. If the cds.txt file does not exist, the selection structure's False path should display the "Can't find the cds.txt file" message in a message box. Type **Else** and then press **Enter**. Now, enter the appropriate MessageBox.Show method.

15. Save the solution and then start the application. The information contained in the cds.txt file appears in the cdsListBox, as shown in Figure 11-32. Click the **Exit** button to end the application.

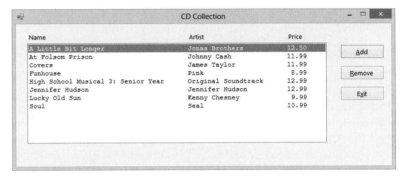

Figure 11-32　Contents of the cds.txt file added to the list box

Coding the addButton_Click Procedure

According to the application's TOE chart, the Add button's Click event procedure should get the CD information from the user and then add it to the cdsListBox. Figure 11-33 shows the procedure's pseudocode.

---

addButton Click event procedure
1. use the InputBox function to get the CD name, artist name, and CD price
2. concatenate the CD name, artist name, and CD price
3. add the concatenated string to the cdsListBox

Figure 11-33　Pseudocode for the addButton_Click procedure
© 2013 Cengage Learning

To code the addButton_Click procedure and then test the code:

1. Open the code template for the addButton's Click event procedure. Type ' **adds CD information to the list box** and then press **Enter** twice.

2. The procedure will use three String variables to store the CD name, artist name, and CD price. It will also use a String variable to store the concatenated string. Enter the appropriate Dim statements, using the names `inputName`, `inputArtist`, `inputPrice`, and `concatenatedInfo`.

3. The procedure will use a Double variable to store the CD price after it has been converted to Double. Type a Dim statement that declares a Double variable named `price` and then press **Enter** twice.

4. The first step in the procedure's pseudocode uses the InputBox function to get the CD name, artist name, and CD price. Type **' get the CD information** and then press **Enter**. Now, enter the appropriate InputBox functions. Assign the functions' return values to the appropriate variables. Press **Enter** twice after typing the last InputBox function.

5. The second step in the pseudocode concatenates the CD name, artist name, and CD price. Enter the following comments:

   ' format the price, then concatenate the
   ' input items, using 40 characters for the
   ' CD name, 25 characters for the artist name,
   ' and 5 characters for the price

6. Now, enter a statement that uses the TryParse method to convert the `inputPrice` variable's value to Double, storing the result in the `price` variable.

7. Next, enter an assignment statement that formats the `price` variable's value to "N2" and assigns the result to the `inputPrice` variable.

8. Now, enter an assignment statement that concatenates the contents of the following three variables: `inputName`, `inputArtist`, and `inputPrice`. Use the PadRight method to ensure that the CD name and artist name contain 40 and 25 characters, respectively. Use the PadLeft method to ensure that the CD price contains five characters. The assignment statement should assign the concatenated string to the `concatenatedInfo` variable. Press **Enter** twice after typing the statement.

9. The third step in the pseudocode adds the concatenated string to the cdsListBox. Type **' add the CD information to the list box** and then press **Enter**. Now, enter a statement that adds the contents of the `concatenatedInfo` variable to the cdsListBox.

10. Save the solution and then start the application.

11. Click the **Add** button. Type **Rolling In The Deep** as the CD name and then press **Enter**. Type **Adele** as the artist name and then press **Enter**. Type **2.99** as the price and then press **Enter**. The addButton_Click procedure adds the CD information to the list box. The list box's Sorted property is set to True, so the information you entered appears in the eighth line of the list box, as shown in Figure 11-34. Click the **Exit** button to end the application.

the CD name appears in alphabetical order

Figure 11-34 New CD information added to the list box

Coding the removeButton_Click Procedure

According to the application's TOE chart, the removeButton_Click procedure should remove the selected CD from the cdsListBox. The procedure's pseudocode is shown in Figure 11-35.

removeButton Click event procedure
if a CD is selected in the cdsListBox
    remove the CD from the cdsListBox
end if

Figure 11-35 Pseudocode for the removeButton_Click procedure
© 2013 Cengage Learning

To code the removeButton_Click procedure and then test the code:

1. Open the code template for the removeButton's Click event procedure. Type ' **removes the selected CD from the list box** and then press **Enter** twice.

2. The procedure will use an Integer variable to store the index of the CD selected in the cdsListBox. Enter a Dim statement that declares an Integer variable named `index`. Initialize the variable using the list box's SelectedIndex property. Press **Enter** twice after typing the Dim statement.

3. The procedure's pseudocode contains a selection structure whose condition determines whether a CD is selected in the cdsListBox. Recall that when no item is selected in a list box, the list box's SelectedIndex property contains the number −1. Enter the following If clause:

   If index <> −1 Then

4. As you learned in the chapter, a list box's Items collection has a RemoveAt method that you can use to remove an item from the list box. Enter the appropriate statement to remove the selected CD from the cdsListBox.

5. If necessary, delete the blank line above the End If clause in the procedure.

6. Save the solution and then start the application. Notice that the CD information you entered in the previous section does not appear in the list box. This is because you haven't yet entered the instructions to save the list box items to the cds.txt file. Those instructions will be entered in the MainForm_FormClosing procedure, which you will code in the next section.

7. Click **Funhouse** in the list box and then click the **Remove** button. The button's Click event procedure removes the Funhouse CD from the list box. Click the **Exit** button to end the application.

Coding the MainForm_FormClosing Procedure

According to the application's TOE chart, the MainForm_FormClosing procedure is responsible for saving the contents of the cdsListBox to the cds.txt file. The procedure's pseudocode is shown in Figure 11-36.

MainForm FormClosing event procedure
1. open the cds.txt file for output
2. repeat for each CD in the list box
         write the CD information to the file
     end repeat
3. close the file

Figure 11-36   Pseudocode for the MainForm_FormClosing procedure
© 2013 Cengage Learning

To code the MainForm_FormClosing procedure and then test the code:

1. Open the code template for the MainForm's FormClosing event procedure. Type **' saves the list box information** and then press **Enter** twice.

2. The procedure will use a StreamWriter variable named `outFile`. Type the appropriate Dim statement and then press **Enter** twice.

3. The first step in the procedure's pseudocode opens the cds.txt file for output. Type **' open the file for output** and then press **Enter**. Now, enter a statement that uses the CreateText method to open the file.

4. The second step in the pseudocode is a loop that repeats its instructions for each CD in the list box. Enter the following comment and For Each clause:

    ' write each CD in the list box
    For Each cd As String In cdsListBox.Items

5. Change the Next clause to **Next cd**.

6. The instruction in the loop body should write the CD information to the file. Click the **blank line** below the For Each clause. Now, enter a statement that uses the WriteLine method to write the contents of the **cd** variable to the cds.txt file.

7. If necessary, delete the blank line above the Next cd clause.

8. The third step in the pseudocode closes the file. Insert a **blank line** between the Next cd and End Sub clauses, and then enter the appropriate statement.

9. Save the solution and then start the application. Click the **Add** button. Use the input dialog boxes to enter the following CD information: **Rolling In The Deep**, **Adele**, and **2.99**. The addButton_Click procedure adds the CD information to the list box.

10. Click the **Exit** button. The computer processes the `Me.Close()` statement in the button's Click event procedure; doing this invokes the form's FormClosing event. The instructions in the MainForm_FormClosing procedure save the contents of the list box to the cds.txt file.

11. Start the application again. Notice that the CD information you entered appears in the list box. Click **Rolling In The Deep** and then click the **Remove** button. The button's Click event procedure removes the selected CD information from the list box.

12. Click the **Exit** button. Start the application again. Notice that the Rolling In The Deep CD does not appear in the list box. Click the **Exit** button.

13. Close the Code Editor window and then close the solution. Figure 11-37 shows the code for the CD Collection application.

```
1 ' Project name:        CD Collection Project
2 ' Project purpose:     Allows the user to add and delete list box entries
3 '                      Reads CD information from a sequential access file
4 '                      Writes CD information to a sequential access file
5 ' Created/revised by:  <your name> on <current date>
6
7 Option Explicit On
8 Option Strict On
9 Option Infer Off
10
11 Public Class MainForm
12
13     Private Sub exitButton_Click(sender As Object,
        e As EventArgs) Handles exitButton.Click
14         Me.Close()
15     End Sub
16
17     Private Sub MainForm_FormClosing(sender As Object,
        e As FormClosingEventArgs) Handles Me.FormClosing
18         ' saves the list box information
19
20         Dim outFile As IO.StreamWriter
21
22         ' open the file for output
23         outFile = IO.File.CreateText("cds.txt")
24         ' write each CD in the list box
25         For Each cd As String In cdsListBox.Items
26             outFile.WriteLine(cd)
27         Next cd
28         outFile.Close()
29
30     End Sub
31
32     Private Sub MainForm_Load(sender As Object,
        e As EventArgs) Handles Me.Load
33         ' fills the list box with data
34         ' stored in a sequential access file
35
36         Dim inFile As IO.StreamReader
37         Dim fileName As String = "cds.txt"
38         Dim cdInfo As String
39
40         ' verify that the file exists
41         If IO.File.Exists(fileName) Then
42             ' open the file for input
43             inFile = IO.File.OpenText(fileName)
44             ' process loop body until end of file
45             Do Until inFile.Peek = -1
46                 ' read a line from the file
47                 cdInfo = inFile.ReadLine
48                 ' add the line to the list box
49                 cdsListBox.Items.Add(cdInfo)
50
```

Figure 11-37   Code for the CD Collection application *(continues)*

(continued)

```
 51              Loop
 52              inFile.Close()
 53              ' select the first line in the list box
 54              cdsListBox.SelectedIndex = 0
 55          Else
 56              MessageBox.Show("Can't find the cds.txt file",
 57                        "CD Collection",
 58                        MessageBoxButtons.OK,
 59                        MessageBoxIcon.Information)
 60
 61          End If
 62      End Sub
 63
 64      Private Sub addButton_Click(sender As Object,
         e As EventArgs) Handles addButton.Click
 65          ' adds CD information to the list box
 66
 67          Dim inputName As String
 68          Dim inputArtist As String
 69          Dim inputPrice As String
 70          Dim concatenatedInfo As String
 71          Dim price As Double
 72
 73          ' get the CD information
 74          inputName = InputBox("CD name:", "CD Collection")
 75          inputArtist = InputBox("Artist:", "CD Collection")
 76          inputPrice = InputBox("Price:", "CD Collection")
 77
 78          ' format the price, then concatenate the
 79          ' input items, using 40 characters for the
 80          ' CD name, 25 characters for the artist name,
 81          ' and 5 characters for the price
 82          Double.TryParse(inputPrice, price)
 83          inputPrice = price.ToString("N2")
 84          concatenatedInfo = inputName.PadRight(40) &
 85              inputArtist.PadRight(25) & inputPrice.PadLeft(5)
 86
 87          ' add the CD information to the list box
 88          cdsListBox.Items.Add(concatenatedInfo)
 89
 90      End Sub
 91
 92      Private Sub removeButton_Click(sender As Object,
         e As EventArgs) Handles removeButton.Click
 93          ' removes the selected CD from the list box
 94
 95          Dim index As Integer = cdsListBox.SelectedIndex
 96
 97          If index <> -1 Then
 98              cdsListBox.Items.RemoveAt(index)
 99          End If
100      End Sub
101 End Class
```

Figure 11-37   Code for the CD Collection application
© 2013 Cengage Learning

PROGRAMMING EXAMPLE

Glovers Industries Application

Glovers Industries stores the item numbers and prices of its products in a sequential access file named itemInfo.txt. Create an application that displays the item numbers in a list box. When the user selects an item number, the application should display the item's price. Use the following names for the solution and project, respectively: Glovers Solution and Glovers Project. Save the application in the VbReloaded2012\Chap11 folder. Change the form file's name to Main Form.vb. You will also need to create the itemInfo.txt sequential access file. Save the itemInfo.txt file in the project's bin\Debug folder. See Figures 11-38 through 11-43.

Task	Object	Event
1. Create a Product structure that has two members: a String member named number and a Decimal member named price	MainForm	Declarations section
2. Declare and initialize a class-level, five-element Product array named items		
1. Fill the items array with the item numbers and prices stored in the itemInfo.txt file		Load
2. Fill the numbersListBox with the item numbers stored in the itemInfo.txt file		
Display the item numbers	numbersListBox	None
Display (in the priceLabel) the price associated with the selected item number		SelectedIndexChanged
End the application	exitButton	Click
Display the price (from numbersListBox)	priceLabel	None

Figure 11-38 TOE chart
© 2013 Cengage Learning

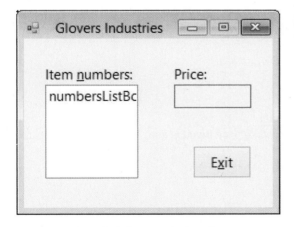

Figure 11-39 MainForm and tab order

Object	Property	Setting
MainForm	Font	Segoe UI, 11pt
	MaximizeBox	False
	StartPosition	CenterScreen
	Text	Glovers Industries
priceLabel	AutoSize	False
	BorderStyle	FixedSingle
	TextAlign	MiddleCenter

Figure 11-40 Objects, properties, and settings
© 2013 Cengage Learning

```
itemInfo.txt  ⊐ ✕
    12AVX,5
    23ABC,8.97
    23TWT,4.69
    34ZAB,12.5
    91BAN,34.67
```

Figure 11-41 Contents of the itemInfo.txt sequential access file
© 2013 Cengage Learning

MainForm Load event procedure
if the itemInfo.txt file exists
    open the file for input
    repeat until the end of the file
        read a line from the file and separate the item number from the price
        assign the item number and price to the current element in the items array
        add the item number to the numbersListBox
        add 1 to the variable that keeps track of the array subscript and list box index
    end repeat
    close the file
    select the first item in the numbersListBox
else
    display an appropriate error message
end if

numbersListBox SelectedIndexChanged event procedure
use the index of the selected item to access the appropriate price from the items array, and then display
the price in the priceLabel

exitButton Click event procedure
close the application

Figure 11-42 Pseudocode
© 2013 Cengage Learning

```vbnet
1  ' Project name:          Glovers Project
2  ' Project purpose:       Display the price of an item
3  ' Created/revised by:    <your name> on <current date>
4
5  Option Explicit On
6  Option Strict On
7  Option Infer Off
8
9  Public Class MainForm
10
11     ' define the Product structure
12     Structure Product
13         Public number As String
14         Public price As Decimal
15     End Structure
16
17     ' declare class-level array
18     Private items(4) As Product
19
20     Private Sub MainForm_Load(sender As Object,
       e As EventArgs) Handles Me.Load
21         ' fills the items array and numbersListBox with
22         ' the data stored in a sequential access file
23
24         Dim inFile As IO.StreamReader
25         Const FileName As String = "itemInfo.txt"
26         Dim x As Integer   ' subscript and index
27         Dim fields(1) As String
28
29         If IO.File.Exists(FileName) Then
30             inFile = IO.File.OpenText(FileName)
31             Do Until inFile.Peek = -1
32                 ' separate item number from price
33                 fields = inFile.ReadLine.Split(","c)
34                 ' assign item number and price to the array
35                 items(x).number = fields(0)
36                 items(x).price = Convert.ToDecimal(fields(1))
37                 ' add item number to the list box
38                 numbersListBox.Items.Add(items(x).number)
39
40                 ' update variable that keeps track of the
41                 ' array subscript and list box index
42                 x += 1
43             Loop
44             inFile.Close()
45             numbersListBox.SelectedIndex = 0
46         Else
47             MessageBox.Show("Can't find " & FileName,
48                 "Glovers Industries", MessageBoxButtons.OK,
49                 MessageBoxIcon.Information)
50         End If
51     End Sub
52
```

Figure 11-43 Code (continues)

(continued)

```
53    Private Sub numbersListBox_SelectedIndexChanged(
      sender As Object, e As EventArgs
      ) Handles numbersListBox.SelectedIndexChanged
54        ' displays the price corresponding to the
55        ' item selected in the list box
56
57        Dim index As Integer = numbersListBox.SelectedIndex
58        priceLabel.Text = items(index).price.ToString("N2")
59    End Sub
60
61    Private Sub exitButton_Click(sender As Object,
      e As EventArgs) Handles exitButton.Click
62        Me.Close()
63    End Sub
64 End Class
```

Figure 11-43   Code
© 2013 Cengage Learning

Summary

- You can use Visual Basic's Structure statement to define a user-defined data type, also called a structure. You typically enter the Structure statement in the form's Declarations section in the Code Editor window.

- After defining a structure, you can use the structure to declare a structure variable. A structure variable contains one or more member variables. You access a member variable using the structure variable's name, followed by the dot member access operator and the member variable's name.

- The member variables contained in a structure variable can be used just like any other variables.

- When a structure variable is passed to a procedure, all of its members are automatically passed.

- You can create an array of structure variables. You access a member variable in an array element using the array's name, followed by the element's subscript enclosed in parentheses, the dot member access operator, and the member variable's name, like this: *arrayName(subscript).memberVariableName*.

- An application can write information to a file (called an output file) and also read information from a file (called an input file).

- The information in a sequential access file (also referred to as a text file) is always accessed sequentially, which means it is accessed in consecutive order from the beginning of the file through the end of the file.

- You can write data to a sequential access file by first declaring a StreamWriter variable, and then using either the CreateText method or the AppendText method to open the file. You assign the appropriate method's return value to the StreamWriter variable. You then use either the Write method or the WriteLine method to write the data to the file.

- You can read data from a sequential access file by first declaring a StreamReader variable. Before opening the file, you should use the Exists method to determine whether the file exists. If the file exists, you use the OpenText method to open the file, assigning the method's return value to the StreamReader variable. You then use the Peek and ReadLine methods to read the data from the file.

- When a procedure is finished using a sequential access file, it should use the Close method to close the file.

- The FormClosing event occurs when a form is about to be closed. You can prevent a form from being closed by setting the Cancel property of the FormClosing event procedure's **e** parameter to True.

- You can use the Items collection's RemoveAt method or its Remove method to remove an item from a list box or combo box.

- You can use the PadLeft and PadRight methods to align columns of information that appear in the interface. You also can use the methods to align information written to a sequential access file.

- You can use the Strings.Space method to include a specific number of space characters in a string.

- When writing records to a file, programmers typically write each record on a separate line in the file. They use a delimiter character to separate the fields in each record.

- You can use the Split function to read delimited records from a file.

Key Terms

AppendText method—used with a StreamWriter variable to open a sequential access file for append

Cancel property—a property of the **e** parameter in the FormClosing event procedure; when set to True, it prevents the form from closing

Close method—used with either a StreamWriter variable or a StreamReader variable to close a sequential access file

CreateText method—used with a StreamWriter variable to open a sequential access file for output

Delimiter character—a character used to separate the fields in a record

Exists method—used to determine whether a file exists

Field—a single item of information about a person, place, or thing

FormClosing event—occurs when a form is about to be closed, which can happen as a result of the computer processing the `Me.Close()` statement or the user clicking the Close button on the form's title bar

Input files—files from which an application reads data

Line—a sequence (stream) of characters followed by the newline character

Member variables—the variables contained in a structure

OpenText method—used with a StreamReader variable to open a sequential access file for input

Output files—files to which an application writes data

Peek method—used with a StreamReader variable to determine whether a file contains another character to read

ReadLine method—used with a StreamReader variable to read a line of text from a sequential access file

Record—a group of related fields that contain all of the necessary data about a specific person, place, or thing

603

Remove method—a method of the Items collection; uses the item's value to remove the item from a list box or combo box

RemoveAt method—a method of the Items collection; uses the item's index to remove the item from a list box or combo box

Sequential access files—files composed of lines of text that are both read and written sequentially; also called text files

Split function—separates (splits) a string into substrings based on a delimiter character and then assigns the substrings to a one-dimensional array

Stream of characters—a sequence of characters

StreamReader object—used to read a sequence (stream) of characters from a sequential access file

StreamWriter object—used to write a sequence (stream) of characters to a sequential access file

Strings.Space method—can be used to include a specific number of spaces in a string

Structure statement—used to create user-defined data types, called structures

Structure variables—variables declared using a structure as the data type

Structures—data types created by the Structure statement; allow the programmer to group related items into one unit; also called user-defined data types

Text files—another term for sequential access files

User-defined data types—data types created by the Structure statement; see Structures

Write method—used with a StreamWriter variable to write data to a sequential access file; differs from the WriteLine method in that it does not write a newline character after the data

WriteLine method—used with a StreamWriter variable to write data to a sequential access file; differs from the Write method in that it writes a newline character after the data

Review Questions

 Each Review Question is associated with one or more objectives listed at the beginning of the chapter.

1. Which of the following declares a Vehicle variable named `car`? (2)

   a. `Private car As Vehicle`

   b. `Dim car As Vehicle`

   c. `Dim Vehicle As car`

   d. both a and b

2. Which of the following assigns the string "Jaguar" to the `maker` member of a Vehicle variable named `car`? (2)

   a. `car.maker = "Jaguar"`

   b. `Vehicle.maker = "Jaguar"`

   c. `Vehicle.car.maker = "Jaguar"`

   d. `maker.car = "Jaguar"`

3. An application uses a structure named Employee. Which of the following statements creates a five-element array of Employee structure variables? (4)

   a. `Dim workers As Employee(4)`

   b. `Dim workers As Employee(5)`

   c. `Dim workers(4) As Employee`

   d. `Dim workers(5) As Employee`

4. Each structure variable in the **states** array contains a String member named **id** and an Integer member named **population**. Which of the following assigns the string "RI" to the first element in the array? (4)

   a. `states(0).id = "RI"`
   b. `states(1).id = "RI"`
   c. `states.id(0) = "RI"`
   d. `states.id(1) = "RI"`

5. Which of the following opens the cities.txt file and allows the computer to write new data to the end of the file's existing data? (5)

   a. `outFile = IO.File.AddText("cities.txt")`
   b. `outFile = IO.File.AppendText("cities.txt")`
   c. `outFile = IO.File.InsertText("cities.txt")`
   d. `outFile = IO.File.OpenText("cities.txt")`

6. If the file to be opened does not exist, the _____ method results in an error when it is processed by the computer. (7)

   a. AppendText
   b. CreateText
   c. OpenText
   d. WriteText

7. Which of the following reads a line of text from a sequential access file and assigns the line (excluding the newline character) to the **lineOfText** variable? (7)

   a. `lineOfText = inFile.ReadLine`
   b. `lineOfText = ReadLine(inFile)`
   c. `inFile.Read(lineOfText)`
   d. `inFile.ReadLine(lineOfText)`

8. What does the Peek method return when the end of the file is reached? (8)

   a. 0
   b. −1
   c. the last character in the file
   d. the newline character

9. Which of the following If clauses determines whether the employ.txt file exists? (8)

   a. `If IO.File.Exists("employ.txt") Then`
   b. `If IO.File("employ.txt").Exists Then`
   c. `If IO.Exists("employ.txt") = True Then`
   d. `If IO.Exists.File("employ.txt") = True Then`

10. The OpenText method creates a _____ object. (7)

    a. File
    b. SequenceReader
    c. StreamReader
    d. StreamWriter

11. The AppendText method creates a _____ object. (5)

    a. File

    b. SequenceReader

    c. StreamReader

    d. StreamWriter

12. Which of the following reads a record from a sequential access file and assigns the fields in each record to the **songs** array? The fields are delimited by a space character. (13, 14)

    a. `songs = inFile.ReadLine.Split(" "c)`

    b. `songs = inFile.ReadLine.SplitBy(" "c)`

    c. `songs = inFile.ReadLine.SplitInto(" "c)`

    d. `songs = inFile.ReadLine.SplitUsing(" "c)`

13. The _____ event occurs when the computer processes the `Me.Close()` statement or when the user clicks the Close button on the form's title bar. (9)

    a. FormClosing

    b. FormFinish

    c. Finish

    d. none of the above

Each Exercise, except the DISCOVERY exercises, is associated with one or more objectives listed at the beginning of the chapter.

Exercises

Pencil and Paper

INTRODUCTORY

1. Write a Structure statement that defines a structure named Book. The structure contains two String member variables named **title** and **author** and a Decimal member variable named **cost**. Then, write a Private statement that declares a Book variable named **fiction**. (1, 2)

INTRODUCTORY

2. Write a Structure statement that defines a structure named Tape. The structure contains three String member variables named **name**, **artist**, and **songLength**. It also contains an Integer member variable named **songNum**. Then, write a Dim statement that declares a Tape variable named **blues**. (1, 2)

INTRODUCTORY

3. An application contains the Structure statement shown here. Write a Dim statement that declares a Computer variable named **homeUse**. Then, write an assignment statement that assigns the string "App75" to the **model** member. Finally, write an assignment statement that assigns the number 1650 to the **cost** member. (1, 2)

```
Structure Computer
    Public model As String
    Public cost As Decimal
End Structure
```

INTRODUCTORY

4. An application contains the Structure statement shown here. Write a Dim statement that declares a MyFriend variable named **school**. Then, write assignment statements that assign the value in the firstTextBox to the **first** member, and assign the value in the lastTextBox to the **last** member. Finally, write assignment statements that assign

the value in the `last` member to the lastLabel and assign the value in the `first` member to the firstLabel. (1, 2)

```
Structure MyFriend
    Public last As String
    Public first As String
End Structure
```

5. Write the code to declare a variable named `outFile` that can be used to write data to a sequential access file. Then, write the statement to open a sequential access file named sales.txt for output. (5)

INTRODUCTORY

6. Write the code to declare a variable named `inFile` that can be used to read data from a sequential access file. Then, write the statement to open a sequential access file named sales.txt for input. (7)

INTRODUCTORY

7. Write the code to close the sequential access file associated with a StreamWriter variable named `outFile`. (6)

INTRODUCTORY

8. Write an If clause that determines whether a sequential access file exists. The file's name is sales.txt. (8)

INTRODUCTORY

9. Write a Do clause that determines whether the end of a sequential access file has been reached. The file is associated with a StreamReader variable named `inFile`. (8)

INTRODUCTORY

10. An application contains the Structure statement shown here. Write a Private statement that declares a 10-element one-dimensional array of Computer variables. Name the array `business`. Then, write an assignment statement that assigns the string "Tosh7400" to the `model` member contained in the first array element. Finally, write an assignment statement that assigns the number 4560 to the `cost` member contained in the first array element. (4)

INTERMEDIATE

```
Structure Computer
    Public model As String
    Public cost As Decimal
End Structure
```

11. An application contains the Structure statement shown here. Write a Private statement that declares a five-element one-dimensional array of Worker variables. Name the array `coWorkers`. Then, write an assignment statement that assigns the value in the name1TextBox to the `first` member contained in the last array element. Finally, write an assignment statement that assigns the value in the name2TextBox to the `last` member contained in the last array element. (4)

INTERMEDIATE

```
Structure Worker
    Public last As String
    Public first As String
End Structure
```

12. A sequential access file named travel.txt contains records whose four fields are delimited by a comma. Write a Dim statement to declare a one-dimensional String array named `travelInfo`. Then, write a statement that reads a line of text from the file and assigns the fields to the `travelInfo` array. The file is associated with a StreamReader variable named `inFile`. (13, 14)

INTERMEDIATE

ADVANCED

13. A sequential access file named vacations.txt contains records whose three fields are delimited by a comma. The application that uses the file defines a structure named TravelInfo. The TravelInfo structure contains three members: a String member named location, an Integer member named lengthOfStay, and a Double member named cost. (4, 13, 14)

   a. Write a Private statement to declare a one-dimensional TravelInfo array named myVacations. The myVacations array should contain 10 elements.

   b. Write a Dim statement to declare a one-dimensional String array named fields.

   c. Write a statement that reads a line of text from the vacations.txt file and assigns the fields to the fields array. The file is associated with a StreamReader variable named inFile.

   d. Write the statements to assign the fields contained in the first element in the fields array to the appropriate members in the first element in the myVacations array.

Computer

MODIFY THIS

14. If necessary, complete the Concentration Game application from this chapter's Programming Tutorial 1, and then close the solution. Use Windows to make a copy of the Concentration Solution folder. Rename the folder Concentration Solution-ModifyThis. Open the Concentration Solution (Concentration Solution.sln) file contained in the Concentration Solution-ModifyThis folder. Create a sequential access file named words5.txt. Save the file in the project's bin\Debug folder. The first eight words in the file as well as the last eight words in the file should be Alabama, Alaska, Arizona, Arkansas, California, Colorado, Connecticut, and Delaware. Modify the application's code so that it also uses the words5.txt file. Save the solution and then start and test the application. Close the solution. (5, 7)

MODIFY THIS

15. If necessary, complete the CD Collection application from this chapter's Programming Tutorial 2, and then close the solution. Use Windows to make a copy of the CD Collection Solution folder. Rename the folder CD Collection Solution-ModifyThis. Open the CD Collection Solution (CD Collection Solution.sln) file contained in the CD Collection Solution-ModifyThis folder. Modify the FormClosing event procedure so that it asks the user whether he or she wants to save the list box items to the cds.txt file. The procedure should take the appropriate action based on the user's response. Also modify the Remove button's Click event procedure so that it verifies that the user wants to remove the selected CD from the list box. Use the message "Do you want to remove the *x* CD?", in which *x* is the name of the CD. The procedure should take the appropriate action based on the user's response. Save the solution and then start and test the application. Close the solution. (9, 10)

MODIFY THIS

16. In this exercise, you will modify the West Coast Emporium application from Figure 11-7 in the chapter. Open the West Coast Solution (West Coast Solution.sln) file contained in the VbReloaded2012\Chap11\West Coast Solution-ModifyThis folder. The modified application should display the number of stores in the selected state and also the name of the regional manager for the state. The names of the regional managers are shown in Figure 11-44. Make the appropriate modifications to the interface and code. Save the solution and then start and test the application. Close the solution. (4)

State	Regional manager
California (CA)	Perry Johanson
Oregon (OR)	Sally Cranston
Washington (WA)	Pat Ippolito

Figure 11-44 Information for Exercise 16
© 2013 Cengage Learning

17. If necessary, complete the Concentration Game application from this chapter's Programming Tutorial 1, and then close the solution. Use Windows to make a copy of the Concentration Solution folder. Rename the folder Concentration Solution-ListBox. Open the Concentration Solution (Concentration Solution.sln) file contained in the Concentration Solution-ListBox folder. Modify the interface and code to allow the user to change the words used in the game by selecting the desired filename (words1.txt, words2.txt, words3.txt, or words4.txt) from a list box while the application is running. The selected file should be used when the New Game button is clicked. Save the solution and then start and test the application. Close the solution. (7, 8)

MODIFY THIS

18. Open the Employee List Solution (Employee List Solution.sln) file contained in the VbReloaded2012\Chap11\Employee List Solution folder. The Write button should write the contents of the employTextBox (excluding any leading or trailing spaces) to a sequential access file named employees.txt. Each name should appear on a separate line in the file. Save the file in the project's bin\Debug folder. The Read button should read the names from the employees.txt file and display each in the list box. Code the appropriate event procedures. Save the solution and then start the application. Test the application by writing five names to the file, and then end the application. Open the employees.txt file to verify that it contains five names. Close the employees.txt window and then close the solution. (5-8)

INTRODUCTORY

19. Open the Memo Solution (Memo Solution.sln) file contained in the VbReloaded2012\ Chap11\Memo Solution folder. The Write button should write the contents of the memoTextBox to a sequential access file named memo.txt. Save the file in the project's bin\Debug folder. Save the solution and then start the application. Test the application by writing the memo shown in Figure 11-45 to the file, and then end the application. Open the memo.txt file to verify that it contains the memo. Close the memo.txt window and then close the solution. (5, 6)

INTRODUCTORY

To all employees:

The annual picnic will be held at Jeffers Park on Saturday, August 21. Bring your family for a day full of fun!

Peter Mulcahey
Personnel Manager

Figure 11-45 Memo for Exercise 19
© 2013 Cengage Learning

INTRODUCTORY

20. Open the Report Solution (Report Solution.sln) file contained in the VbReloaded2012\ Chap11\Report Solution folder. The application stores three state names and sales amounts in an array. Code the application so that it creates the report shown in Figure 11-46. Save the report in a sequential access file named report.txt. Use hyphens for the underline. Use an accumulator to total the sales amounts. Save the solution and then start and test the application. End the application. Open the report.txt file to verify that it contains the report. Close the report.txt window and then close the solution. (5, 6)

```
Siranna Inc. Sales Report
State              Sales
Arizona            25,500
New Mexico         10,300
Texas               9,900
                   -------
Total sales:       $45,700
```

Figure 11-46 Report for Exercise 20
© 2013 Cengage Learning

INTERMEDIATE

21. Open the Name Solution (Name Solution.sln) file contained in the VbReloaded2012\ Chap11\Name Solution folder. Open the names.txt file contained in the project's bin\ Debug folder. The sequential access file contains five names. Close the names.txt window. The Display button should read the five names from the names.txt file and store each in a five-element array. It should sort the array in descending order and then display the contents of the array in the list box. Code the button's Click event procedure. Save the solution and then start and test the application. Close the solution. If you need to recreate the names.txt file, open the file in a window in the IDE, delete the contents of the file (if necessary), and then enter the following five names: Joanne, Zelda, Abby, Ben, and Linda. (6-8)

INTERMEDIATE

22. Open the Carver Solution (Carver Solution.sln) file contained in the VbReloaded2012\ Chap11\Carver Solution folder. The application should display a grade based on the number of points entered by the user. The grading scale is shown in Figure 11-47. Create a structure that contains two members: an Integer variable for the minimum points and a String variable for the grades. Use the structure to declare a five-element array. Store the minimum points and grades in the array. The application should search the array for the number of points earned and then display the appropriate grade from the array. Be sure to verify that the user wants to exit the application. Code the application. Save the solution and then start and test the application. Close the solution. (4, 9)

Minimum points	Grade
0	F
300	D
350	C
400	B
450	A

Figure 11-47 Grading scale for Exercise 22
© 2013 Cengage Learning

23. If necessary, complete Computer Exercise 18, and then close the solution. Use Windows to make a copy of the Employee List Solution folder. Rename the folder Employee List Solution-Intermediate. Open the Employee List Solution (Employee List Solution.sln) file contained in the Employee List Solution-Intermediate folder. (5, 6, 8)

    a. Use Windows to delete the employees.txt file contained in the project's bin\Debug folder.

    b. The first time the Write button's Click event procedure is processed, it should determine whether the employees.txt file exists. If the file exists, the procedure should use the MessageBox.Show method to ask the user whether the existing file should be replaced. Include Yes and No buttons in the message box. If the user clicks the Yes button, replace the existing file; otherwise, append to the existing file.

    c. Save the solution and then start the application. Type Helen in the Name box and then click the Write button. End the application.

    d. Start the application again. Type Ginger in the Name box and then click the Write button. The application should ask whether you want the existing file replaced. Click the No button and then end the application.

    e. Open the employees.txt file. The file should contain two names: Helen and Ginger. Close the employees.txt window.

    f. Start the application again. Type George in the Name box and then click the Write button. Click the Yes button and then end the application.

    g. Open the employees.txt file. The file should contain one name: George. Close the employees.txt window and then close the solution.

24. Open the Salary Solution (Salary Solution.sln) file contained in the VbReloaded2012\Chap11\Salary Solution folder. Open the Code Editor window and study the existing code. The application displays the salary amount associated with the code entered by the user. Currently, the Private statement stores the six salary amounts in the `salaries` array. Modify the application so that it reads the salary amounts from the salary.txt file contained in the project's bin\Debug folder and stores each in the array. Save the solution and then start and test the application. Close the solution. (6-8)

25. If necessary, complete the CD Collection application from this chapter's Programming Tutorial 2, and then close the solution. Use Windows to make a copy of the CD Collection Solution folder. Rename the folder CD Collection Solution-Undo. Open the CD Collection Solution (CD Collection Solution.sln) file contained in the CD Collection Solution-Undo folder. Add an Undo Remove button to the interface. Set its Enabled property to False. The button's Click event procedure should restore the last line removed by the Remove button. Make the necessary modifications to the code. Save the solution and then start and test the application. Close the solution. (10)

26. If necessary, complete the CD Collection application from this chapter's Programming Tutorial 2, and then close the solution. Use Windows to make a copy of the CD Collection Solution folder. Rename the folder CD Collection Solution-Structure. Open the CD Collection Solution (CD Collection Solution.sln) file contained in the CD Collection Solution-Structure folder. Create a structure and then use the structure in the Add button's Click event procedure. Save the solution and then start and test the application. Close the solution. (1, 2)

27. Open the Friends Solution (Friends Solution.sln) file contained in the VbReloaded2012\Chap11\Friends Solution folder. The Add button should add the name entered in the text portion of the combo box control to the list portion of the control, but only if the

name is not already in the list. The Remove button should remove (from the list portion of the combo box) the name either entered in the text portion or selected in the list portion. The form's FormClosing event procedure should save the combo box items in a sequential access file named myFriends.txt. The form's Load event procedure should read the names from the myFriends.txt file and add each name to the combo box. Code the application. Save the solution and then start and test the application. Close the solution. (5-10)

ADVANCED

28. Open the Numbers Solution (Numbers Solution.sln) file contained in the VbReloaded2012\Chap11\Numbers Solution folder. The Display button's Click event procedure should read the five numbers stored in the numbers.txt file and display the numbers in the list box. The numbers.txt file is contained in the project's bin\Debug folder. Currently, the file contains the numbers 1 through 5. The Update button's Click event procedure should read the five numbers from the numbers.txt file and store the numbers in an array. It then should increase each number in the array by 1 and write the array contents to an empty numbers.txt file. Code the appropriate procedures. Save the solution and then start the application. Click the Display button. The numbers 1 through 5 appear in the list box. Click the Update button and then click the Display button. The numbers 2 through 6 appear in the list box. Close the solution. If you need to recreate the numbers.txt file, open the file in a window in the IDE, delete the contents of the file (if necessary), and then enter the numbers 1 through 5. (5-8)

ADVANCED

29. Open the Test Scores Solution (Test Scores Solution.sln) file contained in the VbReloaded2012\Chap11\Test Scores Solution folder. The Save button should save the contents of the nameTextBox and scoreTextBox to a sequential access file named scores.txt. Save each student's record on a separate line. The Display button should use the InputBox function to prompt the user to enter a test score. It then should display the names of the students earning that test score. Save the solution and then start the application. Test the application by entering the student records shown in Figure 11-48. Click the Save button after entering each record. Then, click the Display button. Enter 95 and then press Enter. The names of the students whose test score is 95 appear in the list box. Close the solution. (5-8, 13, 14)

Name	Test score
John Jones	80
Phillip Hawking	95
Kevin Carley	83
Ellie Mayfield	78
Rachael Smith	95
Susan Carkley	99
Harriet Chu	95

Figure 11-48 Student records for Exercise 29

© 2013 Cengage Learning

DISCOVERY

30. If necessary, complete the CD Collection application from this chapter's Programming Tutorial 2, and then close the solution. Use Windows to make a copy of the CD Collection Solution folder. Rename the folder CD Collection Solution-No Duplicate. Open the CD Collection Solution (CD Collection Solution.sln) file contained in the CD Collection Solution-No Duplicate folder. Before prompting the user to enter the artist name and CD price, the Add button's Click event procedure should determine whether the CD name already appears in the list box. If the list box contains the CD name, the procedure should display an appropriate message and then *not* add the CD to the list. Save the solution and then start and test the application. Close the solution.

31. Open the Grades Solution (Grades Solution.sln) file contained in the VbReloaded2012\Chap11\Grades Solution folder. The application should display a student's name and the grades earned on two tests. **DISCOVERY**

    a. Open the Code Editor window. Create a structure named StudentInfo. The structure should contain two members: a String variable for the student's name and a String array for the grades. An array contained in a structure cannot be assigned an initial size, so you will need to include an empty set of parentheses after the array name.

    b. In the getButton_Click procedure, use the StudentInfo structure to declare a structure variable.

    c. Research the Visual Basic ReDim statement. Use the ReDim statement to declare the array's size in the getButton_Click event procedure. In this case, the array should have two elements. (Keep in mind that the array belongs to the structure variable.)

    d. The getButton_Click procedure should use three InputBox functions to get the student's name and both grades. (Store each grade in the array.)

    e. The getButton_Click procedure should display the student's name and grades in the reportLabel.

    f. Save the solution and then start the application. Enter your name and the grades A and B. Your name and both grades appear in the reportLabel. Close the solution.

32. If necessary, complete Computer Exercise 31, and then close the solution. Use Windows to make a copy of the Grades Solution folder. Rename the folder Grades Solution-Modified. Open the Grades Solution (Grades Solution.sln) file contained in the Grades Solution-Modified folder. The getButton_Click procedure should allow the user to enter the names and grades for five students. (Hint: You will need to use an array of structure variables.) Display the five student names and their grades in the reportLabel. You will need to make the reportLabel larger. Save the solution and then start and test the application. Close the solution. **DISCOVERY**

33. Open the Debug Solution (Debug Solution.sln) file contained in the VbReloaded2012\Chap11\Debug Solution folder. Open the Code Editor window and review the existing code. Start the application and then test it using Sue and 1000, and then using Pete and 5000. A run time error occurs. Read the error message. If you are using the Express edition, click the Break button. Click DEBUG on the menu bar and then click Stop Debugging. Open the bonus.txt file contained in the project's bin\Debug folder. Notice that the file is empty. Close the bonus.txt window. Locate and then correct the errors in the code. When the application is working correctly, close the solution. (5, 6) **SWAT THE BUGS**

Case Projects

Warren High School

This year, three students are running for senior class president: Mark Stone, Sheima Patel, and Sam Perez. Create an application that keeps track of the voting. Save the voting information in a sequential access file. The application should display the number of votes per candidate. Use the following names for the solution and project, respectively: Warren Solution and Warren Project. Save the application in the VbReloaded2012\Chap11 folder. Change the form file's name to Main Form.vb. You can either create your own interface or create the one shown in Figure 11-49. (5-8)

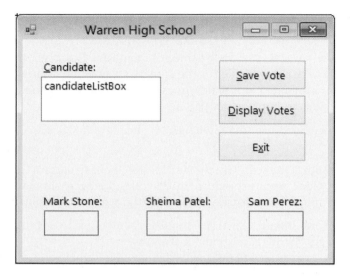

Figure 11-49 Sample interface for the Warren High School application

 WKRK-Radio

Each year, WKRK-Radio polls its audience to determine the best Super Bowl commercial. The choices are as follows: Budweiser, FedEx, E*TRADE, and Pepsi. Create an application that the station manager can use to save each caller's choice in a sequential access file. The application should display the number of votes for each commercial. Use the following names for the solution and project, respectively: WKRK Solution and WKRK Project. Save the application in the VbReloaded2012\Chap11 folder. Change the form file's name to Main Form.vb. You can either create your own interface or create the one shown in Figure 11-50. (5-8)

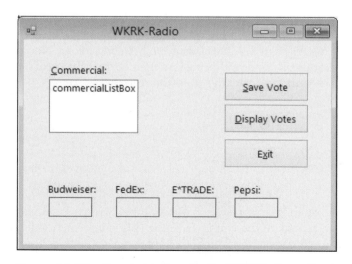

Figure 11-50 Sample interface for the WKRK-Radio application

Political Awareness Organization

During July and August of each year, the Political Awareness Organization (PAO) sends a questionnaire to the voters in its district. The questionnaire asks the voter for his or her political party (Democratic, Republican, or Independent) and age. From the returned questionnaires, the organization's secretary tabulates the number of Democrats, Republicans, and Independents in the district. The secretary wants an application that she can use to save each respondent's information (political party and age) to a sequential access file. The application should calculate and display the number of voters in each political party. When the user clicks the Exit button, the application should verify that the user wants to exit the application. Use the following names for the solution and project, respectively: PAO Solution and PAO Project. Save the application in the VbReloaded2012\Chap11 folder. Change the form file's name to Main Form.vb. You can either create your own interface or create the one shown in Figure 11-51. (5-9)

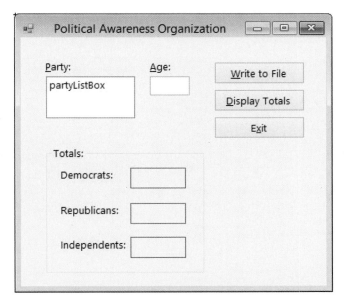

Figure 11-51 Sample interface for the Political Awareness Organization application

 Revellos

Revellos has stores located in several states. Create an application that the sales manager can use to enter the following information for each store: the store number, the state in which the store is located, and the store manager's name. The application should save the information in a sequential access file. Each store's information should appear on a separate line in the file. In other words, the first store's number, state name, and manager name should appear on the first line in the file. The application should allow the sales manager to enter a store number, and then display both the state in which the store is located and the store manager's name. The store information is shown in Figure 11-52. Use the following names for the solution and project, respectively: Revellos Solution and Revellos Project. Save the application in the VbReloaded2012\ Chap11 folder. Change the form file's name to Main Form.vb. (5-8, 13, 14)

Number	State	Manager
1004	Texas	Jeffrey Jefferson
1005	Texas	Paula Hendricks
1007	Arizona	Jake Johansen
1010	Arizona	Henry Abernathy
1011	California	Barbara Millerton
1013	California	Inez Baily
1015	California	Sung Lee
1016	California	Lou Chan
1017	California	Homer Gomez
1019	New Mexico	Ingrid Nadkarni

Figure 11-52   Information for the Revellos application

© 2013 Cengage Learning

CHAPTER 12

Access Databases and LINQ

After studying Chapter 12, you should be able to:

1. Define the terms used when talking about databases
2. Connect an application to a Microsoft Access database
3. Bind table and field objects to controls
4. Explain the purpose of the DataSet, BindingSource, TableAdapter, TableAdapterManager, and BindingNavigator objects
5. Customize a DataGridView control
6. Handle errors using the Try...Catch statement
7. Position the record pointer in a dataset
8. Access the value stored in a field object
9. Query a dataset using LINQ
10. Customize a BindingNavigator control
11. Use the LINQ aggregate operators

Reading and Study Guide

Before you begin reading Chapter 12, view the Ch12_ReadingStudyGuide.pdf file. You can open the file using Adobe Reader, which is available for free on the Adobe Web site at *www.adobe.com/downloads/*.

Database Terminology

In order to maintain accurate records, most businesses store information about their employees, customers, and inventory in computer databases. A **computer database** is an electronic file that contains an organized collection of related information. Many products exist for creating computer databases; such products are called database management systems (or DBMS). Some of the most popular database management systems are Microsoft Access, Microsoft SQL Server, and Oracle. You can use Visual Basic to access the data stored in databases created by these database management systems. As a result, companies can use Visual Basic to create a standard interface that allows employees to access information stored in a variety of database formats. Instead of learning each DBMS's user interface, the employee needs to know only one interface. The actual format of the database is unimportant and will be transparent to the user.

In this chapter, you will learn how to access the data stored in Microsoft Access databases. Databases created using Microsoft Access are relational databases. A **relational database** is one that stores information in tables composed of columns and rows, similar to the format used in a spreadsheet. The databases are called "relational" because the information in the tables can be related in different ways.

Each column in a relational database's table represents a field and each row represents a record. As you learned in Chapter 11, a field is a single item of information about a person, place, or thing—such as a name, a salary amount, a Social Security number, or a price. A record is a group of related fields that contain all of the necessary data about a specific person, place, or thing. The college you are attending keeps a student record on you. Examples of fields contained in your student record include your Social Security number, name, address, phone number, credits earned, and grades earned. A group of related records is called a **table**. Each record in a table contains the same fields.

A relational database can contain one or more tables. A one-table database would be a good choice for storing information about the college courses you have taken. An example of such a table is shown in Figure 12-1. Each record in the table contains four fields: an ID field that indicates the department name and course number, a course title field, a field listing the number of credit hours, and a grade field.

ID	Title	Hours	Grade
ACC110	Accounting Procedures	3	A
ENG101	English Composition I	3	B
CIS156	Visual Basic 2012	3	A
BIO111	Environmental Biology	3	C

Figure 12-1 Example of a one-table relational database
© 2013 Cengage Learning

Most tables have a **primary key**, which is a field that uniquely identifies each record. In the table shown in Figure 12-1, you could use either the ID field or the Title field as the primary key because the data in those fields will be unique for each record.

You might use a two-table database to store information about a CD (compact disc) collection. You would store the general information about each CD, such as the CD's name and the artist's name, in the first table. The information about the songs on each CD, such as their title and track number, would be stored in the second table. You would need to use a common field—for example, a CD number—to relate the records contained in both tables.

Figure 12-2 shows an example of a two-table database that stores CD information. The first table is referred to as the **parent table**, and the second table is referred to as the **child table**. The CdNum field is the primary key in the parent table because it uniquely identifies each record in the table. The CdNum field in the child table is used solely to link the song title and track information to the appropriate CD in the parent table. In the child table, the CdNum field is called the **foreign key**.

Parent and child tables are also referred to as master and detail tables, respectively.

Figure 12-2   Example of a two-table relational database
© 2013 Cengage Learning

Storing data in a relational database offers many advantages. The computer can retrieve data stored in a relational format both quickly and easily, and the data can be displayed in any order. The information in the CD database, for example, can be arranged by artist name, song title, and so on. You also can control the amount of information you want to view from a relational database. You can view all of the information in the CD database, only the information pertaining to a certain artist, or only the names of the songs contained on a specific CD.

Mini-Quiz 12-1

The answers to Mini-Quiz questions are located in Appendix A. Each question is associated with one or more objectives listed at the beginning of the chapter.

1. A _____ is an organized collection of related information stored in a computer file. (1)

    a.   database

    b.   dataset

    c.   field

    d.   record

2. A _____ database stores information in tables. (1)

    a.   columnar

    b.   relational

    c.   sorted

    d.   tabular

3. Which of the following statements is true about a relational database? (1)

a. Data stored in a relational database can be retrieved both quickly and easily by the computer.

b. Data stored in a relational database can be displayed in any order.

c. A relational database stores data in a column and row format.

d. all of the above

Connecting an Application to a Microsoft Access Database

In the concepts portion of this chapter, you will use a Microsoft Access database named Employees. The database contains one table, which is named tblEmploy. The table data is shown in Figure 12-3. The table contains seven fields and 17 records. The Emp_Number field is the primary key because it uniquely identifies each record in the table. The Status field contains the employment status, which is either the letter F (for full-time) or the letter P (for part-time). The Code field identifies the employee's department: 1 for Accounting, 2 for Advertising, 3 for Personnel, and 4 for Inventory.

field names

records

Emp_Number	Last_Name	First_Name	Hired	Rate	Status	Code
100	Benton	Jack	3/5/2001	$15.00	F	2
101	Jones	Carol	4/2/2001	$15.60	F	2
102	Ismal	Asaad	1/15/2002	$10.00	P	1
103	Rodriguez	Carl	5/6/2002	$12.00	P	3
104	Iovanelli	Rebecca	8/15/2002	$20.00	F	1
105	Nyugen	Thomas	10/20/2002	$11.00	P	3
106	Vine	Martha	2/5/2003	$9.50	P	2
107	Smith	Jefferson	5/14/2003	$17.50	F	2
108	Gerber	Sarah	9/24/2004	$21.00	F	3
109	Jones	Samuel	1/10/2005	$13.50	F	4
110	Smith	John	5/6/2005	$9.00	P	4
111	Krutchen	Jerry	5/7/2006	$9.00	P	4
112	Smithson	Jose	6/27/2009	$14.50	F	1
113	Johnson	Leshawn	7/20/2009	$10.00	P	4
114	Jerod	James	4/9/2010	$10.00	P	4
115	Simons	Pam	6/8/2011	$9.00	P	2
116	Sorenson	Harry	3/4/2012	$15.00	F	3

Figure 12-3   Data contained in the tblEmploy table

Before an application can access the data stored in a database, it needs to be connected to the database. You can make the connection using the Data Source Configuration Wizard. The basic procedure for doing this is shown in Figure 12-4. (More detailed steps can be found in Programming Tutorial 1.) The wizard also allows you to specify the data you want to access. The computer makes a copy of the specified data and stores the copy in its internal memory. The copy of the data you want to access is called a **dataset**.

HOW TO Connect an Application to an Access Database

1. Open the application's solution file.

2. If necessary, open the Data Sources window by clicking VIEW on the menu bar, pointing to Other Windows, and then clicking Data Sources.

3. Click Add New Data Source in the Data Sources window to start the Data Source Configuration Wizard, which displays the Choose a Data Source Type screen. If necessary, click Database.

4. Click the Next button to display the Choose a Database Model screen. If necessary, click Dataset.

5. Click the Next button to display the Choose Your Data Connection screen. Click the New Connection button. If the Choose Data Source dialog box opens, click Microsoft Access Database File, select the Always use this selection check box, and then click the Continue button.

6. If Microsoft Access Database File (OLE DB) does not appear in the Data source box, click the Change button, click Microsoft Access Database File, and then click the OK button.

7. Click the Browse button in the Add Connection dialog box to open the Select Microsoft Access Database File dialog box. Locate and then click the database filename. Click the Open button.

8. Click the Test Connection button, and then close the message box.

9. Click the OK button to close the Add Connection dialog box. Click the Next button, and then click the Yes button to add the database file to the application's project folder.

10. If necessary, select the "Yes, save the connection as" check box in the Save the Connection String to the Application Configuration File screen.

11. Click the Next button to display the Choose Your Database Objects screen. Select the appropriate table and/or field objects, and then click the Finish button.

Figure 12-4 How to connect an application to an Access database
© 2013 Cengage Learning

Figure 12-5 shows the result of using the wizard to connect the Morgan Industries application to the Employees database. The database file's name appears in the Solution Explorer window, and the dataset's name appears in the Data Sources window. The EmployeesDataSet contains one table object and seven field objects.

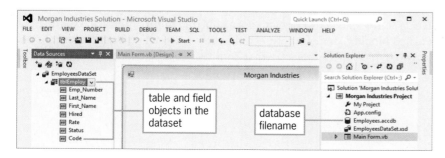

Figure 12-5 Result of running the Data Source Configuration Wizard

After an application is connected to a database, you can use the procedure shown in Figure 12-6 to view the fields and records stored in the dataset. The figure also includes a sample Preview Data window showing the contents of the EmployeesDataSet. Notice the information that appears in the Select an object to preview box. EmployeesDataSet is the name of the dataset in the application, and tblEmploy is the name of the table included in the dataset. Fill and GetData are methods. The Fill method populates an existing table with data, while the GetData method creates a new table and populates it with data.

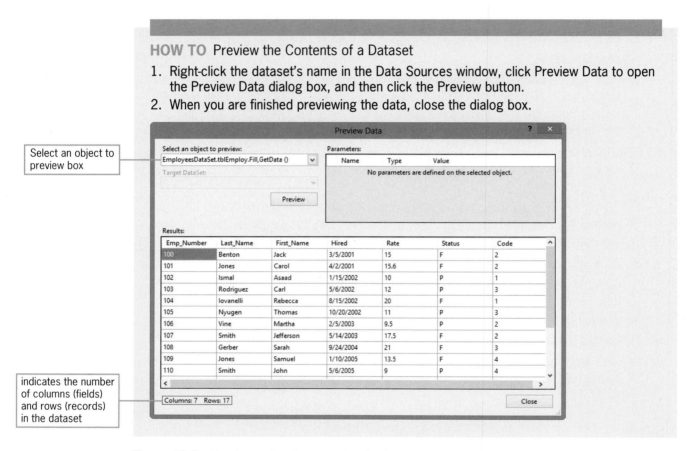

HOW TO Preview the Contents of a Dataset
1. Right-click the dataset's name in the Data Sources window, click Preview Data to open the Preview Data dialog box, and then click the Preview button.
2. When you are finished previewing the data, close the dialog box.

Select an object to preview box

indicates the number of columns (fields) and rows (records) in the dataset

Figure 12-6   How to preview the contents of a dataset
© 2013 Cengage Learning

Binding the Objects in a Dataset

For the user to view the contents of a dataset while an application is running, you need to connect one or more objects in the dataset to one or more controls in the interface. Connecting an object to a control is called **binding**, and the connected controls are called **bound controls**. As indicated in Figure 12-7, you can bind the object either to a control that the computer creates for you or to an existing control in the interface.

 Bound controls are also referred to as data-aware controls.

HOW TO Bind an Object in a Dataset

To have the computer create a control and then bind an object to it:
In the Data Sources window, click the object you want to bind. If necessary, use the object's list arrow to change the control type. Drag the object to an empty area on the form and then release the mouse button.

To bind an object to an existing control:
In the Data Sources window, click the object you want to bind. Drag the object to the control on the form and then release the mouse button. Alternatively, you can click the control on the form and then use the Properties window to set the appropriate property or properties. (Refer to the *Binding to an Existing Control* section later in this chapter.)

Figure 12-7 How to bind an object in a dataset
© 2013 Cengage Learning

Having the Computer Create a Bound Control

When you drag an object from a dataset to an empty area on the form, the computer creates a control and automatically binds the object to it. The icon that appears before the object's name in the Data Sources window indicates the type of control the computer will create. For example, the icon next to tblEmploy in Figure 12-8 indicates that a DataGridView control will be created when you drag the tblEmploy table object to the form. A DataGridView control displays the table data in a row and column format, similar to a spreadsheet. You will learn more about the DataGridView control in the next section. The icon next to each of the seven field objects, on the other hand, indicates that the computer will create a text box when a field object is dragged to the form.

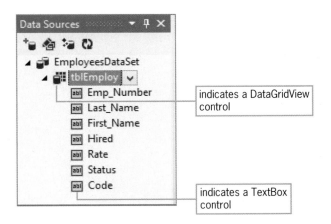

Figure 12-8 Icons in the Data Sources window

When an object is selected in the Data Sources window, you can use the list arrow that appears next to the object's name to change the type of control the computer creates. For example, to display the table data in separate text boxes rather than in a DataGridView control, you click tblEmploy in the Data Sources window and then click the tblEmploy list arrow, as shown in Illustration A in Figure 12-9. Clicking Details in the list tells the computer to create a separate control for each field in the table. Similarly, to display the Last_Name field's data in a label control rather than in a text box, you first click Last_Name in the Data Sources window. You then click the field's list arrow, as shown in Illustration B in Figure 12-9, and then click Label in the list.

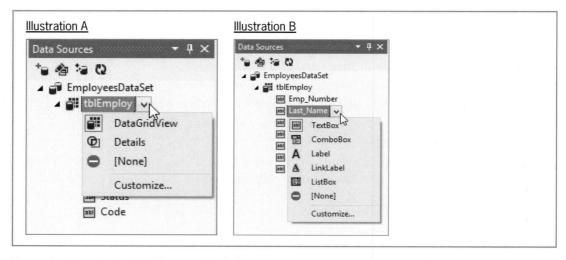

Figure 12-9   Result of clicking an object's list arrow

Figure 12-10 shows the result of dragging the tblEmploy object from the Data Sources window to the MainForm, using the default control type for a table. Besides adding a DataGridView control to the form, the computer also adds a BindingNavigator control. When an application is running, you can use the **BindingNavigator control** to move from one record to the next in the dataset, as well as to add or delete a record and save any changes made to the dataset. The computer also places five objects in the component tray: a DataSet, BindingSource, TableAdapter, TableAdapterManager, and BindingNavigator. As you learned in Chapter 2, the component tray stores objects that do not appear in the user interface while an application is running. An exception to this is the BindingNavigator object, which appears as the BindingNavigator control during both design time and run time.

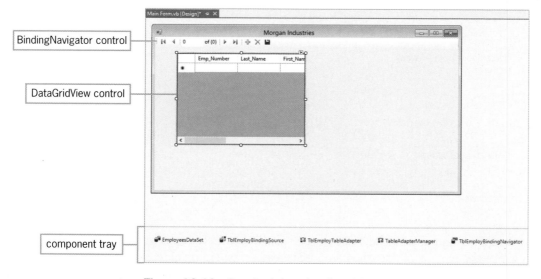

Figure 12-10   Result of dragging the table object to the form

The **TableAdapter object** connects the database to the **DataSet object**, which stores the information you want to access from the database. The TableAdapter is responsible for retrieving the appropriate information from the database and storing it in the DataSet. It also can be used to save to the database any changes made to the data contained in the DataSet. The **TableAdapterManager object** provides the functionality to save the changes made in datasets that contain multiple tables.

The **BindingSource object** provides the connection between the DataSet and the bound controls on the form. The TblEmployBindingSource in Figure 12-10 connects the EmployeesDataSet to two bound controls: a DataGridView control and a BindingNavigator control. The TblEmployBindingSource allows the DataGridView control to display the data contained in the EmployeesDataSet. It also allows the BindingNavigator control to access the records stored in the EmployeesDataSet. Figure 12-11 illustrates the relationships among the database, the objects in the component tray, and the bound controls on the form.

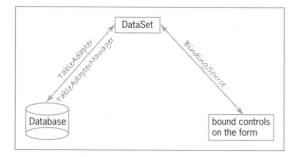

Figure 12-11 Illustration of the relationships among the database, the objects in the component tray, and the bound controls
© 2013 Cengage Learning

If a table object's control type is changed from DataGridView to Details, the computer automatically provides the appropriate controls (such as text boxes, labels, and so on) when you drag the table object to the form. It also adds the BindingNavigator control to the form and the five objects to the component tray. The appropriate controls and objects are also automatically included when you drag a field object to an empty area on the form.

The DataGridView Control

The **DataGridView control** is one of the most popular controls for displaying table data because it allows you to view a great deal of information at the same time. The control displays the data in a row and column format, similar to a spreadsheet. Each row represents a record, and each column represents a field. The intersection of a row and a column in a DataGridView control is called a **cell**.

Like the PictureBox control, the DataGridView control has a task list. The task list is shown in Figure 12-12 along with a description of each task.

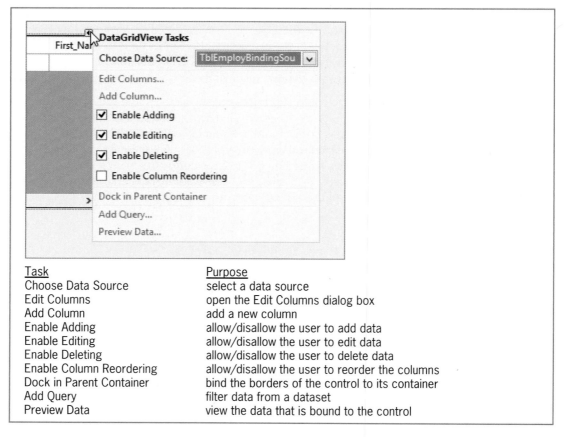

Task	Purpose
Choose Data Source	select a data source
Edit Columns	open the Edit Columns dialog box
Add Column	add a new column
Enable Adding	allow/disallow the user to add data
Enable Editing	allow/disallow the user to edit data
Enable Deleting	allow/disallow the user to delete data
Enable Column Reordering	allow/disallow the user to reorder the columns
Dock in Parent Container	bind the borders of the control to its container
Add Query	filter data from a dataset
Preview Data	view the data that is bound to the control

Figure 12-12   DataGridView control's task list
© 2013 Cengage Learning

Figure 12-13 shows the Edit Columns dialog box, which opens when you click Edit Columns on the DataGridView control's task list. You can use the Edit Columns dialog box during design time to add columns to the control, remove columns from the control, and reorder the columns. You can also use it to set the properties of the bound columns. For example, you can use a column's DefaultCellStyle property to format the column's data, and also to change the column's width and alignment. You can use a column's HeaderText property, on the other hand, to change a column's heading.

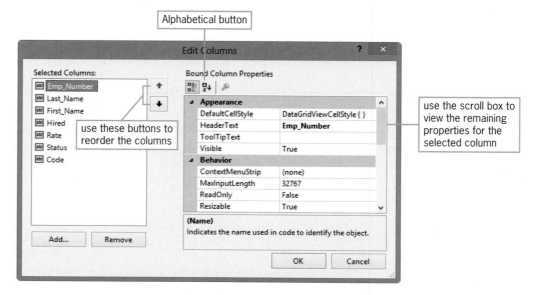

Figure 12-13   Edit Columns dialog box

Some properties of a DataGridView control are listed only in the Properties window. One such property is AutoSizeColumnsMode. The AutoSizeColumnsMode property has seven different settings that determine the way the column widths are sized in the DataGridView control. The Fill setting automatically adjusts the column widths so that all of the columns exactly fill the display area of the control. The ColumnHeader setting, on the other hand, automatically adjusts the column widths based on the header text.

Figure 12-14 shows the DataGridView control docked in its parent container, which is the MainForm in the Morgan Industries application. The Edit Columns dialog box was used to change the header text in several columns. It was also used to format and align the data in the Pay Rate column. However, you won't see the effect of the formatting and aligning until the application is started. The Properties window was used to set the control's AutoSizeColumnsMode property to Fill.

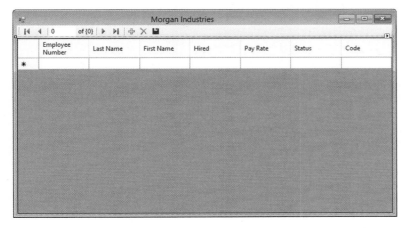

Figure 12-14 DataGridView control after setting some of its properties

Visual Basic Code

In addition to adding the appropriate controls and objects to the application when a table or field object is dragged to the form, the computer also enters two event procedures in the Code Editor window; the procedures are shown in Figure 12-15.

```
Private Sub TblEmployBindingNavigatorSaveItem_Click(sender As Object,
            e As EventArgs) Handles TblEmployBindingNavigatorSaveItem.Click
    Me.Validate()
    Me.TblEmployBindingSource.EndEdit()
    Me.TableAdapterManager.UpdateAll(Me.EmployeesDataSet)

End Sub

Private Sub MainForm_Load(sender As Object, e As EventArgs) Handles MyBase.Load
    'TODO: This line of code loads data into the
    'EmployeesDataSet.tblEmploy' table. You can move, or remove it, as needed.
    Me.TblEmployTableAdapter.Fill(Me.EmployeesDataSet.tblEmploy)

End Sub
```

Figure 12-15 Procedures automatically entered in the Code Editor window

The MainForm_Load procedure uses the TableAdapter object's Fill method to retrieve the data from the database and store it in the EmployeesDataSet. In most applications, the code to fill a dataset belongs in this procedure. However, as the comments in the procedure indicate, you can either move or delete the code. The data will appear in the DataGridView control because the control is bound to the dataset's tblEmploy object. Figure 12-16 shows the result of starting the Morgan Industries application. Notice that the first cell in the DataGridView control is highlighted (selected). You can use the arrow keys on your keyboard to move the highlight to a different cell in the control. When a cell is highlighted, you can modify its contents by simply typing the new data.

Save Data button

Employee Number	Last Name	First Name	Hired	Pay Rate	Status	Code
100	Benton	Jack	3/5/2001	15.00	F	2
101	Jones	Carol	4/2/2001	15.60	F	2
102	Ismal	Asaad	1/15/2002	10.00	P	1
103	Rodriguez	Carl	5/6/2002	12.00	P	3
104	Iovanelli	Rebecca	8/15/2002	20.00	F	1
105	Nyugen	Thomas	10/20/2002	11.00	P	3
106	Vine	Martha	2/5/2003	9.50	P	2
107	Smith	Jefferson	5/14/2003	17.50	F	2
108	Gerber	Sarah	9/24/2004	21.00	F	3
109	Jones	Samuel	1/10/2005	13.50	F	4
110	Smith	John	5/6/2005	9.00	P	4
111	Krutchen	Jerry	5/7/2006	9.00	P	4
112	Smithson	Jose	6/27/2009	14.50	F	1
113	Johnson	Leshawn	7/20/2009	10.00	P	4

Figure 12-16   Dataset displayed in the DataGridView control

The TblEmployBindingNavigatorSaveItem_Click procedure shown earlier in Figure 12-15 is processed when you click the Save Data button (the disk) on the BindingNavigator control. The procedure's code validates the changes made to the data before saving the data to the database. Two methods are involved in the save operation: the BindingSource object's EndEdit method and the TableAdapterManager's UpdateAll method. The EndEdit method applies any pending changes (such as new records, deleted records, or changed records) to the dataset. The UpdateAll method commits the dataset changes to the database. Because it is possible for an error to occur when saving data to a database, you should add error handling code to the Save Data button's Click event procedure.

Handling Errors in the Code

An error that occurs while an application is running is called an **exception**. If your code does not contain specific instructions for handling the exceptions that may occur, Visual Basic handles them for you. Typically, it does this by displaying an error message and then abruptly terminating the application. You can prevent your application from behaving in such an unfriendly manner by taking control of the exception handling in your code; you can do this using the **Try...Catch statement**.

Figure 12-17 shows the basic syntax of the Try...Catch statement and includes examples of using the syntax. The basic syntax contains a Try block and a Catch block. Within the Try block, you place the code that could possibly generate an exception. When an exception occurs in the Try block's code, the computer processes the code contained in the Catch block; it then skips to the code following the End Try clause. A description of the exception that occurred is stored in the Message property of the Catch block's ex variable. You can access the description using the code ex.Message, as shown in Example 2 in the figure. Keep in mind that the Catch block's code is processed only when an error occurs in the Try block.

When an error occurs in a procedure's code during run time, programmers say that the procedure "threw an exception."

HOW TO Use the Try...Catch Statement

<u>Basic syntax</u>
Try
> *one or more statements that might generate an exception*
Catch ex As Exception
> *one or more statements to execute when an exception occurs*
End Try

<u>Example 1</u>
```
Private Sub displayButton_Click(sender As Object,
e As EventArgs) Handles displayButton.Click
    Dim inFile As IO.StreamReader
    Dim line As String

    Try
        inFile = IO.File.OpenText("names.txt")
        Do Until inFile.Peek = -1
            line = inFile.ReadLine
            namesListBox.Items.Add(line)
        Loop
        inFile.Close()
    Catch ex As Exception
        MessageBox.Show("File error", "JK's",
            MessageBoxButtons.OK, MessageBoxIcon.Information)
    End Try
End Sub
```

<u>Example 2</u>
```
Private Sub TblEmployBindingNavigatorSaveItem_Click(
sender As Object, e As EventArgs
) Handles TblEmployBindingNavigatorSaveItem.Click
    Try
        Me.Validate()
        Me.TblEmployBindingSource.EndEdit()
        Me.TableAdapterManager.UpdateAll(Me.EmployeesDataSet)
        MessageBox.Show("Changes saved", "Morgan Industries",
            MessageBoxButtons.OK, MessageBoxIcon.Information)
    Catch ex As Exception
        MessageBox.Show(ex.Message, "Morgan Industries",
            MessageBoxButtons.OK, MessageBoxIcon.Information)
    End Try
End Sub
```

The Try...Catch statement also has a Finally block, whose code is processed whether or not an exception is thrown within the Try block.

Figure 12-17 How to use the Try...Catch statement
© 2013 Cengage Learning

If an exception occurs in Example 1's Try block in Figure 12-17, the computer will display the message "File error" and then skip to the code following the End Try clause. If an error occurs in Example 2's Try block, the computer will display a description of the exception; otherwise, it will display the "Changes saved" message.

The Copy to Output Directory Property

When the Data Source Configuration Wizard connected the Morgan Industries application to the Employees database, it added the database file (Employees.accdb) to the application's project folder. (You can verify this by referring to the Solution Explorer window shown earlier in Figure 12-5.) A database file contained in a project is referred to as a local database file. The way changes are saved to a local database file is determined by the file's **Copy to Output Directory property**. Figure 12-18 lists the values that can be assigned to the property.

HOW TO Use the Copy to Output Directory Property

Property setting	Meaning
Do not copy	The file in the project folder is not copied to the bin\Debug folder when the application is started.
Copy always	The file in the project folder is copied to the bin\Debug folder each time the application is started.
Copy if newer	When an application is started, the computer compares the date on the file in the project folder with the date on the file in the bin\Debug folder. The file from the project folder is copied to the bin\Debug folder only when its date is newer.

Figure 12-18   How to use the Copy to Output Directory property
© 2013 Cengage Learning

 If you want to experiment with the DataGridView version of the Morgan Industries application, open the solution contained in the Try It 1! folder. In the solution, the database file's Copy to Output Directory property is set to Copy if newer.

When a file's Copy to Output Directory property is set to its default setting, Copy always, the file is copied from the project folder to the project folder's bin\Debug folder each time you start the application. In this case, for example, the Employees.accdb file is copied from the Morgan Industries Project folder to the Morgan Industries Project\bin\Debug folder. As a result, the file will appear in two different folders in the solution. When you click the Save Data button on the BindingNavigator control, any changes made in the DataGridView control are recorded only in the file stored in the bin\Debug folder; the file stored in the project folder is not changed. The next time you start the application, the file in the project folder is copied to the bin\Debug folder, overwriting the file that contains the changes. You can change this behavior by setting the database file's Copy to Output Directory property to Copy if newer. The Copy if newer setting tells the computer to compare the dates on both files to determine which file has the newer (more current) date. If the database file in the project folder has the newer date, the computer should copy it to the bin\Debug folder; otherwise, it shouldn't copy it.

Binding to an Existing Control

As indicated earlier in Figure 12-7, you can bind an object in a dataset to an existing control on the form. The easiest way to do this is by dragging the object from the Data Sources window to the control. However, you can also click the control and then set one or more properties in the Properties window. The appropriate property (or properties) to set depends on the control you are binding. For example, you use the DataSource property to bind a DataGridView control. However, you use the DataSource and DisplayMember properties to bind a ListBox control, and use the DataBindings/Text property to bind label and text box controls.

When you drag an object from the Data Sources window to an existing control, the computer does not create a new control; instead, it binds the object to the existing control. Because a new control does not need to be created, the computer ignores the control type specified for the object in the Data Sources window. Therefore, it is not necessary to change the control type in the Data Sources window to match the existing control's type. In other words, you can drag an object that is associated with a text box in the Data Sources window to a label control on the form. The computer will bind the object to the label, but it will not change the label to a text box.

Figure 12-19 shows a different version of the Morgan Industries application. In this version, the Emp_Number, Last_Name, Status, and Code field objects were dragged from the Data Sources window to the numberLabel, lastNameLabel, statusLabel, and codeLabel controls, respectively; doing this binds each field object to its respective label control. In addition to binding the field objects to the controls, the computer also adds the DataSet, BindingSource, TableAdapter, and TableAdapterManager objects to the component tray.

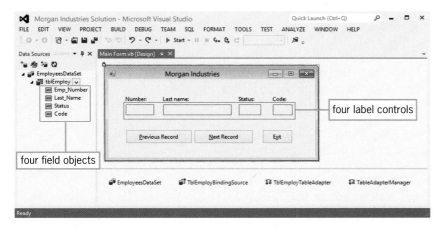

Figure 12-19   Result of dragging field objects to existing label controls

Notice that when you drag an object from the Data Sources window to an existing control, the computer does not add a BindingNavigator object to the component tray, nor does it add a BindingNavigator control to the form. You can use the BindingNavigator tool, which is located in the Data section of the toolbox, to add a BindingNavigator control and object to the application. You then would need to set the control's DataSource property to the name of the BindingSource object (in this case, TblEmployBindingSource).

Besides adding the objects shown in Figure 12-19 to the component tray, the computer also enters (in the Code Editor window) the Load event procedure shown earlier in Figure 12-15. Recall that the procedure uses the TableAdapter object's Fill method to retrieve the data from the database and store it in the DataSet object.

Figure 12-20 shows a sample run of this version of the Morgan Industries application. Only the first record in the dataset appears in the interface. Because the interface does not contain a BindingNavigator control, which would allow you to move from one record to the next, you will need to code the Next Record and Previous Record buttons to view the remaining records.

Figure 12-20   First record displayed in the interface

Coding the Next Record and Previous Record Buttons

The BindingSource object uses an invisible record pointer to keep track of the current record in the dataset. It stores the position of the record pointer in its **Position property**. The first record is in position 0; the second is in position 1, and so on. Figure 12-21 shows the Position property's syntax and includes examples of using the property.

HOW TO Use the BindingSource Object's Position Property

Syntax
bindingSourceName.**Position**

Example 1
`recordNum = TblEmployBindingSource.Position`
assigns the current record's position to the `recordNum` variable

Example 2
`TblEmployBindingSource.Position = 4`
moves the record pointer to the fifth record in the dataset

Example 3
`TblEmployBindingSource.Position += 1`
moves the record pointer to the next record in the dataset; you can also write the statement as follows: `TblEmployBindingSource.Position = TblEmployBindingSource.Position + 1`

Figure 12-21   How to use the BindingSource object's Position property
© 2013 Cengage Learning

Rather than using the Position property to position the record pointer in a dataset, you can use the BindingSource object's Move methods. The **Move methods** move the record pointer to the first, last, next, or previous record in the dataset. Figure 12-22 shows each Move method's syntax and includes examples of using two of the methods.

HOW TO Use the BindingSource Object's Move Methods

Syntax
bindingSourceName.**MoveFirst()**
bindingSourceName.**MoveLast()**
bindingSourceName.**MoveNext()**
bindingSourceName.**MovePrevious()**

Example 1
`TblEmployBindingSource.MoveFirst()`
moves the record pointer to the first record in the dataset

Example 2
`TblEmployBindingSource.MoveNext()`
moves the record pointer to the next record in the dataset

Figure 12-22   How to use the BindingSource object's Move methods
© 2013 Cengage Learning

When the user clicks the Next Record button in the Morgan Industries interface, the button's Click event procedure should move the record pointer to the next record in the dataset. Similarly, when the user clicks the Previous Record button, the button's Click event procedure should move the record pointer to the previous record in the dataset. You can use the TblEmployBindingSource object's MoveNext and MovePrevious methods to code the procedures, as shown in Figure 12-23.

If you want to experiment with the Labels version of the Morgan Industries application, open the solution contained in the Try It 2! folder. In the solution, the database file's Copy to Output Directory property is set to Copy always.

```
Private Sub nextButton_Click(sender As Object, e As EventArgs) Handles
    ' moves the record pointer to the next record

    TblEmployBindingSource.MoveNext()
End Sub

Private Sub previousButton_Click(sender As Object, e As EventArgs) Han
    ' moves the record pointer to the previous record

    TblEmployBindingSource.MovePrevious()
End Sub
```

Figure 12-23   nextButton_Click and previousButton_Click procedures

Accessing the Value Stored in a Field

At times, you may need to access the value stored in a field in a dataset. You can do so using the syntax shown in Figure 12-24. The figure also includes examples of accessing some of the fields in the EmployeesDataSet.

HOW TO Access the Value Stored in a Field

Syntax
dataSetObjectName.tableName(recordNumber).fieldName

Example 1
```
Dim last As String
last = EmployeesDataSet.tblEmploy(0).Last_Name
```
assigns the value stored in the first record's Last_Name field (Benton) to the last variable

Example 2
```
Dim payRate As Double
payRate = EmployeesDataSet.tblEmploy(4).Rate
```
assigns the value stored in the fifth record's Rate field (20) to the payRate variable

Figure 12-24   How to access the value stored in a field
© 2013 Cengage Learning

Mini-Quiz 12-2

1. Which of the following objects connects a database to a DataSet object? (4)

    a. BindingSource

    b. DataBase

    c. DataGridView

    d. TableAdapter

2. An application contains the following objects: FriendsDataSet, TblNamesBindingSource, TblNamesTableAdapter, TableAdapterManager, and TblNamesBindingNavigator. Which of the following statements retrieves data from the Friends database and stores it in the FriendsDataSet? (4)

    a. `Me.FriendsDataSet.Fill(Friends.accdb)`

    b. `Me.TblNamesBindingSource.Fill(Me.FriendsDataSet)`

    c. `Me.TblNamesBindingNavigator.Fill(FriendsDataSet.tblNames)`

    d. `Me.TblNamesTableAdapter.Fill(Me.FriendsDataSet.tblNames)`

3. If an application contains the `Catch ex As Exception` clause, which of the following can be used to access the exception's description? (6)

    a. `ex.Description`

    b. `ex.Exception`

    c. `ex.Message`

    d. `Exception.Description`

4. If the current record is the second record in the dataset, which of the following statements will position the record pointer on the first record? (7)

    a. `TblEmployBindingSource.Position = 0`

    b. `TblEmployBindingSource.Position -= 1`

    c. `TblEmployBindingSource.MoveFirst()`

    d. all of the above

Creating a Query

You can arrange the records stored in a dataset in any order. For example, the records in the EmployeesDataSet can be arranged by employee number, pay rate, status, and so on. You can also control the number of records you want to view at any one time. You can view all of the records in the EmployeesDataSet; or, you can choose to view only the records for the part-time employees. You use a **query** to specify both the records to select in a dataset and the order in which to arrange the records. You can create a query in Visual Basic using a feature called **Language Integrated Query** or, more simply, **LINQ**.

Figure 12-25 shows the basic syntax of LINQ when used to select and arrange records in a dataset. In the syntax, *variableName* and *elementName* can be any names you choose, as long as the name follows the naming rules for variables. In other words, there is nothing special about the `records` and `employee` names used in the examples. The Where and Order By clauses are optional parts of the syntax. You use the **Where clause**, which contains a *condition*, to limit the records you want to view. Similar to the condition in the If...Then...Else and Do...Loop statements, the condition in a Where clause specifies a requirement that must be met for a record to be selected. The **Order By clause** is used to arrange (sort) the records in either ascending (the default) or descending order by one or more fields.

HOW TO Use LINQ to Select and Arrange Records in a Dataset
Basic syntax
Dim *variableName* = **From** *elementName* **In** *dataset.table*
      [**Where** *condition*]
      [**Order By** *elementName.fieldName1* [**Ascending** | **Descending**]
          [, *elementName.fieldNameN* [**Ascending** | **Descending**]]]
      Select *elementName*

Example 1
```
Dim records = From employee In EmployeesDataSet.tblEmploy
              Select employee
```
selects all of the records in the dataset

Example 2
```
Dim records = From employee In EmployeesDataSet.tblEmploy
              Order By employee.Code
              Select employee
```
selects all of the records in the dataset and arranges them in ascending order by the Code field

Example 3
```
Dim records = From employee In EmployeesDataSet.tblEmploy
              Where employee.Status.ToUpper = "P"
              Select employee
```
selects only the part-time employee records in the dataset

Example 4
```
Dim records = From employee In EmployeesDataSet.tblEmploy
              Where employee.Last_Name.ToUpper Like "J*"
              Order By employee.Code Descending
              Select employee
```
selects from the dataset only the employee records whose last name begins with the letter J, and arranges them in descending order by the Code field

Figure 12-25 How to use LINQ to select and arrange records in a dataset
© 2013 Cengage Learning

Notice that the syntax shown in Figure 12-25 does not require you to specify the data type of the variable in the Dim statement. Instead, the syntax allows the computer to infer the data type from the value being assigned to the variable. However, for this inference to take place, you must set Option Infer to On (rather than to Off, as you have been doing). You can do this by entering the `Option Infer On` statement in the General Declarations section of the Code Editor window.

Figure 12-25 also includes examples of using the LINQ syntax. The statement in Example 1 selects all of the records in the dataset and assigns the records to the `records` variable. The statement in Example 2 performs the same task; however, the records are assigned in ascending order by the Code field. If you are sorting records in ascending order, you do not need to include the keyword `Ascending` in the Order By clause because `Ascending` is the default sort order. The statement in Example 3 assigns only the records for part-time employees to the `records` variable. The statement in Example 4 uses the Like operator and the asterisk pattern-matching character to select only records whose Last_Name field begins with the letter J, followed by zero or more characters. (You learned about the Like operator and pattern-matching characters in Chapter 10.) The statement sorts the records in descending order by the Code field.

The syntax and examples in Figure 12-25 merely assign the selected and/or arranged records to a variable. To actually view the records, you need to assign the variable's contents to the DataSource property of a BindingSource object. The syntax for doing this is shown in Figure 12-26, along with an example of using the syntax. Any control that is bound to the BindingSource object will display the appropriate field(s) when the application is started.

If you want to experiment with the examples shown in Figures 12-25 and 12-26, open the solution contained in the Try It 3! folder.

HOW TO Assign the Contents of a LINQ Variable to a BindingSource Object

Basic syntax
bindingSource.**DataSource** = *variableName*.**AsDataView**

Example
```
TblEmployBindingSource.DataSource = records.AsDataView
```
assigns the contents of the `records` variable (from Figure 12-25) to the TblEmployBindingSource object

---

Figure 12-26   How to assign the contents of a LINQ variable to a BindingSource object
© 2013 Cengage Learning

Personalizing a BindingNavigator Control

The BindingNavigator control contains buttons that allow you to move to a different record in the dataset, add or delete a record, and save any changes made to the dataset. At times, you may want to include additional items—such as another button, a text box, or a drop-down button—on the BindingNavigator control. Figure 12-27 lists the steps for adding items to and deleting items from the BindingNavigator control.

Ch12-DropDown Button

HOW TO Customize a BindingNavigator Control

To add an item to a BindingNavigator control:
1. Click the BindingNavigator control's task box and then click Edit Items to open the Items Collection Editor window.
2. If necessary, click the "Select item and add to list below" arrow, and then click the item you want to add to the BindingNavigator control.
3. Click the Add button.
4. Click the Alphabetical button to display the property names in alphabetical order. Provide appropriate values for the item's Name, DisplayStyle, and Text properties.
5. If necessary, you can use the up and down arrows in the Items Collection Editor window to reposition the item.

To delete an item from a BindingNavigator control:
1. Click the BindingNavigator control's task box and then click Edit Items to open the Items Collection Editor window.
2. In the Members list, click the item you want to remove and then click the *X* button.

Figure 12-27   How to customize a BindingNavigator control *(continues)*

(continued)

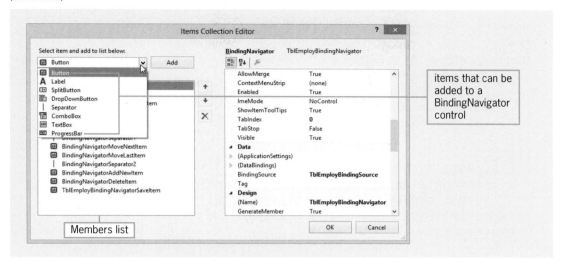

Figure 12-27   How to customize a BindingNavigator control
© 2013 Cengage Learning

Figure 12-28 shows a DropDownButton on the Morgan Industries BindingNavigator control during design time. The DropDownButton, whose caption is Average Pay Rate, offers a menu that contains three items. The menu items allow the user to determine the average pay rate for all employees, part-time employees, or full-time employees. You will learn how to calculate these values in the next section.

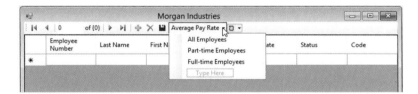

Figure 12-28   DropDownButton added to the BindingNavigator control

Using the LINQ Aggregate Operators

In addition to using LINQ to sort and select the records in a dataset, you can use it to perform arithmetic calculations on the fields in the records. The calculations are performed using the LINQ aggregate operators. The most commonly used aggregate operators are Average, Count, Max, Min, and Sum. An **aggregate operator** returns a single value from a group of values. The Sum operator, for example, returns the sum (total) of the values in the group, whereas the Min operator returns the smallest value in the group. You include an aggregate operator in a LINQ statement using the syntax shown in Figure 12-29. The figure also includes examples of using the syntax.

638

HOW TO Use the LINQ Aggregate Operators

Syntax
Dim *variableName* [**As** *dataType*] =
  Aggregate *elementName* **In** *dataset.table*
  [**Where** *condition*]
  Select *elementName.fieldName*
  Into *aggregateOperator*( )

Example 1
```
Dim avgRate As Double =
    Aggregate employee In EmployeesDataSet.tblEmploy
    Select employee.Rate Into Average()
```
calculates the average of the pay rates in the dataset and assigns the result to the
`avgRate` variable

Example 2
```
Dim maxRate As Double =
    Aggregate employee In EmployeesDataSet.tblEmploy
    Where employee.Status.ToUpper = "P"
    Select employee.Rate Into Max()
```
finds the highest pay rate for a part-time employee and assigns the result to the
`maxRate` variable

Example 3
```
Dim counter As Integer =
    Aggregate employee In EmployeesDataSet.tblEmploy
    Where employee.Code = 2
    Into Count()
```
counts the number of employees whose department code is 2 and assigns the result to
the `counter` variable (The Count operator doesn't need the Select clause.)

Figure 12-29 How to use the LINQ aggregate operators
© 2013 Cengage Learning

 If you want to experiment with the code shown in Figure 12-29, open the solution contained in the Try It 4! folder.

Figure 12-30 shows the code associated with the three menu items shown earlier in Figure 12-28. It also includes a sample run of the Morgan Industries application when the user selects the Part-time Employees item from the DropDownButton.

```
Private Sub avgAllItem_Click(sender As Object,
e As EventArgs) Handles avgAllItem.Click
    ' displays the average pay rate for all employees

    Dim avgRate As Double =
        Aggregate employee In EmployeesDataSet.tblEmploy
        Select employee.Rate Into Average()

    MessageBox.Show("Average pay rate for all employees: " &
        avgRate.ToString("C2"), "Morgan Industries",
        MessageBoxButtons.OK, MessageBoxIcon.Information)
End Sub

Private Sub avgParttimeItem_Click(sender As Object,
e As EventArgs) Handles avgParttimeItem.Click
    ' displays the average pay rate for part-time employees

    Dim avgRate As Double =
        Aggregate employee In EmployeesDataSet.tblEmploy
        Where employee.Status.ToUpper = "P"
        Select employee.Rate Into Average()

    MessageBox.Show("Average pay rate for part-time employees: " &
        avgRate.ToString("C2"), "Morgan Industries",
        MessageBoxButtons.OK, MessageBoxIcon.Information)
End Sub

Private Sub avgFulltimeItem_Click(sender As Object,
e As EventArgs) Handles avgFulltimeItem.Click
    ' displays the average pay rate for full-time employees

    Dim avgRate As Double =
        Aggregate employee In EmployeesDataSet.tblEmploy
        Where employee.Status.ToUpper = "F"
        Select employee.Rate Into Average()

    MessageBox.Show("Average pay rate for full-time employees: " &
        avgRate.ToString("C2"), "Morgan Industries",
        MessageBoxButtons.OK, MessageBoxIcon.Information)
End Sub
```

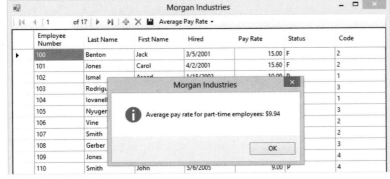

If you want to experiment with the LINQ aggregate operator version of the Morgan Industries application, open the solution contained in the Try It 5! folder.

Figure 12-30   Code associated with the three items on the DropDownButton
© 2013 Cengage Learning

Mini-Quiz 12-3

1. Which of the following statements selects all of the records in the tblStates table? (9)

    a. ```
        Dim records = From state In StatesDataSet.tblStates
                Select All state
        ```

    b.  ```
        Dim records = From state In StatesDataSet.tblStates
                Select state
        ```

    c. `Dim records = Select state From StatesDataSet.tblStates`

    d. ```
        Dim records = From StatesDataSet.tblStates
                Select tblStates.state
        ```

2.  The tblCities table contains a numeric field named Population. Which of the following statements calculates the total population of all the cities in the table? (11)

    a.  ```
        Dim total As Integer =
                Aggregate city In CitiesDataSet.tblCities
                Select city.Population Into Sum()
        ```

    b. ```
        Dim total As Integer =
                Sum city In CitiesDataSet.tblCities
                Select city.Population Into total
        ```

    c.  ```
        Dim total As Integer =
                Aggregate CitiesDataSet.tblCities.city
                Select city.Population Into Sum()
        ```

    d. ```
        Dim total As Integer =
                Sum city In CitiesDataSet.tblCities.population
        ```

3.  In a LINQ statement, which clause is used to sort the selected records? (9)

    a.  Arrange
    b.  Order By
    c.  Sort
    d.  Where

You have completed the concepts section of Chapter 12. The Programming Tutorial section is next.

## PROGRAMMING TUTORIAL 1

*Completing the Trivia Game Application*

In this tutorial, you will complete an application that displays trivia questions and answers. The questions and answers are stored in a Microsoft Access database named Trivia.accdb. The database contains one table, which is named tblGame. The table contains nine records. Each record has six fields named Question, AnswerA, AnswerB, AnswerC, AnswerD, and CorrectAnswer. The application keeps track of the number of incorrect responses made by the user, and it displays that information after all nine questions have been answered. Figures 12-31 and 12-32 show the application's TOE chart and MainForm, respectively.
        ```

Task	Object	Event
End the application	exitButton	Click
Fill the dataset with data	MainForm	Load
1. Compare the user's answer with the correct answer 2. Keep track of the number of incorrect answers 3. Display the next question and answers from the dataset 4. Display the number of incorrect answers	submitButton	Click
Display questions from the dataset	questionTextBox	None
Display answers from the dataset	aTextBox, bTextBox, cTextBox, dTextBox	None
Get the user's answer	aRadioButton, bRadioButton, cRadioButton, dRadioButton	None

Figure 12-31   TOE chart for the Trivia Game application
© 2013 Cengage Learning

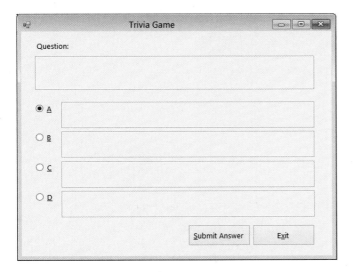

Figure 12-32   MainForm for the Trivia Game application

Connecting the Application to the Trivia Database

First, you need to open the Trivia Game application and connect it to the Trivia database.

To open the application and then connect it to the database:

1. Start Visual Studio. Open the **Trivia Game Solution (Trivia Game Solution.sln)** file contained in the VbReloaded2012\Chap12\Trivia Game Solution folder. If necessary, open the designer window.

2. If necessary, open the Data Sources window by clicking **VIEW** on the menu bar, pointing to **Other Windows**, and then clicking **Data Sources**.

3. Click **Add New Data Source** in the Data Sources window to start the Data Source Configuration Wizard. If necessary, click **Database** on the Choose a Data Source Type screen.

4. Click the **Next** button to display the Choose a Database Model screen. If necessary, click **Dataset**.

5. Click the **Next** button to display the Choose Your Data Connection screen. Click the **New Connection** button. At this point, you will see either the Choose Data Source dialog box or the Add Connection dialog box.

6. If the Add Connection dialog box opens, skip to Step 7. However, if the Choose Data Source dialog box opens, click **Microsoft Access Database File** in the Data source box, select the **Always use this selection** check box, and then click the **Continue** button to open the Add Connection dialog box.

7. If Microsoft Access Database File (OLE DB) does not appear in the Data source box, click the **Change** button to open the Change Data Source dialog box, click **Microsoft Access Database File**, and then click the **OK** button.

8. Click the **Browse** button in the Add Connection dialog box. Open the VbReloaded2012\ Chap12\Access Databases folder and then click **Trivia.accdb** in the list of filenames. Click the **Open** button. Figure 12-33 shows the completed Add Connection dialog box.

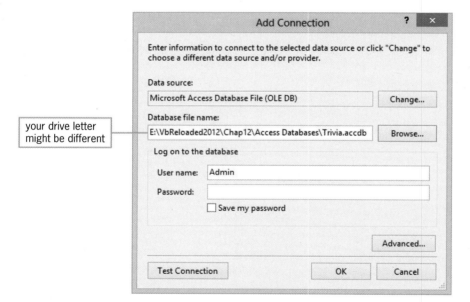

your drive letter might be different

Figure 12-33   Completed Add Connection dialog box

9. Click the **Test Connection** button. The "Test connection succeeded." message appears in a message box. Close the message box.

10. Click the **OK** button to close the Add Connection dialog box. Trivia.accdb appears in the Choose Your Data Connection screen. Click the **Next** button. The message box shown in Figure 12-34 opens. The message asks whether you want to include the database file in the current project. By including the file in the current project, you can more easily copy the application and its database to another computer.

Figure 12-34 Message regarding copying the database file

11. Click the **Yes** button to add the Trivia.accdb file to the application's project folder in the Solution Explorer window. The Save the Connection String to the Application Configuration File screen appears next. The name of the connection string, TriviaConnectionString, appears on the screen. If necessary, select the **Yes, save the connection as** check box.

12. Click the **Next** button to display the Choose Your Database Objects screen. You use this screen to select the table and/or field objects to include in the dataset, which is automatically named TriviaDataSet.

13. Expand the Tables node and then expand the tblGame node. (You expand a node by clicking the small triangle next to it.) In this application, you need the dataset to include all of the fields. Click the **empty box** next to tblGame. Doing this selects the table and field check boxes, as shown in Figure 12-35.

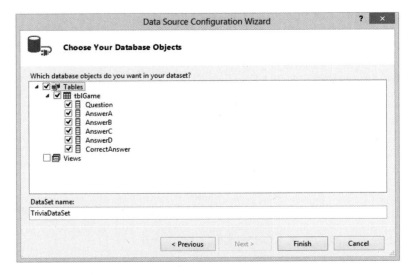

Figure 12-35 Objects selected in the Choose Your Database Objects screen

14. Click the **Finish** button. The computer adds the TriviaDataSet to the Data Sources window. Expand the tblGame node in the Data Sources window. As shown in Figure 12-36, the dataset contains one table object and six field objects.

table and field objects
in the dataset

Figure 12-36   Result of running the Data Source Configuration Wizard

15. Now, preview the data contained in the dataset. Right-click **TriviaDataSet** in the Data Sources window, and then click **Preview Data** to open the Preview Data dialog box. Click the **Preview** button. See Figure 12-37.

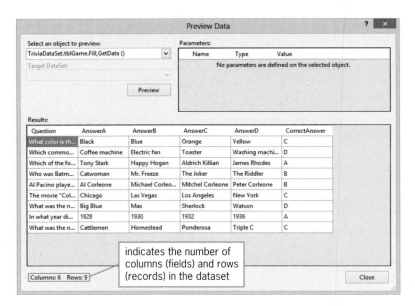

indicates the number of columns (fields) and rows (records) in the dataset

Figure 12-37   Data displayed in the Preview Data dialog box

16. Click the **Close** button to close the Preview Data dialog box.

Note: In this application, the user will not be adding, deleting, or modifying the records in the dataset, so you do not need to change the database file's Copy to Output Directory property from "Copy always" to "Copy if newer."

Binding the Field Objects to the Text Boxes

Next, you will bind the field objects in the dataset to the appropriate text boxes on the form.

To bind the field objects to the text boxes and then test the application:

1. Click the **Question** field object in the Data Sources window and then drag the field object to the questionTextBox, but don't release the mouse button. See Figure 12-38.

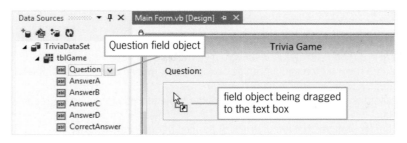

Figure 12-38   Question field object being dragged to the questionTextBox

2. Release the mouse button. The computer binds the Question field object to the questionTextBox. It also adds the TriviaDataSet, TblGameBindingSource, TblGameTableAdapter, and TableAdapterManager objects to the component tray.

3. Drag the AnswerA, AnswerB, AnswerC, and AnswerD field objects to the appropriate text boxes.

4. Save the solution and then start the application. The first record in the dataset appears in the interface, as shown in Figure 12-39.

Figure 12-39   Interface showing the first record

5. Click the **Exit** button to end the application. If necessary, auto-hide the Data Sources, Solution Explorer, and Properties windows.

Coding the Trivia Game Application

According to the application's TOE chart (shown earlier in Figure 12-31), only three event procedures need to be coded: the exitButton's Click event procedure, the MainForm's Load event procedure, and the submitButton's Click event procedure. When you open the Code Editor window, you will notice that the exitButton's Click event procedure has already been coded for you. The MainForm's Load event procedure also contains the appropriate code. Recall that the computer automatically enters the code in the Load event procedure when you drag an object from the Data Sources window to the interface. Therefore, the only procedure you need to code is the submitButton's Click event procedure. The procedure's pseudocode is shown in Figure 12-40.

submitButton Click event procedure
1. store the position of the record pointer in a variable
2. determine the selected radio button and assign its Text property (without the leading ampersand that designates the access key) to a variable named userAnswer
3. if the value in the userAnswer variable does not match the value stored in the current record's CorrectAnswer field
    add 1 to a counter variable that keeps track of the number of incorrect answers
end if
4. if the record pointer is not pointing to the last record
    move the record pointer to the next record in the dataset
else
    display the number of incorrect answers in a message box
end if

Figure 12-40   Pseudocode for the submitButton_Click procedure
© 2013 Cengage Learning

To code the submitButton_Click procedure and then test the code:

1. Open the Code Editor window. In the General Declarations section, replace <your name> and <current date> in the comments with your name and the current date, respectively.

2. Open the code template for the submitButton's Click event procedure. Enter the following comments. Press **Enter** twice after typing the last comment.

   ' determines whether the user's answer is correct
   ' and the number of incorrect answers

3. The procedure will use an Integer variable to keep track of the record pointer's position in the dataset. It will also use a String variable to store the user's answer (A, B, C, or D) to the current question. Enter the following Dim statements:

   Dim ptrPos As Integer
   Dim userAnswer As String

4. The procedure will use a static Integer variable to keep track of the number of incorrect answers made by the user. Type the following Static statement and then press **Enter** twice:

   Static numIncorrect As Integer

5. The first step in the pseudocode stores the record pointer's position in a variable. Enter the following comment and assignment statement. Press **Enter** twice after typing the assignment statement.

   ' store record pointer's position
   ptrPos = TblGameBindingSource.Position

6. Next, the procedure needs to determine the selected radio button and then assign its Text property (without the leading ampersand) to the userAnswer variable. Enter the following comment and Select Case statement:

   ' determine selected radio button
   Select Case True
   **   Case aRadioButton.Checked**
   **   userAnswer = aRadioButton.Text.Substring(1, 1)**
   **   Case bRadioButton.Checked**
   **   userAnswer = bRadioButton.Text.Substring(1, 1)**

```
        Case cRadioButton.Checked
                userAnswer = cRadioButton.Text.Substring(1, 1)
        Case Else
                userAnswer = dRadioButton.Text.Substring(1, 1)
    End Select
```

7. The next step in the pseudocode is a single-alternative selection structure that compares the value in the userAnswer variable with the value in the current record's CorrectAnswer field. If both values are not the same, the procedure should add the number 1 to the value in the numIncorrect variable. Insert **two blank lines** between the End Select and End Sub clauses. Beginning in the blank line above the End Sub clause, enter the following comment and selection structure:

```
' if necessary, update the number of incorrect answers
If userAnswer <>
        TriviaDataSet.tblGame(ptrPos).CorrectAnswer Then
        numIncorrect += 1
End If
```

8. The last step in the pseudocode is a dual-alternative selection structure that determines whether the record pointer is pointing to the last record in the dataset. If it's not, the procedure should move the record pointer to the next record; doing this will display that record's question and answers. However, if the record pointer is pointing to the last record, it means that there are no more questions and answers to display. In that case, the procedure should display the number of incorrect answers made by the user. Insert **two blank lines** between the End If and End Sub clauses. Beginning in the blank line above the End Sub clause, enter the following comment and selection structure:

```
' determine position of record pointer
If ptrPos < 8 Then
        TblGameBindingSource.MoveNext()
Else
        MessageBox.Show("Number incorrect: " &
                        numIncorrect.ToString, "Trivia Game",
                        MessageBoxButtons.OK,
                        MessageBoxIcon.Information)
End If
```

9. Save the solution and then start the application. You will answer the first question correctly. Click the **C** radio button and then click the **Submit Answer** button.

10. You will answer the second question incorrectly. Click the **A** radio button and then click the **Submit Answer** button.

11. Answer the remaining seven questions on your own. When you have submitted the answer for the last question, the submitButton_Click procedure displays the number of incorrect responses in a message box.

12. Close the message box and then click the **Exit** button. Close the Code Editor window and then close the solution. Figure 12-41 shows the Trivia Game application's code.

```
1 ' Project name:        Trivia Game Project
2 ' Project purpose:     Displays trivia questions and
3 '                      answers and the number of incorrect
4 '                      answers made by the user
5 ' Created/revised by:  <your name> on <current date>
6
7 Option Explicit On
8 Option Strict On
9 Option Infer Off
```

Figure 12-41 Code for the Trivia Game application *(continues)*

(continued)

```
10
11  Public Class MainForm
12
13      Private Sub exitButton_Click(ByVal sender As Object,
        ByVal e As System.EventArgs) Handles exitButton.Click
14          Me.Close()
15      End Sub
16
17      Private Sub MainForm_Load(sender As Object,
        e As EventArgs) Handles MyBase.Load
18          'TODO: This line of code loads data into the
            'TriviaDataSet.tblGame' table. You can move,
            or remove it, as needed.
19          Me.TblGameTableAdapter.Fill(Me.TriviaDataSet.tblGame)
20
21      End Sub
22
23      Private Sub submitButton_Click(sender As Object,
        e As EventArgs) Handles submitButton.Click
24          ' determines whether the user's answer is correct
25          ' and the number of incorrect answers
26
27          Dim ptrPos As Integer
28          Dim userAnswer As String
29          Static numIncorrect As Integer
30
31          ' store record pointer's position
32          ptrPos = TblGameBindingSource.Position
33
34          ' determine selected radio button
35          Select Case True
36              Case aRadioButton.Checked
37                  userAnswer = aRadioButton.Text.Substring(1, 1)
38              Case bRadioButton.Checked
39                  userAnswer = bRadioButton.Text.Substring(1, 1)
40              Case cRadioButton.Checked
41                  userAnswer = cRadioButton.Text.Substring(1, 1)
42              Case Else
43                  userAnswer = dRadioButton.Text.Substring(1, 1)
44          End Select
45
46          ' if necessary, update the number of incorrect answers
47          If userAnswer <>
48              TriviaDataSet.tblGame(ptrPos).CorrectAnswer Then
49              numIncorrect += 1
50          End If
51
52          ' determine position of record pointer
53          If ptrPos < 8 Then
54              TblGameBindingSource.MoveNext()
55          Else
56              MessageBox.Show("Number incorrect: " &
57                          numIncorrect.ToString, "Trivia Game",
58                          MessageBoxButtons.OK,
59                          MessageBoxIcon.Information)
60          End If
61      End Sub
62  End Class
```

Figure 12-41   Code for the Trivia Game application

© 2013 Cengage Learning

PROGRAMMING TUTORIAL 2

Coding the Academy Award Winners Application

In this tutorial, you will code an application that uses a Microsoft Access database named Movies to keep track of the Academy Award winners for Best Picture. The database stores the title of each movie, the year the movie won the award, the name(s) of the director(s), and the movie's running time. The application will allow the user to modify the existing records, as well as add records to the database and also delete records from the database. In addition, it will allow the user to display the average running time. Figure 12-42 shows the contents of the tblMovies table in the Movies database.

YearWon	Title	DirectedBy	RunningTime
2000	Gladiator	Ridley Scott	155
2001	A Beautiful Mind	Ron Howard	135
2003	The Lord of the Rings: The Return of the King	Peter Jackson	201
2004	Million Dollar Baby	Clint Eastwood	132
2005	Crash	Paul Haggis	112
2006	The Departed	Martin Scorsese	151
2007	No Country for Old Men	Joel Cohen, Ethan Cohen	122
2008	Slumdog Millionaire	Danny Boyle	120
2009	The Hurt Locker	Kathryn Bigelow	131
2010	The King's Speech	Tom Hooper	118
2011	The Artist	Michel Hazanavicius	100

Figure 12-42   Contents of the tblMovies table in the Movies database

Connecting the Application to the Movies Database

First, you need to open the Academy Award Winners application and connect it to the Movies database.

To open the application and then connect it to the database:

1. Start Visual Studio. Open the **Academy Awards Solution (Academy Awards Solution.sln)** file contained in the VbReloaded2012\Chap12\Academy Awards Solution folder. If necessary, open the designer and Data Sources windows.

2. Click **Add New Data Source** in the Data Sources window to start the Data Source Configuration Wizard. Use the wizard to connect the application to the Movies database, which is stored in the Movies.accdb file. The file is contained in the VbReloaded2012\Chap12\Access Databases folder. In this application, you need the dataset to include all of the fields in the tblMovies table.

The user will be allowed to add, delete, and modify the records in the dataset, so you will need to change the database file's Copy to Output Directory property.

To change the database file's Copy to Output Directory property:

1. Click **Movies.accdb** in the Solution Explorer window, and then use the Properties window to change the Copy to Output Directory property to **Copy if newer**.

Next, you will display the records in a DataGridView control.

To display the records in a DataGridView control:

1. Drag the tblMovies table object from the Data Sources window to the upper-left corner of the form and then release the mouse button.

2. In the Properties window, set the TblMoviesDataGridView control's AutoSizeColumnsMode to **Fill**.

3. Click the **TblMoviesDataGridView** control, click its **task box**, and then click **Dock in Parent Container** on the task list.

4. Now, click **Edit Columns** on the task list to open the Edit Columns dialog box. Click the **Alphabetical** button to display the properties in alphabetical order.

5. Change the YearWon column's HeaderText property to **Year Won**. Also change its AutoSizeMode property to **ColumnHeader**.

6. Click **Title** in the Selected Columns list. Change the column's AutoSizeMode property to **DisplayedCells**.

7. Now, change the DirectedBy column's AutoSizeMode and HeaderText properties to **DisplayedCells** and **Directed By**, respectively.

8. Finally, change the RunningTime column's HeaderText property to **Running Time**.

9. Click the **OK** button to close the Edit Columns dialog box, and then lock the controls on the form.

In the next set of steps, you will begin coding the application.

To begin coding the application:

1. Open the Code Editor window. In the comments that appear in the General Declarations section, replace <your name> and <current date> with your name and the current date, respectively.

2. Include an appropriate Try...Catch statement in the TblMoviesBindingNavigatorSaveItem_Click procedure. If an error occurs in the procedure, display a description of the error in a message box; otherwise, display the "Changes saved" message in a message box.

3. Save the solution and then start the application to display the records in the DataGridView control. Click the **Year Won column** in the empty row at the bottom of the control. Type **2012** and press **Tab**. Now, type **Argo** and press **Tab**. Next, type **Grant Heslov, Ben Affleck, George Clooney** and press **Tab**. Finally, type **130** and press **Enter**.

4. Click the **Save Data** button (the disk) on the BindingNavigator control. The "Changes saved" message appears in a message box. Close the message box, and then close the application by clicking the **Close** button on the form's title bar.

5. Start the application again. The record you entered appears as the last record in the DataGridView control. Now, click the **empty box** that appears to the left of the last record; doing this highlights (selects) the record. Click the **Delete** button (the **X**) on the BindingNavigator control and then click the **Save Data** button.

6. Close the message box, and then close the application. Now, start the application again. The record you deleted no longer appears in the TblMoviesDataGridView control. Close the application.

Adding an Item to the BindingNavigator Control

In the next set of steps, you will add a button to the BindingNavigator control. The button will allow the user to display the average running time of the movies in the dataset.

To add a button to the BindingNavigator control:

1. Make the designer window the active window, and then unlock the controls on the form. Click an **empty area** on the TblMoviesBindingNavigator control and then click the control's **task box**.

2. Click **Edit Items** on the task list to open the Items Collection Editor dialog box. Click the **Add** button. ToolStripButton1 appears at the bottom of the Members list. Click the **Alphabetical** button to display the property names in alphabetical order. Click **(Name)** in the properties list. Type **avgTimeButton** and press **Enter**. Change the **DisplayStyle** property to **Text**, and then change the **Text** property to **Average Time**. See Figure 12-43.

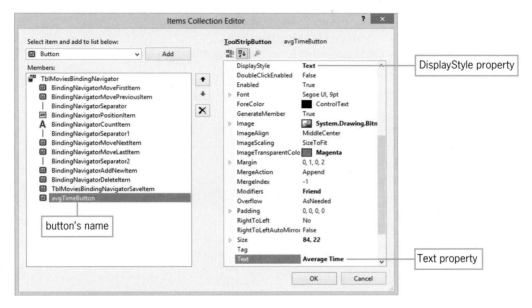

Figure 12-43 avgTimeButton added to the Items Collection Editor dialog box

3. Close the Items Collection Editor dialog box. Lock the controls on the form and then save the solution. The Average Time button appears on the BindingNavigator control, as shown in Figure 12-44.

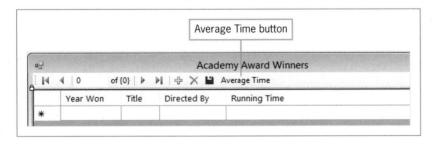

Figure 12-44 Average Time button added to the BindingNavigator control

Coding the Average Time Button's Click Event Procedure

The avgTimeButton_Click procedure will use a LINQ aggregate operator—namely, Average—to calculate the average running time of the movies in the dataset.

To code the avgTimeButton_Click procedure and then test the code:

1. Make the Code Editor window the active window. Open the code template for the avgTimeButton's Click event procedure. Type the following comment and then press **Enter** twice:

    ' display the average running time

2. Enter a LINQ statement that uses the Average aggregate operator to calculate the average running time. Assign the aggregate operator's result to a Double variable named avgRunningTime. Press **Enter** twice after typing the Dim statement.

3. Finally, enter the following statement:

   MessageBox.Show("Average running time: " &
   avgRunningTime.ToString("N1"),
   "Academy Award Winners",
   MessageBoxButtons.OK,
   MessageBoxIcon.Information)

4. Save the solution and then start the application. Click the **Average Time** button. The average running time appears in a message box, as shown in Figure 12-45.

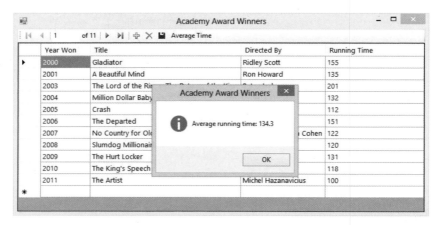

Figure 12-45 Message box showing the average running time

5. Close the message box and then close the application. Close the Code Editor window and then close the solution. Figure 12-46 shows the code for the Academy Award Winners application.

```
 1 ' Project name:      Academy Awards Project
 2 ' Project purpose:   Allows the user to modify, add,
 3 '                    and delete records, and also to
 4 '                    display the average running time
 5
 6 Option Explicit On
 7 Option Strict On
 8 Option Infer Off
 9
10 Public Class MainForm
11
12     Private Sub TblMoviesBindingNavigatorSaveItem_Click(
        sender As Object, e As EventArgs
        ) Handles TblMoviesBindingNavigatorSaveItem.Click
13         Try
14             Me.Validate()
15             Me.TblMoviesBindingSource.EndEdit()
16             Me.TableAdapterManager.UpdateAll(Me.MoviesDataSet)
17             MessageBox.Show("Changes saved",
18                         "Academy Award Winners",
19                         MessageBoxButtons.OK,
20                         MessageBoxIcon.Information)
```

Figure 12-46 Code for the Academy Award Winners application *(continues)*

(continued)

```
21          Catch ex As Exception
22              MessageBox.Show(ex.Message, "Academy Award Winners",
23                              MessageBoxButtons.OK,
24                              MessageBoxIcon.Information)
25          End Try
26      End Sub
27
28      Private Sub MainForm_Load(sender As Object,
        e As EventArgs) Handles MyBase.Load
29              'TODO: This line of code loads data into the
                'MoviesDataSet.tblMovies' table. You can move,
                or remove it, as needed.
30              Me.TblMoviesTableAdapter.Fill(Me.MoviesDataSet.tblMovies)
31
32      End Sub
33
34      Private Sub avgTimeButton_Click(sender As Object,
        e As EventArgs) Handles avgTimeButton.Click
35          ' display the average running time
36
37          Dim avgRunningTime As Double =
38              Aggregate movie In MoviesDataSet.tblMovies
39              Select movie.RunningTime Into Average()
40
41          MessageBox.Show("Average running time: " &
42                          avgRunningTime.ToString("N1"),
43                          "Academy Award Winners",
44                          MessageBoxButtons.OK,
45                          MessageBoxIcon.Information)
46      End Sub
47 End Class
```

Figure 12-46   Code for the Academy Award Winners application
© 2013 Cengage Learning

PROGRAMMING EXAMPLE

Cartwright Industries Application

The sales manager at Cartwright Industries records the item number, name, and price of the company's products in a database named Items. The Items database is stored in the Items.accdb file, which is contained in the VbReloaded2012\Chap12\Access Databases folder. The tblItems table in the database contains 10 records, each composed of three fields. The ItemNum and ItemName fields contain text, and the Price field contains numbers. Create an application that displays the records in a DataGridView control. The application should allow the user to select records whose ItemNum field matches the one or more characters entered by the user. Use the following names for the solution and project, respectively: Cartwright Solution and Cartwright Project. Save the application in the VbReloaded2012\Chap12 folder. Change the form file's name to Main Form.vb. See Figures 12-47 through 12-50.

ItemNum	ItemName	Price
ABX12	Chair	$45.00
CSR14	Desk	$175.00
JTR23	Table	$65.00
NRE09	End Table	$46.00
OOE68	Bookcase	$100.00
PPR00	Coffee Table	$190.00
PRT45	Lamp	$30.00
REZ04	Love Seat	$200.00
THR98	Side Chair	$133.00
WKP10	Sofa	$273.00

Figure 12-47   Contents of the tblItems table in the Items database

Figure 12-48   MainForm

Object	Property	Setting
MainForm	Font	Segoe UI, 10pt
	MaximizeBox	False
	StartPosition	CenterScreen
	Text	Cartwright Industries
TblItemsDataGridView	AutoSizeColumnsMode	Fill
ItemNum column	HeaderText	Number
ItemName column	HeaderText	Name
Price column	DefaultCellStyle	Format: N2
		Alignment: MiddleRight
Number button	Name	numberButton
	DisplayStyle	Text
	Text	Number

Figure 12-49   Objects, properties, and settings
© 2013 Cengage Learning

```vb
1  ' Project name:        Cartwright Project
2  ' Project purpose:     Displays all records from a dataset
3  '                      or those matching an item number
4  ' Created/revised by:  <your name> on <current date>
5
6  Option Explicit On
7  Option Strict On
8  Option Infer On
9
10 Public Class MainForm
11
12     Private Sub TblItemsBindingNavigatorSaveItem_Click(
        sender As Object, e As EventArgs
        ) Handles TblItemsBindingNavigatorSaveItem.Click
13         Try
14             Me.Validate()
15             Me.TblItemsBindingSource.EndEdit()
16             Me.TableAdapterManager.UpdateAll(Me.ItemsDataSet)
17
18             MessageBox.Show("Changes saved",
19                             "Cartwright Industries",
20                             MessageBoxButtons.OK,
21                             MessageBoxIcon.Information)
22         Catch ex As Exception
23             MessageBox.Show(ex.Message,
24                             "Cartwright Industries",
25                             MessageBoxButtons.OK,
26                             MessageBoxIcon.Information)
27         End Try
28     End Sub
29
30     Private Sub MainForm_Load(sender As Object,
        e As EventArgs) Handles MyBase.Load
31         'TODO: This line of code loads data into the
           'ItemsDataSet.tblItems' table. You can move, or
           remove it, as needed.
32         Me.TblItemsTableAdapter.Fill(Me.ItemsDataSet.tblItems)
33
34     End Sub
35
36     Private Sub numberButton_Click(sender As Object,
        e As EventArgs) Handles numberButton.Click
37         ' displays records matching an item number
38
39         Dim itemNum As String
40         Const Prompt As String = "One or more characters " &
41             "(leave empty to retrieve all records):"
42
43         ' get item number
44         itemNum = InputBox(Prompt, "Item Number")
45         itemNum = itemNum.ToUpper.Trim
46
47         ' select records matching item number
48         Dim records = From item In ItemsDataSet.tblItems
49             Where item.ItemNum.ToUpper Like itemNum & "*"
50             Select item
51
52         TblItemsBindingSource.DataSource = records.AsDataView
53     End Sub
54 End Class
```

Figure 12-50 Code
© 2013 Cengage Learning

Summary

- You can use Visual Basic to access the data stored in databases created by many different database management systems.

- Databases created by Microsoft Access are relational databases. A relational database can contain one or more tables. Each table consists of rows and columns.

- Most tables contain a primary key that uniquely identifies each record.

- The data in a relational database can be displayed in any order, and you can control the amount of information you want to view.

- To access the data stored in a database, you first connect an application to the database. Doing this creates a dataset that contains objects, such as table objects and field objects.

- You can display the information contained in a dataset by binding one or more of the objects in the dataset to one or more controls in the application's interface.

- A TableAdapter object connects a database to a DataSet object.

- A BindingSource object connects a DataSet object to the bound controls on a form.

- The DataGridView control displays data in a row and column format, similar to a spreadsheet. The intersection of a column and a row is called a cell.

- In most applications, the statement to fill a dataset with data is entered in the form's Load event procedure.

- You can use the Try...Catch statement to handle any exceptions that occur while an application is running. A description of the exception is stored in the Message property of the Catch block's **ex** parameter.

- A database file's Copy to Output Directory property determines when and if the file is copied from the project folder to the project folder's bin\Debug folder each time the application is started.

- The BindingSource object uses an invisible record pointer to keep track of the current record in the dataset. The location of the record pointer is stored in the object's Position property.

- You can use the BindingSource object's Move methods to move the record pointer in a dataset.

- You can access the value stored in a field object in a dataset.

- You can use LINQ to select and arrange the records in a dataset. LINQ also provides the Average, Sum, Count, Min, and Max aggregate operators.

- You can include additional items, such as text boxes and drop-down buttons, on a BindingNavigator control. You also can delete items from the control.

Key Terms

Aggregate operator—an operator that returns a single value from a group of values; LINQ provides the Average, Count, Max, Min, and Sum aggregate operators

Binding—the process of connecting an object in a dataset to a control on a form

BindingNavigator control—can be used to move the record pointer from one record to another in a dataset, as well as to add, delete, and save records

BindingSource object—connects a DataSet object to the bound controls on a form

Bound controls—the controls connected to an object in a dataset

Cell—the intersection of a row and a column in a DataGridView control

Child table—a table linked to a parent table

Computer database—an electronic file that contains an organized collection of related information

Copy to Output Directory property—a property of a database file; determines when and if the file is copied from the project folder to the project folder's bin\Debug folder

DataGridView control—displays data in a row and column format

Dataset—a copy of the data (database fields and records) that can be accessed by an application

DataSet object—stores the information you want to access from a database

Exception—an error that occurs while an application is running

Foreign key—the field used to link a child table to a parent table

Language Integrated Query—LINQ; the query language built into Visual Basic 2012

LINQ—an acronym for Language Integrated Query

Move methods—methods of a BindingSource object; used to move the record pointer to the first, last, next, or previous record in a dataset

Order By clause—used in LINQ to arrange (sort) the records in a dataset

Parent table—a table linked to a child table

Position property—a property of a BindingSource object; stores the position of the record pointer

Primary key—the field that uniquely identifies each record in a table

Query—specifies the records to select in a dataset and the order in which to arrange the records

Relational database—a database that stores information in tables composed of columns (fields) and rows (records)

Table—a group of related records

TableAdapter object—connects a database to a DataSet object

TableAdapterManager object—handles saving data to multiple tables in a dataset

Try...Catch statement—used for exception handling in a procedure

Where clause—used in LINQ to limit the records you want to view in a dataset

Review Questions

Each Review Question is associated with one or more objectives listed at the beginning of the chapter.

1. The _____ property stores an integer that represents the location of the record pointer in a dataset. (4, 7)

   a. BindingNavigator object's Position

   b. BindingSource object's Position

   c. BindingSource object's Location

   d. TableAdapter object's Location

2. If the record pointer is positioned on record number 5 in a dataset, which of the following will move the record pointer to record number 4? (4, 7)

   a. `TblBooksBindingSource.GoPrevious()`

   b. `TblBooksBindingSource.Move(4)`

   c. `TblBooksBindingSource.MovePrevious()`

   d. `TblBooksBindingSource.PositionPrevious()`

3. The _____ object provides the connection between a DataSet object and a control on a form. (3, 4)

   a. Bound   c. BindingSource

   b. Binding   d. Connecting

4. The process of connecting a control to an object in a dataset is called _____. (3)

   a. assigning   c. joining

   b. binding   d. none of the above

5. Which of the following will select only records whose LastName field begins with an uppercase letter A? (9)

   a.
```
Dim records = From name In NamesDataSet.tblNames
        Where name.LastName Like "A*"
        Select name
```

   b.
```
Dim records = From NamesDataSet.tblNames
        Select LastName Like "A*"
```

   c.
```
Dim records = From tblNames
        Where tblName.LastName Like "A*"
        Select name
```

   d.
```
Dim records = From name In NamesDataSet.tblNames
        Where tblName.LastName Like "A*"
        Select name
```

6. Which of the following calculates the sum of the values stored in a numeric field named JulySales? (11)

   a.
```
Dim total As Double =
        From sales In SalesDataSet.tblSales
        Select sales.JulySales Into Sum()
```

   b.
```
Dim total As Double =
        Aggregate sales In SalesDataSet.tblSales
        Select sales.JulySales Into Sum()
```

   c.
```
Dim total As Double =
        From sales In SalesDataSet.tblSales
        Aggregate sales.JulySales Into Sum()
```

   d.
```
Dim total As Double =
        From sales In SalesDataSet.tblSales
        Sum sales.JulySales
```

7. The tblCities table contains a numeric field named Population. Which of the following statements selects all cities having a population that exceeds 15,000? (9)

   a.
```
Dim records = From city In CitiesDataSet.tblCities
        Where Population > 15000
        Select city
```

b. ```
Dim records = From city In CitiesDataSet.tblCities
      Select city.Population > 15000
```

c. ```
Dim records = From city In CitiesDataSet.tblCities
      Where city.Population > 15000 Select city
```

d. ```
Dim records = Select city.Population > 15000
      From tblCities
```

8. Which clause is used in a LINQ statement to limit the records that will be selected? (9)

   a. Limit
   b. Order By
   c. Select
   d. Where

9. Which of the following determines the number of records in the tblBooks table? (11)

   a. ```
Dim num As Integer =
      Aggregate book In BooksDataSet.tblBooks
      In Count()
```

   b. ```
Dim num As Integer =
      Aggregate book In BooksDataSet.tblBooks
      Into Count()
```

   c. ```
Dim num As Integer =
      Aggregate book In BooksDataSet.tblBooks
      Into Sum()
```

   d. ```
Dim num As Integer =
      Aggregate book From BooksDataSet.tblBooks
      Into Counter()
```

10. An application's BindingSource, BindingNavigator, DataSet, and table objects are named TblCustsBindingSource, TblCustsBindingNavigator, CustomersDataSet, and tblCusts, respectively. Which of the following assigns the value stored in the first record's City field to the cityName variable? (8)

   a. ```
cityName =
      TblCustsBindingNavigator.tblCusts(0).City
```

   b. ```
cityName = tblCusts(0).City
```

   c. ```
cityName = TblCustsBindingSource.City(0)
```

   d. ```
cityName = CustomersDataSet.tblCusts(0).City
```

# Exercises

 *Pencil and Paper*

Each Exercise is associated with one or more objectives listed at the beginning of the chapter.

1. Write a statement that assigns the location of a dataset's record pointer to an Integer variable named **recNum**. The BindingSource object's name is TblCityBindingSource. (7)

   **INTRODUCTORY**

2. Write a statement that moves the record pointer to the last record in the dataset. The BindingSource object's name is TblCityBindingSource. (7)

   **INTRODUCTORY**

3. The tblMagInfo table contains three fields. The Code and Cost fields are numeric. The Magazine field contains text. The dataset's name is MagsDataSet. (9)

   **INTRODUCTORY**

   a. Write a LINQ statement that arranges the records in descending order by the Cost field.

   b. Write a LINQ statement that selects records having a code of 9.
```

c. Write a LINQ statement that selects records having a cost of at least $3.

d. Write a LINQ statement that selects the Daily Food Guide magazine.

4. Using the information from Pencil and Paper Exercise 3, write a LINQ statement that selects magazines whose name begins with the letter G (in either uppercase or lowercase). Also write a LINQ statement that calculates the average cost of a magazine. (9, 11)

 Computer

5. Open the Morgan Industries Solution (Morgan Industries Solution.sln) file contained in the VbReloaded2012\Chap12\Morgan Industries Solution-Labels folder. Modify the Next Record and Previous Record buttons' Click event procedures to use the Position property rather than the MoveNext and MovePrevious methods. Save the solution and then start and test the application. Close the solution. (4, 7)

6. If necessary, complete the Trivia Game application from this chapter's Programming Tutorial 1, and then close the solution. Use Windows to make a copy of the Trivia Game Solution folder. Rename the folder Trivia Game Solution-ModifyThis. Open the Trivia Game Solution (Trivia Game Solution.sln) file contained in the Trivia Game Solution-ModifyThis folder. Display the question number (from 1 through 9) along with the word "Question" in a label control in the interface. Add another button to the interface. The button should allow the user to start a new game. Allow the user to click the New Game button only after he or she has answered all nine questions. Save the solution and then start and test the application. Close the solution. (2-4, 7, 9)

7. Open the Morgan Industries Solution (Morgan Industries Solution.sln) file contained in the VbReloaded2012\Chap12\Morgan Industries Solution-ListBox folder. Unlock the controls and then delete the numberLabel control from the form. Also delete the Previous Record and Next Record buttons and their Click event procedures. Add a list box to the form. Set the list box's Name, DataSource, and DisplayMember properties to numberListBox, TblEmployBindingSource, and Emp_Number, respectively. Lock the controls and then reset the tab order. Save the solution and then start and test the application. Close the solution. (4)

8. Open the Morgan Industries Solution (Morgan Industries Solution.sln) file contained in the VbReloaded2012\Chap12\Morgan Industries Solution-DropDownButton folder. (9-11)

   a. Add a DropDownButton to the BindingNavigator control. Change the DropDownButton's Name, DisplayStyle, and Text properties to deptDropDownButton, Text, and Department, respectively.

   b. Use the DropDownItems property to add four items to the DropDownButton: Accounting (Code 1), Advertising (Code 2), Personnel (Code 3), and Inventory (Code 4). Be sure to change each menu item's name, as well as its DisplayStyle and Text properties. Each item should display (in a message box) the number of employees in the department. Code each item's Click event procedure. Save the solution and then start and test the application. Close the solution.

9. Sydney Industries records the item number, name, and price of each of its products in a database named Products. The Products database is stored in the VbReloaded2012\Chap12\Access Databases folder. The database contains a table named tblProducts. The table contains 10 records, each composed of three fields. The ItemNum and ItemName fields contain text; the Price field contains numbers. Open the Sydney Solution (Sydney Solution.sln) file contained in the VbReloaded2012\Chap12\Sydney

Solution-DataGridView folder. Connect the application to the Products database. Change the database file's Copy to Output Directory property to Copy if newer. Bind the table to a DataGridView control and then make the necessary modifications to the control. Enter the Try...Catch statement in the Save Data button's Click event procedure. Include appropriate messages. Save the solution and then start and test the application. Close the solution. (2-6)

10. Sydney Industries records the item number, name, and price of each of its products in a database named Products. The Products database is stored in the VbReloaded2012\ Chap12\Access Databases folder. The database contains a table named tblProducts. The table contains 10 records, each composed of three fields. The ItemNum and ItemName fields contain text; the Price field contains numbers. Open the Sydney Solution (Sydney Solution.sln) file contained in the VbReloaded2012\Chap12\Sydney Solution-Labels folder. Connect the application to the Products database. Bind the appropriate objects to the existing label controls. Code the Click event procedures for the Next Record and Previous Record buttons. Save the solution and then start and test the application. Close the solution. (2-4, 7)

11. Open the Magazine Solution (Magazine Solution.sln) file contained in the VbReloaded2012\Chap12\Magazine Solution-Introductory folder. The application is connected to the Magazines database, which is stored in the Magazines.accdb file. The database contains a table named tblMagazine; the table has three fields. The Cost field is numeric. The Code and MagName fields contain text. Start the application to view the records contained in the dataset, and then stop the application. Open the Code Editor window. The codeButton_Click procedure should display the record whose Code field contains EX33. The nameButton_Click procedure should display only the Visual Basic record. The allButton_Click procedure should display all of the records. Code the three procedures. Save the solution and then start and test the application. Close the solution. (4, 9)

12. The MusicBox database is stored in the VbReloaded2012\Chap12\Access Databases\ MusicBox.accdb file. The database contains a table named tblBox. The table contains 10 records, each composed of four text fields. Open the MusicBox Solution (MusicBox Solution.sln) file contained in the VbReloaded2012\Chap12\MusicBox Solution-DataGridView folder. Connect the application to the MusicBox database. Change the database file's Copy to Output Directory property to Copy if newer. Bind the table to a DataGridView control and then make the necessary modifications to the control. Enter the Try...Catch statement in the Save Data button's Click event procedure. Include appropriate messages. Save the solution and then start and test the application. Close the solution. (2-6)

13. The MusicBox database is stored in the VbReloaded2012\Chap12\Access Databases\ MusicBox.accdb file. The database contains a table named tblBox. The table contains 10 records, each composed of four text fields. Open the MusicBox Solution (MusicBox Solution.sln) file contained in the VbReloaded2012\Chap12\MusicBox Solution-Labels folder. Connect the application to the MusicBox database. Bind the appropriate objects to the existing label controls. Code the Click event procedures for the Next Record and Previous Record buttons. Save the solution and then start and test the application. Close the Code Editor window and then close the solution. (2-4, 7)

14. Open the Addison Playhouse Solution (Addison Playhouse Solution.sln) file contained in the VbReloaded2012\Chap12\Addison Playhouse Solution folder. Connect the application to a Microsoft Access database named Play. The database is stored in the VbReloaded2012\Chap12\Access Databases\Play.accdb file. The Play database contains one table named tblReservations. The table has 20 records. Each record has three fields: a numeric field named Seat, and two text fields named Patron and Phone. The application

should display the contents of the dataset in a DataGridView control. It should also allow the user to add, delete, modify, and save records. Enter the Try...Catch statement in the Save Data button's Click event procedure. Include appropriate messages. Save the solution and then start and test the application. Close the solution. (2-6)

INTERMEDIATE

662

15. Open the Magazine Solution (Magazine Solution.sln) file contained in the VbReloaded2012\Chap12\Magazine Solution-Intermediate folder. The application is connected to the Magazines database stored in the Magazines.accdb file. The database contains a table named tblMagazine; the table has three fields. The Cost field is numeric. The Code and MagName fields contain text. Start the application to view the records contained in the dataset, and then stop the application. The allButton_Click procedure should display all of the records. The costButton_Click procedure should display records having a cost of at least $4. The nameButton_Click procedure should display only magazines whose name begins with the letter C (in either uppercase or lowercase). The avgButton_Click procedure should display the average cost of a magazine in a message box. Code the four procedures. Save the solution and then start and test the application. Close the solution. (9, 11)

INTERMEDIATE

16. Open the MusicBox Solution (MusicBox Solution.sln) file contained in the VbReloaded2012\Chap12\MusicBox Solution-LINQ folder. The application is connected to the MusicBox database stored in the MusicBox.accdb file. The database contains a table named tblBox. The table contains 10 records, each composed of four text fields. Start the application to view the records contained in the dataset, and then stop the application. The allButton_Click procedure should display all of the records. The shapeButton_Click procedure should display the records for music boxes having the shape selected by the user. The sourceButton_Click procedure should display either the records for music boxes received as gifts, or the records for music boxes that were purchased by the user. The countButton_Click procedure should display the number of music boxes in the dataset. Code the four procedures. Save the solution and then start and test the application. Close the solution. (9, 11)

INTERMEDIATE

17. In this exercise, you use a Microsoft Access database named Trips. The database keeps track of a person's business and pleasure trips. The database is stored in the VbReloaded2012\Chap12\Access Databases\Trips.accdb file. The database contains one table named tblTrips. The table has 10 records. Each record has the following four text fields: TripDate, Origin, Destination, and BusinessPleasure. The user should be able to display the number of trips from a specific origin to a specific destination, such as from Chicago to Nashville. He or she should also be able to display the total number of business trips and the total number of pleasure trips. (7, 9)

   a. Create a Visual Basic Windows application. Use the following names for the solution and project, respectively: Trips Solution and Trips Project. Save the application in the VbReloaded2012\Chap12 folder. Change the form file's name to Main Form.vb.

   b. Connect the application to the Trips database and then drag the tblTrips object to the form. Make the appropriate modifications to the interface.

   c. Open the Code Editor window and code the application. Be sure to enter the Try...Catch statement in the Save Data button's Click event procedure. (Hint: While coding the application, keep in mind that you can use a logical operator in the Where clause.) Save the solution and then start the application. Use the application to answer the following questions:

      How many trips were made from Chicago to Nashville?
      How many trips were made from Atlanta to Los Angeles?
      How many business trips were taken?
      How many pleasure trips were taken?

   d. Close the solution.

18. Open the Debug Solution (Debug Solution.sln) file contained in the VbReloaded2012\Chap12\Debug Solution folder. The application is connected to the Friends database stored in the Friends.accdb file. The database contains one table named tblFriends. The table contains nine records. Open the Code Editor window and review the existing code. Correct the code to remove the jagged line that appears below one of the lines of code. Save the solution and then start and test the application. Click the Fill button and then click the Next and Previous buttons. Notice that the application is not working correctly. Correct the application's code. When the application is working correctly, close the solution. (7)

Case Projects

Modified Trivia Game

If necessary, complete the Trivia Game application from this chapter's Programming Tutorial 1, and then close the solution. Use Windows to make a copy of the Trivia Game Solution folder. Rename the folder Trivia Game Solution-Case Project. Open the Trivia Game Solution (Trivia Game Solution.sln) file contained in the Trivia Game Solution-Case Project folder. Modify the application to allow the user to answer the questions in any order and also to change his or her answers. (You can modify the interface to include additional buttons.) The modified application should display the number of incorrect answers only when the user requests that information. Make the appropriate modifications to the code. Save the solution and then start and test the application. Close the solution. (2-4, 7, 8)

College Courses

In this Case Project, you use a Microsoft Access database named Courses. The database is stored in the VbReloaded2012\Chap12\Access Databases\Courses.accdb file. The database contains one table named tblCourses. The table has 10 records. Each record has the following four fields: ID, Title, CreditHours, and Grade. The CreditHours field is numeric; the other fields contain text. Create an application that allows the user to display the records for a specific grade (A, B, C, D, or F). The user should also be able to display all of the records. Display the records in a DataGridView control. The application should not allow the user to add or delete records. Include a Calculate GPA button on the BindingNavigator control. The button's Click event procedure should display the student's GPA. An A grade is worth 4 points, a B is worth 3 points, and so on. Use the following names for the solution and project, respectively: College Courses Solution and College Courses Project. Save the application in the VbReloaded2012\Chap12 folder. Change the form file's name to Main Form.vb. (2-11)

Political Awareness Organization

During July and August of each year, the Political Awareness Organization (PAO) sends a questionnaire to the voters in its district. The questionnaire asks the voter for his or her political party (Democratic, Republican, or Independent) and age. From the returned questionnaires, the organization's secretary tabulates the number of Democrats, Republicans, and Independents in the district. The secretary wants an application that she can use to save each respondent's information (political party and age) in a database named PAO. The PAO database is stored in the VbReloaded2012\Chap12\Access Databases\PAO.accdb file. The database contains one table named tblQuestionnaire. The table has 15 records. Each record has a text field named Party, and two numeric fields named Id and Age. The application should also allow the secretary to edit and delete records, as well as to calculate and display the number of voters in each political party. Use a DataGridView control in the interface. Use the following names for the solution and project, respectively: PAO Solution and PAO Project. Save the application in the VbReloaded2012\Chap12 folder. Change the form file's name to Main Form.vb. (2-6, 9, 11)

 ## The Fiction Bookstore

Jerry Schmidt, the manager of the Fiction Bookstore, uses a Microsoft Access database named Books to keep track of the books in his store. The database is stored in the VbReloaded2012\ Chap12\Access Databases\Books.accdb file. The database has one table named tblBooks. The table has five fields. The BookNumber, Price, and QuantityInStock fields are numeric. The Title and Author fields contain text. Mr. Schmidt wants an application that he can use to enter an author's name (or part of a name) and then display only the titles of books written by the author. Display the information in a DataGridView control; however, don't allow the user to add, delete, modify, or save records. In this application, you need to allow the user to specify the records he or she wants to select while the application is running. Add a text box and a button to the BindingNavigator control. Mr. Schmidt will use the text box to specify the records he wants to select. He will use the button to tell the computer to display the selected records. Mr. Schmidt also wants to display the total value of the books in his store. Use the following names for the solution and project, respectively: Fiction Bookstore Solution and Fiction Bookstore Project. Save the application in the VbReloaded2012\Chap12 folder. Change the form file's name to Main Form.vb. (2-6, 9-11)

 ## Counting Calories

In this Case Project, you use a Microsoft Access database named Calories. The database is stored in the VbReloaded2012\Chap12\Access Databases\Calories.accdb file. The database contains one table named tblCalories. The table has 10 records. Each record has the following six fields: Day, Breakfast, Lunch, Dinner, Dessert, and Snack. The Day field contains text; the other fields are numeric. Create an application that allows the user to display the total number of calories consumed in the entire dataset. The user should also be able to add, delete, and edit records, as well as to display the total calories consumed for a specific meal, such as the total calories consumed for breakfasts, lunches, dinners, desserts, or snacks. In addition, the user should be able to display the total calories consumed on a specific day, the number of days in which more than 1200 calories were consumed, and the average number of calories consumed per day. Use the following names for the solution and project, respectively: Calorie Counter Solution and Calorie Counter Project. Save the application in the VbReloaded2012\Chap12 folder. Change the form file's name to Main Form.vb. Use the application to answer the questions listed below. (2-6, 9, 11)

How many calories were consumed in the entire dataset?
How many calories were consumed for desserts?
How many calories were consumed on 12/21/2013?
On how many days were more than 1200 calories consumed?
What is the average number of calories consumed per day?

CHAPTER 3

Creating Simple Web Applications

After studying Chapter 13, you should be able to:

1 Define basic Web terminology

2 Create a Web site project

3 Add Web pages to a Web site project

4 Customize a Web page

5 Code a control on a Web page

6 View a Web page in full screen view

7 Start a Web site project

8 Close and open a Web site project

9 Use image and link button controls (Programming Tutorial 1)

10 Use label, text box, button, and validator controls (Programming Tutorial 2)

Reading and Study Guide

Before you begin reading Chapter 13, view the Ch13_ReadingStudyGuide.pdf file. You can open the file using Adobe Reader, which is available for free on the Adobe Web site at *www.adobe.com/downloads/*.

666

Web Site Projects

The Internet is the world's largest computer network, connecting millions of computers located all around the world. One of the most popular features of the Internet is the World Wide Web, often referred to simply as the Web. The Web consists of documents called **Web pages** that are stored on Web servers. A **Web server** is a computer that contains special software that "serves up" Web pages in response to requests from client computers. A **client computer** is a computer that requests information from a Web server. The information is requested and subsequently viewed through the use of a program called a Web browser or, more simply, a **browser**. Currently, the most popular browsers are Microsoft Internet Explorer, Google Chrome, and Mozilla Firefox.

Many Web pages are static. A **static Web page** is a document whose purpose is merely to display information to the viewer. Static Web pages are not interactive. The only interaction that can occur between static Web pages and the viewer is through links that allow the viewer to "jump" from one Web page to another. Figures 13-1 and 13-2 show examples of static Web pages created for the Barclay Bakery store. The Web page in Figure 13-1 shows the store's name, address, and telephone number. The page also provides a link to the Web page shown in Figure 13-2. That page shows the store's business hours and provides a link for returning to the first Web page. You will create both Web pages in Programming Tutorial 1.

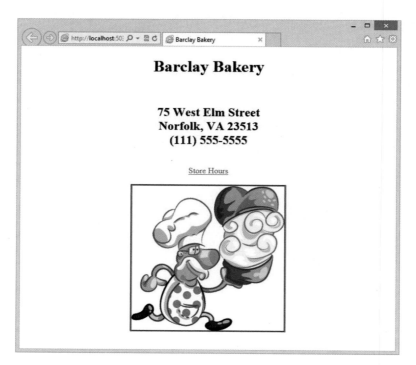

Figure 13-1   Example of a static Web page
OpenClipArt.org/Przylga

Figure 13-2 Another example of a static Web page

Although static Web pages provide a means for a store to list its location and hours, a company wanting to do business on the Web must be able to do more than just list information: It must be able to interact with customers through its Web site. The Web site should allow customers to submit inquiries, select items for purchase, and submit payment information. It should also allow the company to track customer inquiries and process customer orders. Tasks such as these can be accomplished using dynamic Web pages.

Unlike a static Web page, a **dynamic Web page** is interactive in that it can accept information from the user and also retrieve information for the user. Examples of dynamic Web pages include forms for purchasing merchandise online and for submitting online résumés. Figure 13-3 shows an example of a dynamic Web page that converts U.S. dollars to Mexican pesos. The Web page provides a text box for the user to enter the number of U.S. dollars. When the user clicks the Submit button, the button's Click event procedure will display the corresponding number of Mexican pesos on the Web page. You will create the Dollars to Pesos Web page in Programming Tutorial 2.

Figure 13-3 Example of a dynamic Web page
OpenClipArt.org/Onsemeliot

The Web site projects created in this chapter use a technology called ASP.NET 4.5. **ASP** stands for "Active Server Pages" and refers to the type of Web page created by the ASP technology. All ASP pages contain HTML (Hypertext Markup Language) tags that tell the client's browser how to render the page on the computer screen. For example, the instruction <h1>Hello</h1> uses the opening <h1> tag and its closing </h1> tag to display the word "Hello" as a heading on the Web page. Many ASP pages also contain ASP tags that specify the controls to include on the Web page. In addition to the HTML and ASP tags, dynamic ASP pages contain code that tells the objects on the Web page how to respond to the user's actions. In this chapter, you will write the appropriate code using the Visual Basic programming language.

When a client computer's browser sends a request for an ASP page, the Web server locates the page and then sends the appropriate HTML instructions to the client. The client's browser uses the instructions to render the Web page on the computer screen. If the Web page is a dynamic one, like the Dollars to Pesos page shown in Figure 13-3, the user can interact with the page by entering data. In most cases, the user then clicks a button on the Web page to submit the data to the server for processing. When the server receives the data, it executes the Visual Basic code associated with the Web page. It then sends back the appropriate HTML, which now includes the result of processing the code and data, to the client for rendering in the browser window. Using the Dollars to Pesos Web page as an example, the user first enters the number of U.S. dollars and then clicks the Submit button, which submits the user's entry to the Web server. The server executes the Visual Basic code to convert the U.S. dollars to Mexican pesos and then sends back the HTML, which now includes the number of pesos. Notice that the Web page's HTML is interpreted and executed by the client computer, whereas the program code is executed by the Web server. Figure 13-4 illustrates the relationship between the client computer and the Web server.

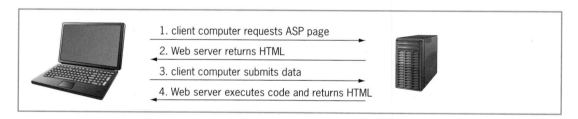

Figure 13-4   Illustration of the relationship between a client computer and a Web server
© 2013 Cengage Learning

Creating a Web Site Project

You can create a Web site project using Visual Studio 2012 for Web, which is available either as a stand-alone product (called Visual Studio Express 2012 for Web) or as part of Visual Studio 2012. You can download a free copy of Visual Studio Express 2012 for Web from Microsoft's Web site. At the time of this writing, the address is *http://www.microsoft.com/visualstudio/eng/products/visual-studio-express-for-web*. Figure 13-5 lists the steps for starting and configuring the Express edition.

HOW TO Start and Configure Visual Studio Express 2012 for Web

1. *Windows 8:* If necessary, tap the Windows logo key to switch to the Windows 8 tile-based mode and then click the VS Express for Web tile.

   Windows 7: Click the Start button on the taskbar, point to All Programs, click Microsoft Visual Studio Express 2012, and then click Visual Studio Express 2012 for Web.

2. Click TOOLS on the menu bar and then point to Settings. If necessary, click Expert Settings to select it.

3. Click TOOLS on the menu bar, click Options, and then click the Project and Solutions node. If necessary, select the following four check boxes: Always show Error List if build finishes with errors, Track Active Item in Solution Explorer, Always show solution, and Save new projects when created. Deselect the remaining check boxes. (See figure below.)

4. Click the OK button to close the Options dialog box.

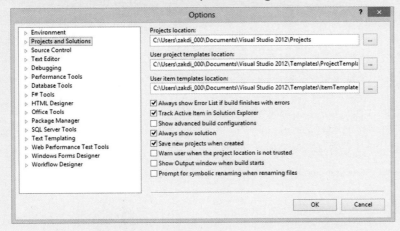

Figure 13-5   How to start and configure Visual Studio Express 2012 for Web
© 2013 Cengage Learning

Figure 13-6 lists the steps for creating an empty Web site project. It also includes an example of a completed New Web Site dialog box. Your dialog box will look slightly different if you are using the Express edition.

HOW TO Create an Empty Web Site Project

1. Start either Visual Studio 2012 or Visual Studio Express 2012 for Web.

2. Click FILE on the menu bar and then click New Web Site to open the New Web Site dialog box. If necessary, click Visual Basic in the Installed Templates list. Click ASP.NET Empty Web Site in the middle column of the dialog box.

3. If necessary, change the entry in the Web location box to File System. The File System selection allows you to store your Web site project in any folder on either your computer or a network drive.

4. In the box that appears next to the Web location box, enter the location where you want the Web site project saved. (See figure below.)

5. Click the OK button to close the New Web Site dialog box.

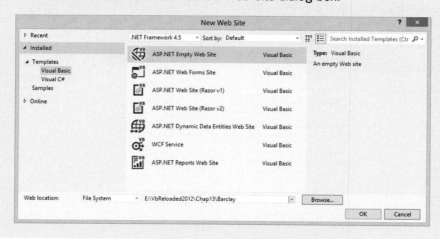

Figure 13-6   How to create an empty Web site project
© 2013 Cengage Learning

Adding a Web Page to the Project

After creating an empty Web site project, you need to add a Web page to it. The default name for the first Web page added to a project is Default.aspx. The .aspx file contains the instructions for rendering the visual elements on the Web page. Figure 13-7 lists the steps for adding a new Web page to a project. It also shows an example of a completed Add New Item dialog box, as well as an example of the Default.aspx Web page in Design view. Your dialog box and screen will look slightly different if you are using the Express edition.

HOW TO Add a New Web Page to a Web Site Project

1. If necessary, open the project. Click WEBSITE on the menu bar and then click Add New Item to open the Add New Item dialog box. (If WEBSITE does not appear on the menu bar, click the project's name in the Solution Explorer window.)

2. If necessary, click Visual Basic in the Installed list and then (if necessary) click Web Form in the middle column of the dialog box. Verify that the Place code in separate file check box is selected, and that the Select master page check box is not selected. (See first figure below.)

3. If necessary, change the name in the Name box.

4. Click the Add button to display the Web page in the Document window. If necessary, click the Design tab that appears at the bottom of the IDE. You can use Design view to add text and controls to the Web page. (See second figure below.)

5. If you need to display the Formatting toolbar, click VIEW on the menu bar, point to Toolbars, and then click Formatting.

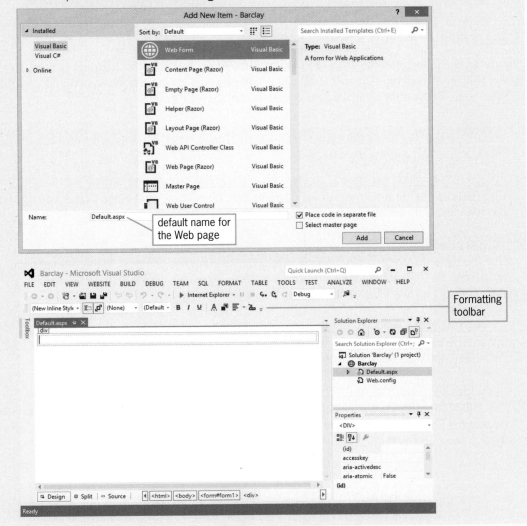

Figure 13-7 How to add a new Web page to a Web site project
© 2013 Cengage Learning

672

Figure 13-8 lists the steps for adding an existing Web page to a Web site project.

HOW TO Add an Existing Web Page to a Web Site Project

1. If necessary, open the project. Click WEBSITE on the menu bar and then click Add Existing Item to open the Add Existing Item dialog box. (If WEBSITE does not appear on the menu bar, click the project's name in the Solution Explorer window.)

2. Locate and then click the name of the file that contains the Web page. The filename will end with .aspx.

3. Click the Add button to display the Web page in the Document window. If necessary, click the Design tab that appears at the bottom of the IDE.

Figure 13-8 How to add an existing Web page to a Web site project
© 2013 Cengage Learning

Customizing a Web Page

Figure 13-9 shows different ways of customizing a Web page. As the figure indicates, you can add a title, controls, and text to a Web page. You can also format the static text and controls on a Web page. **Static text** is text that the user is not allowed to edit.

HOW TO Customize a Web Page

<u>To add a title, which will appear on the page's tab in the browser window:</u>
Click DOCUMENT in the Properties window's Object box, click Title in the Properties list, type the title, and then press Enter.

<u>To add a control:</u>
Use the tools provided in the Toolbox window. Like Windows controls, Web controls have properties that are listed in the Properties window. However, unlike Windows controls, Web controls have an ID property rather than a Name property.

<u>To add static text, which is text the user cannot edit:</u>
Either type the text directly on the Web page, or drag a label control from the toolbox to the Web page and then set the control's Text property.

<u>To format the static text or controls:</u>
Use either the FORMAT menu or the Formatting toolbar (shown in the figure below). You can display the Formatting toolbar by clicking VIEW on the menu bar, pointing to Toolbars, and then clicking Formatting.

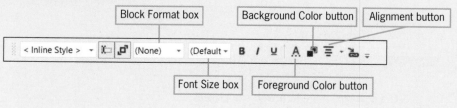

Figure 13-9 How to customize a Web page
© 2013 Cengage Learning

Coding the Controls on a Web Page

Like the controls on a Windows form, the controls on a Web page can be coded to perform tasks when a specific event occurs. The submitButton_Click procedure shown in Figure 13-10, for example, will display the message "The Submit button was clicked." in the messageLabel when the user clicks the Submit button on the Web page. You enter the code in the Code Editor window. The code is saved in a file whose filename extension is .aspx.vb. The .aspx.vb extension indicates that the file contains the Visual Basic code for a Web page. The .aspx.vb file is commonly referred to as the code-behind file because it contains the code "behind" the Web page.

```
Protected Sub submitButton_Click(sender As Object,
                e As EventArgs) Handles submitButton.Click
    messageLabel.Text = "The Submit button was clicked."
End Sub
```

Figure 13-10   Code entered in the Submit button's Click event procedure

Viewing a Web Page in Full Screen View

While you are designing a Web page, you can periodically view the page in full screen view to determine how it will appear to the user. Full screen view provides a quick and easy way to verify the placement of controls and text on the Web page. Figure 13-11 lists the steps for viewing a Web page in full screen view. The figure also includes an example of a Web page displayed in full screen view.

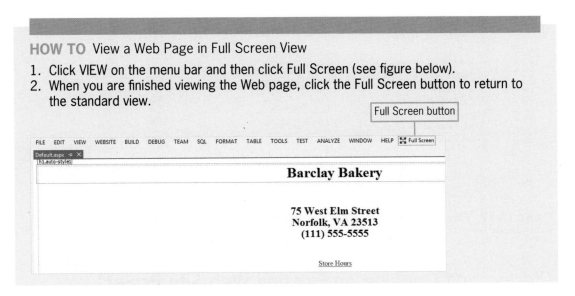

HOW TO View a Web Page in Full Screen View

1. Click VIEW on the menu bar and then click Full Screen (see figure below).
2. When you are finished viewing the Web page, click the Full Screen button to return to the standard view.

Full Screen button

FILE   EDIT   VIEW   WEBSITE   BUILD   DEBUG   TEAM   SQL   FORMAT   TABLE   TOOLS   TEST   ANALYZE   WINDOW   HELP   Full Screen

Barclay Bakery

75 West Elm Street
Norfolk, VA 23513
(111) 555-5555

Store Hours

Figure 13-11   How to view a Web page in full screen view
© 2013 Cengage Learning

Starting a Web Site Project

Typically, you start a Web site project either by pressing Ctrl+F5 or by clicking the Start Without Debugging option on the DEBUG menu. If you prefer to use the menu option, you might need to add it to the menu. The steps for doing this are listed in Figure 13-12, along with an example of a completed Customize dialog box.

HOW TO Add the Start Without Debugging Option to the DEBUG Menu

1. Click TOOLS on the menu bar and then click Customize to open the Customize dialog box.

2. Click the Commands tab. The Menu bar radio button should be selected. Click the down arrow in the Menu bar list box. Scroll down the list until you see Debug, and then click Debug.

3. Click the Add Command button to open the Add Command dialog box, and then click Debug in the Categories list. Scroll down the Commands list until you see Start Without Debugging, and then click Start Without Debugging. Click the OK button to close the Add Command dialog box.

4. Click the Move Down button until the Start Without Debugging option appears below the Start / Continue option (see figure below). Your dialog box will look slightly different if you are using Visual Studio Express 2012 for Web.

5. Click the Close button to close the Customize dialog box.

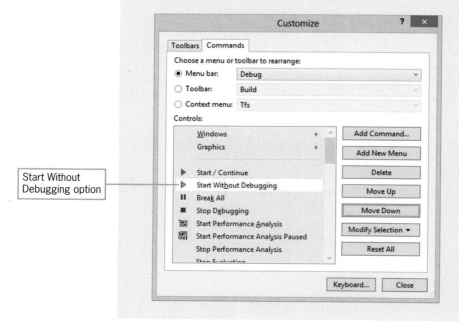

Start Without Debugging option

Figure 13-12 How to add the Start Without Debugging Option to the DEBUG menu
© 2013 Cengage Learning

Closing and Opening an Existing Web Site Project

You can use the FILE menu to close and also open an existing Web site project. Figure 13-13 lists the steps for performing both tasks.

HOW TO Close and Open an Existing Web Site Project

To close an existing Web site project:

Click FILE on the menu bar and then click Close Solution.

To open an existing Web site project:

1. Click FILE on the menu bar and then click Open Web Site to open the Open Web Site dialog box. If necessary, click the File System button.

2. Click the name of the Web site and then click the Open button.

3. If a message box appears and asks whether you want to use IIS Express or the Visual Studio Development Server, click the Yes button to use IIS Express.

4. If necessary, right-click the Web page's name in the Solution Explorer window and then click View Designer.

Figure 13-13 How to close and open an existing Web site project
© 2013 Cengage Learning

Mini-Quiz 13-1

1. A computer that requests an ASP page from a Web server is called a _____ computer. (1)

    a. browser

    b. client

    c. requesting

    d. none of the above

2. A _____ is a program that uses HTML to render a Web page on the computer screen. (1)

    a. browser

    b. client

    c. server

    d. none of the above

3. A Web page's HTML instructions are processed by the _____. (1)

    a. client computer

    b. Web server

4. What name is automatically assigned to the first Web page added to a new Web site project? (3)

    a. Form1.aspx

    b. Default.vb

    c. Default.aspx

    d. WebForm1.vb

The answers to Mini-Quiz questions are located in Appendix A. Each question is associated with one or more objectives listed at the beginning of the chapter.

5.　The code entered in a Web page's Code Editor window is stored in a file whose filename extension is ——————. (5)

    a.　.asp

    b.　.aspx

    c.　.aspx.vb

    d.　.vb.aspx

You have completed the concepts section of Chapter 13. The Programming Tutorial section is next.

PROGRAMMING TUTORIAL 1

Creating the Barclay Bakery Web Site Project

In this tutorial, you will create a Web site project for the Barclay Bakery store. The project contains the two Web pages shown earlier in Figures 13-1 and 13-2 in the chapter. The Web pages contain static text, an image control, and two link button controls.

To create the Web site project:

1.　*If you are using Visual Studio 2012*, start Visual Studio 2012.

　　If you are using Visual Studio Express 2012 for Web, follow the instructions shown earlier in Figure 13-5 to start and (if necessary) configure the Express edition.

2.　If necessary, open the Solution Explorer and Properties windows, and auto-hide the Toolbox window.

3.　Click **FILE** on the menu bar and then click **New Web Site** to open the New Web Site dialog box. If necessary, click **Visual Basic** in the Installed Templates list, and then click **ASP.NET Empty Web Site** in the middle column of the dialog box.

4.　If necessary, change the entry in the Web location box to **File System**. The File System selection allows you to store your Web site project in any folder on either your computer or a network drive.

5.　In this step, you will be instructed to store the Web site project in the VbReloaded2012\Chap13 folder on the E drive; however, you should use the drive letter that contains your data files. In the box that appears next to the Web location box, replace the existing text with **E:\VbReloaded2012\Chap13\Barclay**. Figure 13-14 shows the completed New Web Site dialog box. Your dialog box will look slightly different if you are using the Express edition.

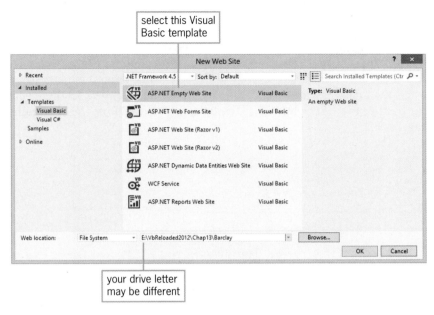

select this Visual
Basic template

your drive letter
may be different

Figure 13-14   New Web Site dialog box

6.   Click the **OK** button to close the dialog box. The computer creates an empty Web site project named Barclay.

Adding a Web Page to the Project

After creating an empty Web site project, you need to add a Web page to it.

To add a Web page to the project:

1.   Click **WEBSITE** on the menu bar and then click **Add New Item** to open the Add New Item dialog box. (If WEBSITE does not appear on the menu bar, click the project's name in the Solution Explorer window.)

2.   If necessary, click **Visual Basic** in the Installed list and then (if necessary) click **Web Form** in the middle column of the dialog box. Verify that the Place code in separate file check box is selected, and that the Select master page check box is not selected. As indicated in Figure 13-15, the Web page will be named Default.aspx.

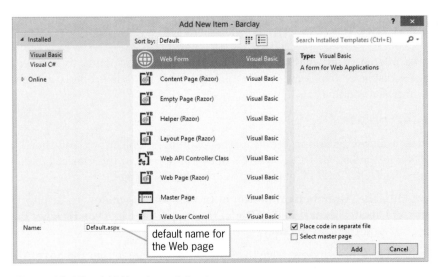

default name for
the Web page

Figure 13-15   Add New Item dialog box

3. Click the **Add** button to display the Default.aspx page in the Document window. If necessary, click the **Design** tab that appears at the bottom of the IDE. When the Design tab is selected, the Web page appears in Design view in the Document window, as shown in Figure 13-16. You can use Design view to add text and controls to the Web page. If the Formatting toolbar does not appear on your screen, click **VIEW** on the menu bar, point to **Toolbars**, and then click **Formatting**. If the div tag does not appear in the Document window, click either the **<div>** button at the bottom of the IDE or the **rectangle** below the body tag.

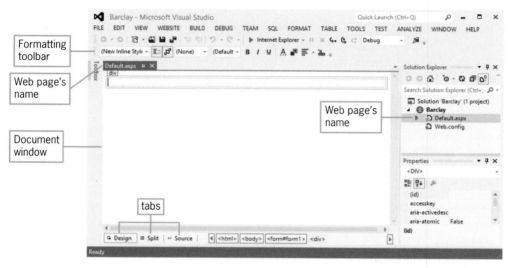

Figure 13-16   Default.aspx Web page shown in Design view

4. Click the **Source** tab to display the Web page in Source view. This view shows the HTML and ASP tags that tell a browser how to render the Web page. The tags are automatically generated for you as you are creating the Web page in Design view. Currently, the Web page contains only HTML tags.

5. Click the **Split** tab to split the Document window into two parts. The upper half displays the Web page in Source view, and the lower half displays it in Design view.

6. Click the **Design** tab to return to Design view, and then auto-hide the Solution Explorer window.

Adding a Title to the Web Page

In the following set of steps, you will change the Web page's Title property to Barclay Bakery. When a Web page is displayed in a browser, the value stored in its Title property appears on the page's tab in the browser window.

To change the Title property:

1. Click the **down arrow** button in the Properties window's Object box and then click **DOCUMENT** in the list. (If DOCUMENT does not appear in the Object box, click the Design tab.) The DOCUMENT object represents the Web page.

2. If necessary, click the **Alphabetical** button in the Properties window to display the properties in alphabetical order. Click **Title** in the Properties list. Type **Barclay Bakery** in the Settings box and then press **Enter**.

3. Auto-hide the Properties window. Save the solution by clicking either the **Save All** button on the Standard toolbar or the **Save All** option on the FILE menu.

Starting a Web Site Project

Typically, you start a Web site project either by pressing Ctrl+F5 or by clicking the Start Without Debugging option on the DEBUG menu. If you prefer to use the menu option rather than the shortcut keys, you may need to add the option to your DEBUG menu; you can do this by performing the next set of steps. If you prefer to use the Ctrl+F5 shortcut keys, you can skip the next set of steps.

To add the Start Without Debugging option to the DEBUG menu:

1. First, you will determine whether your DEBUG menu already contains the Start Without Debugging option. Click **DEBUG** on the menu bar. If the menu contains the Start Without Debugging option, close the menu by clicking **DEBUG** again, and then skip the remaining steps in this set of steps.

2. If the DEBUG menu does *not* contain the Start Without Debugging option, close the menu by clicking **DEBUG** again. Click **TOOLS** on the menu bar and then click **Customize** to open the Customize dialog box.

3. Click the **Commands** tab. The Menu bar radio button should be selected. Click the **down arrow** in the Menu bar list box. Scroll down the list until you see Debug, and then click **Debug**.

4. Click the **Add Command** button to open the Add Command dialog box, and then click **Debug** in the Categories list. Scroll down the Commands list until you see Start Without Debugging, and then click **Start Without Debugging**. Click the **OK** button to close the Add Command dialog box.

5. Click the **Move Down** button until the Start Without Debugging option appears below the Start / Continue option, as shown in Figure 13-17. (Your dialog box may look slightly different if you are using the Express edition.)

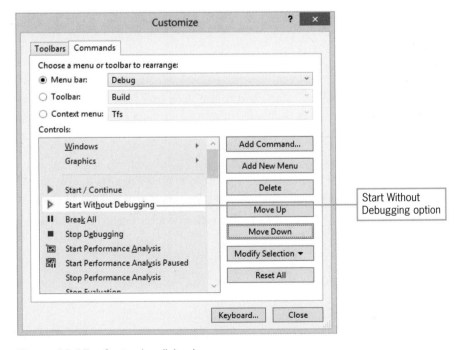

Figure 13-17   Customize dialog box

6. Click the **Close** button to close the Customize dialog box.

When you start a Web site project in either Visual Studio 2012 or Visual Studio Express 2012 for Web, the computer creates a temporary Web server that allows you to view your Web page in a browser. Keep in mind, however, that your Web page will need to be placed on an actual Web server for others to view it.

To start a Web site project:

1. Start the Web site project either by pressing **Ctrl+F5** or by clicking the **Start Without Debugging** option on the DEBUG menu. (If the message "Intranet settings are turned off by default." appears, click the Don't show this message again button.) Your browser requests the Default.aspx page from the Web server. The server locates the page and then sends the appropriate HTML instructions to your browser for rendering on the screen. The value in the page's Title property appears on the page's tab in the browser window. See Figure 13-18.

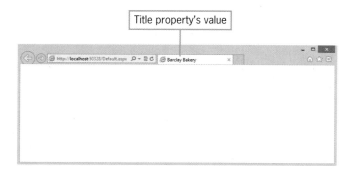

Figure 13-18 Web page displayed in Internet Explorer

2. Close the browser window by clicking the **Close** button on its title bar.

Customizing a Web Page

In the following set of steps, you will add static text to the Web page. Recall that static text is text that the user is not allowed to edit. You then will use the Formatting toolbar to format the text.

To add static text to the Web page:

1. If necessary, click **inside the rectangle** that appears below the div tag at the top of the Document window. The div tag defines a division in a Web page. (If the div tag does not appear in the Document window, click the <div> button at the bottom of the IDE.)

2. Enter the following four lines of text. Press **Enter** twice after typing the last line.

   Barclay Bakery
   75 West Elm Street
   Norfolk, VA 23513
   (111) 555-5555

3. Save the project.

4. Select (highlight) the Barclay Bakery text on the Web page. Click the **down arrow** in the Block Format box on the Formatting toolbar. (If the Formatting toolbar does not appear on your screen, click VIEW on the menu bar, point to Toolbars, and then click Formatting.) See Figure 13-19.

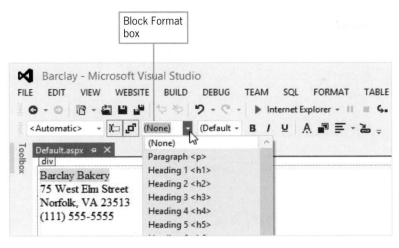

Figure 13-19   Result of clicking the arrow in the Block Format box

5. Click **Heading 1 <h1>**.

6. Select (highlight) the address and phone number text on the Web page. Click the **down arrow** in the Block Format box and then click **Heading 2 <h2>**.

7. Now, you will use the Formatting toolbar's Alignment button to center all of the static text. Select all of the static text on the Web page and then click the **down arrow** on the Alignment button. See Figure 13-20.

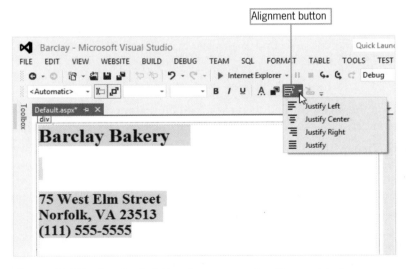

Figure 13-20   Result of clicking the arrow on the Alignment button

8. Click **Justify Center**. The selected text appears centered, horizontally, on the Web page. Click **anywhere below the phone number** to deselect the text, and then save the project.

Viewing a Web Page in Full Screen View

While you are designing a Web page, you can use the Full Screen option on the VIEW menu to determine how the Web page will appear to the user.

To view the Web page using the Full Screen option:

1. Click **VIEW** on the menu bar and then click **Full Screen**. See Figure 13-21. Although not identical to viewing in a browser window, full screen view provides a quick and easy way to verify the placement of controls and text on the Web page.

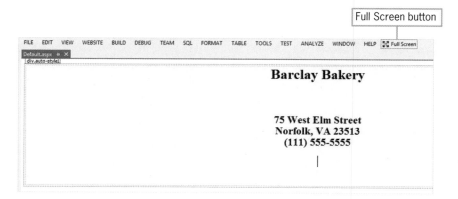

Figure 13-21   Default.aspx Web page displayed in full screen view

2. Click the **Full Screen** button to return to the standard view. (If you mistakenly clicked the window's Close button, click the Full Screen button, right-click Default.aspx in the Solution Explorer window, and then click View Designer.)

Adding Another Web Page to the Project

In the next set of steps, you will add a second Web page to the project. The Web page will display the store's hours of operation.

To add another Web page to the project:

1. Click **WEBSITE** on the menu bar and then click **Add New Item**. (If WEBSITE does not appear on the menu bar, click the project's name in the Solution Explorer window.)

2. If necessary, click **Visual Basic** in the Installed list and then (if necessary) click **Web Form** in the middle column of the dialog box. Change the filename in the Name box to **Hours** and then click the **Add** button. The computer appends the .aspx extension to the filename and then displays the Hours.aspx Web page in the Document window. (If necessary, click the Design tab to view the page in Design view.)

3. Temporarily display the Solution Explorer window. Notice that the window now contains the Hours.aspx filename.

4. Click the **Hours.aspx** tab and then temporarily display the Properties window. Click the **down arrow** button in the Properties window's Object box and then click **DOCUMENT** in the list. Change the Web page's Title property to **Barclay Bakery**.

5. Click the **Hours.aspx** tab. The blinking insertion point should be inside the rectangle that appears below the div tab. (If the div tag does not appear in the Document window, click the <div> button at the bottom of the IDE.) Type **Please visit us during these hours:** and then press **Enter** twice.

6. Now, enter the following three lines of text. Press **Enter** twice after typing the last line.

   Monday - Friday 7am - 5pm
   Saturday 7am - noon
   Sunday 9am - noon

7. Select the Please visit us during these hours: text. Click the **down arrow** in the Font Size box and then click **x-large (24pt)**. Also click the *I* (Italic) button on the Formatting toolbar.

8. Select the three lines of text that contain the store hours. Click the **down arrow** in the Font Size box and then click **large (18pt)**. Also click the **B** (Bold) button on the Formatting toolbar.

9. Now, you will change the color of the selected text. Click the **Foreground Color** button on the Formatting toolbar to open the More Colors dialog box. Click **any red hexagon** and then click the **OK** button.

10. Select all of the static text on the Web page. Click the **down arrow** on the Alignment button and then click **Justify Center**.

11. Click the **second blank line** below the store hours to deselect the text, and then save the project.

Adding a Link Button Control to a Web Page

In the next set of steps, you will add a link button control to both Web pages. The link button control on the Default.aspx page will display the Hours.aspx page. The link button control on the Hours.aspx page will return the user to the Default.aspx Web page.

To add a link button control to both Web pages:

1. First, you will add a link button control to the Hours.aspx page. Permanently display the Toolbox window. Expand the **Standard** node, if necessary, and then click the **LinkButton** tool. Drag your mouse pointer to the location shown in Figure 13-22.

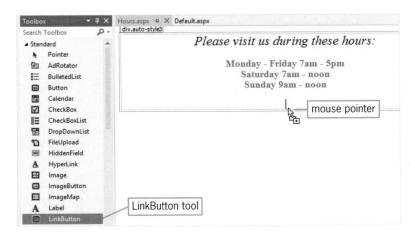

Figure 13-22　Link button control being dragged to the Hours.aspx page

2. Release the mouse button to add a link button control to the Web page.

3. Temporarily display the Properties window. Change the control's Text property to **Home Page** and then press **Enter**. Click **PostBackUrl** in the Properties list and then click the **...** (ellipsis) button to open the Select URL dialog box. Click **Default.aspx** in the Contents of folder list. See Figure 13-23.

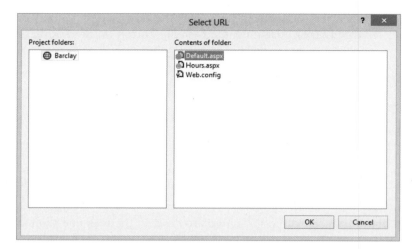

Figure 13-23   Select URL dialog box

4. Click the **OK** button to close the dialog box, and then click the **Web page**.

5. Now, you will add a link button control to the Default.aspx page. Click the **Default.aspx** tab. Click the **LinkButton** tool. Drag your mouse pointer to the location shown in Figure 13-24.

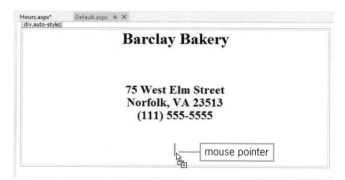

Figure 13-24   Link button control being dragged to the Default.aspx page

6. Release the mouse button to add a link button control to the Web page.

7. Temporarily display the Properties window. Change the control's Text property to **Store Hours** and then change its PostBackUrl property to **Hours.aspx**. Click the **OK** button to close the Select URL dialog box.

8. Click the **Web page** and then save the project.

9. Start the project. The Default.aspx page appears in the browser window. See Figure 13-25.

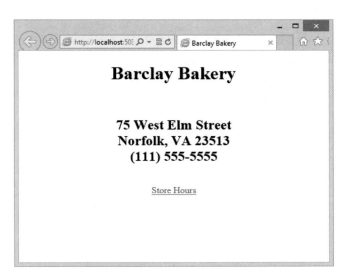

Figure 13-25   Default.aspx Web page displayed in a browser window

10.   Click the **Store Hours** link to display the Hours.aspx page. See Figure 13-26.

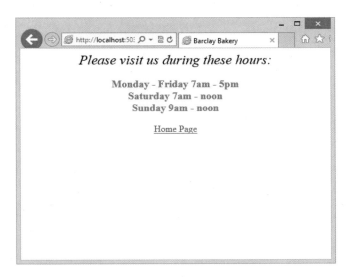

Figure 13-26   Hours.aspx Web page displayed in a browser window

11.   Click the **Home Page** link to display the Default.aspx page, and then close the browser window.

Adding an Image Control to a Web Page

In the next set of steps, you will add an image control to the Default.aspx page. The control will display the image stored in the VbReloaded2012\Chap13\Bakery.png file.

To add an image control to the Web page:

1.   First, you need to add the Bakery.png file to the project. Click **WEBSITE** on the menu bar and then click **Add Existing Item**. Open the VbReloaded2012\Chap13 folder. Click the **down arrow** in the box that controls the file types and then click **All Files (*.*)** in the list. Click **Bakery.png** in the list of filenames and then click the **Add** button.

2. If necessary, insert a **blank line** below the Store Hours link button control. Click the **blank line** below the control and then press **Enter** to insert another blank line. Click the **Image** tool in the toolbox and then drag your mouse pointer to the location shown in Figure 13-27.

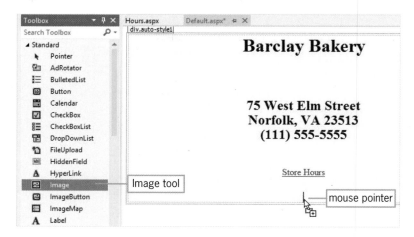

Figure 13-27   Image control being dragged to the Default.aspx page

3. Release the mouse button to add an image control to the Web page.

4. Temporarily display the Properties window. Click **ImageUrl** in the Properties list, if necessary, and then click the **...** (ellipsis) button to open the Select Image dialog box. Click **Bakery.png** in the Contents of folder section and then click the **OK** button.

5. Next, you will put a grooved border around the image control. Change the image control's BorderStyle property to **Groove**.

6. Now, you will change the color of the image's border to red. Click **BorderColor** in the Properties list and then click the **...** (ellipsis) button. When the More Colors dialog box opens, click **any red hexagon**. Click the **OK** button to close the dialog box and then click the **Web page**.

7. Auto-hide the toolbox. Save and then start the project. See Figure 13-28.

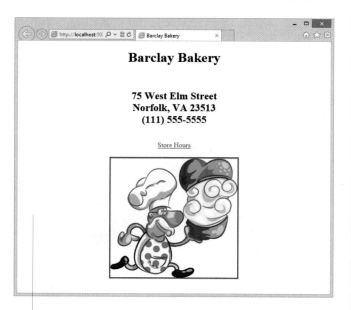

Figure 13-28   Browser window showing the Default.aspx page
OpenClipArt.org/Przylga

8. Verify that the browser window is not maximized. Place your mouse pointer on the window's right border and then drag the border to the left to make the window narrower. Notice that the text and image remain centered in the visible portion of the window. Now, drag the right border to the right to make the window wider. Here again, the text and image remain centered in the visible portion of the window.

9. Close the browser window.

10. Click **FILE** on the menu bar and then click **Close Solution** to close the project.

Repositioning a Control on a Web Page

At times, you may want to reposition a control on a Web page. In this section, you will move the image and link button controls to different locations on the Default.aspx Web page. First, however, you will create a new Web site project and then copy the Barclay Bakery files to the project.

To create a new Web site project and then copy files to the project:

1. Use the New Web Site option on the FILE menu to create an empty Web site project named **Barclay2**. Save the project in the VbReloaded2012\Chap13 folder.

2. Now, close the Barclay2 project by clicking **FILE** on the menu bar and then clicking **Close Solution**.

3. Use Windows to open the Barclay2 folder. Delete the Web.config file.

4. Use Windows to open the Barclay folder. Select the folder's contents, which include six files (Default.aspx, Default.aspx.vb, Hours.aspx, Hours.aspx.vb, Bakery.png, and Web.config. Copy the six files to the Barclay2 folder.

Now, you will open the Barclay2 project and move the two controls to different locations on the Default.aspx Web page.

To open the Barclay2 project and then move the controls:

1. Click **FILE** on the menu bar and then click **Open Web Site** to open the Open Web Site dialog box. If necessary, click the **File System** button. If necessary, click the **Barclay2** folder, which is contained in the VbReloaded2012\Chap13 folder. Click the **Open** button. If a message box appears and asks whether you want to use IIS Express or the Visual Studio Development Server, click the **Yes** button to use IIS Express.

2. If the Default.aspx Web page is not open in the Document window, right-click **Default.aspx** in the Solution Explorer window and then click **View Designer**.

3. First, you will move the image control from the bottom of the page to the top of the page. If necessary, position the insertion point immediately before the first letter B in the Barclay Bakery heading, and then press **Enter** to insert a blank line above the heading.

4. Click the **image control** on the Web page. Drag the image control to the blank line immediately above the heading, and then release the mouse button.

5. Next, you will move the link button control to the empty area below the store's name. Click the **link button control**. Drag the control to the empty area below the store's name, and then release the mouse button.

6. Click **FILE** on the menu bar and then click **Save Default.aspx**.

7. Start the project. See Figure 13-29.

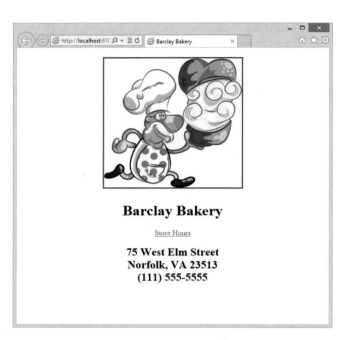

Figure 13-29 Browser window showing the modified Default.aspx page

OpenClipArt.org/Przylga

8. Close the browser window. Close the project by clicking **FILE** on the menu bar and then clicking **Close Solution**. If you are prompted to save the solution, click the **No** button.

PROGRAMMING TUTORIAL 2

Creating the Dollars to Pesos Web Site Project

In this tutorial, you will create a Web site project that converts U.S. dollars to Mexican pesos. The project contains the dynamic Web page shown earlier in Figure 13-3. The Web page contains static text, a text box, a label, and a button.

To create the Web site project and then add a Web page to it:

1. *If you are using Visual Studio 2012,* start Visual Studio 2012.

   If you are using Visual Studio Express 2012 for Web, follow the instructions shown earlier in Figure 13-5 to start and (if necessary) configure the Express edition.

2. If necessary, open the Solution Explorer, Properties, and Toolbox windows.

3. Use the New Web Site option on the FILE menu to create an empty Web site project named DollarsToPesos. Save the project in the VbReloaded2012\Chap13 folder. If you need help, refer to the How To box shown earlier in Figure 13-6.

4. Use the Add New Item option on the WEBSITE menu to add a Web page named Default.aspx to the project. If you need help, refer to the How To box shown earlier in Figure 13-7.

In the next set of steps, you will customize the Web page.

To customize the Web page:

1. If necessary, click **DOCUMENT** in the Properties window's Object box. Change the DOCUMENT object's Title property to **Dollars to Pesos**.

2. If necessary, click the **Design** tab to view the page in Design view and then click **inside the rectangle** that appears below the div tag at the top of the Document window. (If the div tag does not appear in the Document window, click the <div> button at the bottom of the IDE.)

3. Next, you will add an image file named DollarsPesos.png to the application. Click **WEBSITE** on the menu bar and then click **Add Existing Item**. Open the VbReloaded2012\Chap13 folder. Click the **down arrow** in the box that controls the file types and then click **All Files (*.*)** in the list. Click **DollarsPesos.png** in the list of filenames and then click the **Add** button.

4. If necessary, permanently display the Toolbox window and expand the Standard node. Drag an image control from the Toolbox into the rectangle that appears below the div tag, and then release the mouse button. Change the image control's ImageUrl property to **DollarsPesos.png**.

5. Click an **empty area** to the right of the image control to deselect the control, and then press **Enter** twice.

6. Type **U.S. Dollars to Mexican Pesos** and then press **Enter** twice.

7. Type **Number of dollars:**, press the **Spacebar** three times, and then press **Enter** twice.

8. Type **Number of pesos:**, press the **Spacebar** three times, and then press **Enter** twice.

9. Click the **Button** tool in the toolbox and then drag the mouse pointer to the Web page. Position the mouse pointer as shown in Figure 13-30, and then release the mouse button.

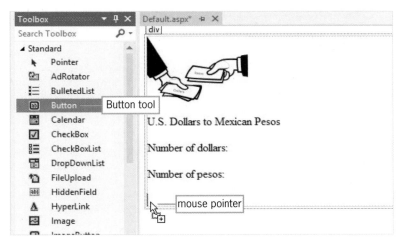

Figure 13-30 Button control being dragged to the Web page
OpenClipArt.org/Onsemeliot

10. Select (highlight) the first line of text on the Web page. Click the **down arrow** in the Block Format box on the Formatting toolbar, and then click **Heading 1 <h1>**. (If the Formatting toolbar does not appear on your screen, click VIEW on the menu bar, point to Toolbars, and then click Formatting.)

11. Select (highlight) the remaining two lines of text on the Web page. Click the **down arrow** in the Font Size box on the Formatting toolbar, and then click **x-large (24pt)**.

12. Click an **empty area** of the Web page.

13. Click the **TextBox** tool in the toolbox and then drag the mouse pointer to the Web page. Position the mouse pointer as shown in Figure 13-31, and then release the mouse button.

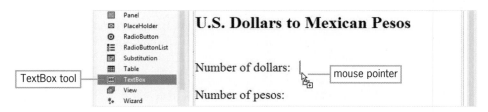

Figure 13-31   Text box being dragged to the Web page

14. Click the **Label** tool in the toolbox and then drag the mouse pointer to the Web page. Position the mouse pointer as shown in Figure 13-32, and then release the mouse button.

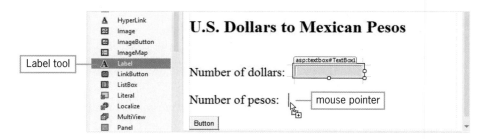

Figure 13-32   Label being dragged to the Web page

15. Auto-hide the Toolbox window and then save the project.

In the next set of steps, you will set the appropriate properties of the controls.

To set the properties of the controls:

1. Unlike Windows controls, Web controls have an ID property rather than a Name property. Permanently display the Properties window. Set the label's ID property (which appears at the top of the Properties list) to **pesosLabel**.

2. Now, set the following properties for the label:

   BorderStyle   **Solid**
   BorderWidth   **1px**
   Text   **0**
   Width   **80px**

3. Click the **label control** on the Web page to return to the designer window. Either click **FORMAT** on the menu bar and then point to **Background Color,** or click the **Background Color** button on the Formatting toolbar. Click **any pale yellow hexagon,** and then click the **OK** button.

4. Click the **text box** on the Web page and then set its ID and Width properties to **dollarsTextBox** and **60px,** respectively.

5. Click the **button control** on the Web page and then set its ID and Text properties to **submitButton** and **Submit,** respectively.

6. Click the **Default.aspx** tab to make the designer window the active window. Auto-hide the Properties window and then save the project. Figure 13-33 shows the completed Web page.

Figure 13-33 Completed Web page
OpenClipArt.org/Onsemeliot

Coding the Submit Button's Click Event Procedure

When the user clicks the Submit button, the button's Click event procedure should convert the number of U.S. dollars to Mexican pesos and then display the result on the Web page. At the time of this writing, a dollar was equivalent to approximately 12.62 pesos. As you do when coding a control on a Windows form, you enter the code for a control on a Web page in the Code Editor window.

To code the submitButton_Click procedure and then test the code:

1. Right-click the **Web page** and then click **View Code** to open the Web page's Code Editor window. As the window's tab indicates, the code entered in this window will be saved in the Default.aspx.vb file. Recall that a Web page's .aspx.vb file is referred to as the code-behind file because it contains code that supports the Web page. Temporarily display the Solution Explorer window. If necessary, expand the **Default.aspx** node. See Figure 13-34.

Figure 13-34 Code Editor and Solution Explorer windows

2. Enter the following comments above the Partial Class clause. Replace <your name> and <current date> with your name and the current date, respectively. Press **Enter** twice after typing the last comment.

   ```
   ' Web site project:      DollarsToPesos
   ' Purpose:               Convert dollars to pesos
   ' Created/revised by:    <your name> on <current date>
   ```

3. Now, enter the following Option statements:

   ```
   Option Explicit On
   Option Strict On
   Option Infer Off
   ```

4. Open the submitButton's Click event procedure. Type the following comment and then press **Enter** twice:

' converts dollars to pesos

5. The procedure will use a Double named constant to store the conversion rate of 12.62. Enter a Const statement to declare and initialize the `PesoRate` named constant.

6. The procedure will use two Double variables to store the number of dollars and the number of pesos. Enter the Dim statements to declare the `dollars` and `pesos` variables. Press **Enter** twice after typing the second Dim statement.

7. Next, enter a statement that uses the TryParse method to convert the contents of the dollarsTextBox to Double, storing the result in the `dollars` variable.

8. Now, enter an assignment statement that converts the dollars to pesos, assigning the result to the `pesos` variable.

9. Finally, enter an assignment statement that assigns the number of pesos to the pesosLabel's Text property. Format the number of pesos using the "N2" format.

10. Save the project and then press **Ctrl+F5** to start the project. Click the **Number of dollars** box and then type **10**. Click the **Submit** button; doing this submits your entry to the Web server, along with a request for additional services. (If the message "Do you want AutoComplete to remember web form entries?" appears, click the No button.) The server processes the code contained in the button's Click event procedure and then sends the appropriate HTML to the browser for rendering on the screen. See Figure 13-35.

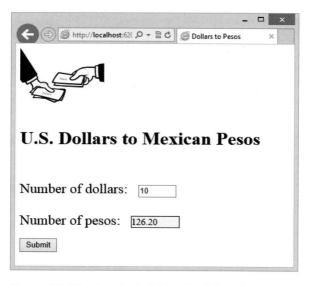

Figure 13-35 Result of clicking the Submit button
OpenClipArt.org/Onsemeliot

11. Close the browser window and then close the Code Editor window.

Validating User Input

The Validation section of the toolbox provides several tools for validating user input. The tools are referred to as validator tools. The name, purpose, and important properties of each validator tool are listed in Figure 13-36. In the Dollars to Pesos project, you will use a RequiredFieldValidator control to verify that the user entered the number of dollars.

HOW TO Use the Validator Tools

Name	Purpose	Properties
CompareValidator	compare an entry with a constant value or the property stored in a control	ControlToCompare ControlToValidate ErrorMessage Operator Type ValueToCompare
CustomValidator	verify that an entry passes the specified validation logic	ClientValidationFunction ControlToValidate ErrorMessage
RangeValidator	verify that an entry is within the specified minimum and maximum values	ControlToValidate ErrorMessage MaximumValue MinimumValue Type
RegularExpressionValidator	verify that an entry matches a specific pattern	ControlToValidate ErrorMessage ValidationExpression
RequiredFieldValidator	verify that a control contains data	ControlToValidate ErrorMessage
ValidationSummary	display all of the validation error messages in a single location on a Web page	DisplayMode HeaderText

Figure 13-36   How to use the validator tools
© 2013 Cengage Learning

To verify that the user entered the number of dollars:

1. Click **to the immediate right of the dollarsTextBox** and then press the **Spacebar** five times.

2. Permanently display the Toolbox window, and then locate and expand its Validation section. Click the **RequiredFieldValidator** tool and then drag the mouse pointer to the Web page. Position the mouse pointer as shown in Figure 13-37, and then release the mouse button.

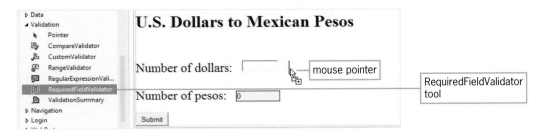

Figure 13-37   RequiredFieldValidator control being dragged to the Web page

3. Auto-hide the Toolbox window, and then temporarily display the Properties window. Set the following properties for the RequiredFieldValidator control:

ControlToValidate   **dollarsTextBox**
ErrorMessage   **Required entry**
ForeColor   choose a red hexagon

4. Auto-hide the Properties window and then save the application.

5. Press **Ctrl+F5** to start the application. Click the **Submit** button without entering a value in the dollarsTextBox. (If a Web page opens and displays the "Server Error in '/' Application." message, refer to the Important note that follows Figure 13-38.) The RequiredFieldValidator control displays the "Required entry" message. See Figure 13-38.

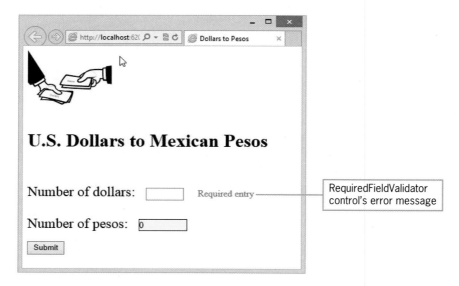

Figure 13-38   Result of clicking the Submit button when both text boxes are empty
OpenClipArt.org/Onsemeliot

Important note: At the time of this writing, there was an unresolved issue with some of the validator controls. Until this problem is fixed, you can use the following workaround: First, close the browser window. Next, right-click Web.config in the Solution Explorer window and then click Open. Change both occurrences of "4.5" (or "4.5.1") to "4.0", and then save the project. Close the Web.config window and then repeat Step 5.

6. Type **20** in the dollarsTextBox and then click the **Submit** button. The error message is removed from the Web page and the number 252.40 appears in the pesosLabel.

7. Close the browser window and then close the application. Figure 13-39 shows the application's code.

```
 1 ' Web site project:      DollarsToPesos
 2 ' Purpose:               Convert dollars to pesos
 3 ' Created/revised by:    <your name> on <current date>
 4
 5 Option Explicit On
 6 Option Strict On
 7 Option Infer Off
 8
 9 Partial Class _Default
10     Inherits System.Web.UI.Page
11
12     Protected Sub submitButton_Click(sender As Object,
        e As EventArgs) Handles submitButton.Click
13         ' converts dollars to pesos
14
15         Const PesoRate As Double = 12.62
16         Dim dollars As Double
17         Dim pesos As Double
18
19         Double.TryParse(dollarsTextBox.Text, dollars)
20         pesos = dollars * PesoRate
21         pesosLabel.Text = pesos.ToString("N2")
22
23     End Sub
24 End Class
```

Figure 13-39   Code for the Dollars to Pesos Web site project
© 2013 Cengage Learning

Modifying a Web Page

In this section, you will create a new Web site project and then copy the Dollars to Pesos files to the project. You then will modify the Dollars to Pesos Web page so it looks like Figure 13-40.

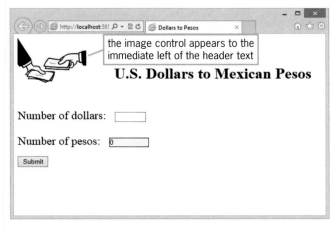

Figure 13-40   Modified Web page
OpenClipArt.org/Onsemeliot

To create a new Web site project and then copy files to the project:

1. Use the New Web Site option on the FILE menu to create an empty Web site project named **DollarsToPesos2**. Save the project in the VbReloaded2012\Chap13 folder.

2. Now, close the DollarsToPesos2 project by clicking **FILE** on the menu bar and then clicking **Close Solution**.

3. Use Windows to open the DollarsToPesos2 folder. Delete the Web.config file.

4. Use Windows to open the DollarsToPesos folder. Select the folder's contents, which include four files (Default.aspx, Default.aspx.vb, DollarsPesos.png, and Web.config). Copy the four files to the DollarsToPesos2 folder.

Now, you will open the DollarsToPesos2 project and modify its Web page.

To open the DollarsToPesos2 project and then modify its Web page:

1. Click **FILE** on the menu bar and then click **Open Web Site** to open the Open Web Site dialog box. If necessary, click the **File System** button. If necessary, click the **DollarsToPesos2** folder, which is contained in the VbReloaded2012\Chap13 folder. Click the **Open** button. If a message box appears and asks whether you want to use IIS Express or the Visual Studio Development Server, click the **Yes** button to use IIS Express.

2. If the Default.aspx Web page is not open in the Document window, right-click **Default.aspx** in the Solution Explorer window and then click **View Designer**.

3. Click to the **immediate left of the U** in the U.S. Dollars to Mexican Pesos header text. Press the **Tab** key five times.

4. Click the **image control**. Now, click **FORMAT** on the menu bar and then click **Position** to open the Position dialog box. See Figure 13-41.

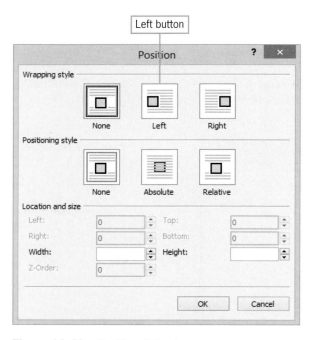

Figure 13-41   Position dialog box

5. Click the **Left** button in the Wrapping style section, and then click the **OK** button to position the image control on the left side of the header text.

6. Save the project, and then press **Ctrl+F5** to start the project. The Web page shown earlier in Figure 13-40 appears in the browser window.

7. Close the browser window and then close the project. If you are prompted to save the solution, click the **No** button.

PROGRAMMING EXAMPLE

Multiplication Calculator Web Site Project

Create an empty Web site project named Multiplication. Save the project in the VbReloaded2012\Chap13 folder. Add a new Web page named Default.aspx to the project. Change the DOCUMENT object's Title property to Multiplication Calculator. Create the Web page shown in Figure 13-42. The calculator image is stored in the VbReloaded2012 \Chap13\Calculator.png file. The Submit button should display the product of the two numbers entered by the user. See Figures 13-42 and 13-43.

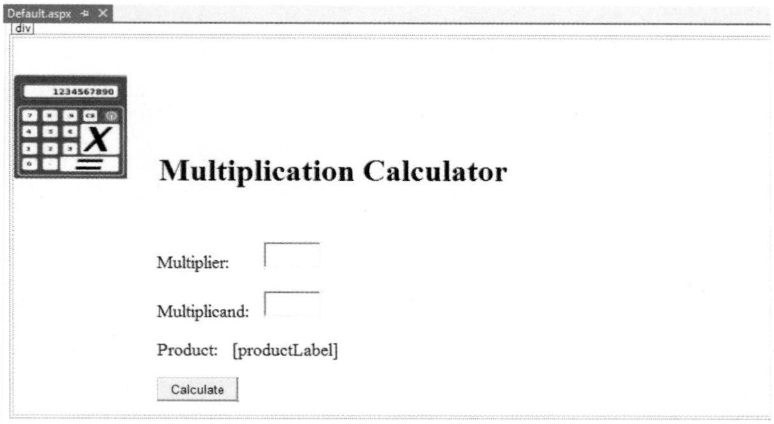

Figure 13-42 Default.aspx Web page
OpenClipArt.org/gsagri04

```
1 ' Web site project:      Multiplication
2 ' Purpose:               Display the product of two numbers
3 ' Created/revised by:    <your name> on <current date>
4
5 Option Explicit On
6 Option Strict On
7 Option Infer Off
8
9 Partial Class _Default
10    Inherits System.Web.UI.Page
11
12    Protected Sub calcButton_Click(sender As Object,
      e As EventArgs) Handles calcButton.Click
13        ' calculates the product of two numbers
14
15        Dim multiplier As Double
16        Dim multiplicand As Double
17        Dim product As Double
18
19        Double.TryParse(multiplierTextBox.Text, multiplier)
20        Double.TryParse(multiplicandTextBox.Text, multiplicand)
21
22        product = multiplier * multiplicand
23        productLabel.Text = product.ToString("N2")
24
25    End Sub
26 End Class
```

Figure 13-43 Code
© 2013 Cengage Learning

Summary

- A client computer uses a browser to request a Web page from a Web server. It also uses the browser to view the Web page.

- Web pages can be either static or dynamic (interactive).

- HTML tags tell the browser how to render a Web page on the computer screen. ASP tags specify the controls to include on a Web page.

- Dynamic Web pages contain code that is processed by the Web server.

- You can add static text and controls to a Web page. Like Windows controls, Web controls have properties, and they can be coded to perform tasks when an action (such as clicking) occurs. However, unlike Windows controls, Web controls have an ID property (rather than a Name property). You use the ID property to refer to the control in code.

- The .aspx file contains the instructions for rendering the visual elements on the Web page. The .aspx.vb file contains the Web page's code and is referred to as the code-behind file.

Key Terms

ASP—stands for "Active Server Pages"

Browser—a program that allows a client computer to request and view Web pages

Client computer—a computer that requests information from a Web server

Dynamic Web page—an interactive document that can accept information from the user and also retrieve information for the user

Static text—text that the user is not allowed to edit

Static Web page—a non-interactive document whose purpose is merely to display information to the viewer

Web pages—the documents stored on Web servers

Web server—a computer that contains special software that "serves up" Web pages in response to requests from client computers

Review Questions

 Each Review Question is associated with one or more objectives listed at the beginning of the chapter.

1. An online form used to purchase a product is an example of a _____ Web page. (1)

    a. dynamic

    b. static

2. ASP stands for _____ . (1)

    a. Always Special Pages   c. Active Server Products

    b. Active Special Pages   d. none of the above

3. Which of the following filenames indicates that the file contains the Visual Basic code associated with a Web page? (2, 3, 5)

    a. Default.aspx.vb   c. Default.vb

    b. Default.aspx   d. Default.vb.aspx

4. In code, you refer to a control on a Web page using the control's _____ property. (5)

   a. Caption   c. Name
   b. ID   d. Text

5. The HTML instructions in a Web page are processed by the _____ . (1, 7)

   a. client computer   b. Web server

6. The Visual Basic code in a Web page is processed by the _____ . (1, 7)

   a. client computer   b. Web server

7. You can use a _____ control to verify that a control on a Web page contains data. (10)

   a. RequiredFieldValidator   c. RequiredValidator
   b. RequiredField   d. none of the above

8. You can use a _____ control to verify that an entry on a Web page is within minimum and maximum values. (10)

   a. MinMaxValidation   c. EntryValidator
   b. MaxMinValidation   d. RangeValidator

9. The text that appears on a Web page's tab in the browser window is determined by the _____ property. (4)

   a. APPLICATION object's Name   c. DOCUMENT object's Tab Name
   b. APPLICATION object's Title   d. DOCUMENT object's Title

10. A _____ is a program that uses HTML to render a Web page on the computer screen. (1)

   a. browser   c. server
   b. client   d. none of the above

Exercises

Pencil and Paper

Each Exercise is associated with one or more objectives listed at the beginning of the chapter.

1. Explain the difference between a static Web page and a dynamic Web page. (1)   INTRODUCTORY

2. Explain the relationship between a client computer and a Web server. (1)   INTRODUCTORY

Computer

3. If necessary, complete the Dollars to Pesos project from this chapter's Programming Tutorial 2, and then close the project. (2- 8, 10)   MODIFY THIS

   a. Create an empty Web site project named ConverterRangeValidator. Save the project in the VbReloaded2012\Chap13 folder. Close the ConverterRangeValidator project.

   b. Use Windows to open the ConverterRangeValidator folder. Delete the Web.config file.

    c. Use Windows to open the DollarsToPesos folder. Select the folder's contents. Copy the selected contents to the ConverterRangeValidator folder.

    d. Open the ConverterRangeValidator Web site. If necessary, click the Yes button to use IIS Express. Right-click Default.aspx in the Solution Explorer window and then click View Designer.

    e. Add a RangeValidator control to the Web page. Change the control's Type property to Double, and set its ControlToValidate property to dollarsTextBox. The control should display an appropriate message when the number of dollars is either less than 1 or greater than 100,000; set the control's MinimumValue, MaximumValue, and Text properties.

    f. Save and then start the project. (If necessary, refer to the Important note that appears after Figure 13-38 in the chapter.) Test the project. Close the browser window and then close the project.

MODIFY THIS 4. If necessary, complete the Multiplication Calculator project from this chapter's Programming Example, and then close the project. (2-8, 10)

    a. Create an empty Web site project named Multiplication2. Save the project in the VbReloaded2012\Chap13 folder. Close the Multiplication2 project.

    b. Use Windows to open the Multiplication2 folder. Delete the Web.config file.

    c. Use Windows to open the Multiplication folder. Select the folder's contents. Copy the selected contents to the Multiplication2 folder.

    d. Open the Multiplication2 Web site. If necessary, click the Yes button to use IIS Express. Right-click Default.aspx in the Solution Explorer window and then click View Designer.

    e. Add two RequiredFieldValidator controls to the Web page. Associate the controls with the two text boxes. The controls should display the message "Required entry" (without the quotes) when their respective text box is empty.

    f. Save and then start the project. (If necessary, refer to the Important note that appears after Figure 13-38 in the chapter.) Test the project. Close the browser window and then close the project.

INTRODUCTORY 5. Create an empty Web site project named Caroline. Save the project in the VbReloaded2012\Chap13 folder. Add a new Web page named Default.aspx to the project. Change the DOCUMENT object's Title property to Caroline's Pet Shoppe. Create a Web page similar to the one shown in Figure 13-44. The static text should be centered, horizontally, on the page. Save and then start the project. Close the browser window and then close the project. (2-4, 6-8)

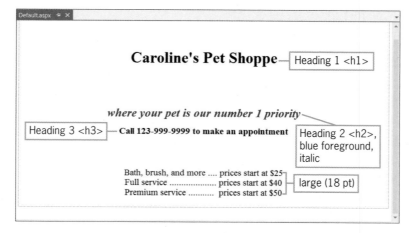

Figure 13-44   Web page for Exercise 5

6. Create an empty Web site project named AppleOrchard. Save the project in the VbReloaded2012\Chap13 folder. Add a new Web page named Default.aspx to the project. Change the DOCUMENT object's Title property to Apple Orchard Farm. Create a Web page similar to the one shown in Figure 13-45. The image on the Web page is stored in the VbReloaded2012\Chap13\Apple.png file. Save and then start the project. Close the browser window and then close the project. (2-4, 6-9)

```
Default.aspx ⊹ ✕
```

Apple Orchard Farm

Bowling Green, Kentucky

270-555-5555

Pick apples with us!

Figure 13-45 Web page for Exercise 6
OpenClipArt.org/Ana Paula

7. Create an empty Web site project named SquareArea. Save the project in the VbReloaded2012\Chap13 folder. (2-10)

   a. Add a new Web page named Default.aspx to the project. Change the DOCUMENT object's Title property to Square Area.

   b. Create the Web page shown in Figure 13-46. The square image is stored in the VbReloaded2012\Chap13\Square.png file. Set the CompareValidator control's ControlToValidate, Operator, Type, and ValueToCompare properties to sideTextBox, Greater Than, Double, and 0, respectively. Also set the control's ErrorMessage and ForeColor properties appropriately.

   c. Open the Code Editor window. Use comments to document the project's name and purpose, as well as your name and the current date. Code the Calculate Area button's Click event procedure. Display the area with two decimal places.

   d. Save and then start the project. (If necessary, refer to the Important note that appears after Figure 13-38 in the chapter.) Test the project using positive and negative numbers, as well as the number 0. Close the browser window. Close the Code Editor window and then close the project.

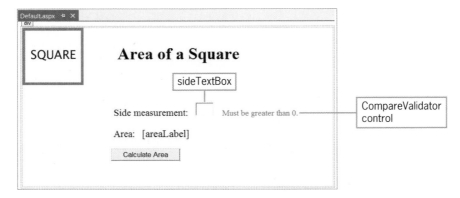

Figure 13-46 Web page for Exercise 7

INTERMEDIATE

8. Create an empty Web site project named Temperature. Save the project in the VbReloaded2012\Chap13 folder. Add a new Web page named Default.aspx to the project. Change the DOCUMENT object's Title property to Temperature Converter. The Web page should allow the user to enter a temperature in degrees Fahrenheit. When the user clicks a button on the Web page, the button's Click event procedure should display the temperature converted to Celsius. Save and then start and test the project. Close the browser window. Close the Code Editor window and then close the project. (2-8, 10)

INTERMEDIATE

9. Create an empty Web site project named Measurement. Save the project in the VbReloaded2012\Chap13 folder. Add a new Web page named Default.aspx to the project. Change the DOCUMENT object's Title property to "Inches to Centimeters". The Web page should provide a text box for the user to enter the number of inches. When the user clicks a button on the Web page, the button's Click event procedure should display the number of inches converted to centimeters. Save and then start and test the project. Close the browser window. Close the Code Editor window and then close the project. (2-8, 10)

INTERMEDIATE

10. Create an empty Web site project named Hearthstone. Save the project in the VbReloaded2012\Chap13 folder. Add two new Web pages named Default.aspx and Message.aspx to the project. Change each DOCUMENT object's Title property to Hearthstone Heating and Cooling. Create Web pages similar to the ones shown in Figures 13-47 and 13-48. The image on the Web page is stored in the VbReloaded2012\Chap13\Thermostat.png file. The static text and link button control on the Default.aspx page should be centered, horizontally, on the page. Save and then start the project. Close the browser window and then close the project. (2-4, 6-9)

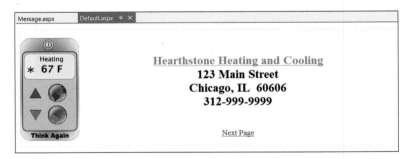

Figure 13-47   Default.aspx Web page for Exercise 10

OpenClipArt.org/motudo

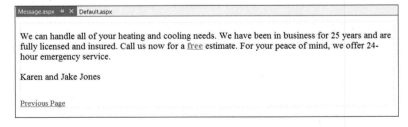

Figure 13-48   Message.aspx Web page for Exercise 10

11. Create an empty Web site project named ZipCode. Save the project in the VbReloaded2012\Chap13 folder. (2-8, 10)

a. Add a new Web page named Default.aspx to the project. Change the DOCUMENT object's Title property to ZIP Code Verifier.

b. Create the Web page shown in Figure 13-49. Use labels for the static text. Also, use the Segoe UI font for the static text and controls. Use a RequiredFieldValidator control to verify that the text box is not empty. Use a RegularExpressionValidator control to verify that the ZIP code is in the appropriate format.

c. Save and then start the project. (If necessary, refer to the Important note that appears after Figure 13-38 in the chapter.) Test the project by clicking the text box and then pressing Enter. The RequiredFieldValidator control should display the "Please enter a ZIP code." message. Now, test it using the following ZIP codes: 606123, 60612, 60611-3, and 60611-3456. The RegularExpressionValidator control should display the "Incorrect format" message for the first and third ZIP codes. Close the browser window. Close the Code Editor window and then close the project.

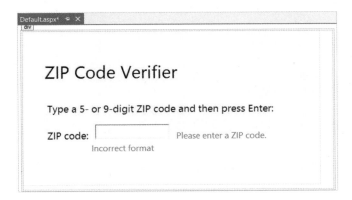

Figure 13-49   Web page for Exercise 11

Case Projects

 Market Foods

Create an empty Web site project named MarketFoods. Save the project in the VbReloaded2012\Chap13 folder. Add a new Web page named Default.aspx to the project. Change the DOCUMENT object's Title property to Market Foods. Create a Web page similar to the sketch shown in Figure 13-50. The DropDownList control should contain the store numbers listed in Figure 13-51. When the user clicks the Submit button, the button's Click event procedure should display the names of the manager and assistant manager on the Web page. Code the procedure. Save and then start and test the project. Close the browser window and then close the project. (2-8, 10)

Market Foods

Store number: [DropDownList]   [Submit]

Manager: [   ]

Assistant: [   ]

Figure 13-50   Sketch for the Market Foods Web page
© 2013 Cengage Learning

Store number	Manager	Assistant manager
101	Carson Jones	Susan Holsteng
102	Janice Leigh	Sung Ho
103	Suman Patel	Linda Lincoln
104	Lou Chan	Ted Yardley
105	Chase Michaels	Joe Petalino

Figure 13-51   Store information for the Market Foods Web page
© 2013 Cengage Learning

 ## Jeremy Antiques

Create an empty Web site project named JeremyAntiques. Save the project in the VbReloaded2012\Chap13 folder. Add a new Web page named Default.aspx to the project. Change the DOCUMENT object's Title property to Jeremy Antiques. Create a Web page that provides a text box for the user to enter a sales amount. Associate a RequiredFieldValidator control with the text box. When the user clicks a button on the Web page, the button's Click event procedure should display both a 5% sales tax and a 6% sales tax. Code the procedure. Save and then start and test the project. Close the browser window and then close the project. (2-10)

 ## Cheap Loans

Create an empty Web site project named Cheap Loans. Save the project in the VbReloaded2012\Chap13 folder. Add a new Web page named Default.aspx to the project. Change the DOCUMENT object's Title property to Cheap Loans. Create a Web page that provides text boxes for the user to enter the amount of a loan, the annual interest rate, and the term of the loan (in years). Associate each text box with its own RequiredFieldValidator control. When the user clicks a button on the Web page, the button's Click event procedure should display the monthly payment. Code the procedure. Save and then start and test the project. Close the browser window and then close the project. (2-10)

Skate-Away Sales

Create an empty Web site project named SkateAway. Save the project in the VbReloaded2012\Chap13 folder. Add a new Web page named Default.aspx to the project. Change the DOCUMENT object's Title property to Skate-Away Sales. The Skate-Away Sales company sells skateboards by phone. The skateboards are priced at $100 each and are available in two colors: yellow and blue. The project should allow the salesperson to enter the customer's name, the number of blue skateboards ordered, and the number of yellow skateboards ordered. When the user clicks a button on the Web page, the button's Click event procedure should calculate the total number of skateboards ordered and the total price of the order, including a 5% sales tax. Create an appropriate Web page, and then code the button's Click event procedure. Save and then start and test the project. Close the browser window and then close the project. (2-10)

Creating Classes and Objects

After studying Chapter 14, you should be able to:

1. Explain the terminology used in object-oriented programming
2. Create a class
3. Instantiate and utilize an object
4. Add Property procedures to a class
5. Include data validation in a class
6. Create default and parameterized constructors
7. Include methods other than constructors in a class
8. Include a ReadOnly property in a class
9. Create an auto-implemented property
10. Overload the methods in a class

Reading and Study Guide

Before you begin reading Chapter 14, view the Ch14_ReadingStudyGuide.pdf file. You can open the file using Adobe Reader, which is available for free on the Adobe Web site at *www.adobe.com/downloads/*.

Object-Oriented Programming Terminology

As you learned in Chapter 1, Visual Basic 2012 is an **object-oriented programming language**, which is a language that allows the programmer to use objects to accomplish a program's goal. Recall that an **object** is anything that can be seen, touched, or used. In other words, an object is nearly any *thing*. The objects used in an object-oriented program can take on many different forms. The text boxes, list boxes, and buttons included in most Windows applications are objects, and so are the application's named constants and variables. An object can also represent something found in real life, such as a wristwatch or a car.

Every object used in an object-oriented program is created from a **class**, which is a pattern that the computer uses to create the object. Using object-oriented programming (**OOP**) terminology, objects are **instantiated** (created) from a class, and each object is referred to as an **instance** of the class. A button control, for example, is an instance of the Button class. The button is instantiated when you drag the Button tool from the toolbox to the form. A String variable, on the other hand, is an instance of the String class and is instantiated the first time you refer to the variable in code. Keep in mind that the class itself is not an object, but the directions on how to create an object. Only an instance of a class is an object.

Every object has **attributes**, which are the characteristics that describe the object. Attributes are also called properties. Included in the attributes of buttons and text boxes are the Name and Text properties. List boxes have a Name property as well as a Sorted property.

In addition to attributes, every object also has behaviors. An object's **behaviors** include methods and events. **Methods** are the operations (actions) that the object is capable of performing. For example, a button can use its Focus method to send the focus to itself. Similarly, a String variable can use its ToUpper method to temporarily convert its contents to uppercase. **Events**, on the other hand, are the actions to which an object can respond. A button's Click event, for instance, allows the button to respond to a mouse click.

A class contains—or, in OOP terms, it **encapsulates**—all of the attributes and behaviors of the object it instantiates. The term "encapsulate" means "to enclose in a capsule." In the context of OOP, the "capsule" is a class.

Creating a Class

In previous chapters, you instantiated objects using classes that are built into Visual Basic, such as the TextBox and Label classes. You used the instantiated objects in a variety of ways in many different applications. In some applications, you used a text box to enter a name, while in other applications you used it to enter a sales tax rate. Similarly, you used label controls to identify text boxes and also to display the result of calculations. The ability to use an object for more than one purpose saves programming time and money—an advantage that contributes to the popularity of object-oriented programming.

You can also define your own classes in Visual Basic and then create instances (objects) from those classes. You define a class using the **Class statement**, which you enter in a class file. Figure 14-1 shows the statement's syntax and lists the steps for adding a class file to an open project. The figure also includes an example of the Class statement entered in a class file. The three Option statements included in the figure have the same meaning in a class file as they have in a form file.

HOW TO Define a Class

<u>Syntax</u>
Public Class *className*
    attributes section
    behaviors section
End Class

<u>Adding a class file to an open project</u>
1. Click PROJECT on the menu bar and then click Add Class. The Add New Item dialog box opens with Class selected in the middle column of the dialog box.
2. Type the name of the class (using Pascal case) followed by a period and the letters vb in the Name box, and then click the Add button.

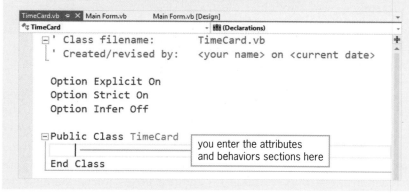

Figure 14-1   How to define a class
© 2013 Cengage Learning

The creation of a good class, which is one whose objects can be used in a variety of ways by many different applications, requires a lot of planning.

Although it is not a requirement, the convention is to use Pascal case for the class name—for example, TimeCard. The names of Visual Basic classes (such as Integer and TextBox) also follow this naming convention. Within the Class statement, you define the attributes and behaviors of the objects the class will create. In most cases, the attributes are represented by Private variables and Public properties. The behaviors are represented by methods, which can be Sub or Function procedures. (You also can include Event procedures in a Class statement. However, that topic is beyond the scope of this book.)

After you define a class, you can use either of the syntax versions in Figure 14-2 to instantiate one or more objects. In both versions, *className* is the name of the class, and *variableName* is the name of a variable that will represent the object. The difference between both versions relates to when the object is actually created. The computer creates the object only when it processes the statement containing the New keyword. (You will learn more about the New keyword later in this chapter.) Also included in Figure 14-2 is an example of using each version of the syntax.

HOW TO Instantiate an Object from a Class

Syntax – Version 1
{**Dim** | **Private**} *variableName* **As** *className*
variableName = **New** *className*[(*argumentList*)]

Syntax – Version 2
{**Dim** | **Private**} *variableName* **As New** *className*[(*argumentList*)]

Example 1 (using syntax version 1)
```
Private hoursInfo As TimeCard
hoursInfo = New TimeCard
```
The Private instruction creates a TimeCard variable named **hoursInfo**. The assignment statement instantiates a TimeCard object and assigns it to the **hoursInfo** variable.

Example 2 (using syntax version 2)
```
Dim hoursInfo As New TimeCard
```
The Dim instruction creates a TimeCard variable named **hoursInfo**. The statement also instantiates a TimeCard object, which it assigns to the **hoursInfo** variable.

Figure 14-2 How to instantiate an object from a class
© 2013 Cengage Learning

In Example 1, the `Private hoursInfo As TimeCard` instruction creates a class-level variable that can represent a TimeCard object; however, it does not create the object. The object isn't created until the computer processes the `hoursInfo = New TimeCard` statement, which uses the TimeCard class to instantiate a TimeCard object. The statement assigns the object to the `hoursInfo` variable. In Example 2, the `Dim hoursInfo As New TimeCard` instruction creates a procedure-level variable named `hoursInfo`. It also instantiates a TimeCard object and assigns it to the variable.

Mini-Quiz 14-1

The answers to Mini-Quiz questions are located in Appendix A. Each question is associated with one or more objectives listed at the beginning of the chapter.

1. A class is considered an object. (1)

   a. True
   b. False

2. In Visual Basic, you enter the Class statement in a class file whose filename extension is _____ . (2)

   a. .cla
   b. .cls
   c. .vb
   d. none of the above

3. Which of the following instantiates an Animal object and assigns it to the **dog** variable? (3)

   a. `Dim dog As Animal`
   b. `Dim dog As New Animal`
   c. `Dim dog As Animal`
      `dog = New Animal`
   d. both b and c

In the remainder of this chapter, you will view examples of class definitions and also examples of code in which objects are instantiated and used. The first example is a class that contains attributes only, with each attribute represented by a Public variable.

Example 1—A Class That Contains Public Variables Only

In its simplest form, the Class statement can be used in place of the Structure statement, which you learned about in Chapter 11. Like the Structure statement, the Class statement groups related items into one unit. However, the unit is called a class rather than a structure. Figure 14-3 shows how you could code the Painters Paradise application from Chapter 11 using a class rather than a structure. As you may remember, the application displays the company's gross profit. Figure 14-3 also includes a sample run of the application.

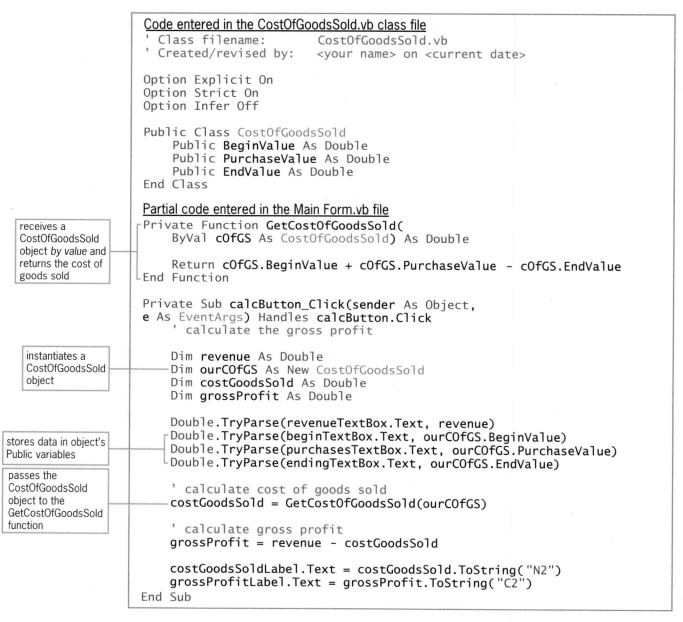

```
Code entered in the CostOfGoodsSold.vb class file
' Class filename:        CostOfGoodsSold.vb
' Created/revised by:    <your name> on <current date>

Option Explicit On
Option Strict On
Option Infer Off

Public Class CostOfGoodsSold
    Public BeginValue As Double
    Public PurchaseValue As Double
    Public EndValue As Double
End Class
```

Partial code entered in the Main Form.vb file

receives a CostOfGoodsSold object *by value* and returns the cost of goods sold

```
Private Function GetCostOfGoodsSold(
    ByVal cOfGS As CostOfGoodsSold) As Double

    Return cOfGS.BeginValue + cOfGS.PurchaseValue - cOfGS.EndValue
End Function

Private Sub calcButton_Click(sender As Object,
e As EventArgs) Handles calcButton.Click
    ' calculate the gross profit
```

instantiates a CostOfGoodsSold object

```
    Dim revenue As Double
    Dim ourCOfGS As New CostOfGoodsSold
    Dim costGoodsSold As Double
    Dim grossProfit As Double
```

stores data in object's Public variables

```
    Double.TryParse(revenueTextBox.Text, revenue)
    Double.TryParse(beginTextBox.Text, ourCOfGS.BeginValue)
    Double.TryParse(purchasesTextBox.Text, ourCOfGS.PurchaseValue)
    Double.TryParse(endingTextBox.Text, ourCOfGS.EndValue)
```

passes the CostOfGoodsSold object to the GetCostOfGoodsSold function

```
    ' calculate cost of goods sold
    costGoodsSold = GetCostOfGoodsSold(ourCOfGS)

    ' calculate gross profit
    grossProfit = revenue - costGoodsSold

    costGoodsSoldLabel.Text = costGoodsSold.ToString("N2")
    grossProfitLabel.Text = grossProfit.ToString("C2")
End Sub
```

Figure 14-3 Painters Paradise application using a class *(continues)*

(continued)

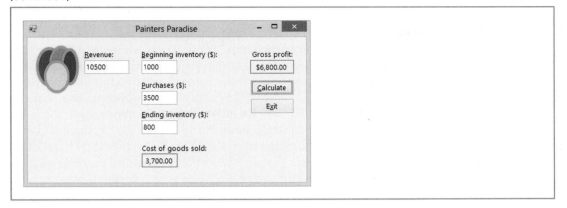

Figure 14-3 Painters Paradise application using a class
© 2013 Cengage Learning

If you want to experiment with the Painters Paradise application, open the solution contained in the Try It 1! folder.

Comparing the original code from Figure 11-6 with the code shown in Figure 14-3, you will notice that the Structure statement has been replaced with the Class statement. Unlike the Structure statement, which is entered in the MainForm's Declarations section, the Class statement is entered in a class file named CostOfGoodsSold.vb. The Class statement defines the three attributes of a CostOfGoodsSold object; each attribute is represented by a Public variable. A class's Public variables can be accessed by any application that contains an instance of the class. Using OOP terminology, the Public variables are "exposed" to the application. The convention is to use Pascal case for the names of the Public variables. This is because the Public variables represent properties that will be seen by anyone using an object instantiated from the class. The properties of Visual Basic objects, such as the Text and StartPosition properties, also follow this naming convention.

When comparing both versions of the code, you will also notice that the `Dim ourCOfGS As CostOfGoodsSold` statement in Figure 11-6 is replaced with the `Dim ourCOfGS As New CostOfGoodsSold` statement in Figure 14-3. (Notice the `New` keyword in the latter statement.) The Dim statement in Figure 11-6 declares a structure variable named `ourCOfGS`, whereas the Dim statement in Figure 14-3 instantiates a CostOfGoodsSold object named `ourCOfGS`.

Before viewing the second example of classes and objects, you will learn about Private variables, Public properties, and methods.

Private Variables and Public Property Procedures

Although you can define a class that contains only attributes represented by Public variables—like the CostOfGoodsSold class shown in Figure 14-3—that is rarely done. The disadvantage of using Public variables in a class is that a class cannot control the values assigned to its Public variables. As a result, the class cannot validate the values to ensure they are appropriate for the variables. Rather than declaring a class's variables using the `Public` keyword, most programmers declare them using the `Private` keyword. The naming convention for a class's Private variables is to use the underscore as the first character in the name and then camel case for the remainder of the name, as in the names `_side`, `_bonus`, and `_annualSales`.

Unlike a class's Public variables, its Private variables are not visible to applications that contain an instance of the class. Using OOP terminology, the Private variables are "hidden" from the application. Because of this, the names of the Private variables will not appear in the IntelliSense list as you are coding the application, nor will they be recognized within the application's code. For an application to assign data to or retrieve data from a Private variable in a class, it must use a Public property. In other words, an application cannot directly refer to a Private variable in a class. Rather, it must refer to the variable indirectly, through the use of a Public property. This is because a class's Private variables can be used only by instructions within the class itself.

You create a Public property using a **Property procedure**, whose syntax is shown in Figure 14-4. A Public Property procedure creates a property that is visible to any application that contains an instance of the class. In most cases, a Property procedure header begins with the keywords `Public Property`. However, as the syntax indicates, the header can also include one of the following keywords: `ReadOnly` or `WriteOnly`. The **ReadOnly keyword** indicates that the property's value can be retrieved (read) by an application, but the application cannot set (write to) the property. The property would get its value from the class itself rather than from the application. The **WriteOnly keyword** indicates that an application can set the property's value, but it cannot retrieve the value. In this case, the value would be set by the application for use within the class.

As Figure 14-4 shows, the name of the property follows the `Property` keyword in the header. You should use nouns and adjectives to name a property and enter the name using Pascal case, as in Side, Bonus, and AnnualSales. Following the property name is an optional *parameterList* enclosed in parentheses, the keyword `As`, and the property's *dataType*. The dataType must match the data type of the Private variable associated with the Property procedure.

HOW TO Create a Property Procedure

Syntax
Public [ReadOnly | WriteOnly] Property propertyName[(parameterList)] **As** dataType
   Get
       [instructions]
       Return privateVariable
   End Get
   Set(value As dataType**)**
       [instructions]
       privateVariable = {**value** | defaultValue}
   End Set
End Property

Example 1 – an application can both retrieve and set the Side property's value

```
Private _side As Integer

Public Property Side As Integer
    Get
        Return _side
    End Get
    Set(value As Integer)
        If value > 0 Then
            _side = value
        Else
            _side = 0
        End If
    End Set
End Property
```

Figure 14-4 How to create a Property procedure *(continues)*

(continued)

<u>Example 2 – an application can retrieve, but not set, the Bonus property's value</u>
```
Private _bonus As Double

Public ReadOnly Property Bonus As Double
    Get
        Return _bonus
    End Get
End Property
```

713

<u>Example 3 – an application can set, but not retrieve, the AnnualSales property's value</u>
```
Private _annualSales As Decimal

Public WriteOnly Property AnnualSales As Decimal
    Set(value As Decimal)
        _annualSales = value
    End Set
End Property
```

Figure 14-4   How to create a Property procedure
© 2013 Cengage Learning

Between a Property procedure's header and footer, you include a Get block of code, a Set block of code, or both Get and Set blocks of code. The appropriate block (or blocks) of code to include depends on the keywords contained in the procedure header. If the header contains the `ReadOnly` keyword, you include only a Get block of code in the Property procedure. The code contained in the **Get block** allows an application to retrieve the contents of the Private variable associated with the property. In the Property procedure shown in Example 2 in Figure 14-4, the `ReadOnly` keyword indicates that an application can retrieve the contents of the Bonus property, but it cannot set the property's value.

If the header contains the `WriteOnly` keyword, on the other hand, you include only a Set block of code in the procedure. The code in the **Set block** allows an application to assign a value to the Private variable associated with the property. In the Property procedure shown in Example 3 in Figure 14-4, the `WriteOnly` keyword indicates that an application can assign a value to the AnnualSales property, but it cannot retrieve the property's contents.

If the Property procedure header does not contain the `ReadOnly` or `WriteOnly` keywords, you include both a Get block of code and a Set block of code in the procedure, as shown in Example 1 in Figure 14-4. In this case, an application can both retrieve and set the Side property's value.

A Property procedure's Get block contains the **Get statement**, which begins with the Get clause and ends with the End Get clause. Most times, you will enter only the `Return` *privateVariable* instruction within the Get statement. The instruction returns the contents of the Private variable associated with the property. In Example 1 in Figure 14-4, the `Return _side` statement returns the contents of the `_side` variable, which is the Private variable associated with the Side property. Similarly, the `Return _bonus` statement in Example 2 returns the contents of the `_bonus` variable, which is the Private variable associated with the Bonus property. Example 3 does not contain a Get statement; this is because the AnnualSales property is designated as a WriteOnly property.

The Length property of a one-dimensional array is an example of a ReadOnly property.

The Set block in a Property procedure contains the **Set statement**, which begins with the Set clause and ends with the End Set clause. The Set clause's `value` parameter temporarily stores the value that is passed to the property by the application. The `value` parameter's *dataType* must match the data type of the Private variable associated with the Property procedure. You can enter one or more instructions between the Set and End Set clauses. One of the instructions should assign the contents of the `value` parameter to the Private variable associated with the property. In Example 3 in Figure 14-4, the `_annualSales = value` statement assigns the contents of the property's `value` parameter to the Private `_annualSales` variable.

In the Set statement, you often will include instructions to validate the value received from the application before assigning it to the Private variable. The Set statement in Example 1 in Figure 14-4 includes a selection structure whose condition determines whether the side measurement received from the application is greater than 0. If it is, the `_side = value` instruction assigns the integer stored in the `value` parameter to the Private `_side` variable. Otherwise, the `_side = 0` instruction assigns a default value (in this case, 0) to the variable.

Notice that the Property procedure in Example 2 in Figure 14-4 does not contain a Set statement. This is because the Bonus property is designated as a ReadOnly property.

Constructors

Most classes contain at least one constructor. A **constructor** is a class method, always named New, whose purpose is to initialize the class's Private variables. Constructors never return a value, so they are always Sub procedures rather than Function procedures. The syntax for creating a constructor is shown in Figure 14-5. Notice that a constructor's *parameterList* is optional. A constructor that has no parameters, like the constructor in Example 1, is called the **default constructor**; a class can have only one default constructor. A constructor that contains one or more parameters, like the constructor in Example 2, is called a **parameterized constructor**. A class can have as many parameterized constructors as needed. However, the parameterList in each parameterized constructor must be unique within the class. The method name (in this case, New) combined with its optional parameterList is called the method's **signature**.

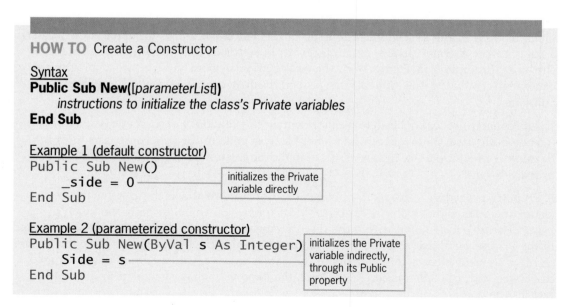

HOW TO Create a Constructor

Syntax
Public Sub New([*parameterList***])**
    instructions to initialize the class's Private variables
End Sub

Example 1 (default constructor)
```
Public Sub New()
    _side = 0 ─── initializes the Private
End Sub          variable directly
```

Example 2 (parameterized constructor)
```
Public Sub New(ByVal s As Integer) ─ initializes the Private
    Side = s                          variable indirectly,
End Sub                               through its Public
                                      property
```

Figure 14-5 How to create a constructor
© 2013 Cengage Learning

A default constructor is allowed to initialize the class's Private variables directly. The default constructor shown in Example 1 in Figure 14-5, for instance, assigns the number 0 to the class's Private _side variable. Parameterized constructors, on the other hand, should use the class's Public properties to access the Private variables indirectly. This is because the values passed to a parameterized constructor come from the application rather than from the class itself. Values that originate outside of the class should always be assigned to the Private variables indirectly, through the Public properties. Doing this ensures that the Property procedure's Set block, which may contain validation code, is processed. The parameterized constructor shown in Example 2 in Figure 14-5, for instance, uses the Public Side property to initialize the Private _side variable indirectly.

When an object is instantiated, the computer uses one of the class's constructors to initialize the class's Private variables. If a class contains more than one constructor, the computer determines the appropriate constructor by matching the number, data type, and position of the arguments in the statement that instantiates the object with the number, data type, and position of the parameters listed in each constructor's parameterList. The statements in Examples 1 and 2 in Figure 14-6 will invoke the default constructor because neither statement contains any arguments. The statements in Examples 3 and 4 will invoke the parameterized constructor because both statements contain an Integer argument.

HOW TO Invoke a Constructor

Example 1 – invokes the default constructor
```
Dim sqShape As New Square
```

Example 2 – invokes the default constructor
```
Dim sqShape As Square
sqShape = New Square
```

Example 3 – invokes the parameterized constructor
```
Dim sqShape As New Square(15)
```

Example 4 – invokes the parameterized constructor
```
Dim sqShape As Square
Integer.TryParse(sideTextBox.Text, sideMeasurement)
sqShape = New Square(sideMeasurement)
```

Recall that the statement containing the **New** keyword instantiates the object.

Figure 14-6 How to invoke a constructor
© 2013 Cengage Learning

Methods Other than Constructors

Except for constructors, which must be Sub procedures, the other methods in a class can be either Sub procedures or Function procedures. Recall from Chapter 8 that the difference between these two types of procedures is that a Function procedure returns a value after performing its assigned task, whereas a Sub procedure does not return a value. Figure 14-7 shows the syntax for a method that is not a constructor. (In other words, a method that does something other than create and initialize an object.) Like property names, method names should be entered using Pascal case. However, unlike property names, the first word in a method name should be a verb, and any subsequent words should be nouns and adjectives. Figure 14-7 also includes two examples of a method that allows a Square object to calculate its area. Notice that you can write the method as either a Function procedure or a Sub procedure.

HOW TO Create a Method That Is Not a Constructor

Syntax
Public {**Sub** | **Function**} *methodName*([*parameterList*]) [**As** *dataType*]
    instructions
End {**Sub** | **Function**}

Example 1 – Function procedure
```
Public Function GetArea() As Integer
    Return _side * _side
End Function
```

Example 2 – Sub procedure
```
Public Sub GetArea(ByRef sqArea As Integer)
    sqArea = _side * _side
End Sub
```

Figure 14-7   How to create a method that is not a constructor
© 2013 Cengage Learning

Example 2—A Class That Contains Private Variables, Public Properties, and Methods

Figure 14-8 shows the definition of the Rectangle class, which the Carpets Galore application uses to instantiate a Rectangle object that represents a floor in a room. The figure also shows the application's calcButton_Click procedure, which displays the floor's area (in square yards) and the cost of carpeting the floor. The figure also includes a sample run of the application.

Class statement entered in the Rectangle.vb class file
```
' Class filename:        Rectangle.vb
' Created/revised by:    <your name> on <current date>

Option Explicit On
Option Strict On
Option Infer Off

Public Class Rectangle
    Private _length As Double
    Private _width As Double

    Public Property Length As Double
        Get
            Return _length
        End Get
        Set(value As Double)
            If value > 0 Then
                _length = value
            Else
                _length = 0
            End If
        End Set
    End Property
End Property
```

Figure 14-8   Carpets Galore application *(continues)*

(continued)

```vb
    Public Property Width As Double
        Get
            Return _width
        End Get
        Set(value As Double)
            If value > 0 Then
                _width = value
            Else
                _width = 0
            End If
        End Set
    End Property

    Public Sub New()
        _length = 0
        _width = 0
    End Sub

    Public Sub New(ByVal len As Double, ByVal wid As Double)
        Length = len
        Width = wid
    End Sub

    Public Function GetArea() As Double
        Return _length * _width
    End Function
End Class
```

calcButton_Click procedure entered in the MainForm.vb file

```vb
Private Sub calcButton_Click(sender As Object,
e As EventArgs) Handles calcButton.Click
    ' displays square yards and cost of carpet

    ' instantiate a Rectangle object
    Dim floor As New Rectangle                          ── instantiates a Rectangle object, using the default constructor

    ' declare variables
    Dim priceSqYd As Double
    Dim sqYards As Double
    Dim cost As Double

    ' assign values to the object's Public properties
    Double.TryParse(lengthListBox.SelectedItem.ToString, floor.Length)   ── uses the object's Public properties to assign values to the Private variables
    Double.TryParse(widthListBox.SelectedItem.ToString, floor.Width)
    Double.TryParse(priceListBox.SelectedItem.ToString, priceSqYd)

    ' calculate the square yards
    sqYards = floor.GetArea / 9            ── invokes the Rectangle object's GetArea method
    ' calculate the carpet cost
    cost = priceSqYd * sqYards
    ' display output
    sqYardsLabel.Text = sqYards.ToString("N1")
    costLabel.Text = cost.ToString("C2")
End Sub
```

Figure 14-8 Carpets Galore application *(continues)*

(continued)

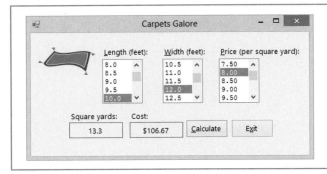

Figure 14-8   Carpets Galore application

OpenClipArt.org/Artmaker; © 2013 Cengage Learning

If you want to experiment with the Carpets Galore application, open the solution contained in the Try It 2! folder.

The `Dim floor As New Rectangle` instruction in the calcButton_Click procedure instantiates a Rectangle object, using the default constructor to initialize the object's Private variables. The first two TryParse methods in the procedure use the object's Public properties to assign values to the object's Private variables. The procedure then uses the object's GetArea method to calculate and return the area of the floor (in square feet).

Figure 14-9 shows how you could code the calcButton_Click procedure using the parameterized constructor rather than the default constructor used in Figure 14-8. The modifications made to the code are shaded in the figure. In this version of the procedure, the `Dim floor As Rectangle` instruction creates a variable that can store a Rectangle object, but it does not create the object. The object is created when the computer processes the `floor = New Rectangle(roomLen, roomWid)` instruction, which passes its two Double arguments (*by value*) to the parameterized constructor (shown earlier in Figure 14-8). The parameterized constructor stores the values it receives in its `len` and `wid` parameters, and then assigns the parameter values to the Rectangle object's Public Length and Width properties.

declares a variable that can store a Rectangle object

instantiates a Rectangle object, using the parameterized constructor

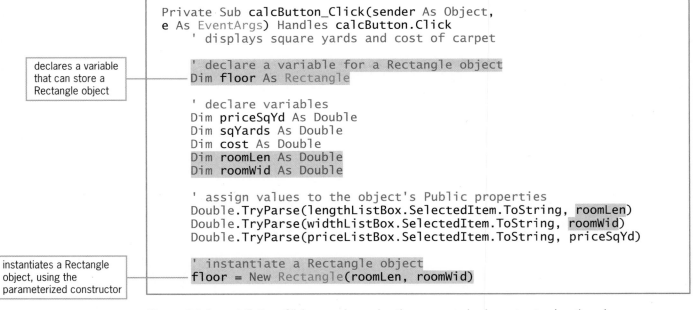

```
Private Sub calcButton_Click(sender As Object,
e As EventArgs) Handles calcButton.Click
    ' displays square yards and cost of carpet

    ' declare a variable for a Rectangle object
    Dim floor As Rectangle

    ' declare variables
    Dim priceSqYd As Double
    Dim sqYards As Double
    Dim cost As Double
    Dim roomLen As Double
    Dim roomWid As Double

    ' assign values to the object's Public properties
    Double.TryParse(lengthListBox.SelectedItem.ToString, roomLen)
    Double.TryParse(widthListBox.SelectedItem.ToString, roomWid)
    Double.TryParse(priceListBox.SelectedItem.ToString, priceSqYd)

    ' instantiate a Rectangle object
    floor = New Rectangle(roomLen, roomWid)
```

Figure 14-9   calcButton_Click procedure using the parameterized constructor *(continues)*

Example 3—Reusing a Class

(continued)

```
     ' calculate the square yards
     sqYards = floor.GetArea / 9
     ' calculate the carpet cost
     cost = priceSqYd * sqYards
     ' display output
     sqYardsLabel.Text = sqYards.ToString("N1")
     costLabel.Text = cost.ToString("C2")
  End Sub
```

Figure 14-9 calcButton_Click procedure using the parameterized constructor
© 2013 Cengage Learning

When you assign a value to a property, the computer passes the value to the property's Set statement, where it is stored in the Set statement's `value` parameter. In this case, the selection structure in the Length property's Set statement (shown earlier in Figure 14-8) compares the value stored in the `value` parameter with the number 0. If the value is greater than 0, the selection structure's True path assigns the value to the Private `_length` variable; otherwise, its False path assigns the number 0 to the variable. Similarly, the selection structure in the Width property's Set statement compares the value stored in the `value` parameter with the number 0. If the value is greater than 0, the selection structure's True path assigns the value to the Private `_width` variable; otherwise, its False path assigns the number 0 to the variable. Notice that a parameterized constructor uses the class's Public properties to access the Private variables indirectly. This is because the values passed to a parameterized constructor come from the application rather than from the class itself. As mentioned earlier, values that originate outside of the class should always be assigned to the Private variables indirectly, through the Public properties. Doing this ensures that the Property procedure's Set block, which typically contains validation code, is processed.

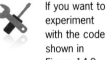

If you want to experiment with the code shown in Figure 14-9, open the solution contained in the Try It 3! folder.

Example 3—Reusing a Class

In Example 2, you used the Rectangle class to instantiate an object that represented the floor in a room. In this example, you will use the Rectangle class to instantiate an object that represents a square pizza. A square is simply a rectangle that has four equal sides. As mentioned earlier, the ability to use an object—in this case, a Rectangle object—for more than one purpose saves programming time and money, which contributes to the popularity of object-oriented programming.

Figure 14-10 shows the calcButton_Click procedure in the Pete's Pizzeria application. The procedure uses the Rectangle class from Figure 14-8. The figure also includes a sample run of the application.

```
Private Sub calcButton_Click(sender As Object,
e As EventArgs) Handles calcButton.Click
    ' displays the number of square pizza slices
    ' that can be cut from a square pizza

    Dim entirePizza As New Rectangle ⎤   instantiates two
    Dim pizzaSlice As New Rectangle ⎦   Rectangle objects
    Dim entireArea As Double
    Dim sliceArea As Double
    Dim slices As Double

    Double.TryParse(entirePizzaTextBox.Text, entirePizza.Length) ⎤   uses the Public
    Double.TryParse(entirePizzaTextBox.Text, entirePizza.Width)  │   properties to assign
    Double.TryParse(pizzaSliceTextBox.Text, pizzaSlice.Length)   │   values to the Private
    Double.TryParse(pizzaSliceTextBox.Text, pizzaSlice.Width) ⎦   variables
```

Figure 14-10 Pete's Pizzeria application *(continues)*

(continued)

invokes each object's GetArea method

```
' calculate areas
entireArea = entirePizza.GetArea
sliceArea = pizzaSlice.GetArea
' calculate number of slices
If sliceArea > 0 Then
    slices = entireArea / sliceArea
Else
    slices = 0
End If
' display number of slices
slicesLabel.Text = slices.ToString("N1")
End Sub
```

720

If you want to experiment with the code shown in Figure 14-10, open the solution contained in the Try It 4! folder.

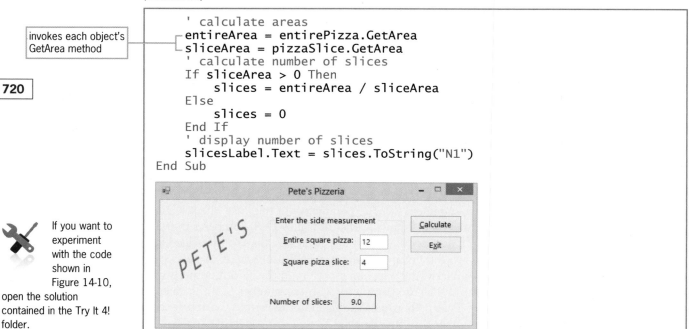

Figure 14-10   Pete's Pizzeria application
© 2013 Cengage Learning

Example 4—A Class That Contains a ReadOnly Property

As you learned earlier, the ReadOnly keyword in a Property procedure's header indicates that the property's value can be retrieved (read) by an application, but the application cannot set (write to) the property. A ReadOnly property gets its value from the class itself rather than from the application. The CourseGrade class shown in Figure 14-11 contains a ReadOnly property named Grade. The property gets its value from the class's DetermineGrade method. The figure also shows the displayButton_Click procedure in the Grade Calculator application. The procedure instantiates a CourseGrade object and then uses the object's DetermineGrade method to determine the student's grade. The procedure displays the grade in the gradeLabel, as shown in the sample run included in the figure.

<u>Class statement entered in the CourseGrade.vb class file</u>
```
' Class filename:      CourseGrade.vb
' Created/revised by:  <your name> on <current date>

Option Explicit On
Option Strict On
Option Infer Off

Public Class CourseGrade
    Private _score1 As Integer
    Private _score2 As Integer
    Private _grade As String

    Public Property Score1 As Integer
        Get
            Return _score1
        End Get
```

Figure 14-11   Grade Calculator application *(continues)*

Example 4—A Class That Contains a ReadOnly Property

721

(continued)

```vb
        Set(value As Integer)
            _score1 = value
        End Set
    End Property

    Public Property Score2 As Integer
        Get
            Return _score2
        End Get
        Set(value As Integer)
            _score2 = value
        End Set
    End Property

    Public ReadOnly Property Grade As String
        Get
            Return _grade
        End Get
    End Property

    Public Sub New()
        _score1 = 0
        _score2 = 0
        _grade = String.Empty
    End Sub

    Public Sub DetermineGrade()
        Select Case _score1 + _score2
            Case Is >= 180
                _grade = "A"
            Case Is >= 160
                _grade = "B"
            Case Is >= 140
                _grade = "C"
            Case Is >= 120
                _grade = "D"
            Case Else
                _grade = "F"
        End Select
    End Sub
End Class
```

ReadOnly property

displayButton_Click procedure entered in the MainForm.vb file
```vb
Private Sub displayButton_Click(sender As Object,
e As EventArgs) Handles displayButton.Click
    ' calculates and displays a letter grade

    ' instantiate a CourseGrade object
    Dim studentGrade As New CourseGrade

    ' assign test scores
    Integer.TryParse(test1ListBox.SelectedItem.ToString,
                studentGrade.Score1)
    Integer.TryParse(test2ListBox.SelectedItem.ToString,
                studentGrade.Score2)

    ' determine the grade
    Call studentGrade.DetermineGrade()

    ' display the grade
    gradeLabel.Text = studentGrade.Grade

End Sub
```

calls the object's DetermineGrade method

accesses the object's ReadOnly Grade property

Figure 14-11 Grade Calculator application *(continues)*

(continued)

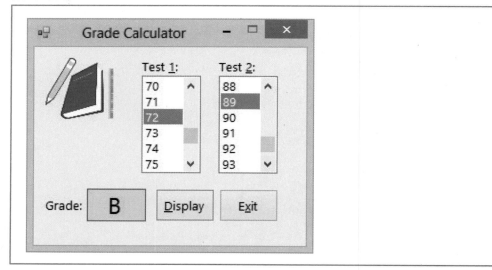

Figure 14-11 Grade Calculator application

OpenClipArt.org/Minduka; © 2013 Cengage Learning

Example 5—A Class That Contains Auto-Implemented Properties

The **auto-implemented properties** feature in Visual Basic enables you to specify the property of a class in one line of code, as shown in Figure 14-12. When you enter the line of code in the Code Editor window, Visual Basic automatically creates a hidden Private variable that it associates with the property. It also automatically creates hidden Get and Set blocks. The Private variable's name will be the same as the property's name, but it will be preceded by an underscore. For example, if you create an auto-implemented property named City, Visual Basic will create a hidden Private variable named _City. The auto-implemented properties feature provides a shorter syntax for you to use when creating a class: You don't need to create the Private variable associated with a property, nor do you need to enter the property's Get and Set blocks of code. However, keep in mind that you will need to use the standard syntax if you want to add validation code to the Set block, or if you want the property to be either ReadOnly or WriteOnly.

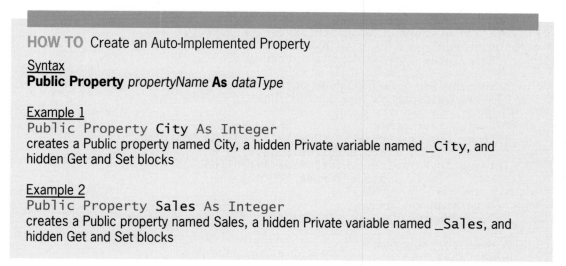

HOW TO Create an Auto-Implemented Property

<u>Syntax</u>
Public Property *propertyName* **As** *dataType*

<u>Example 1</u>
`Public Property City As Integer`
creates a Public property named City, a hidden Private variable named _City, and hidden Get and Set blocks

<u>Example 2</u>
`Public Property Sales As Integer`
creates a Public property named Sales, a hidden Private variable named _Sales, and hidden Get and Set blocks

Figure 14-12 How to create an auto-implemented property

© 2013 Cengage Learning

Example 6—A Class That Contains Overloaded Methods

Figure 14-13 shows how you could use the auto-implemented properties feature in the CourseGrade class from the previous section. The code pertaining to the two auto-implemented properties (Score1 and Score2) is shaded in the figure. You cannot use the auto-implemented properties feature for the class's Grade property because that property is ReadOnly. (You will create this class in Programming Tutorial 1.)

```vb
' Class filename:       CourseGrade.vb
' Created/revised by:   <your name> on <current date>

Option Explicit On
Option Strict On
Option Infer Off

Public Class CourseGrade
    Public Property Score1 As Integer          auto-implemented
    Public Property Score2 As Integer          properties
    Private _grade As String

    Public ReadOnly Property Grade As String    a ReadOnly
        Get                                     property cannot
            Return _grade                       be an auto-
        End Get                                 implemented
    End Property                                property

    Public Sub New()
        _Score1 = 0
        _Score2 = 0
        _grade = String.Empty
    End Sub

    Public Sub DetermineGrade()
        Select Case _Score1 + _Score2
            Case Is >= 180
                _grade = "A"
            Case Is >= 160
                _grade = "B"
            Case Is >= 140
                _grade = "C"
            Case Is >= 120
                _grade = "D"
            Case Else
                _grade = "F"
        End Select
    End Sub
End Class
```

Figure 14-13 CourseGrade class using auto-implemented properties
© 2013 Cengage Learning

Example 6—A Class That Contains Overloaded Methods

In this example, you will use a class named Employee to instantiate an object. Employee objects have the attributes and behaviors listed in Figure 14-14.

Attributes of an Employee object
employee number
employee name

Behaviors of an Employee object
1. An Employee object can initialize its attributes using values provided by the class.
2. An Employee object can initialize its attributes using values provided by the application in which it is instantiated.
3. An Employee object can calculate and return the gross pay for salaried employees, who are paid twice per month. The gross pay is calculated by dividing the salaried employee's annual salary by 24.
4. An Employee object can calculate and return the gross pay for hourly employees. The gross pay is calculated by multiplying the number of hours the employee worked during the week by his or her pay rate.

Figure 14-14   Attributes and behaviors of an Employee object
© 2013 Cengage Learning

Figure 14-15 shows the Employee class defined in the Employee.vb file. The class contains two auto-implemented properties and four methods. The two New methods are the class's default and parameterized constructors. The default constructor initializes the class's Private variables directly, while the parameterized constructor uses the class's Public properties to initialize the Private variables indirectly. As you learned earlier, using a Public property in this manner ensures that the computer processes any validation code associated with the property. Even though the Number and EmpName properties in Figure 14-15 do not have any validation code, you should use the properties in the parameterized constructor in case validation code is added to the class in the future.

```vb
' Class filename:        Employee.vb
' Created/revised by:    <your name> on <current date>

Option Explicit On
Option Strict On
Option Infer Off

Public Class Employee
    Public Property Number As String
    Public Property EmpName As String

    Public Sub New()
        _Number = String.Empty
        _EmpName = String.Empty
    End Sub

    Public Sub New(ByVal num As String, ByVal name As String)
        Number = num
        EmpName = name
    End Sub
```

auto-implemented properties

overloaded constructors

Figure 14-15   Employee class definition (*continues*)

Example 6—A Class That Contains Overloaded Methods

(continued)

```
      Public Function GetGross(ByVal salary As Double) As Double
            ' calculates the gross pay for salaried
            ' employees, who are paid twice per month

            Return salary / 24
      End Function

      Public Function GetGross(ByVal hours As Double,
                               ByVal rate As Double) As Double
            ' calculates the weekly gross pay for hourly employees

            Return hours * rate
      End Function
   End Class
```

overloaded GetGross methods

Figure 14-15   Employee class definition
© 2013 Cengage Learning

When two or more methods have the same name but different parameters, the methods are referred to as **overloaded methods**. The two constructors in Figure 14-15 are considered overloaded methods because each is named New and each has a different parameterList. You can overload any of the methods contained in a class, not just constructors. The two GetGross methods in the figure are also overloaded methods because they have the same name but a different parameterList.

You already are familiar with overloaded methods because you have used several of the ones built into Visual Basic. Examples of such methods include ToString, TryParse, Convert.ToDecimal, and MessageBox.Show. The Code Editor's IntelliSense feature displays a box that allows you to view a method's signatures, one signature at a time. Recall that a method's signature includes its name and optional parameterList. The box shown in Figure 14-16 displays the first of the ToString method's four signatures. You use the up and down arrows in the box to display the other signatures. If a class you create contains overloaded methods, the signatures of those methods will also be displayed in the IntelliSense box.

```
grossLabel.Text = gross.ToString(
                  ▲ 1 of 4 ▼  ToString() As String
                              Converts the numeric value of this instance to its equivalent string representation.
```

Figure 14-16   First of the ToString method's four signatures

Overloading is useful when two or more methods require different parameters to perform essentially the same task. Both overloaded constructors in the Employee class, for example, initialize the class's Private variables. However, the default constructor does not need to be passed any information to perform the task, while the parameterized constructor requires two items of information (the employee number and name). Similarly, both GetGross methods in the Employee class calculate and return a gross pay amount. However, the first GetGross method performs its task for salaried employees and requires an application to pass it one item of information: the employee's annual salary. The second GetGross method performs its task for hourly employees and requires two items of information: the number of hours the employee worked and his or her rate of pay.

Rather than using two overloaded GetGross methods in the Employee class, you could have used two methods having different names, such as GetSalariedGross and GetHourlyGross. The advantage of overloading the GetGross method is that you need to remember the name of only one method.

The Employee class is used in the Woods Manufacturing application, which displays the gross pay for salaried and hourly employees. It also displays a report showing each employee's number, name, and gross pay. Salaried employees at the company are paid twice per month. Therefore, each salaried employee's gross pay is calculated by dividing his or her annual salary by 24. Hourly employees are paid weekly. The gross pay for an hourly employee is calculated by multiplying the number of hours the employee worked during the week by his or her hourly pay rate. Figure 14-17 shows the application's calcButton_Click procedure and includes a sample run of the application.

declares a variable to store an Employee object

instantiates an Employee object

calculates the gross pay for an hourly employee

calculates the gross pay for a salaried employee

```
Private Sub calcButton_Click(sender As Object,
e As EventArgs) Handles calcButton.Click
    ' displays the gross pay and a report

    ' declare variables
    Dim ourEmployee As Employee
    Dim annualSalary As Double
    Dim hours As Double
    Dim hourRate As Double
    Dim gross As Double

    ' instantiate an Employee object
    ourEmployee =
        New Employee(numTextBox.Text, nameTextBox.Text)

    ' determine the selected radio button
    If hourlyRadioButton.Checked Then
        ' calculate the gross pay for an hourly employee
        Double.TryParse(hoursListBox.SelectedItem.ToString, hours)
        Double.TryParse(rateListBox.SelectedItem.ToString, hourRate)
        gross = ourEmployee.GetGross(hours, hourRate)
    Else
        ' calculate the gross pay for a salaried employee
        Double.TryParse(salaryListBox.SelectedItem.ToString,
                        annualSalary)
        gross = ourEmployee.GetGross(annualSalary)
    End If

    ' display the gross pay and report
    grossLabel.Text = gross.ToString("C2")
    reportTextBox.Text = reportTextBox.Text &
        ourEmployee.Number.PadRight(6) &
        ourEmployee.EmpName.PadRight(25) &
        gross.ToString("N2").PadLeft(9) & ControlChars.NewLine

    numTextBox.Focus()
End Sub
```

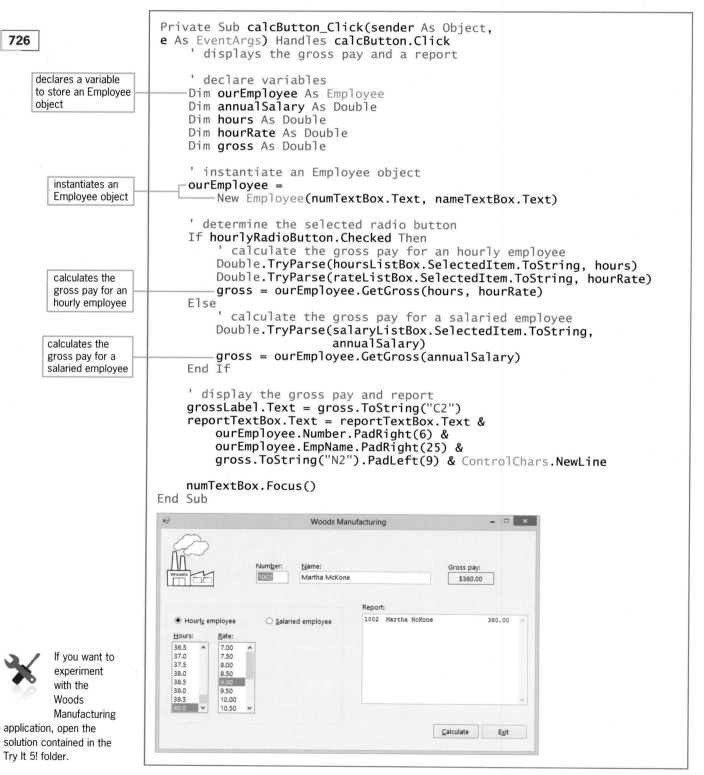

If you want to experiment with the Woods Manufacturing application, open the solution contained in the Try It 5! folder.

Figure 14-17 calcButton_Click procedure

OpenClipArt.org/Improulx; © 2013 Cengage Learning

Mini-Quiz 14-2

1. Some constructors return a value. (6)

   a. True

   b. False

2. A Private variable in a class can be accessed directly by a Public method in the same class. (6, 7)

   a. True

   b. False

The answers to Mini-Quiz questions are located in Appendix A. Each question is associated with one or more objectives listed at the beginning of the chapter.

3. The name of the default constructor for a class named Animal is —————— . (6)

   a. Animal

   b. AnimalConstructor

   c. Constructor

   d. none of the above

4. The validation code is entered in the —————— block in a Property procedure. (5)

   a. Assign

   b. Get

   c. Set

   d. Validate

You have completed the concepts section of Chapter 14. The Programming Tutorial section is next.

PROGRAMMING TUTORIAL 1

Coding the Grade Calculator Application

In this tutorial, you will create an application that displays a student's grade. The grade is based on two tests whose scores can be from 0 through 100. The grading scale is shown in Figure 14-18. Figures 14-19 and 14-20 show the application's TOE chart and MainForm, respectively. The interface contains four labels, two list boxes, a picture box, and two buttons.

Points	Grade
at least 180	A
160 – 179	B
140 – 159	C
120 – 139	D
less than 120	F

Figure 14-18 Grading scale for the Grade Calculator application
© 2013 Cengage Learning

Task	Object	Event
1. Fill the list boxes with test scores from 0 through 100	MainForm	Load
2. Select test score 75 in each list box		
End the application	exitButton	Click
Get the two test scores	test1ListBox, test2ListBox	None
Clear the gradeLabel		SelectedValueChanged
Display the letter grade in gradeLabel	displayButton	Click
Display the letter grade (from displayButton)	gradeLabel	None

Figure 14-19 TOE chart for the Grade Calculator application
© 2013 Cengage Learning

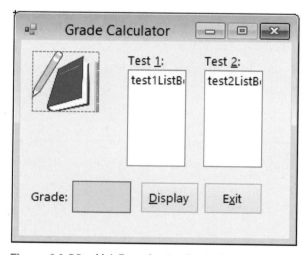

Figure 14-20 MainForm for the Grade Calculator application
OpenClipArt.org/Minduka

Creating the CourseGrade Class

First, you will open the Grade Calculator application and then create the CourseGrade class shown earlier in Figure 14-13. The CourseGrade class contains three attributes: two test scores and a letter grade. It also contains a default constructor that initializes the test scores to 0 and initializes the letter grade to the empty string. In addition, it contains the DetermineGrade method, which determines the appropriate letter grade based on the sum of both test scores.

To open the application and create the CourseGrade class:

1. Start Visual Studio. Open the **Grade Solution (Grade Solution.sln)** file contained in the VbReloaded2012\Chap14\Grade Solution folder. If necessary, open the designer window.

2. Click **PROJECT** on the menu bar and then click **Add Class**. The Add New Item dialog box opens with Class selected in the middle column. Change the entry in the Name box to **CourseGrade.vb** and then click the **Add** button.

3. Press **Enter** to insert a blank line above the Public Class clause. Beginning in the blank line, enter the following two comments, replacing <your name> and <current date> with your name and the current date, respectively. Press **Enter** twice after typing the second comment.

```
' Class filename:      CourseGrade.vb
' Created/revised by:  <your name> on <current date>
```

4. Now, enter the following three Option statements:

```
Option Explicit On
Option Strict On
Option Infer Off
```

5. Click the **blank line** below the Public Class clause. The class will not need to validate its two test score attributes, so you can define them using the auto-implemented properties feature. Enter the following lines of code:

```
Public Property Score1 As Integer
Public Property Score2 As Integer
```

6. The third attribute is the letter grade, which will be determined by the class itself. The user should not be allowed to change the letter grade after it has been determined, so you will need to define the attribute using a Private variable and a Public ReadOnly property. Type the following line of code and then press **Enter** twice:

```
Private _grade As String
```

7. Next, enter the following Property procedure header. When you press Enter, the Code Editor will automatically include the Get block of code and the End Property clause in the procedure. (The Set block will not be included because the header contains the ReadOnly keyword.)

```
Public ReadOnly Property Grade As String
```

8. As you learned in the chapter, the Get statement typically contains an instruction that returns the contents of the property's Private variable. Type the following statement, but don't press Enter:

```
Return _grade
```

9. Next, you will enter the default constructor. Insert **two blank lines** above the End Class clause. Beginning in the blank line immediately above the clause, enter the following default constructor:

```
Public Sub New()
    _Score1 = 0
    _Score2 = 0
    _grade = String.Empty
End Sub
```

10. Finally, you will enter the DetermineGrade method, which will assign the appropriate grade to the _grade variable. The method will be a Sub procedure because it will not need to return a value to the application that calls it. Insert **two blank lines** above the End Class clause, and then enter the following procedure header in the blank line immediately above the clause:

```
Public Sub DetermineGrade()
```

11. Now, enter the following Select Case statement:

```
Select Case _Score1 + _Score2
    Case Is >= 180
        _grade = "A"
    Case Is >= 160
        _grade = "B"
    Case Is >= 140
        _grade = "C"
    Case Is >= 120
        _grade = "D"
    Case Else
        _grade = "F"
End Select
```

12. Save the solution and then close the CourseGrade.vb window.

Coding the displayButton's Click Event Procedure

According to the application's TOE chart (shown earlier in Figure 14-19), the following procedures need to be coded: the MainForm's Load event procedure, the Click event procedures for the two buttons, and the SelectedValueChanged procedure for the two list boxes. All but the displayButton_Click procedure have already been coded for you.

To code the displayButton_Click procedure and then test the code:

1. Open the MainForm's Code Editor window. In the comments that appear in the General Declarations section, replace <your name> and <current date> with your name and the current date, respectively.

2. Locate the displayButton_Click procedure, and then click the **blank line** below the `' instantiate a CourseGrade object` comment. Enter the following Dim statement:

    Dim studentGrade As New CourseGrade

3. Now you will use the object's Public properties to assign the test scores, which are selected in the list boxes, to the object's Private variables. Click the **blank line** below the `' assign test scores` comment. Enter the following assignment statements:

    **Integer.TryParse(test1ListBox.SelectedItem.ToString,
                 studentGrade.Score1)
    Integer.TryParse(test2ListBox.SelectedItem.ToString,
                 studentGrade.Score2)**

4. Next, you will use the object's DetermineGrade method to determine the appropriate grade. Click the **blank line** below the `' determine the grade` comment, and then enter the following Call statement:

    Call studentGrade.DetermineGrade()

5. Finally, you will use the object's ReadOnly Grade property to display the grade stored in the Private _grade variable. Click the **blank line** below the `' display the grade` comment, and then enter the following line of code:

    gradeLabel.Text = studentGrade.Grade

6. Save the solution and then start the application. Click **72** in the Test 1 box and then click **89** in the Test 2 box. Click the **Display** button. The letter B appears in the Grade box. See Figure 14-21.

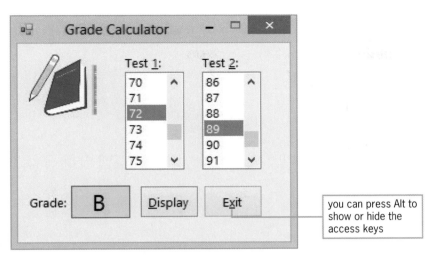

Figure 14-21 Grade shown in the interface
OpenClipArt.org/Minduka

label: you can press Alt to show or hide the access keys

7. On your own, test the application using different test scores. When you are finished, click the **Exit** button. Close the Code Editor window and then close the solution. Figure 14-22 shows the application's code. It also includes the code entered in the CourseGrade.vb file.

<u>Class statement entered in the CourseGrade.vb class file</u>

```
1  ' Class filename:        CourseGrade.vb
2  ' Created/revised by:    <your name> on <current date>
3
4  Option Explicit On
5  Option Strict On
6  Option Infer Off
7
8  Public Class CourseGrade
9      Public Property Score1 As Integer
10     Public Property Score2 As Integer
11     Private _grade As String
12
13     Public ReadOnly Property Grade As String
14         Get
15             Return _grade
16         End Get
17     End Property
18
19     Public Sub New()
20         _Score1 = 0
21         _Score2 = 0
22         _grade = String.Empty
23     End Sub
24
25     Public Sub DetermineGrade()
26         Select Case _Score1 + _Score2
27             Case Is >= 180
28                 _grade = "A"
29             Case Is >= 160
30                 _grade = "B"
31             Case Is >= 140
32                 _grade = "C"
33             Case Is >= 120
34                 _grade = "D"
```

Figure 14-22 Code for the Grade Calculator application *(continues)*

(continued)

```
35              Case Else
36                  _grade = "F"
37          End Select
38      End Sub
39 End Class
```

Code entered in the MainForm.vb file

```
 1 ' Project name:         Grade Project
 2 ' Project purpose:      Displays a grade based on two test scores
 3 ' Created/revised by:   <your name> on <current date>
 4
 5 Option Explicit On
 6 Option Strict On
 7 Option Infer On
 8
 9 Public Class MainForm
10
11      Private Sub MainForm_Load(sender As Object,
        e As EventArgs) Handles Me.Load
12          ' fills the list boxes with values
13
14          For score As Integer = 0 To 100
15              test1ListBox.Items.Add(score.ToString)
16              test2ListBox.Items.Add(score.ToString)
17          Next score
18
19          test1ListBox.SelectedItem = "75"
20          test2ListBox.SelectedItem = "75"
21      End Sub
22
23      Private Sub exitButton_Click(sender As Object,
        e As EventArgs) Handles exitButton.Click
24          Me.Close()
25      End Sub
26
27      Private Sub ClearLabel(sender As Object,
        e As EventArgs
        ) Handles test1ListBox.SelectedValueChanged,
        test2ListBox.SelectedValueChanged
28          gradeLabel.Text = String.Empty
29      End Sub
30
31      Private Sub displayButton_Click(sender As Object,
        e As EventArgs) Handles displayButton.Click
32          ' calculates and displays a letter grade
33
34          ' instantiate a CourseGrade object
35          Dim studentGrade As New CourseGrade
36
37          ' assign test scores
38          Integer.TryParse(test1ListBox.SelectedItem.ToString,
39                           studentGrade.Score1)
40          Integer.TryParse(test2ListBox.SelectedItem.ToString,
41                           studentGrade.Score2)
42
43          ' determine the grade
44          Call studentGrade.DetermineGrade()
45
46          ' display the grade
47          gradeLabel.Text = studentGrade.Grade
48
49      End Sub
50 End Class
```

Figure 14-22   Code for the Grade Calculator application

PROGRAMMING TUTORIAL 2

Modifying the Roll 'Em Game Application

In this tutorial, you will modify the Roll 'Em Game application from Chapter 6's Programming Tutorial 1. The modified application will use a class named PairOfDice.

To open the application and create the PairOfDice class:

1. Start Visual Studio. Open the **Roll Em Game Solution (Roll Em Game Solution.sln)** file contained in the VbReloaded2012\Chap14\Roll Em Game Solution folder. If necessary, open the designer window.

2. Use the PROJECT menu to add a new Class file to the project. Name the class file PairOfDice.vb.

3. Insert a **blank line** above the Public Class clause. Enter the following comments, replacing <your name> and <current date> with your name and the current date, respectively. Press **Enter** twice after typing the second comment.

   ' Class filename: PairOfDice.vb
   ' Created/revised by: <your name> on <current date>

4. Now, enter the appropriate Option statements.

5. The PairOfDice class should contain two Private Integer variables named _die1 and _die2. Click the **blank line** below the Public Class clause and then enter the appropriate statements. Press **Enter** twice after typing the last statement.

6. Enter Public Property procedures for the two Private variables. The properties should be ReadOnly. Name the properties Die1 and Die2.

7. Enter the default constructor, which should initialize the Private variables to 0.

8. Enter a Public method named RollDice. The method should be a Sub procedure that generates two random integers from 1 through 6. The random integers should be assigned to the class's Private variables.

9. Save the solution and then close the PairOfDice.vb window.

Now, you will modify the code contained in the Roll 'Em button's Click event procedure.

To modify the rollButton_Click procedure:

1. Open the MainForm's Code Editor window. In the comments that appear in the General Declarations section, replace <your name> and <current date> with your name and the current date, respectively.

2. Locate the rollButton's Click event procedure. Replace the Dim random1 As Integer and Dim random2 As Integer statements with a Dim statement that declares a PairOfDice variable named dice. The Dim statement should also instantiate a PairOfDice object.

3. Replace the two statements that assign values to the random1 and random2 variables with a statement that calls the PairOfDice object's RollDice procedure.

4. Replace random1 in the first Select Case clause with the PairOfDice object's Die1 property.

5. Replace random2 in the second Select Case clause with the PairOfDice object's Die2 property.

6. Replace random1 and random2 in the first If clause with the appropriate properties.

7. Save the solution and then start the application. Click the **Roll 'Em** button. See Figure 14-23. Because random numbers determine the images assigned to the two picture boxes, your application might display different images than those shown in the figure. In addition, the "Congratulations, player 1!" message, rather than the "Player 1 rolled:" message, may appear on your screen.

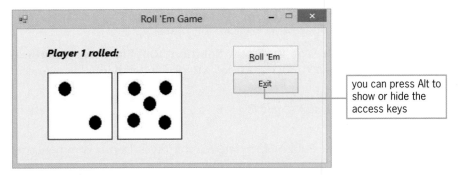

you can press Alt to show or hide the access keys

Figure 14-23   Sample run of the Roll 'Em Game application

8. Click the **Exit** button. Close the Code Editor window and then close the solution. Figure 14-24 shows the code entered in the PairOfDice.vb file. It also shows the modified rollButton_Click procedure. The changes made to the original procedure are shaded in the figure.

```
Class statement entered in the PairOfDice.vb class file
 1 ' Class filename:       PairOfDice.vb
 2 ' Created/revised by:   <your name> on <current date>
 3
 4 Option Explicit On
 5 Option Strict On
 6 Option Infer Off
 7
 8 Public Class PairOfDice
 9     Private _die1 As Integer
10     Private _die2 As Integer
11
12     Public ReadOnly Property Die1 As Integer
13         Get
14             Return _die1
15         End Get
16     End Property
17
18     Public ReadOnly Property Die2 As Integer
19         Get
20             Return _die2
21         End Get
22     End Property
23
24     Public Sub New()
25         _die1 = 0
26         _die2 = 0
27     End Sub
28
29     Public Sub RollDice()
30         Dim randGen As New Random
31         _die1 = randGen.Next(1, 7)
32         _die2 = randGen.Next(1, 7)
33     End Sub
34 End Class
```

Figure 14-24   PairOfDice class and rollButton_Click procedure *(continues)*

(continued)

rollButton Click event procedure entered in the MainForm.vb file

```vb
15  Private Sub rollButton_Click(sender As Object,
    e As EventArgs) Handles rollButton.Click
16    ' simulates the Roll 'Em game
17
18    Dim randGen As New Random
19    Dim dice As New PairOfDice
20    Static player As Integer = 1
21
22    ' clear images and display message
23    firstDiePictureBox.Image = Nothing
24    secondDiePictureBox.Image = Nothing
25    msgLabel.Text = "Player " &
26        player.ToString & " rolled:"
27
28    ' disable Roll 'Em button
29    rollButton.Enabled = False
30
31    ' refresh form and then delay execution
32    Me.Refresh()
33    System.Threading.Thread.Sleep(1000)
34
35    ' generate two random integers from 1 through 6
36    Call dice.RollDice()
37
38    ' display appropriate image in firstDiePictureBox
39    Select Case dice.Die1
40        Case 1
41            firstDiePictureBox.Image = dot1PictureBox.Image
42        Case 2
43            firstDiePictureBox.Image = dot2PictureBox.Image
44        Case 3
45            firstDiePictureBox.Image = dot3PictureBox.Image
46        Case 4
47            firstDiePictureBox.Image = dot4PictureBox.Image
48        Case 5
49            firstDiePictureBox.Image = dot5PictureBox.Image
50        Case Else
51            firstDiePictureBox.Image = dot6PictureBox.Image
52    End Select
53
54    ' display appropriate image in secondDiePictureBox
55    Select Case dice.Die2
56        Case 1
57            secondDiePictureBox.Image = dot1PictureBox.Image
58        Case 2
59            secondDiePictureBox.Image = dot2PictureBox.Image
60        Case 3
61            secondDiePictureBox.Image = dot3PictureBox.Image
62        Case 4
63            secondDiePictureBox.Image = dot4PictureBox.Image
64        Case 5
65            secondDiePictureBox.Image = dot5PictureBox.Image
66        Case Else
67            secondDiePictureBox.Image = dot6PictureBox.Image
68    End Select
```

Figure 14-24 PairOfDice class and rollButton_Click procedure *(continues)*

(continued)

```
69
70      ' check if there is a winner
71      If dice.Die1 = dice.Die2 Then
72          msgLabel.Text = "Congratulations, player " &
73              player.ToString & "!"
74          Dim count As Integer = 1
75          Do While count <= 10
76              msgLabel.Visible = Not msgLabel.Visible
77              Me.Refresh()
78              System.Threading.Thread.Sleep(100)
79              count += 1
80          Loop
81      End If
82
83      ' reset the current player
84      If player = 1 Then
85          player = 2
86      Else
87          player = 1
88      End If
89
90      ' enable Roll 'Em button
91      rollButton.Enabled = True
92
93  End Sub
```

Figure 14-24   PairOfDice class and rollButton_Click procedure
© 2013 Cengage Learning

PROGRAMMING EXAMPLE

Kessler Landscaping Application

Create an application that estimates the cost of laying sod. Use the following names for the solution and project, respectively: Kessler Solution and Kessler Project. Save the application in the VbReloaded2012\Chap14 folder. Change the form file's name to Main Form.vb. Add a new class file named Rectangle.vb to the project. See Figures 14-25 through 14-30.

Task	Object	Event
1. Calculate the area of the rectangle 2. Calculate the total price 3. Display the total price in the totalLabel	calcButton	Click
End the application	exitButton	Click
Display the total price (from calcButton)	totalLabel	None
Get the length in feet	lengthTextBox	None
Get the width in feet	widthTextBox	None
Get the price of the sod per square yard	priceTextBox	None
Clear the contents of the totalLabel	lengthTextBox, widthTextBox, priceTextBox	TextChanged
Select the existing text		Enter

Figure 14-25   TOE chart
© 2013 Cengage Learning

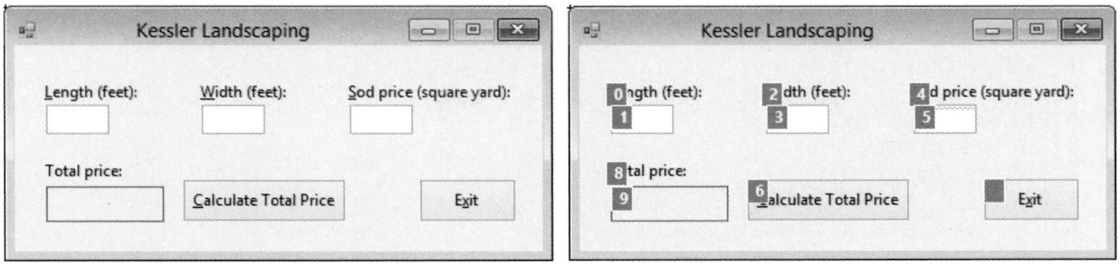

Figure 14-26 MainForm and tab order

Object	Property	Setting
MainForm	Font	Segoe UI, 9pt
	MaximizeBox	False
	StartPosition	CenterScreen
	Text	Kessler Landscaping
totalLabel	AutoSize	False
	BorderStyle	FixedSingle
	TextAlign	MiddleCenter

Figure 14-27 Objects, properties, and settings
© 2013 Cengage Learning

---

exitButton Click event procedure
close the application

calcButton Click event procedure
1. instantiate a Rectangle object
2. store the length and width entries in the Rectangle object's Public properties
3. store the sod price in a variable
4. use the Rectangle object's GetArea method to calculate the rectangle's area in square feet
5. calculate the rectangle's area in square yards
6. calculate the total price of the sod
7. display the total price of the sod in the totalLabel

lengthTextBox, widthTextBox, and priceTextBox TextChanged event procedures
clear the contents of the totalLabel

lengthTextBox, widthTextBox, and priceTextBox Enter event procedures
select the text box's existing text

Figure 14-28 Pseudocode
© 2013 Cengage Learning

```
 1 ' Class filename:        Rectangle.vb
 2 ' Created/revised by:    <your name> on <current date>
 3
 4 Option Explicit On
 5 Option Strict On
 6 Option Infer Off
 7
 8 Public Class Rectangle
 9     Private _length As Double
10     Private _width As Double
11
12     Public Property Length As Double
13         Get
14             Return _length
15         End Get
16         Set(value As Double)
17             If value > 0 Then
18                 _length = value
19             Else
20                 _length = 0
21             End If
22         End Set
23     End Property
24
25     Public Property Width As Double
26         Get
27             Return _width
28         End Get
29         Set(value As Double)
30             If value > 0 Then
31                 _width = value
32             Else
33                 _width = 0
34             End If
35         End Set
36     End Property
37
38     Public Sub New()
39         _length = 0
40         _width = 0
41     End Sub
42
43     Public Sub New(ByVal l As Double, ByVal w As Double)
44         Length = l
45         Width = w
46     End Sub
47
48     Public Function GetArea() As Double
49         Return _length * _width
50     End Function
51 End Class
```

Figure 14-29   Code for the Rectangle.vb file

© 2013 Cengage Learning

```
1  ' Project name:         Kessler Project
2  ' Project purpose:      Displays the cost of laying sod
3  ' Created/revised by:   <your name> on <current date>
4
5  Option Explicit On
6  Option Strict On
7  Option Infer Off
8
9  Public Class MainForm
10
11     Private Sub SelectText(sender As Object,
       e As EventArgs) Handles lengthTextBox.Enter,
       widthTextBox.Enter, priceTextBox.Enter
12         Dim thisTextBox As TextBox
13         thisTextBox = TryCast(sender, TextBox)
14         thisTextBox.SelectAll()
15     End Sub
16
17     Private Sub ClearLabel(sender As Object,
       e As EventArgs
       ) Handles lengthTextBox.TextChanged,
       widthTextBox.TextChanged, priceTextBox.TextChanged
18         totalLabel.Text = String.Empty
19     End Sub
20
21     Private Sub exitButton_Click(sender As Object,
       e As EventArgs) Handles exitButton.Click
22         Me.Close()
23     End Sub
24
25     Private Sub calcButton_Click(sender As Object,
       e As EventArgs) Handles calcButton.Click
26         ' calculates the cost of laying sod
27
28         Dim lawn As New Rectangle
29         Dim sodPrice As Double
30         Dim area As Double
31         Dim totalPrice As Double
32
33         Double.TryParse(lengthTextBox.Text, lawn.Length)
34         Double.TryParse(widthTextBox.Text, lawn.Width)
35         Double.TryParse(priceTextBox.Text, sodPrice)
36
37         ' calculate the area (in square yards)
38         area = lawn.GetArea / 9
39
40         ' calculate and display the total price
41         totalPrice = area * sodPrice
42         totalLabel.Text = totalPrice.ToString("C2")
43     End Sub
44 End Class
```

Figure 14-30 Code for the MainForm.vb file
© 2013 Cengage Learning

Summary

- The objects used in an object-oriented program are instantiated (created) from classes.

- A class encapsulates (contains) the attributes that describe the object it creates. The class also contains the behaviors that allow the object to perform tasks and respond to actions.

- You use the Class statement to define a class. Class names are entered using Pascal case. You enter a class definition in a class file, which you can add to the current project using the PROJECT menu.

- The `Option Explicit On`, `Option Strict On`, and `Option Infer Off` statements have the same meaning in a class file as they do in a form file.

- The names of the user-defined Private variables in a class usually begin with the underscore character. Subsequent characters in the name are entered using camel case. The names of the Private variables created by auto-implemented properties also begin with the underscore. However, the underscore is followed by the name of the Public property defined by the user.

- When an object is instantiated in an application, the Public members of the class are exposed to the application. The Private members, on the other hand, are hidden from the application.

- An application must use a Public property to either assign data to or retrieve data from a Private variable in a class. You create a Public property using a Public Property procedure. The names of the properties in a class should be entered using Pascal case and consist of nouns and adjectives.

- In a Property procedure header, the `ReadOnly` keyword indicates that the property's value can be retrieved (read), but not set. The `WriteOnly` keyword, on the other hand, indicates that the property's value can be set, but not retrieved.

- The Get block in a Property procedure allows an application to access the contents of the Private variable associated with the property. The Set block, on the other hand, allows an application to assign a value to the Private variable. The Set block can contain validation code.

- A class can have one or more constructors. All constructors are Sub procedures that are named New. Each constructor must have a different parameterList (if any).

- A constructor that has no parameters is the default constructor. A class can contain only one default constructor. Constructors that contain parameters are called parameterized constructors.

- The computer processes the constructor whose parameters match (in number, data type, and position) the arguments contained in the statement that instantiates the object.

- The names of the methods in a class should be entered using Pascal case. You should use a verb for the first word in the name, and nouns and adjectives for any subsequent words in the name.

- Values that originate outside of a class should always be assigned to the class's Private variables indirectly, through the Public properties.

- When you create an auto-implemented property, Visual Basic automatically creates the property's Private variable and its Get and Set blocks of code.

- You can overload the methods in a class.

Key Terms

Attributes—the characteristics that describe an object

Auto-implemented properties—the feature that enables you to specify the property of a class in one line of code

Behaviors—an object's methods and events

Class—a pattern that the computer follows when instantiating (creating) an object

Class statement—the statement used to define a class in Visual Basic

Constructor—a method whose instructions are automatically processed each time the class instantiates an object; initializes the class's variables; always a Sub procedure named New

Default constructor—a constructor that has no parameters; a class can have only one default constructor

Encapsulates—an OOP term that means "contains"

Events—the actions to which an object can respond

Get block—the section of a Property procedure that contains the Get statement

Get statement—appears in a Get block in a Property procedure; contains the code that allows an application to retrieve the contents of the Private variable associated with the property

Instance—an object created from a class

Instantiated—the process of creating an object from a class

Methods—the actions that an object is capable of performing

Object—anything that can be seen, touched, or used; an instance of a class

Object-oriented programming language—a programming language that allows the use of objects to accomplish a program's goal

OOP—an acronym for object-oriented programming

Overloaded methods—two or more class methods that have the same name but different parameterLists

Parameterized constructor—a constructor that contains parameters

Property procedure—used to create a Public property that an application can use to indirectly access a Private variable in a class

ReadOnly keyword—used when defining a Property procedure; indicates that the property's value can only be retrieved (read) by an application

Set block—the section of a Property procedure that contains the Set statement

Set statement—appears in a Set block in a Property procedure; contains the code that allows an application to indirectly assign a value to the Private variable associated with the property; may also contain validation code

Signature—a method's name combined with its optional parameterList

WriteOnly keyword—used when defining a Property procedure; indicates that an application can only set the property's value

Review Questions

Each Review Question is associated with one or more objectives listed at the beginning of the chapter.

1. Two or more methods that have the same name but different parameterLists are referred to as _____ methods. (1, 7, 10)

   a. loaded

   b. overloaded

   c. parallel

   d. signature

2. The Product class contains a Private variable named _price. The variable is associated with the Public Price property. An application instantiates a Product object and assigns it to a variable named item. Which of the following can be used by the application to assign the number 45 to the _price variable? (3, 4)

   a. _price = 45

   b. Price = 45

   c. _price.item = 45

   d. item.Price = 45

3. The Product class in Review Question 2 also contains a Public method named GetNewPrice. The method is a Function procedure. Which of the following can be used by the application to invoke the GetNewPrice method? (3, 7)

   a. newPrice = Call GetNewPrice()

   b. newPrice = Price.GetNewPrice

   c. newPrice = item.GetNewPrice

   d. newPrice = item.GetNewPrice(_price)

4. An application can access the Private variables in a class _____. (2-4)

   a. directly

   b. using properties created by Public Property procedures

   c. through Private procedures contained in the class

   d. none of the above

5. To expose a variable or method contained in a class, you declare the variable or method using the keyword _____. (1, 2)

   a. Exposed

   b. Private

   c. Public

   d. Viewable

6. The method name combined with the method's optional parameterList is called the method's _____. (1, 6, 7)

   a. autograph

   b. inscription

   c. signature

   d. statement

7. A constructor is _____. (6)

   a. a Function procedure

   b. a Property procedure

   c. a Sub procedure

   d. either a Function procedure or a Sub procedure

8. An application instantiates an Animal object and assigns it to the dog variable. Which of the following calls the DisplayBreed method contained in the Animal class? (3, 7)

   a. Call Animal.DisplayBreed()

   b. Call DisplayBreed.Animal()

   c. Call DisplayBreed.Dog

   d. Call dog.DisplayBreed()

9. An application instantiates a MyDate object and assigns it to the `payDate` variable. The MyDate class contains a Public Month property that is associated with a Private String variable named `_month`. Which of the following can be used by the application to assign the number 12 to the Month property? (3, 4)

   a. `payDate.Month = "12"`   c. `payDate._month = "12"`

   b. `payDate.Month._month = "12"`   d. `MyDate.Month = "12"`

10. The Return statement is entered in the _____ block in a Property procedure. (4)

    a. Get   b. Set

11. A class contains a Private variable named `_capital`. The variable is associated with the Public Capital property. Which of the following is the best way for a parameterized constructor to assign the value stored in its `capName` parameter to the variable? (2, 6)

    a. `_capital = capName`   c. `_capital.Capital = capName`

    b. `Capital = capName`   d. none of the above

12. A class can contain only one constructor. (2, 6)

    a. True   b. False

13. The Purchase class contains a ReadOnly property named Tax. The property is associated with the Private `_tax` variable. A button's Click event procedure instantiates a Purchase object and assigns it to the `currentSale` variable. Which of the following is valid in the Click event procedure? (4, 8)

    a. `taxLabel.Text = currentSale.Tax.ToString("C2")`

    b. `currentSale.Tax = sales * .1`

    c. `currentSale.Tax = 50`

    d. all of the above

14. A class contains an auto-implemented property named Title. Which of the following is the correct way for the default constructor to assign the string "Unknown" to the variable associated with the property? (2, 9)

    a. `_Title = "Unknown"`   c. `Title._Title = "Unknown"`

    b. `_Title.Title = "Unknown"`   d. none of the above

15. A ReadOnly property can be an auto-implemented property. (2, 8, 9)

    a. True   b. False

Exercises

 Each Exercise is associated with one or more objectives listed at the beginning of the chapter.

 Pencil and Paper

1. If a class contains more than one constructor, how does the computer determine the appropriate one to use when an object is instantiated? (3, 6)   INTRODUCTORY

2. What are overloaded methods and why are they used? (10)   INTRODUCTORY

3. Write a Class statement that defines a class named Book. The class contains three Public variables named `Title`, `Author`, and `Cost`. The `Title` and `Author` variables are String variables. The `Cost` variable is a Decimal variable. Next, use the syntax shown in Version 1 in Figure 14-2 to declare a variable that can store a Book object; name the variable `fiction`. Also write a statement that instantiates a Book object and assigns it to the `fiction` variable. (2, 3)   INTRODUCTORY

INTRODUCTORY

4. Rewrite the Class statement from Pencil and Paper Exercise 3 so that it uses Private variables rather than Public variables. Be sure to include the Property procedures and default constructor. Next, rewrite the Class statement using auto-implemented properties. (2, 4, 6, 9)

INTRODUCTORY

5. Write a Class statement that defines a class named Tape. The class contains four Private String variables named _tapeName, _artist, _songNumber, and _length. Name the corresponding properties TapeName, Artist, SongNumber, and Length. Be sure to include the default constructor. Then, use the syntax shown in Version 2 in Figure 14-2 to create a Tape object, assigning it to a variable named blues. (2-4, 6)

INTRODUCTORY

6. The Television class definition is shown in Figure 14-31. Write a Dim statement that uses the default constructor to instantiate a Television object in an application. The Dim statement should assign the object to a variable named flatScreen. Next, write assignment statements that the application can use to assign the string "14AB4" and the number 459.99 to the Model and Price properties, respectively. Finally, write an assignment statement that the application can use to invoke the GetNewPrice function. Assign the function's return value to a variable named newPrice. (3)

```
Public Class Television
    Private _model As String
    Private _price As Double

    Public Property Model As String
        Get
            Return _model
        End Get
        Set(value As String)
            _model = value
        End Set
    End Property

    Public Property Price As Double
        Get
            Return _price
        End Get
        Set(value As Double)
            _price = value
        End Set
    End Property

    Public Sub New()
        _model = String.Empty
        _price = 0
    End Sub

    Public Sub New(ByVal m As String, ByVal p As Double)
        Model = m
        Price = p
    End Sub

    Public Function GetNewPrice() As Double
        Return _price * 1.08
    End Function
End Class
```

Figure 14-31 Television class definition
© 2013 Cengage Learning

7. Using the Television class definition shown in Figure 14-31, write a Dim statement that uses the parameterized constructor to instantiate a Television object. Pass the parameterized constructor the string "25JFB5" and the number 729.99. The Dim statement should assign the object to a variable named myTv. (3)

INTRODUCTORY

8. An application contains the statement Dim myNewTv As Television. Using the Television class definition shown in Figure 14-31, write an assignment statement that instantiates a Television object and initializes it using the modelName and modelPrice variables. The statement should assign the object to the myNewTv variable. (3)

INTRODUCTORY

745

9. Write the Property procedure for a ReadOnly property named BonusRate. The property's data type is Decimal. (4, 8)

INTERMEDIATE

10. Write the class definition for a class named Worker. The class should have two attributes: a worker's name and his or her salary. The salary may contain a decimal place. Use auto-implemented properties. The class should also contain two constructors: the default constructor and a constructor that allows an application to assign values to the Private variables. (2, 6, 9)

INTERMEDIATE

11. Add a method named GetNewSalary to the Worker class from Pencil and Paper Exercise 10. The method should calculate a Worker object's new salary, which is based on a raise percentage provided by the application using the object. Before calculating the new salary, the method should verify that the raise percentage is greater than or equal to 0. If the raise percentage is less than 0, the method should assign the number 0 as the new salary. (5, 7)

INTERMEDIATE

Computer

12. Open the Painters Solution (Painters Solution.sln) file contained in the VbReloaded2012\ Chap14\Painters Solution folder. Modify the CostOfGoodsSold class so that it uses Public auto-implemented properties rather than Public variables. Include a default constructor in the class. Save the solution and then start and test the application. Close the solution. (6, 9)

MODIFY THIS

13. Open the Pizzeria Solution (Pizzeria Solution.sln) file contained in the VbReloaded2012\ Chap14\Pizzeria Solution. Modify the calcButton_Click procedure to use the Rectangle class's parameterized constructor. Save the solution and then start and test the application. Close the solution. (3)

MODIFY THIS

14. Open the Square Solution (Square Solution.sln) file contained in the VbReloaded2012\ Chap14\Square Solution folder. Add a new class file named Square.vb to the project. The Square class should have one attribute: a side measurement. The side measurement may contain a decimal place and should always be greater than or equal to 0. The class should also have three behaviors: a default constructor, a function that calculates and returns the square's area, and a function that calculates and returns the square's perimeter. Code the Square class. Then, open the form's Code Editor window and complete the calcButton_Click procedure. Display the calculated results with two decimal places. Save the solution and then start and test the application. (2-7)

INTRODUCTORY

15. Open the Sweets Solution (Sweets Solution.sln) file contained in the VbReloaded2012\ Chap14\Sweets Solution folder. Add a new class file named Salesperson.vb to the project. The Salesperson class should have two attributes: a salesperson's ID and a sales amount. The ID and sales amount should have the String and Decimal data types, respectively. The class should also have a default constructor. Code the Salesperson class. Then, open the form's Code Editor window and complete the saveButton_Click procedure. The procedure

INTRODUCTORY

should save the ID and sales amount in a sequential access file. Save the solution and then start and test the application. Be sure to verify that the sales.txt file contains the IDs and sales amounts that you entered. Close the solution. (2-6)

INTRODUCTORY

16. Open the Salary Solution (Salary Solution.sln) file contained in the VbReloaded2012\ Chap14\Salary Solution folder. Open the Worker.vb class file and then enter the class definition from Pencil and Paper Exercises 10 and 11. Save the solution and then close the Worker.vb window. Open the MainForm's Code Editor window. Use the comments to enter the missing instructions. Save the solution and then start the application. Test the application by entering your name, a current salary amount of 54000, and a raise percentage of 10 (for 10%). The new salary should be $59,400.00. Close the solution. (2-7)

INTERMEDIATE

17. Open the Circle Area Solution (Circle Area Solution.sln) file contained in the VbReloaded2012\Chap14\Circle Area Solution folder. (2-7)

   a. Add a new class file named Circle.vb to the project. The Circle class should contain one attribute: the circle's radius. It should also contain a default constructor, a parameterized constructor, and a method that calculates and returns the circle's area. Use the following formula to calculate the area: $3.141592 * radius^2$. Code the Circle class. Save the solution and then close the Circle.vb window.

   b. Open the form's Code Editor window. The calcButton_Click procedure should display the circle's area, using the radius entered by the user. Display the area with two decimal places. Code the procedure.

   c. Save the solution and then start and test the application. Close the solution.

INTERMEDIATE

18. In this exercise, you will create an application that can be used to calculate the cost of installing a fence around a rectangular area. (2-7)

   a. Create a Visual Basic Windows application. Use the following names for the solution and project, respectively: Fence Solution and Fence Project. Save the application in the VbReloaded2012\Chap14 folder. Change the form file's name to Main Form.vb.

   b. Use Windows to copy the Rectangle.vb file from the VbReloaded2012\Chap14 folder to the Fence Solution\Fence Project folder. Use the PROJECT menu to add the Rectangle.vb class file to the project. Add a method named GetPerimeter to the Rectangle class. The method should calculate and return the perimeter of a rectangle. To calculate the perimeter, the method will need to add together the length and width measurements and then multiply the sum by 2.

   c. Create the interface shown in Figure 14-32. The image for the picture box is stored in the VbReloaded2012\Chap14\Fence.png file.

   d. Open the form's Code Editor window and then code the application, which should calculate and display the cost of installing the fence.

   e. Save the solution and then start the application. Test the application using 120 feet as the length, 75 feet as the width, and 10 as the cost per linear foot of fencing. The installation cost should be $3,900.00. Close the solution.

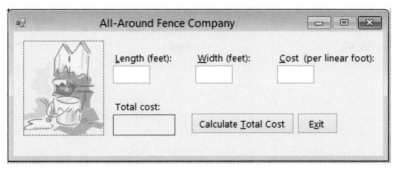

Figure 14-32 Interface for Exercise 18
OpenClipArt.org/liftarn

19. In this exercise, you will define a Triangle class. You will also create an application that allows the user to display either a Triangle object's area or its perimeter. The formula for calculating the area of a triangle is 1/2 * *base* * *height*. The formula for calculating the perimeter of a triangle is $a + b + c$, where a, b, and c are the lengths of the sides. (2-7)

INTERMEDIATE

a. Create a Windows application. Use the following names for the solution and project, respectively: Math Triangle Solution and Math Triangle Project. Save the application in the VbReloaded2012\Chap14 folder. Change the form file's name to Main Form.vb.

b. Create the interface shown in Figure 14-33. The image for the picture box is stored in the VB2012\Chap14\Triangle.png file.

c. Add a class file to the project. Name the class file Triangle.vb. The Triangle class should verify that the dimensions are greater than 0 before assigning the values to the Private variables. Include a default constructor in the class. The class should also include a method to calculate the area of a triangle, and a method to calculate the perimeter of a triangle. Save the solution and then close the Triangle.vb window.

d. Open the MainForm's Code Editor window. Use the InputBox function to get the appropriate data from the user. Save the solution and then start and test the application. Close the solution.

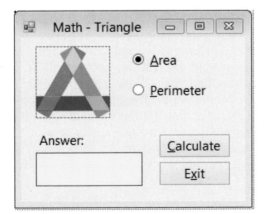

Figure 14-33 Interface for Exercise 19
OpenClipArt.org/10binary

ADVANCED

20. If necessary, complete the Grade Calculator application from this chapter's Programming Tutorial 1, and then close the solution. Use Windows to make a copy of the Grade Solution folder. Rename the folder Grade Solution-Advanced. Open the Grade Solution (Grade Solution.sln) file contained in the Grade Solution-Advanced folder. (2-7)

a. Open the CourseGrade.vb file. Currently, the maximum number of points a student can earn is 200 (100 points per test). Modify the DetermineGrade method so that it accepts the maximum number of points a student can earn. For an A grade, the student must earn at least 90% of the maximum points. For a B, the student must earn at least 80%. For a C, the student must earn at least 70%. For a D, the student must earn at least 60%. If the student earns less than 60% of the maximum points, the grade is F. Make the appropriate modifications to the class's code. Save the solution and then close the CourseGrade.vb window.

b. The application should use the InputBox function to get the maximum number of points per test. Each list box should display numbers from 0 through the maximum number of points per test.

c. Open the MainForm's Code Editor window and make the necessary modifications to the code. Save the solution and then start and test the application. Close the solution.

SWAT THE BUGS

21. Open the Debug Solution (Debug Solution.sln) file contained in the VbReloaded2012\Chap14\Debug Solution folder. (The image in the picture box was downloaded from the Open Clip Art Library at *http://openclipart.org*.) Open the form's Code Editor window and the class's Code Editor window. Correct the calcButton_Click procedure to remove the jagged lines. Save the solution and then start and test the application. Notice that the application is not working correctly. Locate and correct the errors in the code. When the application is working correctly, close the solution. (2-7)

Case Projects

 Glasgow Health Club

Each member of Glasgow Health Club must pay monthly dues that consist of a basic fee and one or more optional charges. The basic monthly fee for a single membership is $50; for a family membership, it is $90. If the member has a single membership, the additional monthly charges are $30 for tennis, $25 for golf, and $20 for racquetball. If the member has a family membership, the additional monthly charges are $50 for tennis, $35 for golf, and $30 for racquetball. The application should display the member's basic fee, additional charges, and monthly dues. Use the following names for the solution and project, respectively: Glasgow Solution and Glasgow Project. Save the application in the VbReloaded2012\Chap14 folder. Change the form file's name to Main Form.vb. You can either create your own interface or create the one shown in Figure 14-34. Be sure to use a class in the application. (2-7)

Figure 14-34 Sample interface for the Glasgow Health Club application

 Serenity Photos

The manager of the Accounts Payable department at Serenity Photos wants an application that keeps track of the checks written by her department. More specifically, she wants to record (in a sequential access file) the check number, date, payee, and amount of each check. Use the following names for the solution and project, respectively: Serenity Solution and Serenity Project. Save the application in the VbReloaded2012\Chap14 folder. Change the form file's name to Main Form.vb. You can either create your own interface or create the one shown in Figure 14-35. The image is stored in the VbReloaded2012\Chap14\Flower.png file. Be sure to use a class in the application. (2-7)

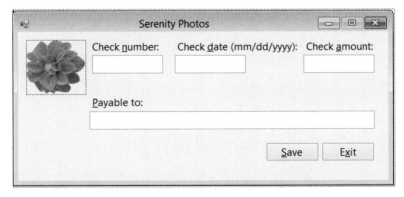

Figure 14-35 Sample interface for the Serenity Photos application

OpenClipArt.org/yves_guillou

 Pennington Book Store

Shelly Jones, the manager of the Pennington Book Store, wants an application that calculates and displays the total amount a customer owes. A customer can purchase one or more books at either the same price or different prices. The application should keep a running total of the amount the customer owes, and display the total in the Total due box. For example, a customer might purchase two books at $6 and three books at $10. To calculate the total due, Shelly will need to enter 2 in the Quantity box and 6 in the Price box, and then click the Add to Sale button. The Total due box should display $12.00. To complete the order, Shelly will need to enter 3 in the Quantity box and 10 in the Price box, and then click the Add to Sale button. The Total due box should display $42.00. Before calculating the next customer's order, Shelly will need to click the New Order button. Use the following names for the solution and project, respectively: Pennington Solution and Pennington Project. Save the application in the VbReloaded2012\Chap14 folder. Change the form file's name to Main Form.vb. You can either create your own interface or create the one shown in Figure 14-36. Be sure to use a class in the application. (2-7)

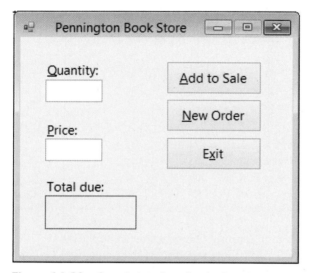

Figure 14-36   Sample interface for the Pennington Book Store application

 Bingo Game

Create an application that simulates the game of Bingo. Use the following names for the solution and project, respectively: Bingo Game Solution and Bingo Game Project. Save the application in the VbReloaded2012\Chap14 folder. You can either create your own interface or create the one shown in Figure 14-37. Be sure to use a class in the application. (2-7)

Figure 14-37   Sample interface for the Bingo Game application

Answers to Mini-Quizzes

Chapter 1

Mini-Quiz 1-1

1. d. all of the above
2. You auto-hide a window by clicking the Auto Hide (vertical pushpin) button on the window's title bar.
3. You temporarily display an auto-hidden window by clicking the window's tab.
4. To reset the windows in the IDE, click WINDOW on the menu bar, click Reset Window Layout, and then click the Yes button.
5. c. Text
6. a. StartPosition

Mini-Quiz 1-2

1. To delete a control from a form, select the control in the designer window and then press the Delete key.
2. c. label
3. d. all of the above
4. b. Image
5. You should select the Label4 control first.

Mini-Quiz 1-3

1. b. Close Solution
2. c. startup
3. b. `Me.Close()`
4. c. `cityLabel.Text = "Nashville"`
5. c. debugging

Chapter 2

Mini-Quiz 2-1

1. d. tasks
2. b. False
3. c. text box

Mini-Quiz 2-2

1. a. book title capitalization
2. d. all of the above
3. b. None, True

Mini-Quiz 2-3

1. a. 0
2. c. 3
3. c. Alt+t
4. b. False

Mini-Quiz 2-4

1. d. all of the above
2. d. all of the above
3. b. `PrintForm1.Print()`
4. c. .wav

Chapter 3

Mini-Quiz 3-1

1. a. only one item
2. c. `commission_rate`
3. `Dim pricePerItem As Double`
4. `Dim counter As Integer = 1`

Mini-Quiz 3-2

1. b. `city = "Paris"`
2. c. `amount = 50`
3. b. `Integer.TryParse(inputPop, population)`
4. a. `cost = Convert.ToDecimal(25.67)`

Mini-Quiz 3-3

1. c. 16
2. b. 32
3. a. `counter += 1`

Mini-Quiz 3-4

1. d. procedure
2. b. Class-level
3. c. `Static score As Integer`
4. a. `Private Const Title As String = "Coach"`

Mini-Quiz 3-5

1. a. `Option Explicit On`
2. c. `Double.TryParse(salesTextBox.Text, sales)`
3. The computer will promote the contents of the `commRate` variable to Double and then multiply the result by the contents of the `sales` variable. It then will assign the product to the `commission` variable.

Mini-Quiz 3-6

1. c. process
2. d. both a and b
3. a. `clearButton.Focus()`
4. b. `commLabel.Text = commission.ToString("N2")`

Chapter 4

Mini-Quiz 4-1

1. b. False
2. c. both its True and False paths
3. b. False
4. a. diamond

Mini-Quiz 4-2

1. d. only the False path in the If...Then...Else statement
2. a. `If sales >= 450.67 Then`
3. a. `"Do they live in " & state & "?"`
4. b. `item.ToLower`
5. a. Checked

Mini-Quiz 4-3

1. a. True
2. False
3. False
4. b. `Dim randGen As New Random`

Chapter 5

Mini-Quiz 5-1

1. a. membership status, day of the week

2. if the golfer is a club member
    display $5
  else
      if the day is Monday through Thursday
          display $15
      else
          display $25
      end if
  end if

3.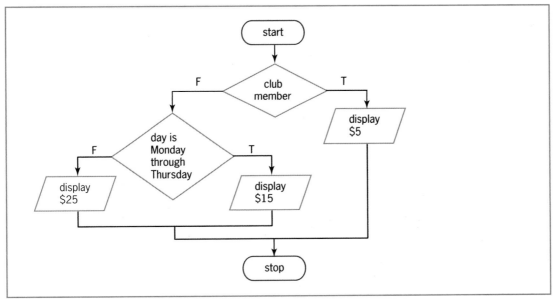

4. ```
   If memberCheckBox.Checked Then
       feeLabel.Text = "$5"
   Else
       If dayNum >= 1 AndAlso dayNum < 5 Then
           feeLabel.Text = "$15"
       Else
           feeLabel.Text = "$25"
       End If
   End If
   ```
   Note: You can also use If memberCheckBox.Checked = True Then.
   ```

Mini-Quiz 5-2

1. b. `Case "1", "2", "3", "4"`
2. a. `Case 10, 11, 12, 13, 14, 15`
3. a. True

Mini-Quiz 5-3

1. d. `ControlChars.Back`
2. a. Checked
3. c. `Windows.Forms.DialogResult.Abort`
4. b. e. `Handled = True`

Chapter 6

Mini-Quiz 6-1

1. b. pretest
2. b. loop exit
3. a. looping

Mini-Quiz 6-2

1. d. all of the above
2. `sum += score` (or `sum = sum + score`)
3. `numValues += 5` (or `numValues = numValues + 5`)
4. `numItems -= 1` (or `numItems += -1` or `numItems = numItems - 1` or `numItems = numItems + -1`)

Mini-Quiz 6-3

1. a. Multiline
2. b. within
3. d. `zip = InputBox("ZIP code:", "ZIP")`

Mini-Quiz 6-4

1. a. Add
2. b. Items
3. c. SelectedIndex
4. c. `System.Threading.Thread.Sleep(2000)`

Chapter 7

Mini-Quiz 7-1

1. d. all of the above
2. c. 13
3. ```
   For num As Integer = 6 To 1 Step –1
       numListBox.Items.Add(num.ToString)
   Next num
   ```

Mini-Quiz 7-2

1. c. either a pretest loop or a posttest loop
2. a. a nested, outer
3. b. outer, nested

Mini-Quiz 7-3

1. c. `–Financial.Pmt(.04 / 12, 24, 5000)`
2. `cityTextBox.SelectAll()`
3. d. all of the above

Mini-Quiz 7-4

1. a. Add
2. b. False
3. c. `stateComboBox.Items.Count`
4. `ImageList1.Images.Item(1)`
   ```

Chapter 8

Mini-Quiz 8-1

1. a. True
2. b. `Private Sub DisplayMessage()`
3. d. `Call DisplayMessage()`

Mini-Quiz 8-2

1. b. `Private Sub Display(ByVal x As String, ByVal y As String)`
2. a. `Private Sub Calc(ByVal x As Integer, ByRef y As Double)`
3. b. `Call Calc(sales, bonus)`

Mini-Quiz 8-3

1. d. `Handles nameTextBox.TextChanged, salesTextBox.TextChanged`
2. a. `Private Function Calc() As Decimal`
3. c. one value only
4. b. `currentLabel = TryCast(sender, Label)`
5. a. Enabled

Chapter 9

Mini-Quiz 9-1

1. a. `Dim letters(3) As String`
2. d. both a and b
3. a. `cities(4) = "Scottsburg"`

Mini-Quiz 9-2

1. b. `For Each scoreElement In scores`
        `total += scoreElement`
    `Next scoreElement`

2. `For subscript As Integer = 0 To 4`
        `total += scores(subscript)`
    `Next subscript`

3. `Dim subscript As Integer`
   `Do While subscript <= 4`
        `total += scores(subscript)`
        `subscript += 1`
   `Loop`

4. `Array.Sort(scores)`

Mini-Quiz 9-3

1. d. all of the above

2. b. `testAnswers(2, 0) = True`

3. b. `highCol = population.GetUpperBound(1)`

Chapter 10

Mini-Quiz 10-1

1. d. `numChars = msgLabel.Text.Length`

2. b. `state = state.Remove(1, 6)`

3. a. `state = state.Insert(0, "South ")`

Mini-Quiz 10-2

1. c. True

2. a. 4

3. b. `footType = restaurant.Substring(8, 7)`

4. d. all of the above

Mini-Quiz 10-3

1. c. `partNum Like "###[A-Z]##"`
2. b. `salesTextBox.Text Like "*,*"`
3. c. `rateTextBox.Text Like "*%"`

Chapter 11

Mini-Quiz 11-1

1. a. Declarations section
2. b. `address.street = "Maple"`
3. d. `inventory(4).quantity = 100`

Mini-Quiz 11-2

1. d. both a and b
2. b. `outFile.WriteLine(cityTextBox.Text)`
3. `outFile.Close()`

Mini-Quiz 11-3

1. c. OpenText
2. b. `msg = inFile.ReadLine`
3. `inFile.Close()`
4. the character

Mini-Quiz 11-4

1. c. `address = city & Strings.Space(10) & state`
2. a. e. `Cancel = True`
3. b. `customer = inFile.ReadLine.Split("$"c)`

Chapter 12

Mini-Quiz 12-1

1. a. database
2. b. relational
3. d. all of the above

Mini-Quiz 12-2

1. d. TableAdapter
2. d. `Me.TblNamesTableAdapter.Fill(Me.FriendsDataSet.tblNames)`
3. c. `ex.Message`
4. d. all of the above

Mini-Quiz 12-3

1. b. `Dim records = From state In StatesDataSet.tblStates`
      `Select state`
2. a. `Dim total As Integer =`
      `Aggregate city In CitiesDataSet.tblCities`
      `Select city.population Into Sum()`
3. b. Order By

Chapter 13

Mini-Quiz 13-1

1. b. client
2. a. browser
3. a. client computer
4. c. Default.aspx
5. c. .aspx.vb

Chapter 14

Mini-Quiz 14-1

1. b. False
2. c. .vb
3. d. both b and c

Mini-Quiz 14-2

1. b. False
2. a. True
3. d. none of the above
4. c. Set

How To Boxes

How to	Chapter	Figure
Access an item in a list box	6	6-22
Access characters in a string	10	10-6
Access the value stored in a field	12	12-24
Add a control to a form	1	1-16
Add a new splash screen to a project	2	2-13
Add a new Web page to a Web Site Project	13	13-7
Add an existing Web page to a Web Site Project	13	13-8
Add images to an image list control's Images collection	7	7-22
Add the Start Without Debugging option to the DEBUG menu	13	13-12
Align columns of information	11	11-22
Align the characters in a string	10	10-4
Assign a value to an existing variable	3	3-5
Assign a value to an object's property during run time	1	1-31
Assign the contents of a LINQ variable to a BindingSource object	12	12-26
Assign the result of an arithmetic expression to a variable	3	3-12
Associate a procedure with different objects and events	8	8-14
Bind an object in a dataset	12	12-7
Change the executable file's name in the Project Designer window	1	1-29
Clear the items from a list box	6	6-20
Clear the Text property of a control	3	3-37
Close a solution	1	1-34
Close an input sequential access file	11	11-18
Close an output sequential access file	11	11-12
Close and open an existing Web Site Project	13	13-13
Concatenate strings	4	4-13
Connect an application to an Access database	12	12-4
Create a constructor	14	14-5
Create a Function procedure	8	8-18
Create a method that is not a constructor	14	14-7
Create a Property procedure	14	14-4
Create a StreamReader object	11	11-14
Create a StreamWriter object	11	11-10
Create a Visual Basic 2012 Windows application	1	1-5

(continues)

(continued)

How to	Chapter	Figure
Create an auto-implemented property	14	14-12
Create an empty Web Site Project	13	13-6
Create and call an independent Sub procedure	8	8-1
Customize a BindingNavigator control	12	12-27
Customize a Web page	13	13-9
Declare a named constant	3	3-20
Declare a one-dimensional array	9	9-2
Declare a StreamReader variable	11	11-13
Declare a StreamWriter variable	11	11-9
Declare a structure variable	11	11-2
Declare a two-dimensional array	9	9-16
Declare a variable	3	3-4
Define a class	14	14-1
Define a structure	11	11-1
Determine the highest subscript in a one-dimensional array	9	9-6
Determine the highest subscripts in a two-dimensional array	9	9-18
Determine the number of characters in a string	10	10-1
Determine the number of elements in an array	9	9-5
Determine the number of items in a list box	6	6-23
Determine the order in which operators are evaluated	4	4-24
Determine whether a file exists	11	11-15
End a running application	1	1-30
Evaluate expressions containing a logical operator	4	4-21
Evaluate expressions containing arithmetic and comparison operators	4	4-8
Evaluate expressions containing operators with the same precedence	3	3-11
Format a number using the ToString method	3	3-32
Generate random integers	4	4-25
Insert characters in a string	10	10-3
Instantiate an object from a class	14	14-2
Invoke a constructor	14	14-6
Invoke a Function procedure	8	8-19
Make a control blink	6	6-39
Manage the windows in the IDE	1	1-10
Manipulate the controls on a form	1	1-17
Name a variable	3	3-2
Open an existing solution	1	1-35
Open the Code Editor window	1	1-20
Plan an application	2	2-1
Play an audio file	2	2-29
Prevent the division by zero run time error	4	4-9
Preview the contents of a dataset	12	12-6
Print the code and interface during design time	1	1-33
Read data from a sequential access file	11	11-16
Read records from a sequential access file	11	11-24
Refer to a member variable in an array element	11	11-8
Refer to an image in the Images collection	7	7-23
Remove an item from a list box or combo box	11	11-21
Remove characters from a string	10	10-2
Save a solution	1	1-24
Search a string	10	10-5
Select the default list box item	6	6-25
Set the TabIndex property using the Tab Order option	2	2-11
Specify a range of values in a Case clause	5	5-10
Specify the splash screen	2	2-16

(continues)

(continued)

Most Commonly Used Properties of Objects

Windows Form

AcceptButton	specify a default button that will be selected when the user presses the Enter key
CancelButton	specify a cancel button that will be selected when the user presses the Esc key
ControlBox	indicate whether the form contains the Control box, as well as the Minimize, Maximize, and Close buttons
Font	specify the font to use for text
FormBorderStyle	specify the appearance and behavior of the form's border
MaximizeBox	specify the state of the Maximize button
MinimizeBox	specify the state of the Minimize button
Name	give the form a meaningful name
Size	specify the form's size
StartPosition	indicate the starting position of the form
Text	specify the text that appears in the form's title bar

Button

Enabled	indicate whether the button can respond to the user's actions
Font	specify the font to use for text
Image	specify the image to display on the button's face
ImageAlign	indicate the alignment of the image on the button's face
Name	give the button a meaningful name
TabIndex	indicate the position of the button in the Tab order
Text	specify the text that appears on the button

CheckBox

Checked	indicate whether the check box is selected or unselected
Font	specify the font to use for text
Name	give the check box a meaningful name
TabIndex	indicate the position of the check box in the Tab order
Text	specify the text that appears inside the check box

ComboBox

DropDownStyle	indicate the style of the combo box
Font	specify the font to use for text
Name	give the combo box a meaningful name
SelectedIndex	get or set the index of the selected item
SelectedItem	get or set the value of the selected item
Sorted	specify whether the items in the list portion are sorted
TabIndex	indicate the position of the combo box in the Tab order
Text	get or set the value that appears in the text portion

DataGridView

AutoSizeColumnsMode	control the way the column widths are sized
DataSource	indicate the source of the data to display in the control
Dock	define which borders of the control are bound to its container
Name	give the data grid view control a meaningful name

GroupBox

Name	give the group box a meaningful name
Padding	specify the internal space between the edges of the group box and the edges of the controls contained within the group box
Text	specify the text that appears in the upper-left corner of the group box

ImageList

ColorDepth	specify the number of bits per pixel allocated for the image color
Images	indicate the collection of images to store in the control
ImageSize	indicate the dimensions for the images
TransparentColor	specify the color to treat as transparent when an image is rendered

Label

AutoSize	enable/disable automatic sizing
BorderStyle	specify the appearance of the label's border
Font	specify the font to use for text
Name	give the label a meaningful name
TabIndex	specify the position of the label in the Tab order
Text	specify the text that appears inside the label
TextAlign	specify the position of the text inside the label

ListBox

Font	specify the font to use for text
Name	give the list box a meaningful name
SelectedIndex	get or set the index of the selected item
SelectedItem	get or set the value of the selected item
SelectionMode	indicate whether the user can select zero choices, one choice, or more than one choice
Sorted	specify whether the items in the list are sorted

Panel

BorderStyle	specify the appearance of the panel's border
Font	specify the font to use for the text and controls inside the panel

PictureBox

Image	specify the image to display
Name	give the picture box a meaningful name
SizeMode	specify how the image should be displayed
Visible	hide/display the picture box

RadioButton

Checked	indicate whether the radio button is selected or unselected
Font	specify the font to use for text
Name	give the radio button a meaningful name
Text	specify the text that appears inside the radio button

TableLayoutPanel

Name	give the table layout panel a meaningful name
CellBorderStyle	specify whether the table cells have a visible border
ColumnCount	indicate the number of columns in the table
Columns	specify the style of each column in the table
Padding	specify the internal space between the edges of the table layout panel and the edges of the controls contained within the table layout panel
RowCount	indicate the number of rows in the table
Rows	specify the style of each row in the table

TextBox

BackColor	indicate the background color of the text box
CharacterCasing	specify whether the text should remain as is or be converted to either uppercase or lowercase
Font	specify the font to use for text
ForeColor	indicate the color of the text inside the text box
Name	give the text box a meaningful name
MaxLength	specify the maximum number of characters the text box will accept
Multiline	control whether the text can span more than one line
PasswordChar	specify the character to display when entering a password
ReadOnly	specify whether the text can be edited
ScrollBars	indicate whether scroll bars appear on a text box (used with a multiline text box)
TabIndex	specify the position of the text box in the Tab order
TabStop	indicate whether the user can use the Tab key to give focus to the text box
Text	get or set the text that appears inside the text box

Timer

Name	give the timer a meaningful name
Enabled	stop/start the timer
Interval	indicate the number of milliseconds between each Tick event

Visual Basic Conversion Functions

This appendix lists the Visual Basic conversion functions. As mentioned in Chapter 3, you can use the conversion functions (rather than the Convert methods) to convert an expression from one data type to another.

Syntax	Return data type	Range for expression
CBool(*expression*)	Boolean	Any valid String or numeric expression
CByte(*expression*)	Byte	0 through 255 (unsigned)
CChar(*expression*)	Char	Any valid String expression; value can be 0 through 65535 (unsigned); only the first character is converted
CDate(*expression*)	Date	Any valid representation of a date and time
CDbl(*expression*)	Double	−1.79769313486231570E+308 through −4.94065645841246544E-324 for negative values; 4.94065645841246544E-324 through 1.79769313486231570E+308 for positive values
CDec(*expression*)	Decimal	+/−79,228,162,514,264,337,593,543,950,335 for zero-scaled numbers, that is, numbers with no decimal places; for numbers with 28 decimal places, the range is +/−7.9228162514264337593543950335; the smallest possible non-zero number is 0.0000000000000000000000000001 (+/−1E-28)
CInt(*expression*) CLng(*expression*)	Integer Long	−2,147,483,648 through 2,147,483,647; fractional parts are Rounded −9,223,372,036,854,775,808 through 9,223,372,036,854,775,807; fractional parts are rounded
CObj(*expression*)	Object	Any valid expression
CSByte(*expression*)	SByte (signed Byte)	−128 through 127; fractional parts are rounded
CShort(*expression*)	Short	−32,768 through 32,767; fractional parts are rounded
CSng(*expression*)	Single	−3.402823E+38 through −1.401298E-45 for negative values; 1.401298E-45 through 3.402823E+38 for positive values
CStr(*expression*)	String	Depends on the expression
CUInt(*expression*)	UInt	0 through 4,294,967,295 (unsigned)
CULng(*expression*)	ULng	0 through 18,446,744,073,709,551,615 (unsigned)
CUShort(*expression*)	UShort	0 through 65,535 (unsigned)

Finding and Fixing Program Errors

After studying Appendix E, you should be able to:

1 Locate syntax errors using the Error List window
2 Locate a logic error by stepping through the code
3 Locate logic errors using breakpoints
4 Fix syntax and logic errors
5 Identify a run time error

Finding and Fixing Syntax Errors

As you learned in Chapter 1, a syntax error occurs when you break one of a programming language's rules. Most syntax errors are a result of typing errors that occur when entering instructions, such as typing `Me.Clse()` instead of `Me.Close()`. The Code Editor detects most syntax errors as you enter the instructions. However, if you are not paying close attention to your computer screen, you may not notice the errors. In the next set of steps, you will observe what happens when you start an application that contains a syntax error.

To start debugging the Total Sales Calculator application:

1. Start Visual Studio 2012. Open the **Total Sales Solution (Total Sales Solution.sln)** file contained in the VbReloaded2012\AppE\Total Sales Solution folder. If necessary, open the designer window. The application calculates and displays the total of the sales amounts entered by the user. See Figure E-1.

Figure E-1 Total Sales Calculator application
OpenClipArt.org/luc

2. Open the Code Editor window. Figure E-2 shows the code entered in the calcButton_Click procedure. The jagged blue lines alert you that three lines of code contain a syntax error.

```
Private Sub calcButton_Click(sender As Object, e As Even
    ' calculates and displays the total sales

    ' declare variables
    Dim jack As Integer
    Dim mary As Integer
    Dim khalid As Integer
    Dim sharon As Integer
    Dim total As Intger            syntax error

    ' assign input to variables
    Integer.TryParse(jackTextBox.Text, jack        syntax error
    Integer.TryParse(maryTextBox.Text, mary)
    Integer.TryParse(khalidTextBox.Text, khalid)
    Integer.TryParse(sharonTextBox.Text, sharon)

    ' calculate total sales
    totl = jack + mary + khalid + sharon
                                    syntax error
    ' display total sales
    totalLabel.Text = total.ToString("C0")
End Sub
```

Figure E-2   calcButton_Click procedure

3. Start the application. If a dialog box similar to the one shown in Figure E-3 appears, click the **No** button. (If you are using the Express Edition, your dialog box's title bar will say Microsoft Visual Studio Express 2012 for Windows Desktop.)

Microsoft Visual Studio ✕

ℹ There were build errors. Would you like to continue and run the last successful build?

Yes   No

☐ Do not show this dialog again

Figure E-3   Dialog box

4. The Error List window opens at the bottom of the IDE, and the Code Editor displays a red rectangle next to each error in the code. If necessary, click the **first error message** in the Error List window. See Figure E-4. The Error List window indicates that the code contains three errors, and it provides a description of each error and the location of each error in the code. The red rectangles indicate that the Code Editor has some suggestions for fixing the errors.

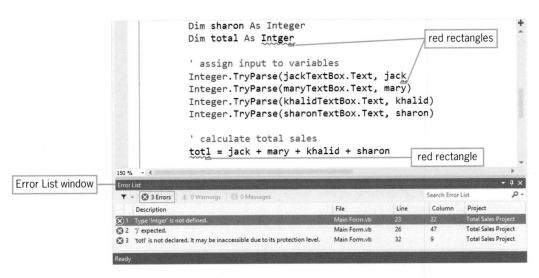

Figure E-4   Error List window

Note: To change the size of the Error List window, position your mouse pointer on the window's top border until the mouse pointer becomes a vertical line with an arrow at the top and bottom. Then press and hold down the left mouse button while you drag the border either up or down.

5. Double-click the **first error message** in the Error List window. The Code Editor opens the Error Correction window shown in Figure E-5.

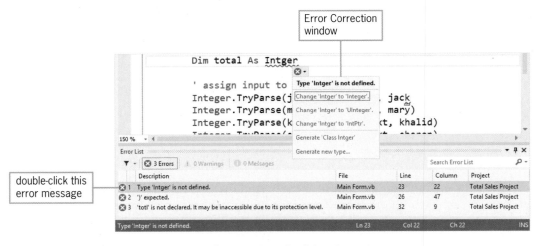

Figure E-5   List of suggestions for fixing the typing error

6. The first error is simply a typing error: The programmer meant to type `Integer`. You can either type the missing **e** yourself or click the appropriate suggestion in the Error Correction window. Click **Change 'Intger' to 'Integer'.** in the list. The Code Editor makes the change in the Dim statement and also removes the error from the Error List window.

7. Double-click the **first error message** in the Error List window. Move the scroll bar in the Error Correction window all the way to the right. The window indicates that the missing parenthesis will be inserted at the end of the assignment statement that contains the syntax error. See Figure E-6.

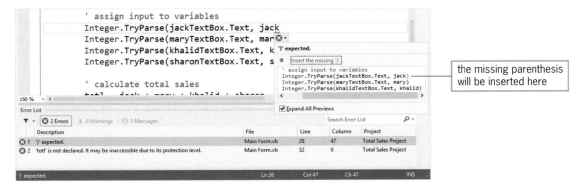

Figure E-6 List of suggestions for fixing the missing parenthesis error

8. Click the **Insert the missing ')'.** suggestion to insert the missing parenthesis. The Code Editor removes the error from the Error List window.

9. Only one error message remains in the Error List window. The error's description indicates that the Code Editor does not recognize the name `totl`. Double-click the **remaining error message** in the Error List window. See Figure E-7.

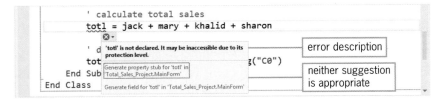

Figure E-7 Error Correction window for the last error message

Neither of the suggestions listed in the Error Correction window in Figure E-7 is appropriate for fixing the error. Therefore, you will need to come up with your own solution to the problem. You do this by studying the line of code that contains the error. First, notice that the unrecognized name (`totl`) appears on the left side of an assignment statement. This tells you that the name belongs to something that can store information—either a control or a variable. It doesn't refer to the Text property, so it's most likely the name of a variable. Looking at the beginning of the procedure, where the variables are declared, you will notice that the procedure declares a variable named `total`. Obviously, the programmer mistyped the variable's name.

To finish debugging the Total Sales Calculator application:

1. Change `totl` to **total** in the assignment statement and then move the insertion point to another line in the Code Editor window. When you move the insertion point, the Code Editor removes the error message from the Error List window.

2. Close the Error List window. Save the solution and then start the application. Test the application using **125600** as Jack's sales, **98700** as Mary's sales, **165000** as Khalid's sales, and **250400** as Sharon's sales. Click the **Calculate** button. The total sales are $639,700. See Figure E-8.

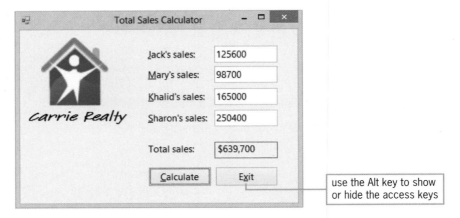

Figure E-8   Sample run of the Total Sales Calculator application
OpenClipArt.org/luc

3. Click the **Exit** button. Close the Code Editor window and then close the solution.

Finding and Fixing Logic Errors

Unlike syntax errors, logic errors are much more difficult to find because they do not trigger an error message from the Code Editor. A logic error can occur for a variety of reasons, such as forgetting to enter an instruction or entering the instructions in the wrong order. Some logic errors occur as a result of calculation statements that are correct syntactically but incorrect mathematically. For example, consider the statement `radiusSquared = radius + radius`, which is supposed to calculate the square of the number stored in the `radius` variable. The statement's syntax is correct, but it is incorrect mathematically because you square a number by multiplying it by itself, not by adding it to itself. In the next two sections, you will debug two applications that contain logic errors.

To debug the Discount Calculator application:

1. Open the **Discount Solution (Discount Solution.sln)** file contained in the VbReloaded2012\AppE\Discount Solution folder. If necessary, open the designer window. See Figure E-9. The application calculates and displays three discount amounts, which are based on the price entered by the user.

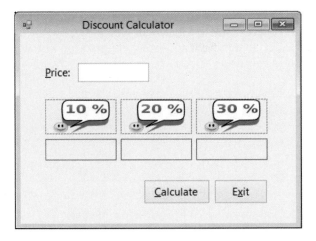

Figure E-9 Discount Calculator application

2. Open the Code Editor window. Figure E-10 shows the code entered in the calcButton_Click procedure.

```
Private Sub calcButton_Click(sender As Object, e As Ev
    ' calculates and displays a 10%, 20%, and
    ' 30% discount on an item's price

    ' declare variables
    Dim price As Decimal
    Dim discount10 As Decimal
    Dim discount20 As Decimal
    Dim discount30 As Decimal

    ' calculate discounts
    discount10 = price * 0.1D
    discount20 = price * 0.2D
    discount30 = price * 0.3D

    ' display discounts
    disc10Label.Text = discount10.ToString("N2")
    disc20Label.Text = discount20.ToString("N2")
    disc30Label.Text = discount30.ToString("N2")
End Sub
```

Figure E-10 calcButton_Click procedure

3. Start the application. Type **100** in the Price box and then click the **Calculate** button. The interface shows that each discount is 0.00, which is incorrect. Click the **Exit** button.

4. You'll use the DEBUG menu to run the Visual Basic debugger, which is a tool that helps you locate the logic errors in your code. Click **DEBUG** on the menu bar. The menu's Step Into option will start your application and allow you to step through your code. It does this by executing the code one statement at a time, pausing immediately before each

statement is executed. Click **Step Into**. Type **100** in the Price box and then click the **Calculate** button. The debugger highlights the first instruction to be executed, which is the calcButton_Click procedure header. In addition, an arrow points to the instruction, as shown in Figure E-11, and the code's execution is paused.

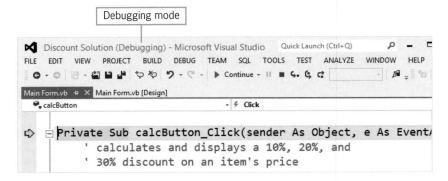

Figure E-11   Result of using the DEBUG menu's Step Into option

5. You can use either the DEBUG menu's Step Into option or the F8 key (F11 key if you are using the Express Edition) on your keyboard to tell the computer to execute the highlighted instruction. Press the **F8** (or **F11**) key. After the computer processes the procedure header, the debugger highlights the next statement to be processed, which is the `discount10 = price * 0.1D` statement. It then pauses execution of the code. (The Dim statements are skipped over because they are not considered executable by the debugger.)

6. While the execution of a procedure's code is paused, you can view the contents of controls and variables that appear in the highlighted statement and also in the statements above it in the procedure. Before you view the contents of a control or variable, however, you should consider the value you expect to find. Before the `discount10 = price * 0.1D` statement is processed, the `discount10` variable should contain its initial value, 0. (Recall that the Dim statement initializes numeric variables to 0.) Place your mouse pointer on `discount10` in the highlighted statement. The variable's name (`discount10`) and current value (0D) appear in a small box, as shown in Figure E-12. The letter D indicates that the data type of the value—in this case, 0—is Decimal. At this point, the `discount10` variable's value is correct.

```
' declare variables
Dim price As Decimal
Dim discount10 As Decimal
Dim discount20 As Decimal
Dim discount30 As Decimal

' calculate discounts
discount10 = price * 0.1D
discoun  discount10 0D   * 0.2D
discount30 = price * 0.3D
```

Figure E-12   Value stored in `discount10` before the highlighted statement is executed

7. Now consider the value you expect the `price` variable to contain. Before the highlighted statement is processed, the `price` variable should contain the number 100, which is the value you entered in the Price box. Place your mouse pointer on `price` in the highlighted statement. As Figure E-13 shows, the `price` variable contains 0D, which is its initial value. Consider why the variable's value is incorrect. In this case, the value is incorrect because no statement above the highlighted statement assigns the Price box's value to the `price` variable. In other words, a statement is missing from the procedure.

```
      ' calculate discounts
⇨     discount10 = price * 0.1D
      discount20 = pri● price 0D ⇐ D
      discount30 = price * 0.3D
```

Figure E-13 Value stored in `price` before the highlighted statement is executed

8. Click **DEBUG** on the menu bar and then click **Stop Debugging** to stop the debugger. Click the **blank line** below the last Dim statement and then press **Enter** to insert another blank line. Now, enter the following comment and TryParse method:

   ' assign price to a variable
   Decimal.TryParse(priceTextBox.Text, price)

9. Save the solution. Click **DEBUG** on the menu bar and then click **Step Into**. Type **100** in the Price box and then click the **Calculate** button. Press **F8** (or **F11** if you are using the Express Edition) to process the procedure header. The debugger highlights the TryParse method and then pauses execution of the code.

10. Before the TryParse method is processed, the priceTextBox's Text property should contain 100, which is the value you entered in the Price box. Place your mouse pointer on `priceTextBox.Text` in the TryParse method. The box shows that the Text property contains the expected value. The 100 is enclosed in quotation marks because it is considered a string.

11. The `price` variable should contain its initial value, 0D. Place your mouse pointer on `price` in the TryParse method. The box shows that the variable contains the expected value.

12. Press **F8** (or **F11**) to process the TryParse method. The debugger highlights the `discount10 = price * 0.1D` statement before pausing execution of the code. Place your mouse pointer on `price` in the TryParse method, as shown in Figure E-14. Notice that after the method is processed by the computer, the `price` variable contains the number 100D, which is correct.

```
      ' assign price to a variable
      Decimal.TryParse(priceTextBox.Text, price)
                                    ● price 100D ⇐

      ' calculate discounts
⇨     discount10 = price * 0.1D
      discount20 = price * 0.2D
```

Figure E-14 Value stored in `price` after the TryParse method is executed

13. Before the highlighted statement is processed, the discount10 variable should contain its initial value, and the price variable should contain the value assigned to it by the TryParse method. Place your mouse pointer on discount10 in the highlighted statement. The box shows that the variable contains 0D, which is correct. Place your mouse pointer on price in the highlighted statement. The box shows that the variable contains 100D, which also is correct.

14. After the highlighted statement is processed, the price variable should still contain 100D. However, the discount10 variable should contain 10D, which is 10% of 100. Press **F8** (or **F11**) to execute the highlighted statement, and then place your mouse pointer on discount10 in the statement. The box shows that the variable contains the expected value. On your own, verify that the price variable in the statement contains the appropriate value.

15. To continue program execution without the debugger, click **DEBUG** on the menu bar and then click **Continue**. This time, the correct discount amounts appear in the interface. See Figure E-15.

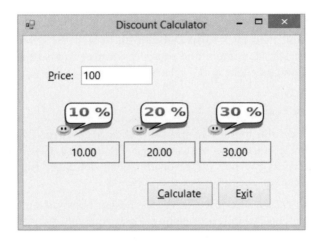

Figure E-15   Sample run of the Discount Calculator application

16. Click the **Exit** button. Close the Code Editor window and then close the solution.

Setting Breakpoints

Stepping through code one line at a time is not the only way to search for logic errors. You also can use a breakpoint to pause execution at a specific line in the code. You will learn how to set a breakpoint in the next set of steps.

To begin debugging the Hours Worked application:

1. Open the **Hours Worked Solution (Hours Worked Solution.sln)** file contained in the VbReloaded2012\AppE\Hours Worked Solution folder. If necessary, open the designer window. See Figure E-16. The application calculates and displays the total number of hours worked in four weeks.

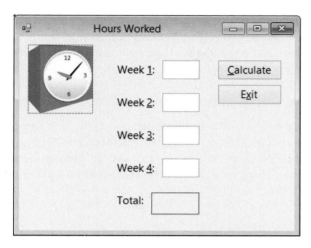

Figure E-16 Hours Worked application
OpenClipArt.org/AirW

2. Open the Code Editor window. Figure E-17 shows the code entered in the calcButton_Click procedure.

```
Private Sub calcButton_Click(sender As Object, e As EventArgs)
    ' calculates and displays the total number
    ' of hours worked during 4 weeks

    ' declare variables
    Dim week1 As Double
    Dim week2 As Double
    Dim week3 As Double
    Dim week4 As Double
    Dim total As Double

    ' assign input to variables
    Double.TryParse(week1TextBox.Text, week1)
    Double.TryParse(week2TextBox.Text, week2)
    Double.TryParse(week3TextBox.Text, week2)
    Double.TryParse(week4TextBox.Text, week4)

    ' calculate total hours worked
    total = week1 + week2 + week3 + week4

    ' display total hours worked
    totalLabel.Text = total.ToString("N1")
End Sub
```

Figure E-17 calcButton_Click procedure

3. Start the application. Type **10.5**, **25**, **33**, and **40** in the Week 1, Week 2, Week 3, and Week 4 boxes, respectively, and then click the **Calculate** button. The interface shows that the total number of hours is 83.5, which is incorrect; it should be 108.5. Click the **Exit** button.

The statement that calculates the total number of hours worked is not giving the correct result. Rather than having the computer pause before processing each line of code in the procedure, you will have it pause only before processing the calculation statement. You do this by setting a breakpoint on the statement.

To finish debugging the Hours Worked application:

1. Right-click the **calculation statement**, point to **Breakpoint**, and then click **Insert Breakpoint**. (You also can set a breakpoint by clicking the statement and then using the Toggle Breakpoint option on the DEBUG menu. Or, you can simply click in the gray margin next to the statement.) The debugger highlights the statement and places a circle next to it, as shown in Figure E-18.

Figure E-18   Breakpoint set in the procedure

2. Start the application. Type **10.5**, **25**, **33**, and **40** in the Week 1, Week 2, Week 3, and Week 4 boxes, respectively, and then click the **Calculate** button. The computer begins processing the code contained in the button's Click event procedure. It stops processing when it reaches the breakpoint statement, which it highlights. The highlighting indicates that the statement is the next one to be processed. Notice that a yellow arrow now appears in the red dot next to the breakpoint. See Figure E-19.

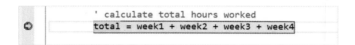

Figure E-19   Result of the computer reaching the breakpoint

3. Before viewing the values contained in each variable in the highlighted statement, consider the values you expect to find. Before the calculation statement is processed, the `total` variable should contain its initial value (0). Place your mouse pointer on `total` in the highlighted statement. The box shows that the variable's value is 0.0, which is correct. (You can verify the variable's initial value by placing your mouse pointer on `total` in its declaration statement.) Don't be concerned that 0.0 appears rather than 0. The .0 indicates that the value's data type is Double.

4. The other four variables should contain the numbers 10.5, 25, 33, and 40, which are the values you entered in the text boxes. On your own, view the values contained in the `week1`, `week2`, `week3`, and `week4` variables. Notice that two of the variables (`week1` and `week4`) contain the correct values (10.5 and 40.0). The `week2` variable, however, contains 33.0 rather than 25.0, and the `week3` variable contains its initial value (0.0) rather than the number 33.0.

5. Two of the TryParse methods are responsible for assigning the text box values to the `week2` and `week3` variables. Looking closely at the four TryParse methods in the procedure, you will notice that the third one is incorrect. After converting the contents of the week3TextBox to a number, the method should assign the number to the `week3` variable rather than to the `week2` variable. Click **DEBUG** on the menu bar and then click **Stop Debugging**.

6. Change week2 in the third TryParse method to **week3**.

7. Now you can remove the breakpoint. Right-click the **statement containing the breakpoint**, point to **Breakpoint**, and then click **Delete Breakpoint**. (Or, you can simply click the breakpoint circle.)

8. Save the solution and then start the application. Type **10.5**, **25**, **33**, and **40** in the Week 1, Week 2, Week 3, and Week 4 boxes, respectively, and then click the **Calculate** button. The interface shows that the total number of hours is 108.5, which is correct. See Figure E-20.

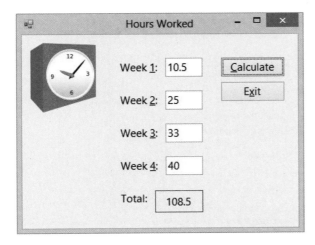

Figure E-20 Sample run of the Hours Worked application
OpenClipArt.org/AirW

9. On your own, test the application using other values for the hours worked in each week. When you are finished testing, click the **Exit** button. Close the Code Editor window and then close the solution.

Run Time Errors

In addition to syntax and logic errors, programs can also have run time errors. A run time error is an error that occurs while an application is running. As you will observe in the following set of steps, an expression that attempts to divide a value by the number 0 will result in a run time error. This is because, as in math, division by 0 is not allowed.

To use the Quotient Calculator application to observe a run time error:

1. Open the **Quotient Solution (Quotient Solution.sln)** file contained in the VbReloaded2012\AppE\Quotient Solution folder. If necessary, open the designer window. See Figure E-21. The interface provides two text boxes for the user to enter two numbers. The Calculate button's Click event procedure divides the number in the numeratorTextBox by the number in the denominatorTextBox and then displays the result, called the quotient, in the quotientLabel.

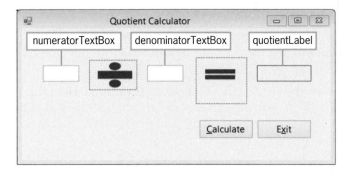

Figure E-21   Quotient Calculator application

2. Open the Code Editor window. Figure E-22 shows the code entered in the calcButton_Click procedure.

```
Private Sub calcButton_Click(sender As Object, e As EventArgs) Ha
    ' display the result of dividing two numbers

    Dim numerator As Decimal
    Dim denominator As Decimal
    Dim quotient As Decimal

    Decimal.TryParse(numeratorTextBox.Text, numerator)
    Decimal.TryParse(denominatorTextBox.Text, denominator)

    quotient = numerator / denominator

    quotientLabel.Text = quotient.ToString("N2")
End Sub
```

Figure E-22   calcButton_Click procedure

3. Start the application. Type **100** and **5** in the numeratorTextBox and denominatorTextBox controls, respectively, and then click the **Calculate** button. The interface shows that the quotient is 20.00, which is correct.

4. Now, delete the 5 from the denominatorTextBox and then click the **Calculate** button. A run time error occurs. The Error Correction window indicates that the highlighted statement, which also has an arrow pointing to it, is attempting to divide by 0. The troubleshooting tips section of the window advises you to "Make sure the value of the denominator is not zero before performing a division operation." See Figure E-23. (If you are using the Express Edition, the error message appears in a box along with a Break button. Click the Break button.)

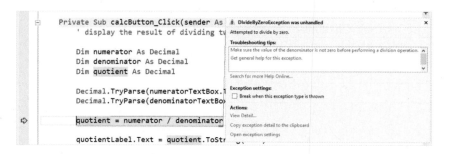

Figure E-23   Run time error caused by attempting to divide by 0

When the denominatorTextBox is empty, or when it contains a character that cannot be converted to a number, the second TryParse method in the procedure stores the number 0 in the denominator variable. If the denominator variable contains 0, the statement that calculates the quotient will produce a run time error because the variable is used as the denominator in the calculation. To prevent this error from occurring, you will need to tell the computer to calculate the quotient only when the denominator variable contains a value other than 0. You do this using a selection structure, which is covered in Chapter 4 in this book.

To add a selection structure to the Quotient Calculator application:

1. Click **DEBUG** on the menu bar and then click **Stop Debugging**.

2. Enter the selection structure shown in Figure E-24. Be sure to move the calculation statement into the selection structure's True path, as shown.

```
Private Sub calcButton_Click(sender As Object, e As EventArgs
    ' display the result of dividing two numbers

    Dim numerator As Decimal
    Dim denominator As Decimal
    Dim quotient As Decimal

    Decimal.TryParse(numeratorTextBox.Text, numerator)
    Decimal.TryParse(denominatorTextBox.Text, denominator)

    If denominator <> 0 Then                          ── enter this selection
        quotient = numerator / denominator            ── structure
    End If ───

    quotientLabel.Text = quotient.ToString("N2")
End Sub
```

Figure E-24   Selection structure entered in the procedure

3. Start the application. Type **100** and **5** in the numeratorTextBox and denominatorTextBox controls, respectively, and then click the **Calculate** button. The interface shows that the quotient is 20.00, which is correct.

4. Now, delete the 5 from the denominatorTextBox and then click the **Calculate** button. Instead of a run time error, the number 0.00 appears in the interface. See Figure E-25.

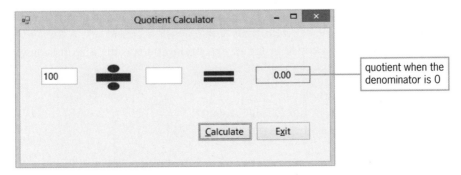

Figure E-25   Result of including the selection structure in the calcButton_Click procedure

5. Click the **Exit** button. Close the Code Editor window and then close the solution.

Summary

- To find the syntax errors in a program, look for jagged lines in the Code Editor window. Or, start the application and then look in the Error List window.

- To find the logic errors in a program, either step through the code in the Code Editor window or set a breakpoint.

- You can step through the code using either the Step Into option on the DEBUG menu or the F8 key (F11 key if you are using the Express Edition) on the keyboard.

- To set a breakpoint, right-click the line of code on which you want to set the breakpoint. Point to Breakpoint and then click Insert Breakpoint. You also can click the line of code and then use the Toggle Breakpoint option on the DEBUG menu. In addition, you can click in the gray margin next to the line of code.

- To remove a breakpoint, right-click the line of code containing the breakpoint, point to Breakpoint, and then click Delete Breakpoint. You also can simply click the breakpoint circle in the margin.

- To determine whether a variable contains the number 0, use a selection structure.

 Each Review Question is associated with one or more objectives listed at the beginning of the chapter.

Review Questions

1. While stepping through code, the debugger highlights the statement that _____. (2)

   a. was just executed
   b. will be executed next
   c. contains the error
   d. none of the above

2. Logic errors are listed in the Error List window. (1, 2)

   a. True
   b. False

3. Which key is used to step through code? (2)

   a. F5
   b. F6
   c. F7
   d. none of the above

4. While stepping through the code in the Code Editor window, you can view the contents of controls and variables that appear in the highlighted statement only. (2)

   a. True
   b. False

5. You use _____ to pause program execution at a specific line in the code. (3)

   a. a breakpoint
   b. the Error List window
   c. the Step Into option on the DEBUG menu
   d. the Stop Debugging option on the DEBUG menu

6. If the `totalScore` and `tests` variables contain the numbers 200 and 0, respectively, the statement `avg = totalScore / tests` will _____. (5)

   a. assign 0 to the `avg` variable
   b. result in a syntax error
   c. result in a logic error
   d. result in a run time error

7. If the `totalScore` and `tests` variables contain the numbers 0 and 10, respectively, the statement `avg = totalScore / tests` will _____. (5)

    a. assign 0 to the `avg` variable
    c. result in a logic error
    b. result in a syntax error
    d. result in a run time error

8. The statement `Constant Rate As Double` is an example of a _____. (1)

    a. correct statement
    c. syntax error
    b. logic error
    d. run time error

9. When entered in a procedure, which of the following statements will result in a syntax error? (1)

    a. `Me.Clse()`
    b. `Integer.TryPars(hoursTextBox.Text, hours)`
    c. `Dim rate as Decimel`
    d. all of the above

Exercises

 Computer

Each Exercise is associated with one or more objectives listed at the beginning of the chapter.

1. Open the Commission Calculator Solution (Commission Calculator Solution.sln) file contained in the VbReloaded2012\AppE\Commission Calculator Solution folder. Use what you learned in the chapter to debug the application. When you are finished debugging the application, close the Code Editor window and then close the solution. (1-5)

    INTRODUCTORY

2. Open the New Pay Solution (New Pay Solution.sln) file contained in the VbReloaded2012\AppE\New Pay Solution folder. Use what you learned in the chapter to debug the application. When you are finished debugging the application, close the Code Editor window and then close the solution. (1-5)

    INTRODUCTORY

3. Open the Hawkins Solution (Hawkins Solution.sln) file contained in the VbReloaded2012\AppE\Hawkins Solution folder. Use what you learned in the chapter to debug the application. When you are finished debugging the application, close the Code Editor window and then close the solution. (1-5)

    INTRODUCTORY

4. Open the Allenton Solution (Allenton Solution.sln) file contained in the VbReloaded2012\AppE\Allenton Solution folder. Use what you learned in the chapter to debug the application. When you are finished debugging the application, close the Code Editor window and then close the solution. (1-5)

    INTRODUCTORY

5. Open the Martins Solution (Martins Solution.sln) file contained in the VbReloaded2012\AppE\Martins Solution folder. Use what you learned in the chapter to debug the application. When you are finished debugging the application, close the Code Editor window and then close the solution. (1-5)

    INTERMEDIATE

6. Open the Average Score Solution (Average Score Solution.sln) file contained in the VbReloaded2012\AppE\Average Score Solution folder. Use what you learned in the chapter to debug the application. When you are finished debugging the application, close the Code Editor window and then close the solution. (1-5)

    INTERMEDIATE

ADVANCED

7. Open the Beachwood Solution (Beachwood Solution.sln) file contained in the VbReloaded2012\AppE\Beachwood Solution folder. Use what you learned in the chapter to debug the application. When you are finished debugging the application, close the Code Editor window and then close the solution. (1-5)

ADVANCED

8. Open the Framington Solution (Framington Solution.sln) file contained in the VbReloaded2012\AppE\Framington Solution folder. Use what you learned in the chapter to debug the application. When you are finished debugging the application, close the Code Editor window and then close the solution. (1-5)

Index

Note: Page numbers in **boldface** indicate key terms.